Fusion

Integrated Reading and Writing **Book 2**

Enhanced Edition

KEMPER / MEYER / VAN RYS / SEBRANEK

Dave Kemper

Verne Meyer
Dordt College

John Van Rys
Redeemer University College

Pat Sebranek

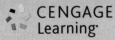

CENGAGE
Learning·

Australia • Brazil • Mexico • Singapore • United Kingdom • United States

CENGAGE
Learning

Fusion: Integrated Reading and Writing, Enhanced Edition, Book 2
Dave Kemper, Verne Meyer, John Van Rys, and Pat Sebranek

Product Director: Annie Todd

Senior Content Developer:
Marita Sermolins

Associate Content Developer: Beth Rice

Product Assistant: Luria Rittenberg

Senior Media Developer: Amy Gibbons

Senior Marketing Manager: Lydia LeStar

Content Project Manager:
Rosemary Winfield

Art Director: Faith Brosnan

Manufacturing Planner: Betsy Donaghey

Rights Acquisition Specialist:
Ann Hoffman

Text and Cover Designer: Sebranek, Inc.

Cover Image: Sebranek, Inc.

Production Service and Compositor:
Sebranek, Inc.

For product information and technology assistance, contact us at
Cengage Learning Customer & Sales Support, 1-800-354-9706.
For permission to use material from this text or product,
submit all requests online at **www.cengage.com/permissions.**
Further permissions questions can be emailed to
permissionrequest@cengage.com.

Library of Congress Control Number: 2011942007

ISBN-13: 978-1-285-46497-8

ISBN-10: 1-285-46497-4

Cengage Learning
200 First Stamford Place, 4th floor
Stamford, CT 06902
USA

Cengage Learning is a leading provider of customized learning solutions with office locations around the globe, including Singapore, the United Kingdom, Australia, Mexico, Brazil, and Japan. Locate your local office at **international.cengage.com/region**.

Cengage Learning products are represented in Canada by Nelson Education, Ltd.

For your course and learning solutions, visit **www.cengage.com**.

Purchase any of our products at your local college store or at our preferred online store **www.cengagebrain.com**.

Instructors: Please visit **login.cengage.com** and log in to access instructor-specific resources.

Printed in the U.S.A.
2 3 4 5 6 7 17 16 15 14

Fusion 2 Brief Contents

Part II: Reading and Writing Essays   **161**

Flashon Studio, 2013 / Used under license from Shutterstock.com

Preface

Fusion: Integrated Reading and Writing, Book 2, is the first text to connect the reading and writing processes in every chapter. *Fusion* uses parallel strategies to teach students how to analyze readings and generate writing. Throughout, grammar instruction is integrated with writing instruction using high-interest readings.

We wanted to find out how instructors expect to teach the combined course, and what they need in order to teach it more effectively. *Fusion* is the direct result of extensive research conducted across the country, which indicated that a textbook addressing instructors' needs would

- provide instructor support, with particular attention paid to teaching reading;
- cover essential reading skills and two levels of writing (paragraph and essay development);
- present lessons following a pattern of reading, writing, analyzing, and grammar;
- provide support for those new to teaching in an integrated reading and writing environment;
- integrate a variety of interesting readings;
- incorporate online technology (**Aplia**™) to promote skill development and allow for tracking of learning outcomes; and
- promote better outcomes, persistence, and retention by giving students a chance to move through the developmental sequence and into credit-bearing courses more quickly.

NEW in the Enhanced Edition

More Reading Strategies to Better Prepare Students. Expanded reading coverage helps students learn and practice the key concepts associated with reading skills.

Chapter 2 "Academic Reading and Learning" coverage now includes
- asking questions as part of prereading;
- understanding the structure of textbooks and textbook chapters;
- drawing inferences with practice opportunities;
- using additional note-taking systems, such as topic outlines, sentence outlines, and clusters;
- understanding deductive and inductive thinking, along with textual examples and guidance for checking each way of thinking; and
- additional vocabulary coverage providing examples of vocabulary notebook entries across disciplines, denotative and connotative meanings, and additional examples of and practice with context clues and word parts.

Chapter 3 "The Traits of Academic Reading" coverage now includes
- identifying the topic with additional practice;
- identifying implied main ideas with additional practice;

- organization of an argument, including discussion about main claim, evidence, counterargument, and receptive and resistant audiences;
- a Diction Glossary that introduces and gives examples of important terms related to diction, like colloquialisms, jargon, and slang;
- a Figures of Speech Glossary that provides definitions and examples of key types of figurative language; and
- the three major types of irony that can contribute to tone.

Additional Readings for Practice. Additional readings that challenge students' critical-thinking skills, enrich their college-ready vocabulary, and reflect the types of reading and writing expected of them in their college courses provide opportunities for practice and interaction.

- **In Part 1, new "Review and Enrichment"** sections allow students to immediately practice reading and writing skills as they are introduced.
- **Part 2 chapters now include three professional essay-length readings.** New apparatus helps students implement the reading process through background information, guiding prereading questions, prompts to annotate and take notes as they read, and vocabulary questions.
- **In Part 2, all "Reading and Reacting"** reading samples now provide **more background information, prereading questions, vocabulary questions, and drawing inference prompts.**

Chapter Features

Fusion reflects the best research on reading, writing, and learning, so students can be confident that following the explanations and guidelines in each chapter will promote success. Here are the key features in the text:

- **Integrated reading and writing guidance in every chapter.** *Fusion's* integrated approach is reciprocal and reinforcing. Parallel reading and writing strategies are introduced in Chapter 1, "The Reading-Writing Connection."
- **Brief, approachable learning units.** Every chapter has several assignments with a clear learning objective and a clear stopping point. This purposeful design allows students to stay focused. Insight boxes sprinkled throughout each chapter explain or reinforce concepts.
- **Grammar instruction in every modes chapter.** *Fusion* integrates relevant grammar coverage in the context of students' reading and writing assignments. Additional practice and instruction appears in the book's "Workshop" sections.
- **Pedagogy that emphasizes critical thinking and vocabulary.** Purposeful use of learning aids, like *Consider the Traits* boxes, thought-provoking quotes, followed by a *"What do you think?"* question, and integrated *Drawing Inference* activities, reinforces key concepts, promotes skill development, and encourages students to think analytically. Challenging words are defined on-page, and integrated vocabulary exercises provide students practice in defining words.

Additional Support for *Fusion*

Aplia™ for *Fusion*. Through diagnostic tests, succinct instruction, and engaging assignments, **Aplia™** for *Fusion: Integrated Reading and Writing* reinforces key concepts and provides students with the practice they need to build fundamental reading, writing, and grammar skills:

- Diagnostic tests provide an overall picture of a class's performance, allowing instructors to instantly see where students are succeeding and where they need additional help.

- Assignments include immediate and constructive feedback, reinforcing key concepts and motivating students to improve their reading and writing skills.

- Grades are automatically recorded in the Aplia grade book, keeping students accountable while minimizing time spent grading.

- **The Individualized Study Path (ISP).** An ISP course generates a personalized list of assignments for each student that is tailored to his or her specific strengths and weaknesses. ISP assignments are randomized, auto-graded problems that correspond to skills and concepts for a specific topic. Students get as much help and practice as they require on topics where they are weak. Conversely, if there are topics they understand well, no remediation is necessary and no additional assignments will be present.

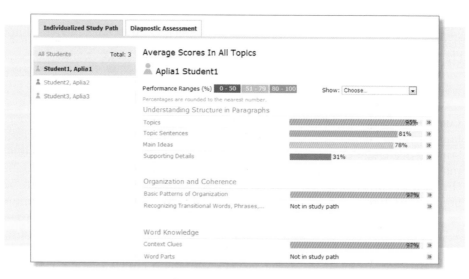

Instructor Manual and Test Bank. The Instructor Manual and Test Bank is located on the Instructor Companion Site in a convenient printable format. This supplement features a wealth of resources for course enrichment, including

- test bank material: chapter quizzes, a midterm exam, and a final exam;
- detailed sample syllabi, including syllabi mapped to North Carolina, Texas, and Virginia state objectives;
- a variety of writing prompts to be used in class or as homework assignments;
- a success story about how Aplia and *Fusion* can be used together in the classroom; and
- a guide to teaching ESL learners using *Fusion*.

Cognero®. Cengage Learning testing powered by Cognero® is a flexible, online system that allows you to author, edit, and manage test-bank content from multiple Cengage Learning solutions, including the quizzes and exams available on Fusion's Instructor Companion Site. Multiple test versions can be created in an instant, and tests can be delivered from your LMS or your classroom.

Instructor Companion Site. Access the Instructor's Manual and Test Bank, and PowerPoint slides organized around topics covered in the book with a high level chapter overview, as well as an opening and closing activity.

Write Experience 2.0. Students need to learn how to write well in order to communicate effectively and think critically. Cengage Learning's Write Experience provides students with additional writing practice without adding to your workload. Utilizing artificial intelligence to score student writing instantly and accurately, it also provides students with detailed revision goals and feedback on their writing to help them improve. Write Experience is powered by e-Write IntelliMetric Within— the gold standard for automated scoring of writing—used to score the Graduate Management Admissions Test (GMAT) analytical writing assessment. Visit www.cengage.com/writeexperience to learn more.

Course Redesign for Developmental Education. Course Redesign is one of the latest trends impacting the landscape of higher education and developmental studies. Cengage Learning's trained consultants, instructional designers, subject matter experts, and educational researchers offer a variety of services to guide you through the process of redesigning your curriculum. Combining that with a wealth of powerful digital and print offerings allows us to personalize solutions to your state or institution's needs. Contact your Learning Consultant to learn more about these services or visit www.cengage.com/services.

Acknowledgements

Many thanks to the many reviewers who have helped to shape *Fusion* into the text you have before you:

Wes Anthony, *Cleveland Community College;* Joe Antinarella, *Tidewater Community College;* Stacey Ariel, *Santa Rosa Junior College*; Margaret Bartelt, *Owens Community College;* Jon Bell, *Pima College;* Christina Blount, *Lewis and Clark Community College;* Mary Boudreaux, *San Jacinto College;* Kimberly Bovee, *Tidewater Community College;* Janice Brantley, *University of Arkansas at Pine Bluff;* Robyn Browder, *Davenport University;* Doris Bryant, *Thomas Nelson Community College;* Jennifer Call, *Cape Fear Community College;* Jana Carter, *Montana State University Great Falls;* Roberta Cohen, *Union County College*; Annette Dammer, *Fayetteville Technical Community College;* Melissa DuBrowa, *Berkeley College;* Arlene Edmundson, *United Tribes Technical College;* Mary Etter, *Davenport University;* Shannon Fernandes, *Yakima Valley Community College;* JoAnn Foriest, *Prairie State College;* Marty Frailey, *Pima Community College;* Johnanna Grimes, *Tennessee State University;* David Harper, *Chesapeake College;* Gina Henderson, *Tallahassee Community College;* Eric Hibbison, *J. Sargeant Reynolds Community College;* Donna Hill, *College of the Ouachitas;* Brent Kendrick, *Lord Fairfax Community College;* Shayna Kessel, *Los Angeles City College;* Sara Kuhn, *Chattanooga State Community College;* Glenda Lowery, *Rappahannock Community College;* Deborah Maness, *Wake Technical Community College;* Katherine McEwen, *Cape Fear Community College;* Carolyn Miller, *Chattanooga State Community College;* Miriam Moore, *Lord Fairfax Community College;* Ann Moser, *Virginia Western Community College;* Ray Orkwis, *Northern Virginia Community College;* Jay Peterson, *Atlantic Cape Community College;* Laura Powell, *Danville Community College;* Pam Price, *Greenville Technical College;* Carole Quine, *Baltimore City Community College;* Janet Rico Everett, *Southern Arkansas University Tech;* David Robinson, *College of Southern Maryland;* Mary S. Leonard, *Wytheville Community College;* Brenda Sickles, *Tidewater Community College;* Virginia Smith, *Carteret Community College;* Suba Subbarao, *Oakland Community College;* Claudia Swicegood, *Rowan-Cabarrus Community College;* Jennifer Taylor Feller, *Northern Virginia Community College-Woodbridge;* Nicole Tong, *Northern Virginia Community College;* Patricia Tymon, *Virginia Highlands Community College;* Kathy Tyndall, *Wake Technical Community College;* Julie Voss, *Front Range Community College;* Michelle Zollars, *Patrick Henry Community College*

Enhanced Edition

Brenda Ashcraft, *Virginia Western Community College;* Teena Boone, *Rowan-Cabarrus Community College;* Mike Coulehan, *El Paso Commuity College;* Kris DeAngelis, *Central Piedmont Community College;* Meribeth Fields, *Central Florida Community College;* Cynthia Gomez, *Hodges University;* Eric Hibbison, *J. Sargeant Reynolds Community College;* Marcia Hines, *Saint Mary's University of Minnesota;* Alice Kimara, *Baltimore City Community College;* Kimberly Koledoye, *Houston Community College;* Kina Lara, *San Jacinto College South;* Alice Leonhardt, *Blue Ridge Community College;* Glenda Lowery, *Rappahannock Community College*; Breanna Lutterbie, *Germanna Community College;* Gail Malone, *South Plains College;* Deborah Maness, *Wake Technical Community College;* Abigail Montgomery, *Blue Ridge Community College;* Miriam Moore, *Lord Fairfax Community College;* Lana Myers, *Lone Star College-Montgomery;* Elizabeth Powell, *Forsyth Technical Community College;* Tony Procell, *El Paso Community College;* Robert Sandhaas, *San Jacinto College South Campus;* Melissa Shafner, *Mitchell College;* Deborah Spradlin, *Tyler Jr. College;* Claudia Swicegood, *Rowan-Cabarrus Community College;* Gene Voss, *Houston Community College;* Shari Waldrop, *Navarro College;* Dawn White, *Davidson County Community College;* Lori Witkowich, *College of Central Florida*

Part I:

Reading and Writing for Success

Part I: Reading and Writing for Success

1

"There's nothing more exciting to me than to read books."
—Toni Morrison

The Reading-Writing Connection

Professional writers know all about the special connection between reading and writing. Stephen King says, "Reading is the creative center of a writer's life." Joan Aiken says, "Read as much as you possibly can." William Faulkner says, "Read, read, read. Read everything. . . ." Writers know that reading helps them write, and that writing influences them to read more.

As a student, you need to make your own special connection between reading and writing. To begin, it is important to understand how academic reading and writing work together to help you learn. Then you'll need strategies for improving your academic reading and writing. The chapters in this section will introduce you to these strategies.

Learning Outcomes

LO1 Understand reading and writing assignments.

LO2 Use the traits for reading and writing.

LO3 Use graphic organizers for reading and writing.

What do you think?

In the above quotation, why might author Toni Morrison find reading so exciting? How do Morrison's feelings about reading compare to your own?

LO1 Understanding Reading and Writing Assignments

> "It's good to rub and polish our brain against that of others."
> —Michel de Montaigne

Being prepared is an important part of making good choices. You would, for example, want to know the basics about a job or an internship before you applied for it. The same holds true for each of your college reading and writing assignments. You should identify the main features before you get started on your work.

The STRAP Strategy

You can use the STRAP strategy to analyze your writing and reading assignments. The strategy consists of answering questions about these five features: *subject*, *type*, *role*, *audience*, and *purpose*. Once you answer the questions, you'll be ready to get to work. This chart shows how the strategy works:

For Reading Assignments		For Writing Assignments
What specific topic does the reading address?	**Subject**	What specific topic should I write about?
What form (*essay, text chapter, article*) does the reading take?	**Type**	What form of writing (*essay, article*) will I use?
What position (*student, responder, concerned individual*) does the writer assume?	**Role**	What position (*student, citizen, employee*) should I assume?
Who is the intended reader?	**Audience**	Who is the intended reader?
What is the goal of the material?	**Purpose**	What is the goal (*to inform, to persuade*) of the writing?

The STRAP Strategy in Action

Suppose you were given the following reading assignment in an environmental studies class.

Assignment: Read the essay "The ABC Daily To-Do List." (See pages 280–281.) Then write a blog entry comparing the advice in the essay with the way you have managed your time in the past. (Below are answers to the STRAP questions for this assignment.)

Subject:	Keeping a daily to-do list
Type:	Process essay
Role:	An educator helping students to achieve
Audience:	Students
Purpose:	To inform students about time-management skills

Respond for Reading Analyze the following reading assignment by answering the STRAP questions below.

Assignment: Read the personal narrative "Codes of Conduct" on pages 194–195. Then in your notebook, respond to the reading noting its key features and your reactions to them.

    Subject: What specific topic does the reading address?

                            _____

    Type: What form (*essay, narrative, text chapter*) does the reading take?

                            _____

    Role: What position (*concerned individual, observer, participant*) does the writer assume?

                            _____

    Audience: Who is the intended audience?

                            _____

    Purpose: What is the goal of the text (*to inform, to persuade, to share*)?

                            _____

Additional Practice: Use the STRAP questions above to analyze the following assignment.

- Read the definition essay "What Is Emotional Intelligence?" on pages 251–252. Identify the main features of this essay.

Respond for Writing Analyze the writing assignment below by answering the STRAP questions that follow it.

Assignment: In a posting on the class blog, reflect on the importance of a specific school-related experience. Consider who was involved, what happened, and why it is significant.

    Subject: What specific topic does the writing assignment address?

                            _____

    Type: What form (*essay, report, blog posting*) should my writing take?

                            _____

    Role: What position (*student, citizen, family member*) should I assume?

                            _____

    Audience: Who is the intended audience?

                            _____

    Purpose: What is the goal of my writing (*to inform, to persuade, to reflect*)?

                            _____

Additional Practice: Use the STRAP questions above to analyze this assignment.

- The ability to work in groups is important in college and in the workplace. Write an essay explaining three or four group skills that students should learn and practice.

LO2 Using the Traits for Reading and Writing

Using the traits of writing can help you gain a full understanding of reading assignments, and they can help you develop your own paragraphs and essays. The traits identify the key elements of written language, including ideas, organization, voice, word choice, sentence fluency, and conventions. Pages 47–102 discuss how to use the traits when reading, and pages 131–160 discuss how to use them when writing.

INSIGHT ————————————————

Using the traits helps you answer these two questions: "What elements should I look for in each of my reading assignments?" and "What elements should I consider when developing my writing assignments?"

The Traits in Action

This chart shows how to use the traits for reading and writing assignments.

Read to identify . . .	The Traits	Write to shape . . .
■ the topic. ■ the thesis (main point). ■ the key supporting details.	**Ideas**	■ a thesis or focus. ■ your thoughts on the topic. ■ effective supporting details.
■ the quality of the beginning, middle, and ending parts. ■ the organization of the supporting details.	**Organization**	■ an effective beginning, middle, and ending. ■ a logical, clear presentation of your supporting details.
■ the level of the writer's interest in and knowledge about the topic.	**Voice**	■ a voice that sounds interesting, honest, and knowledgeable.
■ the quality of the words. (Are they interesting and clear?)	**Word Choice**	■ words that are specific, clear, and fitting for the assignment.
■ the effectiveness of the sentences. (Do they flow smoothly, and are they clear?)	**Sentence Fluency**	■ smooth-reading, clear, and accurate sentences.
■ to what degree the writing follows conventions (and why or why not).	**Conventions**	■ paragraphs or essays that follow the conventions or rules.

Note   Design, or the appearance of a text, is sometimes included in a list of the traits. The key consideration of design is readability: Does the design add to or take away from the reading of a text?

Respond for Reading To get a feel for using the traits for reading, answer the questions below for the essay "Herbivore, Carnivore, or Omnivore?" (page 348).

Tip

The questions on this page cover the first three traits of effective reading and writing.

Questions to Answer for Reading

Ideas: What is the topic of this essay?

What main point is made about the topic? (Look for a thesis statement.)

What details stand out? Name two.

Organization: How does it start?

What happens in the middle?

How does it end?

What part do you like best and why?

Voice: Does the writer seem interested in and knowledgeable about the topic? Why or why not?

Extra Practice: Answer the questions above for "Two Tastes of Asia" (page 376).

Respond for Writing To get a feel for using the traits for writing, answer the questions below for this assignment:

- In a posting on the class blog, reflect on the importance of a specific school-related experience. Consider who was involved, what happened, and why it is significant.

Questions to Answer for Writing

Ideas: What topic will you write about?

What main point about the topic could you focus on? (Did the experience help you, change you, etc.?)

What types of details could you include (explanations, examples, descriptions, personal thoughts, conversations, etc.)? Name two.

Organization: How might you start your writing?

What happens in the middle?

How might you end your writing?

Voice: What kind of writing voice and language will best fit this assignment?

Extra Practice: Answer the questions above for this writing assignment:

- The ability to work in groups is important in college and in the workplace. Write an essay explaining three or four group skills that students should learn and practice.

LO3 Using Graphic Organizers for Reading and Writing

Graphic organizers help you map out your thinking for writing and reading assignments. You can, for example, use a Venn diagram or a T-chart to arrange your thoughts for a comparison essay assignment or to take notes about an essay you have just read. Other common graphics help you organize your thinking for problem-solution, cause-effect, and narrative writing and reading assignments. (See page 9 for common graphic organizers.)

Using a Time Line

Provided below is a time line charting the main actions in the narrative essay starting on page 194. (A time line identifies the key actions and events, without the related details and explanations.)

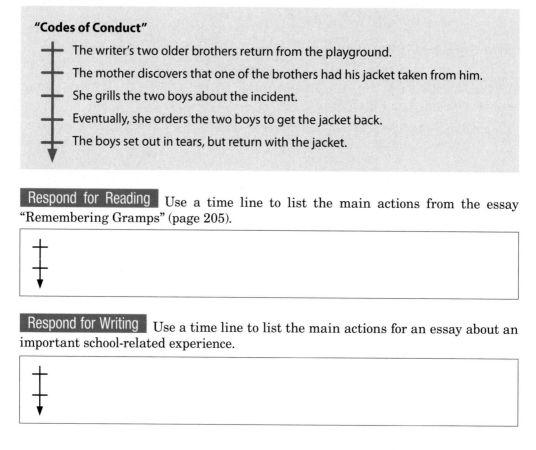

"Codes of Conduct"

The writer's two older brothers return from the playground.

The mother discovers that one of the brothers had his jacket taken from him.

She grills the two boys about the incident.

Eventually, she orders the two boys to get the jacket back.

The boys set out in tears, but return with the jacket.

Respond for Reading Use a time line to list the main actions from the essay "Remembering Gramps" (page 205).

Respond for Writing Use a time line to list the main actions for an essay about an important school-related experience.

Sample Graphic Organizers

Time Line Use for personal narratives to list actions or events in the order they occurred.

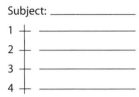

Line Diagram Use to collect and organize details for informational essays.

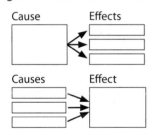

Cause-Effect Organizer Use to collect and organize details for cause-effect essays.

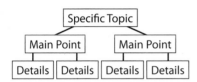

Evaluation Chart Use to collect supporting details for essays of evaluation.

Subject: _____

Points to Evaluate	Supporting Details
1	
2	
3	
4	

Process Diagram Use to collect details for science-related writing, such as the steps in a process.

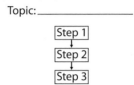

Venn Diagram Use to collect details to compare and contrast two topics.

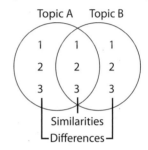

Problem-Solution Web Use to map out problem-solution essays.

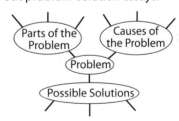

Cluster Use to collect details for informational essays.

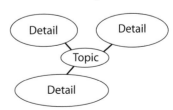

Review and Enrichment

Complete these activities as needed to help you better understand the reading-writing connection.

Understand the STRAP Strategy   Answer these questions about the STRAP strategy. (See pages 4–5.)

- What is the STRAP strategy? _____
- What does each letter in STRAP stand for? _____

Assignment: Use the STRAP strategy to analyze the essay "To Work Out or Not to Work Out" on page 318.

Subject: _____

Type: _____

Role: _____

Audience: _____

Purpose: _____

Use the Traits   Answer these questions about the traits of writing. (See pages 6–7.)

- What traits of writing should you identify in reading and writing assignments?

  _____

- Which trait deals with the main point of the writing?

  _____

- Which trait deals with the rules for using the language correctly?

  _____

Use the Traits   Answer the "Questions to Answer for Writing" on page 7 for the following assignment:

Assignment: Write an essay explaining how to do or make something. Choose a topic that you know well, and be sure to include all of the necessary steps.

Ideas: _____

_____

Organization: _____

_____

Voice: _____

_____

2

> "The books that help you the most are those which make you think the most."
>
> —Theodore Parker

Academic Reading and Learning

Technology is "simply irresistible," especially with the immediate connections that it allows you to make. One minute you are texting a friend, and the next minute you are watching something on YouTube. Because of electronic gadgetry, the world truly is at your fingertips. Unfortunately, this fast action can be a problem, especially when it comes to college-level reading and learning.

Rather than skimming and surfing, your instructors will expect you to become thoughtfully involved in each reading assignment. In other words, they want you to be a critical reader, entirely focused on the material in front of you. The guidelines and strategies presented in this chapter will help you do just that for all types of reading assignments, from textbook chapters to published articles and essays.

Learning Outcomes

LO1 Read to learn.

LO2 Understand the reading process.

LO3 Understand the structure of textbooks.

LO4 Use basic reading strategies (annotating, note taking, outlining, summarizing).

LO5 Read critically.

LO6 Draw inferences.

LO7 Improve vocabulary.

LO8 Read graphics.

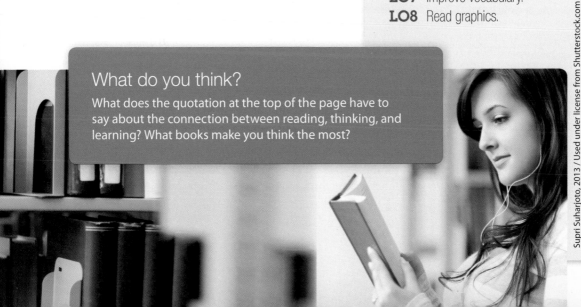

What do you think?

What does the quotation at the top of the page have to say about the connection between reading, thinking, and learning? What books make you think the most?

Supri Suharjoto, 2013 / Used under license from Shutterstock.com

> "Meaning doesn't reside ready-made in the text. . . . It happens during the transaction between reader and text."
>
> —Louise Rosenblatt

LO1   Reading to Learn

Reading and learning logically go hand in hand. You read to learn about new concepts and ideas; you read to learn how to do something; and you read to understand the past, the present, and the future. In college, reading is an essential learning tool, and you will learn the most by becoming an active reader.

> **CONSIDER THE TRAITS**
>
> In effective text, the reader will find strong ideas, logical organization, a clear voice, precise words, and smooth sentences. These traits are the working parts of a text.

Effective Academic Reading

Follow the guidelines listed below for all of your reading assignments.

1. **Divide the assignment into doable parts.** Don't try to read long texts all at once. Instead, try to read for 15–30 minutes at a time.

2. **Find a quiet place.** You'll need space to read and write without distractions. (Quiet background music is okay if it helps you stay on task.)

3. **Gather your materials.** Have on hand a notebook, related handouts, Web access, and so on.

4. **Approach your reading as a process.** Academic reading requires that you do a number of things, usually in a certain order. (See pages 13–15.)

5. **Use proven reading strategies.** For example, taking notes and annotating a text get you actively involved in your reading. (See pages 20–26.)

6. **Know what to look for when you read.** There are key ideas or elements that you need to identify in order to understand a text. (See pages 27–29.)

7. **Summarize what you have learned.** Also note any concepts or explanations that you don't understand. (See page 25.)

8. **Review your reading from time to time.** Doing this will help you internalize the information so you can apply it in your writing and class work.

Practice   Choose the star below that best describes your academic reading skills. Then, in a brief paragraph, explain your choice. In your paragraph, consider which of the guidelines above you do or do not follow.

Weak   ★ ★ ★ ★ ★   Strong

LO2 Understanding the Reading Process

Reading a sport or fashion magazine can be quick and easy because you are reading for enjoyment. Reading an academic text is entirely different because you are reading to gain information. Always approach your academic reading carefully, following the steps in an effective process, so you don't miss important facts and details.

Think about it.

Reading allows you to discover what other people are thinking about important subjects.

The Steps in the Process

The process described below helps you pace yourself and read thoughtfully. See pages 14–15 for a closer look.

Process	Activities
Prereading	First become familiar with the text and establish a starting point for reading.
Reading	Read the assignment once to get a basic understanding of the text. Use reading strategies such as the ones on pages 20–26.
Rereading	Complete additional readings and analysis as needed until you have a clear understanding of the text's key elements or traits.
Reflecting	Evaluate your reading experience: *What have you learned? What questions do you have about the material? How has this reading changed or expanded what you know about the topic?*

The Process in Action

This graphic presents the reading process in action. The arrows show how you may move back and forth between the steps. For example, after beginning your reading, you may refer back to something in your prereading.

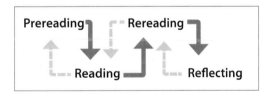

Practice What observations can you make about the reading process after reviewing the information above? One observation is provided below; list three or four additional ones on your own paper.

Academic reading can't be done quickly.

A CLOSER LOOK at the Process

Each step in the reading process requires a special type of thinking and planning. Following these steps will help you become a more confident reader and learner.

Prereading addresses what you should do *before* your actual reading. A cook reviews a recipe in order to have everything in place before starting; prereading serves a similar purpose. Here are the basic prereading tasks.

- **Review the title.** Many readers give the title very little thought. Bad move. The title often identifies the topic of the reading and helps you understand the author's attitude or feeling about it.

- **Learn about the author.** Read the brief biography about the author if it is provided with the text. Otherwise, check online for information about the writer. This information may help you appreciate the author's approach or point of view taken in the text.

- **Preview the text.** To do so, complete the following actions: Read the first paragraph or two to get a general idea about the topic, the level of language used, the writer's tone, and so on. Next, skim the text for headings, bold words, and graphics. Then read the final paragraph or two to see how the text ends. Finally, consider the author's purpose and audience.

- **Establish a starting point for reading.** Once you have done all of these things, write down your first thoughts about the text. Consider what you already know about the topic, what questions you have, and what you expect to learn.

- **Ask questions.** Forming a set of prereading questions will help you stay on task as you read. A common practice is to base your questions on information that you've gleaned while previewing the text's title, objectives, headings, subheadings, first sentences in paragraphs, bold-faced terms, and visuals. Here are three possible prereading questions.
  - The learning objective **"Explain when searches can be made without a warrant"** can be turned into this question: **When can searches be made without a warrant?**
  - The heading **"The Fourth Amendment"** can be turned into this question: **How does the Fourth Amendment protect the rights of the people?**
  - The bold-faced term **"Probable cause"** can be turned into this question: **What is meant by probable cause?**

Reading a text requires your undivided attention. These are your goals during the first reading.

- **Confirm the author's purpose and audience.** Is the material intended to explain, describe, or persuade? And does it address general readers, college students, professionals, or some other audience?
- **Identify the thesis or the main idea** of the text. (See pages 52–64.)
- **Locate the evidence**—the facts and details that support the main idea. (See pages 65–66.)
- **Consider the conclusion**—the closing thoughts of the writer.
- **Answer the questions** you posed during prereading.

Rereading a text helps you to better understand its main points. These are your goals during your rereading.

- **Confirm your basic understanding of the text.** Are you still sure about the thesis and support? If not, adjust your thinking as needed.
- **Analyze the development of the ideas.** Is the topic timely or important? Does the thesis seem reasonable? What types of support are provided—facts, statistics, or examples? Does the conclusion seem logical?
- **Consider the organization of the material.** How does the writer organize his or her support? (See page 75.)
- **Check the voice and style of the writing.** Does the writer seem knowledgeable about the topic and interested in it? Are the ideas easy to follow?

Reflecting helps you fine-tune your thinking about the material. Writing about your reading is the best way to reflect on it. These are your goals during this step.

- **Explain what you have learned.** What new information have you gained? How will you use it? Does this new information change your thinking in any way? Explain.
- **Explore your feelings about the reading.** Did the reading surprise you? Did it disappoint you? Did it answer your questions?
- **Identify what questions you still have.** Then try to answer them.

Apply Use this process for your next reading assignment. Afterward discuss the experience with your classmates.

Other Reading Processes

Two other reading processes—KWL and SQ3R—are variations on the reading process described on the previous pages.

KWL

KWL stands for what I *know*, what I *want* to know, and what I *learned*. Identifying what you know (K) and want to know (W) occurs during prereading. Identifying what you learned (L) occurs after your reading, rereading, and reflecting.

Using a KWL Chart

1. Write the topic of your reading at the top of your paper. Then divide the paper into three columns and label them **K, W,** and **L.**
2. In the **K** column, identify what you already know.
3. In the **W** column, identify the questions you want answered.
4. In the **L** column, note what you have learned.

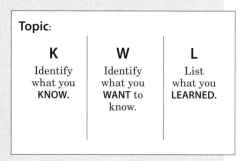

SQ3R

SQ3R is a thorough reading process, very similar to prereading, reading, rereading, and reflecting. The letters SQ3R stand for *survey, question, read, recite,* and *review.*

Using SQ3R

Survey: When you survey, you skim the title, headings, graphics, and first and last paragraphs to get a general idea about the text.

Question: During this step, you ask questions that you hope the text will answer about the topic.

Read: While you do the reading, you take careful notes, reread challenging parts, and so on.

Recite: At the end of each page, section, or chapter, you should state out loud what you have learned. (This could involve answering the 5 W's and H—*who? what? when? where? why?* and *how?*) Reread as necessary.

Review: After reading, you study your notes, answer questions about the reading, summarize the text, and so on.

LO3 Understanding the Structure of Textbooks

In many of your college courses, you will be assigned a textbook, and your instructor will regularly ask you to read particular chapters as background for class lectures and discussions.

Since reading textbooks plays such an important role in your coursework, it is important that you first recognize and understand the main parts they usually include.

Parts of a Textbook

- The **title page** is usually the first printed page in a book. It provides the full title of the book, the authors' names, the publisher's name, and the place of publication.
- The **copyright page** comes right after the title page. This page gives the year in which a copyright was issued, which is usually the same year the book was published. The copyright gives an author or publisher the legal right to the production, publication, and use of the text.
- The **table of contents** shows the major divisions (units, parts, chapters, and topics) in the textbook. It contains page numbers to locate the different divisions. (Many textbooks precede the full table of contents with a table of contents in brief used as a quick guide to the text.)
- A **preface, foreword,** and/or **introduction** often follows the table of contents and introduces the reader to the book.
- The **body** is the main part of the book, containing the actual text.
- Following the body, an **appendix** is sometimes included. This section gives extra information, often in the form of charts, tables, letters, or copies of official documents.
- If included, the **glossary** follows the appendix and serves as the dictionary portion of the book. It is an alphabetical listing of key terms, with an explanation or definition for each one.
- Some textbooks then provide a **reference** section identifying the books or articles the author used during the development of the text.
- The **index** at the end of a textbook lists alphabetically the important topics, terms, and names appearing in the book and the page location for each one.

Practice Locate the different parts of each of your textbooks, including this one. Do any of your textbooks not contain all of these parts, and do any of them contain other parts?

From Schmidt/Shelley/Bardes/Ford, American Government and Politics Today, 2013–2014 Edition, 16E. © 2014 Cengage

AMERICAN GOVERNMENT
AND POLITICS TODAY

Schmidt | Shelley | Bardes | Ford
2013–2014 EDITION

Parts of a Textbook Chapter

As you approach each textbook reading assignment, be aware that most chapters share common features. These features are designed to help you carry out your reading, so it's important that you know what they are and that you use them.

Key features in a chapter from *American Government and Politics Today* are identified and explained. Each one is an important part of the text.

- The **chapter title** identifies the topic of the chapter.
- **Learning outcomes** identify the different things that you can expect to learn from that chapter.
- Many chapters provide **special opening text** to prompt you to think about the chapter.
- **Key terms** are often highlighted and defined.
- **Main headings** are the largest headings and announce each main part of the topic to be discussed.
- **Subheadings** are similar headings and help direct the reading of each main part. (There can be different levels of subheadings. As they get more detailed, they are reduced in size.)
- **Graphics** provide visual representations of important facts and figures.
- **Photographs** and **captions** enhance the discussion in the main text.
- **Side notes** can have a variety of uses depending on the textbook. They can define key terms, identify learning outcomes, or provide interesting facts or ideas, among other things.
- **Summaries** at the end of chapters review the main ideas and details covered in the reading.
- **Resources** to additional reading or viewing may also be provided at the end of a chapter.

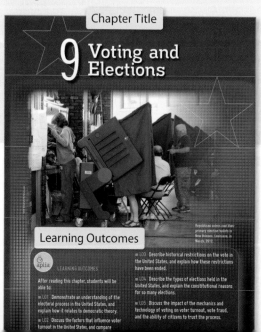

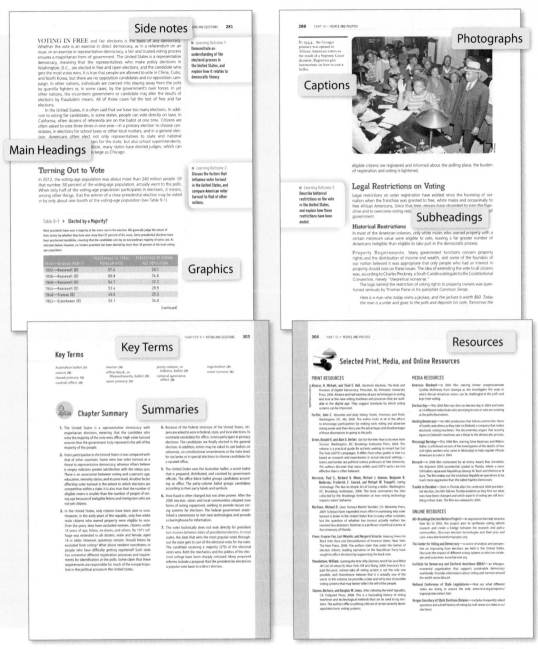

From Schmidt/Shelley/Bardes/Ford, *American Government and Politics Today,* 2013-2014 Edition, 16E. © 2014 Cengage Learning.

Practice   Review the parts of one chapter from one of your textbooks as well as this one. How are they similar or different from the parts you just learned about? Be prepared to discuss the makeup of one textbook chapter with your classmates.

LO4 Using Basic Reading Strategies

To make sure that you gain the most from each reading assignment, carry out the reading strategies on the next few pages.

Annotating a Text

To annotate means "to add comments or make notes in a text." Annotating a text allows you to interact with the ideas in a reading selection. Here are some suggestions:

- Write questions in the margins.
- Underline or highlight important points.
- Summarize key passages.
- Define new terms.
- Make connections to other parts.

> **NOTE:**
> Annotate reading material only if you own the text or if you are reading a photocopy.

Annotating in Action

**Los Chinos Discover el Barrio
by Luis Torres**

There's a colorful mural on the asphalt playground of Hillside Elementary School, in the neighborhood called Lincoln Heights.

Contrasting images are interesting.

Painted on the beige handball wall, the mural is of life-sized youngsters holding hands. Depicted are Asian and Latino kids with bright faces and ear-to-ear smiles.

Reflection

The mural is a mirror of the makeup of the neighborhood today: Latinos living side by side with Asians. But it's not all smiles and happy faces in the Northeast Los Angeles community, located just a *contrast* couple of miles up Broadway from City Hall. On the surface there's harmony between Latinos and Asians. But there are indications of

The writer makes a personal connection.

simmering ethnic-based tensions.

That became clear to me recently when I took a walk through the old neighborhood—the one where I grew up. As I walked along North Broadway, I thought of a joke that comic Paul Rodriguez

Find out about Paul Rodriguez.

often tells on the stage. He paints a picture of a young Chicano walking down a street on LA's East Side. He comes upon two Asians having an animated conversation . . .

Luis Torres, "Los Chinos Discover El Barrio." *Los Angeles Times*, November 14, 1987. Reprinted by permission of the author.

Annotate   Carefully read the excerpt below from an essay by Stephen King. Then, if you own this book, annotate the text according to the following directions:

- Circle the main idea of the passage.
- In the first paragraph, underline or highlight one idea that you either agree with, question, or are confused by. Then make a comment about this idea in the margin.
- Do the same for one idea in the third paragraph and one idea in the final paragraph.
- Circle one or two words that you are unsure of. Then define or explain these words.

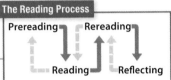

Why We Crave Horror Movies

I think that we're all mentally ill; those of us outside the asylums only   *1*
hide it a little better—and maybe not all that much better, after all. We've
all known people who talk to themselves, people who sometimes squinch
their faces into horrible grimaces when they believe no one is watching,
people who have some hysterical fear—of snakes, the dark, the tight   *5*
place, the long drop . . . and, of course, the final worms and grubs that are
waiting so patiently underground.

When we pay our four or five bucks and seat ourselves at tenth-row
center in a theater showing a horror movie, we are daring the nightmare.

Why? Some of the reasons are simple and obvious. To show that we   *10*
can, that we are not afraid, that we can ride this roller coaster. Which
is not to say that a really good horror movie may not surprise a scream
out of us at some point, the way we may scream when the roller coaster
twists through a complete 360 or plows through a lake at the bottom of the
dip. And horror movies, like roller coasters, have always been the special   *15*
province of the young; by the time one turns 40 or 50, one's appetite for
double twists or 360-degree loops may be considerably depleted.

We also go to reestablish our feelings of essential normality; the
horror movie is innately conservative, even reactionary. Freda Jackson as
the horrible melting woman in *Die, Monster, Die!* confirms for us that no   *20*
matter how far we may be removed from the beauty of a Robert Redford or
a Diana Ross, we are still light-years from true ugliness.

And we go to have fun.

Ah, but this is where the ground starts to slope away, isn't it? Because
this is a very peculiar sort of fun, indeed. The fun comes from seeing   *25*
others menaced—sometimes killed. One critic suggested that if pro football
has become the voyeur's version of combat, then the horror film has become
the modern version of the public lynching. . . .

Taking Effective Notes

Taking notes helps you to focus on reading material and understand it more fully. Notes change information you have read about to information that you are working with. Of course, taking effective notes makes studying for an exam much easier.

Note-Taking Tips

- Use your own words as much as possible.
- Record only key points and details rather than complicated sentences.
- Consider **boldfaced** or *italicized* words, graphics, and captions as well as the main text.
- Employ abbreviations and symbols to save time (vs., #, &, etc.).
- Decide on a system to organize or arrange your notes so they are easy to follow.

Using Two-Column Notes

To make your note taking more active, use a two-column system called the Cornell Method. One column (two-thirds of the page) is for your main notes, and the other column (one-third of the page) is for questions and key terms. Fill in this column after you're done with your main notes.

INSIGHT

To review your notes, cover the main notes and answer the questions in the left column.

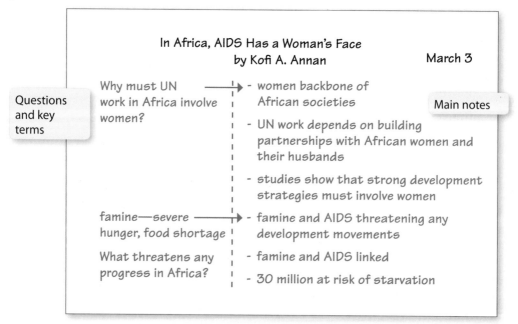

Note: Save space at the bottom of the page to summarize the notes after class.

Using an Outline

An outline shows how ideas fit together in a reading. The ideas in a *topic outline* are expressed in words and phrases. The ideas in a *sentence outline* are expressed in sentences. In a traditional outline, each new division represents another level of detail. As shown below, if you have a "I," you should have at least a "II." If you have an "A," you should at least have a "B," and so on.

Topic Outline

Suppose you have read a chapter about North American trees. Here's the start of a topic outline for this chapter.

Chapter subject: Common North American trees
  I. Trees used in landscaping
      A. Cold climate trees
          1. Hardy evergreens
              a. Norway pine
              b. Scotch pine
          2. Colorful maple trees
              a. Red maple
              b. Silver maple
      B. Warm climate trees
  II. Trees used in agriculture

Important: Unless your instructor says otherwise, adapt your outline to meet your needs, rather than worry whether or not you've followed all of the rules.

Sentence Outline

Here is a portion of a sentence outline for the process essay "The ABC Daily To-Do List" on pages 280–281. (The opening and closing paragraphs are not included in the outline.)

  I. The following steps present one method for creating and using to-do lists.
      A. Brainstorm tasks.
          1. List all the tasks you need to complete for the next day.
          2. Don't worry about the order of your list.
      B. Estimate the time for the tasks.
          1. Note the time needed for each task.
          2. If you are unsure, overestimate rather than underestimate.
          3. Add up the time needed, and compare to your unscheduled time.

Practice Outline the selection "There Are Three Types of Deserts" on pages 308–309. For a special challenge, also outline "Causes of Tropical Deforestation Are Varied and Complex" on pages 337–338.

Using Clusters or Webs

Clustering or webbing is a more graphic way to collect and organize the key points in a reading assignment. Begin a cluster with a nucleus word or idea—most often, the main idea in the reading. Then cluster key points and supporting details around the nucleus concept. Circle each point or detail and connect it to the closest related word. The end result should be a structure that graphically shows you at a glance all the important information in a reading selection. (See page 9 for other graphic organizers.)

Clustering in Action

"The Regulation of Time," pages 185–186, describes how life has become so time-dependent. The cluster that follows presents the key facts and details in this essay. Study it to see how it shows how the important information fits together.

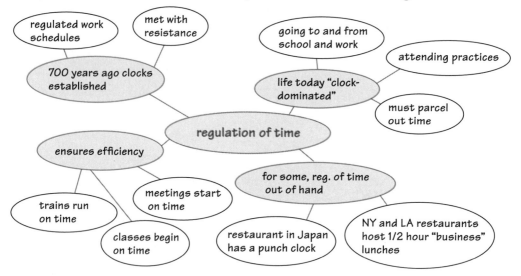

Tip Suppose you want to explore your thoughts and feelings about a text. You can do so in a cluster, or as it is sometime called—a **mind map**. Simply start with an appropriate nucleus word (perhaps the title of the selection) and record and connect your ideas. Clustering in this way may help you gain a firmer understanding of the text.

Practice Read the essay "Why Thinner?" on pages 126–127 in your book. (Or read another selection recommended by your instructor.) Then use a cluster to gather and connect the important information in the text. Afterward, share clusters and discuss the value of this reading strategy.

Summarizing a Text

Summarizing a reading assignment will tell you how well you understand the information. Summarizing means "to present the main points in a clear, concise form using your own words." Generally speaking, a summary should be about one-third as long as the original. (See pages 441–460 for more information.)

Summarizing Tips

- Start by clearly stating the main point of the text.
- Share only the essential supporting facts and details (names, dates, times, and places) in the next sentences.
- Present your ideas in a logical order.
- Tie all of your points together in a closing sentence.

Example Summary

The example below summarizes a two-page essay by Kofi A. Annan concerning the suffering caused by AIDS and famine in southern Africa.

The Face of AIDS

Main ideas (underlined)

Essential supporting details

Closing sentence (underlined)

Famine and AIDS are threatening the agricultural   1
societies in southern Africa. Tragically, women, the main
unifying force in African societies, make up 59 percent of
individuals worldwide infected by the HIV virus. With so
many women suffering from AIDS, the family structure   5
and the agricultural infrastructure are suffering severely.
These conditions have significantly contributed to the famine
conditions and resulting starvation. Any traditional survival
techniques used by African women in the past won't work for
these twin disasters. International relief is needed, and it   10
must provide immediate food and health aid. A key focus of
health aid must be the treatment of women infected with HIV
and preventative education to stop the spread of the disease.
The future of southern Africa depends on the health and
leadership of its women.   15

Practice On your own paper, summarize one of the professional essays in this book or an essay provided by your instructor. Use the tips above as a guide.

Forming Personal Responses

To thoughtfully interact with a text, you need to write about it. Reserve part of your class notebook for these personal responses. Personal responses to a text help you think about it—to agree with it, to question it, to make connections with it. The following guidelines will help you do this:

- **Write several times,** perhaps once before you read, two or three times during the reading, and one time afterward.
- **Write freely and honestly** to make genuine connections with the text.
- **Respond to points of view** that you like or agree with, information that confuses you, connections that you can make with other material, and ideas that seem significant.
- **Label and date your responses.** You can use these entries to prepare for exams or complete other assignments.
- **Share your discoveries.** Your entries can provide conversation starters in discussions with classmates.

> **INSIGHT** —————
>
> If you are a visual person, you may understand a text best by clustering or mapping its important points. (See pages 24 and 133 for sample clusters.)

Types of Personal Responses

Here are some specific ways to respond to a text:

Discuss Carry on a conversation with the author or a character to get to know her or him and yourself a little better.

Illustrate Create graphics or draw pictures to help you figure out parts of the text.

Imitate Continue the article or story line, trying to write like the author.

Express Share your feelings about the text, perhaps in a poem.

Practice Follow the guidelines on this page to explore your thoughts about one of your next reading assignments. Afterward, assess the value of forming personal responses to a text.

LO5 Reading Critically

Critical reading involves a lot of analyzing and evaluating. Analyzing refers to, among other things, classifying and comparing ideas as well as looking for cause-effect relationships. Evaluating refers to weighing the value of a text and considering its strengths and weaknesses.

An educational psychologist named Benjamin Bloom created a list of thinking skills, moving from simple, surface thinking to deeper levels of thinking. In this taxonomy, analyzing and evaluating are clearly deeper levels of thinking.

Bloom's New Taxonomy

Whenever you are asked to . . .	Be prepared to . . .
Remember	collect basic information, identify key terms, and remember main points.
Understand	explain what you have learned, give examples, and restate information.
Apply	identify crucial details, organize key points, and model or show understanding.
Analyze	carefully examine the topic, classify the main points, show cause-effect relationships, and make comparisons.
Evaluate	judge the value of information, identify strengths and weaknesses, and argue for or against the ideas.
Create	develop something new from what you have learned.

Practice Study the chart above. Then explain in a brief paragraph how many of these thinking skills you apply in your own academic reading.

_____

_____

_____

_____

A CLOSER LOOK at Critical Reading

When reading critically, you are, in effect, asking and answering thoughtful questions about a text. Here are some thoughtful questions that a critical reader may ask about a nonfiction text:

Asking Critical Questions

- What is the purpose of the reading (to inform, to entertain, to persuade)?
- Who is the intended audience (general readers, students, professionals)?
- What parts does the text include (title, headings, graphics, introduction, etc.)?
- What logical pattern of reasoning does it follow? (See below.)
- What is the thesis or main idea in the reading? (See pages 52–64.)
- How is the thesis supported or developed (facts, examples, definitions, etc.) ?
- What parts of the text seem especially important and why?
- What questions do you still have about the topic?
- How will you use this information?

Deductive and Inductive Thinking

Almost all texts that you read will follow either deductive or inductive patterns of reasoning. **Deductive thinking** moves from a general thesis to specific supporting details. Most texts follow this form of thinking. **Inductive thinking** moves from specific examples and facts to a general conclusion. Understanding these two basic patterns will be helpful when you are reading academic texts. The graphic that follows shows how the two patterns of thinking move in different directions.

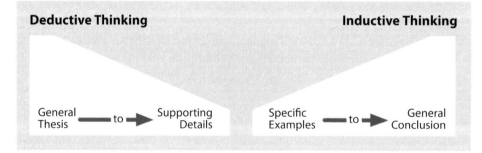

Deductive Thinking   **Inductive Thinking**

General Thesis —to→ Supporting Details   Specific Examples —to→ General Conclusion

Deductive Thinking

Here is an example of a paragraph that is arranged deductively. The main idea (underlined) is followed by specific details.

It's hard to say how humpback whales find their way. They may rely on their excellent sense of hearing to pick up low-frequency sound waves that bounce off common ocean features such as rock and coral. Scientists also believe that they may look for familiar landforms. Two researchers recently detected a small amount of magnetic material in humpbacks, which may allow them to migrate by sensing the earth's magnetic field. This may explain why whales get stranded. Some researchers think it's because they are drawn to coasts with low magnetic forces, thinking they are clear waterways. This would also explain how they could follow such precise migration paths.

Use these questions to check for deductive thinking.

- Does the text start with a thesis (main idea or claim)?
- Do the details logically support or follow from the thesis?
- Does the conclusion logically follow the ideas that come before it?

Inductive Thinking

Here is an example of a paragraph that is arranged inductively. It begins with specific examples leading to a general conclusion (underlined).

Arctic air masses dipped repeatedly across the nation's midsection. The results were reported on the nightly news. In the Texas panhandle, pipes burst as cloudless skies brought a rare hard freeze. In Tennessee, some 200 cars piled up in a dense fog, and many lives were lost. Many were injured and one was killed in New York City as a short circuit caused by melting snow led to an underground train derailment. In California, old-timers couldn't remember a colder spell than the one that this year ruined nearly 85 percent of the citrus crop, most of the avocados, the strawberries, and the broccoli. The winter of 2000-01 will be remembered as a costly one.

Use these questions to check for inductive thinking.

- Does the text start with a series of facts, examples, and explanations?
- Do they logically lead up to the general conclusion?
- Does the general conclusion make sense in terms of the preceding evidence (facts, examples, etc.)?

Apply Use this information as a guide when considering the general pattern of thinking used in a text.

LO6   Drawing Inferences

An *inference* is a logical conclusion that you make about something that is not actually said or stated in a text. A thoughtful inference results from a careful reading of a text. Once you understand the main claim and supporting evidence, then and only then can you make worthy inferences.

Steps to Follow

To make thoughtful inferences, follow these steps:

- Carefully read and reread the text, using the reading process.
- Identify the main idea and supporting details.
- Then ask yourself: *What other conclusions can I draw from the reading?*

Inferring in Action

The following passage comes from the Bureau of Labor Statistics Web site. Among other things, the bureau provides economic news releases summarizing regional and state unemployment and employment figures. Note the inferences below that were drawn after a careful reading of the passage.

> Regional and state unemployment rates were little changed in February.   *1*
> Twenty-two states had unemployment rate decreases, 12 states had increases, and 16 states and the District of Columbia had no change, the US Bureau of Labor Statistics reported today. Thirty-seven states and the District of Columbia had unemployment rate decreases from a year earlier, 10 states   *5*
> had increases, and 3 states had no change. The national jobless rate, 7.7 percent, edged down from January and was 0.6 percentage point lower than in February 2012.
>
> In February, the West continued to have the highest regional unemployment rate, 8.5 percent, while the South had the lowest rate,   *10*
> 7.3 percent. No region had a statistically significant over-the-month unemployment rate change.
>
> "Regional and State Employment and Unemployment—February 2013" *Bureau of Labor Statistics*, 29 Mar. 2013. Web. 31 Mar. 2013.

1. What is the main idea in the passage?

   Regional and state unemployment did not change much in February 2013.

2. What details support the main idea?

   (1) While 22 states had lower unemployment, 12 states had increases and 16 states plus DC had no change. (2) There was only a 0.6 percentage decrease in February compared to January.

3. What inferences (conclusions) can you draw from the passage?

   (1) The recovery from a major recession is a slow process. (2) All parts of the country, to some degree, are feeling the effects of unemployment due to the recession.

Practice   To practice drawing inferences, carefully read each passage below. Then answer the questions following each passage.

1.   In the early 1980's, very few Americans had ever heard of acquired   *1*
immune deficiency (AIDS). By 2000, however, AIDS had become the
leading infectious cause of death in the world. More than sixty million
people worldwide have been infected with HIV. Since 1981 AIDS has
claimed twenty-five million lives, or more than 890,000 people each year.   *5*
That is about half as many deaths as in all of World War II, and it is not
over. Today there are thirty-three million people in the world living with
HIV, the virus that causes AIDS. Tragically, 95 percent of all new AIDS
cases are in the poorest countries that are least equipped to handle the
epidemic.   From Ferraro/Andreatta, *Cultural Anthropology*, 9E. © 2012 Cengage Learning.   *10*

   a. What is the main idea in the passage?

   _____

   b. What key type of detail supports the main idea? Circle one: definitions,
statistics, quotations.

   c. What inferences (conclusions) can you draw from the passage?

   _____

2.   The report also documents for the first time an emerging "app gap" in   *1*
which affluent children are likely to use mobile educational games while
those in low-income families are the most likely to have televisions in
their bedrooms.
         The study, by Common Sense Media, a San Francisco nonprofit   *5*
group, is the first of its kind since apps became widespread, and the first
to look at screen time from birth. It found that almost half the families
with incomes above $75,000 had downloaded apps specifically for their
young children, compared with one in eight of the families earning less
than $30,000. More than a third of those low-income parents said they   *10*
did not know what an "app"—short for application—was.
   From Biagi. *Media Impact: An Introduction to Mass Media*, 10E © 2011 Cengage Learning.

   a. What is the main idea in this passage? (Hint: Focus on the first paragraph.)

   _____

   b. What details support this idea? Name two.

   _____

   _____

   c. What inferences (conclusions) can you draw from this passage? Name two.

   _____

   _____

3.

The Other Half of Humanity

In 1964, a French wife and mother had to obtain the written permission *1* of her husband to open a bank account in her own name. Ten years later, after a ferocious verbal battle, the French parliament legalized abortions upon the request of the pregnant women. Twenty years after that, women outnumbered men in the parliament. These three facts are as useful as *5* any to symbolize the changes in the status of women brought about by the struggle for women's liberation in the last several decades.

The Second Sex, as Simone de Beauvoir's influential book called women, has been steadily closing the vast gap that once stood between them and men in the social and economic arenas of the Western world. Many if not most *10* countries now have laws on the books (sometimes unenforced) that prohibit paying women less than men for the same work, discriminating on the basis of gender for promotions or entry into a profession, refusing credit to women, denying them contractual rights, denying women custody of minors, and so on. In 2009, women made up 60 percent of all US university graduates—up *15* from 20 percent in the 1950s. Forty-six percent of the students entering US law schools are women, a number that has approximately quadrupled since 1980. By the time this volume appears on the students' desks, it is estimated that females will make up more than one-third of the total numbers of lawyers. *20*

These indications of rapid change are by no means limited to the economic and labor sectors. The formerly normal status of marriage for young women has been radically questioned. About one-quarter of American women between eighteen and forty-five were single (that is, divorced or unmarried) in 1960, whereas more than half were by 2006. More than half *25* of all first marriages end in divorce. In the United States, one-third of all babies are born to unmarried women—up from 8 percent forty years earlier.

From Adler/Pouwels, *World Civilizations*, 6E. © 2012 Cengage Learning.

a. What is the main idea in this passage?

_____

_____

b. What details from the passage support this main idea? Name two.

_____

_____

c. What inferences (conclusions) can you draw from the passage? Name two.

_____

_____

LO7 Improving Vocabulary

To understand and truly benefit from your academic reading, you need to build a fairly strong reading vocabulary, which you will do if you become a regular reader. You also need strategies right now to unlock the meaning of new words, which you are sure to find in college-level texts. Referring to a dictionary is one such strategy, but that can disrupt your reading if you use it too much. Here are other more reader-friendly strategies for understanding new words.

Keeping a Vocabulary Notebook

Proactive means "acting in advance" or "acting before." Keeping a vocabulary notebook is proactive because you are taking control of your vocabulary building. This strategy will prove especially helpful in challenging courses, when you are introduced to many new words. The note cards below show the kinds of information to include for words you list in your notebook.

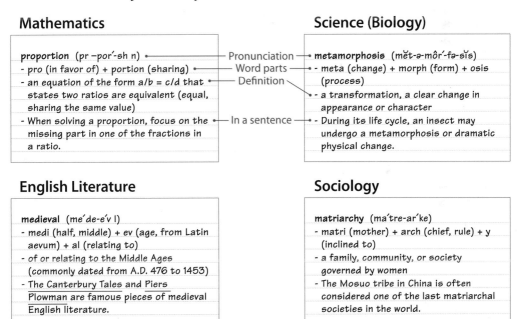

Mathematics

proportion (pr –por´-sh n)
- pro (in favor of) + portion (sharing)
- an equation of the form *a/b = c/d* that states two ratios are equivalent (equal, sharing the same value)
- When solving a proportion, focus on the missing part in one of the fractions in a ratio.

Pronunciation
Word parts
Definition
In a sentence

Science (Biology)

metamorphosis (mĕt-ə-môr´-fə-sĭs)
- meta (change) + morph (form) + osis (process)
- a transformation, a clear change in appearance or character
- During its life cycle, an insect may undergo a metamorphosis or dramatic physical change.

English Literature

medieval (me´de-e´v l)
- medi (half, middle) + ev (age, from Latin aevum) + al (relating to)
- of or relating to the Middle Ages (commonly dated from A.D. 476 to 1453)
- The Canterbury Tales and Piers Plowman are famous pieces of medieval English literature.

Sociology

matriarchy (ma´tre-ar´ke)
- matri (mother) + arch (chief, rule) + y (inclined to)
- a family, community, or society governed by women
- The Mosuo tribe in China is often considered one of the last matriarchal societies in the world.

Identify For each of the following words, create a vocabulary entry like the ones above. Identify the pronunciation and helpful word parts, give a primary definition, and use the word in a sentence. (For assistance, refer to a dictionary and the glossary of word parts on pages 668–676 in your book.)

- censorship
- pathogen
- asteroid
- concentric

Using Context

Instead of skipping new words in your reading, try to figure out what they mean in context—or by looking for clues in the other words and ideas around them. Here is how using context can work:

In some cases, the context clues can be very easy to identify. In the following passage, the word "affiliates" is defined right after the word is mentioned (underlined).

> Broadcast networks can have as many *affiliates* as they want.   *1*
> Affiliates <u>are stations that use network programming but are owned by</u>
> <u>companies other than the networks.</u> No network, however, can have two
> affiliates in the same geographic broadcast area.

In other cases, you must study a text more carefully for context clues. In this passage, an antonym (opposite) suggested in the first part of a sentence (underlined) helps you understand the word "exemptions" in the second part.

> The French peasants slowly became aware of the contrasts between   *1*
> <u>the taxes they had to bear</u> and the *exemptions* enjoyed by the clergy and
> the nobility. When that discontent was later joined by the resentment
> [anger] of the middle-class townspeople, the potential for revolution
> would exist.   *5*

Types of Context Clues

There are many types of context clues, as you will see in the list that follows.

- **Cause-effect relationships:** Suggesting the use of seat belts didn't work, so the state officials made seat-belt use *mandatory*.
- **Definitions built into the text:** Dr. Williams is an *anthropologist*, a person who scientifically studies the physical, social, and cultural development of humans.
- **Comparisons and contrasts:** Lynn Dery lives in New York, so she is used to a fast-paced life; Mandy Williams lives in the country, so she is used to a more *serene* lifestyle.
- **Words in a series:** Spaghetti, lasagna, and *ziti* all have their own special shape.
- **Synonyms (words with the same meaning):** Hector's essay contains too many *banal*, overused phrases.
- **Antonyms (words with the opposite meaning):** Mrs. Wolfe still seemed strong and energetic after the storm, but Mr. Wolfe looked *haggard*.
- **The tone of the text:** The street was filled with *bellicose* protesters who pushed and shoved their way through the crowd. The scene was no longer peaceful and calm, as the marchers promised it would be.

Define Define or explain the italicized word or term in each passage that follows. Also indicate the type of context clue that helped you understand the word.

1.   In 2001 the Federal Bureau of Investigation recorded 9,730 *hate*   *1*
         crimes, or criminal incidents motivated by a person's race, religion, or
         ethnicity. Each incident may involve multiple offenses, such as assault
         and property damage. From Brym/Lie, *Sociology*, 2E. © 2007 Cengage Learning.

Definition/explanation: _____

Type of context clue: _____

2.   To prevent future frostbite incidents, the administration intends   *1*
         to convert several of the existing sidewalks to protected walkways, so
         that students can go from any building on campus to any other building
         without being exposed to *inclement* weather.
         From Parks et al., *A Mathematical View of Our World*, 1E © 2007 Cengage Learning.

Definition/explanation: _____

Type of context clue: _____

3.   The president is the *ultimate* decision maker in military matters and,   *1*
         as such, has the final authority to launch a nuclear strike using missiles
         or bombs. Everywhere the president goes, so too goes the "Football"—a
         briefcase filled with all the codes necessary to order a nuclear attack.
         From Schmidt et al., *American Government and Politics Today, 2013-2014 Edition*, 16E. © 2014 Cengage Learning.

Definition/explanation: _____

Type of context clue: _____

4.   The Blackfoot River flows among beautiful mountain ranges in the   *1*
         west-central part of the US state of Montana. This large *watershed* is
         home to more than 600 species of plants, 21 species of waterfowl, bald
         eagles, peregrine falcons, grizzly bears, and rare species of trout. Some
         species, such as the Howell's gumweed and the bull trout, are threatened   *5*
         with extinction. In other words, this watershed is a precious jewel of
         biodiversity.   From Miller, *Living in the Environment*, 17E. © 2012 Cengage Learning.

Definition/explanation: _____

Type of context clue: _____

Understanding Word Parts

You may have heard of the following terms: *roots* (base words), *prefixes*, and *suffixes*. Many words in our language are made up of combinations of these word parts. (See pages 668–676 for a listing of common word parts.)

- **Roots** like *liber* (as in <u>liber</u>ate) or *rupt* (as in inter<u>rupt</u>) are the starting points for most words.
- **Prefixes** like *anti* (as in <u>anti</u>biotic) or *un* (as in <u>un</u>real) are word parts that come before roots to form new words.
- **Suffixes** like *dom* (as in bore<u>dom</u>) or *ly* (as in hour<u>ly</u>) are word parts that come after roots to form new words.

Sample Words

The following examples show how multiple word parts can be combined to form words.

Transportation combines . . .
- the prefix *trans* meaning "across" or "beyond,"
- the root *port* meaning "carry," and
- the suffix *tion* meaning "act of."

So, *transportation* means "the act of carrying across or beyond."

Biographic combines . . .
- the root *bio* meaning "life,"
- the root *graph* meaning "write," and
- the suffix *ic* meaning "nature of" or "relating to."

So, *biographic* means "relating to writing about real life."

Micrometer combines . . .
- the root *micro* meaning "small" and
- the root *meter* meaning "measure."

So, a *micrometer* is "a device for measuring small distances."

Identify   Using the examples above as a guide, analyze and define the words below.
- mediate (medi + ate)
- portable (port + able)
- interrupt (inter + rupt)
- retrospective (retro + spec + tive)

Within a Text

Note the word *rearmament* in the following passage from a history textbook. You may already know the meaning of this word. If not, studying its parts can help you unlock its meaning.

> The huge road construction and public works programs he [Hitler]   *1*
> began in 1934 absorbed a large portion of the pool of unemployed. With
> *rearmament*, the military was greatly enlarged, and munitions factories
> and their suppliers received government orders.
>
> From Adler/Pouwels, *World Civilizations*, 6E. © 2012 Cengage Learning.

Analysis of the word *rearmament*:

Word parts:

- *Re* is a prefix meaning "again" (see page 669).
- To *arm* is a root or base word meaning "equip or supply with weapons."
- The suffix *ment* basically means "act of" (see page 670).

Definition/explanation of the word:

- *Rearmament* then logically means "the act of arming again."

Practice   Study the italicized word in each of the following passages. Break it into recognizable word parts, explain what each part means, and then define the word. Use the example above as a guide. (Also see pages 668–676.)

1.   Criminologist Travis Hirschi focuses on the reasons why individuals   *1*
do not engage in criminal acts. . . . According to Hirschi, social bonds
promote *conformity* to social norms. The stronger these social bonds . . .
the less likely that any individual will commit a crime.

From Gaines/Miller, *Cengage Advantage Books: Criminal Justice in Action*, 6E. © 2011 Cengage Learning.

Analysis of the word *conformity*:

Word parts: _____

Definition/explanation of the word: _____

2.   Youngsters whose mothers smoked during pregnancy also tend to   *1*
have problems with *hyperactivity*. . . . Some of these behavior problems
persist through the teenage years and even into adulthood.

From Hales, *An Invitation to Health*, 7E. © 2012 Cengage Learning.

Analysis of the word *hyperactivity*:

Word parts: _____

Definition/explanation of the word: _____

Understanding Denotation and Connotation

Denotation

Denotation is the literal or dictionary meaning of a word. For example, the dictionary denotes or defines these words as follows:

- **Abandon** means "to give up or leave."
- **Sag** means "to bend under weight."
- **Fatigue** means "physical weariness."
- **Seeped** means "entered or exited slowly."

Connotation

Connotation refers to the feelings or emotions a word can arouse, such as the negative or bad feelings associated with the word *pig* or the positive or good feelings associated with the word *love*. Note that the underlined words in this passage connote a feeling of disuse, decay, and deterioration:

> The small factory has been <u>abandoned</u> long ago. The roof <u>sags</u> and the walls bow with <u>fatigue</u>. Years have darkened the bricks to the color of <u>dried blood</u>, as though the life of the building has <u>seeped</u> out through the walls. The windows are <u>cracked</u> or <u>broken</u>. . . .   *1*

Practice Read the following passage. Then analyze the underlined words denotatively and connotatively as directed below.

> The <u>rake-thin</u> models who populate modern ads are not promoting good   *1*
> health. They are promoting <u>extreme</u> body shape that is virtually <u>unattainable</u>
> for most people. They do so because it is good business. The fitness, <u>diet</u>,
> <u>low-caloric</u> food, and <u>cosmetic</u> surgery industries do tens of billions of dollars
> of business every year (Hesse-Biber, 1996). Bankrolled by these industries,   *5*
> advertising in the mass media blankets us with images of <u>slim</u> bodies and
> makes these body types appealing.
>
> From Brym/Lie, *Sociology*, 2E. © 2007 Cengage Learning.

Denotative Meaning: Provide dictionary definitions for these three words. (Use the examples above as a guide.)

- unattainable _____
- low-caloric _____
- cosmetic _____

Connotative Meaning: Explain what feeling all the underlined words suggest.

_____

LO8 Reading Graphics

In many of your college texts, a significant portion of the information will be given in charts, graphs, diagrams, and drawings. Knowing how to read these types of graphics, then, is important to your success as a college student. Follow the guidelines below to help you understand graphics.

- **Scan the graphic.** Consider it as a whole to get an overall idea about its message. Note its type (bar graph, pie graph, diagram, table, and so forth), its topic, its level of complexity, and so on.

- **Study the specific parts.** Start with the main heading or title. Next, note any additional labels or guides (such as the horizontal and vertical guides on a bar graph). Then focus on the actual information displayed in the graphic.

- **Question the graphic.** Does it address an important topic? What is its purpose (to make a comparison, to show a change, and so on)? What is the source of the information? Is the graphic out of date or biased in any way?

- **Reflect on its effectiveness.** Explain in your own words the main message of the graphic. Then consider its effectiveness, how it relates to the surrounding text, and how it matches up to your previous knowledge of the topic.

Analysis of a Graphic

Review the bar graph below. Then read the discussion to learn how all of the parts work together.

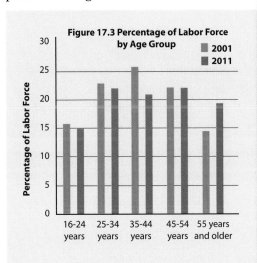

Figure 17.3 Percentage of Labor Force by Age Group

Discussion: This bar graph compares the labor force in 2001 to the labor force in 2011 for five specific age groups. The heading identifies the subject or topic of the graphic. The horizontal line identifies the different age groups, and the vertical line identifies the percentage of the labor force for each group. The key in the upper right-hand corner of the graphic explains the color-coded bars. With all of that information, the graphic reads quite clearly—and many interesting comparisons can be made.

React   Read and analyze the following graphics, answering the questions about each one on your own paper. Use the information on the previous page as a guide.

Graphic 1

1. This graphic is called a pictograph rather than a bar graph. What makes it a "pictograph"?

   _____

   _____

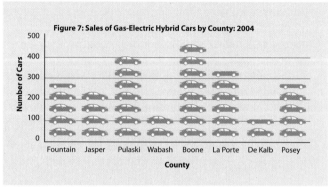

sabri deniz kizil, 2013 / Used under license from Shutterstock.com

2. What is the topic of this graphic?

   _____

3. What information is provided on the horizontal line? On the vertical line?

   _____

4. What comparisons can a reader make from this graphic?

   _____

Graphic 2

1. This graphic is called a line diagram, and it maps a structure. What structure does this diagram map?

   _____

   _____

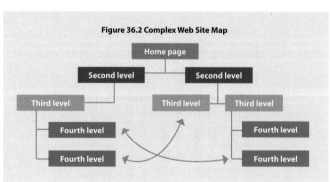

2. From the following items, choose the two working parts in this diagram: *words, lines, symbols.*

3. How are the different navigational choices on a complex Web site shown on this graphic?

   _____

Review and Enrichment

On the next six pages you will review and enrich your understanding of the concepts in this chapter.

Reviewing the Chapter

On your own paper, respond to each set of directions to review the concepts covered in this chapter.

Read to Learn Explain in a few sentences how you should approach your academic reading to get the most out of each assignment. (See page 12.)

_____

_____

Understand the Reading Process List the four steps in the reading process. Identify two things that you should do during each step. (See pages 13–15.)

1. _____

2. _____

3. _____

4. _____

Use Reading Strategies What does it mean to summarize a text? (See page 25.)

_____

Read Critically What does it mean to evaluate a text? (See page 27.)

_____

_____

Draw Inferences What are inferences? (See page 30.)

_____

Improve Vocabulary Explain what it means to use word parts to figure out the meaning of new words. (See page 36.)

_____

_____

Reading

In this section, you will read and react to a personal essay entitled "What Makes a Hero?" Use the steps in the reading process as your reading guide. Also be sure to apply one or more of the reading strategies introduced in this chapter to help you gain a full understanding of the text.

> "As I get older, it is harder to have heroes, but it is sort of necessary."
> —Ernest Hemingway

About the Author

Ted Tollefson is a writer whose essay "Is a Hero Really Nothing but a Sandwich?" appeared in *Utne Reader*, May/June 1993. The selection on the next page comes from this essay.

Prereading

At different points in your life, there's a very good chance you have held certain people in very high regard, perhaps even idolized them as heroes. List a few of your personal heroes, early on and now. Discuss some of your choices.

_____

_____

_____

Identify   Before you read, answer these three questions:

1. What do the title and beginning two paragraphs tell you about the text?

_____

2. Do you think that the author intends to inform, entertain, or persuade?

_____

3. What do you expect to learn?

_____

What do you think?

Consider the quotation at the top of the page: What does it mean to you? Why would heroes be hard to come by with age? Are they necessary?

Reading and Rereading

The author identifies many of the heroes in his life, some of whom you may not be aware of. So be sure to refer to the explanations of the boldfaced words.

As you read the essay, make it your goal to (1) identify the main idea, (2) locate the supporting evidence, and (3) note any secondary ideas that are developed. Consider annotating the text (page 20) during your reading.

What Makes a Hero?

For several years a picture of Warren Spahn of the Milwaukee   *1*
Braves [now the Atlanta Braves] hung on my closet door, one leg poised
in midair before he delivered a smoking fastball. Time passed and
Spahn's picture gave way to others: Elvis, John F. Kennedy, **Carl Jung**,
Joseph Campbell, **Ben Hogan**. These heroic images have reflected back   *5*
to me what I hoped to become: a man with good moves, a sex symbol, an
electrifying orator, a plumber of depths, a teller of tales, a graceful golfer.
Like serpents, we keep shedding the skins of our heroes as we move
toward new phases in our lives.

Like many of my generation, I have a weakness for hero worship. At   *10*
some point, however, we all begin to question our heroes and our need for
them. This leads us to ask: What is a hero? Despite immense differences
in cultures, heroes around the world generally share a number of traits
that instruct and inspire people.

A hero does something worth talking about. A hero has a story of   *15*
adventure to tell and a community who will listen. But a hero goes
beyond mere fame or celebrity. *Heroes serve powers or principles larger
than themselves.* Like high-voltage transformers, heroes take the energy
of higher powers and step it down so that it can be used by ordinary
mortals. *The hero lives a life worthy of imitation.* Those who imitate a   *20*
genuine hero experience life with new depth, zest, and meaning. A sure
test for would-be heroes is what or whom do they serve? What are they
willing to live and die for? If the answer or evidence suggests they serve
only their own fame, they may be celebrities but not heroes. Madonna
and Michael Jackson [now deceased] are famous, but who would claim   *25*
that their adoring fans find life more abundant?

Heroes are catalysts for change. They have a vision from the
mountaintop. They have the skill and the charm to move the masses.
They create new possibilities. Without **Gandhi**, India might still be part
of the British Empire. Without **Rosa Parks** and Martin Luther King Jr.,   *30*
we might still have segregated buses, restaurants, and parks. It may
be possible for large-scale change to occur without charismatic leaders,
but the pace of change would be glacial, the vision uncertain, and the
committee meetings endless.

Though heroes aspire to universal values, most are bound to   35
the culture they came from. The heroes of the Homeric Greeks wept
loudly for their lost comrades and exhibited their grief publicly. A later
generation of Greeks under the **tutelage** of **Plato** disdained this display of
grief as "unmanly."

Though the heroic tradition of white Americans is barely three   40
hundred years old, it already shows some unique and unnerving
features. While most traditional heroes leave home, have an adventure,
and return home to tell the story, American heroes are often homeless.
They come out of nowhere, right what is wrong, and then disappear into
the wilderness. Throughout most of the world, it is acknowledged that   45
heroes need a community as much as a community needs them.

And most Americans seem to prefer their heroes **flawless**, innocent,
forever wearing a white hat or airbrushed features. Character flaws
are held as proof that our heroes aren't really heroes. Several heroes
on my own list have provided easy targets for the purveyors of heroic   50
perfectionism. . . .

American heroes lack a sense of home that might limit and ground
their grandiose ambitions. American heroes avoid acknowledging their
own vices, which makes them more likely to look for somebody else to
blame when things go wrong. Our national heroes seem to be stuck   55
somewhere between **Billy Budd** and the **Lone Ranger**: **pious**, armed
cowboys who are full of energy, hope, and dangerous **naiveté**.

From *Is a Hero Really Nothing but a Sandwich?* by Ted Tollefson, as appeared in *Utne Reader*, May/June 1993, pp 102–103.

Carl Jung
Swiss psychologist

Joseph Campbell
a collector of myths who
was influenced by Jung

Ben Hogan
a great golfer

Gandhi
Indian leader who, through
nonviolent means, gained
India's independence from
Great Britain

Rosa Parks
refused to give up her bus
seat to a white man; helped
trigger the civil rights
movement

tutelage
teaching

Plato
Greek philosopher

flawless
perfect

Billy Budd
a character in a Herman
Melville story whose
innocence arouses the
hatred of the ship's master-
of-arms

Lone Ranger
hero of a television western

pious
religious, devout

naiveté
the state of being
unsophisticated, simple

Reflecting

Practice   Once you complete your reading, answer these questions. Afterward share your responses with your classmates.

1. What main idea is developed in the text?

   _____

   _____

   _____

2. What details support this idea? (Name two.)

   _____

   _____

   _____

3. Is there a secondary important idea that is developed? If so, identify it.

   _____

   _____

   _____

4. What American heroes are mentioned? Name two.

   _____

   _____

5. Has this reading changed or expanded your understanding of the topic? Explain.

   _____

   _____

   _____

6. How would you rate this reading and why?

   Weak ★ ★ ★ ★ ★ Strong

   _____

   _____

Vocabulary Practice

Identify Create a notebook entry for each of the following words. Identify the pronunciation and helpful word parts, give a primary definition, and use the word in a sentence. (See pages 33–37 for help.)

1. catalysts   (line 27)

_____

_____

2. charismatic   (line 32)

_____

_____

3. grandiose   (line 53)

_____

_____

Thinking Critically

Explain Authors often use metaphorical language in their essays and articles, which means they make important points through comparisons. Explain the comparisons made in these sentences from the essay.

1. "Like serpents, we keep shedding the skins of our heroes as we move toward new phases in our lives."

_____

_____

2. "Like high-voltage transformers, heroes take the energy of higher powers and step it down so that it can be used by ordinary mortals."

_____

_____

3

> "The qualities the reader brings to a book can have as much to do with its worth as anything the author puts into it."
> —Norman Cousins

The Traits of Academic Reading

Almost all informational texts are built upon a basic foundation: The writer . . .

- **identifies** a main idea or reason for writing in the opening part;
- **supports, explains,** or **explores** this point in the middle part; and
- **summarizes** or **clarifies** what has been said in the closing part.

There is nothing more essential for you to remember when it comes to your academic reading.

This chapter discusses the traits, or building blocks, of this foundation. Once you understand these traits, you will become a better academic reader, no matter if you are reading an essay, an article, or a textbook chapter. Along the way, you will learn strategies for identifying main ideas, recognizing supporting ideas and patterns of organization, plus much more.

Learning Outcomes

LO1 Topics, main ideas, and supporting details

LO2 Organization

LO3 Voice (tone)

LO4 Word choice and sentences

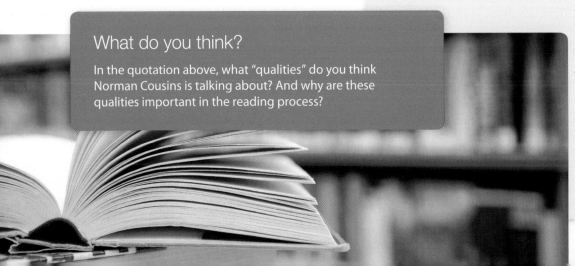

What do you think?

In the quotation above, what "qualities" do you think Norman Cousins is talking about? And why are these qualities important in the reading process?

Falconia, 2013 / Used under license from Shutterstock.com

LO1 Topics, Main Ideas, and Supporting Details

Ideas are the key trait in everything that you read. Every other trait—*organization, voice, word choice*—depends on the ideas. In this section you will learn about identifying the topic, main idea, and supporting details in a text.

Identifying the Topic

Any paragraph, essay, article, or textbook chapter has to be about something, and that something is called the topic. A topic may be a specific person (*Hillary Clinton*), place (*Ellis Island*), object (*vinyl records*), or idea (*trust*). Identifying the topic is naturally one of the important first steps when carrying out a reading assignment. In essence, you need to know what the reading is about.

Luckily, this task is seldom complicated, because the topic is often stated in the title or heading, in the first sentence in a paragraph, or in one of the first few paragraphs in a longer piece of writing. Even when the topic isn't directly stated, you won't have to look too far for clues to help you identify it.

Steps to Follow

1. For paragraphs, read the title and first sentence. If you're still not sure, check the closing sentence, too.

2. For essays, read the title, any headings, and the first paragraph. If you're still not sure, simply keep reading. As you go along, you're sure to identify the topic.

Topics in Context

Topic Stated in a Heading and First Sentence: Here is a passage from a text on criminal justice. The topic—the concept of harm—is stated in the heading and the first sentence. It is also referred to regularly as the text progresses.

Harm

For most crimes to occur, some harm must have been done to a person or   *1*
to a property. A certain number of crimes are actually categorized depending on the harm done to the victim, regardless of the intent behind the criminal act. Take two offenses, both of which involve one person hitting another in the back of the head with a tire iron. In the first instance, the victim dies,   *5* and the offender is charged with murder. In the second, the victim is only knocked unconscious, and the offender is charged with battery. Because the harm in the second instance was less severe, so was the crime with which the offender was charged.

From Gaines/Miller, *Cengage Advantage Books: Criminal Justice in Action,* 6E. © 2011 Cengage Learning.

Topic Stated in the First Sentence: Here is a paragraph from a textbook about cultural anthropology. As you will see, the topic—language—is stated in the first sentence.

> Every language has a logical structure. When people encounter an *1*
> unfamiliar language for the first time, they are confused and disoriented, but
> after becoming familiar with the language, they eventually discover its rules
> and how the various parts are interrelated. All languages have rules and
> principles governing what sounds are to be used and how those sounds are to be *5*
> combined to convey meaning. . . .
>
> From Ferraro/Andreatta, *Cultural Anthropology*, 9E. © 2012 Cengage Learning.

Topic Stated at the End of the First Paragraph in an Essay: In the following excerpt from an essay, the topic—cancer—is identified at the end of the first paragraph.

> Imagine a room containing a large group of people all working hard *1*
> toward the same goal. Each person knows his or her job, does it carefully, and
> cooperates with other group members. Together, they function efficiently and
> smoothly—like a well-oiled machine. Then one worker stops his work and
> steps into someone else's workstation, using those materials to make little *5*
> reproductions of himself. Soon the reproductions spill into other workstations,
> get in the way, and continue to multiply. A human body is like this room, and
> the body's cells are like these workers. If the body is healthy, each cell has a
> necessary job and does it correctly. When a cell begins to function abnormally,
> it can initiate a process that results in cancer. *10*

Delayed Identification of a Topic: In this personal essay, the writer doesn't state his topic—childhood deaths by starvation—until the middle of his essay.

> In two days Kamal would have been four years old, but his wasted body *1*
> now lies under a pile of rocks behind his family's hut.
> Why did Kamal die? The too-easy answer is malnutrition. A lack of
> vitamins and protein opened him to intestinal infection and diarrhea. He could
> have been saved with a simple solution of boiled water, salts, and sugar which *5*
> the UNICEF distributes in a free kit called "oral rehydration therapy" (ORT).
> But Kamal's mother, forced to work 18-hour days at home and in the fields, had
> missed the rural health-care worker's demonstration in the village.
> Why was Kamal malnourished in the first place? He and his six brothers
> and sisters had known hunger all their lives. His father and mother scraped at *10*
> five dry acres of government land, earning no more than $500.00 (US) even in
> a good year. For the past seven years, an unrelenting drought had dried up the
> wells and withered the crops.
> Around the world, according to Roy Prosterman (*The Hunger Project
> Papers*), 18 children like Kamal die of hunger every 60 seconds. In the two *15*
> minutes it may have taken you to read these words, another 36 children died.
> Of all of today's global problems, none can be more tragic than childhood
> deaths by starvation and disease.

Practice Identify the topic in each of the following texts by circling the correct choice. Also state where the topic is first stated.

1.

Ethnicity

Ethnicity can be a powerful draw in terms of customer loyalty and   *1*
community development. Restaurants identified as purveyors of ethnic foods
may appeal to members of a cuisine's ethnic group as well as to others who
are interested in enjoying foods from different cultures. Ethnically based food
service offers comfort and familiarity by providing foods that are considered to   *5*
be part of a culture. From Chon/Maier, *Welcome to Hospitality*, 3E. © 2010 Cengage Learning.

  a. best ethnic restaurants

  b. ethnicity

  c. specialty foods

_____

_____

2.

We Have Been Here Before

Columbus, an Italian, arrived in the New World with a crew of more than   *1*
100 composed of Spaniards, Portuguese, some Jews who had been expelled
from Spain, some convicts, and an Arab brought along to translate anticipated
conversations with Chinese and Japanese—remember where Columbus thought
he was going. Now, about this new American thing, "diversity."   *5*
   Concerning which, Michael Barone says, "We have been here before." As
when Benjamin Franklin, a worrywart, doubted that the Germans who were 40
percent of Pennsylvanians could be assimilated [made similar]. It is generally
wise to believe Barone, the author every two years of "The Almanac of American
Politics," and now of a new book, *The New Americans: How the Melting Pot*   *10*
Can Work Again. To those who say that traditionally white-bread America has
suddenly become multigrain, Barone says: Fiddlesticks.
   American, he says has always been multigrain. . . .

From "We Have Been Here Before" by George Will, *Newsweek*, June 11, 2001.

  a. diversity

  b. Columbus

  c. "The Almanac of American Politics"

_____

_____

3.   Bridewealth is the compensation given upon marriage by the family of the groom to the family of the bride. According to Murdock's "Ethnographic Atlas" (reported in Stephens 1963: 211), approximately 46 percent of all societies give substantial bridewealth payment as a normal part of the marriage process. Although bridewealth is practiced in most regions of the world, it is perhaps most widely found in Africa. . . .

1

5

From Ferraro/Andreatta, *Cultural Anthropology*, 9E. © 2012 Cengage Learning.

a. dowry payments
b. marriage in Africa
c. bridewealth

4.

From *The Big Burn*

On one of the last days of Teddy Roosevelt's time in the White House, the president called in his handpicked successor to talk about plans to run the nation in the second decade of the American century. Despite his girth, William H. Taft was always the smaller man when in Roosevelt's presence, or so he felt. Roosevelt was the human volcano; Taft was a putting green. Roosevelt sucked the air out of a room; Taft tried to be invisible. Roosevelt barked; Taft had a low monotone, punctuated by a random and annoying chuckle. Roosevelt burned two thousand calories before noon and drank his coffee with seven lumps of sugar; Taft was the picture of sloth: multiple chins, a zest for five-course meals and long baths. Sleeping Beauty was the nickname his wife, Nellie, gave him, and oh, how he loved to nap. But to the question of how and where to lead the country, they did not differ, the president believed.

Taft had spent the past three years observing Roosevelt's likes and dislikes, his private quirks and public persona. He took it all in carefully and then projected it back to him, hitting the right notes as Roosevelt probed him on his political beliefs. As such, he seemed to be the perfect successor. Roosevelt was full of energy, at the peak of his power and popularity, but he felt duty-bound to keep the promise he had made to serve only two terms. More than any guiding principle, Will Taft simply was driven by the desire to please the man he considered his closest friend. And so when Roosevelt asked him to the White House in late 1908, after a campaign in which Taft won with the full backing and expert advice of the still-young Roosevelt, the incoming president again said all the right things. Taft had won in a landslide, crushing the perennial Democratic populist William Jennings Bryan.

1

5

10

15

20

From Egan, Timothy. *The Big Burn*. Boston: Houghton Mifflin Harcourt., 2010. Print.

a. Teddy Roosevelt
b. Teddy Roosevelt and William H. Taft
c. William H. Taft

Identifying the Main Idea

Almost every text that you read—be it an essay, an article, or a textbook chapter—develops a **main idea**. The main idea in most paragraphs is stated in the topic sentence. In many essays or articles, the main idea is given in a thesis statement in one of the opening paragraphs. The main idea consists of the topic and usually a particular feeling or idea about that topic.

However, there are times when the main idea is expressed in a summary statement near the closing part of the text. To make things more challenging, the main idea in some essays is implied or suggested rather than directly stated. And some longer, more complicated essays may have more than one main point depending on your **interpretation** of the material. Whatever the case, identifying the main idea (or ideas) is a key task in all of your academic reading.

What the Main Idea Tells You

INSIGHT

An essay needs a specific concept or focus that is developed in the text. A main idea or thesis serves this purpose.

In a *narrative text,* the main idea will tell you what experience the writer is going to share:

> "She told me my grandfather had suffered a stroke during the night and didn't make it."

In an *informational text,* the main idea will tell you what the author is going to explain, illustrate, or discuss:

> "On the surface there's harmony between Latinos and Asians. But there are indications of simmering ethnic-based tensions."

In a *persuasive text,* the main idea will tell you what claim the writer is going to prove or argue for:

> "Barbed hooks should be banned from lure fishing to protect fish that are not yet ready for anglers to keep."

SPECIAL NOTE: The wording of a statement may signal it as the main idea: "This is a tale of two sisters. . . .," "Study after study has shown that . . . ," or "Surprisingly, both [sides] discovered that . . ."

---

interpretation
the act of explaining

Steps to Follow

Follow the steps below to help you identify the main idea or thesis in an essay, an article, or a chapter. In paragraphs, you usually need to look no further than the first sentence.

1. Review the title, any headings, and the first and last paragraphs of the text.

2. Then read the opening part, perhaps the first few paragraphs, to gain a general understanding of the topic.

3. Next, look for a sentence or two in one of the opening paragraphs that seems to direct the writing. (Often, this sentence will come at the end of one of these paragraphs.)

4. Write this statement down, or underline it if you own the text or are reading a copy. (If you can't find such a sentence, try to state the main idea in your own words.)

5. Then continue your initial reading to see if this statement makes sense as the main idea (or at least one of them). Each new paragraph should support or develop it with facts, statistics, examples, and so on.

6. If your thinking changes, identify or write down what you now consider to be the main point.

Topic Sentences and Thesis Statement

A topic sentence or thesis statement usually has two working parts: (1) a specific topic plus (2) a specific feature, feeling, or opinion about it. Here are two examples:

- "Tact (*topic*) is the sensitive handling of situations, even those that are potentially hurtful (*feature*)."
- "Fatherlessness (*topic*) is the most harmful demographic of this generation (*opinion*)."

In Context

Example 1

Study the following paragraph in which the writer describes the sense of taste.

<u>All the flavors that a person can taste are made up of a few taste sensations.</u> In the Western world, people are used to thinking about four tastes: salty, sweet, sour, and bitter. The salty taste comes from substances that include sodium, such as snacks like potato chips or pretzels. The sweet sensation comes from sugars, whether in processed foods like sweetened cereals or naturally occurring in fruit or honey. Sour tastes come from acidic foods such as lemons and grapefruits, and bitter tastes come from alkaline foods such as coffee or dark chocolate. But in the Eastern world, two other taste sensations are recognized. A savory taste comes from amino acids, which are a basic part of meats and proteins. And a spicy taste comes from substances like the capsaicin in hot peppers. Given the savory and spicy nature of Indian, Thai, Chinese, and other Eastern foods, its no wonder that these tastes are recognized. With all the sensations to appeal to, chefs can make every dish a unique and tasty work of art.

1

5

10

Discussion: A paragraph, by definition, is a group of sentences sharing details about a main idea, which is usually stated in the topic sentence. The topic sentence in the above paragraph is underlined. The sentences in the body of the paragraph explain the topic.

Example 2

Examine the first part of this student essay, in which the writer explores alcohol consumption by young adults.

A Shot: The All-Too-Common Cure

Drinking is a serious problem affecting millions of people in the United States. There are, of course, many individual professional people and common workers who come home and relax with a drink or two. For some, these occasional drinks pose no threat; but for others, they lead to serious drinking problems, and eventually to alcoholism, a deadly disease that ruins lives and causes undue suffering. No group seems to be more negatively influenced by drinking than young adults. They often use alcohol for all the wrong reasons.

First, there's the universal understanding that young adults are, by nature, rebellious. Some teens drink to get back at their families. . . .

Conversely, young adults also like to go with the crowd, and drinking is their ticket to acceptance. . . .

Drinking also provides them with the "buzz" that makes social gatherings more fun. . . .

1

5

10

Discussion: In the opening paragraph, general comments about the topic (drinking) introduce the logical thesis (underlined). Each of the next three paragraphs identifies one of the "wrong reasons" for drinking by young adults. So clearly, the underlined statement is the thesis of the essay.

Example 3

Study the title and opening part of the following article in which the writer explores the changes in his childhood neighborhood.

Los Chinos Discover el Barrio

There's a colorful mural on the asphalt playground of Hillside Elementary School, in the neighborhood called Lincoln Heights. Painted on the beige handball wall, the mural is of life-sized youngsters holding hands. Depicted are Asian and Latino kids with bright faces and ear-to-ear smiles. *1*

5

The mural is a mirror of the makeup of the neighborhood today: Latinos living side by side with Asians. But it's not all smiles and happy faces in the Northeast Los Angeles community, located just a couple of miles up Broadway from City Hall. <u>On the surface there's harmony between Latinos and Asians. But there are indications of simmering ethnic-based tensions.</u> *10*

That became clear to me when . . .

Luis Torres, "Los Chinos Discover El Barrio." *Los Angeles Times*, November 14, 1987. Reprinted by permission of the author.

Discussion: The opening paragraph serves as an effective backdrop (contrast) for the underlined idea—that all may not be "smiles" and good times between the Latino and Asian neighbors. The start of the third paragraph indicates that the underlined point will be explored, which, upon reading the essay, proves to be true. So this point is the thesis of the essay.

Example 4

Finally, study the title and opening part of the following article in which the author explores intelligence.

What Is Emotional Intelligence?

Many experts believe that intelligence takes many forms. Rather than a narrow definition of intelligence, they believe in Multiple Intelligences: Linguistic, Logical-Mathematical, Spatial, Kinesthetic, Musical, Interpersonal, Intrapersonal, and Naturalistic. Emotional Intelligence may well be a combination, at least in part, of **intrapersonal** and **interpersonal** intelligences.   5

Emotional intelligence is a set of skills that determines how well you cope with the demands and pressures you face every day. How well do you understand yourself, **empathize** with others, draw on your inner resources, and encourage the same qualities in people you care about? Emotional   10 intelligence involves having people skills, a positive outlook, and the capacity to adapt to change. Emotional intelligence can propel you through difficult situations.

The bottom line? New research links emotional intelligence to college success, and learning about the impact of EI in the first year of college   15 helps students stay in school. . . .

From Staley/Staley, *Annotated Instructor's Edition for Staley's FOCUS on College and Career Success*, 1E. © 2012 Cengage Learning.

Discussion: The underlined statement in the second paragraph answers the question in the title—which suggests that it is the main idea of the text. The third paragraph indicates that the underlined idea will be explored in the main part of the text.

intrapersonal
having to do with a person's inner thoughts and feelings

interpersonal
having to do with the relationships between people

empathize
imagine what another person feels

Practice Identify the main idea or thesis in each essay that follows. Remember that the thesis can appear anywhere in the opening part, and it may be more than one sentence. If you can't find such a statement, state it below in your own words. Then explain each of your choices.

Tip

Refer to the guidelines on page 53 to help you find the main point in each essay.

Practice 1

Ancient Times

In primitive times, the common belief was that disease and illness *1*
were caused by evil spirits and demons. Treatment was directed toward
eliminating the evil spirits. As civilizations developed, changes occurred as
people began to study the human body and make observations about how it
functions. *5*

Religion played an important role in health care. A common belief was
that illness and disease were punishments from the gods. Religious rites
and ceremonies were frequently used to eliminate evil spirits and restore
health. Exploring the structure of the human body was limited because
most religions did not allow dissection, or cutting apart of the body. For *10*
this reason, animals were frequently dissected to learn about different
body parts.

The ancient Egyptians were the first people to record health
records. It is important to remember that many people could not read;
therefore, knowledge was limited to an educated few. Most of the records *15*
were recorded on stone and were created by priests, who also acted as
physicians. . . .

From Simmers, *Diversified Health Occupations*, 7E. © 2009 Cengage Learning.

Main point (thesis): _____

_____

_____

_____

Explain your choice: _____

_____

Practice 2

One-of-a-Kind Character(s)

Mystery books are hugely popular. In fact, they are so popular that a   *1*
reader can find a mystery set in just about any time and place. There are
mysteries that seem very real, and others that are more imaginative. What
all mysteries have in common is a main detective or investigator that leads
the reader through the mystery. The most famous mysteries have a one-of-   *5*
a-kind main character leading the investigation.

Many mystery experts feel that Arthur Conan Doyle created the most
famous detective of all, Sherlock Holmes. The mysterious Holmes hides
out in his flat on Baker Street in London where he conducts experiments,
reads, and occasionally goes into a funk (and smokes opium). His only   *10*
friend and companion is the understanding Dr. Watson. Holmes is a very
serious man with dark hair and piercing eyes. Holmes uses his great
powers of observation and deduction to solve each mystery.

Another British writer, Agatha Christie, invented the famous amateur
detective Jane Marple in the 1920s. Miss Marple is an elderly woman   *15*
residing in a small village in England. She has the personality of a sweet
aunt or grandmother. Miss Marple is a loner like Holmes, but she is very
personable and understanding in social situations. While Holmes busies
himself in his laboratory, Miss Marple works in her garden. Christie
develops each mystery so Miss Marple just happens to appear at the site   *20*
of crime. She snoops around, listens, asks questions, and eventually solves
each crime. . . .

These examples show that the most popular mysteries begin and end
with a special investigator. Each new mystery allows this individual to put
his or her special talents into action to solve a crime that no one else can   *25*
figure out. Readers enjoy each new opportunity to see how their favorite
investigator does the job.

Main point (thesis): _____

_____

_____

_____

Explain your choice: _____

_____

Practice 3

"When Greed Gives Way to Giving"

In the flurry of life, you probably missed this story. I almost did. And   *1*
that would have been too bad.

Over in Belleville, Minnesota, a 67-year-old man named Bob
Thompson sold his road-building company for $422 million back in July. He
did not, as we would expect, buy himself a jet or an island, not even a new   *5*
home. Instead, Thompson decided to share the wealth.

He divided $128 million among his 550 workers. Some checks exceeded
annual salaries. And for more than 80 people, the bonus went beyond their
wildest expectations. They became millionaires. Thompson even included
some retirees and widows in his plan. What's more, he paid the taxes on   *10*
those proceeds—about $25 million.

Employees were so flabbergasted that the wife of an area manager
tearfully said: "I think the commas are in the wrong place."

The commas were right where they belonged. Thompson had made
sure of that, had made sure, too, that not one of the workers would lose   *15*
their jobs in the buyout.

I sat at the breakfast table stunned. I just don't know too many people
or companies that would do something like that. Sure, many employers
offer profit-sharing and stock-option plans. But outright giving? Nah . . .

Main Point: _____

_____

_____

_____

Explain your choice: _____

_____

Implied Main Ideas

As is mentioned on page 52, there are times when the main idea is implied or suggested rather than directly stated. You will know that this is the case if no one sentence seems to direct the writing. When this occurs, follow these steps:

Steps to Follow

1. Identify the topic in the first reading.

2. Pay close attention to each set of details in additional readings.

3. Write down the important idea that can "cover" all of the details.

4. Read the paragraph again to make sure that this idea accurately covers the details. (Revise your statement as needed.)

Implied Main Idea in Context: Example 1

This paragraph is about an eating disorder, but the main idea about this topic is not stated. Read this text and then see below how the implied main idea is identified.

> Every fiber and cell of my body was obsessed with the numbers on the scale   1
> and how much fat I could pinch on my thigh. I fought my sisters for control of the TV
> to do my exercise programs. The cupboards were stacked with cans of diet mixes,
> the refrigerator full of diet drinks. Hidden in my underwear drawer were stacks of
> diet pills that I popped along with my vitamins. At my worst, I would quietly excuse   5
> myself from family activities to turn on the bathroom faucet full blast and vomit
> into the toilet. Every day I stood in front of the mirror, a ritual not unlike brushing
> my teeth, and studied my body. I was never, ever small enough.

- **Topic:** Eating disorder (anorexia)

- **Key details:** Weight a worry, insistent about exercising, using diet products

- **Idea that covers the details:** The person suffered from a serious eating disorder (anorexia).

- **Implied main idea:** I became a victim of anorexia.

Example 2

Here is a multi-paragraph text about physical activity. While the topic is easy to identify, the main idea isn't directly stated. Read this text and then see below how the implied main idea is identified.

To Work Out or Not to Work Out

The Greek philosopher Plato once said, "Lack of activity destroys the good condition of every human being." The American comedian Phyllis Diller once joked, "My idea of exercise is a good brisk sit." ¹

Diller's attitude aligns with someone living a sedentary lifestyle. A person with a sedentary lifestyle exercises fewer than three times per week. This type of lifestyle is linked to weight gain and an increased risk of developing diseases such as type 2 diabetes. ⁵

A second level of physical activity is known simply as "lifestyle active." This level describes a person who performs everyday lifestyle activities such as walking to and from the grocery store, doing yard work, or playing pick-up basketball. Engaging in regular lifestyle activities can help control cholesterol levels and reduce body fat. ¹⁰

Someone who follows a cardiorespiratory exercise program for 20 to 60 minutes, three to five days per week, lives a moderate physical lifestyle, a third level of physical activity. This type of person might be a regular runner, weight lifter, or power walker. A moderate physical lifestyle helps a person become physically fit while reducing the risk of chronic diseases. ¹⁵

Finally, the highest level of physical activity is a vigorous physical lifestyle. People on this level exercise 20 to 60 minutes most days of the week and follow a routine of aerobic exercises, strength training, and stretching exercises. A vigorous physical lifestyle achieves the same benefits of moderate physical activities, while also promoting a greater level of fitness. ²⁰

Many factors contribute to a person's level of physical activity—work environment, family obligations, and other personal responsibilities. Depending on the time of year, a person may live a moderate physical lifestyle one week and a sedentary lifestyle the next week. What's important, of course, is to live a healthy lifestyle. ²⁵

- **Topic:** Physical activity practiced by people

- **Key details:** Explanations of sedentary lifestyle, "lifestyle active," moderate physical lifestyle, and vigorous physical lifestyle

- **Idea that covers the details:** There are different levels of physical activity.

- **Implied main idea:** Different people pursue different levels of physical activity.

Practice   Carefully read the following excerpts. Then identify the implied main idea by filling in the chart that follows. (See the example on the previous page for help.)

1.   The most frequently thrown pitch is a fastball. As its name suggests,   *1*
fastballs travel at the highest velocity of any pitch. Generally speaking, a
fastball travels on a straight line. A second type of pitch, a changeup, is used
to trick hitters into thinking it is a fastball. However, a changeup is thrown
much slower and tails slightly downward. The curveball is a third pitch. It is   *5*
hard to hit because it travels with topspin that it causes it to break sharply
both laterally and downward. A curveball is slower than a fastball but faster
than a changeup. Another common pitch called the slider breaks laterally and
downward. However, its break is shorter than a curve and it is faster. A skilled
pitcher will master at least two of these pitches.   *10*

Topic: _____

Key details: _____

Implied idea that "covers" the details: _____

Implied main idea: _____

2.   The word *ethics* derives from the Greek word *ethos*, meaning the guiding   *1*
spirit or traditions that govern a culture. Part of America's culture is the
unique protection offered to journalists by the First Amendment of the US
Constitution, so any discussion of ethics and the American media acknowledges
the cultural belief that the First Amendment privilege carries with it special   *5*
obligations. Among these obligations are professional ethics, the rules or
standards governing the conduct of the members of a profession. . . . When
journalists make the wrong ethical choices, the consequences can be very
damaging and very public. "It may well be that if journalism loses touch with
ethical choices, it will then cease to be of use to society, and cease to have any   *10*
real reason for being," writes media ethics scholar John Hulteng. "But that, for
the sake of all of us, must never be allowed to happen." Journalists sometimes
make poor ethical judgments because they work quickly and their actions
can be haphazard because the lust to be first with a story can override the
desire to be right . . . and because journalists sometimes are insensitive to the   *15*
consequences of their stories for the people they cover.

From Biagi. *Media Impact: An Introduction to Mass Media*, 10E © 2011 Cengage Learning.

Topic: _____

Key details: _____

Implied idea that "covers" the details: _____

Implied main idea: _____

3.   Many young people socialize in groups until a couple pairs off into a   *1*
romantic relationship. Rather than the conventional dinner and a movie,
college students may just get together to hang out. Is one person interested in
something more? Is the other? Often it can take a while for couples to figure
out if they are in fact dating. With more people remaining single longer, the   *5*
search for a good date has become more complex. Singles bars have become
less popular; cafes, Laundromats, health clubs, and bookstores have become
more acceptable as places to meet new people.

By dating, you can learn how to make conversation, get to know more
about others as well as yourself, and share feelings, opinions, and interests.   *10*
In adolescence and young adulthood, dating also provides an opportunity for
exploring your sexual identity. Some people date for months and never share
more than a good-night kiss. Others may fall into bed together before they fall
in love or even "like" [one another].

Separating your emotional feelings about someone you're dating from your   *15*
sexual desire is often difficult. The first step to making responsible sexual
decisions is respecting your sexual values and those of your partner. If you
care about the other person—not just his or her body—and the relationship
you're creating, sex will be an important, but not the all-important, factor
while you're dating.   From Hales, *An Invitation to Health*, 7E. © 2012 Cengage Learning.   *20*

Topic: _____

Key details: _____

Implied idea that "covers" the details: _____

Implied main idea: _____

4.   The incubator at the University of Northern Iowa invites student   *1*
entrepreneurs to apply for a semester of on-campus assistance, including legal
and accounting services, management training, and access to seed funds.
Carlos Arguello was the first student entrepreneur to "graduate" from this
incubator. . . .   *5*

At the University of Wisconsin-Madison, student entrepreneurs compete
for six spaces in the on-campus incubator by submitting a written application
and making a presentation to the Student Business Incubator Board. At
the University of Michigan, the TechArb incubator houses up to 12 student-
owned high-tech businesses at a time. One recent tenant was Mobil33t,   *10*
which designed the iPhone app DoGood to encourage people to do a good deed
everyday.   From Pride/Hughes/Kapoor, *Foundations of Business*, 3E. © 2013 Cengage Learning

Topic: _____

Key details: _____

Implied idea that "covers" the details: _____

Implied main idea: _____

Recognizing and Analyzing Supporting Details

While the main idea or thesis directs a text, the supporting information determines its effectiveness. As author Donald Murray states, "The writer writes with information, and if there is no information, there will be no effective writing." To appreciate the value of a reading assignment, you need to recognize and analyze the supporting ideas.

Recognizing the Types of Support

The information on the next two pages identifies the types of support that is often included in informational and persuasive texts. The examples come from "Yes, Accidents Happen. But Why?" by Robert Strauss. The main point of the article is that it is hard to determine the cause of automobile accidents.

- **Facts and statistics** give specific details about a main point or topic.

> Drivers ages 18 to 20 were up to four times more likely to have an inattention-related accident than older drivers.

- **Anecdotes** provide a slice of life to illustrate something.

> When Fred Mannering takes his vintage MG sports car out for a spin, he always leaves plenty of room between the car in front of him and the MG. He brakes slowly and deliberately. He rarely speeds, and if he were to go fast, it would be only on a superhighway with little traffic.

- **Quotations** share the specific thoughts of people knowledgeable about the main point.

> "My other car is newer, with good antilock brakes and air bags, so I don't take nearly as much care," said Dr. Mannering, a Purdue University professor of civil engineering who studies the causes and results of traffic accidents.

Inara Prusakova, 2013 / Used under license from Shutterstock.com

■ **References** to experts or studies add authority to an essay.

> Dr. Mannering's study of accidents in Washington State from 1992 to 1997, a period during which air bags and antilock brakes became prevalent, showed that . . .

■ **Analysis** shows the author's critical thinking about a topic.

> In that way, he may reflect the behavior of the average driver, governed by hard-to-quantify influences.

■ **Explanations** move the discussion along.

> Insurance companies, carmakers, inventors, safety advocates and clearly drivers themselves all have an interest in learning about what might reduce the number of accidents.

■ **Examples** demonstrate or show something.

> A driver is unlikely, for one, to tell an officer that he was using a cell phone, especially if he thinks it will increase his liability.

Additional Support

Listed below are other types of support that you may find in your reading assignments.

■ **Analogies** compare something unfamiliar with something familiar.
■ **Definitions** explain complex terms.
■ **Descriptions** or observations show how something or someone appears.
■ **Reasons** answer the question "Why?" about something.
■ **Experiences** share events in the writer's life.
■ **Reflections** offer the writer's personal thoughts or feelings.

INSIGHT ——————————————————————————————

A text may contain any number and combination of supporting details. Knowing this will help you follow its development.

Supporting Details in Context

This paragraph from an essay entitled "Chinese Place, American Space" by Yi-Fu Tuan develops a main point about the traditional Chinese home using *description, explanation,* and *analysis.*

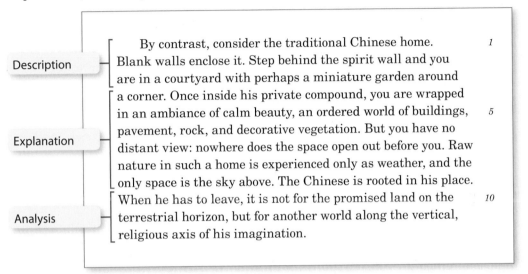

Description

> By contrast, consider the traditional Chinese home.   *1*
> Blank walls enclose it. Step behind the spirit wall and you
> are in a courtyard with perhaps a miniature garden around

Explanation

> a corner. Once inside his private compound, you are wrapped
> in an ambiance of calm beauty, an ordered world of buildings,   *5*
> pavement, rock, and decorative vegetation. But you have no
> distant view: nowhere does the space open out before you. Raw
> nature in such a home is experienced only as weather, and the
> only space is the sky above. The Chinese is rooted in his place.

Analysis

> When he has to leave, it is not for the promised land on the   *10*
> terrestrial horizon, but for another world along the vertical,
> religious axis of his imagination.

This paragraph from a student essay entitled "Nuclear Is Not the Answer" develops the main point about the advantages of nuclear power using *statistics, examples,* and a *quotation.*

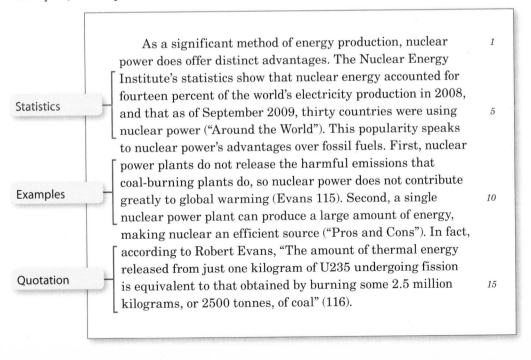

> As a significant method of energy production, nuclear   *1*
> power does offer distinct advantages. The Nuclear Energy

Statistics

> Institute's statistics show that nuclear energy accounted for
> fourteen percent of the world's electricity production in 2008,
> and that as of September 2009, thirty countries were using   *5*
> nuclear power ("Around the World"). This popularity speaks
> to nuclear power's advantages over fossil fuels. First, nuclear

Examples

> power plants do not release the harmful emissions that
> coal-burning plants do, so nuclear power does not contribute
> greatly to global warming (Evans 115). Second, a single   *10*
> nuclear power plant can produce a large amount of energy,
> making nuclear an efficient source ("Pros and Cons"). In fact,

Quotation

> according to Robert Evans, "The amount of thermal energy
> released from just one kilogram of U235 undergoing fission
> is equivalent to that obtained by burning some 2.5 million   *15*
> kilograms, or 2500 tonnes, of coal" (116).

Lastly, the beginning of an essay by Patricia O'Hara illustrates how she developed her attitude and approach to a particular group of people. Notice how she uses examples to draw the reader in and introduce her topic, then transitions to analysis.

Charity Means You Don't Pick and Choose

Examples

"If you're not going to eat that, little boy, I will," said the man sitting [1] on the sidewalk to my son, who was holding a doggie bag of restaurant leftovers. It was the first time my son had ever seen a homeless person. He was 5 years old, and we were spending the weekend visiting museums in Washington, D.C. It was a March night of unusually raw [5] weather—not a night to be sitting on a cold, hard sidewalk. I tightened my grasp on my son's hand as I made eye contact with the man.

"Spare anything, ma'am?"

My son looked up at me uneasily, so I left him with my husband and went over to the man, dollar extended. He thanked me and asked my son [10] again for his doggie bag. I motioned him over, nodding my assurances. "I didn't finish my steak sandwich," my son told him proudly, as he handed the man his bag. The man thanked him and said, "Be good to your mommy."

At just that moment a father and his two teenage sons walked past and, without breaking his stride, barked out: "It'd be better if they got a [15] job!"

Transition

I was startled by the intensity of the man's disapproval, but I, too, have had doubts about offering handouts to the homeless. Under the watchful eyes of my child, I chose the action that I hoped would speak to my son about the principles of charity I hold dear, but the truth is, my [20] decision to give has seldom been clear-cut.

Analysis

Like most people, I'm more comfortable giving when the people on the receiving end are anonymous. I happily participate in the clothing drives sponsored by my son's school, and I drop my spare change in the big metal kettle at the mall, where a man dressed like Santa Claus rings [25] his bell and smiles at shoppers.

Giving directly to the street person shambling across my pathway— well, that's another matter. Hollywood tends to portray the homeless as lovable rogues (think Eddie Murphy in *Trading Places*), but in real life, the person asking for money is often suffering the effects of mental [30] illness or addiction. I'm not proud to admit it, but even the few seconds it takes to look the other person in the eye, extend my hand and offer some change can feel like more of a connection than I want to make.

Practice In each excerpt below, identify the type of support illustrated by the underlined information. Use pages 65–66 as a guide. (The first answer is provided for you.)

1. Slavery in the United States is the granting of that power by which one man exercises and enforces a right of property in the body and soul of another. The condition of a slave is simply that of the brute beast. . . .

    —Frederick Douglass

    <u>Definition</u>

2. All vegetarians are unique, with unique reasons for eating what they eat. For example, many see animals as more than meat—but as creatures with intelligence and feelings.

    —Rob King

3. But the sun's rays do not present an unmitigated threat. As it falls on the skin, sunshine converts a fatty substance in the epidermis into vitamin D. The blood carries vitamin D from the skin to the intestines where it plays a vital role in the absorption of calcium. . . .

    —Marvin Harris

4. In Iowa City in 1963, I married a fellow student, an American of Canadian parentage. . . . I was prepared for (and even welcomed) the emotional strain that came with marrying outside my ethnic community. In 33 years of marriage, we have lived in every part of North America. By choosing a husband who was not my father's selection, I was opting for fluidity, self-invention, blue jeans and T-shirts, and renouncing 3,000 years (at least) of caste-observant, "pure culture" marriage in the Mukherjee family. . . .

    —Bharati Mukherjee

5. Plants can't run away from a threat but they can stand their ground. "They are very good at avoiding getting eaten," said Linda Walling of the University of California, Riverside. . . .

    —Natalie Angier

Practice   In the following essay, Rob King discusses an invasive species in the Florida Everglades. Try to identify different types of support used in each paragraph. (Work on this activity with a classmate if your instructor allows it.)

Ban Burmese Pythons

Reports show some 144,000 pythons have been imported into the   1
United States, many of which end up in homes of irresponsible pet owners.
"All of the Burmese pythons that we see in the park are a product of the
international pet trade," said Skip Snow, a wildlife biologist at Everglades
National Park. The problem is many pet owners don't fully understand the   5
responsibility of taking care of a python. Often the python, which grows up
to between 10 and 20 feet, becomes too big and too expensive to be kept in
a home. In the end, the owner releases the pet into the wild.

_____

_____

It is in the wild where Burmese pythons are causing havoc. The
tropical environment of the Everglades provides perfect conditions for the   10
pythons to breed and feed. With no natural competitor, the strong and
stealthy python is feeding at will on native Everglades species. Scientists
worry that the ecological effects could be devastating. Second to habitat
loss, invasive species are the leading cause of species endangerment.

_____

_____

To be fair, there are no doubt thousands of responsible pet owners   15
across the United States. But the drawbacks of owning Burmese pythons
outweigh the benefits. These species are not meant to be pets. If the United
States wants to maintain its fragile Southern ecosystem, it should take a
hard look at making the importation of Burmese pythons illegal. . . .

_____

_____

Analyzing the Support

Recognizing the different details in a text is only half the story. You also need to determine their effectiveness. Reading without careful analysis of the details is like attempting to bake something without thoughtful consideration of the ingredients and the process: The outcome will be questionable at best.

A Guide to Careful Analysis

Use the following questions to guide your analysis of the support in a particular text. Your answers will help connect you to the reading and judge its worthiness.

Questions to Ask

1. What supporting evidence is especially strong? Why?
   _____

2. Does this information seem reliable and well researched? Explain.
   _____

3. What evidence, if any, is not very effective? Why?
   _____

4. How would you rate the overall quality of the supporting information and why?

   Weak ★ ★ ★ ★ ★ Strong
   _____

5. What have you learned from this text?
   _____

6. What questions do you still have about the topic?
   _____

INSIGHT

Asking and answering questions like those above engages you in the reading and learning process. But you must consider each one carefully.

> "The book to read is not the one [that] thinks for you, but the one [that] makes you think."
> —Harper Lee

Analysis in Action

Here is a paragraph that explores and defines the term *utopia*. The main idea or topic sentence is underlined. The analysis follows the paragraph.

Looking for Utopia

Definition

Everyone wishes to find a perfect place—a utopia that has no crime and no disease, where everyone is happy, healthy, wealthy, and wise. In fact, the word "utopia" would seem to mean "good place," coming from the Greek "eu" (good) and "topos" (place). However, the prefix in Greek is not "eu" but "ou," which means "not" or "no." That's right; "utopia" means "no place." Sir Thomas More   *1*

Reference to an expert

coined the term in 1516, writing a book about a perfect place that didn't exist. His book was a satire, trying to show that a utopia wasn't possible. That didn't stop a number of utopian movements   *5*

Example

from springing up. In fact, one utopian community established in New Harmony, Indiana, proudly announced that it was based on ideas commended by Sir Thomas More. This 2,000-person communal city banned money but quickly dissolved due to   *10*

Quotation

quarreling. Nathaniel Hawthorne tells in *The Scarlet Letter* why such utopians are bound to fail: "The founders of any new colony, whatever Utopia of human virtues and happiness they originally project, have invariably recognized it among their earliest practical necessities to allot a portion of the virgin soil as a cemetery, and another portion as the site of a prison." In other words, no utopia can exist as long as any humans are in it.   *15*

Sample Analysis

Main idea as stated in the topic sentence (underlined above): Everyone desires a perfect place, a utopia.

1. What supporting information is especially strong? Why?

   At the start, the writer explains the history of the term. A reference to Sir Thomas More, the person that coined the term, supports the idea that a utopia is impossible. A real-life example of a failed utopia in New Harmony, Indiana, reinforces the true meaning of the term. Then a quotation from Nathaniel Hawthorne adds further support and authority.

2. Is this information reliable and well researched? Explain.

    Yes, all of the information appears worthy and believable. The

    history of the word and its first use is accurate (as a collegiate

    dictionary shows). The story of New Harmony is accurate

    as well and can be checked on the Internet. In addition, the

    quotation from Nathaniel Hawthorne can be verified online.

3. What evidence, if any, is not very effective? Why?

    There are no apparent weaknesses in the supporting

    information. Each new detail is important and trustworthy.

4. How would you rate the overall quality of the supporting
    information and why?

    Weak ★   ★   ★   ★ (★) Strong

    The supporting information is strong because it presents a

    thoughtful and believable picture of an unfamiliar term. I now

    have a better understanding of "utopia"—an idea that I have

    heard before but never really thought about.

5. What have you learned from this text?

    I learned that the idea of a utopia or perfect world has a

    long history, and that great thinkers like Sir Thomas More

    and Nathaniel Hawthorne have believed that such a place is

    impossible as long as it is populated by normal people.

6. What questions do you still have about the topic?

    What other important attempts have been made? What is there

    about experimental groups that leads to disharmony?

Practice   Analyze the following paragraph about the use of wind farms for energy. To get started, carefully read the paragraph; then underline the topic sentence (main point) and study the different types of support. Finally, answer the analysis questions below.

Support Wind Farm Energy

To counteract its dependence on fossil fuels, the United States must   1
invest in wind farms for its energy needs. A wind farm is made up of a
group of large wind turbines, which convert wind into energy. The benefits
of wind farms are numerous. First, wind is a free and renewable source of
energy. In comparison, fossil fuels like oil and coal are limited in supply   5
and cost money to extract from the earth. Second, wind farms are a clean
energy source. Unlike power plants, which emit dangerous pollutants,
wind farms release no pollution into the air or water, meaning less smog,
less acid rain, and fewer greenhouse emissions. And then there's this:
the American Wind Energy Association reports that running a single   10
wind turbine has the potential to displace 2,000 tons of carbon dioxide,
or the equivalent of one square mile of forest trees. But despite being the
fastest growing energy source in the US, wind energy accounts for only
1.5 percent of power supplied in the country. If the United States wants to
limit carbon emissions and lessen its dependence on fossil fuels, it must act   15
now and invest more money in wind farms. The answer is in the air.

Analysis Questions

1. What main idea is stated in the topic sentence or thesis statement?

   _____

2. What supporting evidence is especially strong? Why?

   _____

3. Is this information reliable and well researched? Explain.

   _____

4. What evidence, if any, is not very effective? Why?

   _____

5. How would you rate the overall quality of the supporting information and why?

   Weak ★ ★ ★ ★ ★ **Strong**

   _____

6. What have you learned from this text? What questions do you still have about the topic?

   _____

Special Challenge   Analyze the essay "To Work Out or Not to Work Out" on page 318 by answering the questions above about it.

LO2 Organization

Ideas and organization work hand in hand to create meaning. It would be almost impossible to understand the ideas in a text if it didn't follow a logical pattern of organization.

Common Patterns of Organization

Factual texts may follow one of these basic patterns. Knowing how these patterns work will help you follow the ideas in a particular text.

- **Chronological:** Essays that recall experiences or explain how something works, or how to do something, usually follow chronological or time order.

- **Spatial:** Essays that describe something or someone are often organized spatially or by location, working from top to bottom, right to left, and so on.

- **Logical:** Essays that simply present supporting ideas in a sensible or reasonable order are organized logically.

- **Cause-effect:** Essays that explain the relationship between causes and effects usually explore the causes first, then the effects.

- **Comparison:** Essays that share the similarities and differences between two ideas may discuss one subject first, then the next subject; may discuss all of the similarities between the two and then their differences; or may make a point-by-point comparison.

- **Problem-solution:** Essays that explore a particular problem often begin with a summary of the problem, follow with possible solutions, and then focus on the best solution.

- **Order of importance (argumentative):** Essays that support a claim may be organized from the most important argument to the least important, or the other way around.

INSIGHT ————————————————————————————————————

While a text usually follows one main pattern, it may use other patterns in a few specific parts.

The Patterns in Action

Each paragraph that follows demonstrates how a common pattern of organization is used to arrange a writer's ideas. (All of the paragraphs come from longer pieces of writing.)

Chronological

This paragraph comes from an essay entitled "Behold the Power of Cheese." The writing explains a process for making cheese. (The words in italics show that time order is used.)

Cheese making starts by heating the milk to kill off any unsafe   *1*
bacteria. *Once* the milk is heated, a starter culture is added to curdle it.
The culture contains different enzymes and bacteria that give cheese its
unique flavor. *Next,* the cheese sits for a day, until the milk has curdled
into solids. The solids are called *curds,* while the leftover liquid is called   *5*
whey. After the cheese maker separates the curds from the whey, the
process continues by reheating the curds, letting them settle, and stirring
away as much liquid as possible. This step is repeated until the cheese
maker believes the cheese is sufficiently solid. *When* the cheese solidifies,
it is poured into molds of different shapes and sizes. *Finally,* the cheese is   *10*
placed in cooler temperatures so that it can ripen.

Cause-Effect

This paragraph by Laura Black identifies the causes of hypothermia in the topic sentence; the rest of the paragraph focuses on the effects of this condition. (The words in italics indicate that cause-effect order is used.)

Even a slight drop in the normal human body temperature of 98.6   *1*
degrees Fahrenheit *causes* hypothermia. Often produced by accidental
or prolonged exposure to cold, the condition forces all bodily functions
to slow down. The heart rate and blood pressure decrease. Breathing
becomes slower and shallower. As the body temperature drops, these *effects*   *5*
become even more dramatic until it reaches somewhere between 88 and 82
degrees Fahrenheit and the person lapses into unconsciousness. When the
temperature reaches between 65 and 59 degrees Fahrenheit, heart action,
blood flow, and electrical brain activity stop. Normally such a condition
would be fatal. However, as the body cools down, the need for oxygen also   *10*
slows down. A person can survive in a deep hypothermic state for an hour
or longer and be revived without serious complications.

Logical

This paragraph comes from "Causes of Tropical Deforestation Are Varied and Complex". (See pages 337–338.) The details are organized logically, meaning that they naturally follow each other.

According to a 2005 study by forest scientists, widespread fires in the   1
Amazon basin are changing weather patterns by raising temperatures and
reducing rainfalls. The resulting droughts dry out the forests and make
them more likely to burn—another example of a runaway positive feedback
loop. This process is converting large deforested areas of tropical forests to   5
tropical grassland (savanna)—another example of an ecosystem reaching
an irreversible ecological tipping point. Models project that if current
burning and deforestation rates continue, 20–30 percent of the Amazon
basin will be turned into savanna in the next 50 years, and most of it could
become savanna by 3980.   10

Patterns in Essays

Of course, essays and other multi-paragraph works also follow common organizational patterns. Below are four examples of essays from this book that follow specific patterns of organization.

- "The ABC Daily To-Do List" on pages 280–281 is a process essay telling someone how to manage daily tasks, and it follows chronological order (step 1, step 2, etc.).

- "Hemispheric Specialization" on pages 366–367 is a comparison essay explaining the differences between the right brain and the left brain. It follows a subject-by-subject pattern of organization.

- "Ancient Times" on pages 222–223 is an illustration essay, providing examples arranged logically, or in a sensible way.

- "Elizabeth I of England" on pages 342–343 is a cause-effect essay discussing the reign of the first Queen Elizabeth. More specifically, the supporting details explore her ascendancy to the throne and the effects of her leadership.

Practice   Identify the main pattern of organization used in the following texts. Use pages 75–77 as a guide for your work. Explain your choices.

1. The production of cement is a complicated process. The raw materials that go into cement consist of about 60 percent lime, 25 percent silica, and 5 percent alumina. The remaining 10 percent is a varying combination of gypsum and iron oxide. First, the mixture is ground up into very fine particles and fed into a kiln. Cement kilns, the largest pieces of moving machinery used in the industry, are colossal steel cylinders lined with firebricks. They can be 25 feet in diameter and up to 750 feet long. The kiln is built at a slant and turns slowly as the cement mix makes its way down from the top end. A flame at the bottom heats the kiln to temperatures of up to 3,000 degrees Fahrenheit. When the melted cement compound emerges from the kiln, it cools into little marble-like balls called clinker. Then the clinker is ground to a consistency finer than flour and packaged as cement.

Pattern of organization:

_____

_____

_____

2. Trees make up an essential part of the earth's ecosystem, but rapid deforestation is having harmful effects on the planet. Deforestation refers to the clearance of forests through logging and burning. The main cause of deforestation is the use of trees for lumber and fuel. Forests are also cut down to make room for farming. But while deforestation can boost struggling economies, it is also causing harm to the environment. Adverse effects of deforestation include erosion of soil, disruption of the water cycle, loss of biodiversity, and flooding and drought. The most harmful effect, though, may be on the climate. Deforestation leads to a greater accumulation of carbon dioxide in the atmosphere, which in turn may warm the planet. Those who practice deforestation must determine if the economic benefits outweigh the negative impact on our earth.

Pattern of organization:

_____

_____

_____

3. Text messaging while driving should be banned in all states because the practice is making US roadways dangerous. Car crashes rank among the leading causes of death in the United States, but many blame the frequency of drinking and driving and ignore the dangers of texting and driving. Studies by the National Highway Traffic Safety Administration show that text messaging while driving is about six times more likely to result in an accident than drunk driving. And according to the US Department of Transportation, mobile devices contribute to almost 6,000 deaths per year. The major danger associated with texting is the distraction it causes to the driver. When a driver's eyes are concentrating on a phone instead of the road, he or she is more likely to get in an accident. Some critics say teenage drivers are the problem, but 20 percent of adults in a recent AAA study admitted regularly sending text messages while driving. At least nineteen states and the District of Columbia understand the aforementioned dangers and have passed bans on texting while driving. All roads would be safer if text messaging were illegal in every state.

Pattern of organization:

_____

_____

_____

4. The essay "Two Tastes of Asia" on page 376.

Main pattern of organization:

_____

_____

5. The essay "Why I Changed My Mind on the Death Penalty" on pages 396–397.

Main pattern of organization:

_____

_____

Other patterns:

_____

_____

Another Approach to Organization

The patterns of organization refer to the middle part of a text, in which the supporting details are presented. There are, of course, opening and closing parts in a text as well. When analyzing a text, keep this three-part structure in mind.

Three-Part Structure

Paragraph Structure

Topic Sentence
- Names the topic and focus

Body Sentences
- Provide supporting sentences
- Follow a pattern of organization

Closing Sentence
- Wraps up the paragraph

Essay Structure

Opening Part
- Introduces the topic
- Provides background information
- Identifies the main point or thesis

Middle Part
- Supports or develops the main point
- Follows one or more patterns of organization

Closing Part
- Summarizes the key ideas
- Restates the thesis
- Provides final thoughts or analysis

Analyzing the Three Parts

Use these questions as a guide when analyzing the beginning, middle, and ending parts in a text. Your answers will contribute to your overall understanding and appreciation of the text.

Questions to Ask

1. What information is given in the opening part—identification of the topic, background information, statement of the main idea or thesis? Explain.

   _____

2. What types of supporting details are included in the middle (main) part?

   _____

3. How are the details in the main part organized?

   _____

4. What information is given in the closing part—summary of key ideas, restatement of the thesis, final thoughts, and so on?

   _____

5. Does the organization make the text easy or hard to follow? Explain.

   _____

Practice Analyze the three parts in the following essays by answering the above questions for each text. (Work on the activity with a classmate if your instructor allows it.)

- "One-of-a-Kind Character" (page 231)

   _____

   _____

- "Making Dirty Water Drinkable" (page 290)

   _____

   _____

David Gilder, 2013 / Used under license from Shutterstock.com

Understanding the Organization of Arguments

Opinions and facts are the working parts of argumentative essays. *The main claim* of an argument presents a point of view or opinion that the writer will defend. The *evidence* in defense of the argument will be factual statements that can be checked, relied upon, and backed up. Argumentative essays often contain *counterarguments* as well, which are opposing points of view or opinions that the writer addresses. (See also pages 393–424.)

The structure of arguments will vary from essay to essay; even so, knowing two basic patterns of organization may help you recognize and understand arguments. The graphics that follow show you these patterns. As you read an argumentative essay, decide if the writer, in one way or another, follows one of these patterns.

Receptive Audience	Resistant Audience
Beginning	Beginning
Most Important Reason	Objection and Answer
Less Important Reason	Less Important Reason
Objection and Answer	Most Important Reason
Ending	Ending

Recognizing Facts and Opinions: An **opinion** is someone's view or belief. A strong opinion is based on facts, but it is not a fact itself. **Facts** are statements that can be checked or proven to be true. They are used to support and explain an opinion.

Opinion: The American public must take greater measures to preserve the country's farmland. (Someone's view)

Fact: From the years 2002 through 2007, America lost more than four million acres of active farmland to development. (A supporting statement that can be checked)

Fact: When development replaces prime farmland, farmers are forced onto nonfertile land, which results in less production. (Another supporting statement that can be checked)

LO3 Voice (Tone)

In addition to ideas and organization, a text also has voice—the special way in which the writer speaks to the reader. Voice is sometimes referred to as tone. Most informational texts will speak to you in one of three ways. Writers of professional material use a serious academic voice, presenting the facts about a topic as they are known. Many personal essayists and bloggers may use a personal voice to help them connect with the reader. And occasionally, some essayists will use a satiric voice when they want to criticize someone or something.

> "What's important is the way we say it."
> —Federico Fellini

INSIGHT

Recognizing the voice is part of understanding and appreciating a text. But be prepared to "read between the lines" in order to recognize it. Think of voice as the personality in the piece of writing.

Types of Voice

Academic Voice

An academic voice used in most textbooks, professional journals, and thoughtful research. An academic voice uses **formal English** and sounds serious and objective (sticking to the facts). The following passage from an informational essay uses an academic voice.

> Wind energy does not pollute. Whether one wind turbine is used by an individual, or a wind farm supplies energy to many people, no air pollutants or greenhouse gases are emitted. California reports that 2.5 billion pounds of carbon dioxide and 15 million pounds of other pollutants have not entered the air because of wind energy.
>
> Unfortunately, wind energy is intermittent. If a wind does not blow, there is little or no electrical power. One way to resolve this problem is to store wind energy in batteries. . . .

1

5

SPECIAL NOTE: Essays in textbooks or professional journals may contain a brief personal introduction or snippets of personal reflection in the closing and still maintain an academic voice.

formal English
a serious, straightforward style used in most academic writing; characterized by objectivity (sticking to the facts)

Stephen Meese, 2013 / Used under license from Shutterstock.com

Personal Voice

A personal voice is used in most personal essays and articles. A personal voice uses **informal English** and sounds somewhat relaxed and subjective (including the writer's thoughts and feelings). The following passage from a blog posting uses a personal voice.

> The interplay between Joe Torre and Brian Cashman in the new book   1
> *The Yankee Years* got me thinking about education as we prepare for a
> new school year. As you know, we are in the midst of serious educational
> discussions focusing on school improvement, standards, and accountability.
> Many say that the future of our nation depends on reinventing our schools.   5
> A tall order to be sure.
>
> But I don't expect this year will be any different from other years, so
> we'll hear about our students' deplorable math skills. We'll also learn that
> they can't problem solve or think critically. . . .

Satiric Voice

A satiric voice is used in essays and commentaries in which the writer speaks humorously or **sarcastically** about someone or something. A satire may be either objective or subjective in its approach. The following passage from a critical essay uses a satiric voice.

> The cafeteria workers mechanically plop portions on the newcomers'   1
> plates. The workers are either oblivious to or maybe just stunned by the
> background noise. Down goes the arm. One scoop of instant mashed
> potatoes lands on a plate. Down goes the arm. One dribble of instant gravy
> splashes on the potatoes. Down goes the arm. Ten green beans join the   5
> group. Next.
>
> The doomed diners clasp their trays, search for a seat, and silently
> swear to bring a lunch tomorrow.

informal English
a relaxed style used in most personal essays; characterized by subjectivity (the writer's personal thoughts and feelings)

satiric
using humor and/or sarcasm

sarcastically
the act of making critical comments

Practice Carefully read the following passages. Then identify the voice used in each one.

1. The first time I created a PowerPoint presentation, I went a little crazy. I overdid all those neat little bells and whistles, so my presentation ended up like a carnival show. . . .

   Voice: _____

   _____

2. Public housing was built in Chicago because of the Great Migration, the name given to the movement of African Americans from the South to the North. The mechanical cotton picker, introduced in the 1920s, replaced field hands in the cotton fields of the South. . . .

   Voice: _____

   _____

3. I met the most wonderful guy this summer. Thick hair. Sparkling eyes. We spent hours talking. I thought for sure we'd end up together. So what happened? Ned, wonderful, handsome Ned, met my cousin. . . . Nancy. I am sure you know Nancy. How incredible to be related to such an amazing person. . . .

   Voice: _____

   _____

4. General Sherman and his men devised ingenious methods for the wrenching of the Southern railroad. They first used a portable rail-lifter that consisted of a chain with a hook on one end and a large iron ring on the other. The hook would be placed under the rail and a small pole put through the ring. Bracing the pole in the ground, a group of soldiers could lift the rail from the ties. . . .

   Voice: _____

   _____

5. Many years ago, after a job change, I received a pocket scheduler to keep track of appointments. Although the calendar is nice, I especially like the blank pages for quick lists, which I make all the time. No longer do I have the nagging feeling that I might be forgetting something. . . .

   Voice: _____

   _____

Diction Glossary

Diction is an author's choice of words based on their correctness, clearness, or effectiveness. This page identifies terms related to diction.

- **Colloquialisms** are expressions usually accepted in informal or casual texts or speaking situations, but not in a formal situations.

    "Anyway, the baby calf was standing underneath its mother, *just kind of* walking around, and the mother cow *took a 'dump'* on the baby calf's head." (Stephan Chbosky, *The Perks of a Wallflower*)

- **Jargon** (technical diction) is a specialized language used by a specific group.

    Computer jargon: *hypertext* (meaning "a system of web-like links among pages on the Internet or within a program")

    Police jargon: *code eight* (meaning "an officer needs immediate help")

    Medical jargon: *agonal* (meaning "a major, negative change in a patient's condition")

    Political jargon: *left wing* (meaning a "liberal, progressive approach")

- **Idioms** are words used in special ways that may be different from their literal meanings.

    as the crow flies (meaning "in a straight line")

    brain drain (meaning "the best graduates moving elsewhere")

    save face (meaning "fix an embarrassing situation")

- **Slang** is the nonstandard language used by a particular group of people among themselves; it is also language used in fiction and special writing situations to lend color and feeling. Slang may have a brief lifespan.

    emo (meaning "to be depressed, moody, and emotional over extended periods of time")

    tope (meaning "something that's beyond cool")

    iceman (meaning "someone with nerves of steel")

- **Trite** language lacks depth or original, fresh thinking.

    After the close call, the manager *leaped* from the dugout and *roared like a lion.*

    The sprinter *ran like a deer.*

    Larisa is a *deep thinker.*

- **Vulgarity** is abusive, vulgar, or disrespectful language.

    bastard (used as a crude insult)

    bitch (a rude reference to a woman)

    prick (an insulting reference for a person considered unpleasant)

Figures of Speech Glossary

Figures of speech are literary devices used to create meaning through a special use of words. Often the meaning is made through a comparison of one form or another. Creative comparisons may contribute to a personal or satiric voice.

- **Metaphor** is a comparison of two unlike things in which no word or comparison (*as* or *like*) is used.
  "When you write, you lay out a line of words. The line of words is a miner's pick, a woodcarver's gouge, a surgeon's probe." —Annie Dillard, *The Writing Life*

- **Simile** is a comparison of two unlike things in which a word of comparison (as or like) is used.
  "She stood in front of the altar, shaking like a freshly caught trout." —Maya Angelou, *I Know Why the Caged Bird Sings*

- **Personification** is a device in which an animal, object, or idea takes on a human characteristic.
  "And what I remember next is how the moon, the pale moon with its one yellow eye … stared through the pink plastic curtains." —Sandra Cisneros, "One Holy Night"

- **Hyperbole** is an extreme exaggeration or overstatement.
  "I have seen this river so wide it had only one bank." —Mark Twain, *Life on the Mississippi*

- **Understatement** is stating an idea with restraint, often for humorous effect.
  "He [our new dog] turned out to be a good traveler, and except for an interruption caused by my wife's falling out of the car, the journey went very well."
  —E. B. White, *A Report in Spring*

Types of Irony

Irony is a twist or surprise in the story line, explanation, or set of circumstances which is designed to make a point. Irony may contribute to the creation of a satiric voice.

- **Verbal irony** occurs when a writer says one thing but really means another.
  A chef critical of a greengrocer's produce might say, "The carrots were so fresh they bent easily to my touch."

- **Dramatic irony** occurs when the reader or viewer observes or knows a critical piece of information that the subject of a text (a character, or individual) can't see him- or herself.
  In the movie *Lincoln*, viewers know that the president will be shot soon after he settles in to enjoy a play in Ford's Theatre. He, obviously, has no idea that this is about to happen.

- **Irony of situation** occurs when there is a great difference between the purpose of an action and the result.
  In *Romeo and Juliet*, Juliet takes a drug to fake her death, while Romeo poisons himself because he thinks Juliet is dead. Juliet awakes and discovers her lover is dead, so she kills herself.

LO4 Word Choice and Sentences

Word choice and sentences are two other important traits to consider when reading assigned texts.

Word Choice

Word choice is closely connected to voice, in that the words used help create the writer's voice. For example, textbook writers will naturally use many specific words associated with the topic. These content-specific words help create the academic voice in the text. Personal essayists, on the other hand, usually rely on more familiar words, which helps create a more personal or conversational voice.

Academic passage using content-specific words (underlined):

Many experts believe that intelligence takes many forms. Rather than   *1*
a narrow definition of intelligence, they believe in Multiple Intelligences:
Linguistic, Logical-Mathematical, Spatial, Kinesthetic, Musical,
Interpersonal, Intrapersonal, and Naturalistic. Emotional intelligence may
well be a combination, at least in part, of intrapersonal and interpersonal   *5*
intelligences.

Passage from a personal essay using mostly familiar words:

Megan and I waited along with everyone else on Kearney Street for   *1*
the San Francisco Chinese New Year Festival and Parade to start. We
bunched together, hip to hip. Little kids sat half on the curb and half on
their toes. Taller people stood in rows behind us, going way back to the
decorated shops.   *5*

Identify Find one passage (two or three sentences) from an essay in *Fusion 2* that uses many content-specific words. Record the passage and underline the content-specific words. Then record a passage from a personal essay that contains very familiar words. Share your work with your classmates.

Word Choice in Academic Texts

The following three features are characteristic of the word choice in academic texts.

Nominalizations In academic texts, you often find **nominalizations**—word formations in which verbs, adjectives, or other parts of speech are used as nouns. These words give the text an academic tone.

Nominal Constructions

- "In all societies, people apply <u>imagination</u> . . ." *(In more direct terms, "In all societies, people imagine. . . .")*

- "The various types of artistic <u>expression</u> include . . ." *(In more direct terms, "People express themselves artistically by . . .")*

- "Art should communicate <u>information</u> by . . ." *(In more direct terms, "Art should inform by . . .")*

- "Among Latinos, Spanglish <u>conversations</u> often flow easily from . . ." *(In more direct terms, "Latinos often converse in . . .")*

Technical Terms Academic texts often contain technical terms. These terms can make academic texts challenging to read. Many texts provide definitions of these words either on the page where they occur or in a glossary. Otherwise, always keep a dictionary handy for reference, and record definitions of important terms in your notes. Here is a passage from an academic essay about the colonists of Roanoke. The technical terms have been underlined.

> Despite centuries of <u>admixing</u>, a modern Catawba Indian was found to be, on average, 50% white and 50% Native American in <u>genetic composition</u> (Pollitzer et al., 1967). The results of the study surprised many who expected the percentage of <u>white genetic attributes</u> to be much higher. . . .

INSIGHT

Very specialized language (often referred to as jargon) is commonly found in professional journals intended for readers who are trained in a particular field.

nominalizations
the use of a verb, an adjective, or an adverb as a noun (*imagination, expression, information*)

Carefully Constructed Language In academic texts, writers choose their words carefully to maintain a certain level of formality. In addition, academic writers will use very few personal pronouns and few, if any, contractions. Notice below how the same idea is stated with carefully constructed language and then personally.

- **Academic, Formal Language:** "One of the best ways to maintain well-being, researchers found, is self-compassion, a healthy form of self-acceptance. . . ."

- **Personal, Informal Language:** Researchers have found that we could be happier if we'd only learn how to accept and deal with life's setbacks.

Word Choice in Personal Essays

The language in personal essays, feature articles, and some reviews is often relaxed and informal.

Relaxed Language Most personal essays will sound somewhat friendly in tone and make the reader feel comfortable and at ease. They may include personal pronouns, in particular first-person pronouns (*I, we, us*), contractions (*it's, can't, weren't*), and perhaps some familiar expressions ("Of course" and "It's too bad that . . ."). And overall, the words will be recognizable to most readers. Notice how easy it is to follow this passage from a personal essay.

- **Personal, Informal Language:** Of course, those were old memories. By the time I reached college, Grandpa wasn't as active anymore. Tired and overworked from his years of hard labor at the steel yard, his back eventually gave out and his joints swelled up with arthritis.

INSIGHT

Language that is even more informal such as slang won't typically be found in your textbooks.

Special Challenge Rewrite one of the academic passages that you identified on page 88, or find another one, so that it reads more personally or informally. Or rewrite the personal passage that you found so that it reads more academically.

_____

_____

_____

_____

Practice Carefully read each of the following passages. Then identify the word choice as *academic* or *personal*.

1. This was not exactly my idea of a fun family vacation. Sweat beads trickled down my brow, and a feeling of dread washed over me as I noticed the low-battery sign blinking on my MP3 player.

   Word choice: _____

   _____

   _____

   _____

2. While vertical farming may seem futuristic, it has roots in the past. A classic example is the Hanging Gardens of Babylon built in 600 BC. These gardens consisted of a series of stackable terraces.

   Word choice: _____

   _____

   _____

   _____

3. When a paragraph is coherent, the parts stay together. A coherent paragraph flows smoothly because each sentence is connected to others by patterns in the language such as repetition and transitions. . . .

   Word choice: _____

   _____

   _____

   _____

4. And then there was Martha. She was a talker, talking openly and frequently, usually about her family—where they were all living and what they were doing. She'd get very excited anytime a relative came to visit.

   Word choice: _____

   _____

   _____

   _____

Sentences

If sentences were a fashion show, here's what you might see: Some sentences might appear perky and preppy; others might appear casual and conversational; and still others might flow more formally in multiple layers of meaning. These "fashions" describe the types of sentences you typically find in different types of informational texts.

Academic Sentences

Academic texts are characterized by longer sentences with multiple layers of meaning. Longer sentences often reveal careful thought and reflection on the part of the writer, who needs to impart information thoroughly and accurately. Here are four longer sentences from academic texts. In each one, the core sentence is underlined. Notice all of the additional information added to each one.

Once a country's forests are gone, <u>the companies move on to another country,</u> leaving ecological devastation behind.

In Indonesia, Malaysia, and other areas of Southeast Asia, <u>tropical forests are being replaced with vast plantations of oil palm</u>, which produces an oil used in cooking, cosmetics, and biodiesel fuel for motor vehicles (especially in Europe).

<u>Spanglish takes on a variety of forms,</u> from the Southern California Anglos who bid farewell with the utterly silly "hasta la bye-bye" to the Cuban-American drivers in Miami who *parquean* their *carros*.

Nevertheless, despite these diverse definitions, <u>any definition of art,</u> if it is to have any cross-cultural comparability, <u>must include five basic elements.</u>

INSIGHT

Longer sentences are complex because they contain multiple clauses and phrases. They require careful reading.

Sentences in Personal Essays

For the most part, the sentences in personal essays are relaxed and conversational in tone. As such, they are usually simple, are easier to follow, and move along at a quicker pace than the sentences in academic texts. In addition, they are generally shorter. Notice how easy it is to read the following passages from personal narratives.

My fate was in my hands—actually my feet. Funny. I had to reach back, do what was needed. I had to realize the future and pass the last runner. . . .

Dad discovered the engine had overheated, and we were stuck. "Is this thing going to blow up?" asked my younger sister Michelle. "I have a bunch of clothes in there. . . ."

Uncle John doesn't believe in candid photos. Instead, he insists on interrupting our activities to get us to pose for pictures. In return, he gets a lot of photos with people smiling through clenched teeth.

I looked down again at the driver hanging from the windowsill. There were six empty beer bottles on the floor of the truck. I could smell the beer through the window.

dragon_fang, 2013 / Used under license from Shutterstock.com

Practice   Carefully read the following sentences. Then identify each one as either academic or personal in structure.

1. While boys suffer from the disease far more frequently than girls do by a ratio of 4 to 1, when girls do develop Legg-Calve-Perthes disease, they tend to suffer more severely from it.

    Sentence style: _____

    _____

2. I love watching the cranes fishing in the river. They look so prehistoric. It's too bad that they stay for such a short time.

    Sentence style: _____

    _____

3. While executions historically demand a certain degree of morbid curiosity, the last meals of the condemned seem to stimulate heightened interest.

    Sentence style: _____

    _____

4. Her face was dirty; her hair greasy and matted. A part of me felt sorry for her.

    Sentence style: _____

    _____

5. The basic unit of the Braille system is called a "cell," which is two dots wide and three dots high.

    Sentence style: _____

    _____

6. Admitting I had a disorder was the hardest thing I've ever done. Now I manage my moods very carefully.

    Sentence style: _____

    _____

Additional Practice   Find two sentences from one or more of the models in *Fusion 2* that are clearly academic in style because of their length and complexity. Then find two sentences that are clearly personal in style. Share these sentences with your classmates.

_____

_____

Review and Enrichment

On the next seven pages you will review and enrich your understanding of the concepts in this chapter.

Reviewing the Chapter

Respond to each set of directions that follow.

Ideas Answer the following questions about ideas in writing. (See pages 48–74.)

1. Where is the main idea located in a paragraph?

_____

2. Where is the main idea located in an essay?

_____

3. Why is finding the main idea an important first step when reading?

_____

4. List four important types of supporting details.

_____

Organization Explain the following three common patterns of organization.

Chronological _____

Logical _____

Cause-effect _____

Explain what is meant by the three-part structure of essays.

_____

Voice Answer the following questions about voice.

1. What is meant by voice in writing?

_____

2. What is the main feature of an academic writing voice?

_____

3. What is the main feature of a personal writing voice?

_____

Word Choice and Sentences Answer the following questions about word choice and sentences.

1. What are the main features of academic word choice and sentences?

_____

2. What are the main features of personal word choice and sentences?

_____

Reading

In this section, you will read and react to the introduction to *The Vertical Farm: Feeding the World in the 21st Century*. Be sure to follow the steps in the reading process as you read. Also be sure to apply one or more of the reading strategies introduced in this chapter to help you understand the text fully.

> "A great city is not to be confused with a populous one."
> —Aristotle

About the Author

Dr. Dickson D. Despommier is a Professor of Public Health in Environmental Health Sciences at Columbia University. He established his vision of a vertical farm with the help of graduate students in one of his classes.

Prereading

Urban dwellers benefit from the employment, entertainment, and cultural opportunities that cities provide. At the same time, this growing segment of the population faces many challenges such as affordable housing, congestion, and crime. If you were "in charge" of a city, what changes would you immediately order? List two or three; then discuss your choices.

CONSIDER THE TRAITS

As you read, pay careful attention to the **ideas**—the main idea or thesis plus the supporting details. Also consider the **organization** of the text—the way in which the author structures the beginning, middle and ending parts.

Identify   Before you read, answer these three questions:

1. What do the title, first few paragraphs, and headings tell you about the text?

2. What do you already know about this topic?

3. What do you expect to learn?

What do you think?

Consider the quotation at the top of the page: What do you think that Aristotle meant? And do you agree with him? Why or why not?

Reading and Rereading

Your image of a farm may be a country setting with a barn, animals grazing in pens, and fields of crops stretching in all directions. This selection introduces you to a completely different type of farm, suitable for city life.

As you read, make it your goal to (1) identify the main idea, (2) locate the key supporting details, and (3) study the closing paragraph.

The Vertical Farm: Feeding the World in the 21st Century: "Introduction"

Fifteen thousand years ago, there was not a single farm on the planet. Fast-forward to the present, when we now farm a landmass the size of South America, which does not include grazing land. Along the way, we invented, among other things, written language, mathematics, music, and, of course, cities. Yet our journey from hunter-gatherers to urban dwellers still hasn't produced a single metropolis that is truly healthy to live in.

As populations grew and urban life became the norm, our habit for producing mountains of waste began to take its toll. Garbage provided sustenance for a wide variety of **peri-domestic** diseases that emerged and then became **endemic**. For example, in the twelfth century, trash of all kinds, strewn carelessly across the European landscape by returning crusaders from the Middle East, attracted hordes of rats. These vermin harbored the plague bacillus, a flea-borne infection. As the rats died, the fleas soon found human hosts to feed on, igniting the first outbreak of the **Black Death** in Europe. It killed more than one-third of all those living there. **Cholera** came to Europe in 1836 by way of trading vessels from the Bay of Bengal, first to London, England. Because of the high nutrient content of the Thames River, due mostly to garbage dumping, cholera became endemic, killing thousands of Londoners every year until John Snow figured out its **modus operandi**.

You'd think we would have learned something from all this. But as late as the nineteenth century, waste on the streets of New York City was still causing massive outbreaks of **diarrheal** disease. To this day, most cities still haven't found a good use for garbage. New York remains plagued by vermin and poor-sanitation-related diseases such as asthma. With landfills for most cities now bulging at the seams, urban communities will have to reinvent waste management. Yet there is hope. All of this is about to change. We now have in our hands the tools and the desire to convert squalid urban blight into places where we'd want to raise our children. Once we have transformed our urban centers, we can turn our attention to renewing the hardwood forests that we destroyed in our zeal to create the farmlands that now produce food for our cities.

Sustainable urban life is technologically achievable, and most important, highly desirable. For example, food waste can easily be converted back into energy employing clean state-of-the-art incineration technologies, and wastewater can be converted back into drinking water. For the first time in history, an entire city can choose to become the functional urban equivalent of a natural ecosystem. We could even generate energy from incinerating human feces if we so desired. We have the ability to create a "cradle to cradle" waste-free economy. All that is needed is the political will to do so. Once we begin the process, cities will be able to live within their means without further damaging the environment.

VERTICAL FARMS

Repairing the environment and still having enough good, healthy food choices may seem like mutually exclusive goals. If the world's population continues to increase, wouldn't we need to cut down even more forest to produce enough food to feed everyone? Not necessarily. One solution lies in vertical farms. These farms would raise food without soil in specially constructed buildings. When farms are successfully moved to cities, we can convert significant amounts of farming back into whatever ecosystem was there originally, simply by leaving it alone.

This plan may sound naïve and impractical. Yet the concept of vertical farming is dead simple. Still, making it happen could require the kind of technical expertise needed for, say, rocket science or brain surgery. Then again, human beings do rocket science and brain surgery quite well. We should not shy away from the challenge of farming vertically simply because it requires cutting-edge engineering, architecture, and agronomy. All of this is within our grasp. We understand the hydroponic and aeroponic farming methodologies needed to grow crops within multistory buildings. Although there are still no examples of functioning vertical farms, many urban planners have become familiar with the concept and are now looking for ways to make it happen. There are already plans on the drawing board by developers in wealthy countries that are running short of arable farmland. In other places where food is becoming scarce and people are going to bed hungry, vertical farms could eventually solve this seemingly intractable problem.

The idea of growing crops in tall buildings might sound strange. But farming indoors is not a new concept. Commercially viable crops such as strawberries, tomatoes, peppers, cucumbers, herbs, and a wide variety of spices have made have made their way from commercial greenhouses to the world's supermarkets in ever-increasing amounts over the last fifteen years. Most of these greenhouses operations are small in comparison to the large commercial farms of the American Midwest, but unlike their outdoor counterparts, greenhouse facilities can produce crops year-

35

40

45

50

55

60

65

70

75

round. Fish, as well as a wide variety of crustaceans and mollusks, have also been raised indoors. Chickens, ducks, and geese could conceivably be raised in indoor farms as well.

Vertical farms are **immune** to weather and other natural elements   80
that can abort food production. Crops can be grown under carefully selected and well-monitored conditions that ensure optimal growth rates for each species of plant and animal year-round. In other words, there are no seasons indoors. The efficiency of each floor of a vertical farm, one acre in **footprint**, could be equivalent to as many as ten to twenty   85
traditional soil-based acres, depending upon the crop. Vertical farms offer many environmental benefit as well. Farming indoors eliminates the need for fossil fuels now used for plowing, applying fertilizer, seeding, weeding, and harvesting.

CITIES WITHOUT WASTE   90

The ingredients in the dinner you just ate at your favorite restaurant likely came from more than fifteen hundred miles away. If you had a vertical farm in your city, all the food on your plate could come from down the block, saving huge amounts of fossil fuel now used to refrigerate and ship produce from all over the world. Also, think of what   95
happens to the food you left on your plate. These leftovers, plus the waste generated in the food-preparation process, are currently nonrecoverable costs—also known as dinner for vermin. Now imagine if this organic waste could be converted back into energy. This would allow restaurants to be paid for the recoverable energy from their waste streams. An   100
industry with a notoriously small (205 percent) profit margin would be able to earn additional income without raising the prices on its menu. . . .

THE END OF POLLUTION

The most pressing case for urban agriculture lies in our failure to handle waste, in particular agricultural runoff (leftover irrigation   105
water laden with pesticides, herbicides, fertilizer, and silt). Agriculture is responsible for more ecosystem disruption than any other kind of pollution. What's more, today's farmers can't do much about it: Floods dictate the timing and extent of runoff.

Some 70 percent of all available freshwater on earth is used for   110
irrigation, and the resulting unused portion is returned to countless rivers and streams. Runoff that reaches the oceans disconnects other ecological systems. Nitrogen fertilizer (ammonium nitrate) has the chemical property of absorbing oxygen from water. Agricultural runoff reduces the vibrant, abundant undersea life of coral reefs to barren   115
remnants. Deforestation for purposes of freeing up farmland reinforces this toxic cycle by adding more nitrogen fertilizer to the mix and by further reducing the earth's capacity to **sequester** carbon from the atmosphere.

In a city with vertical farms, waste will be replaced with the *120* recovery of unrealized energy. In nature, there is no waste. In the new eco-city, discarding anything without finding another use for it would be quite unthinkable. Imagine how absurd it would be to siphon off a gallon's worth of gasoline from the family car and pour it down the sewer. Yet this is equivalent to what we are doing with everything we *125* now throw away. . . .

Science has led the way in helping us to understand the toll we are taking on the planet. Satellites report on the status of many of the factors that contribute to climate change. Ground-based and satellite observations of coal-burning power plants, for example, support the *130* unavoidable conclusion that we are the root cause of it. Now that we've identified the problem, we can devote our energy to finding a set of solutions. Producing food crops in mass quantities within the city limits would be a step in the right direction. The good news is that many of us are already trying to repair the environment through scientific research *135* and **philanthropic** support. This is good evidence of our ability to behave in a selfless and **altruistic** manner when we have the opportunity to do so.

It's time to accept our connectedness to the rest of the natural world. There is only so much natural capital out there, and we are on the verge of exhausting it. Building self-sustaining cities now will allow the land *140* to heal itself, thereby restoring balance between our lives and the rest of nature.

From VERTICAL FARM: FEEDING THE WORLD IN THE 21st CENTURY © 2010 by Dickson Despommier. Reprinted by permission of St. Martin's Press. All Rights Reserved.

peri-domestic
of or pertaining to living in or around human dwellings

endemic
particular in or common to a particular area

Black Death
a disease or plague that killed more than 50 million people in the 14th century

cholera
disease of the small intestines

modus operandi
method of doing something (Latin)

diarrheal
related to a disorder of the stomach and small intestines

sustainable
the ability to maintain or keep going

incineration
the act of burning

ecosystem
a community of organisms and their environments

hydroponic
growing plants in liquid nutrients

immune
not subject to or affected

footprint
in outline

sequester
to set apart

philanthropic
showing kindness, charitable, giving aid

altruistic
selfless, unselfish

Reflecting

Practice   After you complete your reading, answer the following questions. Share your responses with your classmates.

1. What main idea is developed in the text?

   _____

   _____

   _____

2. What supporting details do you find most important? (Name three.)

   _____

   _____

   _____

3. What is the author's purpose—to inform, to entertain, to persuade?

   _____

   _____

   _____

4. Has this text introduced you to a new topic, confirmed what you already knew about the topic, or expanded your understanding of it? Explain.

   _____

   _____

   _____

5. What questions do you still have about vertical farming?

   _____

   _____

6. How would you rate this reading and why?

   Weak ★ ★ ★ ★ ★ Strong

   _____

   _____

Vocabulary Practice

Identify   Use context clues to explain or define the following words. (See pages 34–35 for help.)

1. **vermin**   (line 13)

   clues:_____

   meaning: _____

2. **squalid**   (line 30)

   clues: _____

   meaning: _____

3. **aeroponic**   (line 61)

   clues: _____

   meaning: _____

4. **runoff**   (line 109)

   clues: _____

   meaning: _____

Drawing Inferences

Explain   Answer the following questions to help you draw inferences from the text. (See pages 30–32 for help.)

1. If vertical farms are a solution, what is the problem?

   _____

   _____

2. How can the creation of vertical farms be part of a bigger environmental plan?

   _____

   _____

4

> "Writing became such a process of discovery that I couldn't wait to get to work in the morning."
> —Sharon O'Brien

Academic Writing and Learning

In college, all of the new information coming your way can seem overwhelming. To succeed, you must be able to retain this new knowledge, connect it to other ideas, and share conclusions with your peers and instructors. Writing can help you do all of these things.

Writing is a tool that can help you become a better, more efficient learner. In fact, no other activity can improve your learning and communication skills as well as writing can. And you'll be happy to know that these skills translate directly to the workplace. Today's employers place a premium on effective writing skills.

The guidelines and strategies presented in this chapter will help you meet the demands of your academic writing. You will learn about writing to learn, the writing process, as well as many helpful writing strategies.

Learning Outcomes

LO1 Write to learn.
LO2 Write to share learning.
LO3 Understand the writing process.
LO4 Use writing strategies.
LO5 Understand strong writing.
LO6 Use Standard English.
LO7 Think critically and logically.

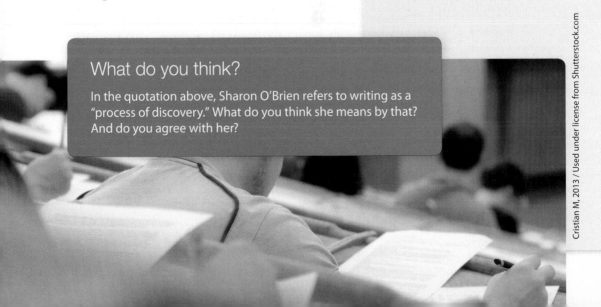

What do you think?

In the quotation above, Sharon O'Brien refers to writing as a "process of discovery." What do you think she means by that? And do you agree with her?

> "Don't think and then write it down. Think on paper."
> —Harry Kemelman

LO1 Writing to Learn

Gertrude Stein made one of the more famous and unusual statements about writing when she said, "To write is to write is to write is to write. . . ." The lofty place that writing held in her life echoes in the line. As far as she was concerned, nothing else needed to be said on the subject.

What would cause someone to become so committed to writing? Was it a desire for fame and recognition? Not really. The real fascination that experienced writers have with writing is the frame of mind it puts them in. The act of filling up a page triggers their thinking and leads to meaningful learning.

Changing Your Attitude

If you think of writing in just one way—as an assignment to be completed—you will never discover its true value. Writing works best when you think of it as a way to learn. A series of questions, a list, or a quick note can be a meaningful form of writing if it helps you think and understand. If you make writing an important part of your learning routine, you'll change your attitude about writing (for the better), and you'll become a better thinker and learner.

Keeping a Class Notebook

Keeping a class notebook or journal is essential if you are going to make writing an important part of your learning routine. Certainly, you can take notes in this notebook, but it is also helpful to reflect on what is going on in the class. These writing activities will help you think about your course work.

- Write freely about anything from class discussions to challenging assignments.
- Explore new ideas and concepts.
- Argue for and against any points of view that came up in class.
- Question what you are learning.
- Record your thoughts and feelings about an extended project.
- Evaluate your progress in the class.

Reflect Write freely for 5 to 10 minutes about your writing experiences. Consider how you feel about writing, your strengths and weaknesses as a writer, if you have ever used writing to learn, and so on. Then share your thoughts with your classmates.

LO2 Writing to Share Learning

The other important function of writing is to share what you have learned. When you write to learn, you are your only audience. But when you write to share learning, your audience expands to include your instructor, your classmates, and others.

All writing projects (paragraphs, essays, blog entries) actually begin with writing to learn as you collect your thoughts and feelings about the topic. But with a first draft in hand, you must make the writing clear, complete, and ready to share with others.

A Learning Connection

As this graphic shows, improved thinking is the link between the two functions of writing. Writing to learn involves exploring and forming your thoughts, and writing to share learning involves clarifying and fine-tuning them.

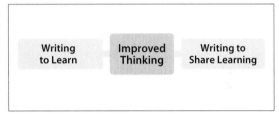

| Writing to Learn | Improved Thinking | Writing to Share Learning |

INSIGHT ——————————————

Following the steps in the writing process is the best way to develop writing to share. This process helps you pace yourself so you don't try to do everything all at once. (See pages 106–111.)

The Range of Writing

The forms of writing to share cover a lot of territory, as you can see in the chart to the right. As a college student, your writing will likely cover the entire spectrum, with a focus on the more formal forms, such as essays and reports.

React Answer these questions about the chart: What forms of writing do you most often engage in? How does your writing approach change at different points along the spectrum?

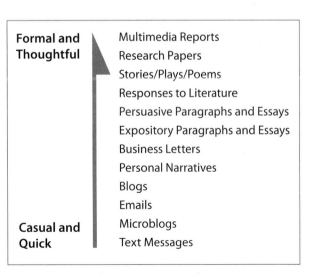

Formal and Thoughtful

Multimedia Reports
Research Papers
Stories/Plays/Poems
Responses to Literature
Persuasive Paragraphs and Essays
Expository Paragraphs and Essays
Business Letters
Personal Narratives
Blogs
Emails
Microblogs
Text Messages

Casual and Quick

LO3 Understanding the Writing Process

When facing an extended writing assignment, most students ask the same question: How will I ever get this done? Even professional writers sometimes labor for the right answer. But have no fear. A writing project is much less imposing when you approach it as a process rather than as an end product. This section will introduce you to the steps in the writing process.

The Steps in the Process

You cannot change a flat tire with one simple action. It takes a number of steps to get the job done right. The same goes for writing. If you expect to complete a paper in one general attempt, you (and your instructor) will be disappointed in the results. On the other hand, if you follow the writing process, you'll complete the job in the right way—one step at a time.

Process	Activities
Prewriting	Start the process by (1) selecting a topic to write about, (2) collecting details about it, and (3) finding a focus or thesis to direct your writing.
Writing	Then write your first draft, using your prewriting plan as a general guide. Writing a first draft allows you to connect your thoughts about a topic.
Revising	Carefully review your first draft and have a classmate read it as well. Change any parts that need to be clearer, and add missing information.
Editing	Edit your revised writing by checking for style, grammar, punctuation, and spelling errors.
Publishing	During the final step, prepare your writing to share with your instructor, your peers, or another audience.

Reasons to Write

Always use the writing process when you are writing to share learning and when you are writing certain personal forms. You don't need to use it when you are simply writing to learn.

Reason	Forms	Purpose
Writing to share learning	Summaries, informational essays	To show your understanding of subjects you are studying
Personal writing	Personal essays, blog postings, short stories, plays	To share your personal thoughts, feelings, and creativity with others

Reflect Explain how the writing process explained above compares with your own way of completing assignments. Consider what you normally do first, second, third, and so on.

"A writer is not so much someone who has something to say as he is someone who has found a process that will bring about new things he would not have thought of if he had not started to say them."
—William Stafford

The Process in Action

As the chart to the right indicates, there can be forward and backward movement between the steps in the writing process. For example, after writing a first draft, you may decide to collect more details about your topic, which is actually a prewriting activity.

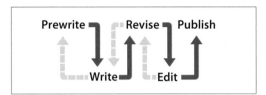

Points to Remember

When using the writing process, you need to understand the following points.

1. All the steps require some type of writing. Prewriting (planning), revising, and editing are as much writing activities as composing the first draft is.

2. It is unlikely that the process will work the same for any two writing assignments. For one assignment, you may struggle with gathering details. For another, you may have trouble starting the first draft. For still another, you may move from step to step with little difficulty.

3. No two writers develop their writing in the same way. Some writers need to talk about their writing early on, while others would rather keep their ideas to themselves. Some writers need to step away from their writing at times to let their thoughts percolate. Other writers can't stop until they produce a first draft. Your own writing personality will develop as you gain more writing experience.

4. All the information about the writing process won't make you a better writer unless you make a sincere effort to use it. You wouldn't expect to play the piano just by reading about it—you must follow the instructions and practice. The same holds true for writing.

INSIGHT

When you respond to a writing prompt on a test, use an abbreviated form of the writing process. Spend a few minutes gathering and organizing your ideas; then write your response. Afterward, read what you have produced and quickly revise and edit it.

Create   Make a chart that shows your own process—the one you described on page 106. Share your chart with your classmates.

A CLOSER LOOK at the Process

Each step in the writing process requires a special type of thinking. Following these steps will help you become a more confident writer and learner.

Prewriting is the first step in the writing process. In many ways, it is the most important step because it involves all of the decisions and planning that come before writing a first draft. If you plan well, you will be well prepared to work through the rest of the process. These are the basic prewriting tasks.

- **Identify a meaningful writing idea.** Pick a topic that meets the requirements of the assignment and that truly interests you. Otherwise, you will have a hard time writing about it. Begin your topic search by writing freely about the assignment or by simply listing your ideas.

- **Collect plenty of details.** Explore your own thoughts and feelings about the topic. Then gather additional information, either through firsthand experience (observations, interviews, and so on) or by reading about the topic in books, magazines, and on the Internet.

- **Establish a focus.** Just as a skilled photographer focuses or centers the subject before taking a photograph, you must identify a special part or feeling about the topic before writing your first draft. This focus, or emphasis, is usually expressed in a thesis statement. (See pages 138–139.)

- **Choose a pattern of arrangement.** Once you have established a focus, decide what details to include in your writing and how to organize them. You can arrange your details chronologically (by time), logically, by order of importance, and so on. (See pages 140–143.)

- **Organize your information.** With a pattern of arrangement in mind, you can organize your details in one of three basic ways:
    - Make a quick list of main points and support.
    - Create an outline—a more formal arrangement of main points and subpoints.
    - Fill in a graphic organizer—arranging main points and details in a chart or diagram. (See page 9.)

INSIGHT

Thorough prewriting is critical when you are writing essays, articles, and reports. It is not as important when you are writing personal blogs and narratives.

Drafting is the next step in the writing process. You have one important task during this step—to connect your thoughts and ideas about your topic. Just put these thoughts on paper so you have something to work with. They do not have to be perfectly worded. Here is a basic guide to drafting.

- **Strike while you're hot.** Write your first draft while your planning is still fresh in your mind.

- **Refer to your prewriting.** Use all of your planning and organizing as a basic writing guide. But also be open to new ideas as they come to mind.

- **Write as much as you can.** Keep writing until you get all of your ideas on paper, or until you come to a natural stopping point. Concentrate on forming your ideas rather than on making everything correct.

- **Form a meaningful whole.** A meaningful whole for a paragraph means a topic sentence, multiple body sentences, and a closing sentence. For an essay, it means an opening paragraph (with a thesis statement), multiple middle paragraphs, and a closing paragraph.

Paragraph	Essay
Topic sentence ⟶	Opening paragraph (with thesis statement)
Body sentences ⟶	Middle paragraphs
Closing sentence ⟶	Closing paragraph

- **Pay special attention to each part.** All three parts—the opening, the middle, and the closing—play important roles in your writing. Give each part special attention. (See pages 112–117.)
  - The opening gets the reader's interest and states your thesis.
  - The middle supports your thesis.
  - The closing offers important final thoughts about the topic.

- **Look back to move forward.** Sometimes it helps to stop and reread what you have written to help you add new ideas.

- **Write naturally and honestly.** "Talk" to your readers, as if a group of classmates were gathered around you.

- **Remember, it's a draft.** A first draft is your first look at a developing writing idea. You will have plenty of opportunities to improve upon it later in the process.

A CLOSER LOOK at the Process (continued)

Revising is the third step in the process. During this step, you shape and improve the ideas in your first draft. You would never expect a musician to record a song after putting lyrics and music together for the first time. The same holds true with your writing. You still have a lot of work ahead of you. Here is a basic guide to revising.

- **Step away from your draft.** Your time away will help you see your first draft more clearly, and with a fresh outlook.

- **Revisit your purpose.** Are you writing to explain, to persuade, to describe, or to share?

- **Read your draft many times.** Read it silently and out loud to get an overall impression of your work.

- **Have peers read it.** Their comments and questions will help you decide what changes to make.

- **Check your overall focus.** Decide if your thesis still works and if you have provided enough support for it.

- **Review each part.** Be sure that the opening sets the proper tone for your writing, the middle part supports your thesis, and the closing provides worthy final thoughts about the topic.

- **Know your basic moves.** There are four basic ways to make changes—adding, cutting, rewriting, or reordering information. Each change or improvement that you make will bring you closer to a strong finished paper.

Add information to . . .
- make a main point more convincing.
- complete an explanation.
- improve the flow of your writing.

Cut information if it . . .
- doesn't support the thesis.
- seems repetitious.

Rewrite information if it . . .
- seems confusing or unclear.
- appears too complicated.
- lacks the proper voice.

Reorder information if it . . .
- seems out of order.
- would make more sense in another spot.

- **Plan a revising strategy.** Decide what you need to do first, second, and third, and then make the necessary changes.

Editing is the fourth step, when you check your revised writing for style and correctness. Editing becomes important *after* you have revised the content of your writing. Editing is like buffing out the smudges and scratches on a newly painted car. The buffing is important, but only after the main work—the actual painting—is complete. Here is a basic guide to editing.

- **Start with a clean copy.** Do your editing on a clean copy of your revised writing; otherwise, things get too confusing.

- **Check first for style.** Make sure that you have used the best words, such as specific nouns and verbs and smooth-reading sentences.

- **Then check for correctness.** Start by checking your spelling, then move on to end punctuation, and so on.

- **For spelling, read from the last word to the first.** This strategy will force you to look at each word. (A spell checker will not catch every error.)

- **Circle punctuation.** This strategy will force you to look at each mark.

- **Refer to an editing checklist.** You'll find an example on page 183. Also refer to pages 483–661 for sentence, grammar, punctuation, and mechanics rules.

- **Use editing symbols.** These symbols provide an efficient way to mark errors.

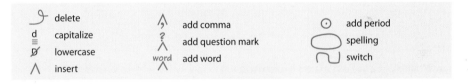

- **Get help.** Ask a trusted classmate to check for errors as well. You are too close to your writing to notice everything.

Publishing is the final step in the writing process. During this step, you prepare your writing before submitting or sharing it.

- **Prepare a final copy.** Incorporate all of your editing changes.

- **Follow design requirements.** Format your final copy according to the requirements established by your instructor.

- **Proofread the text.** Check your writing one last time for errors.

LO4 Using Writing Strategies

The writing strategies and instruction on the next ten pages will help you write strong essays and reports.

Creating an Effective Opening

In many situations, first impressions are important—say, for instance, when you're interviewing for a job or introducing yourself to a roommate or coworker. First impressions are important in writing, too, because the first few ideas help set the tone for the rest of the piece. (Tone refers to the writer's attitude toward her or his topic.) The information that follows will help you make a positive first impression in your essays.

The Basic Parts

The opening paragraph should (1) identify the topic, (2) gain the reader's interest, and (3) state the thesis. You may also include a sentence or two of background information.

Listed here are strategies to help you gain the reader's interest.

- Begin with a surprising or little-known fact about the topic.

  Thousands of babies are born each year with alcohol-related defects, making fetal alcohol syndrome one of the leading causes of mental retardation.

- Ask an interesting or challenging question about the topic.

  What exactly do the signs held up by homeless people tell us?

- Start with a revealing quotation.

  "We live here and they live there," Bigger Thomas says in *Native Son*. "We black and they white. They got things and we ain't. They do things and we can't."

- Share a brief, dramatic story.

  It was May 1945. World War II had just ended and Yugoslavia had been overtaken. The town of Vrhnika, Yugoslavia, was no longer safe. Russian and communist troops would break into houses, take what they wanted, and even kill.

- Open with a bold statement.

  Barbie's boobs and spacious mansion helped cause the decay of today's youth, or so say some experts.

Example Opening Paragraph

Analyze   Carefully read the following opening paragraph from an essay about a degenerative bone disease called Legg-Calve-Perthes (pronounced leg-cal-VAY-PER-theez). Then answer the questions below.

> Allie Mason acted like a typical high school freshman. She was *1*
> bubbly, energetic, and extremely friendly. She was also a conscientious
> student, belonged to the Honors Art Club, and enjoyed golfing. What set
> Allie apart was a debilitating physical condition that caused one of her
> legs to be noticeably shorter than the other one and forced her to limp. *5*
> As a result, she had to endure endless medical procedures and missed
> out on typical school activities such as gym and dances. She also had to
> endure more than her share of insensitive remarks. She remembered, "My
> classmates would tease me and call me names." Their comments obviously
> hurt, especially those made by her friends. The reason for Allie's suffering *10*
> was Legg-Calve-Perthes, a painful bone disease that truly challenges the
> sufferer.

1. What strategy does the writer use to introduce the topic and engage the reader? (See the previous page.)

   _____

2. What, if any, background information is provided about the topic?

   _____

3. What is the thesis statement in this paragraph?

   _____

4. What special part or feeling about the topic is identified in this statement?

   _____

5. How would you rate this opening and why?

   Weak ★ ★ ★ ★ ★ Strong

   _____

Developing the Middle Part

In the middle paragraphs, you develop all of the main points that support your thesis statement. Use your planning (quick list, outline, graphic organizer) as a general guide when you develop this part of an essay. Here are a few tips for getting started.

- **Keep your thesis statement in mind as you write.** All of your main points should support or explain this statement.
- **Develop each main point in a separate paragraph (or two).** State the main point in the form of a topic sentence and follow with detail sentences that support it.
- **Use plenty of details** to fully explain your ideas.
- **Use your own words,** except on those few occasions when you employ a quotation to add authority to your writing.
- **Be open to new ideas that occur to you,** especially if they will improve your essay.
- **Try any of the basic writing moves** that are appropriate to your topic.

Basic Writing Moves

The paragraphs in the middle part of an essay should, among other things, *explain, describe, define, classify,* and so on. What follows is a list and definitions of these basic writing moves.

Narrating — sharing an experience or a story

Describing — telling how someone or something appears, acts, or operates

Explaining — providing important facts, details, and examples

Analyzing — carefully examining a subject or breaking it down

Comparing — showing how two subjects are similar and different

Defining — identifying or clarifying the meaning of a term

Reflecting — connecting with or wondering about

Evaluating — rating the value of something

Arguing — using logic and evidence to prove something is true

Special Challenge   Read two different essays in this book. On your own paper, list the different moves that the writers use in the middle paragraphs of the essays. For example, a writer may *explain* in one or more paragraphs, *reflect* in another, and so on.

Example Middle Paragraph

Analyze   Carefully read the following middle paragraph from an essay on Legg-Calve-Perthes. Then answer the questions below.

> Legg-Calve-Perthes is both rare and mysterious. The disease affects   *1*
> only 5 of every 100,000 children, usually when they are between the ages
> of five and twelve. While boys suffer from the disease far more frequently
> than girls do by a ratio of 4 to 1, when girls do develop Legg-Calve-Perthes,
> they tend to suffer more severely from it. At this point, researchers are not   *5*
> really sure of the cause of the disease. They are, however, fairly certain
> that it is not genetic. They also know that a reduction of blood flow at the
> hip joint contributes to the disease and causes the bone tissue to collapse
> or react in other strange ways. Usually, the rounded part of the femur
> bone that fits into the hip joint becomes deformed. In Allie's case, the top   *10*
> of her femur bone grew to double its normal size, a condition that produced
> extreme pain when she tried to walk. It's hard to imagine how Allie or
> anyone else is able to deal with this condition during the active childhood
> years.

1. What is the topic sentence in this paragraph?

   _____

2. What special feature about the topic is emphasized in this
   sentence?

   _____

3. What basic writing move (or moves) does the writer use in this
   paragraph? (See the previous page.)

   _____

4. How would you rate this paragraph and why?

   Weak ★ ★ ★ ★ ★ Strong

   _____

Writing a Strong Closing

While the opening part of your writing offers important *first* impressions, the closing part offers important *final* impressions. More specifically, the closing helps the reader better understand and appreciate the importance of your topic or thesis.

The Basic Parts

Consider the strategies below when writing your closing. In most cases, you will want to use more than one of these strategies; but whatever you choose to do, your closing must flow smoothly from your last middle paragraph.

- Remind the reader of the thesis.

  Legg-Calve-Perthes is like a cancer in how it affects an individual and her or his family.

- Summarize the main points or highlight one or two of them.

  Ultimately, both Alan and Bigger (two literary characters) fail to gain real control over the outside forces in their lives. Alan forfeits his interest in life, and Bigger forfeits life itself.

- Reflect on the explanation or argument you've presented in the middle part.

  It would be a shame to lose these amazing creatures (humpback whales). We don't want their mysterious song to be a thing of the past. And we can't turn to zoos when the numbers shrink to a precious few.

- Offer a final idea to keep the reader thinking about the topic.

  If the country waits until an agroterrorist attack happens, people may become ill, the overall economy could be damaged, and the agricultural economy may never recover.

INSIGHT —————

You may need to write two or three versions of your closing before it says exactly what you want it to say.

Example Closing Paragraph

Analyze Carefully read the following closing paragraph from an essay on Legg-Calve-Perthes. Then answer the questions below.

Legg-Calve-Perthes is like a cancer in how it affects an individual and her family. In Allie's case, the debilitating effects started with her painful efforts to walk and has continued with attempts to address the condition with operations, therapy, and braces. Through all of this, she and her family have missed out on so much. Her mother had to quit her job, and her sister felt ignored. As Allie recalled, "My sister has always felt jealous of all of the attention I get from my parents." But knowing that the condition should, in time, resolve itself certainly must help sufferers like Allie meet each new challenge. It must also help them to know that young people suffering from Legg-Calve-Perthes usually do quite well in the long term. Unfortunately, the chance of permanent hip damage exists as well.

1. In what way does the first sentence remind the reader of the thesis statement?

   ____

2. What other strategy or strategies does the writer use?

   ____

3. How would you rate this paragraph and why?

   Weak ★ ★ ★ ★ ★ Strong

   ____

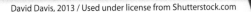

David Davis, 2013 / Used under license from Shutterstock.com

LO5 Understanding Strong Writing

The traits (ideas, organization, voice, and so on) are the key ingredients in writing. Each one contributes to a successful essay or report. (See pages 131–160.)

The traits-based checklist below serves as a guide to strong writing. Your writing will be clear and effective when it can "pass" each point. This checklist is especially helpful during revising, when you are deciding how to improve your writing.

> "There is no such thing as good writing, only good rewriting."
> —Louis Brandeis

INSIGHT ————————————————————————————————

Word choice and sentence fluency are not as important early on in the revising process, when you are focused on content. But they do become important later on, during editing.

A Guide to Strong Writing

Ideas

- [ ] **1.** Does an interesting and relevant topic serve as a starting point for the writing?
- [ ] **2.** Is the writing focused, addressing a specific feeling about or a specific part of the topic? (Check the thesis statement.)
- [ ] **3.** Are there enough specific ideas, details, and examples to support the thesis?
- [ ] **4.** Overall, is the writing engaging and informative?

Organization

- [ ] **5.** Does the writing form a meaningful whole—with opening, middle, and closing parts?
- [ ] **6.** Does the writing follow a logical pattern of organization?
- [ ] **7.** Do transitions connect ideas and help the writing flow?

Voice

- [ ] **8.** Does the writer sound informed about and interested in the topic?
- [ ] **9.** Does the writer sound sincere and genuine?

Word Choice

- [ ] **10.** Does the word choice clearly fit the purpose and the audience?
- [ ] **11.** Does the writing include specific nouns and verbs?

Sentence Fluency

- [ ] **12.** Are the sentences clear, and do they flow smoothly?
- [ ] **13.** Are the sentences varied in their beginnings and length?

React Carefully read the following paragraphs from a persuasive essay. Then answer the questions below.

Learn to Earn

Lack of student motivation is a main topic of discussion when it comes   *1*
to today's underachieving schools. The experts ask, how can we motivate
our students to learn? And how can we keep them in school long enough
to prepare for the twenty-first century workplace? These questions are
especially important in urban areas, where the dropout rate is alarming,   *5*
especially among nonnative English students. One answer appears quite
logical: Give them money. In other words, if we want our students to
succeed in school, we should pay them.

Students, in one way, are already bribed to attend school. The whole
point of academic scholarships is based on receiving a monetary reward for   *10*
being a good student. Calling a cash award a "scholarship" doesn't alter the
fact that what's being offered is money. Presently, only the best students or
the best athletes pick up all the cash. That does not seem fair. What about
the student that doesn't want to go to college? Why not pay everyone for
going to school the same way they would get paid for doing any other job?   *15*

Many students drop out of school because they are forced to work to
help support their families. When it comes to choosing between going to
school or going to work, the latter usually wins out for practical reasons.
If these same students were paid a minimum wage for attending school,
they wouldn't have to worry about choosing between education and keeping   *20*
their jobs. In the long run, it would probably be less expensive to keep
these students in school by paying them than to have them drop out of
school with no skills.

Ideas

☐ **1.** Is the topic relevant and interesting?

☐ **2.** Is the focus, or thesis, of the essay clear?

☐ **3.** Does the essay contain a variety of specific details?

Organization

☐ **4.** Does the first paragraph include the key elements of an effective opening?

☐ **5.** Do the paragraphs follow a logical pattern of organization?

Voice

☐ **6.** Does the writer sound informed and interested in the topic?

☐ **7.** Does the writer sound sincere and honest?

LO6 Using Standard English

Standard English (SE) is English that is considered appropriate for school, business, and government. You have been learning SE throughout your years in school. The chart that follows shows the basic differences between non-Standard English (NS) and SE.

Differences in . . .	NS	SE
1. Expressing plurals after numbers	10 mile	10 miles
2. Expressing habitual action	He always be early.	He always is early.
3. Expressing ownership	My friend car . . .	My friend's car . . .
4. Expressing the third-person singular verb	The customer ask . . .	The customer asks . . .
5. Expressing negatives	She doesn't never . . .	She doesn't ever . . .
6. Using reflexive pronouns	He sees hisself . . .	He sees himself . . .
7. Using demonstrative adjectives	Them reports are . . .	Those reports are . . .
8. Using forms of *do*	He done it.	He did it.
9. Avoiding double subjects	My manager he . . .	My manager . . .
10. Using *a* or *an*	I need new laptop. She had angry caller.	I need a new laptop. She had an angry caller.
11. Using the past tense of verbs	Carl finish his . . .	Carl finished his . . .
12. Using *isn't* or *aren't* versus *ain't*	The company ain't . . .	The company isn't . . .

> "Standard English is not a language—
> but a variety of English among many."
> —Peter Trudgill

Read Carefully read the following descriptive essay. As you will see, it contains underlined examples of non-standard variations of American English (NS).

My <u>grandparents they used</u> to babysit for me when my mom had to   *1*
work weekends. They were never too busy to have me. Whenever I <u>be bored</u>
with playing outside, I would head into the two-car garage and "help"
Grandpa. His garage was really just a collection place for all of his old
machines. He <u>be always putzing</u> around with something in there. I think   *5*
<u>Grandpa saw hisself</u> as a master repairman.

When I walked into that old garage, the burnt smell of oil <u>were</u> the
first thing I would notice. Once my eyes adjusted to the gloom, I could
start making out different parts of the collection. On the right wall, he <u>had</u>
<u>picture</u> of everyone in the Smith family. On certain days I had to stand   *10*
<u>four inch</u> from the picture to see the grinning faces. Glaring sunbeams
would shoot through <u>them dusty, yellowish curtains</u> covering the one
window.

In one corner, there <u>were</u> a dirty old refrigerator <u>load up</u> with cans of
soda and new canisters of snuff, just in case he <u>run</u> out while working on   *15*
a project. You see, <u>Grandpa he</u> always had a pinch of snuff in his mouth.
Because of that nasty habit, he would sometimes spit into an old coffee
can. I <u>didn't never</u> touch that can for sure. Other than that, he was a great
person to be around because he <u>be so patient and interested</u> in working
with me.   *20*

Discuss In small groups or as a class, identify the number that describes each underlined NS form, using the chart on page 120 as a guide. Then explain how to express each one using Standard English (SE).

LO7 Thinking Critically and Logically

Critical thinking is careful, logical thinking—the kind of thinking that you should use for your academic essays and reports. Here are some questions that will help you to think critically and logically about your writing projects.

Asking Critical Questions

- What is the purpose of my writing (to inform, to entertain, to persuade)?
- Who is my intended audience (general readers, my instructor, my peers)?
- Can my topic be separated into parts? If so, what are they?
- How well do I know my topic?
- What will the reader gain from reading about this topic?
- What logical pattern of thinking should I follow? (See below.)
- What will be the focus, or thesis, of my writing? (See pages 138–139.)
- How will I support my thesis?

Deductive and Inductive Thinking

Most of your academic writing will follow either a deductive or an inductive pattern of thinking. **Deductive thinking** moves from a general thesis to specific supporting details. This is the most common pattern of thinking that you will use. **Inductive thinking** moves from specific facts and details to a general conclusion.

Use these questions to check for deductive thinking.

- Do I include a thesis in my opening part?
- Do the details logically support or follow from my thesis?
- If the writing is persuasive, do I address any obvious limitations or opposing points of view? (See page 395.)
- Does the conclusion logically follow the ideas that come before it?

Use these questions to check for inductive thinking.

- Do I start with a series of facts, examples, and explanations?
- Do the details logically lead up to a general conclusion?
- If the writing is persuasive, do I address any obvious limitations or opposing points of view? (See page 395.)
- Is the general conclusion reasonable?

Apply For your next writing assignment, use the questions on this page as a general guide to critical and logical thinking.

A CLOSER LOOK at Logic

Logic is the science of reasonable and accurate thinking. Your writing will be logical if it contains relevant and provable evidence.

Reliable and Logical Evidence

If you were writing a paper about the aurora borealis, the following types of evidence would be provable:

Observation: I saw the northern lights for the first time last week.

Quotation: Carl Sagan once said, "Somewhere, something incredible is waiting to be known."

Statistic: It takes the solar wind 104 hours to reach earth.

Comparison: The aurora borealis works much like the excited gases in a fluorescent light bulb.

Explanation: According to the latest reports from NASA . . .

Inference: For the aurora borealis to appear, there must have been solar flares within the previous 24 hours.

Faulty Logic

The opposite of logical evidence is evidence that is illogical or exaggerated like the examples below. Be sure to avoid these types of faulty logic in your own writing.

Exaggerating the facts: Eating chocolate can cause all kinds of diseases, even if you eat only one or two pieces a day.

Distracting the reader: Chocolate is not only bad for your health, but it also costs a lot of money, and the wrappers add to the problem of littering.

Offering extremes: Either people should give up chocolate, or we are going to face incredible increases in heath-care costs.

Telling only part of the truth: The new increase in tuition is a good idea because it will lower taxes for county residents.

Appealing to a popular position: The new tuition increase is a good idea because it passed unanimously at the last board meeting.

Practice Write two or three of your own examples of faulty logic (without naming the type). Then exchange your work with a partner and discuss each other's examples.

Review and Enrichment

On the next seven pages you will review and enrich your understanding of the concepts in this chapter.

Reviewing the Chapter

Respond to each set of directions that follows.

Write to Learn Answer the following questions about writing to learn. (See page 104.)

1. How is writing to learn different from traditional writing assignments?

_____

2. What are two ways you can write to learn using a class notebook?

_____

Understand the Writing Process Answer the following questions about the writing process. (See pages 106–111.)

1. What are the steps in the writing process?

_____

2. Explain the forward and backward movement of this process.

_____

Use Writing Strategies Answer the following questions about the writing strategies and instruction covered in this chapter. (See pages 112–121.)

1. What are the three main parts of an academic essay?

_____

2. What is Standard English?

_____

3. How can the guide to strong writing help you?

_____

Think Critically and Logically Answer the following questions about critical and logical thinking. (See pages 122–123.)

1. What is critical thinking?

_____

2. What is meant by faulty logic? Give one example.

_____

Reading

In the first part of this section, you will read and react to "Why Thinner?" from the textbook *Sociology: Your Compass to a New World*. Use the steps in the reading process as your guide. In the second part, you will find writing ideas to choose from for a paragraph or essay of your own.

> "We delight in beauty of the butterfly, but rarely admit the changes it has gone through to achieve that beauty."
> —Maya Angelou

About the Authors

Robert J. Brym received a PhD from the University of Toronto, and he teaches sociology at the same university. Brym has authored many books on political sociology, race, and ethnic relations. **John Lie** received his PhD from Harvard University and has served as Dean of International and Area Studies at the University of California at Berkley. Lie has authored many books on a wide range of topics, from contemporary East Asia to race and ethnicity.

Prereading

As you well know, body image is an important issue for many people. That is why so many individuals exercise, diet, and keep up with the latest fashions. Think about your involvement with and feelings about "body image." Then list a few of your thoughts for discussion.

CONSIDER THE TRAITS

As you read, pay careful attention to the **ideas**—the main idea or thesis and the supporting details. Also consider the **organization** of the text—how the authors structure the beginning, middle, and ending parts. Finally, determine the **voice** of the writing—does the writing speak to highly educated readers or to a more general audience?

_____

_____

_____

_____

What do you think?

Consider the quotation at the top of the page: Is Maya Angelou talking specifically about butterflies, or does her idea apply to something else? Explain. Do you agree with what she says?

Identify   Before you read, answer these three questions:

1. What do the title and the first few lines in each paragraph tell you about the text?

   _____

2. What might be the author's purpose?

   _____

3. What do you expect to learn?

   _____

Reading and Rereading

This selection makes some interesting comparisons between the past and present understanding of body image. As you read, make it your goal to (1) identify the main idea, (2) locate the supporting evidence and the comparisons, and (3) assess the value of the selection. Consider annotating the text (page 20) during your reading.

The Reading Process

Prereading → Rereading
↑ ↓ ↑ ↓
Reading → Reflecting

Why Thinner?

The human body has always served as a sort of personal billboard   _1_
that advertises gender. However, historian Joan Jacobs Brumberg (1997)
makes a good case for the view that the importance of body image to
our **self-definition** has grown over the past century. Just listen to the
difference in emphasis on the body in the diary resolutions of two typical   _5_
white, middle-class American girls, separated by a mere 90 years. From
1892: "Resolved, not to talk about myself or feelings. To think before
speaking. To work seriously. To be self-restrained in conversation and
actions. Not to let my thoughts wander. To be dignified. Interest myself
more in others." From 1982: "I will try to make myself better in any way   _10_
I possibly can with the help of my budget and babysitting money. I will
lose weight, get new lenses, already got new haircut, good makeup, new
clothes and accessories" (quoted in Brumberg, 1997: xxi).

As body image became more important for one's self-definition in
the course of the 20th century, the ideal body image became thinner,   _15_
especially for women. Thus, the first American "glamour girl" was
Mrs. Charles Dana Gibson, who was famous in advertising and society
cartoons in the 1890s and 1900s as the "Gibson Girl." According to
the Metropolitan Museum of Art's Costume Institute, " Every man in
America wanted to win her" and "every woman in America wanted to be   _20_

her. Women stood straight as poplars and tightened their **corset** strings to show off tiny waists" (Metropolitan Museum of Art, 2000).

As featured in the *Ladies Home Journal* in 1905, the Gibson Girl measured 38-27-45—certainly not slim by today's standards. During the 20th century, however, the ideal female body type thinned out. The "White Rock Girl," featured on the logo of the White Rock Beverage Company, was 5 feet 4 inches and weighed 140 pounds in 1894. In 1947 she had slimmed down to 125 pounds. By 1970 she was 5 feet 8 inches and 118 pounds (Peacock, 2000).

Why did body image become more important to people's self-definition during the 20th century? Why was slimness stressed? Part of the answer to both questions is that more Americans grew overweight as their lifestyles became more sedentary. As they became better educated, they became increasingly aware of the health problems associated with being overweight. The desire to slim down was, then, partly a reaction to bulking up. But that is not the whole story.

The rake-thin models who populate modern ads are not promoting good health. They are promoting an extreme body shape that is virtually unattainable for most people. They do so because it is good business. The fitness, diet, low-caloric food, and cosmetic surgery industries do tens of billions of dollars of business every year (Hesse-Biber, 1996). Bankrolled by these industries, advertising in the mass media blankets us with images of slim bodies and makes these body types appealing. Once people become convinced that they need to develop bodies like the ones they see in ads, many of them are really in trouble because these body images are very difficult for most people to attain.

From Brym/Lie, *Sociology*, 2E. © 2007 Cengage Learning.

self-definition
evaluating one's worth as an individual

corset
a close-fitting undergarment worn to support and shape the waistline

Reflecting

Practice After you complete your reading, answer the following questions. Share your responses with your classmates.

1. What main idea is developed in the text?

_____

_____

_____

2. What supporting details do you find most interesting and important? (Name two.)

_____

_____

_____

3. Has this text confirmed or changed your understanding of the topic? Explain.

_____

_____

_____

4. What questions, if any, do you still have about the topic?

_____

_____

_____

5. How would you rate this reading and why?

Weak ★ ★ ★ ★ ★ Strong

_____

_____

_____

Vocabulary Practice

Identify For each word below, define the identified word parts. Then try to explain the meaning of the complete word. (See pages 36–37 and 668–676 for help.)

1. self-restrained (line 8) self + restrain + ed

_____

_____

2. sedentary (line 33) sed + en + (t)ary

_____

_____

3. unattainable (line 39) un + attain + able

_____

_____

Drawing Inferences

Explain Answer the following questions to help you draw inferences from the text. (See pages 30–32 for help.)

1. Why do glamour and beauty seem so important? What value do they have?

_____

_____

_____

_____

2. To what degree is modern life influenced by mass media and advertising? Explain.

_____

_____

_____

_____

Writing

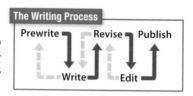

The Writing Process
Prewrite → Revise → Publish
Write → Edit

What follows are possible writing activities to complete in response to the reading. Use the writing process (pages 106–111) to help you develop your paragraph or essay.

Prewriting

Choose one of the following writing ideas. Or decide upon an idea of your own making related to the reading.

Writing Ideas

1. **Writing to Learn:** In an email message or personal letter, explain modern beauty and glamour to someone from long ago or to someone in the future.
2. **Paragraph Writing:** Share the details of a personal weight-loss experience.
3. Describe the most glamorous person you know.
4. **Essay Writing:** Write an extended definition of *beauty*. Consider dictionary definitions, the word's history, specific examples, quotations containing the word, and so on. (See pages 33–38 for help.)

When planning . . .

Refer to page 108 to help with your prewriting and planning. Also refer to the tips below.

- Choose a topic that truly interests you.
- Collect plenty of details and ideas so that you have a lot to say.
- Decide on an interesting way (your focus) to write about your topic.

Writing and Revising

Refer to pages 109–110 to help you write and revise your first draft. Also refer to the tips below.

When writing . . .

- Explore your ideas fully.
- Form a meaningful whole with a beginning, middle, and ending.
- Don't worry about getting everything just right in your first draft.

When revising . . .

- Let your first draft sit unread for a bit. Then review it carefully.
- Then check your ideas for clarity and completeness.
- Ask a classmate to react to your first draft.

Editing

Refer to the checklist on page 183 when you are ready to edit your writing for style and correctness.

5

> "Good writing is writing that works. It says just enough and no more."
>
> —Patricia T. O'Conner

The Traits of Academic Writing

Looking at a writing assignment, you may wonder, "How will I ever complete it?" To answer this question, remember that writing is a process, and if you follow the steps in this process, you will have a manageable blueprint to follow. (See pages 106–111.) In addition, realize that effective writing is characterized by certain traits or elements, including strong ideas and clear organization.

Taken together, the writing process and the traits of writing serve as a sure guide for completing writing assignments. As you become comfortable with using both, your writing will improve.

This chapter will introduce you to the traits and show you how to apply them in the paragraphs and essays that you write. The traits include ideas, organization, voice, word choice, sentence fluency, and conventions.

Learning Outcomes

LO1 Ideas
LO2 Focus or thesis
LO3 Organization
LO4 Voice (tone)
LO5 Word choice and sentences
LO6 Conventions

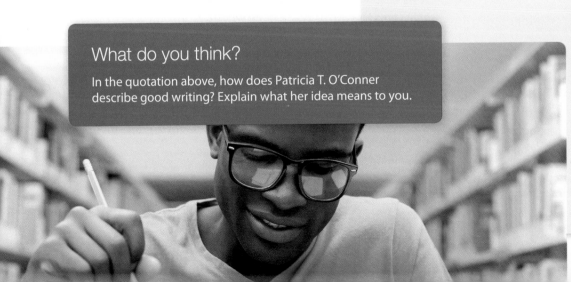

What do you think?

In the quotation above, how does Patricia T. O'Conner describe good writing? Explain what her idea means to you.

Diego Cervo, 2013 / Used under license from Shutterstock.com

LO1 Ideas

The key writing trait is ideas. Ideas are the fuel that powers your writing. Without strong ideas, you are running on vapors, meaning that you won't get very far. When selecting ideas, first consider your topic; then collect details to support it.

> "Find a subject you care about and which you in your heart feel others should care about."
> —Kurt Vonnegut

Choosing a Topic

Personal essayist Andy Rooney of *60 Minutes* fame stated, "I don't pick subjects so much as they pick me." He is lucky that he can write about anything that interests him. You are not so lucky in most of your writing assignments because your choices are usually rather limited. Even so, always try to select a topic that interests you; otherwise, you will find it difficult to do your best work.

Narrowing Your Choices

Some assignments will tell you specifically what you should write about, but in most cases, they will identify a general subject area that serves as a starting point for a topic search. This graphic shows how the selecting process should work from the general subject area to a specific topic.

INSIGHT

A topic for a research report must be broad enough to offer plenty of information. For a more limited assignment (a one- or two-page essay), the topic should be more specific.

Assignment: Analyze the cause and effects of an urban health problem.

General subject area	urban health problem
Narrowing the subject	related to living conditions
Specific topic	exposure to lead paint

Choose Identify a specific topic for the following assignment. (Use the example above as a guide.)

Assignment: In a persuasive essay, argue for or against a new or proposed mode of transportation.

1. General subject area

2. Narrow the subject

3. Specific topic

Selecting Strategies

If you can't think of a suitable topic for an assignment, review your class notes, your textbook, and Web sites for ideas. You may also want to use these selecting strategies to help you identify possible topics.

■ **Clustering** Begin a cluster with the general subject area or a narrowed subject. Cluster related words around it. Write about one of these ideas.

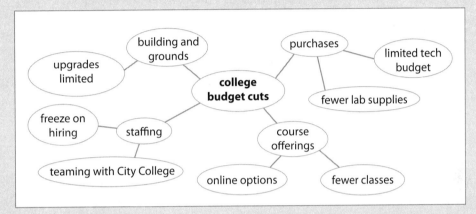

■ **Freewriting** Write nonstop for 5–10 minutes about your assignment to discover possible topics. Begin by writing down a particular thought about the assignment. Then record whatever comes to mind without stopping to judge, edit, or correct your writing.

■ **Developing a Dialogue** Create a dialogue or conversation between yourself and another person to identify possible topics for a writing assignment.

Practice Create a dialogue for the writing assignment below. Afterward, circle any possible writing ideas. (Use your own paper to continue the conversation.)

Assignment: Write a brief personal essay in which you reflect on something that really bugs you about school life or the workplace.

You: _So what is one thing that really bugs you about this school?_

Other person: _____

You: _____

Other person: _____

Gathering Details

Writing your first draft will go smoothly if you have collected plenty of details to support your topic, so use strategies like those below and on the next page to gather facts and details.

Deciding What You Already Know

To review what you already know about a topic, try one of these strategies:

- **Five W's of Writing** Answer the five W's (*who? what? when? where?* and *why?*) to identify basic information about your subject. Add *how?* to the list for more coverage.
- **Listing** List your first thoughts about your topic as well as questions about it. Record ideas nonstop for as long as you can.
- **Clustering** Create a cluster with your specific topic as the starting point. (See page 133.)
- **Focused Freewriting** Write freely about your specific topic for at least 5 minutes to see what thoughts and feelings you can uncover. Keep writing for as long as you can.
- **Dialoguing** Discuss your specific topic in a creative dialogue between you and another person of your choice.

Explore   Using one of the strategies above, collect your first thoughts about a topic you identified on the previous page, or one of the topics listed here.

- the benefits (or drawbacks) of taking online college courses
- a promising career choice
- a particular trend in fashion or music

_____

_____

_____

_____

"Writing comes more
easily if you have
something to say."
—Sholem Asch

Collecting Additional Information

For most writing assignments, gathering your own thoughts will just be a starting point. You will also need to research your topic to learn more about it. Your research may consist of reading about a topic or learning about it through firsthand experiences.

Questioning

Questions can guide your search for additional information about a topic. Whether your topic is a **problem** *(school budget cuts)*, a **policy** *(graduation requirements)*, or a **concept** *(a weight-training program)*, the questions in the following chart will lead you to related facts and details.

	Description	Function	History	Value
Problems	What is the problem?	Who or what is affected by it?	What or who caused it?	What is its significance?
Policies	What are the most important features?	What is the policy meant to do?	What brought this policy about?	What are its advantages and disadvantages?
Concepts	What is the concept or idea?	Why is it important?	When did it start?	What value does it have?

Collect   Fill in the first blank below with a specific topic. (See the previous activities in this chapter for ideas.) Then indicate the topic's category—either a problem, policy, or concept. Finally, choose two appropriate questions from the chart above and answer them. (You may have to do some quick research to answer your questions.)

Topic: _____

Category: _____

Question 1: _____

Question 2: _____

Understanding Supporting Details

Your college instructors expect you to support your ideas with strong details. Details help you develop complete explanations and arguments.

Types of Details

The following list identifies the common types of details.

- **Facts and statistics** give specific information that can be checked.

  > Legg-Calve-Perthes affects only 5 of every 100,000 people, usually when they are between the ages of five and twelve.

- **Examples** demonstrate or show something.

  > **Main point:** Donald has always been more daring.
  >
  > **Example:** When we were younger, he was the first to jump off the cliffs at the quarry.

- **Definitions** explain new terms.

  > The *American Heritage College Dictionary* defines sexual harassment as "unwanted and offensive sexual advances or negative sexual remarks."

- **Quotations** provide the thoughts of people knowledgeable about the topic.

  > Ms. Sandra Williams, the community service advisor, said, "Working in the community shows students that a lot of other people need their help."

- **Reflections** offer the writer's thoughts.

  > I wonder if he ever knew how frightened I was and how I imagined there to be all types of evil on the other side of that half-opened door.

Identify List two or three different types of details that you could use to support the topic you've been working with in this chapter.

_____

_____

_____

Levels of Details

Strong essays contain different levels of details to explain or develop each main point. Here are the three basic levels of detail in writing.

- **Level 1:** A **controlling sentence** names a topic (usually a topic sentence) or makes a main point.
- **Level 2:** A **clarifying sentence** explains a level 1 sentence.
- **Level 3:** A **completing sentence** adds details to complete the point.

Details in Action

In the passage that follows, the level 1 sentence (a topic sentence) is supported by three level 2 sentences. The last level 2 sentence is supported by two level 3 sentences.

> **(Level 1)** Legg-Calve-Perthes is both rare and mysterious. **(Level 2)**   1
> The disease affects only 5 of every 100,000 children, usually when they are
> between the ages of five and twelve. **(Level 2)** Boys suffer from the disease
> far more frequently than girls do, by a ratio of 4 to 1, which makes Allie's
> experience all the more unusual. **(Level 2)** At this point, researchers are   5
> not really sure of the cause of the disease. **(Level 3)** They are, however,
> fairly certain that it is not genetic. **(Level 3)** They also know that a
> reduction of blood flow . . .

Identify   Carefully read the following passage; then label its levels of detail. (Work on this activity with a partner if your instructor allows it.)

> (_____) Plato, an ancient Greek philosopher and   1
> educator, was the first to write a book about the lost continent of Atlantis.
> (_____) Most people agree that Plato's book includes only legends,
> not real history. (_____) When Plato described Atlantis, he
> painted a picture of a people of fabulous wealth who ruled over a great and   5
> wonderful empire. (_____) He also claimed that the continent of
> Atlantis sank beneath the sea in one day's time.

Special Challenge   Write a brief paragraph about your best piece of technology or your favorite type of music. Afterward, label your sentences with a 1, 2, or 3, depending on the level of detail they include.

LO2 Focus or Thesis

Identifying a focus is not one of the basic traits, but it is included here because it helps you plan how to use the ideas you collect.

Choosing a Special Part of a Topic

A skilled photographer decides to focus or center a subject before taking a photograph. You should do the same before you begin writing. A strong focus helps you decide what information to include in your writing.

To decide on a focus, consider your feelings about your topic and the information that you have collected. For example, if you are writing an essay about a person, you could focus on your feelings about this person. The following example identifies the focus for an essay on an important happening or event.

> Suppose you were writing an essay on the effects of the 2010 Gulf oil leak on a local shrimping community. You could focus on the effects on one specific family.
>
> **Topic:** Effects of 2010 Gulf oil spill on (name of local shrimping community)
>
> **Focus:** The spill's effect on a particular family or business

Evaluating a Focus

Without a clear focus, writing can ramble and even lose the reader. For example, a story that shares every detail about a local festival lacks focus. But one that shares the writer's unique impression of the event with a few key details has a strong focus.

Review Rate the effectiveness of each focus below by circling the appropriate star. Consider whether the focus is clear, reasonable, and worth developing. Explain each of your choices.

1. **Topic:** My personal ambitions **Focus:** A direct result of my mother's influence

   weak ★ ★ ★ ★ ★ strong _____

   _____

2. **Topic:** Dog food **Focus:** Who makes it?

   weak ★ ★ ★ ★ ★ strong _____

   _____

3. **Topic:** Scooters **Focus:** Have been around a while

   weak ★ ★ ★ ★ ★ strong _____

   _____

Forming a Thesis Statement

State your focus in a thesis statement for an essay and in a topic sentence for a paragraph. The following formula can be used to write a thesis statement or a topic sentence.

A specific topic		A particular feeling, feature, or part		An effective thesis statement or topic sentence
wearing *hijab*—Islamic covering	**+**	Mixed feelings about it	**=**	To wear *hijab*—Islamic covering—invites mixed feelings in me.

INSIGHT ————————————————————————————
You may have to write two, three, or even four versions of a thesis statement before it says what you want it to say.

Create   Identify a focus and then write a topic sentence or thesis statement for each of the following assignments. The first one is done for you.

1. **Writing assignment:** Paragraph describing a specific type of exercise

   Specific topic: Pilates

   Focus: _a thoughtful approach to fitness_

   Topic sentence: _Pilates provides a thoughtful approach to physical fitness._

2. **Writing assignment:** Paragraph explaining a type of ethnic food

   Specific topic: Tex-Mex cuisine

   Focus: _____

   Topic sentence: _____

3. **Writing assignment:** Essay reflecting on a modern social problem

   Specific topic: Affordable living spaces

   Focus: _____

   Thesis statement: _____

4. **Writing assignment:** Essay analyzing a favorite or important movie

   Specific topic: (Your choice)

   Focus: _____

   Thesis statement: _____

LO3 Organization

After identifying your thesis, you'll need to decide how to organize the information that supports it. Start by studying your thesis; then review the information you have gathered.

1. **Study your thesis statement.** It may identify how to organize your ideas. For example, consider the following thesis statement:

   > After all of these years, *The Simpsons* continues to entertain American viewers.

   This thesis suggests arranging the information by order of importance or deductive organization. (See below.)

2. Then **review the information you have gathered.** Decide which ideas support your thesis and arrange them according to the best method of organization.

Patterns of Organization

Listed below are some of the common patterns that you will use in your writing.

- Use **chronological order** (time) when you are sharing a personal experience, telling how something happened, or explaining how to do something.

- Use **spatial order** (location) for descriptions, arranging information from left to right, top to bottom, from the edge to the center, and so on.

- Use **order of importance** when you are taking a stand or arguing for or against something. Arrange your reasons either from most important to least important or the other way around.

- Use **deductive organization** if you want to follow your thesis statement with basic information—supporting reasons, examples, and facts.

- Use **inductive organization** when you want to present specific details first and conclude with your thesis statement.

- Use **comparison organization** when you want to show how one topic is different from and similar to another one.

JeniFoto, 2013 / Used under license from Shutterstock.com

Choose Study each of the following thesis statements. Then choose the method of organization that the thesis suggests. Explain each of your choices. The first one is done for you.

1. **Thesis statement:** The boardwalk makes Coney Island different from any other New York neighborhood.

   Appropriate method of organization: _spatial order_

   Explain: _The thesis suggests that the writer will describe the boardwalk, so_

   spatial organization makes sense.

   _____

2. **Thesis statement:** I am a Korean, but I am an American, too.

   Appropriate method of organization: _____

   Explain: _____

   _____

   _____

3. **Thesis statement:** Multicultural education is vital to a society made up of many different peoples.

   Appropriate method of organization: _____

   Explain: _____

   _____

   _____

4. **Thesis statement:** I did something totally out of character for me; I jumped off a bridge with nothing more than a giant rubber band attached to my ankles.

   Appropriate method of organization: _____

   Explain: _____

   _____

   _____

5. **Thesis statement:** (Choose one that you wrote on page 139.)

   Appropriate method of organization: _____

   Explain: _____

   _____

   _____

Arranging Details

Here are three basic strategies for arranging your supporting details after identifying an appropriate pattern of organization.

- **Make a quick list** of main points.
- **Create an outline**—an organized arrangement of main points and subpoints.
- **Fill in a graphic organizer,** arranging main points and details in a chart or diagram. (See page 9.)

Using a Quick List

A quick list works well when you are writing a short essay or paragraph, or when your planning time is limited. Here is a quick list for an essay about comets. (The main pattern of organization is chronological.)

Sample Quick List

Thesis statement: The appearance of comets in the night skies has puzzled people for thousands of years.

- very early on, thought to be planets
- Aristotle, the result of air escaping from atmosphere
- by 15th & 16th centuries, thought to be heavenly bodies
- all along, considered a sign of impending disaster
- really a gaseous body around a core of ice and dust
- head, hundreds of miles in diameter; tail millions of miles in length

Create   Write a thesis statement and a quick list for an essay explaining why a certain television show is one of your favorites.

Thesis statement:

_____

_____

Quick list:

_____

_____

_____

_____

Using an Outline

An effective outline carefully arranges ideas for your writing. Topic and sentence outlines follow specific guidelines: If you have a "I," you must have at least a "II." If you have an "A," you must have at least a "B," and so on. You can also change or simplify an outline to meet your needs.

Simplified Outline

What follows is the first part of a simplified outline that includes main points in complete sentences and supporting details in phrases.

Thesis statement: Charlotte Perkins Gilman rejected common beliefs about male dominance.

1. Gilman's beliefs did little to prepare her for married life.
    – in 1884, married Charles W. Stetson
    – gave birth to a daughter
    – visited CA shortly after to mentally and emotionally heal
    – wrote a book about a pregnant woman locked in a room

2. During the next stage in her life, Gilman became a leading feminist.
    – delivered speeches on women's rights
    – edited *Impress* for Women's Press Associate
    – from 1895-1900, continued lecturing
    – in 1896, a delegate to the National Socialist and Labor Congress in London

Create   Develop the first part of a simplified outline for an essay about television viewing. A thesis statement and two main points are provided. Put the main points in a logical order and make up two or three details to support each one.

Thesis statement: Unregulated television viewing has harmful effects on young viewers.

Main points: Television is passive, requiring almost no skill or thinking. Television viewing takes away from study and reading time.

1. _____
    – _____
    – _____
    – _____

2. _____
    – _____
    – _____
    – _____

LO4 Voice (Tone)

Voice is the way you express yourself or sound in your writing. In most cases, college instructors will expect you to use an academic voice. At other times, a more personal voice will be more appropriate.

- **Academic voice:** Academic voice is preferable for most academic writing, especially informational essays and reports. The voice reflects interest in and knowledge about your topic and uses language appropriate for college-level course work. This means it follows the rules of Standard English. (See pages 120–121.) This passage demonstrates an academic voice.

> Ella Fitzgerald is one of the most famous jazz vocalists in music history. Known as "the First Lady of Song," Fitzgerald made her singing debut at 17 in the renowned Apollo Theater in Harlem, New York. . . . *(The writer sounds interested in and knowledgeable about her topic and follows the rules for Standard English.)*

INSIGHT

Other features of an academic voice include the following: Generally, presenting information in the third-person (*he, she, her,* and so on); maintaining objectivity (excluding personal thoughts and feelings); and choosing words that sound more formal (*he would* rather than *he'd*).

- **Personal voice:** The personal voice is less formal, almost like conversation. It is useful for writing narratives or personal essays, Of course, it should still reflect an interest in the topic and try to follow the rules of Standard English. This passage demonstrates a personal voice.

> When I was five or six, I discovered that circuses aren't all they're supposed to be. We were going to a circus for a class trip, and I couldn't wait. For starters, my friend Connie Lee told me her mom fainted when she first saw the lion tamer. . . . *(The writer sounds interested and conversational but still follows the rules for Standard English.)*

INSIGHT

Other features of a personal voice include the following: Generally, speaking in the first person (*I, my, we,* and so on); using a subjective tone (including personal thoughts and feelings); and offering a more relaxed word choice (*they're* instead *of they are*).

Create   Write two passages about someone you admire or about an important event. In the first passage, use an academic voice; in the second, use a personal voice. Be prepared to share and discuss your work with your classmates.

Developing a Writing Voice

When it comes to developing your writing voice, experience is the best teacher. So don't expect to write with "voice" just by learning about it. Here are a few things that you can do to work on your voice:

- **Practice writing.** Write nonstop for at least 10 minutes daily. Write about anything and everything. A neighbor really bugs you. Write about him or her. You've heard about a new policy at your school. Write about it. This practice will help you become more comfortable with writing, which will help you write with more personality.

- **Become a regular reader.** Read anything and everything. Read newspapers, magazines, mysteries, blogs, box tops. As you read, you will learn about different ways to express ideas.

- **Model good writing.** If you really like the sound of an essay or article, try to write passages like it.

- **Know what you're talking about.** If you know a lot about a topic, it's easier to write about it and sound interested and knowledgeable. So be sure to do research before you start your writing.

- **Know your purpose and assignment.** Research reports will require an academic voice; narratives and other informal types of writing will require a personal voice. (See the previous page.)

- **Be honest.** Never try to sound like someone that you're not. Keep things simple and real. This may be easier said than done. As editor Patricia T. O'Conner says, "Simplicity takes practice."

Practice   Write nonstop for 5–10 minutes (time yourself) about any topic, but be sure not to stop. (If necessary, write "I'm drawing a blank" over and over until a new idea comes to mind.) Afterward, count the number of words you have written. The number of words that you write each time will increase dramatically.

_____

_____

_____

_____

_____

LO5 Word Choice and Sentences

Your words and sentences must fit the type of writing that you are doing. As you learned on the previous two pages, the language that you use in a report will be different from the language you use in personal writing.

Choosing the Best Words

In most cases, specific words (*Godzilla roars*) are better to use than general ones (*the creature yells*). And fresh words (a *belly* laugh) are better than overused ones (a *loud* laugh).

Specific Nouns and Verbs

It's especially important to use specific nouns and verbs because they carry the most meaning in your writing. The charts below show different examples of general versus specific nouns and verbs.

General nouns:	hybrid	idea	headache	writer
Specific nouns:	Prius	memory	migraine	Mark Twain

General verbs:	talk	move	think	draw
Specific verbs:	debate	slink	reflect	sketch

Analyze Study the photograph to the right. Then list examples of specific nouns and verbs that could be associated with it. Afterward, compare lists with your classmates.

Paul Cowan, 2013 / Used under license from Shutterstock.com

Specific Nouns	Specific Verbs

What to Watch for with Words

If the words you use help to create clear and interesting paragraphs, essays, and reports, then you have probably used the right ones. The following information discusses word-related issues to consider:

Watch for . . .

- **vague adjectives** (modifiers of nouns) such as *neat, big, pretty, small, cute, fun, bad, nice, good, great,* and *funny.* Use more specific adjectives instead.

> **Vague adjective:** Gerald delivered a nice tribute to his mother.
>
> **Specific adjective:** Gerald delivered a heartwarming tribute to his mother.

- **too many adjectives in general.** Being "adjective happy" detracts from rather than adds to writing.

> **Too many adjectives:** Part-time help can complete high-profile, high-impact workplace tasks without adding full-time employees.
>
> **Fewer adjectives:** Part-time help can complete essential tasks without adding full-time employees. (simpler and clearer)

- **too many "be" verbs** (*is, are, was, were,* and so on). Instead, use specific action verbs.

> **"Be" verb:** Carlos is a persuasive debater about politics.
>
> **Specific action verb:** Carlos debates persuasively about politics.

- **the same word used over and over.** Such repetition calls undue attention to the word.

> **Overuse of a word:** I noticed a woman dressed in a crisp, navy blue suit. The woman appeared to be in charge. I soon realized that the woman was the owner.
>
> **Variety added:** I noticed a woman dressed in a crisp, navy blue suit who appeared to be in charge. I soon realized that she was the owner.

- **words used incorrectly.** Words such as *their, they're,* and *there,* or *it* and *it's,* are commonly misused.

> Presidents consult with their (not they're or there) advisors.
>
> Every branch of the military offers its (not it's) wartime help.

Create Write your own example for each one of the problems discussed above. For each problem, provide an alternative with improved word choice. Afterward, share your work with your classmates.

Writing Strong Sentences

Writing clear, correct sentences leads to effective paragraphs and essays. By definition, a simple sentence expresses a complete thought and contains a subject and a verb. But not all sentences are "simple." There are compound sentences and complex sentences, as well as other types.

The most common sentence errors include fragments (*incomplete sentences*), comma splices (*two sentences connected only with a comma*), and run-on sentences (*two sentences joined without punctuation or a connecting word*). The examples at the bottom of the chart demonstrate these errors. (See pages 531–550 for more explanations and practice activities.)

A Basic Guide to Sentences

Correct Sentences

Simple sentence:	Jackson chews his fingernails. (*one complete idea*)
Compound sentence:	Max watches the presentation, but his mind is really somewhere else. (*two complete ideas*)
Complex sentence:	Sonja takes quick notes, while Connie sketches tiny flowers. (*one main idea and one subordinate or lesser idea*)

Sentence Errors

Fragment:	Popcorn all over the floor. (*no verb*)
Complete:	Popcorn *spilled* all over the floor. (*verb added*)
Fragment:	Couldn't help laughing. (*no subject*)
Complete:	We couldn't help laughing. (*subject added*)
Comma Splice:	Josie and I ordered coffee, we decided to split a cookie. (*missing a connecting word or end punctuation*)
Correct:	Josie and I ordered coffee, *and* we decided to split a cookie. (*connecting word added*)
Run-on:	Taking my dog for a walk frustrates me he has to sniff every tree and shrub in front of him. (*no punctuation*)
Correct:	Taking my dog for a walk frustrates me. He has to sniff every tree and shrub in front of him. (*punctuation added*)

Create   Write for 5–10 minutes about your favorite piece of technology. Then use the information above to check your sentences. Ask a classmate to check them as well. Correct any sentence errors that you find.

What to Watch for with Sentences

Understanding basic sentences and common errors is a critical first step. But there are other issues to consider when it comes to writing effective sentences. The information that follows identifies three of them.

Watch for . . .

■ **short, choppy sentences.** Too many short sentences in a row will sound choppy. To correct this problem, combine some of the ideas.

> **Choppy sentences:** A Harley roared past us. The cycle was jet black. It stopped in front of a food stand. The food stand sells fresh fish tacos.
>
> **Combined sentences:** A jet-black Harley roared past us and stopped in front of a food stand that sells fresh fish tacos.

■ **sentences with the same beginning.** This problem often creates choppy sentences. To correct this problem, vary some of your sentence beginnings and lengths.

> **Sentences with no variety:** Keeping a daily planner is important. It keeps track of your schedule. It lists your assignments. It helps you plan your time.
>
> **Varied sentences:** Keeping a daily planner is important. In addition to keeping track of your schedule, it lists your assignments and helps you plan your time.

■ **sentences with passive verbs.** With a passive verb, the subject is acted on rather than doing the action. (See page 584 for more information and activities.) To fix this problem, change the passive verbs into active ones.

> **Passive verb:** The 16-ounce porterhouse steak *was attacked* by the Chihuahua.
>
> **Active verb:** The Chihuahua *attacked* the 16-ounce porterhouse steak.

Evaluate   Use the following strategy to evaluate the sentences that you used in the activity on page 148.

1. List the opening words in your sentences. Decide if you need to vary some sentence beginnings.

   _____

2. List the number of words in each sentence. Decide if you need to vary sentence lengths.

   _____

3. List the main verbs used. Decide if you need to replace any passive verbs with action verbs.

   _____

LO6 Conventions

The conventions are the rules for grammar, usage, and mechanics that you need to follow in order to produce clear, correct academic writing. However, this is the final element that you should address in a piece of writing. If you pay undue attention to correctness too early in the process, you may shortchange other important steps, such as fully developing your ideas.

Getting Started

If you're working on a computer, correct your writing on a printout of your work. Then key in the changes. Be sure to save the edited printout so you have a record of the changes you've made.

If you're working with pen and paper, do your editing on a neat copy of your revised writing. Then make a new copy of your writing and save the edited copy. Once you develop a final copy, be sure to proofread it for correctness before you submit it.

Strategies for Editing

When checking for errors, examine your writing word for word and sentence by sentence. The following strategies will help you edit thoroughly and effectively.

- Work with a clean copy of your writing, one that incorporates your revisions and stylistic changes.
- Check one element at a time—spelling, punctuation, and so on.
- For spelling, start at the bottom of the page to force yourself to look at each word. (Remember that your spell-checker will not catch all errors.)
- For punctuation, circle all the marks to force yourself to look at each one.
- Read your work aloud at least once, noting any errors as you go along.
- Have an editing guide (see pages 483–661 in this text) and a dictionary handy.
- Ask a trusted classmate to check your work as well.

Preview   When you have questions about punctuation, grammar, or any other convention, turn to pages 483–661. This part of the book is divided into three major workshops. Answer the following questions about this section.

1. What are the names of the three workshops in this section?

   _____

2. How will these workshops prove helpful when you are editing your writing?

   _____

3. Which one or two of these workshops will you probably turn to more than the others? Why?

   _____

Using Editing Symbols

You can use editing symbols to mark errors in your writing. Listed below are some of the most common symbols.

C̲hicago	Capitalize a letter.	my ⌄speech *first*	Insert here.
F̸all	Make lowercase.	⌄ ⌄ ⌄	Insert a comma, a colon, or a semicolon.
Mr⊙Ford	Insert (add) a period.	⌄ ⌄ ⌄	Insert an apostrophe or quotation marks.
Sp. or recieve	Correct spelling.	? !	Insert a question mark or an exclamation point.
Mr. Lott he	Delete (take out) or replace.	possible worst	Switch words or letters.

Edit Use the editing symbols above to mark and correct errors in this writing sample. The first error has been marked for you.

During the last few decades⌃this Nation has become obsessed with   *1*
dieting and caloric intake. While many of us are counting calories, not
everyone understands what it is were are counting. by definition, a calorie
is a measure of the heat similar to that required to raise the temperature
of one gram of water by one degree. Our bodies can be thought of as   *5*
biocemical machines that burn the food we eat for fuel The amount of
burning that takes place is measured in calories. how much energy is
produced by burning calories is determined by how active we are. By just
sitting and resting we burn about a calorie a minute. Just to stay alive
our body it must burn 1440 calories per day. The more active we are, the   *10*
more calories we will up burn. How many calories do we burn up when we
engage in hard exercise.

Review and Enrichment

On the next nine pages you will review and enrich your understanding of the concepts in this chapter.

Reviewing the Chapter

On your own paper, respond to each set of directions below.

Ideas   Answer the following questions about writing ideas. (See pages 132–137.)

- What does it mean to narrow a subject? _____
- What are four different types of supporting details? _____

Focus or Thesis   Explain the importance of a focus or thesis in an essay. (See pages 138–139.)

_____

_____

Organization   Identify the first four patterns of organization listed in this section. Explain each one. (See pages 140–143.)

1. _____

2. _____

3. _____

4. _____

Voice   Explain the following two types of writing voices. (See pages 144–145.)

- Academic voice: _____

_____

- Personal voice: _____

_____

Word Choice and Sentences   Answer the following questions about this section. (See pages 146–149.)

- Why is it important to use specific nouns and verbs? _____

_____

- Why should you vary your sentence beginnings and lengths? _____

_____

Conventions   Explain when in the writing process you should check for conventions and why the "timing" is important. (See pages 150–151.)

_____

_____

Reading

In the first part of this section, you will read and react to a personal essay entitled "My Accidental Jihad." In this essay, the writer reflects upon her husband's month-long observance of a sacred religious practice. Use the reading process as a guide as you read. In the second part, you will choose from a series of writing ideas to develop a paragraph or essay of your own.

> "For those who believe, no proof is necessary. For those who don't believe, no proof is possible."
> —Stuart Chase

About the Author

Krista Bremer is an essayist whose writing has appeared in many magazines, including *O, The Oprah Magazine*, *MORE*, and *The Sun*. Her award-winning essay has led to a memoir with the same title.

Prereading

No matter where you work, live, or go to school in the United States, you are bound to meet and interact with people with customs and beliefs different from your own. This set of circumstances makes life interesting, stimulating, and, at times, challenging. One way to connect with your ethnic diversity is with the restaurants and/or food you enjoy. List two or three of your favorite ethnic restaurants. Then share your thoughts about them with your classmates.

CONSIDER THE TRAITS

As you read, pay careful attention to the **ideas**—especially the details that you learn about the husband's observance of Ramadan and the writer's thoughts about it. Also consider the writer's **voice**—the way in which she speaks about the topic. Upon completion of your reading, ask yourself to what degree the text engages you.

What do you think?

Consider the quotation at the top if the page: What is author Stuart Chase's point and do you agree with it?

Identify   Before you read, answer these three questions:

1. What do the title, the first paragraph, and the first lines in some of the other paragraphs tell you about the text?

_____

2. What might be the author's purpose?

_____

3. What do you expect to learn?

_____

Reading and Rereading

"My Accidental Jihad," which first appeared in a magazine called *The Sun*, was cited in a book called *Best American Spiritual Writing*. The author's husband is a practicing Muslim; she is not.

As you read, make it your goal to (1) identify the main idea of the essay, (2) note the supporting details, and (3) compare the author's thoughts and feelings with her husband's actions. Consider using a graphic organizer such as a T-chart or a Venn diagram to help you make the comparison. (See page 9.)

From *My Accidental Jihad*

Early one morning in September, when our house is pitch-dark and the entire family is still asleep, my husband, Ismail, sits upright at the first sound of his alarm, dresses quickly, and leaves our bedroom. Later, after I've woken up and made my way downstairs for a cup of coffee, I find him standing at the counter, stuffing the last of his breakfast into his mouth, his eye on the clock as if he were competing in a pie-eating contest at the fair. The minute hand clicks forward, and, on cue, Ismail drops the food he's holding. I'm momentarily confused. My husband and I usually sit down together over or first cup of coffee, and he rarely eats breakfast. Then I realize: Ramadan has begun.

For the next month, nothing will touch my husband's mouth between sunup and sundown: Not food. Not water. Not my lips. A chart posted on our refrigerator tells him the precise minute when his fast must begin and end each day. I will find him in front of this chart again this evening, staring at his watch, waiting for it to tell him he may eat.

Ramadan is the ninth month of the lunar calendar, the month during which the **Koran** was revealed to the Prophet Mohammed through the angel Gabriel. Each year, more than one billion Muslims observe Ramadan by fasting from dawn to dusk. In addition to avoiding food and drink during daylight hours, Muslims are expected to refrain from all

1

5

10

15

20

other indulgences: sexual relations, gossip, evil thoughts—even looking at "corrupt" images on television, in magazines, or on the Internet. Ramadan is a month of purification, during which Muslims are called upon to make peace with enemies, strengthen ties with family and friends, cleanse themselves of impurities, and refocus their lives on God.   *25*
It's like a month-long spiritual tune-up.

My husband found fasting easier when he lived in Libya, surrounded by fellow Muslims. Everyone's life changes there during the fast: people work less (at least those who work outside the home), take long naps during the day, and feast with family and friends late into the night.   *30*
Now, with a corporate job and an American wife who works full time, my husband has a totally different experience of Ramadan. He spends most of his waking hours at work, just as he does every other month of the year. He still picks up our son from day care and shares cooking and cleaning responsibilities at home. Having no Muslim friends in   *35*
our Southern college town, he breaks his fast alone, standing at our kitchen counter. Here in the United States, Ramadan feels more like an extreme sport than a spiritual practice. Secretly I've come to think of it as "Ramathon."

I try to be supportive of Ismail's fast, but it's hard. The rules seem   *40*
unnecessarily harsh to me, an American raised in the seventies by parents who challenged the status quo. The humility required to submit to such a grueling, seemingly illogical exercise is not in my blood. In my family, we don't submit. We question the rules. We debate. And we do things our own way. I resent the fact that Ismail's life is being   *45*
micromanaged by the chart in the kitchen. Would Allah really hold it against him if he finished his last bit of toast, even if the clock says it's a minute past sunrise? The no-water rule seems especially cruel to me, and I find the prohibition against kissing a little **melodramatic**. I'm tempted to argue with Ismail that the rules are outdated, but he   *50*
has a billion Muslims in his corner, whereas I have yet to find another disgruntled American wife who feels qualified to rewrite one of the five pillars of **Islam**. . . .

When my husband fasts, our relationship becomes a bland, lukewarm concoction that I find difficult to swallow. I'm not proud of this   *55*
fact. After all, he isn't the only one in our house with a spiritual practice: I stumble out of bed in the dark most mornings and meditate in the corner of our room with my back to him, trying to find that bottomless truth beyond words. Once in a great while, I'll drag him to church on Sunday. Whenever I suggest we say grace at the table, he reaches   *60*
willingly for my hand, and words of gratitude flow easily from him. He has never criticized my practices, even when they are wildly inconsistent or **contradictory**. But Ramadan is not ten minutes of meditation or an hour-long sermon: it's an entire month of deprivation. Ismail's God is the old-fashioned kind, omnipresent and stern, uncompromising with his   *65*

demands. During Ramadan this God expects him to pray on time, five times a day—and to squeeze in additional prayers of forgiveness as often as he can. My God would never be so demanding. My God is a **flamboyant** and **fickle** friend with a biting wit who likes a good party. My God is transgendered and tolerant to a fault; he/she shows up unexpectedly *70* during peak moments, when life feel glorious and **synchronous**, then disappears for long stretches of time.

But Ramadan leaves little room for dramatic flair. There is no chorus of voices or public celebration—just a quiet and steady submission to Allah in the privacy of one's home. For some Muslims who live in the *75* West, the holiday becomes even more private, since their friends and colleagues are not even aware of their fast.

During the early days of Ramadan, Ismail deals with his hunger by planning his next meal and puttering around the kitchen. In the last half-hour before the sunsets, he rearranges the food in our refrigerator *80* or wipes down our already-clean counters. At night in bed, as I drift off to sleep, he reviews each ingredient in the baklava he intends to make the following evening. "Do you think I should replace the walnuts with pistachios?" he whispers. In the middle of the workday, when I call his cell phone, I hear the beeping of a cash register in the background. He is *85* wandering the aisles of our local grocery store. "I needed to get out of the office," he says matter-of-factly, as if all men escaped to the grocery store during lunch. . . .

I thought I understood the rules of Ramadan: the timetable on the refrigerator, the five daily prayers. But I didn't understand that *90* the real practice is addressing a toddler's temper tantrum or a wife's hostile silence when you haven't eaten or drunk anything in ten hours. I was like the children of Israel in the Bible, who once complained that, despite their dutiful fasting, God still wasn't answering their prayers. The children of Israel had it all wrong: God doesn't count calories. The *95* fast itself only sets the stage. God is interested in our behavior and intentions while we are hungry. Through his prophet Isaiah, God gave the children of Israel peace of mind. . . .

The purpose of fasting during Ramadan is not simply to suffer hunger, thirst, or desire, but to bring oneself closer to *taqwa*: a state of *100* sincerity, discipline, generosity, and surrender to Allah; the sum total of all Muslim teachings. When, in a moment of frustration, I grumble to my husband about his bad breath, he responds in the spirit of taqwa: He listens sympathetically and then apologizes and promises to keep his distance. He offers to sleep on the couch if that would make me more *105* comfortable. He says he wishes I had told him earlier so he could have spared me any discomfort. His humility catches me off guard and makes my resentment absurd.

This month of Ramadan has revealed to me the limits of my compassion. I recall a conversation I had with Ismail in the aftermath of *110*

September 11, 2001, when the word jihad often appeared in news stories about Muslim extremists who were hell-bent on destroying the United States. According to Ismail, the Prophet Mohammed taught that the greatest jihad, or struggle, of our lives is not the one that takes place on a battlefield, but the one that takes place within our hearts—the *115* struggle to increase self-discipline and become a better person. This month of Ramadan has thrown me into my own accidental jihad, forcing me to wrestle with my intolerances and self-absorption. And I have been losing ground in this battle, forgetting my husband's intentions and focusing instead on the petty ways I am inconvenienced by his practice. *120*

Ramadan is meant to break our rigid habits of overindulgence, the ones that slip into our lives as charming guests and then refuse to leave, taking up more and more space and stealing our attention away from God. And it's not just the big habits, the ones that grab us by the throat—alcohol, coffee, cigarettes—but the little ones that take us gently *125* by the hand and lead us stealthily away from the truth. I begin to notice my own compulsions, the small and socially acceptable ones that colonize my day: The way I depend on regular exercise to bolster my mood. The number of times I check my email. The impulse to watch a movie with my husband after our children are in bed, rather than let the silence *130* envelop us both. And the words: all the words in books, in magazines, on the computer; words to distract me from the mundane truth of the moment. I begin to notice how much of my thinking revolves around what I will consume next. . . .

In the evening, just before sundown, Ismail arranges three dates on *135* a small plate and pours a tall glass of water, just as the Koran instructs him to do, just as the Prophet Mohammed himself did long ago. Then he sits down next to me at the kitchen counter while I thumb through cookbooks, wondering what to make for dinner. He waits dutifully while the phone rings, while our daughter practices scales on the piano, while *140* our son sends a box of LEGOs crashing onto our wood floor. Then, at the moment the sun sets, he lifts a date to his mouth and closes his eyes.

Jihad
an individual's attempt at spiritual self-perfection; a Muslim holy war or struggle

Koran
the sacred text of Muslims

melodramatic
exaggerated behavior, showing lots of emotion

Islam
Muslim religion

contradictory
illogical; a statement that disagrees with something

flamboyant
showy, bright, colorful

fickle
likely to change

synchronous
happening at the same time

Reflecting

Practice After you complete your reading, answer these questions. Afterward share your responses with your classmates.

1. What is the main idea in the text? Is it directly stated or implied? (See page 52.)

_____

_____

_____

2. What supporting details do you find most interesting? (Name two or three.)

_____

_____

_____

3. How is the text organized—chronologically, logically, or spatially? Explain.

_____

_____

_____

4. What voice does the author project—academic or personal? Explain.

_____

_____

_____

5. How would you rate this selection and why?

  Weak ★ ★ ★ ★ ★ Strong

_____

_____

_____

Vocabulary Practice

Identify   Use context clues to help you define or explain the following words from the text. (See pages 34–35 for help.)

1. **fast**   (line 13)

   clues: _____

   meaning: _____

2. **indulgences**   (line 21)

   clues: _____

   meaning: _____

3. **concoction**   (line 55)

   clues: _____

   meaning: _____

4. **self-absorption**   (line 117)

   clues: _____

   meaning: _____

Drawing Inferences

Explain   Answer these questions to help you draw inferences from the text. (See pages 30–32 for help.)

1. What two words come to mind when you think of the husband? Explain your choices.

   _____

   _____

2. What two words come to mind when you think of the author? Explain your choices.

   _____

   _____

3. What does the author mean when she says, "This month of Ramadan has thrown me into my own accidental jihad"?

   _____

Writing

What follows are possible writing activities to complete in response to the reading. Use the writing process (pages 106–111) to help you develop your paragraph or essay.

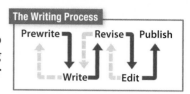

Prewriting

Choose one of the following writing ideas. Or decide on an idea of your own making related to the reading.

Writing Ideas

1. **Writing to Learn:** Write freely and rapidly for 5–10 minutes about the author of "My Accidental Jihad": Can you relate to her thoughts and feelings completely, in some ways, or not at all? Underline one or two ideas in your writing that interest or surprise you.

2. **Paragraph Writing:** Share one of your own experiences in which you abstained (denied yourself) from something for an extended period of time.

3. **Essay Writing:** Develop an extended definition of the word *sacrifice*. Consider the dictionary definition, the history of the word, and what the word means to you.

4. Develop an essay in which you compare the husband and wife in "My Accidental Jihad."

When planning . . .

Refer to page 108 to help with your prewriting and planning. Also use the tips below.

- Choose a topic that you truly want to explore.
- Gather your thoughts about the topic, and complete the necessary research.
- Decide on a special way to write about your topic.

Writing and Revising

Refer to pages 109–110 to help you write and revise your first draft. Also refer to the tips below.

When writing . . .

- Don't worry about getting everything just right in your first draft.
- Include a beginning, middle, and ending

When revising . . .

- Check your first draft for clarity and completeness.
- Ask a classmate to react to your first draft.

Editing

Refer to the checklist on page 183 to edit your writing for style and correctness.

Part II:

Reading and Writing Essays

Part II: Reading and Writing Essays

6

> "Words, when well chosen, have so great a force in them that a description often gives us more lively ideas than the sight of things themselves."
> —Joseph Addison

Description

What sets human beings apart from other animals is, among other things, our curiosity. We have a deep-seated need to know what things look like and what is going on around us. It is not an exaggeration to say that the world as we know it would not exist if people weren't extremely curious.

The focus of descriptive writing is essentially what people, places, and things look like. An essay in a science text may describe an endangered species, or the devastation caused by an earthquake. A historical article may describe the scene of a famous battle, or the appearance of an important person. A personal essay may describe a favorite family gathering, or a cherished pet.

In the first part of this chapter, you will learn about description and then read and react to professional descriptive essays. In the second part, you will write your own description.

Learning Outcomes

LO1 Understand description.

LO2 Learn reading strategies (identifying the details and considering the organization).

LO3 Read and react to a professional description.

LO4 Read and react to a second professional description.

LO5 Plan your description essay.

LO6 Write the first draft.

LO7 Revise the writing.

LO8 Edit the writing.

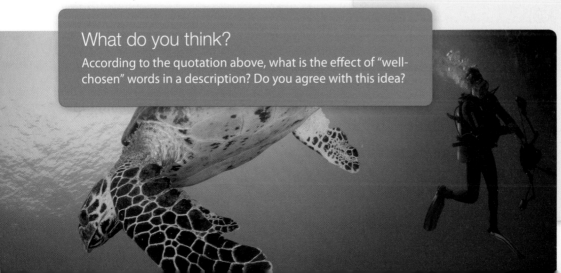

Mark Doherty, 2013 / Used under license from Shutterstock.com

What do you think?

According to the quotation above, what is the effect of "well-chosen" words in a description? Do you agree with this idea?

LO1 Understanding Description

Writing that captures the appearance of someone or something is descriptive. Writing that recounts an event or recreates the feeling or mood associated with a time and place is also descriptive. Even writing that shares experiment results can be descriptive. Description covers a lot of territory.

Descriptive writing helps readers visualize (see in their minds) the topic—a person, a place, an object, or an event. To that end, descriptive writing almost always contains plenty of specific details. The following passages show the power of specific details in descriptive writing.

> "Description is what makes the reader a sensory participant in the story."
> —Stephen King

Without specific details: Ryan and I walked to the wire fence around the gravestones. The stones were old and had no markings on them.

With specific details: Ryan and I waded through the grass and peered past the wire mesh that caged the gravestones. Because they were worn smooth by countless storms, any writing on the stones was long gone.

Description in Academic Texts

An academic text may be pure description from start to finish, although most texts have other goals: to inform, to explain, or to analyze. Even within a typical explanation or analysis, however, there's a good chance some description will occur. For example, in an analysis of the traditional nuclear family, a sociologist may describe a day in the life of such a family. In an explanation of gender differences, a physiologist may describe each gender at a certain point in life.

INSIGHT

No matter where or when a description occurs, it should contain specific details; otherwise, it will not provide a clear picture for the reader.

Practice Find two or three descriptive passages in your textbooks or in online articles. Be prepared to share one of these passages and to explain why you chose it as a good example of description.

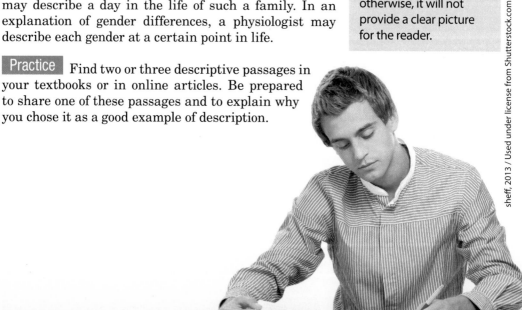

sheff, 2013 / Used under license from Shutterstock.com

Reading

Reading descriptions can be entertaining and enlightening. They can create pleasing images in your mind and help you better understand a particular person, place, object, or event.

LO2 Learning Reading Strategies

When you analyze a description, you need to focus on the quality and the arrangement of the details. These two strategies will help you do that.

Identifying the Details

You can use a sensory chart like the one below to keep track of and analyze the details in a description. Sensory means "related to the senses." A description may not address all of the senses. For example, a writer wouldn't include "taste details" in a description of an important historical site.

Sensory Chart

Sights	Sounds	Smells	Tastes	Textures

Considering Organization

To be effective, descriptive details must be easy to follow. The arrangement or organization a writer uses depends on the topic. Here is a guide to the organizational patterns used most often in descriptions.

- **Spatial Organization:** Details are arranged according to location—top to bottom, right to left, foreground to background, and so on. This arrangement is often used in physical descriptions of people and places.
- **Chronological Organization:** Details are presented according to the passage of time. This arrangement works well in travel writing, in which the writer records details as he or she observes them.
- **Logical Order:** The details simply follow one another predictably or naturally. This arrangement is common in academic texts, which are part explanation and part description.

Follow Up: Review the descriptive passages you chose for the practice activity on page 164. For each one, identify the sensory details and organization pattern.

LO3 Reading and Reacting to a Professional Description

In this selection, the author describes the unique sensations associated with a motorcycle vacation. Using the reading process will help you gain a full understanding of the text.

About the Author

Lester Smith is a writer and technologist for an educational publisher in Wisconsin. He got his first motorcycle license at age 48 and since that time has ridden to the southern border of New Mexico and back, through the Rockies, and completely around Lake Superior.

Preread Before you read, answer these three questions:

1. What do the title, first paragraph, and first lines of other paragraphs tell you about the text?

_____

2. What do you already know about the topic?

_____

3. What do you expect to learn?

_____

Read and Reread As you read make it your goal to (1) identify the main idea, (2) pay careful attention to the sensory details, and (3) study the final few lines. Completing a sensory chart (page 165) will help you keep track of the details.

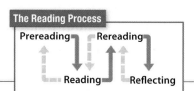

The Reading Process

Prereading — Rereading

Reading — Reflecting

Zen and the Art of a Motorcycle Vacation

You know how the centerline on a road can be hypnotizing when you're   1
driving? Well, it has a similar effect when you're motorcycling a long
distance. Plus the asphalt itself is more visible, streaming underneath
like an endless gray river. Add to these the rushing wind, the powerful
vibration of the engine, and the result is like some sort of dream.   5

But motorcycling keeps you alert, too. Without the "bubble" of a car
around you, you're more conscious of changes in temperature. You can tell
without even seeing it when a stream is nearby, just by the sudden coolness

in the air. You're also more aware of changes in the light, from the shadow $\qquad$ 10
of tiny clouds passing overhead during the day to the glow of a distant
town at night shining into the sky. That dark column of storm clouds up
ahead is more of a threat when you're motorbiking. (I once got caught in a
hailstorm in Texas, with no shelter visible for miles. Not even a roadside
tree!) $\qquad$ 15

    Also, some part of your brain has to remain alert for drivers who
might run into you, for gravel or litter or branches on the road, for deer
and wildlife that might suddenly jump out, and for possible malfunctions
of your bike itself. You have to listen for changes in the engine's roar or in
the hiss of your tires on the pavement. Some part of your brain even pays $\qquad$ 20
attention to the smells of the bike. (Is that burning oil, or maybe a leak of
overheated coolant?)

    Then there is the constant stimulation of new sights, especially if
you're traveling unfamiliar roads. Every hilltop reveals a new landscape.
Vegetation changes as you leave the city, going from carefully trimmed $\qquad$ 25
and watered lawns, to green and brown weeds along country roadsides,
to open fields of corn or soybeans or onions or whatever, to trees of all
sizes and colors. Even the color of the dirt changes as you travel. Illinois,
for example, has rich black dirt that fades to a dark gray when it's dry.
Missouri's soil is red clay, with lots of crumbly white rock in it. Get to $\qquad$ 30
Arizona, and the "dirt" is yellow-gray dust or sand.

    On a long road trip, this combination of hypnotic road, constant
vigilance for danger, and changing scenery creates a sort of **Zen** condition.
Your conscious mind can't focus on one thought for long, because it has to
keep the bike upright, on the road, and out of trouble. So your brain begins $\qquad$ 35
to mull things over at a lower level. Whatever worries you might have had
at home slip off your shoulders as you begin to realize that for however
long this trip is scheduled, you are on your own, with just your thoughts
and sensations for companions. Then, at the end of a day of riding, you get
off your bike, physically tired and a little deafened and still vibrating, and $\qquad$ 40
you sleep soundly. It is the very best way to travel.

Lester Smith, "Zen and the Art of a Motorcycle Vacation." Used by permission of the author.

vigilance
alert watchfulness

Zen
a school of Mahayang Buddhism that
says true understanding can be attained
through meditation and thoughtful study

Reflect   After you read, answer these questions. Then share your responses with your classmates.

1. What is the main idea? Is this main idea directly stated or implied?

   _____

2. What sensory details seem especially helpful or effective? (Name two.)

   _____

3. How is this description organized—spatially, chronologically, or logically? Explain.

   _____

4. How would you rate this essay and why?

   Weak ★ ★ ★ ★ ★ Strong

   _____

Vocabulary Practice

Identify   Define the word parts as indicated. Then try to explain the meaning of the complete word. (See pages 36–37 and 668–676 for help.)

1. **conscious**   (line 7)   con + sci + ous

   _____

   _____

2. **malfunction**   (line 17)   mal + function

   _____

   _____

Drawing Inferences

Explain   Answer the following question to help you draw an inference about the text. (See pages 30–32 for help.)

■   How can there be an "art" to a motorcycle vacation?

   _____

   _____

LO4 Reading and Reacting to a Second Professional Description

This description examines the plight of the Inuit people as their traditional lifestyle has given way to a modern one. The authors integrate a great deal of description with explanation and narration. Use the reading process to help you gain a full understanding of the text.

About the Authors

The wife and husband team of **Yva Momatiuk** and **John Eastcott** are photojournalists whose work has appeared in *National Geographic*, *Audubon*, and *Smithsonian*, among many other periodicals. They have also published six books.

Preread   Before you read, answer these three questions:

1. What do the title, the opening two paragraphs, and the first lines of other paragraphs tell you about the text?

_____

2. What might be the authors' purpose?

_____

3. What do you expect to learn?

_____

Read and Reread   As you read, make it your goal to (1) identify the main idea and (2) note the before and after details about the Inuit lifestyle for both men and women. Consider annotating the text (page 20) during your reading.

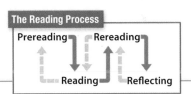

The Reading Process

Prereading → Rereading → Reading → Reflecting

Our Land: Nunavut's Inuit Women

Mabel Angulalik ties the dead bird's feet to the top of a makeshift post.   1
She spreads its wings to warn other seagulls patrolling the beach: leave
my drying fish alone. Around the post, wooden racks bend under slabs of
Arctic char curing in the weak July sun. Its warmth has only just begun
to melt the sea ice around Victoria Island in Canada's new territory of   5
Nunavut, *Our Land* in Inktitut, the language of the Inuit.

Angulalik watches the shifting ice, and the lines in her old face
deepen. After she was born, her mother—paralyzed from the waist down—

put her baby daughter in the snow to freeze. "My mother was crawling on her hands and knew she couldn't look after me," Angulalik says quietly. *10* "But another family camping nearby found me and took me in. And here I am."

Indeed she is. Yet her memories of the nomadic life following animals across tundra and ice are full of hardship: Hardly any food. No oil for lamps. A husband chosen for her, as required by custom. Babies born in *15* snow houses. Caribou hides to sew, fish to dry, blubber to preserve.

Today Angulalik lives in a warm house in the nearby town of Ikaluktitiak, which means Good Fishing Place. She spends her summers in a cabin by the sea, tending to fish racks and smelling the salty air. But when a young relative arrives to collect her, she hikes up her wolverine- *20* trimmed parka, climbs aboard the all-terrain vehicle, and holds tight as they bump back to Ikaluktitiak.

The town, like most Arctic settlements, has an airport, a nurses' station, several stores, schools, hotels, and churches. The political **entity** of Nunavut was created on April 1, 1999, and constitutes about one-fifth *25* of Canada's landmass. Eighty-five percent of its inhabitants, some 15,500 people, are Inuit. It took them twenty years to negotiate independence, and now the Inuit want to plan the future on their terms. Yet things have changed in twenty years.

Change has brought forth a new Inuit woman. Today she is more likely *30* to drive a truck than a dogsled, visit a tanning salon than her fishing net, and worry about her children's grades rather than food for them. If she is forty-five or older, she may be **fluent** in her ancestors' tongue as well as in English; if she is younger, her Inuktitut maybe limited to a few phrases. She is a bridge between her traditional parents and the thoroughly modern *35* youngsters. She is the glue of her family and at times the sole wage earner.

One of the earliest debates in Nunavut, was over equal representation of women and men in the new government. It failed, but today the Pauktuutit Inuit Women's Association funds job-training programs, helps women fighting custody battles, and builds shelters for abused wives. *40*

Eva Otokiak is the manager of Ikaluktitiak's seven-bed shelter and a former victim of domestic violence. "I endured because of my five children," she says, stroking her short hair. She explains that as families left the open land for settlements, many became troubled. The men discovered that their legendary survival and hunting skills were useless. Unless they *45* attended school, learned English, and joined the market economy, they had to survive on government handouts. Welfare covered necessities but killed pride; alcohol and drugs obliterated pain but destroyed whole families. Nunavut's suicide rate is seven times that of southern Canada.

In some families, men who once hunted take care of the children while the women work. Women aren't just chasing better jobs, however; they have also emerged as a healing force. Most Inuit women try to ensure the kind of robust family life, communal ties, and connection to the land that social researchers say are necessary for emotional health.   50

"I have to say no to my children more often than if we still lived on the land," Otokiak says. "I say no to big parties, no to getting pregnant early." To cope with the new life, she learned to be more assertive than her ancestors, a difficult task if you come from an intrinsically cooperative culture.   55

Nunavut women credit the men with much of their strength. Brenda Jencke decided to return north from her husband's home province of Ontario, so their three children would grow up close to her Inuit roots. He supported her all the way, and today she heads their construction company in Ikaluktitiak.   60

A slender woman with a dazzling smile, Margo Kadlun works for a caribou research project. She remembers how much she wanted to go hunting when she was small. "My father warned me: 'You cannot go if you are whining, and I won't bring you back if you get tired,'" she recalls. "We walked miles and miles across the tundra until be got a couple caribou. Brought back several leg bones and cached the rest. But my father never told me I couldn't go because I was a girl. And he taught me not to whine but to stick to what I want to do. He gave me that."   65   70

"Our Land: Nunavut's Inuit Women" by Yva Momtiuk and John Eastcott. From *The World & I* (July 2000). Reprinted by permission of the authors.

Nunavut a territory of northern Canada	**entity** object, something that exists	**assertive** bold, confident
Inuit members of the Eskimo peoples of North America	**fluent** polished, skilled	**intrinsically** the quality of being essential or basic
char an arctic fish	**obliterated** wiped out, erased	**cached** hid

Reflect   Answer the following questions about the selection. Then discuss your responses with your classmates.

1. What is the main idea of the selection? How far into the text did you have to go before you could identify it?

_____

_____

2. Is the essay organized spatially, chronologically, or logically? Or is more than one pattern employed? Explain.

_____

_____

3. Do the descriptive details focus on one sense or on many of them (sight, sounds, smells, etc.)? Explain.

_____

_____

4. What are two descriptions that you find interesting, important, or surprising?

_____

_____

_____

5. In what way is there a before-and-after element in this essay?

_____

_____

_____

6. How would you rate this essay and why?
   Weak ★ ★ ★ ★ ★ Strong

_____

_____

_____

Vocabulary Practice

Identify Use context clues to explain or define the following words. (See pages 34–35 for help.)

1. **nomadic** (line 13)

   clues: _____

   definition: _____

2. **legendary** (line 45)

   clues: _____

   definition: _____

3. **robust** (line 53)

   clues: _____

   definition: _____

Drawing Inferences

Explain Answer the following questions to help you draw inferences from the text. (See pages 30–32 for help.)

1. Does the fate of the Inuit people reflect the fate of any other people?

   _____

   _____

2. What should women take away from this essay? What about men?

   _____

   _____

3. Is there a sense of inevitably or predictability about this situation?

   _____

   _____

Writing

In your own descriptive essay, you will describe an event, an activity, or a journey. Be sure to use the writing process to help you do your best work. (See pages 106–111.)

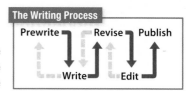

LO5 Planning Your Description

The information on these two pages will help you complete all of the important prewriting tasks before you develop your first draft.

Selecting a Topic

For your description, consider an event you recently participated in or witnessed, a brief journey you took, or an activity that you regularly carry out. Your description will focus on the sights and sounds related to your topic.

Select List two or three possible topics for each of the categories below. (A sample topic is provided for each.) Circle the one you would most like to describe.

	Event	Activity	Journey
1.	attending a concert	doing laundry	kayaking
2.			
3.			

Thinking About Your Topic

Before you get too involved in your planning, think about your topic—why you chose it, what you hope to discover about it, and so on.

Reflect Write freely about your topic, answering the following types of questions in your writing.

- Why did you choose this topic? _____
- What do you hope to discover in your writing? _____
- How will you gather details for your writing (from memory, from firsthand experience)? _____
- What special feeling or part of the topic would you like to emphasize? _____
- How would you like the reader to react to your description? _____

Follow Up: Underline ideas in your free writing that you especially like. Share these ideas with your classmates.

Gathering Details

At the core of your description will be the details that you include. As you learned on page 165, it's important to consider a variety of sensory details—sights, sounds, smells, tastes, and textures. The following chart identifies many of the sensory details in the description on page 176.

Sensory Chart

Sights	Sounds	Smells	Tastes	Textures
-gray fog	-silence	-foul algae		-blooms of algae
-jumping fish	-splash of water			
-circular ripples				
-bald eagle				

Collect Complete a sensory chart for your chosen topic. Include details only in the categories that apply to your topic.

Considering the Organization

The best descriptive writing does more than simply share what something or someone looks like. Instead, descriptions are used to enrich a story or an explanation. For example, the professional model on pages 166–167 describes the landscape during a journey. The model on pages 169–171 describes a way of life. Use this same method in your own description of an event, activity, or journey.

Arrange List the sensory details that you have collected in the order that you want to include them in your essay. Consider this arrangement as a starting point; you can change the order of details as necessary during your writing.

INSIGHT

An observation report is a special type of descriptive writing. In it, you simply record sensory details as you perceive them, one after another, in a specific location. See page 176 for an example.

LO6 Writing the First Draft

After you have completed your prewriting and planning, you are ready to write your first draft. Writing a first draft is your first opportunity to connect all of your ideas about your topic.

Read Before you begin your draft, read the following descriptive essay, paying careful attention to the opening, middle, and closing parts.

Paddling Bliss

Earlier in the morning, a light gray fog blanketed the lake. I could just   1
make out the boats docked in the marina and a faint outline of trees to the
side. Not a sound could be heard. But now, a few hours later, the fog has
lifted, which means it's time for me to get on the water. Most mornings, I
kayak for exercise and enjoyment.   5

I start out from O'Dell's Bay, just 30 yards from my grandfather's
cottage. By habit, I check the water quality soon after I start, looking for
any patches of nasty algae that sometimes blooms on the surface. At its
best, the lake water is a very light brown color, almost looking like root
beer in the wake of a motorboat. At its worst, in the dog days of August, the 10
water can shimmer with smelly, blue-green algae.

Once I'm out of the bay, I usually turn left, staying fairly close to the
shoreline. On a good day, I'll see a lot of fish jumping, or at least I'll hear
their splash and see the circular ripples that they've caused. Last year, for
the first time, I saw a bald eagle flying away from its nest, which looked   15
pretty much like a junk pile in the tree. I once came upon a crane with
a fish in its mouth. As I paddled closer, it would move on, a few yards at
a time. We played tag like this for a few moments before the crane had
enough and took to the air to find a quiet spot for dinner.

At different points, I'll mark out a spot, say a boat docked 100 yards   20
away, and paddle like crazy until I reach it. This really gets my heart
pumping and gives my arms and shoulders a good workout. At other times,
I'll just lazily drift along, taking in the quiet and calm that can only be felt
on the water.

The lake is big enough that it makes me feel pretty small sometimes. If 25
the wind happens to pick up, the waves can build up a lot of power, making
kayaking feel more like riding a roller coaster. And I swear that the sky
is bigger here than it is back in city. I like it best when it is partly cloudy,
because the clouds look huge against the blue sky.

Once I reach Half Moon Bay, I usually turn around and head back. The   30
trip home might be easier or harder, depending on the wind's direction. I
almost always focus less on nature and more on exercise on the return trip.
I guess that's because I'm seeing the same things again. Once I make my
last paddle and glide to a stop on the beach, I'm tired, but happy for the
experience.   35

Creating an Opening Paragraph

The opening paragraph should gain your reader's attention, introduce your topic, and state your thesis. Here are three strategies for gaining the reader's interest.

- Establish a mood or feeling.
   Earlier in the morning, a light gray fog blanketed the lake. I could just make out the boats docked in the marina and a faint outline of trees to the side.
- Set the scene for the description.
   Saturday morning at the Laundromat hums with activity.
- Ask a question.
   Why are most of us so attracted to water?

Writing a Thesis Statement

To create a thesis statement for your essay, follow this formula.

Topic		Special Feeling About It		Thesis Statement
kayaking on a lake	**+**	for exercise and enjoyment	**=**	Most mornings, I kayak for exercise and enjoyment.

Developing the Middle Paragraphs

In the middle paragraphs, describe your topic according to your planning and prewriting.

- Use sensory details to help the reader visualize your topic.
- Organize your description so it is easy to follow.

Writing a Closing Paragraph

Your closing paragraph should bring your description to a natural stopping point and provide a final thought about the topic.

Example final thoughts:

- Once I make my last paddle and glide to a stop on the beach, I'm tired, but happy for the experience.
- The Laundromat is clearly a meeting place for all kinds: family members, friends, and total strangers.

Write Write your first draft, using the information above and on the previous pages as a guide.

LO7 Revising the Writing

Revising your first draft involves adding, deleting, rearranging, and reworking parts of your writing. Revision can begin with a peer review.

Peer Review

Sharing your writing at various stages is important, especially when you review and revise a first draft. The feedback that you receive will help you improve and strengthen your essay.

Peer Review Sheet

Essay title: _____

Writer: _____

Reviewer: _____

1. Which part of the essay seems to work best—opening, middle, or closing? Why?

    _____

    _____

2. Which part of the essay needs work—opening, middle, or closing? Why?

    _____

    _____

3. Do the middle paragraphs effectively describe the topic? Explain.

    _____

    _____

4. Can you clearly imagine the event or activity being described?

    _____

    _____

5. Identify a phrase or two that show the writer's level of interest.

    _____

    _____

Respond Complete a response sheet like this one after reading the first draft of a classmate's essay. Then share the sheet with the writer. (Keep your comments positive and helpful.)

Using Figures of Speech

Adding sensory details is the main way to improve a description. A closely related technique, using figures of speech, can also enrich a description. Figures of speech involve the creative use of words. One common figure of speech is personification.

Personification is a technique in which a writer speaks of or describes an animal, idea, or object as if it were human. Here are a few examples from a professional passage.

- "Towards noon a yellowish haze crept up the horizon." *(Haze is described as having the ability to crawl.)*
- "The flying sand clawed at the man's face." *(Sand is described as having the ability to claw.)*
- "A plastic bag danced in the breeze." *(A bag is described as having the ability to dance.)*

Revising in Action

Read aloud the first draft and then the revised version of the following passage. Note how personification enriches the description by creating a more effective image for the reader.

> **First draft:** The Laundromat is noisy on Saturday morning.
>
> **Revised:** Saturday morning at the Laundromat hums with activity.

Revise Improve your writing, using the following checklist and your partner's comments on the response sheet. Continue revising until you can check off each item in the list.

Using a Revising Checklist

Ideas

☐ 1. Do I focus on one specific topic to describe?

☐ 2. Do I establish a focus or thesis for my description?

☐ 3. Do I include plenty of sensory details to describe my topic?

☐ 4. Do I use any examples of personification in my description?

Organization

☐ 5. Does my essay have effective opening, middle, and closing parts?

☐ 6. Have I arranged my details in an effective and clear way?

Voice

☐ 7. Do I sound knowledgeable and interested in my topic?

LO8   Editing the Writing

Editing your revised draft is a matter of correcting the style and accuracy issues that can distract the reader.

Commas Used in Compound Sentences

A compound sentence is made up of simple sentences joined by a coordinating conjunction: *and, but, or, nor, for, so,* or *yet.* (See pages 508–509.)

- When a compound sentence contains two simple sentences, place a comma before the coordinating conjunction.

  Two weeping willows stand on one end of the pond**, and** these trees provide cooling shade.

- When a compound sentence joins three or more short sentences in a series, place commas after each thought. The final comma should come before the coordinating conjunction. (See the next page.)

  Stately oak trees dot the south pasture**,** proud pine trees flank the hillside**, and** multicolored bushes border the pond.

- A semicolon can also be used to connect the simple thoughts in a compound sentence.

  The clouds above caught the reflection of the sunset**;** they soon turned a brilliant pink.

INSIGHT

Turning a series of short, choppy sentences into a compound sentence can make the sentences read more smoothly.

Practice   Turn the following sets of short sentences into compound sentences. Be sure to punctuate each new sentence correctly.

1. In the morning, fog often covers the lush green hills below. It covers only my ankles here on the deck.
2. There is one dirt road working its way down the hill. The road leads into the main village.
3. My grandfather slowly trudges up the road. He would much rather travel by car.
4. One brother herds sheep along a ridge. Another brother carries a basket of fruit. Their father checks a wheat field.

Apply   Check the punctuation of any compound sentences in your descriptive essay. Also look for series of short sentences that you could combine into compound sentences.

Commas Used in a Series

Use commas to separate individual words, phrases, or clauses in a series. A series contains at least three items.

- **Connecting words in a series:** Our dog Benson is *friendly, observant, and obedient.*

- **Connecting phrases in a series:** Daily, Benson gets *a morning and evening walk, three small meals, and plenty of additional attention.*

- **Connecting clauses in a series:** As far as complaints go, *my dad wishes Benson wouldn't bark so much, my mom wishes he wouldn't shed so much, and I wish he wouldn't follow me around.*

Practice   Rewrite the following sentences, adding commas as needed.

1. Around the food stalls at the flea market, you will find chewed-up ears of corn greasy kebab sticks and half-eaten candy apples.

2. The hot dog stand is littered with napkins smeared with ketchup mustard and relish.

3. Every Saturday morning, vendors set up their stalls shoppers arrive in droves and the neighborhood comes alive.

Special Challenge: Combine each of the following series of sentences into a longer sentence containing items in a series. Use commas correctly.

4. Homeless people want a safe shelter. They want a good meal. They want warm clothes.

5. The homeless often live under bridges. They make fires for warmth. They eat whatever food they can find.

Apply   Check the punctuation of any items in a series in your descriptive essay. Also watch for short, choppy sentences that you could combine into longer sentences containing items in a series.

Gary Paul Lewis, 2013 / Used under license from Shutterstock.com

Marking an Essay

Before you edit your revised essay, practice editing the following description.

Practice   Edit the following description, using the checklist on page 183 as a basic guide. Correct any sentence or convention errors that you find, using the marks listed below.

Paricutin

The story of Paricutin, a Volcano that formed in Mexico last century,   *1*
is an interesting one. On February 20, 1943, a farmer near the town of
paricutin was startled by a column of column of smoke rising from the
middle of his cornfield. Thinking he had somehow started a fire, he rushed
to put it out, he found that the smoke was coming from a small hole in the   *5*
ground, not from an open "fire."

The farmer thought about how for a moment to smother the fire, and
he decided to plug the hole with a rock. Later, when he checced back, he
was alarmed by the increased escape of dense, black smoke. Recalling that
the ground had trembled recently, and noticing that the soil felt hot under   *10*
his bare feet, he hurried to town to tell the mayor and to bring some people
back with him. When they all returned, black was smoke billowing from a
hole 30 feet deep.

The first explosion came that very night, shoting a thick column of
smoke, cinders, and ash more than a mile into the air. More explosions   *15*
followed every few seconds, throwing masses of rock that varied from the
size of a walnut to size of a house. Lava began to flow two days later, and
the newborn volcano continued to erupt for many months.

The lava flows and ash shower's obliterated surrounding farms,
forests, and villages. Paricutin, the first town destroyed, gave up its very   *20*
name to the new "mountain of fire."

Correction Marks

⌐ delete	⌃ add comma	^{word} ⌃ add word			
d capitalize	? add question	⊙ add period			
∅ lowercase	⌃ mark	⬭ spelling			
⌃ insert	⌄ insert an apostrophe	⤳ switch			

Using an Editing Checklist

Now it's time to correct your own descriptive essay.

Edit Prepare a clean copy of your revised essay and use the following checklist to look for errors. Continue working until you can check off each item in the list.

Words

☐ 1. Have I used specific nouns and verbs? (See page 146.)

☐ 2. Have I used more action verbs than "be" verbs? (See page 147.)

Sentences

☐ 3. Have I avoided improper shifts in sentences? (See pages 544–545.)

☐ 4. Have I avoided fragments and run-ons? (See pages 532–535, 538–539.)

Conventions

☐ 5. Do I use correct verb forms (*he saw*, not *he seen*)? (See page 588.)

☐ 6. Do my subjects and verbs agree (*she speaks*, not *she speak*)? (See pages 516–525.)

☐ 7. Have I used the right words (*their, there, they're*)?

☐ 8. Have I capitalized first words and proper nouns and adjectives? (See page 626.)

☐ 9. Have I used commas after long introductory word groups and to separate items in a series? (See pages 638–639.)

☐ 10. Have I used commas correctly in compound sentences? (See pages 636–637.)

☐ 11. Have I used apostrophes correctly in contractions and to show possession? (See pages 652–653.)

Adding a Title

Add an appropriate title to your description. Here are three simple strategies for creating one.

- Use a key phrase from the essay:

  Pushing Onward

- Identify or suggest your focus:

  Pastoral Pond

- Use alliteration, the repetition of a consonant sound:

  Fluff and Fold

Enrichment: Reading

On pages 185–186 you will find an essay entitled "The Regulation of Time" to read and react to. As you read this selection, which comes from the textbook *Sociology: Your Compass for a New World*, be sure to follow the steps in the reading process. The reading activities are followed by a number of writing ideas to choose from to write a descriptive paragraph or essay of your own.

> "Don't overwrite description in a story—you haven't got time."
> —Elizabeth Spencer

About the Authors

Robert J. Brym received a PhD from the University of Toronto, and he teaches sociology at the same university. Brym has authored many books on politics, sociology, race, and ethnic relations. **John Lie** received his PhD from Harvard University and has served as Dean of International and Area Students at the University of California at Berkeley. Lie has authored many books on a wide range of topics, from contemporary East Asia to race and ethnicity.

Prereading

The passage of time, losing time, and traveling through time are common themes in literature. Time is the subject of many songs. Science and technology attempt to save us time. Write freely for 5 minutes about time. Consider questions like these: Are you usually early or late and why? Do you wish you had more time? Are you always aware of time?

CONSIDER THE TRAITS

As you read the essay starting on the next page, focus first on the **ideas**—the specific topic and the details that are used to describe it. Also consider the **organization**—the way the opening, middle, and closing parts are constructed. The organization should help you follow the ideas.

What do you think?

In the quotation above, what do you think it means to "overwrite" a description?

Identify Before you read, answer these three questions:

1. What do the title, first paragraph, and first lines of other paragraphs tell you about the text?

2. What are your first thoughts about the author's purpose?

3. What questions would you like answered in your reading?

Reading and Rereading

The essay combines description with explanation and analysis. You will learn how the concept of time has changed over "time"—and why the change has occurred.

As you read, make it your goal to (1) identify the topic, (2) pay careful attention to the descriptive and explanatory details, and (3) consider the importance of the final few lines. Take notes (see page 22) to help you keep track of important information.

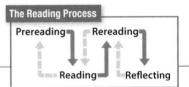

The Regulation of Time

People did not always let the clock determine the pace of daily life. *1*
When the first mechanical clocks were installed in public squares in
Germany nearly 700 years ago to signal the beginning of the workday,
the timing of meals, and quitting time, workers resisted. They were
accustomed to enjoying many holidays and a flexible and vague work
schedule **regulated** only approximately by the seasons and the rising and *5*
setting of the sun. The strict **regime** imposed by the work clocks made their
lives harder. They staged uprisings to silence the clock but to no avail.
City officials sided with employers and imposed fines for ignoring the work
clocks. Harsher penalties, including death, were imposed on anyone trying
to use the clocks' bells to signal a revolt (Thompson, 1967). *10*

Today, nearly 700 years later, many people seem like slaves of the work
clock. This is especially true of urban North American couples who are
employed full time in the paid labor force and have preteen children. For
them, life often seems an endless round of waking up at 6:30 a.m.; getting
everyone washed and dressed; preparing the kids' lunches; getting them *15*
out the door in time for the school bus or the car pool; driving to work
through rush-hour traffic; preparing dinner; taking the kids to their soccer
game; returning home to clean up the dishes and helping with homework;
getting the kids washed, their teeth brushed, and then into bed; and (if
they have not brought some office work home) grabbing an hour of TV *20*
before collapsing, exhausted, for approximately 6 ½ hours' sleep before the
story repeats itself.

At the end of the 1990s, married couples with children younger
than 6 years worked for pay 16 hours a week longer than they did in
the late 1960s (US Department of Labor, 1999c: 100). Managers were *25*
more likely than any other category of workers to be working for pay 49

hours a week or more. Next came sales personnel who earn **commissions**, transportation workers (especially truck drivers), and professionals (Rones, Ilg, and Gardner, 1997: 9). Life is less hectic for residents of small towns, unmarried people, couples without small children, retirees, and the unemployed. But the lives of many people are so packed with activities that they must carefully regulate time and **parcel out** each moment precisely so that they may tick off item after item from an ever-growing list of tasks that need to be completed on schedule (Schor, 1992). After 700 years of conditioning, it is unusual for people to rebel against the clock anymore, . . . 35

The precise regulation of time is a rational means of **ensuring** efficiency. Minding the clock maximizes how much work you get done in a day. The regulation of time makes it possible for trains to run on schedule, university classes to begin punctually, and business meetings to start on time. But even if we allow that minding the clock is **rational** as a means of achieving efficiency, is it rational as an end in itself? For many people, it is not. They complain that the precise regulation of time has gotten out of hand. Life has simply become too hectic for many people to enjoy. How rational is it that a restaurant in Japan has installed a punch-clock for its customers? The restaurant offers all you can eat for 35 yen per minute. As a result, "The diners rush in, punch the clock, load their trays from the buffet table, and concentrate intensely on efficient chewing and swallowing, trying not to waste time talking to their companions before rushing back to punch out" (Gleick, 2000 [1999]: 244). Meanwhile, in New York and Los Angeles some upscale restaurants have gotten in on the act. 50 An increasingly large number of business clients are so pressed for time, they pack in two half-hour lunches with successive guests. The restaurants **oblige**, making the resetting of tables "resemble the pit-stop activity at the Indianapolis 500" (Gleick, 2000 [1999]: 155). Arguably, as these examples illustrate, a rational means (the use of the work clock) has been applied to 55 a given goal (maximizing work) but has led to an irrational end (a too-hectic life).

From Brym/Lie, *Sociology*, 2E. © 2007 Cengage Learning.

30

40

45

regulated controlled	**ensuring** making sure
regime regular pattern	**rational** logical
commissions a fee or percentage earned by a sales representative	**oblige** to do service for
parcel out to divide into parts	

Reflecting

Practice   After you read, answer the questions on this page. Share your responses with your classmates.

1. What is the main idea in the text?

    _____

    _____

2. What is described in the first paragraph? The second paragraph? The final paragraph?

    _____

    _____

    _____

3. How is the essay organized—spatially, chronologically, or logically? (See pages 75–77.) Or does it utilize more than one pattern? Explain.

    _____

    _____

4. What is one idea or detail that you found especially surprising, interesting, or important? Explain.

    _____

    _____

5. How would you explain the last sentence?

    _____

    _____

6. How would you rate this essay and why?

    Weak ★ ★ ★ ★ ★ Strong

    _____

    _____

Vocabulary Practice

Identify   Define the following words using your understanding of context clues as a guide. (See pages 34–35 for help.)

1. **hectic**   (line 29)

   clues: _____

   definition: _____

2. **maximize**   (line 37)

   clues: _____

   definition: _____

3. **punctually**   (line 39)

   clues: _____

   definition: _____

Drawing Inferences

Explain   Answer the following questions to help you draw inferences from the text. (See pages 30–32 for help.)

1. What cultures or parts of the world are most affected by the regulation of time?

   _____

   _____

2. How important will the regulation of time be in the future?

   _____

   _____

3. Is there a sense of inevitably or predictability about this situation?

   _____

   _____

   _____

Writing

What follows are writing activities to complete in response to the reading. Use the writing process (pages 106–111) to help you develop your writing.

Prewriting

Choose one of the following writing ideas for your own descriptive writing, or decide upon an idea of your own making related to the reading.

Writing Ideas

1. **Writing to Learn:** Complete a cluster or web with "time" as your starting point. (See pages 24 and 133.) Make as many connections as you can. Put a star (★) next to one or two ideas in your cluster that you could write about.

2. **Essay Writing:** Write an essay about one of the ideas you starred.

3. Describe what life would be like today if, suddenly, time was not regulated.

4. Write a descriptive essay based on a favorite photograph. Attach a copy of the photograph to the essay.

5. Write an essay that describes a common scene, perhaps in a subway, Laundromat, or coffee shop.

> ### When planning ...
> Refer to pages 174–175 to help you plan your essay. Also use these tips.
> - Consider all of the senses as you collect details for your writing.
> - Establish a focus for your description to help you know which details to include, and which ones to leave out.

Writing and Revising

Refer to pages 176–179 to help you write and revise your first draft. Also use the tips that follow.

> ### When writing ...
> - Pay special attention to each part of your essay—the opening, the middle, and the closing.
> - Use details that help the reader visualize the topic.
>
> ### When revising ...
> - Arrange your details spatially, chronologically, or logically so they are easy to follow.
> - Do not over describe in your essay. Readers may get confused if they are confronted with too many details.

Editing

Refer to the checklist on page 183 when you are ready to edit your work for style and correctness.

Reflecting on Descriptive Writing

Answer the following questions about your reading and writing experiences in this chapter.

1. What is the purpose of a descriptive essay?

   _____

2. How is description often handled in academic texts?

   _____

3. What is your favorite description in this chapter? Explain.

   _____

4. What reading strategy in this chapter is the most helpful? Explain.

   _____

5. What do you like best about your descriptive essay?

   _____

6. What is one thing you would like to change in it?

   _____

7. What is the most important thing you have learned about descriptions?

   _____

   _____

   _____

Key Terms to Remember

When you read and write descriptive essays, it's important to understand the following terms.

- **Description**—the creation of an image of a person, a place, a thing, or an idea
- **Sensory details**—details that address sights, sounds, smells, tastes, and textures
- **Spatial organization**—the arrangement of descriptive details according to location—top to bottom, right to left, background to foreground, and so on

7

> "The narrative impulse is always with us; we couldn't imagine ourselves through a day without it."
> —Robert Coover

Narration

In his book *On Writing Well,* William Zinsser says that the one subject all writers know better than anything else is themselves. Their thoughts and feelings about their past actions and present lives shape who they are and how they see the world. And no matter if they write nonfiction, fiction, or poetry, all writers' personal thoughts and experiences will influence their work. It can really be no other way.

When writing directly about their own experiences, writers are involved in autobiographical writing. An autobiography shares the key experiences in a writer's life, and each shared experience can be considered a personal narrative, the subject of this chapter. A personal narrative shares one memorable experience and covers a brief span of time, anywhere from a few minutes to a few hours.

In the first part of this chapter, you will learn about personal narratives and read and react to professional examples. In the second part, you will write your own narrative.

Learning Outcomes

LO1 Understand narration.

LO2 Learn reading strategies (using a time line and following the story line).

LO3 Read and react to a professional narrative.

LO4 Read and react to a second professional narrative.

LO5 Plan a personal narrative.

LO6 Write the first draft.

LO7 Revise the writing.

LO8 Edit the writing.

What do you think?

What is the "narrative impulse" that Robert Coover identifies in the quotation? And why couldn't we "imagine ourselves through a day without it"?

Krivosheev Vitaly, 2013 / Used under license from Shutterstock.com

LO1 Understanding Narration

Writers are essentially storytellers (to *narrate* means "to tell a story"), and as you learned in the introduction, the stories they know best are their own. Writing about their experiences also helps writers to better understand themselves. Writer Catherine Drinker Bower said that writing is "a kind of double living," allowing a person to experience the actual moment and then revisit it by writing about it.

A personal narrative usually shares an event in a writer's life that has some heightened importance. Surprises, setbacks, turning points—these are common subjects for personal narratives. For example, the first professional narrative on pages 194–195 shares a surprising experience about life on the streets. The second narrative on pages 198–200 shares a turning point in the writer's life.

Depending on the subject, a narrative will draw out different responses. Some narratives will simply entertain you. Others will encourage you, inspire you, or even shock you. Of course, it is always fun to compare the writer's experience with your own: "I know just how he's feeling," "I've never experienced anything like that," and so on.

> "I love the freedom that the narrative form provides."
> —Sidney Sheldon

Personal Narratives Versus Narrative Essays

A personal narrative focuses on recreating an experience by answering the 5 W's and H (*who? what? when? where? why?* and *how?*) about it. A narrative essay goes a step further by analyzing the experience, trying to explain what it means. A bit of analysis may work its way into a personal narrative, but that is not the writing's main purpose. Even so, college instructors usually expect you to provide some analysis or interpretation of your experiences, no matter which writing form you use.

INSIGHT

It's almost impossible to recall every last detail or conversation from a past experience, but writers can still capture the spirit of the time and place by sharing realistic moments.

Practice   List three or four people, famous or not so famous, whose personal stories interest you. Provide a brief explanation for each choice. Share your choices with your classmates. (Follow up: Check online to see if the person has written her or his autobiography.)

_____

_____

_____

_____

Reading

Since personal narratives are stories, reading them is not difficult. However, using reading strategies can certainly enhance the experience.

LO2 Learning Reading Strategies

When reading a personal narrative, you can use a time line to keep track of the important events and a plot line to help you analyze the narrative.

Using a Time Line

Part of the challenge when reading a narrative is keeping track of the key actions in the order that they occur. A graphic organizer called a time line works well for this purpose because narratives are almost always organized chronologically, or by time.

Time Line	
Order	Main Actions or Conversations
1.	
2.	
3.	

CONSIDER

When completing a time line, focus on the essential actions in a story. You don't need to include all the specific details.

Following the Story Line

A personal narrative is essentially a story. And like the plot in a fictional story, a narrative should create suspense as it moves along. The chart that follows shows the parts of the plot and how the level of reader interest should build as the story progresses. The parts of the plot are also explained below.

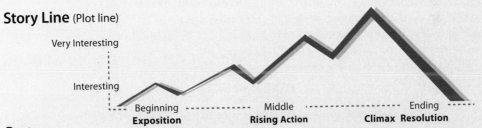

Story Line (Plot line)

Very Interesting

Interesting

Beginning ----- Middle ----- Ending
Exposition   Rising Action   Climax Resolution

Parts:

Exposition: The characters (people) are introduced, the setting (time and place of the action) is established, and a conflict or problem is identified.

Rising action: A series of actions and conversations build suspense.

Climax: The main character faces the conflict, either overcoming it or learning from it. This is the most exciting part.

Resolution: The narrative wraps up quickly after the climax. Sometimes the climax and resolution are wrapped up in one action.

LO3 Reading and Reacting to a Professional Narrative

The narrative below comes from *Fist Stick Knife Gun*, a memoir about growing up in the middle of urban violence. Use the reading process to help you gain a full understanding of the text. (See below.)

About the Author

Geoffrey Canada spent his early years in the South Bronx amid violence, poverty, and broken families. Later, in high school, he lived with an aunt in Long Island and, eventually, earned undergraduate and graduate degrees. He now serves as CEO and president of the Harlem Children's Zone, an organization that helps students in Harlem graduate from high school and college. *Fist Stick Knife Gun* is his first book.

Preread   Before you read, answer these two questions:

1. What do the title, first paragraph, and first lines of other paragraphs tell you about the text?

   _____

2. What type of experience will be shared?

   _____

3. What might be the author's purpose for this narrative?

   _____

Read and Reread   As you read, make it your goal to (1) identify the main idea or focus on the narrative and (2) follow the story line.

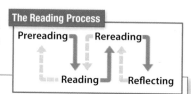

The Reading Process

Prereading   Rereading

Reading   Reflecting

Codes of Conduct

Down the block from us was a playground. It was nearby and we   *1*
didn't have to cross the street to get there. We were close in age. My oldest
brother, Daniel, was six, next came John who was five, I was four, and my
brother Reuben was two. Reuben and I were unable to go to the playground
by ourselves because we were too young. But from time to time my two   *5*
oldest brothers would go there together and play.

I remember them coming inside one afternoon having just come back
from the playground. There was great excitement in the air. My mother
noticed right away and asked, "Where's John's jacket?"

My brother responded, "This boy . . . this boy he took my jacket."   *10*

Well, we all figured that was the end of that. My mother would have to go and get the jacket back. But the questioning continued. "What do you mean, he took your jacket?"

"I was playing on the sliding board and I took my jacket off and left it on the bench, and this boy he tried to take it. And I said it was my jacket, and he said he was gonna take it. And he took it. And I tried to take it back, and he pushed me and said he was gonna beat me up."

To my mind John's explanation was clear and convincing; this case was closed. I was stunned when my mother turned to my older brother, Daniel, and said, "And what did you do when this boy was taking your brother's jacket?"

Daniel looked shocked. What did he have to do with this? And we all recognized the edge in my mother's voice. Daniel was being accused of something and none of us knew what it was.

Daniel answered, "I didn't do nuthin; I told Johnny not to take his jacket off. I told him."

My mother exploded, "You let somebody take your brother's jacket and you did nothing? That's your younger brother. You can't let people just take your things. You know I don't have money for another jacket. You better not ever do this again. Now you go back there and get your brother's jacket."

My mouth was hanging open. I couldn't believe it. What was my mother talking about, go back and get it? Dan and Johnny were the same size. If the boy was gonna beat up John, he certainly could beat up Dan. We wrestled all the time and occasionally hit one another in anger, but none of us knew how to fight. We were all equally incompetent when it came to fighting. So it made no sense to me. If my mother hadn't had that look in her eye, I would have protested. Even at four years old I knew this wasn't fair. But I also knew that look in my mother's eye. A look that signified a line not to be crossed.

My brother Dan was in shock. He felt the same way I did. He tried to protest. "Ma, I can't beat that boy. It's not my jacket. I can't get it. I can't."

My mother gave him her ultimatum. "You go out there and get your brother's jacket or when you get back I'm going to give you a beating that will be ten times as bad as what that little thief could do to you. And John, you go with him. Both of you better bring that jacket back here."

The tears began to flow. Both John and Dan were crying. My mother ordered them out. Dan had this look on his face that I had seen before. A stern determination showed through his tears. For the first time I didn't want to go with my brothers to the park. I waited a long ten minutes and then, to my surprise, John and Dan triumphantly strolled into the apartment. Dan had John's jacket in his hand.

From *Fist Stick Knife Gun: A Personal History of Violence in America*, pages 4–6. Boston: Beacon Press, 1995. Permission conveyed through Copyright Clearance Center.

Reflect After you complete your reading, answer these questions. Then share your responses with your classmates.

1. What are the main actions and conversations in the narrative? List them on a time line.

_____

_____

_____

_____

_____

2. What stands out in the development of the essay—the explanations, the dialogue, and/or the sensory details? Explain.

_____

_____

_____

3. How much time is covered?

_____

_____

4. What is the purpose of the narrative? (Choose one.) Explain your choice.
   a. to entertain   **b.** to persuade   **c.** to inform   **d.** to humor

_____

_____

5. How would you rate this essay and why?
   Weak ★ ★ ★ ★ ★ Strong

_____

_____

Vocabulary Practice

Identify Define or explain the following words by using context clues and your understanding of word parts. List any clues or word parts that help you. (See pages 36–37 and 668–676.)

1. **edge** (line 23)

2. **incompetent** (line 35)

3. **ultimatum** (line 42)

Drawing Inferences

Explain Answer the following questions to help you draw inferences from the text. (See pages 30–32.)

1. Who learned the most from this experience?

2. What can you infer about the mother's actions, beliefs, etc.?

3. What feelings does this narrative elicit in you and why?

Yes -Royalty Free, 2013 / Used under license from Shutterstock.com

LO4 Reading and Reacting to a Second Professional Narrative

In the narrative below, the subject shares an important turning point in her life, when she decided to become a dedicated student of learning. Use the reading process to help you gain a full understanding of the text.

About the Author

Thomas J. Cottle is a psychologist whose writing shares his thoughts about people, social issues, education, and justice. He has authored many books, and his writing also appears in periodicals.

Preread   Before you read, answer these three questions:

1. What do the title, the first two paragraphs, and the first lines of other paragraphs tell you about the narrative?

_____

2. What might be the author's purpose in sharing this story?

_____

3. What do you expect to learn?

_____

Read and Reread   As you read, make it your goal to (1) identify the main idea of the narrative and (2) follow Lucille Elmore's thoughts and ideas. Consider annotating the text (page 20) during your reading.

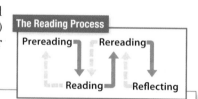

Overcoming an Invisible Handicap

On her thirtieth birthday, Lucille Elmore informed her husband that   *1*
she was going through a crisis. "I was thirty years old, active, in good
health—and I was illiterate," she recalls. "I didn't know books, I didn't
know history, I didn't know science. I had the barest understanding of
the arts. Like a physical condition, my knowledge limped, my intelligence   *5*
limped."

She was not only the mother of two young children but also was
working full time as an administrative assistant in a business-consulting

firm. Nevertheless, at age thirty, with her husband's agreement, Lucille
Elmore enrolled in college. "I thought getting in would be difficult," she   *10*
says. "It was easy. I thought I couldn't discipline myself, but that came.
Half the people in the library the first day thought I was the librarian, but
that didn't **deter** me."

For Lucille, the awareness of her invisible limp came only gradually.
As a young woman, she had finished high school, but she had chosen   *15*
not to go on with her education. Her parents, who had never completed
high school themselves, urged her to go to college but she refused. At the
time, she was perhaps a bit timid and lacked a certain confidence in her
own intellectual or academic abilities. Besides, a steady job was far more
important at that point to Lucille than schooling; she felt she could read on   *20*
her own to make up for any lack of education.

At twenty, working full time, she married Ted Elmore, a salesman
for a foodstore chain, a man on his way to becoming more than modestly
successful. There was no need for her to work, but she did so until her first
child was born; she was then twenty-two. A second child was born two   *25*
years later, and three years after that, she went back to work. With her
youngest in a day-care program, she felt no reservations about working,
but her lack of education began to nag at her as she approached the age of
thirty. She thus gave up her job, entered a continuing-education program
at a nearby university, and began what she likens to a love affair.   *30*

"I'm carrying on an open affair with books, but like a genuinely good
lover, I'm being guided. Reading lists, suggested reading, recommended
readings—I want them all. I must know what happened in the twelfth,
thirteenth, and eighteenth centuries. I want to know how the world's
major religions evolved. Papal history, I know nothing of papal history and   *35*
succession, or the politics involved. I read the Bible, but I never studied it.
It's like music: I listened, but it wasn't an informed listening. Now all of
this is changing.

"I must tell you, I despise students when they talk about 'the real
world,' as if college were a dream world. They simply don't understand   *40*
what the accumulation of knowledge and information means. Maybe you
have to be thirty at least, and going through a personal crisis, to fully
appreciate what historical connections are.

"A line of Shakespeare challenges me more than half the jobs I'll be equipped for when I'm finished. I'm having an affair with him, too, only   *45* it's called Elizabethan Literature 606. I think many people prefer the real world of everyday work because it's less frightening than the larger-than-life world of college.

"There's a much more important difference between the rest of the students and me. We don't agree at all on what it means to be a success.   *50* They think in terms of money, things. I suppose that's normal. They don't understand that, with a nice home, and decent job prospects, and two beautiful children, I know I am a failure. I'm a failure because I'm ignorant. I'm a failure until I have knowledge, until I can work with it, be excited by and play with ideas.   *55*

"I don't go to school for the rewards down the line. I want to reach the point at which I don't measure knowledge by anything but itself. An idea has value or it doesn't. This is how I now determine success and failure.

"'How can I use it?' That's what students ask. 'What good will this do me?' They don't think about what the question says about them, even   *60* without an answer attached to it. Questions like that only build up competition. But competition is the bottom line for so many students. I guess, getting ahead, getting a bit of a step up on the other guy. I know, it's my husband's life.

"I'll tell what I think I like most about my work: the library. I can   *65* think of no place so **exclusive** and still so open and public. Millions of books there for the taking. A chair to sit in, a row of books, and you don't need a penny. For me, the library is a religious center, a shrine.

"Students talk about the real world out there. What about the free world in here? Here, no one arrests you for what you're thinking. In the   *70* library, you can't talk, so you have to think. I never knew what it meant to think about something, to really think it through. I certainly never understood what you had to know to even begin to think. I always thought it was normal to limp."

"Overcoming an Invisible Handicap" by Thomas Cottle. From *Psychology Today*, January 1980. Reprinted by permission of the author.

deter	**exclusive**
prevent, stop	special

Reflect   After you complete your reading, answer these questions. Then share your responses with your classmates.

1. What is the purpose of this narrative—to inform, to entertain, or to persuade? (Choose one.) Explain your choice.

   _____

   _____

2. As the narrative unfolds, what element does the author rely on the most—explanation, dialogue, or action scenes?

   _____

   _____

3. How does the author tie the ending to the beginning of the narrative?

   _____

   _____

   _____

4. How would you describe Lucille Elmore?

   _____

   _____

   _____

5. What, if anything, surprises you about Elmore's thoughts or ideas?

   _____

   _____

6. How would you rate this narrative and why?
   Weak ★ ★ ★ ★ ★ Strong

   _____

   _____

   _____

Vocabulary Practice

Identify   Use context clues to explain or define the following words. (See pages 34–35 for help.)

1. **illiterate**   (line 3)

   clues: _____

   definition: _____

2. **papal**   (line 35)

   clues: _____

   definition: _____

3. **accumulation**   (line 41)

   clues: _____

   definition: _____

4. **shrine**   (line 68)

   clues: _____

   definition: _____

Drawing Inferences

Explain   Answer the following questions to help you draw inferences from the text. (See pages 30–32.)

1. How does your concept of education compare with Lucille's?

   _____

   _____

2. How does your concept of success compare with Lucille's?

   _____

   _____

3. What is "real life" for Lucille?

   _____

Writing

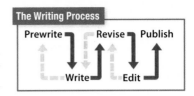

In this part of the chapter, you will write a narrative about a memorable experience from your past. Be sure to use the writing process to help you do your best work. (See pages 106–111.)

LO5 Planning a Personal Narrative

These two pages will help you gather and focus your thoughts for writing.

Selecting a Topic

Select List four experiences from your own life to consider for a personal narrative. Identify important experiences that covered a brief span of time, from a few minutes to a few hours. Then choose one of the experiences to write about.

1. _____
2. _____
3. _____
4. _____

Identifying the Key Actions

Think carefully about the actions and conversations related to your experience.

Identify Use a time line to list the main actions in chronological order.

Time Line
1. _____
2. _____
3. _____

CONSIDER THE PAST ————————————————————————

If you have trouble recalling details about the experience, complete one of these activities.

- Talk about the experience with a classmate or with someone else associated with it.

- Review any photographs or videos of the experience.

- Write nonstop about the experience for 5–7 minutes to see what actions and details come to mind.

Gathering Details

The most vivid narrative essays use plenty of sensory details that allow the reader to picture, hear, and touch what you describe. The following chart identifies the sensory details in the narrative on page 205.

> "Storytelling is the most powerful way to put ideas into the world today."
> —Robert McKee

Sights	Sounds	Smells	Tastes	Textures
ceiling fan	buzz of the phone	eggs frying	burn of the bourbon drink	lump in the throat
egg in the frying pan	conversation with Mom			watery eyes
sparkle of brown eyes	Grandpa's deep laugh			
arthritic hands				

Complete On your own paper, complete a sensory chart by listing the sights, sounds, smells, tastes, or textures related to your experience. (Your experience may not have details in every category.)

Renata Osinska, 2013 / Used under license from Shutterstock.com

Showing Details

Sensory details help you recreate an experience rather than simply tell about it. Other details that help you show rather than tell include the following:

Dialogue shares conversations between people.
> "Are you awake?" she asked, her voice cracking.
> Sensing her distress, I asked, "What's wrong?"

Personal reflections reveal your thoughts and feelings at the time.
> I felt thankful for the times we had together . . .

References to the setting (time and place of the action) help the reader visualize the experience.
> It was sometime after eight o'clock on a Saturday morning . . .

Consider Think about how you might include dialogue, personal reflections, and references to the setting in your narrative.

LO6 Writing the First Draft

In a first draft, you follow your plan and organize your details to create a narrative. The sample narrative below is about a memorable moment in the writer's life.

Read Read the narrative, noting how the writer created effective opening and closing parts. Also note how he developed his ideas in the middle part. Are all of the details arranged chronologically? Does the writer include any personal thoughts and feelings about the experience?

Remembering Gramps

Opening paragraph

It was sometime after eight o'clock on a Saturday morning   1
when I received the call about my grandfather's death. I was
already awake, cracking eggs into a skillet, when my cell
phone buzzed on the countertop. A little early for a phone call,
I thought. It was my mom. "Are you awake?" she asked, her   5
voice cracking. Sensing her distress, I asked, "What's wrong?"
She told me my grandfather had suffered a stroke during the
night and didn't make it.

Middle paragraph 1

After talking through the funeral plans, I wobbled over to
my cushy, leather couch and stared blankly at the circulating   10
blades on the ceiling fan. Memories of my grandfather spun
around in my head, like the time he taught me how to throw
a curveball, and the fishing trip we took together on the
Gulf Coast, and the day he poured me a Coke, but instead
mistakenly handed me his glass of bourbon and ice.   15

Middle paragraph 2

Of course, those were old memories. By the time I
reached college, Grandpa wasn't as active anymore. Tired and
overworked from his years of hard labor at the steel yard,
his back eventually gave out and his joints swelled up with
arthritis. He lived alone in the modest two-bedroom home he   20
built for my grandmother after they married. But even after
she was gone, he never lost the sparkle in his brown eyes. Nor
did he lose his sense of humor, punctuated by a deep baritone
laugh.

Closing paragraph

And so I sat there, staring at the ceiling and reminiscing   25
about Grandpa. Sure, I had a lump in my throat, and tears
filled my eyes; but I felt thankful for the times we had together
and hopeful that one day I could be as good a grandfather as
he had been to me. I owed him that much—and so much more.

Creating an Opening Paragraph

The opening part should capture the readers' attention and lead them into the story. Here are three strategies for beginning a story:

- **Jump right into things:** Jammed in our aging royal blue Chevy Astro van with no air conditioning, no radio, and limited legroom sat my parents, my two sisters, and our beloved golden retriever, Max.
- **Set the stage:** It was sometime after eight o'clock on a Saturday morning when I received the call about my grandfather's death.
- **Offer an interesting thought:** I should have listened to my brother and never walked into that room.

Creating the Middle Paragraphs

In the middle part of your narrative, you share the main details about the experience. In other words, this is where you tell your story. Here are some reminders:

- Be sure to follow your time line from page 203.
- Try to include explanations, sensory details, and dialogue to build the excitement. (See page 204.)
- When necessary, use transition words that show time. (See the list on this page.)

Time Transitions

after, before, later, now, soon, suddenly, when, while, first, second, finally

Creating a Closing Paragraph

The closing part can wrap up the experience after the most exciting action has happened, or it can provide an analysis of the experience by explaining its value and importance. Here are three strategies to consider:

- **Include a final piece of dialogue:** We did eventually make it to the Grand Canyon, but not before Mom admitted, "A pool would feel really nice right now."
- **Conclude with the last important action:** John and Dan triumphantly strolled into the apartment. Dan had John's jacket in his hand.
- **Offer a final analysis of the experience:** I felt thankful for the times we had together and hopeful that one day I could be as good a grandfather as he had been to me.

Write Write your first draft, using your planning (pages 203–204) and the information above to guide you.

LO7 Revising the Writing

Revising your first draft involves adding, deleting, rearranging, and reworking parts of your writing. Revision often begins with a peer review.

Peer Review

Sharing your writing is especially important when you are reviewing and revising a first draft. The feedback will help you change and improve your essay.

Peer Review Sheet

Narrative title: Remembering Gramps

Writer: Colin Lindau

Reviewer: Colleen Belmont

1. Which part of the narrative seems to work best—opening, middle, or closing? Why?

   Opening, because it makes you want to read the rest and find out what is going to happen.

2. Which part of the narrative needs work—opening, middle, or closing? Why?

   Middle, because you want more details about the relationship between the writer and the grandfather.

3. Which details in the story caught your attention? Name three.

   a. buzzing phone

   b. cracking voice

   c. modest two-bedroom home

4. Does the writer include appropriate dialogue? Explain.

   Yes, a short exchange between mother and son gets the reader's attention.

5. Identify a phrase or two that show the writer's level of interest in his or her story.

   Lines 9 and 10 in the essay

Respond Complete a response sheet like the one above after reading the first draft of a classmate's narrative. Then share the sheet with the writer. (Keep your comments helpful and positive.)

Adding Specific Verbs and Modifiers

You can strengthen your narrative by adding specific verbs and modifiers. Such improvements energize your writing.

Verbs		Modifiers	
General	Specific	General	Specific
grew	swelled	baseball (cap)	flat-billed New York Yankees (cap)
came	advanced	curly (hair)	wavy auburn (hair)
run	sprint	sweet (sauce)	tangy barbecue (sauce)
lives	roams		
wear	don		

Revising in Action

Read aloud the first draft and then the revised version of the following excerpt. Using specific verbs and adjectives adds life to the writing.

> wobbled   cushy, leather   circulating   ceiling
> I walked over to my couch and stared blankly at the blades on the fan.

Revise Improve your writing, using the following checklist and a classmate's comments on the response sheet. Continue working until you can check off each item in the list.

Using a Revising Checklist

Ideas

☐ 1. Do I focus on one specific experience or memory?

☐ 2. Do I include sensory details and dialogue?

☐ 3. Do I use specific verbs and modifiers?

Organization

☐ 4. Does the narrative have an opening, a middle, and a closing?

☐ 5. Is the story organized chronologically?

☐ 6. Have I used transitions to connect my sentences?

Voice

☐ 7. Is my interest in the story obvious to the reader?

☐ 8. Does my writing voice sound natural?

LO8 Editing the Writing

The main work of editing is correcting your revised first draft.

Quotation Marks and Dialogue

Dialogue enlivens a story and reveals the personalities of its characters. When you write conversations between people, using their exact words, place quotation marks before and after the **direct quotation.** However, when you write *about* what someone has said, not using the speaker's exact words, omit the quotation marks before and after the **indirect quotation**. See the examples that follow.

Direct Quotation

Before we left class, Mr. Lopez said, **"Next week's final will be comprehensive."**

Indirect Quotation

Mr. Lopez told the class **that the final will be comprehensive.**

Note: The word *that* often indicates dialogue that is being reported rather than quoted.

Practice   Read the sentences below. Indicate where quotation marks ("") should be placed before and after the speaker's exact words in direct quotations. If the sentence contains no direct quotations, write "C" for correct on the blank following the sentence. The first example has been done for you.

1. "On my way out today," Jessie said, "I forgot my cell phone." _____
2. Who is your favorite actress? asked Veronica. _____
3. The salesperson suggested that I should take the truck for a test-drive. _____
4. Frank said that if we want to make it in time, we should leave by noon. _____
5. Pull over to the side of the road, said the police officer. _____
6. After glancing at her test score, Jillian said, Spring break can't come soon enough. _____
7. And with this new car model, said the salesperson, you will save money on gas. _____
8. Jana said that she is in love with her new summer dress. _____

Apply   Read your narrative. If you included any dialogue (with direct quotations), make sure that it is properly marked with quotation marks. If you did not include any dialogue, consider adding some.

Punctuation of Dialogue

As you edit your narrative writing, check all dialogue for punctuation errors. Here are three rules you should follow:

- When a period or comma follows the quotation, place the period or comma *before* the quotation mark.

  "You should check your voice messages," advised Mr. Lee.

  "As you will soon discover," Reggie said, "the wrap station in the cafeteria is the best choice for lunch."

- When a question mark or an exclamation point follows the quotation, place it before the quotation mark if it belongs with the quotation. Otherwise, place it after.

  Sheryl asked, "Where can I get some good soul food?"

  Did you hear Veronica say, "I quit"?

- When a semicolon or colon follows the quotation, place it after the quotation mark.

  Trey simply said, "I have other plans"; he didn't mention his fear of heights.

Practice Correct the punctuation of the dialogue in each of the following sentences.

1. "Let's focus on solutions, not problems", offered Haley.
2. Jack promised he would "try my best to make it;" however, I know he's not coming.
3. "It's not the size of the dog in the fight", suggested Mark Twain ", it's the size of the fight in the dog."
4. "It's about time you showed up"! exclaimed Karen.
5. "Should I apply for the job"? asked my roommate.
6. What did you mean when you said, "There is more to the story than you think?"
7. "We are doing everything in our power to regain your trust", said the company spokesperson.

Apply Review your narrative closely for the punctuation of any dialogue.

Marking a Narrative

Before you correct your revised draft, practice editing the following model.

Practice   Read this narrative, looking for problems listed in the checklist on the next page. Then correct the model using the marks listed below. One correction has been done for you.

Whale Watchers

On a sunny afternoon off the coast of San Diego, my friend Natalie and I set off on our great whale watching adventure. In the winter months some 20,000 gray whales migrate through the Pacific waters along the coast of california, and we wanted to see the majestic creatures in there natural habitat.

As we stepped aboard the 100-foot tour boat nicknamed *"Night and Day"*, Natalie reminded me to take some medication to prevent seasickness. Good thing she did, because the captain announced we would hit 6-foot swells on our journey. Their were about 40 other passengers onboard with us.

About 15 minutes off the shoreline, a passenger shouted, "There she blows"! Indeed, about 20 yards ahead of us, I seen a spray of white water rocket vertically from the ocean surface we had spotted our first whale! As the boat crept closer, we could see the bumpy gray backs of two more whales rising above the undulating waves. I was so excited that I high-fived Natalie so hard it made my hand sting.

We ended up seeing five diffrant gray whales two packs of dolphins, and too many pelicans to count. seeing this beautiful sea life in the wild was an experience I'll never forget. Learning that the whales are endangered goes to show that we must boost our efforts to protect them from extinction.

1

5

10

15

20

Correction Marks

⌇⧸ delete	⋀⸴ add comma	ʷᵒʳᵈ⋀ add word
d̲̲ capitalize	? ⋀ add question mark	⊙ add period
ⅅ̸ lowercase		⬭ spelling
⋀ insert	⩔⸴ insert an apostrophe	⬭ switch

Using an Editing Checklist

Now it's time to correct your own narrative.

Edit   Prepare a clean copy of your revised narrative and use the following checklist to look for errors. Continue working until you can check off each item in the list.

Words

☐ **1.** Have I used specific nouns and verbs? (See page 146.)

☐ **2.** Have I used more action verbs than "be" verbs? (See page 147.)

Sentences

☐ **3.** Have I used sentences with varying beginnings and lengths? (See page 149.)

☐ **4.** Have I avoided improper shifts in sentences? (See pages 544–545.)

☐ **5.** Have I avoided fragments and run-ons? (See pages 532–535, 538–539.)

Conventions

☐ **6.** Do I use correct verb forms (*he saw*, not *he seen*)? (See page 588.)

☐ **7.** Do my subjects and verbs agree (*she speaks*, not *she speak*)? (See pages 516–525.)

☐ **8.** Have I used the right words (*their, there, they're*)?

☐ **9.** Have I capitalized first words and proper nouns and adjectives? (See page 626.)

☐ **10.** Have I used commas after long introductory word groups and to separate items in a series? (See pages 638–639.)

☐ **11.** Have I correctly punctuated any dialogue? (See pages 209–210.)

☐ **12.** Have I carefully checked my spelling?

Adding a Title

Make sure to add an attention-getting title. Here are three simple strategies for writing narrative titles.

- Use a phrase from the piece:

  Remembering Gramps

- Use alliteration, the repetition of a consonant sound:

  Whale Watchers

- Use a play on words:

  Tripped Up Road Trip

> "All writers who have produced anything have done it out of their specific experience, and making that experience reverberate in other people."
> —Gloria Naylor

Enrichment: Reading

On the following two pages you will find another professional narrative to read and react to. This work is followed by a number of narrative writing ideas to choose from. The reading and writing that you do in this section reinforces and enriches the work you have already completed in this chapter.

About the Author

Ben Carson, MD, is a graduate of Yale University and the University of Michigan Medical School and currently directs pediatric neurosurgery at Johns Hopkins University Hospital.

Prereading

If you've ever experienced or witnessed unfairness, injustice, or racism, you will never forget it. Perhaps you've been treated unfairly by a teacher or employer or witnessed someone preyed upon or harassed in some way. List below two or three examples of such treatment that you've experienced or seen.

_____

_____

_____

_____

CONSIDER THE TRAITS

As you read the selection that begins on the next page, focus on the **ideas** as they unfold. Also pay careful attention to the writer's **voice**—the way in which he shares his story. Then ask yourself if the selection produces an enriching reading experience.

What do you think?

What does Gloria Naylor's quotation say about the importance of personal experiences in a writer's life?

Identify   Before you read, answer these three questions:

1. What do the first paragraph and the first lines in other paragraphs tell you about the text?

_____

2. Who might be the author's intended audience?

_____

3. What do you expect to learn in this reading?

_____

Reading and Rereading

It will become clear to you why these two experiences were unforgettable for the author. Either one could have adversely affected Carson.

As you read, make it your goal to (1) follow the story lines, (2) note the types of detail used (explanations, dialogue, sensory details), and (3) note the way in which the writer deals with each experience. Consider annotating the text (page 20) during your reading.

The Reading Process

Prereading   Rereading

Reading   Reflecting

From *Gifted Hands*

At the end of each school year the principal and teachers handed out   *1*
certificates to the one student who had the highest academic achievement
in the seventh, eighth, and ninth grade and that same year Curtis [the
author's brother] won for the ninth grade. By the end of eighth grade,
people had pretty much come to accept the fact that I was a smart kid. I   *5*
won the certificate again the following year. At the all-school assembly
one of the teachers presented my certificate. After handing it to me she
remained up in front of the entire student body and looked out across the
auditorium. "I have a few words I want to say right now," she began, her
voice unusually high. Then to my embarrassment, she bawled out the   *10*
white kids because they had allowed me to be number one. "You're not
trying hard enough," she told them.

While she never quite said it in words, she let them know that a black
person shouldn't be number one in a class where everyone else was white.

As the teacher continued to berate the other students, a number of   *15*
things tumbled about inside my mind. Of course, I was hurt. I had worked
hard to be the top of my class—probably harder than anyone else in the
school—and she was putting me down because I wasn't the same color.
On the one hand I thought, *What a turkey this woman is!* Then an angry
determination welled up inside. *I'll show you and all the others too!*   *20*

I couldn't understand why this woman talked the way she did. She had taught me herself in several classes, had seemed to like me, and she clearly knew that I had earned my grades and merited the certificate of achievement. Why would she say all these harsh things? Was she so ignorant that she didn't realize that people are just people? That their skin or their race doesn't make them smarter or dumber? It also occurred to me that, given enough situations, there are bound to be instances where minorities are smarter. Couldn't she realize that?

Despite my hurt and anger, I didn't say anything. I sat quietly while she railed. Several of the white kids glanced over at me occasionally, rolling their eyes to let me understand their disgust. I sensed they were trying to say to me, "What a dummy she is!"

Some of those very kids, who, three years earlier, had taunted me, had become my friends. They were feeling embarrassed, and I could read resentment on several faces . . . .

[Another] incident that stands out in my memory centered around the football team. In our neighborhood we had a football league. When I was in the seventh grade, playing football was the big thing in athletics.

Naturally, both Curtis and I wanted to play. Neither of us Carsons were large to begin with. In fact, compared to the other players, we were quite small. But we had one advantage. We were fast—so fast that we could outrun everybody else on the field. Because the Carson brothers made such a good showing, our performance apparently upset a few of the white people.

One afternoon when Curtis and I left the field after practice, a group of white men, none of them over 30 years old, surrounded us. Their menacing anger showed clearly before they said a word. I wasn't sure if they were part of the gang that had threatened me at the railroad crossing. I only knew I was scared.

Then one man stepped forward. "If you guys come back, we're going to throw you into the river," he said. Then they turned and walked away from us.

Would they have carried out their threat? Curtis and I weren't as concerned about that as we were with the fact that they didn't want us in the league.

As we walked home, I said to my brother, " Who wants to play football when your own supporters are against you?"

"I think we can find better things to do with our time," Curtis said. . . .

We decided to say nothing to Mother about the threat, knowing if we did, she'd be worried sick about us.

Reflecting

Practice After you complete your reading, answer the following questions. Afterward, share your responses with your classmates.

1. Why does Carson share these two experiences?

   _____

   _____

2. What are the primary types of details used in this selection—dialogue, explanations, or sensory details? Circle one.

3. How would you rate this selection and why?
   Weak ★ ★ ★ ★ ★ Strong

   _____

   _____

Vocabulary Practice

Identify Use context clues to explain or define the following words from the text. (See pages 34–35 for help.)

1. **berate** (line 15)

   clues: _____

   definition: _____

2. **taunted** (line 34)

   clues: _____

   definition: _____

Drawing Inferences

Explain Answer these questions to help you draw inferences from the text.

1. What do these two experiences illustrate or demonstrate to you?

   _____

   _____

2. Are you surprised by the experiences? Explain.

   _____

   _____

Writing

What follows are possible writing activities to complete in response to the reading. Use the writing process (pages 106–111) to help you develop your writing.

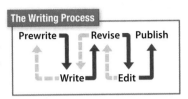

Prewriting

Choose one of the following writing ideas. Or decide upon an idea of your own making related to the reading.

Writing Ideas

1. **Writing to Learn:** Suppose you had witnessed the scene in which the teacher acted so insensitively toward Ben Carson. Write an email message or letter to the teacher in response to her actions.
2. **Narrative Writing:** Share one of your experiences from page 213.
3. Write about a time in which you had to make a quick decision.
4. Share a personal medical emergency.
5. Develop a narrative about a character-building experience.

> **When planning . . .**
> - Make sure that your topic is specific enough for a personal narrative.
> - Include effective details (sensory details, dialogue, and/or actions) to make the story come alive for the reader.

Writing and Revising

Use the tips that follow and the information on pages 205–208 to help you with your drafting and revising.

> **When writing . . .**
> - Include an opening, a middle, and a closing in your narrative.
> - Understand that you don't have to describe or show everything. You can leave some things to the reader's imagination.
>
> **When revising . . .**
> - Ask yourself if your story contains any dead spots that need more detail or should be cut.
> - Determine if readers will be able to visualize (see in their minds) the experience as it unfolds.
> - Decide if the dialogue seems realistic.

Editing

Refer to pages 209–211 when you are ready to edit your narrative for style and accuracy. Use the checklist on page 212 as your final editing guide.

Reflecting on Narrative Writing

Answer the following questions about your narrative reading and writing experiences in this chapter.

1. Why do writers find it valuable to write about their personal experiences?

2. What makes reading a personal narrative enjoyable?

3. Which is your favorite narrative in this chapter? Explain.

4. Which is the most helpful reading strategy in the chapter? Explain.

5. What do you like the most about the narrative you wrote in this chapter? Explain.

6. What one thing would you like to change in it?

7. What is the most important thing you have learned about narrative writing?

Key Terms to Remember

When you read and write narratives, it's important to understand the following terms.

- **Personal narrative**—an account of a memorable experience covering a brief span of time
- **Plot**—the different parts of a story that create suspense (exposition, rising action, climax, resolution)
- **Sensory details**—specific sights, sounds, smells, textures, and tastes
- **Dialogue**—conversation between characters
- **Chronological order**—organized according to time

8

Illustration

"Writing comes more easily if you
have something to say."
—Sholem Asch

A basketball coach may say to her team, "We were sloppy with our footwork in last night's game," and follow up with a video showing different examples. A business instructor may stress the importance of creating a positive working environment and then talk about different ways this can be done. A friend may say how much he or she likes a new apartment and then explain why.

As these brief scenarios show, illustrating a main idea with examples is a fundamental way to share information. Most of the informational reading you will do as a student—everything from textbook chapters to helpful Web sites—will be structured this way. Your understanding and familiarity with the illustrating process will help you with your academic reading and writing.

In the first part of this chapter, you will read and react to two professional texts that illustrate. In the second part, you will write an illustration essay of your own.

Learning Outcomes

LO1 Understand illustration.

LO2 Learn reading strategies. (using a line diagram and recognizing signal words).

LO3 Read and react to a professional illustration.

LO4 Read and react to a second professional illustration.

LO5 Plan an illustration essay.

LO6 Write the first draft.

LO7 Revise the writing.

LO8 Edit the writing.

What do you think?

According to the quotation above, what makes writing easier? Do you agree? Why or why not?

violetkaipa, 2013 / Used under license from Shutterstock.com

LO1 Understanding Illustration

By definition, illustration means "the act of clarifying and explaining." When a chapter or an essay effectively illustrates a main point, it shows that the writer has a good understanding of the topic. The following passage demonstrates illustration; it begins with a main idea followed by three examples that clarify or explain it:

> *(Main idea)* Members of the "Elsewhere Generation" will often ignore people in the same room while virtually interacting with people elsewhere. *(First example)* A teenage boy plays a massively multiplayer online role-playing game with people in a different country while his brothers beg him to play basketball in the driveway. *(Second example)* A group of friends sit in a café, but instead of talking to each other, they are texting people who are miles away. *(Third example)* A student is listening to a lecture while typing a status update on Facebook. . . .

> "A writer writes with information, and if there is no information, there will be no effective writing."
> —Donald Murray

Main points and clarifying examples are the yin and yang of informational writing. One naturally follows the other. If the writer of the passage above hadn't illustrated his main point, readers would learn very little about how the "Elsewhere Generation" interacts. In another example, if an author writes, "On his march to Atlanta, General Sherman devised creative methods for wrecking the Southern railroad," readers would expect examples to follow. How else would they fully understand the writer's point?

A Familiar Structure

Almost all illustration writing follows a familiar structure. Paragraphs that illustrate generally state the main idea in the topic sentence followed by supporting examples. Essays that illustrate often state the thesis (main idea) in the opening paragraph and develop supporting examples in the middle paragraphs. Thus, they follow deductive reasoning. (See pages 28–29.) The best illustration writing begins and ends with good information—an interesting main idea supported by meaningful examples.

INSIGHT

Examples help a writer illustrate, or support, a main point. Other common types of support in informational writing include facts, statistics, reasons, quotations, and definitions. (See pages 65–66.)

Identify   Find a passage in one of your textbooks or on a Web site in which the writer illustrates a main idea. Identify the main idea and supporting examples in the text, and share the passage with your classmates.

Reading

Reading a text that illustrates a main idea boils down to identifying two key components: the thesis (main idea) and the examples that support it. The strategies that follow will help you carry out your reading.

LO2 Learning Reading Strategies

Using a Line Diagram

To keep track of the key components, consider using a line diagram. Identify the main idea at the top of the diagram, the key supporting points on the next level, and more specific details on the next. (Use phrases rather than complete sentences when identifying these components of an essay.)

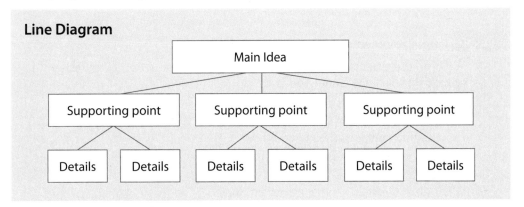

Line Diagram

Recognizing Signal Words

Writers often use signal words or phrases to identify examples. One common signal phrase is "for example." The chart below lists other signal words. Whenever you see one of these words or phrases, an example will most likely follow.

INSIGHT

While illustrating a main point, a writer may employ other types of thinking and analysis, including making comparisons, adding personal reflections, and so on.

Words that signal examples:

for example	another	for instance
also	moreover	additionally
next	in addition	along with

Practice Using a line diagram, identify the key components of the passage that you found for the activity on page 220. Remember to use phrases rather than complete sentences to name the different parts.

LO3 Reading and Reacting to a Professional Illustration

The selection starting below illustrates ways in which health care changed in ancient times. It comes from *Diversified Health Occupations*, a college textbook exploring careers in health care. Use the reading process to help you gain a full understanding of the text.

About the Authors

Louise Simmers has worked in a variety of nursing-related positions, from a public-health nurse to a medical-surgical nurse. **Karen Simmers-Nartker** has worked as an intensive-care nurse, most recently as a coordinator in an open-heart intensive-care unit. **Sharon Simmers-Kobelak** has worked in a variety of capacities in the educational publishing industry.

Preread Before you read, answer these questions:

1. What do the title, the first paragraph, and the first sentences of other paragraphs tell you about the text?

   _____

2. How might illustration be used by the authors?

   _____

3. What do you already know about the topic?

   _____

Read and Reread As you read, make it your goal to (1) identify the main idea, (2) note the supporting illustrative details, and (3) review any parts as needed to gain a full understanding of the text. Consider using a line diagram to identify the illustrative details. (See page 221.)

The Reading Process

Prereading   Rereading

Reading   Reflecting

Ancient Times

In primitive times, the common belief was that disease and illness were caused by evil spirits and demons. Treatment was directed toward eliminating the evil spirits. As civilizations developed, changes occurred as people began to study the human body and make observations about how it functions.

1

5

Religion played an important role in health care. A common belief was that illness and disease were punishments from the gods. Religious rites and ceremonies were frequently used to eliminate evil spirits and restore health. Exploring the structure of the human body was limited because most religions did not allow dissection, or cutting apart of the body. For *10* this reason, animals were frequently dissected to learn about different body parts.

The ancient Egyptians were the first people to record health records. It is important to remember that many people could not read; therefore, knowledge was limited to an educated few. Most of the records *15* were recorded on stone and were created by priests, who also acted as physicians.

The ancient Chinese had a strong belief in the need to cure the spirit and nourish the entire body. This form of treatment remains important today, when holistic health methods stress treating the entire patient— *20* mind, body, and soul.

Hippocrates (ca. 460–377 BC), called the "Father of Medicine," was one of the most important physicians in ancient Greece. The records that he and other physicians created helped establish that disease is caused by natural causes, not by supernatural spirits and demons. The ancient *25* Greeks were also among the first to stress that a good diet and cleanliness would help to prevent disease.

With knowledge obtained from the Greeks, the Romans realized that some diseases were connected to filth, contaminated water, and poor sanitation. They began the development of sanitary systems by building *30* sewers to carry away waste and aqueducts (waterways) to deliver clean water. They drained swamps and marshes to reduce the incidence of malaria. They created laws to keep streets clean and eliminate garbage. The first hospitals were also established in ancient Rome when physicians began caring for injured soldiers or ill people in their homes. *35*

Although many changes occurred in health care during ancient times, treatment was still limited. The average person had poor personal hygiene, drank contaminated water, and had unsanitary living conditions. Diseases such as typhoid, cholera, malaria, dysentery, leprosy, and smallpox infected many individuals. Because the causes of these diseases had not *40* been discovered, the diseases were usually fatal. The average life span was 20–25 years. Today, individuals who die at this age are considered to be young people.

Reflect After you complete you reading, answer these questions. Then share your responses with your classmates.

1. What is the main idea of this text?

   _____

   _____

2. What supporting illustrations do you find especially interesting? Name two.

   _____

   _____

3. How are the supporting details organized—spatially, chronologically, or logically? (See pages 75–77 for help.)

   _____

4. How would you rate this essay and why?

   Weak ★ ★ ★ ★ ★ Strong

   _____

   _____

Vocabulary Practice

Identify Use context clues to explain or define the following words. (See page 34–35 for help.)

1. **holistic**   (line 20)

   clues: _____

   definition: _____

2. **contaminated**   (line 29)

   clues: _____

   definition: _____

Drawing Inferences

Explain Draw an inference from the text by answering the question below.

■ Why would ancient societies rely so on religion for health-care solutions?

   _____

   _____

LO4 Reading and Reacting to a Second Professional Illustration

This essay below from a biology textbook entitled *Biology Today and Tomorrow* uses one example to illustrate life-saving procedures. Use the reading process to help you gain a full understanding of the text.

About the Authors

Cecie Starr, Christine A. Evers, and **Lisa Starr** are best-selling authors of biology textbooks.

Preread   Before you read, answer these questions:

1. What do the title, the first paragraph, and the first lines of other paragraphs tell you about the text?

_____

2. What do you already know about topic?

_____

3. What do you expect to learn?

_____

Read and Reread   As you read, make it your goal to (1) identify the main idea, (2) follow the illustrative story, and (3) reread any parts as needed.

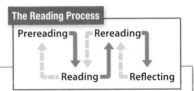

The Reading Process

Prereading   Rereading

Reading   Reflecting

A Shocking Save

The heart is the body's most durable muscle. It begins to beat during   1
the first month of human development and keeps at it for a lifetime.
A natural pacemaker in the heart wall generates electrical signals
that stimulate contraction of heart muscle. This pacemaker sometimes
malfunctions. When it does, electrical signaling becomes disrupted, the   5
heart stops beating, and blood flow halts. Such an event, called a sudden
cardiac arrest, occurs in more than 300,000 people per year in the United
States. An inborn heart defect causes most cardiac arrests in people under
age 36. Heart disease causes most in older people.

The chance of surviving sudden cardiac arrest rises by 50 percent   10 when the affected person receives **cardiopulmonary resuscitation** (CPR) within four to six minutes of the event. A rescuer who carries out traditional CPR alternates mouth-to-mouth respiration that forces air into an affected person's lungs with chest compressions that keep the victim's blood moving. CPR can ensure that essential oxygen reaches the brain, *15* but it cannot restart the heart. That requires a **defibrillator**, a device that resets the natural pacemaker by delivering an electric shock to the chest. You have probably seen this procedure depicted in hospital dramas.

Matt Nader learned about the importance of CPR and defibrillation when he experienced sudden cardiac arrest during a high school football *20* game. He came off the field after a play, sat on the bench to talk to his coach, and felt a burning pain in his chest. His vision suddenly blurred, then he passed out. Nader's parents, who are physicians, were watching the game and rushed from their seats. They quickly determined that Matt did not have a pulse and, as they examined him, he stopped breathing. *25*

Matt's parents began CPR on their son. At the same time, someone ran to get the school's automated external defibrillator (AED), a device about the size of a laptop computer. The AED provides simple voice commands that direct the user to attach electrodes to a person in distress. It then determines whether the person has a heartbeat and, if required, shocks *30* the heart.

In Nader's case, the AED restarted his heart, quite likely saving his life. Cardiologists determined that his sudden cardiac arrest had been caused by a **genetic** heart defect. To protect him, they implanted a small defibrillator inside his body. This device will provide a lifesaving shock if *35* his heart stops again.

After his recovery, Matt Nader appeared before the Texas State Legislature to testify about his experience and advocate for wider availability of AEDs in schools. Thanks in part to his efforts, Texas has passed a law requiring that all high schools have an AED available at *40* athletic events and practices.

From Starr/Evers/Starr, *Biology Today and Tomorrow with Physiology*, 4E. © 2013 Cengage Learning.

malfunction
to fail to function or work

cardiac
heart-related

cardiopulmonary resuscitation
emergency technique to revive someone
whose heart has stopped

defibrillator
electric-shock machine; administers a
controlled electric shock to the chest to
correct a critically irregular heartbeat that
cannot drive the circulation

genetic
related to the genes

Reflect   After you complete your reading, answer these questions. Then share your responses with your classmates.

1. What is the main idea? Is it directly stated or implied? (See page 52.)

   _____

   _____

   _____

2. What story illustrates the main idea?

   _____

   _____

   _____

3. What have you learned from this essay? Name one thing.

   _____

   _____

   _____

4. What questions, if any, do you still have about the topic?

   _____

   _____

   _____

5. How would you rate this essay and why?

   Weak ★ ★ ★ ★ ★ Strong

   _____

   _____

   _____

Vocabulary Practice

Identify For each term below, define the word parts; then define or explain the complete word. (See pages 36–37 and 668–676 for help.)

1. **durable** (line 1) dur + able

   clues: _____

   definition: _____

2. **contraction** (line 4) con + tract + ion

   clues: _____

   definition: _____

3. **implanted** (line 34) im + plant + ed

   clues: _____

   definition: _____

Drawing Inferences

Explain Draw inferences about the text by answering the following questions and/ or by making a thoughtful observation of your own.

1. Whose responsibility is it when it comes to the health and well being of individuals in an organization (school, business, etc.)?

   _____

   _____

2. How does this essay illustrate a larger issue about athletics in school?

   _____

   _____

3. (Your own observation)

   _____

   _____

Writing

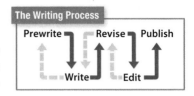

In your own essay, you will illustrate some aspect of modern culture or life. Be sure to use the writing process to help you do your best work. (See pages 106–111.)

LO5 Planning an Illustration Essay

Selecting a Topic

For your essay topic, choose a favorite type of television show, movie, music, Internet site, or so on.

Select List possible topics under at least three of the categories below. (One example is provided for you.) Then circle the topic you want to write about in an illustration essay.

Favorite type of...					
book	movie	television show	music	Internet site	other
mysteries					

Deciding on a Focus

Next, decide on a feature or part of this topic that you could illustrate in your essay. For example, in the essay on pages 222–223, the writers focus on key ancient civilizations to illustrate the early state of medicine. To write about favorite mystery books, a writer could focus on the unique or interesting detectives that popular mystery writers have created.

Explain In the space below, explain your focus, the feature or part of the topic that you will illustrate in your essay.

_____

_____

INSIGHT ———————————————————————

Finding a focus for your writing is a critical part of prewriting, or planning. It helps you choose which details to include and which to leave out. Writing that is not focused usually leads to an essay that spreads all over like a spilled glass of water.

Identifying Your Examples

Once you have established a focus, you need to identify the examples that will illustrate this feature.

Identify   List three or four examples to illustrate your focus. The writer of an essay about unique mystery detectives listed these four.

Sherlock Holmes

Jane Marple

Philip Marlowe

Spenser

Gathering Details

Each example that you share must be developed or explained with appropriate details. The writer of the essay on page 231 gathered details about each detective's personality, appearance, and way of solving mysteries.

Collect   Identify details that explain or develop each one of your examples. You may have to do some research to complete this part of your plan.

Writing a Thesis Statement

Your thesis statement should state your topic and identify your focus. The following formula will help you write this statement.

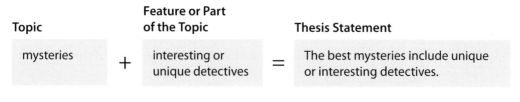

Topic		Feature or Part of the Topic		Thesis Statement
mysteries	+	interesting or unique detectives	=	The best mysteries include unique or interesting detectives.

Create   Write your thesis statement using the formula above as a guide. If necessary, write two or three versions and then choose the best one.

  +   =

LO6 Writing the First Draft

After you have completed your prewriting and planning, you are ready to write your first draft.

Read Before you begin your draft, read the following illustration essay, paying careful attention to the opening, middle, and closing parts. (Three middle paragraphs appear here.)

One-of-a-Kind Character

Mystery books are hugely popular. In fact, they are so popular that a   1
reader can find a mystery set in just about any time and place. There are
mysteries that seem very real, and others that are more imaginative. What
all mysteries have in common is a main detective or investigator that leads
the reader through the mystery. The most famous mysteries have a one-of-   5
a-kind main character leading the investigation.

Many mystery experts feel that Arthur Conan Doyle created the most
famous detective of all, Sherlock Holmes. The mysterious Holmes hides
out in his flat on Baker Street in London where he conducts experiments,
reads, and occasionally goes into a funk (and smokes opium). His only   10
friend and companion is the understanding Dr. Watson. Holmes is a very
serious man with dark hair and piercing eyes. Holmes uses his great
powers of observation and deduction to solve each mystery.

Another British writer, Agatha Christie, invented the famous amateur
detective Jane Marple in the 1920s. Miss Marple is an elderly woman   15
residing in a small village in England. She has the personality of a sweet
aunt or grandmother. Miss Marple is a loner like Holmes, but she is very
personable and understanding in social situations. While Holmes busies
himself in his laboratory, Miss Marple works in her garden. Christie
develops each mystery so Miss Marple just happens to appear at the site   20
of crime. She snoops around, listens, asks questions, and eventually solves
each crime.

In the late 1930s, mystery writer Raymond Chandler created one of the
first great American private investigators, Philip Marlowe. Marlowe is a
hard-drinking tough guy who works in Los Angeles. He carries a gun and   25
is not afraid of a fight, but he is also very intelligent. He learned to be an
investigator by working for the District Attorney's Office and an insurance
company. He often puts his life at risk against some real lowlifes during
his investigations. . . .

These examples show that the most popular mysteries begin and end   30
with a special investigator. Each new mystery allows this individual to put
his or her special talents into action to solve a crime that no one else can
figure out. Readers enjoy each new opportunity to see how their favorite
investigator does the job.

Creating an Opening Paragraph

The opening paragraph in your essay should gain the reader's attention, introduce your topic, and state your thesis. Here are three strategies for beginning an illustration essay.

- **Make a direct statement or two:** Mystery books are hugely popular. In fact, they are so popular that a reader can find a mystery set in just about any time or place.

- **Set the scene:** No matter if it is early in the morning or late at night, J. J.'s Café buzzes with activity.

- **Ask a dramatic question:** Why did Kamal die? The easy answer is malnutrition, but his poor diet was only a small part of the problem.

Developing the Middle Paragraphs

The middle part of your essay must offer supporting examples and explanations. Here are a few tips to help you develop this part.

- Focus on one example per paragraph, starting with a topic sentence that introduces the example.
- Include the details that you have gathered (see page 230) to develop each example.
- Arrange the examples in an order that makes the best sense.
- When necessary, use transitional words or phrases to move from one example to the next.

Writing a Closing Paragraph

The closing paragraph brings your essay to a logical stopping point. Here are three strategies that are often used to bring an illustration to an effective close.

- **Remind the reader of the thesis:** These examples show that the most popular mysteries begin and end with a special investigator.

- **Add another important idea:** Each new mystery allows this individual to put his or her special talents into action to solve a crime that no one else can figure out.

- **Provide a final, meaningful thought:** Readers enjoy each new opportunity to see how their favorite investigator does the job.

Write Write your first draft, using your planning (pages 229–230) and the information above as a guide.

LO7 Revising the Writing

Revising your first draft involves adding, deleting, rearranging, and reworking parts of your writing. Revision often begins with a peer review.

Peer Review

Sharing your writing is especially important when you are reviewing and revising a first draft. The feedback will help you change and improve your essay.

Peer Review Sheet

Essay title: _____

Writer: _____

Reviewer: _____

1. Which part of the essay seems to work best—opening, middle, or closing? Why?

   _____

   _____

2. Which part of the essay needs work—opening, middle, or closing? Why?

   _____

   _____

3. Which example caught your attention? Why?

   _____

   _____

4. Does the writer include enough detail to develop each example? Explain.

   _____

   _____

5. Do you have any questions about any part of the essay?

   _____

   _____

6. Identify a phrase or two that show the writer's level of interest in his or her story.

   _____

   _____

Respond Complete a response sheet like the one above after reading the first draft of a classmate's essay. Then share the sheet with the writer. (Keep your comments helpful and positive.)

Cutting Unnecessary Ideas

A first draft is your first look at your developing writing ideas. Some of your ideas will be fine just as they are, others may need to be clearer, and still others may need to be cut. Unnecessary ideas can weaken the unity and flow of your writing by repeating what was already said or by including unrelated or inaccurate information.

Repeated Idea: The most famous mysteries have a one-of-a-kind main character leading the investigation. ~~This person is always special.~~

Unrelated Idea: Miss Marple has the personality of a sweet aunt or grandmother. ~~But not all elderly people are sweet and nice. . . .~~

Inaccurate Information: Holmes is a very serious man with dark hair and piercing eyes. ~~On the streets, he usually wears a hunting cap with small visors in front and back.~~ (*This is untrue; he usually wears a bowler hat.*)

Revising in Action

Read aloud the unrevised and then the revised version of the following passage. Notice that an unrelated and a repeated idea have been cut.

Grant's first important success came in February of 1862 at the Battle of Fort Donelson in Tennessee. ~~Grant was said to have a drinking problem.~~ The Confederate troops had entered the fort to regroup after a battle at Fort Henry ~~where they had been.~~ Grant ordered his men to make minor attacks on the fort, . . .

Revise   Improve your writing using your classmate's comments on the response sheet and the following checklist. Continue working until you can check off each item in the list.

Using a Revising Checklist

Ideas

- [ ] 1. Have I selected an interesting topic?
- [ ] 2. Have I created a thesis for my essay?
- [ ] 3. Do I include at least three examples to illustrate the thesis?
- [ ] 4. Do I develop each example with enough details?

Organization

- [ ] 5. Does my essay have effective opening, middle, and closing paragraphs?
- [ ] 6. Do I use transitions, if necessary, between paragraphs?

Voice

- [ ] 7. Do I sound knowledgeable and interested in my topic?

LO8 Editing the Writing

The main work of editing is to check the effectiveness of individual words and sentences and correct any errors in your revised writing.

Capitalizing Proper Nouns and Adjectives

In addition to capitalizing the first word in a sentence, here are three other capitalization rules to remember.

- **Sections of the country** are capitalized, but words that indicate direction are not: Josie loves living in the **Southwest**. She lives **west** of Tucson.

- **Titles used with the name of a person** are capitalized, but titles used by themselves are not: **Senator Lee** voted for an extension of benefits; my **senator** voted against it.

- **The first word in a direct quotation** is capitalized, but only if it begins a full sentence: "**We** need to follow hand-washing rules," warned Ms. Banks, "**especially** during flu season."

Practice   Correct the capitalization errors in the following sentences, using the correction marks on page 237. The first sentence has been corrected for you.

1. Horace Greeley once said, "go west, young man."
2. Someday I would like to live in the southwest, which is about 500 miles South of my hometown.
3. During the last presidential election, one of the candidates was senator John McCain from Arizona. He has been a Senator for many years.
4. the climate in the Southwest is totally different from the climate in the northwest.
5. Flagstaff is in the Northern part of Arizona and is much cooler than Phoenix or Tucson.
6. The Pastor of our church said, "faith will guide those who travel."
7. My mother grew up in the midwest in a farming community.
8. her family moved Northwest to Seattle when she was in high school.
9. She once said, "life in Seattle has been much easier than life on the farm."

Apply   Check to see that you have followed the rules above in your illustration essay. (For more information, see pages 625–634.)

Additional Capitalization Rules

Here are three more capitalization rules to keep in mind as you edit your writing.

- **Specific names of special events** (historic events, holidays, sporting events, and so on) are capitalized, but general terms for the events are not: The **Civil War** produced many great leaders. The **war** also ruined many men.
- **Specific names of landforms and places** (mountains, rivers, buildings, bridges, and so on) are capitalized, but general references to them are not: Key battles were fought along the **Mississippi River;** both sides wanted control of the **river.**
- **Specific names of organizations** (military groups, sports teams, political parties, and so on) are capitalized, but general references to them are not: The **Confederate Army** fought bravely against the better-equipped **Union Army.** In the end, both **armies** suffered huge loses.

NOTE: In specific names of holidays, places, and organizations, capitalize the first and last words and other important words, but do not capitalize words such as *of, on, for, the,* or *a* within the name.

Fourth of July   Tavern on the Green   People for the Ethical Treatment of Animals (PETA)

Practice   Rewrite the following sentences, correcting capitalization as needed.

1. Racine, Wisconsin, has a great parade on the fourth of July.

2. The Parade runs along Main Street, starting by the Racine zoo.

3. members of the veterans of foreign wars (VFW) are in the parade.

4. Many companies such as sc johnson build floats for the parade.

5. several drum and bugle corps perform during the parade.

6. The kilties drum and bugle corps originated in Racine.

7. a float commemorating the battle of Iwo Jima is always a hit.

8. The American legion is also well represented in the festivities.

9. Spectators along monument square usually hear a good performance.

10. The fourth of July is also known as Independence day.

Apply   Check to see that you have followed the rules above in your illustration essay. (For more information, see pages 625–634.)

Marking an Essay

Before you finish editing your revised illustration essay, practice editing the following model.

Practice Read this illustration essay, looking for the problems listed in the checklist on the next page. Then correct the model using the marks listed below. One correction has been done for you.

Unconditional Leader

A surprising story in the Civil War is the rise to power of Ulysses s. Grant. At the start of the War. he was a lowly brigadier general of the Illinois volunteers. By 1864, he were appointed by President Lincoln to lead all of the troops in the Union Army. Grant earned this position by succeeding in important battles in the West.

Grant's first important success came in February of 1862 at the Battle of Fort Donelson in Tennessee. The Confederate troops had entered the fort to regroup after a battle at Fort Henry. Grant ordered his men to make miner attacks on the fort, and they also stopped an attempt by the Confederates to break out. Eventually, the Confederate troops agreed to Grant's terms of an unconditional surrender

During the spring of 1862, Grant led his troops in the Battle of shiloh, also in Tennessee. The Confederates made a surprise attack on the first day and pushed Grant's men back. Before the end of the day Grant and General Sherman rallied their troops. Then on the next day, the Union Army forced the Confederates to retreat. Many people criticized Grant for loosing so many troops during the fighting, but President Lincoln supported him by saying, "I can't spare this man; he fights."

Grant's success at Vicksburg, Mississippi, in 1863 really made him famous. the Confederate troops were fortified in Vicksburg, which rose above the Mississippi River. Grant had his men make a few charges into the Confederate battlements, but each one failed. He then decided to trapp the Confederates in the city until they ran out of supplies. Eventually, the Southern troops surrendered, this success gave the Union army free travel up and down the Mississippi River.

When Grant becomes the chief general of the army, he moved East to take on General Lee and his Confederate Army Of Northern Virginia. Grant fought General Lee and his troops until they surrendered. The battles weren't easy, and Grant lost thousands of troops. Yet he never once hesitated; he never once stopped fighting.

Correction Marks

- delete
- capitalize
- lowercase
- insert
- add comma
- add question mark
- insert an apostrophe
- word — add word
- add period
- spelling
- switch

Using an Editing Checklist

Now it's time to correct your own illustration essay.

Edit Prepare a clean copy of your revised essay and use the following checklist to edit it. Continue working until you can check off each item in the list. (For more rules, see pages 483–661.)

Words

☐ 1. Have I used specific nouns and verbs? (See page 146.)

☐ 2. Have I used more action verbs than "be" verbs? (See page 147.)

Sentences

☐ 3. Have I avoided improper shifts in sentences? (See pages 544–545.)

☐ 4. Have I avoided fragments and run-ons? (See pages 532–535, 538–539.)

Conventions

☐ 5. Do I use correct verb forms (*he saw*, not *he seen*)? (See page 588.)

☐ 6. Do my subjects and verbs agree (*she speaks*, not *she speak*)? (See pages 516–525.)

☐ 7. Have I used the right words (*their, there, they're*)?

☐ 8. Have I capitalized first words and proper nouns and adjectives? (See page 626.)

☐ 9. Have I used commas after long introductory word groups and to separate items in a series? (See pages 638–639.)

☐ 10. Have I used commas correctly in compound sentences? (See pages 636–637.)

☐ 11. Have I used apostrophes correctly in contractions and to show possession? (See pages 652–653.)

Adding a Title

Make sure to add an appropriate title for your essay. Here are three strategies to try.

■ Highlight the thesis:

One-of-a-Kind Character

■ Think creatively:

Two Eggs Over Easy

■ Make a direct statement:

Pursuing the Enemy

Enrichment: Reading

In the first part of this section, you will find the essay "Charity Means You Don't Pick and Choose" to read and react to. Be sure to follow the steps in the reading process as you read. In the second part, you will find a number of writing ideas to choose from to write an illustrative essay of your own.

> "The first great gift we can [give to] others is a good example."
> — Thomas Morell

About the Author

Dr. Patricia O'Hara is a professional writer and English professor at Franklin & Marshall College in Pennsylvania.

Prereading

Throughout your life, you will meet many types of people. Some may serve as role models, both good and bad. Write freely for a few minutes about who you are, where you come from, and what you like to do. Then write for another few minutes about one or two people who have influenced you.

CONSIDER THE TRAITS

As you read the essay, focus first on the **ideas**—the main idea and the examples that are used to illustrate it. Also note the author's **voice**—her special way of speaking to the reader. Then ask yourself if the ideas and voice contribute to a satisfying reading experience.

What do you think?

The quotation above refers to a good example as a "great gift." How is an example a gift, especially in an essay that illustrates?

Before you read, answer these three questions:

1. What do the title, first two paragraphs, and first lines of other paragraphs tell you about the essay?

_____

2. What are your first thoughts about the author's purpose and audience?

_____

3. What questions would you like answered in your reading?

_____

Reading and Rereading

In this essay, the author uses personal experiences to illustrate her thesis. As you read, make it your goal to (1) identify the main idea or thesis, (2) note the examples that illustrate the main idea, and (3) study the message in the closing paragraph. Consider annotating the text (page 20) during your reading.

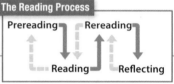

The Reading Process

Prereading ┐ ┌ Rereading

Reading ┘ └ Reflecting

Charity Means You Don't Pick and Choose

"If you're not going to eat that, little boy, I will," said the man sitting on   *1*
the sidewalk to my son, who was holding a doggie bag of restaurant leftovers.
It was the first time my son had ever seen a homeless person. He was 5 years
old, and we were spending the weekend visiting museums in Washington, DC.
It was a March night of unusually raw weather—not a night to be sitting on   *5*
a cold, hard sidewalk. I tightened my grasp on my son's hand as I made eye
contact with the man.

"Spare anything, ma'am?"

My son looked up at me uneasily, so I left him with my husband and went
over to the man, dollar extended. He thanked me and asked my son again for   *10*
his doggie bag. I motioned him over, nodding my assurances. "I didn't finish
my steak sandwich," my son told him proudly, as he handed the man his bag.
The man thanked him and said, "Be good to your mommy."

At just that moment a father and his two teenage sons walked past and,
without breaking his stride, barked out: "It'd be better if they got a job!"   *15*

I was startled by the intensity of the man's disapproval, but I, too, have
had doubts about offering handouts to the homeless. Under the watchful
eyes of my child, I chose the action that I hoped would speak to my son about
the principles of charity I hold dear, but the truth is, my decision to give has
seldom been clear-cut.   *20*

Like most people, I'm more comfortable giving when the people on the
receiving end are **anonymous**. I happily participate in the clothing drives
sponsored by my son's school, and I drop my spare change in the big metal
kettle at the mall, where a man dressed like Santa Claus rings his bell and
smiles at shoppers.

Giving directly to the street person shambling across my pathway—well,   *25*
that's another matter. Hollywood tends to portray the homeless as lovable
rogues (think Eddie Murphy in *Trading Places*), but in real life, the person
asking for money is often suffering the effects of mental illness or addiction.
I'm not proud to admit it, but even the few seconds it takes to look the other
person in the eye, extend my hand and offer some change can feel like more of   *30*
a connection than I want to make.

I've heard the intellectual arguments against giving handouts: the money
will be used to buy drugs or alcohol, handouts breed **dependency**, giving money
discourages the homeless from going to shelters. I don't want to undermine
the efforts of the mental-health professionals who work to get the homeless off   *35*
the streets. But what I know in my head doesn't square with what I feel in my
heart. Pretending that people don't exist and withholding a couple of quarters
or a dollar bill feels like the wrong thing to do.

Several years after our encounter with the homeless man in Washington,
my son and I visited New York City. As we walked down the street, a thin,   *40*
drugged-out young man approached us and asked us for change. It was
midtown at midday, so there was nothing particularly threatening about the
circumstances. Nevertheless, the man was, by anyone's standards, unsavory-
looking with his dirty clothes and unhealthy skin. I passed him by. Half a
block later, my son stopped walking and asked: "Why didn't you give him   *45*
anything?" I fumbled through a rationale about how we hadn't had time to
stop and why we couldn't possibly give to everyone. My son interrupted and
said, "Yeah, I don't think you should give money to people like that."

"People like that."

In his words and his tone of voice were echoes of the man who told the   *50*
panhandler to get a job. I had shown my son that it was acceptable to classify
people as the deserving and the undeserving poor.

Last spring I traveled to London to do some work-related research. Each
day on the way to the library, I passed a group of homeless men lying on the
steps of St. Pancras Old Church. Perhaps spending time in one of Charles   *55*
Dickens' old neighborhoods set me thinking about his righteous anger
at society's neglect of its poor. Or maybe I finally accepted that I'm in no
position—and who is?—to judge another person's worthiness of a small act of
kindness. Whatever the reason, I decided that I would always give when asked,
even when it means weathering the sidelong glances of those who think I'm a   *60*
fool or worse.

My son is now a teenager and will have to decide for himself if and how
he'll give to the poor. For all of my inconsistencies, I hope that I've taught him
that it's better to set the needle of his compass to the magnetic pull of kindness
than to contempt. But time alone will tell.   *65*

anonymous
unnamed

dependency
the state of needing something

Reflecting

Practice   After you complete your reading, answer the following questions. Then share your responses with your classmates.

1. What is the main idea or thesis of the essay? Is it directly stated or implied? (See page 52.)

   _____

   _____

2. What two experiences does the author discuss in detail?

   _____

   _____

3. How do these experiences differ?

   _____

   _____

4. What logical pattern of reasoning does the writer use—deductive or inductive? (See pages 28–29.)

   _____

   _____

5. How does the title relate to the essay's closing or conclusion?

   _____

   _____

6. What part of the essay do you like the most (or the least)?

   _____

   _____

7. How would you rate this essay and why?

   Weak ★ ★ ★ ★ ★ **Strong**

   _____

   _____

Vocabulary Practice

Identify   Explain or define the following words using your understanding of context clues and word parts as your guide. Also list the words or word parts that help you define the terms. (See pages 36–37 and 668–676 for help.)

1. **assurances**   (line 11)

_____

_____

2. **unsavory**   (line 44)

_____

_____

3. **inconsistencies**   (line 64)

_____

_____

Drawing Inferences

Explain   Draw inferences about the essay by answering the following questions and/or by making your own thoughtful observations.

1. After reading this essay, what conclusions can you draw about the author?

_____

_____

2. In addition, what conclusions can you draw about forming personal attitudes and beliefs?

_____

_____

3. (Your own observation)

_____

_____

Writing

What follows are possible writing activities to complete in response to the reading. Use the writing process (pages 106–111) to help you develop your writing.

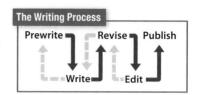

Prewriting

Choose one of the following writing ideas, or decide upon an idea of your own making related to the reading.

Writing Ideas

1. **Writing to Learn:** At the end of the essay, O'Hara states, "For all my inconsistencies, I hope that I've taught him [her son] that it's better to set the needle of his compass to the magnetic pull of kindness than to contempt." Examine this idea in a personal journal or blog entry; base your thoughts on your understanding of the essay and on your own experiences.

2. **Essay Writing:** Write an illustrative essay about one of the ideas (a particular type or group of people) that you listed on page 239.

3. Write an essay in which you explore the concept of "charity."

4. Write about another one of the topics that you identified on page 229.

5. Write an essay or paragraph of illustration related to a photograph in this text.

When Planning . . .

Refer to pages 229–230 to help you plan your essay. Also use these tips.

- Choose a topic that truly interests you and that you know about or can easily research.

- Be able to identify at least two or three worthy examples to illustrate the topic.

Writing and Revising

Refer to pages 231–234 to help you write and revise your first draft. Also use the tips that follow.

When Writing . . .

Refer to pages 231–232 to help you write your first draft. Also use the tips that follow.

- Pay special attention to each part of your essay—the opening, the middle, and the closing.
- Develop each one of the examples with plenty of details.

When Revising . . .

Refer to pages 233–234 to help you revise your first draft. Also use the tips that follow.

- Determine if your essay answers key questions the reader might have about your topic.
- Be prepared to research your topic further if you need more examples or details.
- If you're dissatisfied with any part of your essay, refer to the models in the chapter for ideas.

Editing

Refer to the checklist on page 238 when you are ready to edit your essay for style and correctness.

Reflecting on Illustration Writing

Answer the following questions about your illustration reading and writing experiences in this chapter.

1. What is illustration writing?

   _____

2. Why are thesis statements and examples so closely related or connected?

   _____

3. What is your favorite essay in this chapter? Explain.

   _____

4. Which reading strategy in this chapter is the most helpful?

   _____

5. How will your understanding of illustrating a topic help you with your academic reading?

   _____

6. What do you like best about your essay?

   _____

7. What is one thing you would like to change in it?

   _____

Key Terms to Remember

When you read and write illustration essays, it's important to understand the following terms.

- **Illustration**—the act of clarifying or explaining in writing
- **Example**—one that is common to a group
- **Line diagram**—a graphic organizer used to identify the main idea and examples in writing

9

> "My definition of a free society is a society where it is safe to be unpopular."
>
> —Adlai E. Stevenson

Definition

You already know the primary meaning of *definition*—"the formal statement of the meaning of a word." You also know how to use a dictionary to find the definition of an unfamiliar word. And you are well aware that defining terms is a common type of test question.

This chapter examines the concept of a definition from a different perspective—as an important form of informational writing. The writer of a definition essay usually explains a word from a number of different angles, starting with the dictionary definition of the word, then providing information about the word's history, offering what others have to say about the word, examining the word in different contexts, and so on.

In the first part of this chapter, you will learn about definition writing and read and react to two professional examples of definition writing. In the second part, you will write a definition essay of your own.

Learning Outcomes

LO1 Understand definition.

LO2 Learn reading strategies (identifying the support and considering the source).

LO3 Read and react to a professional definition.

LO4 Read and react to a second professional definition.

LO5 Plan a definition essay.

LO6 Write the first draft.

LO7 Revise the writing.

LO8 Edit the writing.

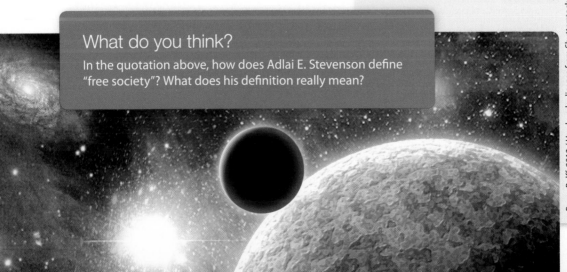

What do you think?

In the quotation above, how does Adlai E. Stevenson define "free society"? What does his definition really mean?

Bruce Rolff, 2013 / Used under license from Shutterstock.com

LO1 Understanding Definition

In one way, a definition essay is a basic form of informational writing that shares facts and details. In another way, it is a mini research paper that may require gathering information from a number of sources, both primary and secondary. A definition essay may also include analysis, comparing a term to others or classifying it. Essays that layer several types of information about a term are called extended definitions.

Extended definition essays are common in academic textbooks, probably because authors have a lot to say about the important terms and concepts related to their areas of expertise. The first professional text in this chapter, which defines *emotional intelligence,* comes from a textbook about succeeding in college. This essay provides a practical definition for incoming students, offers a scale for measuring one's own emotional intelligence, and discusses its importance in daily life.

The second professional text, which examines *globalization*, comes from an American government textbook. This selection defines and discusses an important concept in terms that make it understandable to most readers. Both selections pay careful attention to the explanations and examples.

> "Let me give you a definition of ethics: It is good to maintain and further life—it is bad to damage and destroy life."
> —Albert Schweitzer

Professional Versus Student Essays

Students like yourself may not have the background to develop extended definitions like the ones described above. They are, after all, written by experts. But you can still explore a word—including common synonyms, an explanation of its function, other people's definitions, and so on. The student essay on page 261 includes such information.

INSIGHT

When reading a definition essay, you benefit from the author's research and analysis; when you write a definition essay, you become the researcher, developing your own understanding of a word.

Identify List two probable topics for definition essays in each of the following disciplines. (One idea is provided.) Afterward, share your ideas with your classmates.

History: *What is emancipation?* _____

Science: _____

Sociology: _____

Art or Music: _____

Reading

Reading definition essays boils down to identifying and understanding the different ways that a word is defined. This section provides valuable reading practice.

LO2 Learning Reading Strategies

Identifying the Support

When reading a definition essay, use a gathering grid such as the one below to help you keep track of the different explanations, examples, and definitions. Make adjustments to the grid to meet your personal needs.

Gathering Grid

Subject: _____

Types of Details	Examples from the Text

INSIGHT

The support in an extended definition essay may include the following types of details: *dictionary definitions, other definitions, background information (history), synonyms, antonyms, comparisons, the word in the context of quotations,* and *other explanations.*

Considering the Source

To fully appreciate a definition essay, consider the source of the information. For example, the definition of art in an anthropology textbook will likely be far different from the definition of art in an art history book. Ask questions like the following ones to help you evaluate the information in a definition essay.

- What is the source of the essay (a textbook, a magazine, and so on)?
- If the source is a textbook, what subject does it cover (art, history, business, anthropology, and so on)?
- Who is the author and what is his or her background?
- Does the definition seem limiting in any way?

LO3 Reading and Reacting to a Professional Definition

The essay on the next two pages explores the concept of emotional intelligence. It comes from a college text entitled *FOCUS on College and Career Success*. Use the reading process to help you gain a full understanding of the text.

About the Authors

Constance Staley is a professor at the University of Colorado, Colorado Springs. During her time in the classroom, she has worked with thousands of students, helping them prepare for and succeed in college. *FOCUS on College* and *Career Success* puts in one place all of the valuable advice that she has shared with students over the years. **Steve Staley** is dean of academics and professor of management and humanities at Colorado Technical University. He has also taught at the Air Force Academy, the Naval War College, and the University of Colorado, and has been an Air Force instructor pilot and served as director of corporate communications and educational development in a high-tech firm.

Preread   Before you read, answer these questions:

1. What do the title, beginning two paragraphs, and headings tell you about the text?

   _____

2. What do you already know about the topic?

   _____

3. What questions do you hope to have answered?

   _____

Read and Reread   As you read make it your goal to (1) identify the main idea, (2) note the details that help define the topic, and (3) study the message in the closing paragraph. Consider annotating the text (page 20) during your reading.

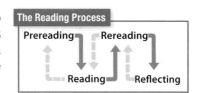

The Reading Process

Prereading   Rereading

Reading   Reflecting

What Is Emotional Intelligence?

Many experts believe that intelligence takes many forms. Rather than *1* a narrow definition of intelligence, they believe in Multiple Intelligences: **Linguistic**, Logical-Mathematical, **Spatial**, **Kinesthetic**, Musical, Interpersonal, Intrapersonal, and Naturalistic. Emotional intelligence may well be a combination, at least in part, of intrapersonal and interpersonal *5* intelligences.

Emotional intelligence is a set of skills that determines how well you cope with the demands and pressures you face every day. How well do you understand yourself, **empathize** with others, draw on your inner resources, and encourage the same qualities in people you care about? Emotional *10* intelligence involves having people skills, a positive outlook, and the capacity to adapt to change. Emotional intelligence can propel you through difficult situations.

The bottom line? New research links emotional intelligence to college success, and learning about the impact of emotional intelligence in the *15* first year of college helps students stay in school.

As you read about the five scales of emotional intelligence, begin thinking about yourself in these areas. As each scale is introduced, ask yourself whether you agree or disagree with the sample statement from a well-known emotional intelligence instrument as it pertains to you. *20*

Intrapersonal Skills (Self-Awareness)

"It's hard for me to understand the way I feel." Agree or disagree?

Are you in tune with your emotions? Do you fully realize when you're anxious, depressed, or thrilled? Or do you just generally feel up or down? Are you aware of layers of emotions . . . ? *25*

Interpersonal Skills (Relating to Others)

"I'm sensitive to the feelings of others." Agree or disagree?

Are you aware of others' emotions and needs? Do you communicate with sensitivity and work to build positive relationships? Are you a good listener . . . ? *30*

Stress Management Skills

"I feel that it's hard for me to control my anxiety." Agree or disagree?

Can you productively manage your emotions so that they work *for* you

and not *against* you? Can you control destructive emotions? Can you work
well under pressure . . . ?   35

Adaptability Skills

*"When trying to solve a problem, I look at each possibility and then
decide on the best way." Agree or disagree?*

Are you flexible? Do you cope well when things don't go according to
plan? Can you switch to a new plan when you need to? Do you manage   40
change effectively . . . ?

General Mood

*"I generally expect things will turn out all right, despite setbacks from
time to time." Agree or disagree?*

Are you optimistic and positive most of the time? Do you feel happy   45
and content with yourself, with others, and your life in general? Are you
energetic and self-motivated . . . ?

Emotional intelligence affects every part of our lives. For example,
researchers study related concepts: **"hardiness," "resilience,"** and "learned
optimism." Some people are more resistant to stress and illness. Hardy,   50
resilient, optimistic people are confident, committed to what they're
doing, feel greater control over their lives, and see hurdles as challenges.
Emotional intelligence is part of the reason why.

From Staley/Staley, *Annotated Instructor's Edition for Staley's FOCUS on College and Career Success*, 1E. © 2012
Cengage Learning.

linguistic	**empathize**
relating to language	understanding another person's feelings
spatial	**hardiness**
related to space or location	able to withstand hardship
kinesthetic	**resilience**
related to the study of movement	the ability to recover quickly

Reflect After you complete your reading, answer these questions. Then share your responses with your classmates.

1. What is the purpose of this selection? (Circle one.) Explain your choice.

   to inform   *to persuade*   *to entertain*   *to humor*

   _____

   _____

2. What is the main idea of this text?

   _____

   _____

3. Use a gathering grid to identify the different ways the term is defined. (See page 249 for help.)

   Subject: _____

Types of Details	Examples from the Text

4. What voice do the authors project—academic or personal? Explain.

   _____

   _____

5. What detail do you find most interesting or valuable? Why?

   _____

   _____

6. How would you rate this selection and why?

   Weak ★ ★ ★ ★ ★ **Strong**

   _____

   _____

Vocabulary Practice

Identify   Define or explain the following words in the selection by using context clues. (See pages 34–35.)

1. **intrapersonal** (line 21)

   clues: _____

   definition: _____

2. **interpersonal** (line 26)

   clues: _____

   definition: _____

3. **adaptability** (line 36)

   clues: _____

   definition: _____

4. **optimistic** (line 51)

   clues: _____

   definition: _____

Drawing Inferences

Explain   Answer the following questions to help you draw inferences from the text. (See pages 30–32 for help.)

1. Would you rather have strong musical or linguistic intelligence? Explain.

   _____

   _____

2. What does the common adage "Know thyself" mean to you, and what value does it have?

   _____

   _____

LO4 Reading and Reacting to a Second Professional Definition

The selection below, which comes from a textbook entitled *American Government and Politics Today*, defines and explains globalization. Use the reading process to help you gain a full understanding of the text.

> "The beginning of wisdom is the definition of terms."
> —Socrates

About the Authors

Steffen W. Schmidt is a professor of political science at Iowa State University and received his PhD at Columbia University. **Mack C. Shelley II** is a professor of political science and statistics at Iowa State University. He received his PhD at the University of Wisconsin. **Barbara A. Bardes** is a professor *emerita* of political science at the University of Cincinnati where she received her PhD. **Lynne E. Ford** is a professor of political science at the College of Charleston and received her PhD at the University of Maryland.

Preread Before you read, answer these questions:

1. What do the title and first paragraph tell you about the text?

   _____

   _____

2. What do you already know about the topic?

   _____

   _____

3. What questions do you hope to have answered?

   _____

   _____

Read and Reread As you read, make it your goal to (1) identify the main idea, (2) note the supporting details, and (3) reread any parts that challenge you. Consider annotating the text (page 20) and/or taking notes (page 22) to help you keep track of the important points.

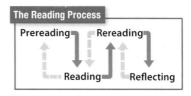

The Reading Process

Prereading → Rereading

Reading → Reflecting

Globalization and World Trade

Most of the consumer electronic goods you purchase—flat-screen   1
television sets, portable media players, cell phones, and digital cameras—
are made in other countries. Many of the raw materials used in
manufacturing in this country are also purchased abroad. Globalization,
which means worldwide distribution of production, marketing, and sales   5
of goods and services, has made it possible for many of the corporations
that are familiar to Americans such as Coca-Cola, Apple, and Procter &
Gamble to sell their products worldwide, manufacture products in many
different nations, and employ hundreds of thousands of people around the
globe.   10

When you go into a store to buy clothing, electronics, or furniture
for your home, you do not usually think about where the item was
manufactured or whose hands manufactured it. Items appear in-store with
English labels and the **appropriate** price tags and care labels you would
expect to see if they were manufactured in the next county. However,   15
they are likely to have been shipped to the United States in a container
and **comprised** of parts manufactured in many different nations. Many
"American-made" cars and trucks contain parts manufactured in Korea or
Mexico or Canada.

While world trade has made our lives easier and products cheaper for   20
consumers, it is a controversial topic. Since 1999, meetings of major trade
bodies such as the World Trade Organization have been marked by large
and sometimes violent demonstrations against globalization. Opponents
of globalization often refer to "slave" wages in developing countries as a
reason to restrict imports from those nations. Others argue that we should   25
restrict imports from countries that do not enforce the same environmental
standards as the United States. There are those who worry that the
United States is no longer able to manufacture some products, such as
computer monitors, and that this could endanger the nation in a time of
war. Most vocal are those who see jobs lost, workers displaced, and towns   30
in economic decline after a factory moves its production overseas. The
United States, at one time, had **flourishing** furniture, textile, and leather
industries. Most of those products are now made overseas.

From Schmidt/Shelley/Bardes/Ford, *American Government and Politics Today,* 2013-2014 Edition, 16E. © 2014
Cengage Learning.

appropriate	comprised	flourishing
suitable, recognizable	consisting of, including	doing very well

Reflect After you complete your reading, answer the questions below. Then share your responses with your classmates.

1. What term is defined in the selection and what does it mean?

_____

_____

2. What other details help explain the term? Identify two.

_____

_____

_____

3. How is the selection organized—chronologically, spatially, or logically? Circle one.

4. How would you characterize the voice of this selection—academic or personal? (See pages 83–84.) Explain.

_____

_____

_____

_____

5. What questions do you still have about the topic?

_____

_____

_____

6. How would you rate this essay and why?

Weak ★ ★ ★ ★ ★ Strong

_____

_____

Vocabulary Practice

Identify For each word below, define the word parts as indicated. Then try to explain the meaning of the complete word. (See pages 36–37 and 668–676 for help.)

1. **controversial** (line 21) contro + vers + (i)al

_____

_____

2. **restrict** (line 26) re + strict

_____

_____

3. **displaced** (line 30) dis + placed

_____

_____

Forming a Personal Response

Express Review any notes and annotations that you have for the selection. Then write freely for 5 minutes exploring your thoughts and feelings about the term. You could organize your writing using the before-and-after structure—starting with your knowledge of the topic before your reading followed by your understanding of it afterward.

_____

_____

_____

_____

_____

_____

_____

Writing

In your own definition essay, you will explore a word or concept that truly interests you. Be sure to use the writing process to help you do your best work. (See pages 106–111.)

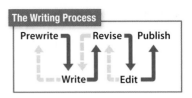

The Writing Process
Prewrite ⎤ ⎡Revise ⎤ Publish
Write ⎦ ⎣Edit ⎦

LO5 Planning a Definition Essay

The next two pages focus on prewriting and planning, starting with selecting a worthy word to define.

Selecting a Topic

The topic for your essay should be an abstract noun like *friendship*. An abstract noun is a word that names an idea or a feeling rather than an object or a thing. An abstract noun is not easy to understand, and it often means different things to different people. Example abstract nouns include *ambition, courage, duty, freedom, justice, prejudice, pride,* and *tradition.*

Select List two or three abstract nouns that interest you. Then circle the one that you want to write about in an essay.

1. _____

2. _____

3. _____

Gathering Details

Once you have selected a topic, you need to collect details that will help you define and explain the word. Here are different types of details to consider.

Types of Details

- dictionary definition(s)
- personal observations (stories)
- synonyms
- antonyms (what it is not)
- the word in action

- explanations of its parts
- comparisons
- quotations using the word
- other people's definitions

Collect Gather details for your essay by identifying at least four or five of the details listed above. Put your information on a gathering grid or some other graphic device. (See page 9.)

Subject: _____	
Types of Details	Examples

Forming a Thesis

Your thesis statement should identify your topic and provide a focus for your essay—a thought or feeling about the topic that you would like to emphasize. The following formula will help you write this statement.

Specific Topic		Thought or Feeling About It		Thesis Statement
Tact	+	the sensitive handling of situations that could be hurtful	=	Tact is the sensitive handling of situations that could be hurtful.

Create Write your thesis statement using the formula above as a guide. If necessary, write two or three versions until your thesis says what you want it to say.

Specific Topic		Thought or Feeling About It		Thesis Statement
	+		=	

Arranging Your Details

Consider how you will arrange the details in your essay. You may want to begin with a basic dictionary definition, or a personal observation that sets the tone for your writing. Then decide on a logical order for the rest of your details, saving one of the most important details for last. Here is the order of the details found in the essay on the next page.

Arrangement of Details

- Observing the lack of tact
- Observing one part of tact—sensitivity
- Tact in action—being truthful
- What tact isn't—avoiding trickery

Arrange List the details you would like to include in your essay in a logical order. You can change the order later if necessary.

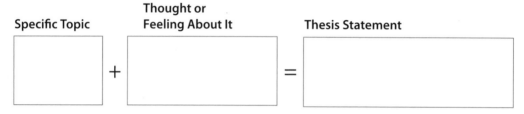

Christo, 2013 / Used under license from Shutterstock.com

LO6 Writing the First Draft

After you have completed your planning, you are ready to write your first draft.

Read Before you begin your draft, read the following definition essay, paying careful attention to the opening, middle, and closing parts.

Break It to 'Em Gently

Opening paragraph

There is a boy in my gym class (I'll call him Bill) who has unbearably yellow, scummy teeth that gross everyone out. Recently, another boy told Bill that he "should go Ajax" his teeth. Bill was crushed. Had the other boy been thinking, he would have realized that there is a better way to handle such a situation. He could have handled it with tact. Tact is the sensitive handling of situations that require conveying a potentially hurtful truth.

Middle paragraph 1

If a person isn't sensitive to another's feelings, there is no way he can be tactful. Children are especially vulnerable and must be handled sensitively. Yesterday, my 5-year-old brother proudly announced that he had cleaned the screen on our television set. Unfortunately, he used Pledge furniture polish, which produced a smeared, oily film on the television screen. My mother smiled and thanked him for his efforts—and then showed him how to clean the screen properly. Her sensitivity enabled my brother to keep his self-respect. Yet, sensitivity alone does not make tact. It is possible for someone to be sensitive but not be tactful.

Middle paragraph 2

A tactful person not only expresses herself sensitively, but truthfully as well. Doctors, for example, must be truthful. If her patient is paralyzed, a tactful doctor will tell the truth—but she will express it with sensitivity. She may try to give the patient hope by telling of new healing techniques under study or of advanced programs for handicapped people. A doctor should use tact with patients' relatives as well. Instead of bluntly saying, "Your husband is dead," a doctor should say, "I'm sorry . . ." or, "He's no longer suffering pain." These are tactful ways of expressing the truth.

Middle paragraph 3

Tact should not be confused with trickery. Trickery occurs when a nurse is about to give a patient an injection and says, "This won't hurt a bit." Trickery occurs in the courtroom when a lawyer phrases his question so as to get the witness to say something he never meant to say. An admiring audience might say, "How tactful he is, this lawyer!" Clever he may be, but tactful he is not.

Closing paragraph

Sensitivity, truthfulness, and careful thought are all necessary components of tact. No one component will do; they must all be utilized in situations where people's feelings are at stake. Tact is a wonderful skill to have, and tactful people are usually admired and respected. Without tact, our society would nurture insensitivity and disregard for others.

1

5

10

15

20

25

30

35

Developing an Opening Paragraph

Your opening paragraph should identify your topic, gain the reader's interest, and state your thesis. Here are three strategies for gaining the reader's interest.

- **Start with a dramatic story:** There is a boy in my gym class (I'll call him Bill) who has unbearably yellow, scummy teeth that gross everyone out. Recently, another boy told Bill that he "should go Ajax" his teeth. Bill was crushed. Had the other boy been thinking, he would have . . .
- **Make a bold statement:** At some point, most nations' histories include periods of either being enslaved or enslaving others.
- **Provide some perspective about the topic:** For centuries, people from a variety of disciplines—including philosophers, anthropologists, politicians, art historians, and professional artists themselves—have proposed definitions of art.

Creating the Middle Paragraphs

In the middle paragraphs, develop your definition with the different types of details you gathered and the planning you did on pages 259–260. Here are more tips.

- Try to include two types of details per middle paragraph, unless you have a lot to say about a particular point, such as what the word means to you.
- Provide enough information to make each point clear to the reader.
- Use transitions to help you move smoothly from one point or detail to the next.

Writing the Closing Paragraph

The closing paragraph should restate the thesis, summarize the main supporting points, or provide a final thought or two about the topic. Here are two strategies to consider.

- **Focus on a key point:** Maybe the best single definition of friendship comes from novelist Laurence Sterne who said, "You can always tell a real friend: When you've made a fool of yourself, he doesn't feel you've done a permanent job."
- **Stress the topic's importance:** Without tact, our society would nurture insensitivity and disregard for others.

Write   Write your first draft, using your planning (pages 259–260) and the information above and on the previous page to guide you.

LO7 Revising the Writing

Revising your first draft involves adding, deleting, rearranging, and reworking parts of your writing. Revision can begin with a peer review.

Peer Review

Sharing your writing at various stages is important, especially when you review and revise a first draft. The feedback that you receive will help you improve and strengthen your essay.

Peer Review Sheet

Essay title: _____

Writer: _____

Reviewer: _____

1. Which part of the essay seems to work best—opening, middle, or closing? Why?

   _____

   _____

2. Which part of the essay needs work—opening, middle, or closing? Why?

   _____

   _____

3. Do the middle paragraphs clearly define the word? Explain.

   _____

   _____

4. Do you understand the word more completely after reading the essay?

   _____

   _____

5. Identify a phrase or two that show the writer's level of interest.

   _____

   _____

Respond   Complete a peer-review sheet like this one after reading the first draft of a classmate's essay. Then share the sheet with the writer. (Keep your comments positive and helpful.)

Adding Clarifying Details

In some cases, it may not be enough to simply state an idea and expect the reader to understand what you mean. You may need to add two or three levels of detail before an idea becomes clear, as in the following example.

Level 1: Courage for a young boy is using the "river swing" on the Black River. (*Not clear enough*)

Level 2: The platform to swing from is about 30 feet up in a huge oak tree, and the rope to grab on to is attached to an even higher tree. (*Clearer*)

Level 3: Once you climb up to the platform, you must grab above a knot on the rope. Then, at the call of " Go," you swing way out and let go right at the top of your swing. (*Much clearer*)

Revising in Action

Read aloud the unrevised and then the revised version of the following passage. Note how the additional details make the information clearer.

Human trafficking is a difficult term to define. To begin with, human trafficking, migration, and smuggling are distinct but related situations, and incorrect understanding of them could wrongly label people. ∧

For example, Public Law 106-386 forbids the US government from jailing victims of human trafficking. On the other hand, illegal immigration subjects many . . .

Revise   Improve your writing, using the following checklist and your partner's comments on the response sheet. Continue revising until you can check off each item in the list.

Using a Revising Checklist

Ideas

☐   **1.** Do I focus on one specific, abstract noun to define?

☐   **2.** Do I state the focus of my essay in a thesis statement?

☐   **3.** Do I include different types of support (definitions, observations, and so on)?

☐   **4.** Do I explain each new main idea with enough detail?

Organization

☐   **5.** Does my essay have effective opening, middle, and closing paragraphs?

☐   **6.** Have I arranged the supporting details in an effective way?

Voice

☐   **7.** Do I sound knowledgeable and interested?

LO8 Editing the Writing

The main work of editing is correcting your revised first draft. Errors can distract the reader and take away from the effectiveness of your writing.

Using Apostrophes in Contractions

A contraction is a shortened form of a word or group of words with the missing letters marked by an apostrophe. Here are some examples.

Common Contractions

I'm (*I* + *am*; the *a* is left out)
don't (*do* + *not*; the *o* is left out)
they're (*they* + *are*; the *a* is left out)
it's (*it* + *is*; the *i* is left out)
should've (*should* + *have*; the *h* and *a* are left out)

wouldn't (*would* + *not*; the *o* is left out)
they'd (*they* + *had*: the *h* and *a* are left out; or *they* + *would*; the *w, o, u,* and *l* are left out)
must've (*must* + *have*: the *h* and *a* are left out)

Missing Letters or Numbers

Letters or numbers are left out in the following types of words and phrases. Apostrophes indicate where the omissions occur.

class of '09 (the number *20* is left out)
peel 'n' eat shrimp (the letters *a* and *d* are omitted)

Practice   Indicate where apostrophes are needed in the following sentences. If no apostrophes are needed, write "c" for "correct" on the blank next to the sentence.

1. To look at me, youd never know that seven years ago I had a mental breakdown. _____
2. Its time for me to admit who I am and what I need to do. _____
3. On the west side of the building, there's a great coffee shop. _____
4. Signs of Turk and Moroccan culture werent so obvious in the Netherlands 15 years ago. _____
5. Preoccupied with her own troubles, Orleanna wouldve been unaware of any troubles in the city. _____
6. Elvis Presley was once considered the king of rock n roll. _____

Apply   Read the sentences in your definition essay, watching for contractions and special words with missing characters. Make sure these words have apostrophes in place to mark the missing letters or numbers. (For more information, see page 652.)

Using Apostrophes to Show Basic Possession

Use apostrophes with nouns to show possession. Possession means "the act of having ownership." The placement of the apostrophe depends on whether the noun is singular or plural. Study the following examples.

Singular Possessives

■ The possessive form of singular nouns is usually made by adding an apostrophe and an *s*.

> my computer**'s** virus   Elena**'s** latest hairstyle   last night**'s** storm

■ When a singular noun of more than one syllable ends with an *s* or *z* sound, the possessive may be formed by adding just an apostrophe, or an apostrophe and an *s*.

> St. Louis**'** best park   or   St. Louis**'s** best park

Plural Possessives

■ The possessive form of plural nouns ending in *s* is made by adding just an apostrophe.

> the instructors**'** offices   the Smiths**'** damaged car

■ For plural nouns not ending in *s,* add an apostrophe and *s*.

> The men**'s** locker room   the children**'s** section of the library

Practice   Indicate where apostrophes are needed in the following sentences. If no apostrophe is needed, write "c" for "correct" on the blank before each sentence.

> 1. North Americas wealth and what it affords are widely known. _____
>
> 2. Because of todays economic problems, more people must do with less. ____
>
> 3. Maria is researching her grandparents childhoods. _____
>
> 4. Diseases that affect plants are an agroterrorist's weapon of choice. _____
>
> 5. My brother backed into Mr. Jones new Buick. _____
>
> 6. The womens investment group provides two scholarships per year. _____

Apply   Read the sentences in your definition essay, paying special attention to nouns that show possession. Be sure that you have correctly placed apostrophes in these words. (For more information, see pages 652–653.)

Marking an Essay

Edit the following model before you edit a revised version of your own essay.

Practice Carefully read the following essay, looking for the problems listed in the checklist on the next page. Correct the model using the marks listed below. The first correction has been done for you.

Trafficking in Slaves

At some point, most nations histories include periods of either being   1
enslaved or enslaving others. Unfortunately, the condition continue today.
In fact, different types of slavery exist today in developing countries as well
as in prosperous countrys such as the United States. Current trends show
that human trafficking or slavery is a very complex problem. With few   5
realistic options for ending it.

Human trafficking is a difficult term to define. To begin with, human
trafficking, migration, and smuggling are distinct but related situations,
and an incorrect understanding of them could wrongly labal people. For
example, Public Law 106-386 forbids the US government from jailing   10
victims of human trafficking. On the other hand, illegal immigration
subjects many people to criminal charges and possible deportation.
Smuggling, the illegal transport of people into a country, is also considered
a matter of immigration rather than human trafficking.

What makes human trafficking different is that it abuses the   15
victims and forces them to travel or work against there will. With this
idea in mind, the United Nations Convention Against Transnational
Organized Crime has developed this definition of human trafficking: "The
recruitment, transportation, transfer, harbouring, or receipt of persons, by
means of the threat or use of force or having control over another person for 20
the purpose of exploitation." under this definition, smuggling can become
trafficking if a smugglers actions include any means of force or threats.

Due to globalization, theres probably no illegal activity more serious
than human trafficking. In fact, human trafficking in todays world can be
summarized as millions of people experiencing multiple forms of slavery,   25
from sexual slavery to debt slavery.

Correction Marks

⤴ delete	⅄ add comma	ʌ̂ word add word
d̳ capitalize	? add question mark	⊙ add period
ⱡ lowercase	∧ mark	⬭ spelling
∧ insert	ⱽ insert an apostrophe	⮎ switch

Using an Editing Checklist

Now it's time to correct your own definition essay.

Edit   Prepare a clean copy of your revised essay and use the following checklist to edit it. Continue working until you can check off each item in the list.

Words

☐   1. Have I used specific nouns and verbs? (See page 146.)

☐   2. Have I used more action verbs than "be" verbs? (See page 147.)

Sentences

☐   3. Have I used sentences with varying beginnings and lengths? (See page 149.)

☐   4. Have I avoided improper shifts in sentences? (See pages 544–545.)

☐   5. Have I avoided fragments and run-ons? (See pages 532–535, 538–539.)

Conventions

☐   6. Do I use correct verb forms (*he saw*, not *he seen*)? (See page 588.)

☐   7. Do my subjects and verbs agree (*she speaks*, not *she speak*)? (See pages 516–525.)

☐   8. Have I used the right words (*their, there, they're*)?

☐   9. Have I capitalized first words and proper nouns and adjectives? (See page 626.)

☐ 10. Have I used commas after long introductory word groups and to separate items in a series? (See pages 638–639.)

☐ 11. Have I correctly punctuated any dialogue? (See pages 209–210.)

☐ 12. Have I used apostrophes correctly in contractions and to show possession? (See pages 265–266.)

Adding a Title

Make sure to add an attention-getting title. Here are three strategies to try.

■ Highlight the thesis:

A Deeper Bond

■ Think creatively:

Break It to 'Em Gently

■ Make a dramatic statement:

Trafficking in Slaves

> "People who urge you to be realistic generally want you to accept their definition of reality."
> —Source unknown

Enrichment: Reading

In the first part of the section, you will find a selection entitled "What Is Art?" to read and react to. As you read this essay, be sure to follow the steps in the reading process. The second part provides a number of writing ideas to choose from for writing a definition paragraph or essay of your own.

About the Authors

Gary Ferraro is Professor Emeritus of Anthropology at the University of North Carolina at Charlotte. He has been involved in research in Kenya and Swaziland, has traveled extensively, and has served as a consultant for organizations such as the Peace Corps and the World Bank. He is the author of many books about anthropology. **Susan Andreatta** is Associate Professor of Anthropology at the University of North Carolina at Greensboro. She has been involved in research in Costa Rica, Jamaica, Barbados, Mexico, Uganda, China, and North Carolina. Andreatta is the director of Project Greenleaf at Greensboro, an organization that provides undergraduate students with valuable research experiences. Her work has been published in many texts.

Prereading

The selection you are about to read discusses a word that you have heard many times: "art." Of course, as a college student, you can expect to be introduced to countless new terms. List a few old or new words associated with the following categories.

television

_____

textbooks

_____

workplace

_____

CONSIDER THE TRAITS

As you read the essay that begins on the next page, focus first on the **ideas**—the word that is being defined and the types of details that are used to define and explain it. Then consider the **organization**—the way that the opening, middle, and closing parts are constructed.

What do you think?

What does the quotation above say about some definitions?

Identify   Before you read, answer these three questions:

1. What do the title, opening paragraph, and first few lines of other paragraphs tell you about the text?

   _____

2. Are the authors trained as artists, historians, or anthropologists and how might that influence the information in the essay?

   _____

3. What questions do you have about the topic?

   _____

Reading and Rereading

"What Is Art?" comes from a textbook entitled _Cultural Anthropology_. The authors provide a very thorough and analytical answer to the question posed in the title. As you read, make it your goal to (1) identify the main definition of art; (2) note the types of information provided in the beginning, middle, and ending parts; and (3) reread any parts as needed to help you understanding the contents.

Consider annotating the text (page 20) and taking notes (page 22) to help you follow the development of the selection.

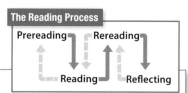

The Reading Process

Prereading · Reading · Rereading · Reflecting

What Is Art?

For centuries, people from a variety of disciplines—including philosophers,   _1_
anthropologists, politicians, art historians, and professional artists
themselves—have proposed definitions of art. George Mills (1957:17) suggested
that "definitions [of art] vary with the purposes of the definers." To illustrate,
the artist might define art in terms of the creative process, the politician's   _5_
definition would emphasize the **communicative** aspects of art that could
mobilize public opinion, the art historian or knowledgeable collector would
focus on the emotional response art produces, and the cultural anthropologist
might define art in terms of the role or function it plays in religious
ceremonies. Nevertheless, despite these diverse definitions, any definition of   _10_
art, if it is to have any cross-cultural comparability, must include five basic
elements:

1. The artistic process should be creative, playful, and enjoyable and need not
   be concerned with the practicality of the object being produced.
2. From the perspective of the consumer, art should produce some type of   _15_
   emotional response, either positive or negative.
3. Art should be **transformational**. An event from nature, such as a cheetah
   running at full speed, may be **aesthetically** pleasing in that it evokes a
   strong emotional response, but it is not art. It becomes art only when
   someone transforms the image into a painting, dance, song, or poem.   _20_

4. Art should communicate information by being **representational**. In other words, once the object of art is transformed, it should make a **symbolic** statement about what is being portrayed.

5. Art implies that the artist has developed a certain level of technical skill not shared equally by all people in a society. . . .   25

Centuries of debate by reasonable people have failed to produce a universally agreed-upon definition of art. Although we will not presume to establish a **universal** definition, it may well be useful, for the purpose of this chapter, to suggest a working definition based on the five elements just listed. Thus art is both the process and the products of applying certain skills to any   30 activity that transforms matter, sound, or motion into a form that is deemed aesthetically meaningful by people in a society.

By using these five features, we can include a wide variety of artistic activities in our definition of art. In all societies people apply imagination, creativity, and technical skills to transform matter, sound, and movement   35 into works of art. The various types of artistic expression include the graphic or plastic arts—such as painting, carving, weaving, basket making, and sculpting out of clay, metal, or glass; the creative manipulation of sounds and words in such artistic forms as music, poetry, and folklore; and the application of skill and creativity to body movement that gives rise to dance.   40

It should be pointed out that these three neatly defined categories of artistic expression sometimes include forms that are not familiar to Westerners. To Westerners the graphic and plastic arts include such media as painting and sculpture, but in the non-Western world people may also include the Nubians' elaborate body decorations (Fairs 1972), Navajo sand painting   45 (Witherspoon 1977), and the Inuits' body tattooing (Birket-Smith 1959). Moreover some activities that in our own society have no particular artistic content may be elevated to an art form in other societies. The Japanese tea ceremony is an excellent case in point. . . .

Every society has a set of standards that distinguish between good art   50 and bad art or between more and less satisfying aesthetic experiences. In some societies, such as our own, what constitutes good art is determined largely by a professional art establishment made up of art critics, museum and conservatory personnel, professors of art, and others who generally make their living in the arts. Other societies may not have professional art   55 establishments, and their artistic standards tend to be more democratic in that they are maintained by the general public. Thus the decoration on a vase, the rhythm of a song, the communicative power of a dance, and the imagery of a painting are subject to the evaluation of artists and non-artists alike.

From Ferraro/Andreatta, *Cultural Anthropology*, 9E. © 2012 Cengage Learning.

anthropologists
people trained to study the origin of human behavior and physical, social, and cultural development

communicative
related to the exchange of thoughts and feelings

transformational
the act of being transformed or changed

aesthetically
of or concerning the appreciation of beauty or good taste

representational
attempting to depict objects, scenes, or figures

symbolic
illustrative, suggestive

universal
common worldwide

Reflecting

Practice   After your reading, answer the following questions. Then share your responses with your classmates.

1. What anthropological definition of art is given? In what part of the text does it appear?

_____

_____

_____

2. What information is provided in the beginning of the selection?

_____

_____

3. What is the purpose of the five elements listed in lines 13–25?

_____

_____

4. Artistic expressions can "transform matter, sound and movement." What does this mean? (See lines 33–40.)

_____

_____

5. What thoughts are communicated in the closing paragraph?

_____

_____

6. Would the authors classify a cheetah running at full speed as art? Why or why not?

_____

_____

7. How would you rate this essay and why?

   Weak ★ ★ ★ ★ ★ Strong

_____

_____

Vocabulary Practice

Identify Explain or define the following words by using your understanding of context clues and word parts. Identify the clues or word parts the help you understand each term. (See pages 34–37 and 668–676 for help.)

1. **diverse** (line 10)

2. **plastic** (line 37)

3. **manipulation** (line 38)

4. **distinguish** (line 50)

Drawing Inferences

Explain Draw inferences from the text by answering the questions below or by making other thoughtful observations.

1. Is the value placed on art different from one culture to the next and from one time period to the next? Explain.

2. Why do people feel the need to engage in artistic expression?

Writing

What follows are possible writing activities to complete in response to the reading. Use the writing process (pages 106–111) to help you develop your work.

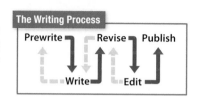

Prewriting

Choose one of the following writing ideas, or decide upon an idea of your own making related to the reading.

Writing Ideas

1. **Writing to Learn:** Complete a cluster or web (page 24) with art as your nucleus word. Make as many connections are you can. Then write freely for five minutes about one of the ideas in your cluster.

2. **Essay Writing**: Write a personal essay exploring art in your life. Consider your own experiences with art, the type of art you enjoy, where you find it, the importance of art in your life, etc.

3. Write a definition essay about one of the words that you listed on page 269.

4. Write an essay in which you illustrate the meaning of a word via one or two examples.

5. Write an essay about an interesting word related to a photograph in this chapter.

When planning . . .

Refer to pages 259–260 to help you plan your essay. Also use these planning tips.

- Choose a word to define that truly interests you.
- Explore the word from a number of different angles.

Writing and Revising

Refer to pages 261–264 to help you write and revise your first draft. Also use the tips that follow.

When writing . . .

Refer to pages 261–262 to help you write your first draft. Also use the tips that follow.

- Pay special attention to each part of your essay—the beginning, the middle, and the closing.

- Use different levels of detail to make your ideas clear. (See page 137.)

When revising . . .

Refer to pages 263–264 to help you revise your first draft. Also use the tips that follow.

- Determine if your essay answers key questions readers might have about the word.

- Be prepared to do some additional research if necessary.

- If you're dissatisfied with any part of your essay, refer to the models in the chapter for ideas.

Editing

Refer to the checklist on page 268 when you are ready to edit your essay for style and correctness.

Sura Nualpradid, 2013 / Used under license from Shutterstock.com

Reflecting on Definition Writing

Answer the following questions about your definition reading and writing experiences in this chapter.

1. What is an extended definition?

   _____

2. What value do definition essays have for the reader?

   _____

3. Which reading strategy in this chapter seems the most helpful? Explain.

   _____

4. Why is it important to know the source of a definition essay?

   _____

5. What do you like best about your definition essay?

   _____

6. What is one thing you would like to change in it?

   _____

Key Terms to Remember

When you read and write definition essays, it's important to understand the following terms.

- **Definition**—the formal statement or explanation of a meaning of a word
- **Gathering grid**—a graphic organizer used to identify or gather different types of defining details (dictionary definitions, synonyms, and so on)
- **Abstract**—referring to an idea or a feeling rather than to something physical

10

> "Knowledge is a process of piling up facts; wisdom lies in their simplification."
>
> —Martin H. Fischer

Process

Explaining a process is a common feature in almost all college textbooks. A science text may explain the carbon or nitrogen cycle. A history text may explain the sequence of events that caused the Black Plague to spread across Europe. An anthropology text may explain the process that has produced out-of-control urban sprawl in developing countries. A linguistics text may explain how new words are added to the language.

By definition, a process is "a series of actions or operations that produces a particular result." Many processes, such as the ones described above, explain how something works or occurs. Then there are process texts that explain how to do or how to make something. This type of essay may, for example, explain how to use a new piece of computer software, how to manage your time, or, as in this textbook, how to use the reading and writing processes.

In this chapter you will read and react to both types of processes. Then you will write a process essay of your own.

Learning Outcomes

LO1 Understand the process form.

LO2 Learn reading strategies (recognizing sequence formats and using graphic organizers).

LO3 Read and react to a professional process.

LO4 Read and react to a second professional process.

LO5 Plan a process essay.

LO6 Write the first draft.

LO7 Revise the writing.

LO8 Edit the writing.

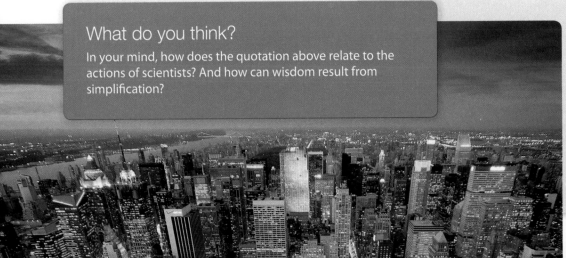

Ilja Mašík, 2013 / Used under license from Shutterstock.com

What do you think?

In your mind, how does the quotation above relate to the actions of scientists? And how can wisdom result from simplification?

> "The process of scientific discovery is, in effect, a continual flight from wonder."
>
> —Albert Einstein

LO1 Understanding the Process Form

Life seems to evolve around processes. You have to follow certain steps to get a driver's license, to graduate, to get a job, to get married, to plant a garden, and on and on. Life without steps to follow would be almost impossible to imagine.

Reading process texts should not be a problem because you have had so much experience with them. They are almost always arranged chronologically (by time) and often include clue words such as *first, next,* and so on. The purpose of a process is to provide an explanation or give directions, so they are usually clear and easy to follow. There are, of course, exceptions, such as instructional manuals written by someone with little understanding of the English language, or essays attempting to explain complicated and advanced processes.

Quite often, a graphic representation of the process will accompany the text. Some graphics include more details than the written explanation. So if the text seems confusing, you can always refer to the graphic for clarification. Pages 13–15 in this book offer a written explanation of the reading process and provide a graphic that shows you how the process works (moving forward and backward between the steps).

Level of Thinking

When working with process essays, you will employ two basic thinking strategies: *understanding* and *applying.* Understanding implies "knowing what the information means." You can show your understanding by restating or summarizing the process. Applying means "putting the information to use." In an essay that explains how to do something, you can show your understanding by demonstrating the process (using the software, changing a tire, and so on).

INSIGHT

Another level of thinking, *analysis,* may come into play with some processes. Analysis is the process of breaking down a topic to increase your understanding of it.

Identify   List three or four processes, sets of directions, or steps to follow that you have read or used recently. Also identify the most frustrating process that you have ever tried to follow. Afterward, share your ideas with your classmates.

1. _____

2. _____

3. _____

Reading

Reading process essays boils down to identifying and understanding the steps that explain how something works or how to do something. These strategies will help you read them.

LO2 Learning Reading Strategies

Recognizing Sequencing Formats

When reading a process essay, you are dealing with a sequence—one step or stage following another. Clue words or transitions often introduce each step so they are easy to identify and follow. Here are a few common sequencing formats that you will find.

Using Graphic Organizers

Since process essays are organized chronologically, you can use a cycle diagram or time line to identify the key details. Cycle diagrams work well for explaining recurring processes, such as the water cycle. Time lines work well for processes that begin and end, with several steps in between.

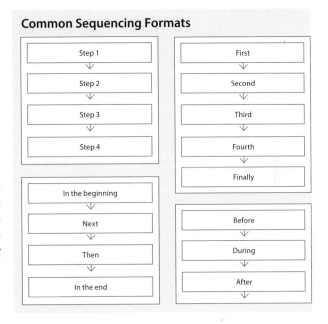

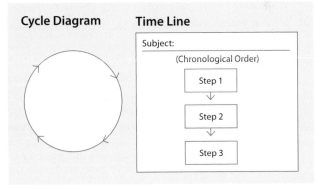

Identify Find an example of process writing in one of your textbooks. Then identify the clue words or transitions used to indicate the steps in the sequence. Next, graph the steps using a cycle diagram or a time line. Afterward, share your work with your classmates.

LO3 Reading and Reacting to a Professional Process

The process selection below, which comes from *Becoming a Master Student*, provides directions for creating and using "to-do" lists to help you manage daily tasks. Use the reading process to help you gain a full understanding of the text.

About the Author

Dave Ellis is an author, an educator, a workshop leader, and a lecturer. His book *Becoming a Master Student* is a best seller in its 15th edition, and it is used by students in the United States and in several other countries. He has coauthored other books on subjects such as human effectiveness and career planning.

Preread   Before you read, answer these questions:

1. What do the title, first paragraph, and bold headings tell you about the text?

_____

2. Who is the intended audience?

_____

3. What do you expect to learn?

_____

Read and Reread   As you read, make it your goal to (1) identify the main idea and (2) follow the steps in the process. Consider annotating the text (page 20) during your reading.

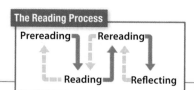

The Reading Process

Prereading   Rereading
Reading   Reflecting

The ABC Daily To-Do List

One advantage of keeping a daily to-do list is that you don't have to remember what to do next. It's on the list. A typical day in the life of a student is full of separate, often unrelated tasks—reading, attending lectures, reviewing notes, working at a job, writing papers, researching special projects, running errands. It's easy to forget an important task on a busy day. When that task is written down, you don't have to rely on your memory.   *1*   *5*

The following steps present one method for creating and using to-do lists. This method involves ranking each item on your list according to three levels of importance—A, B, and C. Experiment with these steps, modify them as you see fit, and invent new techniques that work for you.   *10*

Step 1 Brainstorm tasks

To get started, list all of the tasks you want to get done tomorrow.

Each task will become an item on a to-do list. Don't worry about putting the entries in order or scheduling them yet. Just list everything you want *15* to accomplish on a sheet of paper or planning calendar, or in a special notebook. . . .

Step 2 Estimate time

For each task you wrote down in Step 1, estimate how long it will take you to complete it. This can be tricky. If you allow too little time, you end *20* up feeling rushed. If you allow too much time, you become less productive. For now, give it your best guess. If you are unsure, overestimate rather than underestimate how long it will take you for each task. . . .

Add up the time needed to complete all your to-do items. Also add up the number of unscheduled hours in your day. Then compare the two *25* totals. The power of this step is that you can spot overload in advance. If you have 8 hours' worth of to-do items but only 4 unscheduled hours, that's a potential problem. To solve it, proceed to Step 3.

Step 3 Rate each task by priority

To prevent over scheduling, decide which to-do items are the most *30* important, given the time you have available. One suggestion for making this decision comes from the book *How to Get Control of Your Time and Your Life* by Alan Lakein: Simply label each task A, B, or C. . . . [The A's are the most critical, then the B's followed by the C's.]

Once you've labeled the items on your to-do list, schedule time for all of *35* the A's. The B's and C's can be done randomly during the day when you are in between tasks and are not yet ready to start the next A.

Step 4 Cross off tasks

Keep your to-do list with you at all times. Cross off activities when you finish them, and add new ones when you think of them. If you're using 3x5 *40* note cards, you can toss away or recycle the cards with completed items. Crossing off tasks and releasing cards can be fun—a visible reward for your diligence. This step fosters a sense of accomplishment.

Step 5 Evaluate

At the end of the day, evaluate your performance. Look for A priorities *45* you didn't complete. Look for items that repeatedly turn up as B's or C's on your list and never seem to get done. Consider changing them to A's or dropping them altogether. Similarly, you might consider changing an A that didn't get done to a B or C priority. When you're done evaluating, start on tomorrow's to-do list. . . . *50*

Keep in mind the power of planning a whole week or even 2 weeks in advance. Planning in this way can make it easier to put activities in context and see how your daily goals relate to your long-term goals. Weekly planning can also free you from feeling that you have to polish off your whole to-do list in 1 day. Instead, you can spread tasks out over the whole *55* week.

In any case, make starting your own to-do list an A priority.

From Ellis, *Becoming a Master Student*, 13E. © 2011 Cengage Learning.

Reflect   Answer the questions below about the process essay on pages 280–281. Then discuss your responses with your classmates.

1. What is the main idea of this text?

   _____

   _____

2. What clue-words or headings are used to identify each part of the process?

   _____

   _____

3. Which graphic organizer on page 279 would work well to list the key points in the text?

   _____

4. What primary type of supporting detail does the writer use—sensory details, quotations, explanations, or definitions? (See pages 65–66.)

   _____

   _____

5. Is the text organized chronologically, spatially, or logically? Explain.

   _____

   _____

6. How would you characterize the writer's voice—knowledgeable but distant, knowledgeable and helpful, uncertain and questioning?

   _____

   _____

7. How would you rate this essay and why?
   Weak ★ ★ ★ ★ ★ Strong

   _____

   _____

Vocabulary Practice

Identify   Explain or define the following words by using context clues and your understanding of word parts. Also list the clues or word parts that help you define each term. (See pages 34–37 and 668–676 for help.)

1. **productive**   (line 21)

   _____

   _____

2. **priority**   (line 29)

   _____

   _____

3. **diligence**   (line 43)

   _____

   _____

4. **fosters**   (line 43)

   _____

   _____

Drawing Inferences

Explain   Answer the following questions to help you draw inferences from the text. (See pages 30–32 for help.)

1. How would you characterize this information—practical, impractical, or somewhere in between? Explain.

   _____

   _____

2. What assumption or belief has the writer made about the readers of his advice?

   _____

   _____

LO4 Reading and Reacting to a Second Professional Process

The selection that follows, which comes from a textbook entitled *Sociology: Your Compass for a New World*, discusses the steps in the research process in sociology. Use the reading process to help you gain a full understanding of the text.

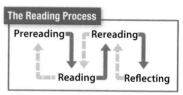
The Reading Process

About the Authors

Robert J. Brym received a PhD from the University of Toronto, and he teaches sociology at the same university. Brym has authored many books on political sociology, race, and ethnic relations. **John Lie** received his PhD from Harvard University and has served as Dean of International and Area Students at the University of California at Berkeley. Lie has authored many books on a wide range of topics, from contemporary East Asia to race and ethnicity.

Preread   Before you read, answer these questions:

1. What do the title, first paragraph, and graphic tell you about the text?

_____

2. What do you expect to learn?

_____

Read and Reread   As you read, make it your goal to (1) identify the main idea, (2) follow the steps in the process, and (3) reread any parts that challenge you.

The Research Cycle

Ideally, sociological research is a **cyclical** process that involves six   *1*
steps. The sociologist's first step is *formulating a research question.*
A research question must be stated so that it can be answered by
systematically collecting and analyzing sociological data.

Sociological research cannot determine whether God exists or what the   *5*
best political system is. Answers to such questions require faith more than
evidence. However, sociological research can determine why some people
are more religious than others and which political system creates more

opportunities for higher education. Answers to such questions require
evidence more than faith.   *10*

The second step involves *reviewing the existing research literature.*
Researchers must **elaborate** their research questions in the clear light
of what other sociologists have already debated and discovered. Why?
Because reading the **relevant** sociological literature stimulates researchers'
sociological imaginations, allows them to refine their initial questions, and   *15*
prevents duplication of effort.

Selecting a research method is the third step in the research cycle. As
we will see later in this chapter, each data collection method has strengths
and weaknesses. Each method is therefore best suited to studying a
different kind of problem. When choosing a method, one must keep these   *20*
strengths and weaknesses in mind.

The fourth stage of the research cycle involves *collecting data* by
observing subjects, interviewing them, reading documents produced by or
about them, and so forth. Many researchers think this is the most exciting
stage of the research cycle because it brings them face to face with the   *25*
puzzling sociological reality that so fascinates them.

Other researchers find the fifth step of the research cycle, *analyzing
the data*, the most challenging. During data analysis you can learn
things that nobody knew before. At this stage, data confirms some of your
expectations and confounds others, requiring you to think creatively about   *30*
familiar issues, reconsider the relevant **theoretical** and research literature,
and abandon pet ideas.

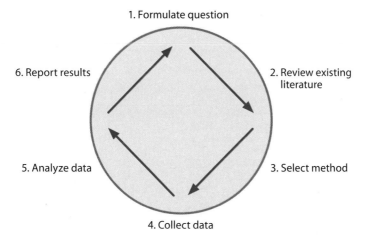

1. Formulate question

6. Report results

2. Review existing
literature

5. Analyze data

3. Select method

4. Collect data

Research is not useful for the sociological community, the subjects of the research, or the wider society if researchers do not complete the sixth step—*publishing the results* in a report, a scientific journal, or a *35* book. Publication serves another important function, too. It allows other sociologists to scrutinize and criticize the research. On that basis, errors can be corrected, and new and more sophisticated research questions can be formulated for the next round of research. Science is a social activity governed by rules defined and enforced by the scientific community. *40*

From Brym/Lie, *Sociology*, 2E. © 2007 Cengage Learning.

cyclical
a sequences that is repeated again and again

systematically
carried out step by step

elaborate
to work out with care, to develop thoroughly

relevant
having significance or importance

theoretical
based on what is possible rather than what is known with certainty

Reflect   After your reading, answer the following questions. Then share your responses with your classmates.

1. What is the main idea of the text?

   _____

   _____

2. How many steps in the process are included?

   _____

3. How do the writers signal each new step?

   _____

   _____

4. How would you rate this essay and why?
   Weak ★ ★ ★ ★ ★ Strong

   _____

   _____

Vocabulary Practice

Identify Use context clues to define the following words. (See pages 34–35.)

1. **duplication**   (line 16)

   clues: _____

   definition: _____

2. **confounds**   (line 30)

   clues: _____

   definition: _____

3. **scrutinize**   (line 37)

   clues: _____

   definition: _____

Drawing Inferences

Explain Draw inferences about the text by answering the questions below. (See pages 30–32 for help.)

1. Why is each step so essential to the process and in the order that they occur?

   _____

   _____

2. The authors conclude with this thought: "Science is a social activity." What does this idea mean to you?

   _____

   _____

3. Are you a process person—someone who relies on directions and steps? Explain.

   _____

   _____

   _____

Writing

In your own process essay, you will explain how something works or is made. Be sure to use the writing process to help you do your best work. (See pages 106–111.)

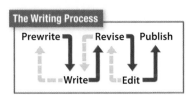

LO5 Planning a Process Essay

The information on these two pages will help you complete the important first steps before you start writing.

Selecting a Topic

Use the following ideas to generate possible process-essay topics.

Consider a process that . . .
- relates to your major or academic concentration.
- keeps you healthy or unhealthy.
- relates to your favorite entertainment—sports, music, theater, and so on.
- impacts the world around you.

Select List four potential topics for your process essay. They may be topics you know a lot about or ones you need to research more thoroughly. Circle the one you would like to write about.

1. _____   3. _____

2. _____   4. _____

Reviewing the Process

Once you have selected a process topic, review what you know about it and, if necessary, supplement your information with additional research.

Reflect Carefully answer these questions to decide if you need to carry out more research or perhaps change your topic.

1. How well do you know this process? _____

2. If necessary, where can you learn more about it? _____

3. Will your readers find this process interesting? _____

INSIGHT ————————————————————————————

When you need to research a topic, you have two main sources of information to choose from: primary and secondary sources. (See pages 428–432.)

Gathering Details

You can use a time line to list the steps in your process. The example to the right lists the steps needed to purify drinking water.

Gather Complete a time line for your essay. Start by writing down your subject. Then fill in the steps involved in the process.

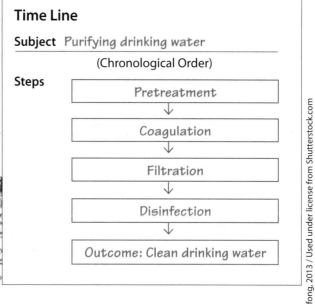

Time Line

Subject Purifying drinking water

(Chronological Order)

Steps

Pretreatment
↓
Coagulation
↓
Filtration
↓
Disinfection
↓
Outcome: Clean drinking water

ifong, 2013 / Used under license from Shutterstock.com

Levels of Detail

In addition to the basic steps in the process, you need to use sufficient details to explain each step. Here is a breakdown of the levels of details included in the second step of "The ABC Daily To-Do List" on pages 280–281.

- **Level 1:** For each task you wrote down in Step 1, estimate how long it will take you to complete it.
    - **Level 2:** This can be tricky.
        - **Level 3:** If you allow too little time, you end up feeling rushed.
        - **Level 3:** If you allow too much time, you become less productive.
    - **Level 2:** For now, give it your best guess.
    - **Level 2:** If you are unsure, overestimate rather than underestimate.

Identify Review the steps that you have identified on your time line. Then decide what details you should include to explain each step. Each new level of detail makes the process clearer for the reader.

LO6 Writing the First Draft

In a first draft, you follow your plan to develop your ideas. Here is another process model to review before you get started.

Read Read the essay, noting how the writer uses the opening paragraph to describe the significance of the process, and then uses the middle paragraphs to explain its steps in chronological order.

Making Dirty Water Drinkable

Opening paragraph

One of the most overlooked luxuries of living in the United States is access to clean drinking water. Statistics show roughly one-eighth of the world's population lack access to safe water supplies, while as many as 2.5 billion people live without sanitized water. Untreated water is full of unhealthy chemicals and contaminants that, if consumed, lead to uncomfortable and sometimes fatal disease, including dysentery and diarrhea. Water purification plants remove these harmful impurities to make our water safe to drink.

Middle paragraph 1

The first step in water purification is pretreatment. During pretreatment, water is pumped in from its source and screened to remove any large twigs, leaves, or other debris before reaching the holding tanks. Next, coagulation begins. Coagulation removes dirt and other particles from the water by adding a chemical that forms sticky particles called "floc." The floc combines with dirt particles as the water moves to a sedimentary basin. Once inside the basin, the combined weight of the dirt and floc causes them to sink to the floor as sedimentation. The sedimentation is then removed from the water, giving water its clear, colorless quality.

Middle paragraph 2

While coagulation removes the sedimentation from the water, the filtration phase pushes the remaining particles and unsettled sedimentation through filters of sand or charcoal. Filtration reduces particles in the water by about 90 to 95 percent. Lastly the water is pumped to a disinfection tank. During disinfection, chlorine is added to kill any lingering viruses or bacteria. Some plants also introduce fluoride into the water to prevent tooth decay. After the process is completed, the water is tested for safety and then released from the treatment plant for safe consumption.

Closing paragraph

Make no mistake: the process of water purification in treatment plants is vitally important to the health of its consumers. By removing dirt and sludge through pretreatment and coagulation, then filtering the lingering particles, and finally disinfecting with chlorine and other chemicals, water purification plants make certain that the water our bodies desperately need to survive will do its job.

Creating an Opening Paragraph

The objective of the opening paragraph is to gain the reader's interest, introduce the topic, and state your thesis. Here are two strategies for gaining the reader's interest.

- **Find an eye-popping statistic:**
  Roughly one-eighth of the world's population lack access to safe water supplies, while as many as 2.5 billion people live without sanitized water.
- **Ask a question:**
  Can you imagine a pizza without mozzarella?

Writing a Thesis Statement

To create a thesis statement for your process essay, follow this formula.

A Specific Process	Outcome	Thesis Statement
water purification **+**	safe water **=**	Water purification plants remove these harmful impurities to make our water safe to drink.

Developing the Middle Paragraphs

In the middle paragraphs, clearly explain each step in the process using the details you identified on page 289. Here are some other tips.

- Try to cover two or three steps per paragraph, unless each step requires a lot of detail.
- Be sure to use transitions or clue words to move from step to step.

Creating a Closing Paragraph

The closing paragraph should restate or summarize the process as a whole and provide a final thought about it. Here are two strategies to consider.

- **Restate the thesis in a new, dramatic way:**
  Water purification plants make certain that the water our bodies desperately need to survive will do its job.
- **Revisit the title to bring your essay full circle:**
  The result is a food as diverse as it is delicious. Behold the power of cheese, indeed.

Write Write your first draft, using your planning (pages 288–289) and the information above and on the previous page to guide you.

LO7 Revising the Writing

Revising your first draft involves adding, deleting, rearranging, and reworking parts of your writing. Revision often begins with a peer review.

Peer Review

Sharing your writing at various stages is important, but it is especially important when you review and revise a first draft. The feedback that you receive will help you change and improve your essay.

Peer Review Sheet

Essay title: _____

Writer: _____

Reviewer: _____

1. Which part of the essay seems to work best—opening, middle, or closing? Why?

    _____

    _____

2. Which part of the essay needs work—opening, middle, or closing? Why?

    _____

    _____

3. Do the middle paragraphs clearly present each step of the process? Explain.

    _____

    _____

4. Do you understand the process after reading the essay?

    _____

    _____

5. Identify a phrase or two that show the writer's level of interest.

    _____

    _____

Respond Complete a peer-review sheet like this one after reading the first draft of a classmate's essay. Then share the sheet with the writer. (Keep your comments helpful and positive.)

Using Transitions That Show Time Order

Transitions or linking words connect ideas by showing the relationships between them. In process writing, time-order transition words link the steps and add coherence to the writing.

Transitions

before	next	second	later	while
during	finally	third	when	at
after	first	then	once	meanwhile

Revising in Action

Read aloud the unrevised and then the revised version of the following excerpt. Note how transitional words improve the flow of the writing.

> The first step in water purification is pretreatment. *During pretreatment,* Water is pumped in from its source. . . . *Next, c* Coagulation begins. Coagulation removes dirt and other particles from the water by adding a chemical that forms sticky particles called "floc." . . . *Once inside the basin,* The combined weight of the dirt and floc causes them to . . .

Revise Improve your writing, using the following checklist and a classmate's comments on the response sheet. Continue revising until you can check off each item in the list.

Using a Revising Checklist

Ideas

☐ **1.** Do I explain an interesting process?

☐ **2.** Do I include all the steps in the process?

Organization

☐ **3.** Does the essay have effective opening, middle, and closing paragraphs?

☐ **4.** Are the steps in a logical time order?

☐ **5.** Have I used clue words and transitions to connect my ideas?

Voice

☐ **6.** Do I use an informed, respectful voice?

☐ **7.** Does my interest in the topic come through?

LO8 Editing the Writing

The main work of editing is checking your revised first draft for style and correctness.

Dangling Modifiers

Dangling modifiers can confuse the reader. Such modifiers describe a word that is not in the sentence.

> **Dangling modifier:**
> After handing in his paper, the teacher began the lecture.
> (It sounds as if the teacher handed in the paper.)
>
> **Corrected:**
> After Landon handed in his paper, the teacher began the lecture.

Practice Correct any dangling modifiers below by rewriting the sentence. If a sentence contains no modifying error, write a C on the line. (The first one has been done for you.)

1. After radioing for clearance, the plane was landed.

   After radioing for clearance, the pilot landed the plane.

2. While scrambling eggs, the mail carrier rang the doorbell.

   _____

3. After waiting in the lobby for hours, the doctor was paged for an update.

   _____

4. After we finished the main course, the server wheeled out the dessert tray.

   _____

5. Stretching under the car, my tennis ball was retrieved.

   _____

Apply Read your essay, looking for dangling modifiers. Correct any that you find by rewriting the sentence so that the modifier clearly describes the correct word.

Misplaced Modifiers

Misplaced modifiers are similar to dangling modifiers in that they create a confusing or illogical idea. They occur when a modifier appears to modify the wrong word in a sentence.

Misplaced modifier:

The tornado siren has **nearly** been **blaring** for an hour.
(Nearly been blaring?)

Corrected:

The tornado siren has been blaring for nearly an hour.

Practice   Underline the misplaced modifier in each of the following sentences. Then correct the error by rewriting the sentence. (The first one has been done for you.)

1. That sedan is my favorite car in the showroom <u>with the shiny blue paint</u>.

   <u>That sedan with the shiny blue paint is my favorite car in the showroom.</u>

2. The soda is my first choice with the most caffeine.

   _____

3. The car's headlights nearly turned on after three miles.

   _____

4. Please review the report on global warming enclosed.

   _____

Apply   Read your essay, checking for misplaced modifiers. Correct any that you find by rewriting the sentence so that the modifier is placed next to the appropriate word.

Eky Studio, 2013 / Used under license from Shutterstock.com

Marking an Essay

Before you finish editing your revised essay, practice editing the following model.

Practice Read this process essay, looking for problems listed in the checklist on the next page. Then correct the model using the marks below. One correction has been done for you.

Fighting the Flu

Flu season is a bummer. For some people, its downright dangerous.   *1*
Every year from November through April, some 60 million Americans will
contract the flu bug. Many people opt to receive a yearly flu vaccine, which
reduces there chances of getting the flu. The type of influenza vaccine
given out each year are created through a multifaceted process.   *5*

The first step is surveyllance. Throughout the year, scientists survey
the globe to predict which strains of the influenza virus will dominate the
next flu season. A vaccine can protect against three different strains, so
this step helps decide which strains to put in the vaccine. Next, the World
Health Organization confirms the dominant strains and submits their   *10*
recommendation to the Food and drug Administration (FDA). The FDA
then distributes seeds of the three strains to manufacturers for production.

After surveillance and strain selection, the manufacturing of vaccines
begins. In this step, each virous strain is produced separately. Later
combined to make one vaccine. Manufacturing begins by injecting millions   *15*
of chicken eggs with the virus strains, which develop. The virus fluid is
then given a chemical treatment, so that the virus is disrupted and will
stop spreading. What's left of the strain is combined. With the other two
strains. Lastly, the FDA tests the vaccine concentrate to make sure it is
acceptable for immunization.   *20*

The result is an influenza vaccine that is distributed in viles and
syringes to clinics throughout the world during flu season. After the
vaccine is injected it takes about two weeks for a body to develop immunity
to the three strains. When flu season ends, the process of creating next
year's vaccine begins again.   *25*

Correction Marks

⌐	delete	⋀	add comma	⋀	add word
d̳ / D̷	capitalize	?	add question mark	⊙	add period
	lowercase			⟳	spelling
⋀	insert	⋁	insert an apostrophe	⤴	switch

Using an Editing Checklist

Now it's time to correct your own essay.

Edit Create a clean copy of your revised essay and use the following checklist to look for errors. Continue working until you can check off each item in the list.

Words

☐ 1. Have I used specific nouns and verbs? (See page 146.)

☐ 2. Have I used more action verbs than "be" verbs? (See page 147.)

Sentences

☐ 3. Have I varied the beginnings and lengths of sentences? (See page 149.)

☐ 4. Have I combined short, choppy sentences? (See page 149.)

☐ 5. Have I avoided improper shifts in sentences? (See pages 544–545.)

☐ 6. Have I avoided fragments and run-ons? (See pages 532–535, 538–539.)

Conventions

☐ 7. Do I use correct verb forms (*he saw*, not *he seen*)? (See page 588.)

☐ 8. Do my subjects and verbs agree (*she speaks*, not *she speak*)? (See pages 516–525.)

☐ 9. Have I used consistent verb tense in all steps? (See page 544.)

☐ 10. Have I used the right words (*their, there, they're*)?

☐ 11. Have I avoided any problems with modifiers? (See pages 542–543.)

☐ 12. Have I used commas after long introductory word groups? (See page 638.)

☐ 13. Have I carefully checked my spelling?

Adding a Title

Make sure to add an attention-getting title. Here are two simple strategies for creating one.

- Use alliteration:

  Fighting the Flu

- Describe the process:

  Making Cheese; Making Dirty Water Drinkable

Create Prepare a clean final copy of your essay and proofread it.

> "Education is not a product: mark, diploma, job, money—in that order; it is a process, a never-ending one."
>
> —Bel Kaufman

Enrichment: Reading

On pages 299–301 you will find an essay that explores the process that has lead to the great diversity in breeds of dogs. Be sure to follow the steps in the reading process to help you gain a full understanding of the text. The reading activities are followed by a number of writing ideas to choose from to develop a process essay of your own.

About the Author

Peter Tyson is a producer for *NOVA Online*. He is also a science writer whose work has appeared in *Atlantic Monthly*, *The New York Times*, and other periodicals.

Prereading

Scientists, engineers, sociologists, and journalists—they all are interested in how things occur. Learning about these processes helps them gain a better understanding of the world around them. What processes do you wonder about? List two for each category below. (A sample for each category is provided.) Then share your ideas with your classmates.

- **Natural processes:**

(growing tomatoes)

- **Job-related processes:**

(publishing a book)

CONSIDER THE TRAITS

As you read this selection, focus first on the **ideas**—the main idea, the explanation of the process, and all of the supporting details. Also note the author's **voice**—how he speaks to you in the text. Does he simply present the facts or does he try to sound interesting and engaged in the topic?

What do you think?

Novelist Bel Kaufman says that education is a process. How is that so? And how is it never-ending?

Identify   Before you read, answer these three questions:

1. What do the title, the first paragraph, and the first lines of other paragraphs tell you about the text?

_____

2. What are your first thoughts about the author's purpose and audience?

_____

3. What questions would you like answered in your reading?

_____

Reading and Rereading

As you will see, the text is not solely the explanation of a process. It also provides a wonderful scientific and historical journey into the evolution of a particular species. Many texts that you read will incorporate multiple methods of development.

As you read, make it your goal to (1) identify the main idea, (2) note the process that is explained, and (3) appreciate the engaging story about the topic. Consider annotating the text (page 20) and/or taking notes (page 22) to help you keep track of the information during your reading.

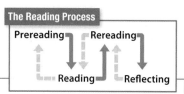

A Potpourri of Pooches

One way to get a feel for just how diverse dogs have become is to jam your   1
fingers down the throat of a Great Dane and then, minutes later, a Chihuahua.
This is what I found myself doing at age 16 during my first full-time summer
job. A large kennel near my home boarded about 100 dogs, and soon after I
started working there I discovered that not only was mine to be the hand that   5
fed and cleaned up after them, but it was also to be the one to administer pills
to those on medication.

Eager to please my first boss, I went at it and soon became a pro at giving
the pills, regardless of the patient's breed, demeanor, or jaw size. Before a dog
knew what was happening, I would slip into its cage, pry its jaws apart, place   10
the pill deep in its throat, retract my saliva-streaked hand, and rub its neck
vigorously to work the pill down. I was bitten only once.

Though my thoughts at the time largely ran to girls and sports, I do
remember thinking how amazing it was that the Dr. Seussian **mélange** of
creatures in my care all belonged to the same species. If I had stopped to   15
wonder why they . . . came in so many flavors, I probably would have told
myself because we've been breeding them for those flavors for thousands of
years.

But I would have been wrong, or at least only somewhat right. The answer,
it turns out, is complicated. In fact, even as scientists know that we humans   20

are the chief instigators of doggie differentiation, they're not really sure how dogs have become so diverse.

The human factor

Why do we know people are the key? Think of your favorite species of wild animal—elephant, eagle, barracuda, whatever. Does its kind come in as wide a range of shapes, sizes, and colors as the dog? Not even remotely. "You never get that kind of variation in wild populations," says animal behaviorist James Serpell of the University of Pennsylvania. "For the most part, selection in the wild is towards one particular type that does best in whatever environment the species has to deal with." 30

Dogs are diverse largely because of artificial rather than natural selection, because of us rather than nature. But just how much of their variety can be laid at our feet versus Mother Nature's remains unclear. **Charles Darwin** suggested that one reason dogs are so variable is that they must have arisen not just from wolves but from other **canids** like jackals and coyotes as well. But recent genetic studies conducted by evolutionary biologist Robert Wayne and colleagues at the University of California at Los Angeles revealed that the **mitochondrial DNA** of dogs and wolves is very similar, while that of jackals and coyotes is distinctly different. Astounding as it seems, all 400 or so recognized breeds today descend directly from the wolf. 40

Even if we can't look to multiple canid ancestors for the dog, there are other ways that natural forces may have contributed to its diversity. Ray Coppinger, a biologist at Hampshire College and author of *Dogs: A Startling New Understanding of Canine Origin, Behavior, and Evolution*, says that "natural" breeds occasionally arise. One way is through simple adaptation to different 45 environmental niches; dogs in northern regions, for example, tend to be bigger because of the cold. Another way is when a catastrophe like rabies wipes out an entire local population of dogs, one isolated in some way from other populations. If just one pregnant female survives the catastrophe, or if a new pair somehow arrives from elsewhere, their descendants will have only that female's or that 50 pair's genes to work with. If that lone female or both the new arrivals have red hair or curly tails, all their descendants may have the same.

The human factor, again

That said, dogs would never have become so diversified without our, well, dogged manipulation of canine mating. It's not known exactly when people 55 and pups first got together, but it was a long time ago. The first archeological evidence of dogs **morphologically** distinct from wolves comes from roughly 12,000 years ago in the Middle East. By that time and perhaps much earlier— Wayne's genetic data hint that dogs split from wolves about 135,000 years ago—dogs appear to have been at least semi-domesticated. By 2000 B.C., 60 dogs resembling the modern pharaoh hound are depicted on Egyptian tombs, implying that both domestication and diversification were well under way.

For the next few thousand years, right up until the late 19th century, people bred dogs for certain skills: running down prey (greyhounds), hunting rodents in holes (terriers), flushing and fetching game (pointers and retrievers). 65 It wasn't until the late 1800s, when kennel clubs first formed, that breeding for

appearance rather than behavior began in earnest. Pure-breeding started then as well: to be registered as a purebred giant schnauzer, both your parents had to be registered as giant schnauzers. Breeders bent on designing the perfect breed are indubitably the reason why today we have dogs as **divergent** as the   70
long-faced borzoi and squashed-faced bulldog, the Mexican hairless and lavishly **hirsute** Pekingese, the 150-pound St. Bernard and two-pound Chihuahua . . . .

But what is it about dogs that makes them so plastic, so genetically malleable? "I don't know of anyone who can answer that question," Serpell told me straightforwardly. When I asked Stephen Budiansky, author of *The Truth*   75
About Dogs, he said, "It may be just one of those things like why do elephants have trunks and others don't? It may just be almost an accident of evolution that dogs are so **plastic** while cats aren't." For his part, Budiansky feels we'll know a lot more once researchers start thoroughly teasing apart the dog genome.

Keeping a watchful eye   80

Dogs are a supremely successful species. There are perhaps 50 million owned dogs in the United States alone, and many millions more running free. (Wolves, by contrast, probably number less than 150,000 worldwide.) But their companionship with man now comes at a cost. Their very **mutability** has resulted in certain breeds having been pushed to the edge of survivability   85
—try breeding bulldogs with even shorter faces, and the resulting puppies may not be able to breathe. Inbreeding has also resulted in increased **susceptibility** of many purebred dogs to diseases and other medical ills.

"Inbreeding can cause a variety of problems, especially if breeders are doing things like breeding down lines—father-daughter kind of stuff," says   90
Stanley Coren, a psychologist at the University of British Columbia and author of several books on dogs. Conscientious breeders select dogs on the basis of their longevity and particular characteristics and don't breed within lines, he says. As long as they do that, there's still a lot of room, Coren feels, to safely breed dogs to our liking   95

Potpourri
a mixed or scrambled collection

mélange
a wide mixture of elements

Charles Darwin
English natural scientist who formulated a theory of evolution based on natural selection

canids
any of the carnivorous mammals of the family Canidae, including foxes, wolves, dogs, jackals, and coyotes

mitochondrial DNA
double-stranded genetic material, maternally inherited

morphologically
involving the branch of biology that deals with form and structure

divergent
tending to be different

hirsute
hairy

plastic
moldable

mutability
changeability

susceptibility
likely to be harmed or influenced by

Reflecting

Practice After your reading, answer the following questions. Then share your responses with your classmates.

1. What main idea is developed?

_____

_____

2. What process is explained?

_____

_____

3. What is one of the most interesting things you learned about the topic?

_____

_____

Vocabulary Practice

Identify Create vocabulary entries for the words below. For each word, identify the pronunciation and helpful word parts, give a primary definition, and use the word in a sentence. (See pages 33–38 and a dictionary for help.)

1. **demeanor** (line 9)

2. **variation** (line 26)

Drawing Inferences

Explain Answer the following question to help you draw an inference from the text. (See pages 30–32 for help.) Also consider making a thoughtful observation of your own.

- Why are people so closely drawn to dogs?

_____

_____

_____

_____

Writing

What follows are possible writing activities to complete in response to the reading. Use the writing process (pages 106–111) to help you develop your work.

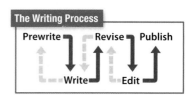

Prewriting

Choose one of the following writing ideas, or decide upon an idea of your own making related to the reading.

1. **Writing to Learn:** Write a personal blog or journal entry in which you explore your own connection with dogs.
2. **Essay Writing:** Develop an essay based on the human connection to another species.
3. Write a process essay about one of the topics you listed on page 288 or 298.
4. Write a process essay based on a photograph in this book.
5. In an essay, compare your relationship with dogs to another people's relationship with them.

When planning . . .

Refer to pages 288–289 to help you with your prewriting and planning. Also consider the tips that follow.

- Make sure that you know the process well before you try to explain it.
- Include different levels of detail as needed to make the process clear. (See page 137.)

Writing and Revising

Refer to pages 290–293 to help you write and revise your first draft. Also use the tips that follow.

When writing . . .

- Include an opening, a middle, and a closing in your essay. (See page 291.)
- Consider how you will identify the steps in the process—with subheadings as in the essay on pages 280–281, with transitions, or so on?

When revising . . .

- Decide if you need to do any additional research on your topic.
- Consider including a graphic representation of the process.

Editing

Refer to pages 294–296 when you are ready to edit your essay for style and correctness. Use the checklist on page 297 as your final editing guide.

Reflecting on Process Writing

Answer the following questions about your process reading and writing experiences in this chapter.

1. Why are process essays so important?

   _____

2. What is your favorite essay in this chapter? Explain.

   _____

3. Which reading strategy in this chapter is most helpful? Explain.

   _____

4. What key elements make a process essay easy to recognize and follow?

   _____

5. What do you like the most about the main essay that you wrote in this chapter?

   _____

6. What is one thing that you would like to change in this essay?

   _____

7. What is the easiest thing about this type of writing? The hardest?

   _____

Key Terms to Remember

When you read and write process essays, it's important to understand the following terms.

- **Process**—a series of actions, steps, or changes bringing about a result
- **Sequencing**—the following of one thing after another
- **Cycle chart**—a graphic organizer that identifies the steps in a recurring process
- **Chronological order**—time order, commonly used in process essays
- **Levels of detail**—details that become progressively more specific to help clarify or complete a main point

11

> "The small part of ignorance that we arrange and classify, we give the name of knowledge."
> —Ambrose Bierce

Classification

Suppose you are planting a flower garden in front of your school's science building. You don't know what type of flowers to plant, and the options are limitless. What should you do? Well, you could try breaking down the wide variety of available flowers into categories, or subgroups—considering the color, shape, style, and growing patterns that would work well in your garden.

Classify means "to arrange or organize according to class or category." Classifications are common in the physical and life sciences. They are also common in many of the social sciences, such as anthropology and sociology. Because of this, you'll find plenty of essays that classify information in your college textbooks. In this chapter, you will read two professional classification selections and then develop one of your own.

Learning Outcomes

LO1 Understand classification.

LO2 Learn reading strategies (understanding the form and diagramming the ideas).

LO3 Read and react to a professional classification.

LO4 Read and react to a second professional classification.

LO5 Plan a classification essay.

LO6 Write the first draft.

LO7 Revise the writing.

LO8 Edit the writing.

What do you think?

Explain what Ambrose Bierce means in the quotation at the top of the page.

E.G.Pors, 2013 / Used under license from Shutterstock.com

> "Science is the systematic classification of experience."
> —George Henry Lewes

LO1 Understanding Classification

A researcher named Benjamin Bloom created a list of thinking skills called Bloom's Taxonomy. The thinking in his list moves from basic levels of thinking such as *remembering* to levels that require deeper thinking such as *analyzing*. Classifying, the subject of this chapter, is a form of analyzing. (See page 27.)

The purpose of classification in the sciences has always been to form new understandings through observations and experiments. For example, in the natural sciences, botanists study plants to add to their understanding of all living things. In the behavior sciences, psychologists study the mind to understand human behavior. Scientists naturally classify what they see and study: "My experiments reveal three specific types of . . ."

Look at a line diagram that shows different types of plants or animals, and you will realize how challenging it can be to form a classification. These diagrams result from years of study and observation, as well they should, because they map out the world as we know it. If they were based on mere guesswork, they would add little to our understanding of things.

Branching Out

However, not all classifications must be held to the thorough standards of scientific analysis. For example, a physical trainer at a fitness center may classify four basic categories of weight lifters. If her or his observations reasonably cover the range of lifters, then they will have value and interest, just not in the true scientific sense of things. In truth, classifying and sorting is a common thinking activity for all people in all aspects of their lives.

INSIGHT

Classifying is a form of analysis that requires observing carefully, making connections, and categorizing.

Ariwasabi, 2013 / Used under license from Shutterstock.com

Identify For each topic below, identify four or five categories or subgroups. This is basic classification. Afterward, share your work with your classmates.

sitcoms   snacks   friends

_____

_____

Reading

LO2 Learning Reading Strategies

Understanding the Form

There are three basic questions for reading and analyzing a classification essay:

1. How does the writer break down the topic into categories?
2. What types of supporting details explain each category?
3. Are the categories equal and logical?

The Process in Action

Here is an analysis of an essay about deserts.

1. How does the writer break down the topic into categories?

   a. Tropical deserts   b. Temperate deserts   c. Cold deserts

2. What types of supporting details explain each category?

   The writer describes the range of temperatures, precipitation, and vegetation unique to each type of desert.

3. Are the categories equal and logical?

   An equal amount of information is provided for each category; the information gives the reader a good understanding of the three main types of deserts.

Diagramming the Ideas

Of all of the essays in your college reading, the classification essay may be the easiest type to follow. First of all, the writer will identify the topic and categories in the beginning part of the essay. Then the writer usually addresses the categories, one after another, with similar types of supporting details.

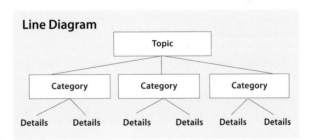

Line Diagram

To help you analyze the categories and supporting details, you can use a line diagram.

Practice Use these strategies for your next reading assignment that classifies information. Afterward, discuss the value of the strategies.

Tip

Creating a line diagram helps you to determine if the categories are logical and equal. It also shows whether enough support is provided for each category.

LO3 Reading and Reacting to a Professional Classification

The following selection, which comes from a textbook entitled *Living in the Environment*, classifies three types of deserts. Use the reading process to help you gain a full understanding of the text.

About the Authors

G. Tyler Miller, Jr., is a textbook writer, specializing in environmental science. He is the current president of Earth Education and Research. **Scott E. Spoolman** is a textbook writer and editor. He is the author of many articles in science, engineering, business, and politics.

Preread   Before you read, answer these questions:

1. What do the title, the first paragraph, and the first sentences in other paragraphs tell you about the text?

_____

2. What are your first impressions of the vocabulary? Do the words seem difficult, easy to follow, or somewhere in between?

_____

3. What do you expect to learn in this reading?

_____

Read and Reread   As you read, make it your goal to (1) identify the main idea, (2) recognize the types or categories that are classified, and (3) note specific details explaining each type. You may want to use a line diagram (see the previous page) to help you keep track of the important information as you read.

The Reading Process

Prereading   Rereading

Reading   Reflecting

There Are Three Major Types of Deserts

In a desert, annual precipitation is low and often scattered unevenly throughout the year. During the day, the baking sun warms the ground and evaporates water from plant leaves and the soil. But at night, most of the heat stored in the ground **radiates** quickly into the atmosphere. Desert soils have little vegetation and moisture to help store the heat and the skies above deserts are usually clear. This explains why in a desert you may roast during the day but shiver at night.   1

                    5

The lack of vegetation, especially in tropical and polar deserts, makes them **vulnerable** to sandstorms driven by winds that can spread sand from one area to another. Desert surfaces are also vulnerable to disruption from vehicles such as SUVs. *10*

A combination of low rainfall and varying average temperatures creates tropical, temperate, and cold deserts.

Tropical deserts such as the Sahara and the Namib in Africa are hot and dry most of the year. They have few plants and a hard, windblown *15* surface **strewn** with rocks and some sand. They are the deserts we often see in the movies.

In *temperate deserts* such as the Sonoran Desert in southeastern California, southwestern Arizona, and northwestern Mexico, daytime temperatures are high in the summer and low in winter and there is *20* more precipitation than in tropical deserts. The sparse vegetation consists mostly of widely dispersed, drought-resistant shrubs and cacti or other **succulents** adapted to the lack of water and temperature variations.

In *cold deserts* such as the Gobi Desert in Mongolia, vegetation is sparse. Winters are cold, summers are warm or hot, and precipitation is *25* low. Desert plants and animals have **adaptations** that help them to stay cool and to get enough water to survive.

Desert ecosystems are fragile. Their soils take from decades to hundreds of years to recover from disturbances such as off-road vehicle traffic. This is because deserts have slow growth, low species **diversity**, *30* slow **nutrient** cycling (due to low bacterial activity in soils), and very little water. Also, off-road vehicle traffic in deserts can destroy the habitats for a variety of animals that live underground in this biome.

From Miller, *Living in the Environment*, 17E. © 2012 Cengage Learning.

Galyna Andrushko, 2013 / Used under license from Shutterstock.com

radiate
to send rays or waves

vulnerable
open to physical or emotional harm

strewn
spread or scattered over an area or surface

succulents
water-retaining plants

adaptations
adjustments made to survive in a certain environment

diversity
differences

nutrient
a source of nourishment; a life-giving substance

Reflect   Answer the questions below about the process essay on pages 308–309. Then discuss your responses with your classmates.

1. What main idea is developed?

_____

_____

2. What three types of deserts are classified?

_____

_____

3. What types of supporting details does the writing include—facts, statistics, quotations, examples, and/or personal reflection? (See pages 65–66.).

_____

_____

Vocabulary Practice

Identify   Use context clues to explain or define the following words. (See pages 34–35 for help.)

1. **annual**   (line 1)

   clues: _____

   definition: _____

2. **fragile**   (line 28)

   clues: _____

   definition: _____

Drawing Inferences

Explain   Answer the following question to draw an inference from this text. (See pages 30–32 for help.)

■ In what ways can you associate the word *extreme* with deserts?

_____

_____

LO4 Reading and Reacting to a Second Professional Classification

The selection below, which comes from a textbook entitled *Criminal Justice in Action*, classifies the written sources of criminal law in the United States. Use the reading process to help you gain a full understanding of the text. (See below.)

About the Authors

Larry K. Gaines is Chair in the Department of Criminal Justice at California State University San Bernardino. He has authored numerous books on criminal justice. **Roger LeRoy Miller** is Director at the Institute of University Studies in Arlington, Texas. He is a legal specialist and has authored numerous books on law and criminal procedure.

Preread   Before you read, answer these questions:

1. What do the title, first paragraph, and headings tell you about the text?

_____

2. What is your first impression of the vocabulary? Does is seem difficult, easy to follow, or somewhere in between?

_____

3. What challenges might the text present as you read?

_____

Read and Reread   As you read, make it your goal to (1) identify the main idea, (2) recognize the categories that are classified, and (3) pay careful attention of the explanation of each category.

Consider annotating the text (page 20) and/or taking notes (page 22) to help you keep track of the important information in the reading.

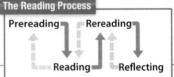

The Reading Process

Prereading → Rereading → Reading → Reflecting

Written Sources of American Criminal Law

Originally, American criminal law was uncodified. That is, it relied   *1*
primarily on judges following previous judicial decisions, and the body
of the law was not written down in any single place. Uncodified law,
however, presents a number of drawbacks. For one, if the law is not
recorded in a manner or place in which the citizenry has access to it,   *5*
then it is difficult, if not impossible, for people to know exactly which acts
are legal and which acts are illegal. Furthermore, citizens have no way
of determining or understanding the procedures that must be followed
to establish innocence or guilt. Consequently, US history has seen the

development of several written sources of American criminal law, also   *10*
known as "**substantive**" criminal law. These sources include the following:
1. The US Constitution and the constitutions of the various states
2. Statues, or laws, passed by Congress and by state legislatures, plus local ordinances
3. Regulations, created by regulatory agencies such as the federal   *15* Food and Drug Administration
4. Case law (court decisions)

We describe each of these important written sources of law in the following pages.

CONSTITUTIONAL LAW   *20*

The federal government and the states have separate written constitutions that set forth the general organization and powers of, and the limits on, their respective governments. Constitutional law is the law as expressed in these constitutions.

The US Constitution is the supreme law of the land. As such, it   *25* is the basis of all law in the United States. Any law that violates the Constitution, as ultimately determined by the United States Supreme Court, will be declared unconstitutional and will not be enforced. The Tenth Amendment, which defines the powers and limitations of the federal government, reserves to the states all powers not granted to the federal   *30* government. Under our system of federalism, each state also has its own constitution. Unless they conflict with the US Constitution or a federal law, state constitutions are supreme within their respective borders.

STATUTORY LAW

Statutes enacted by legislative bodies at any level of government make   *35* up another source of law, which is generally referred to as statutory law. *Federal statues* are laws that are enacted by the US Congress. *State statues* are laws enacted by state legislatures, and statutory law also includes the ordinances passed by cities and counties. A federal statute, of course, applies to all states. A state statue, in contrast, applies only within that   *40* state's borders. City or county ordinances (statues) apply only to those jurisdictions where they are enacted.

Legal Supremacy

It is important to keep in mind that there are essentially fifty-two different criminal codes in this country—one for each state, the District   *45* of Columbia, and the federal government. Originally, the federal criminal code was quite small. The US Constitution mentions only three federal crimes: **treason, piracy,** and **counterfeiting**. Today, according to a recent study, federal law includes about 4,500 offenses that carry criminal penalties. Inevitably, these federal criminal statues are bound to overlap   *50* or even contradict state statutes. In such cases, thanks to the supremacy clause of the Constitution, federal law will almost always prevail. Simply put, the supremacy clause holds that federal law is the "supreme law of the land. . . ."

Ballot Initiatives   *55*

On a state and local level, voters can write or rewrite criminal statutes through a form of direct democracy known as the ballot initiatives. In this process, a group of citizens draft a proposed law and then gather a certain number of signatures to get the proposal on that year's ballot. If a majority of the voters approve the measure, it is enacted into law. Currently, twenty-four states and the District of Columbia accept ballot initiatives, and these special elections have played a crucial role in shaping criminal law in those jurisdictions. *60*

ADMINISTRATIVE LAW

A third source of American criminal law consists of administrative law—the rules, orders, and decisions of regulatory agencies. A regulatory agency is a federal, state, or local government agency established to perform a specific function. The Occupational Safety and Health Administration, for example, oversees the safety and health of American workers. The Environmental Protection Agency (EPA) is concerned with protecting the natural environment, and the Food and Drug Administration regulates food and drugs produced in the United States. *65* *70*

Disregarding certain laws created by regulatory agencies can be a criminal violation. Federal statutes, such as the Clean Water Act, authorize a specific regulatory agency, such as the EPA, to enforce regulations to which criminal sanctions are attached. So, in February 2012, following a criminal investigation led by the EPA, a North Carolina hog farm was found guilty of discharging waste into the Waccamaw River watershed. As punishment, a federal judge sentenced the company to pay $1.5 million in fines and sent its president to prison for six months. *75* *80*

CASE LAW

Another basic source of American law consists of the rules of law announced in court decisions, or **precedents**. These rules of law include interpretations of constitutional provisions, of statutes enacted by legislatures, and of regulations created by administrative agencies. Today, this body of law is referred to variously as the common law, judge-made law, or case law. *85*

Case law relies to a certain extent on how courts interpret a particular statute. If you wanted to learn about the coverage and applicability of a particular statute, for example, you would need to locate the statute and study it. You would also need to see how the courts in your jurisdiction have interpreted the statue—in other words, what precedents have been established in regard to that statute. The use of precedent means that judge-made law varies from jurisdiction to jurisdiction. *90*

From Gaines/Miller, *Cengage Advantage Books: Criminal Justice in Action*, 6E. © 2011 Cengage Learning.

substantive
with practical importance

statutory
controlled by law enacted by legislature

treason
betrayal of country

piracy
robbery on high seas

counterfeiting
making a copy of something in order to defraud or deceive people

initiatives
plans or strategies designed to deal with problems

precedents
the fact of being more important

Reflect   After you complete your reading, answer these questions. Share your responses with your classmates.

1. What main idea is developed?

   _____

   _____

   _____

2. What categories are classified in the reading?

   _____

   _____

3. Are the categories equal and logical? Explain.

   _____

   _____

   _____

4. What details did you find most interesting or important? Name two.

   _____

   _____

   _____

5. What questions, if any, does this text bring to mind?

   _____

   _____

   _____

6. How would you rate this selection and why?

   Weak ★ ★ ★ ★ ★ Strong

   _____

   _____

Vocabulary Practice

Identify Define the following words by using context clues and your understanding of word parts. Also list the clues or word parts that help you define each term. (See pages 34–37 and 668–676 for help.)

1. **uncodified** (line 1)

2. **supreme** (line 25)

3. **violates** (line 26)

4. **interpret** (line 88)

Drawing Inferences

Explain Answer the following questions to help you draw inferences from the text. (See pages 30–32 for help.)

1. After reading this selection, what does it mean to "follow the law"?

2. Why are court decisions dependent on written law?

Writing

LO5 Planning a Classification Essay

In your own classification essay, you will explore the categories, or subgroups, of a topic of your choice. Use the writing process to help you complete your work. (See pages 106–111.)

The Writing Process

Prewrite → Write → Revise → Edit → Publish

Explore Read through the "Essentials of Life" list below. Select four general subject areas you would like to explore.

Essentials of Life

food	intelligence	resources
clothing	personality	energy
shelter	senses	money
education	emotions	government
work	goals	laws
entertainment	health	rights
recreation	environment	science
religion	plants	measurement
family	animals	machines
friends	land	tools
community	literature	agriculture
communication	arts	business

1. Subject area: _____

2. Subject area: _____

3. Subject area: _____

4. Subject area: _____

Select Review the subjects that you have listed above and select one that interests you the most. Then list possible topics that you could classify. (Brainstorm for topic ideas with a partner if your instructor allows it.) Circle the topic that seems most promising.

Subject area: _health_____

Topics: _types of diets, types of exercise, types_

_of vaccines, types of weight lifting_____

_____

picamaniac, 2013 / Used under license from Shutterstock.com

Researching Your Topic

Once you have selected a topic, you may need to learn more about it. Search Internet sites, reference books, textbooks, and other sources as necessary. Look for different ways to classify the topic.

The categories for your topic should be . . .

- **equal,** meaning they are similar in importance or value.
- **exclusive,** meaning they are separate and do not overlap.
- **consistent,** meaning they share the same traits or types of details.

Identify   Using a graphic like the one below, list three to five categories for your topic. In the next column, list key details that are unique to each category. (If you can't think of three or four categories, choose another topic.)

Tip
Whenever you conduct research, be sure to use reliable and up-to-date resources.

Categories or types of _____	Details

Creating Your Thesis Statement

Your thesis should name your topic and provide an overview of the categories in your essay. The following formula will help you create a thesis statement.

The specific topic	an overview of the categories	an effective thesis statement.
The armed forces	includes five branches with distinct roles	The armed forces includes five branches, each one carrying out a distinct role.

+ (between first two)   **=** (before third)

Create   Write your thesis statement, using the formula above as a guide. If you need to, write another version or two until your thesis says what you want it to say.

LO6 Writing the First Draft

After you are finished planning, you are ready to write your first draft. Provided below is another sample classification essay.

Read Read the essay, noting how the writer classified the topic, physical activity, into four distinct subgroups.

To Work Out or Not to Work Out

Opening paragraph

The Greek philosopher Plato once said, "Lack of activity destroys the good condition of every human being." The American comedian Phyllis Diller once joked, "My idea of exercise is a good brisk sit." Clearly, different people pursue different levels of physical activity.   1   5

Subgroup 1

Diller's attitude best aligns with someone living a "sedentary lifestyle." A person with a sedentary lifestyle exercises fewer than three times per week. This type of lifestyle is linked to weight gain and an increased risk of developing diseases such as type 2 diabetes.   10

Subgroup 2

A second level of physical activity is known simply as "lifestyle active." This level describes a person who performs everyday lifestyle activities such as walking to and from the grocery store, doing yard work, or playing pick-up basketball. Engaging in regular lifestyle activities can help control cholesterol levels and reduce body fat.   15

Subgroup 3

Someone who follows a cardiorespiratory exercise program for 20 to 60 minutes, three to five days per week, lives a "moderate physical lifestyle," the third level of physical activity. This type of person might be a regular runner, weight lifter, or power walker. A moderate physical lifestyle helps a person become physically fit while reducing the risk of chronic diseases.   20

Subgroup 4

Finally, the highest level of physical activity is a "vigorous physical lifestyle." People on this level exercise 20 to 60 minutes most days of the week and follow a routine of aerobic exercises, strength training, and stretching exercises. A vigorous physical lifestyle achieves the same benefits of moderate physical activities, while also promoting a greater level of fitness.   25   30

Closing paragraph

Many factors contribute to a person's level of physical activity—work environment, family obligations, and other personal responsibilities. Depending on the time of year, a person may live a moderate physical lifestyle one week and a sedentary lifestyle the next week. What's most important, though, is to live a healthy lifestyle. And a healthy lifestyle requires some level of exercise.   35

Creating an Opening Paragraph

Your opening paragraph should gain the reader's attention, introduce the topic, and state your thesis. (See page 112.) Here are three strategies for beginning your essay.

- **Set the mood:** They serve on land, in the air, and at sea. Their bases reside in at least 135 countries. They are made up of 1.4 million brave men and women, protecting the freedom and ideals of the United States.
- **Start with a question:** What makes a baseball so hard to hit?
- **Use one or two quotations:** The Greek philosopher Plato once said, "Lack of activity destroys the good condition of every human being."

Developing the Middle Paragraphs

Keep these four points about middle paragraphs in mind: (1) Present the categories in the most logical order, (2) explain each category in a separate paragraph, (3) include the same types of details for each category, and (4) consider using transitional words or phrases (the _first_ level, the _second_ level, and so on) to connect the paragraphs.

Creating the Closing Paragraph

Your closing paragraph should do one or more of these things: (1) Restate the thesis, (2) make some summary statements about the categories, and (3) leave the reader with a final important thought.

- **Restate the thesis:** Together, the Army, Navy, Marine Corps, Air Force, and Coast Guard make up the United States armed forces.
- **Make some summary statements about the categories:** Many factors contribute to a person's level of physical activity—work environment, family obligations, and other personal responsibilities.
- **Leave the reader with a final important thought.** What's most important, though, is to live a healthy lifestyle. And a healthy lifestyle requires some level of exercise.

Write On your own paper, write your first draft, using the information above as a guide.

LO7 Revising the Writing

Revising your first draft involves adding, deleting, rearranging, and reworking parts of your writing. Revision can begin with a peer review.

Peer Review

Sharing your writing at various stages is important, especially when you review and revise a first draft. The feedback that you receive will help you change and improve your essay.

Respond Complete a response sheet like this one after reading the first draft of a classmate's essay. Then share the sheet with the writer. (Keep your comments helpful and positive.)

Essay title: _____

Writer: _____

Reviewer: _____

1. Which part of the essay seems to work best—opening, middle, or closing? Why?

   _____

   _____

2. Which part of the essay needs work—opening, middle, or closing? Why?

   _____

   _____

3. Do the middle paragraphs include key details unique to the subgroups? Explain.

   _____

   _____

4. Name two of your favorite details.

   _____

   _____

5. Identify a phrase or two that show the writer's level of interest in the topic.

   _____

   _____

Explaining Special Terms

Depending on the topic, your essay may contain special terms or words that are unfamiliar to your reader. Always explain such terms in the text of your essay. Consider the following strategies:

- **Define the word.**
  A person with a sedentary lifestyle exercises fewer than three times per week.

- **Use an appositive before or after the term.**
  The pitcher threw a slider, a pitch that breaks sideways and downward at a slower speed than a straight fastball. (The appositive is set off with a comma and defines the term *slider* in this example.)

- **Give clues.**
  The African vuvuzelas blared throughout the stadium, a collective buzz from thousands of plastic horns. (Words like *African, blared, buzz, plastic,* and *horns* help the reader understand what *vuvuzelas* are.)

Revising in Action

Read aloud the unrevised and then the revised version of the following excerpt. Note how possibly unfamiliar terms are explained with appositives.

> *, an extremely slow pitch with little to no spin*
> Some baseball pitchers will throw a knuckleball. ∧
> *, a pitcher for the Boston Red Sox,*
> Tim Wakefield is known for throwing mostly knuckleballs. Many batters ∧
> are fooled by this specialty pitch because of its wacky movement.

Revise Improve your writing, using the following checklist and your classmate's comments on the response sheet. Continue working until you can check off each item in the list.

Using a Revising Checklist

Ideas
- [ ] 1. Do I focus on one specific topic?
- [ ] 2. Do I name and explain the categories, or subgroups, of the topic?
- [ ] 3. Do I provide an equal number of details about each category?
- [ ] 4. Have I explained any special terms?

Organization
- [ ] 5. Does my essay have effective opening, middle, and closing paragraphs?
- [ ] 6. Do I use transitions to connect the paragraphs?

Voice
- [ ] 7. Does my voice sound knowledgeable and interested?

LO8 Editing the Writing

The main work of editing is correcting your revised draft.

Commas Used with Extra Information

When words add information that can be removed from a sentence without changing its basic meaning, those words should be set off with commas. Here are three examples:

- Marc Jacobs, a famous American designer, is the creative director for the Louis Vuitton fashion line.
  (The appositive adds information about Marc Jacobs.)
- The road construction barrels, which were orange with white stripes, littered the side of the interstate for miles.
  (The clause adds a description of the barrels.)
- A cannoli, found at many Italian-American delis, is a popular Sicilian pastry.
  (The phrase adds a tip about where you might find cannolis.)

Practice Indicate where commas are needed in the following sentences. If no commas are needed, write "correct" on the blank next to the sentence.

1. Internship coordinators found at most colleges and universities help students apply for and gain valuable internship experience.   _____

2. Shakira a Colombian recording artist has enjoyed crossover success in the Latin and American pop markets.   _____

3. The famous American architect Frank Lloyd Wright was born in a small farming community in Wisconsin.   _____

4. In *Slumdog Millionaire* which won 10 Academy Awards a young man from the slums wins the Indian version of *Who Wants to Be a Millionaire?*   _____

Apply Read the sentences in your classification essay and watch for extra information that ought to be set off with commas. If you find any errors, correct them. (For more information, see page 642.)

Commas After Introductory Phrases

Use a comma after a long introductory phrase.

Introductory Phrase

Despite her craving for ice cream, Candace opted for an apple.

Note: The comma is usually omitted if the phrase comes at the end of the sentence.

Candace opted for an apple despite her craving for ice cream.

Note: You may omit the comma after a short (four or fewer words) introductory phrase, unless it is needed to ensure clarity.

At 6:30 a.m. Rita would brew her favorite coffee.

Practice   Indicate where commas are needed in the following sentences. If no commas are needed, write "correct" on the blank next to the sentence.

1. Even before turning around to check Vince sensed someone was following him. _____

2. At risk of sounding outlandish the smell of chocolate-covered bacon is making my mouth water. _____

3. At midnight Willis decided to call it a night. _____

4. After the concert we stopped at a late-night diner for some grub. _____

5. On the left side of the tool shed I found the circular saw. _____

6. Eventually this rain should subside. _____

7. Before making any harsh judgments you should know I considered all options prior to deciding. _____

8. Based on her preliminary research Hanna felt she was ready to begin drafting an essay. _____

Apply   Read the sentences in your classification essay, paying special attention to long introductory phrases that ought to be set off with commas. If you find any errors, correct them. (For more information, see page 638.)

Marking an Essay

Edit an electronic version of the following model before you edit the revised version of your own essay.

Practice   Read the following classification essay, looking for problems listed in the checklist on the following page. Correct the model using the marks listed below. The first correction has been done for you.

Fast Ballers

What makes a baseball so hard to hit? Well, besides being the size of   *1*
an orange and traveling at faster velocities than vehicles on an interstate,
baseballs do funny things in the air depending on the way their thrown.
There are four main types of pitches thrown by baseball players. Each with
different speeds and trajectories.   *5*

The most frequently thrown pitch is a fastball. As its name suggests,
fastball travel at the highest velocity of any pitch. Generally a fastball's
trajectry is straight through the air and into the catcher's glove.

A second type of pitch, a changeup, is used to trick hitters into
thinking its a fastball. However, the changeup is thrown at a much slower   *10*
speed and tails slightly downward as it reaches the plate.

A third pitch is called a curveball. It is hard to hit because it travels
with topspin that causes it to curve sharply both laterally and downward.
A hitter might think a curveball is coming right at them before it curves
over the plate and into the strike zone. Because of a curveball's trajectory, *15*
its slower than a fastball but faster than a changeup.

A fourth comman pitch is called a slider. The slider is similar to a
curveball in that it break laterally and downward as it reaches the batter.
However, a slider's break is shorter than a curveball's. A slider is also
thrown at a faster speed than a curveball.   *20*

When a pitcher is able to throw all four of these pitches hitting
becomes a guessing game for the batter. if the batter is expecting a fastball
but receives a changeup, he or she might swing to early. No wonder
baseballs is so hard to hit.

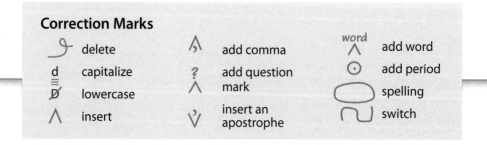

Correction Marks

ℱ delete	⅄ add comma	word∧ add word
d̲ capitalize	?∧ add question mark	⊙ add period
Ø lowercase		spelling
∧ insert	⌄ insert an apostrophe	⊓⊔ switch

Using an Editing Checklist

Now it's time to correct your own essay.

Edit Prepare a clean copy of your revised essay and use the following checklist to look for errors. Continue working until you can check off each item in the list.

Words

☐ **1.** Have I used specific nouns and verbs? (See page 146.)

☐ **2.** Have I used more action verbs than "be" verbs? (See page 147.)

Sentences

☐ **3.** Have I used sentences with varying beginnings and lengths? (See page 149.)

☐ **4.** Have I combined short, choppy sentences? (See page 149.)

☐ **5.** Have I avoided improper shifts in sentences? (See pages 544–545.)

☐ **6.** Have I avoided fragments and run-ons? (See pages 532–535, 538–539.)

Conventions

☐ **7.** Do I use correct verb forms (*he saw*, not *he seen*)? (See page 588.)

☐ **8.** Do my subjects and verbs agree (*she speaks*, not *she speak*)? (See pages 516–525.)

☐ **9.** Have I used the right words (*their, there, they're*)?

☐ **10.** Have I capitalized first words and proper nouns and adjectives? (See page 626.)

☐ **11.** Have I used commas after long introductory word groups and to set off extra information? (See pages 638–639 and 642–643.)

☐ **12.** Have I carefully checked my spelling?

Adding a Title

Make sure to add an attention-getting title. Here are three simple strategies for creating one.

- Describe the classification:

  Five Branches of the United States Armed Forces

- Think creatively:

  To Work Out or Not to Work Out

- Use a play on words:

  Fast Ballers

Create Prepare a clean final copy of your essay and proofread it.

> "To be beyond any existing classification has always pleased me."
> —Annie Jump Cannon

Enrichment: Reading

On pages 327–328 you will find the essay "Dance Moves Can Reveal Your Personality" to read and react to. As you read, be sure to follow the steps in the reading process. The reading activities are followed by a number of ideas for writing your own classification essay.

About the Author

Richard Gray is science reporter for *The Sunday Telegraph*. His stories address many scientific, technological, and environmental topics, including the human impact on climate change.

Prereading

In school, you learn by reading, listening to lectures, and completing assignments and projects. Outside of school, you gain knowledge primarily through firsthand experience and observation. List two or three things you have learned in each way. For example, you may have learned how hybrid cars work through reading and how to parallel park through experience.

CONSIDER THE TRAITS

As you read this essay, focus first on the **ideas**—the topic of the classification, the categories, and the details that explain each category. Then consider the **organization**—the types of information presented in the beginning, middle, and closing parts. Then ask yourself if the presentation of the information produces a satisfying reading experience.

Reading and Lectures

_____

_____

Firsthand Experience and Observation

_____

_____

What do you think?

The quotation above refers to being "beyond any classification." What does this mean to you, and why would that "please" the author?

Identify   Before you read, answer these three questions:

1. What do the title, the first two paragraphs, and the list tell you about the text?

   _____

2. What are your first impressions about the vocabulary? Does it seem difficult, easy to understand, or somewhere in between?

   _____

3. What questions do you hope to be answered?

   _____

Reading and Rereading

This essay appeared as a feature story in *The Sunday Telegraph,* a popular newspaper in Great Britain.

As you read, make it your goal to (1) identify the main idea, (2) locate the types being classified, and (3) study the explanation and analysis of the types. Consider annotating the text (page 20) and/or taking notes (page 22) to help you keep track of the facts and details presented.

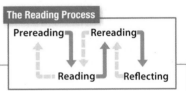

The Reading Process

Prereading → Rereading

Reading → Reflecting

Dance Moves Can Reveal Your Personality

It is where many couples first set eyes on one another—and now research suggests that the dance floor is the perfect place to gauge a **prospective** partner's personality. Scientists have claimed that the way a person **gyrates** in time to music can betray secrets of their character. *1*

Using personality tests, the researchers assessed volunteers into one of *5* five "types." They then observed how each member of each group danced to different kinds of music. They found that:

- **Extroverts** moved their bodies around most on the dance floor, often with energetic and exaggerated movements of their head and arms.
- **Neurotic individuals** danced with sharp, jerky movements of their *10* hands and feet—a style that might be recognized by clubbers and wedding guests as the "shuffle."
- Agreeable personalities tended to have smoother dancing styles, making use of the dance floor by moving side to side while swinging their hands. *15*
- Open-minded people tended to make rhythmic up-and-down movements, and did not move around as much as most of the others.
- People who were conscientious or dutiful moved around the dance floor a lot, and also moved their hands over larger distances than other dancers. *20*

Dr. Geoff Luck of the University of Jyvaskyla in Finland, who led the research, said: "Music is known to evoke strong emotions in people, and emotions can be expressed through bodily movement. People use body motions as reliable indicators of others' personality types, and even the movements of robots have been shown to elicit attributes of 'personality' by   *25* observers."

The researchers studied the dance moves of 60 volunteers who had been selected from 900 people who conducted personality tests. The dancers were picked due to having strong scores in one of the five main personality traits being studied. Each of the volunteers was asked to dance   *30* **spontaneously** to 30 different tracks from six different genres of music— rock, techno, Latin, jazz, funk and pop. Using motion capture technology, the researchers recorded the dance styles of all the volunteers as they were played each musical clip, before analyzing the movements using computer software.   *35*

The researchers found strong correlations between certain dancing styles and each of the personalities. They also discovered that different personalities danced in different ways depending on the music. Rock music tended to bring out stereotypical head-banging moves, particularly among those with an extrovert personality. Those with open-minded personalities   *40* seemed to make more rhythmical limb movements than anyone else during techno music. Agreeable individuals seemed to move around more confidently than the others during Latin music, while the conscientious participants changed from moving around the dance floor to making smaller jerkier movements while listening to techno music. Rock music   *45* appeared to be the only genre that brought neurotics out of their shells; otherwise they tended to make small, nervous movements. . . .

Dr. Peter Lovatt, a psychologist at the University of Hertfordshire and a former professional dancer, said dancing and movement could convey subtle messages about the way people are feeling and thinking, which has   *50* its routes deep in our evolutionary history. He said: "There is a common train of thought that dancing is related to sexual selection and is part of the mate selection process. We have done some work asking 14,000 people to describe their dancing styles and we saw that dancing changes with age as their confidence in dancing changes. Confidence plays an important role   *55* in the way people dance. **Self-esteem** also plays an important role, and this can influence a person's personality."

Richard Gray, "Dance Moves Can Reveal Your Personality," from *The Sunday Telegraph*, November 14, 2010. Copyright © The Daily Telegraph. Reprinted by permission.

prospective	**extroverts**	**spontaneously**
possible, potential	outgoing people	performed without
gyrates	**neurotic individuals**	thinking
moves	people who are easily	**self-esteem**
	stressed	respect for oneself

Reflecting

Practice   After you read, answer the following questions. Then share your responses with your classmates.

1. What is the main idea?

_____

_____

2. What is the basis of the "five types" in this classification?

_____

_____

3. What background information is provided about this classification? Identify two details.

_____

_____

4. Which type best describes you and why?

_____

_____

5. What questions, if any, do you still have about the topic?

_____

_____

6. How would you rate this essay and why?

   Weak ★ ★ ★ ★ ★ Strong

_____

_____

_____

Vocabulary Practice

Identify   Use context clues to define or explain the following words. (See pages 34–35 for help.)

1. **betray** (line 4)

   clues: _____

   definition: _____

2. **evoke** (line 22)

   clues: _____

   definition: _____

3. **genres** (line 31)

   clues: _____

   definition: _____

4. **subtle** (line 50)

   clues: _____

   definition: _____

Drawing Inferences

Explain   Answer the following questions to draw inferences from the text. (See pages 30–32 for help.) Consider adding your own thoughtful observation as well.

1. In what other public arenas can body movements be an indicator of individual personalities? Explain.

   _____

   _____

2. What is the value of such a study? And what are its limitations?

   _____

   _____

3. (Your own observation)

   _____

   _____

Writing

What follows are possible writing activities to complete in response to the reading. Use the writing process (pages 106–111) to help you develop your writing.

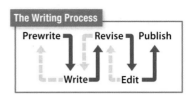

The Writing Process

Prewriting

Choose one of the following writing ideas. Or decide upon an idea of your own making related to the reading.

Writing Ideas

1. **Writing to Learn:** Write a personal blog or journal entry about your experiences with dancing. As you write, make connections between your own experiences and the selection you have just read.

2. **Essay Writing:** Write a classification essay about one of the topics that you identified on page 316.

3. Write a classification essay based on one of the photographs in this book.

4. In an essay, classify the most popular types of music with your age group.

5. In an essay, classify the most popular types of food with your age group.

When planning . . .

Refer to pages 316–317 to help you with your prewriting and planning. Also use the tips that follow.

- Choose a topic that you understand well or can easily learn about.
- Collect similar types of details for each category.
- Decide on a logical order for your categories.

Writing and Revising

Refer to pages 318–321 to help you write and revise your first draft. Also use the tips that follow.

When writing . . .
- Follow your planning notes, but also consider new ideas.
- Include opening, middle, and closing parts.
- Introduce each new category in the same basic way.

When revising . . .
- Check the order of your categories using logical, clear organization.
- Ask a trusted peer to react to your classification.

Editing

Refer to the checklist on page 325 when you are ready to edit your work for style and correctness.

Reflecting on Classification Writing

Answer the following questions about your classification reading and writing experiences in this chapter.

1. Why do writers and researchers attempt to classify information?

_____

2. What is there about classification essays that make them easy to identify and read?

_____

3. What is your favorite essay in this chapter? Explain.

_____

4. What reading strategy in this chapter seems the most helpful? Explain.

_____

5. What is a main benefit of reading a classification essay?

_____

6. What is the easiest thing about classification writing? The hardest?

_____

7. What do you like best about your classification essay?

_____

8. What is one thing you would like to change in it?

_____

Key Terms to Remember

When you read and write classification essays, it's important to understand the following terms.

- **Classification**—the act of arranging or organizing according to classes or categories
- **Categories**—specifically defined divisions; general types or classes of ideas
- **Line diagram**—a graphic organizer that can be used to show main categories and supporting details

12

> "While we are free to choose our actions, we are not free to choose the consequences of those actions."
> —Stephen Covey

Cause-Effect

Why? It's such a simple question, but it leads to much deeper questions about the causes and effects of things. And people certainly have different expectations when they ask it. A mother may ask why her son has cancer because she is worried and protective. The physician may ask the same question because he or she needs a clinical understanding of the condition.

This chapter is all about asking *why* in cause-effect texts. You'll read professional texts that explore the causes and effects of various situations. Then you will write a cause-effect essay yourself. All the while, keep asking *why*.

When you read a cause-effect text, you are getting a behind-the-scenes look at a topic, which naturally improves your understanding of it. When you write this type of essay, you do the behind-the-scenes thinking yourself and share it with your readers.

Learning Outcomes

LO1 Understand cause-effect.

LO2 Learn reading strategies (recognizing causal connections and cause-effect patterns).

LO3 Read and react to a professional cause-effect.

LO4 Read and react to a second professional cause-effect.

LO5 Plan a cause-effect essay.

LO6 Write the first draft.

LO7 Revise the writing.

LO8 Edit the writing.

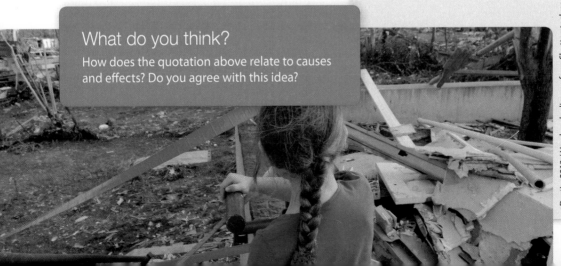

What do you think?

How does the quotation above relate to causes and effects? Do you agree with this idea?

Dustie, 2013 / Used under license from Shutterstock.com

> "Life is a perpetual instruction in cause and effect."
> —Ralph Waldo Emerson

LO1 Understanding Cause-Effect

After examining the results of deforestation (effect), a scientist sets out to determine why it has happened (causes). In a history textbook, the authors highlight the rise to power of a unique sixteenth century leader (causes) and the results of her rule (effects). A journalist notices Spanglish (a blend of Spanish and English) becoming more common (effect) and investigates its development (causes).

Not surprisingly, cause-effect is a common mode of writing and thinking in academic texts. For example, literature anthologies discuss the causes and effects of different developments in literature. Science texts explore the causes and effects of natural phenomena, and psychology texts examine the causes and effects of different types of behavior. This kind of analysis increases your knowledge about the topics you study.

Identifying the causes and effects of a topic may be challenging at times, but careful reading can uncover them. One or both of the terms, *cause* and *effect,* may appear right in the text. And even if they don't, you can discover the causes and effects by looking for the essay's two-part pattern: One part usually develops the set of circumstances that has produced the topic (its origins or causes), and the other part usually explores the results of these circumstances (their impact or effect).

INSIGHT

Like comparing and classifying, identifying causes and effects is a form of analysis. All of these forms require you to carefully examine a topic, and ask *why* again and again.

Cause Versus Effect

By definition, a cause is "the reason for an action or a condition." An effect is "something brought about by a cause or an action." Some cause-effect essays focus more on the causes; others focus more on the effects. Still other essays balance the analysis with equal numbers of causes and effects. It all depends on the information the writer has discovered—and the key points she or he wants to emphasize.

Identify List two or three examples of cause-effect writing from one of your textbooks. Provide a brief explanation of each example, and share your work with your classmates.

1. _____

2. _____

3. _____

Reading
LO2 Learning Reading Strategies

A starting point to understanding a cause-effect essay is identifying the relationship between the causes and effects of a topic or an occurrence. In this part of the chapter, you will discover reading strategies to help you process this relationship.

Recognizing Causal Connections

The thesis in a cause-effect essay usually states or suggests the connection—either good or bad, positive or negative—between the causes and effects. Recognizing this relationship alerts you to the writer's approach or slant as you read the essay. Two cause-effect thesis statements follow; the causal connection for each is identified.

- As the Muslim population grows in the Netherlands, tension between the ethnic Dutch—long known for their progressive attitudes—and their new neighbors has increased.
  Causal Connection: problems between the two groups
- Vegetarians may choose a meat-free diet for different reasons, but their diet has the same basic benefits.
  Causal Connection: different reasons, same benefits

Recognizing Cause-Effect Patterns

As stated earlier, a writer may give more emphasis to the causes or to the effects, depending on the topic. A balanced approach may also be used. These graphics show the three common patterns of arrangement used in cause-effect essays: The first one emphasizes the causes, the second emphasizes the effects, and the third emphasizes causes and effects equally.

Cause-Focused	Effect-Focused	Balanced
Beginning	Beginning	Beginning
Causes	Causes	Causes
Effects	Effects	Effects
Ending	Ending	Ending

INSIGHT

Not all cause-effect essays follow any one of these patterns exactly. Some essays may, in fact, move back and forth between causes and effects according to the writer's decision.

LO3 Reading and Reacting to a Professional Cause-Effect

In this reading selection, the authors explore the causes and effects of deforestation. Use the reading process to help you gain a full understanding of the text.

About the Authors

G. Tyler Miller, Jr., has a PhD from the University of Virginia and has written 59 environmental textbooks. Before becoming a full-time writer, he taught for 20 years and created one of this nation's first environmental programs. Miller is the current president of Earth Education and Research, a group striving to improve environmental education. **Scott E. Spoolman** is a textbook writer and editor and has worked with Miller since 2003. He holds a master's degree in science journalism from the University of Minnesota. Spoolman is the author of many articles in science, engineering, business, and politics.

Preread   Before you read, answer these questions:

1. What do the title, the first paragraph, and the first few lines in other paragraphs tell you about the text?

_____

2. What is your first impression of the vocabulary? Does it seem difficult, easy to follow, or somewhere in between?

_____

3. What do you already know about the topic?

_____

4. What questions do you have about it?

_____

_____

Read and Reread   As you read, make it your goal to (1) identify the main idea, (2) pay careful attention to the causes and effects, and (3) reread any parts as needed. Consider using a cause-effect chart (page 346) to help you keep track of the important details.

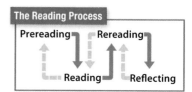

The Reading Process

Prereading   Rereading

Reading   Reflecting

Causes of Tropical Deforestation Are Varied and Complex

Tropical deforestation results from a number of underlying and direct   *1*
causes. Underlying causes, such as pressures from population growth
and poverty, push subsistence farmers and the landless poor into tropical
forests, where they try to grow enough food to survive. Government
subsidies can accelerate the direct causes such as logging and ranching by   *5*
reducing the costs of timber harvesting, cattle grazing, and the creation of
vast plantations.

The major direct causes of deforestation vary in different tropical
areas. Tropical forests in the Amazon and other South American countries
are cleared or burned mostly for cattle grazing and large soybean   *10*
plantations. But clearing these forests for tropical hardwood lumber and
other products, used domestically and sold in the global marketplace, also
plays a role.

In Indonesia, Malaysia, and other areas of Southeast Asia, tropical
forests are being replaced with vast plantations of oil palm, which produces   *15*
an oil used in cooking, cosmetics, and biodiesel fuel for motor vehicles
(especially in Europe). In Africa, the primary direct cause of tropical
deforestation and degradation is individuals struggling to survive by
clearing plots for small-scale farming and by harvesting wood for fuel.
However, women in the Green Belt Movement have helped to reestablish   *20*
forest areas in several African countries.

The degradation of a tropical forest usually begins when a road is cut
deep into the forest interior for logging and settlement. Loggers then use
selective cutting to remove the largest and best trees. When these big trees
fall, many other trees fall with them because of their shallow roots and the   *25*
network of vines connecting the trees in the forest's canopy. This method
causes considerable ecological damage in tropical forests, but much less
than that from burning or clear-cutting forests.

Burning is widely used to clear forest areas for agriculture, settlement,
and other purposes. Healthy rain forests do not burn naturally. But roads,   *30*
settlements, and farming, grazing, and logging operations fragment them.
The resulting patches of forest dry out and readily ignite.

According to a 2005 study by forest scientists, widespread fires in the
Amazon basin are changing weather patterns by raising temperatures
and reducing rainfalls. The resulting droughts dry out the forests and   *35*
make them more likely to burn—another example of a runaway positive
feedback loop. This process is converting large deforested areas of tropical

forests to tropical grassland (savanna)—another example of an ecosystem reaching an irreversible ecological tipping point. Models project that if current burning and deforestation rates continue, 20–30% of the Amazon basin will be turned into savanna in the next 50 years, and most of it could become savanna by 3980. *40*

Foreign corporations operating under government concession contracts do much of the logging in tropical countries. Once a country's forests are gone, the companies move on to another country, leaving ecological devastation behind. For example, the Philippines and Nigeria have lost most of their once-abundant tropical hardwood forests and now are net importers of forest products. Several other tropical countries are following this ecologically and economically unsustainable path. *45*

After the best timber has been removed, timber companies or the local government often sell the land to ranchers who burn the remaining timber to clear the land for cattle grazing. Within a few years, their cattle typically overgraze the land and the ranchers move their operations to another forest area. Then they sell the degraded land to farmers who plow it up for large plantations of crops such as soybeans (largely used for cattle feed), or to settlers who have migrated to tropical forests hoping to grow enough food on a small plot of land to survive. In tropical rain forests, plant nutrients are stored mostly in the quickly decomposed vegetation instead of in the soil. Thus, after a few years of crop growing and erosion from rain, the nutrient-poor soil is depleted of nutrients. Then the farmers and settlers move on to newly cleared land to repeat this environmentally destructive process. *50* *55* *60*

From *Miller, Living in the Environment*, 17E. © 2012 Cengage Learning.

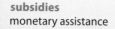

subsidies
monetary assistance

Reflect After you complete your reading, answer these questions. Share your responses with your classmates.

1. What is the main idea?

_____

_____

_____

2. What are the main causes of the topic?

_____

_____

3. What are the significant effects?

_____

_____

_____

4. How would you describe the text's coverage of the topic—regional or global? Explain.

_____

_____

_____

5. How would you rate this paragraph and why?

Weak ★ ★ ★ ★ ★ Strong

_____

_____

Vocabulary Practice

Identify   Define the following words by using context clues and your understanding of word parts. Also list the clues or word parts that help you define each term. (See pages 34–37 and 668–676.)

1. **degradation**   (line 18)

_____

_____

2. **droughts**   (line 35)

_____

_____

3. **unsustainable**   (line 49)

_____

_____

Drawing Inferences

Explain   Answer these questions to help you draw inferences from the text. (See pages 30–32 for help.) Also consider adding a thoughtful observation of your own.

1. What justification, if any, is there for widespread tropical deforestation?

_____

_____

2. Why should anyone care about this situation?

_____

_____

3. (Your own observation)

_____

_____

LO4 Reading and Reacting to a Second Professional Cause-Effect

The selection below, which comes from a history text entitled *World Civilizations*, explores the effects of Elizabeth I's reign as queen of England. Use the reading process to help you gain a full understanding of the text.

About the Authors

Philip J. Adler taught courses in world history for nearly thirty years. He has published widely in the historical journals of this country and German-speaking Europe. **Randall L. Pouwels** has published widely. His book *Horn and Crescent: Cultural Change and Traditional Islam on the East African Coast, 8001900* has become a standard work on African history. He taught for many years at LaTrobe University in Melbourne, Australia, and at UCLA.

Preread Before you read, answer these questions:

1. What do the title, first paragraph, and first sentences in a few other paragraphs tell you about the text?

_____

2. What do you already know about the topic?

_____

3. What questions would you like answered?

_____

Read and Reread As you read, make it your goal to (1) identify the topic, (2) locate the key supporting details, and (3) reread any parts that confuse you. Consider using a cause-effect organizer to help you keep track of the causes and effects. (As you will discover, there is really just one cause, but many effects.)

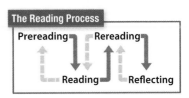

The Reading Process

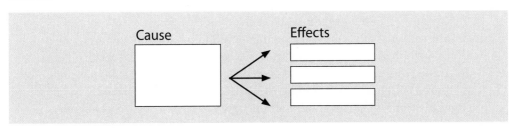

Cause

Effects

Elizabeth I of England

In the late sixteenth century, England became for the first time a   *1*
power to be reckoned with in world affairs. What had been an island
kingdom with little direct influence on any other country except its
immediate neighbors across the Channel gradually reached equality with
the other major Western military and naval powers: France and Spain. But   *5*
England's achievement was not just in military affairs. It also experienced
a magnificent flowering of the arts and a solid advance in the economy,
which finally lifted the nation out of the long depression that had followed
the fourteenth-century plague and the long, losing war with France.

The guiding spirit for this comeback was Elizabeth I, queen of England   *10*
from 1558 until her death in 1603. The daughter of Henry VIII and his
second wife, the ill-fated Anne Boleyn, Elizabeth emerged from a heavily
shadowed girlhood to become one of the most beloved of British lawgivers.
Elizabeth was an intelligent, well-educated woman with gifts in several
domains. One of her most remarkable achievements was that she managed   *15*
to retain her powers without a husband, son, or father in the still very
male-oriented world in which she moved.

Born in 1533, she was only three years old when her mother was
executed. She was declared **illegitimate** by order of the disappointed
Henry, who had wished for a son. But after her father's death, parliament   *20*
established her as third in line to the throne, behind her half-brother,
Edward, and her Catholic half-sister, Mary. During Mary's reign (1553-
1558), Elizabeth was imprisoned for a time, but she was careful to stay
clear of the hectic Protestant-Catholic struggles of the day. By doing so, she
managed to stay alive until she could become ruler in her own right.   *25*

Her rule began amid many internal dangers. The Catholic party in
England opposed her as a suspected Protestant. The **Calvinists** opposed her
as being too much like her father Henry, who never accepted Protestant
theology. The Scots were becoming rabid Calvinists who despised the
English's halfway measures in religious affairs. On top of this, the   *30*
government was deeply in debt.

Elizabeth showed great insight in selecting her officials and
maintained good relations with Parliament. She conducted **diplomatic**
affairs with farsightedness and found she could use her status as an
unmarried queen to definite advantage.   *35*

Philip of Spain, widower of her half-sister, Mary, made several
proposals of marriage and political unity that Elizabeth cleverly held off

without ever quite saying no. She kept England out of the religious wars
that were raging in various parts of Europe for most of her reign, but in
one of these wars, against her ex-suitor Philip, the Virgin Queen led her
people most memorably.   *40*

In 1588, after long negotiations failed, Philip sent the Spanish Armada
to punish England for aiding the rebellious Dutch Calvinists across the
Channel. The queen rallied her sailors in a stirring visit before the battle.
The resulting defeat of the Armada not only signaled England's rise to   *45*
naval equality with Spain but also made Elizabeth the most popular
monarch England had ever seen.

A **golden age** of English literature coincided with Elizabeth's rule,
thanks in some part to her active support of all the arts. Her well-known
vanity induced her to spend large sums to ensure the **splendor** of her court *50*
despite her equally well-known miserliness. The Elizabethan Age produced
Shakespeare, Marlowe, Spenser, and Bacon. By the end of the sixteenth
century, English literature for the first time could hold a place of honor in
any assembly of national arts.

Elizabeth's version of Protestant belief—the Church of England—   *55*
proved acceptable to most of her subjects and finally settled the stormy
waves of sixteenth-century church affairs. By the end of her long reign,
"Good Queen Bess" had become a stock phrase that most people believed
in, from barons to peasants.

From Adler/Pouwels, *World Civilizations*, 6E. © 2012 Cengage Learning.

domains
areas of influence

illegitimate
born to parents who are not married

Calvinists
religious doctrine of John Calvin, maintains salvation comes through faith and that God has already chosen who will believe and be saved

theology
study of religion, especially the Christian faith

diplomatic
showing skill in dealing with people

golden age
an era of great achievement

splendor
great and impressive beauty

Reflect Once you complete your reading, answer the following questions. Then share your responses with your classmates.

1. What main idea is developed in the selection? In what paragraph is it stated?

   _____

   _____

2. What effects of Elizabeth's rule are discussed? Name three.

   _____

   _____

   _____

3. Is the essay organized spatially, chronologically, or logically? Or is there more than one method used? Explain.

   _____

   _____

4. What voice do the authors project—academic or personal? Explain.

   _____

   _____

5. What questions, if any, do you still have about the topic?

   _____

   _____

6. How would you rate this essay and why?

   Weak ★ ★ ★ ★ ★ Strong

   _____

   _____

Vocabulary Practice

Identify Use content clues to define or explain the following words. (See pages 34–35 for help.)

1. **reckoned**   (line 2)

   clues: _____

   definition: _____

2. **ill-fated**   (line 12)

   clues: _____

   definition: _____

3. **reign**   (line 22)

   clues: _____

   definition: _____

4. **monarch**   (line 47)

   clues: _____

   definition: _____

5. **vanity**   (line 50)

   clues: _____

   definition: _____

Drawing Inferences

Explain Answer the questions below to help you draw inferences from the text. (See pages 30–32 for help.)

1. Why have movies been made about Elizabeth I?

   _____

   _____

2. Who should be inspired by her and why?

   _____

   _____

Writing

In this part of the chapter, you will write a cause-effect essay about a certain lifestyle choice. Be sure to use the writing process to help you do your best work. (See pages 106–111.)

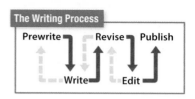

The Writing Process

Prewrite → Revise → Publish
Write → Edit

LO5 Planning a Cause-Effect Essay

Selecting a Topic

You need a topic that interests you—one that you either know a good deal about or are willing to find out about. Your topic must also involve specific causes and effects.

Brainstorm In each column below, brainstorm possible topics for your cause-effect essay. Sample topics have been provided in each category. Try to think of three or four more topics in each category. Then select one topic to write about.

Lifestyle Choices				
Eating	**Activities**	**Style**	**Pastimes**	**Habits**
vegetarianism	rock climbing	dreadlocks	sudoku	smoking

Gathering Details

As you gather details about your topic, think of what you already know and what you need to find out. Do research to find out more about your topic. Then complete a cause-effect chart like the one below.

Cause-Effect Chart

Topic: *Vegetarianism*

Causes	Effects
Concern for animals	Vegans vs. ovo-lacto
Opposition to "factory farming"	Greater awareness
Healthful lifestyle	Greater health
Homegrown food	More sustainable lifestyle
Personal preference	Need for proteins
Peer pressure/social reasons	Struggles in society

Writing a Thesis Statement

After gathering cause-effect details, decide on the main point, or thesis statement, for your essay. Your thesis statement should identify the topic and the causal connection that links the causes and effects.

Topic   **Causal Connection**   **Thesis Statement**

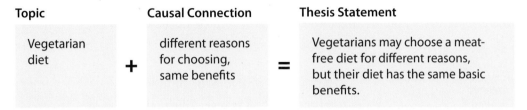

| Vegetarian diet | + | different reasons for choosing, same benefits | = | Vegetarians may choose a meat-free diet for different reasons, but their diet has the same basic benefits. |

Create Develop a thesis statement for your cause-effect essay using the formula above as a guide. If necessary, write two or three versions until your statement says what you want it to say.

Topic   **Causal Connection**   **Thesis Statement**

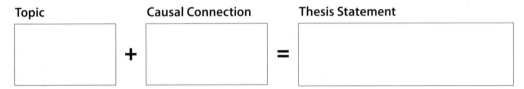

Organizing Your Essay

To organize the details in your cause-effect essay, consider two things:

1. The pattern of arrangement you will use. (See page 335.)

2. The order of the specific causes and effects within the essay. (Will you write about them in the order that you listed them in your chart on page 346, or in some other order?)

Identify Decide on the best pattern of arrangement and order of causes and effects for your essay. Refer to the information above and to the sample essays for help.

1. **Pattern of arrangement:**

_____

_____

2. **Order of causes and effects:**

_____

_____

LO6 Writing the First Draft

After you have completed your planning, you are ready to develop the first draft of your essay. Below is another student essay to consider before you get started.

Read Read the following essay, noting how the writer created effective opening and closing parts and arranged the causes and effects of the topic.

Opening paragraph

Thesis statement

Middle paragraph: Causes

Middle paragraph: Effects

Closing paragraph

Herbivore, Carnivore, or Omnivore?

"We've spent thousands of years getting to the top of the food chain, so why go back to eating leaves?" That's what people sometimes ask vegans and vegetarians, wondering why anyone would choose that kind of diet. Vegetarians may choose a meat-free diet for different reasons, but their diet has the same basic benefits.   1

Every vegetarian is unique, with unique reasons for eating what they eat. Many see animals as more than meat—creatures with intelligence and feelings. These vegetarians don't like the idea of killing animals for food, especially not in the overcrowded   10
and inhumane factory farms of today. Other vegetarians reject modern American eating habits, with too much meat and too few vegetables. The US Department of Agriculture recommends that people "go lean on protein" and eat even less fat. However, the average American eats 16 percent of calories in proteins   15
and 44 percent in fat. Vegetarians seek a better diet and a more sustainable lifestyle. And for some, it's just a matter of personal preference. They just would rather have a salad.

For most vegetarians, their choice has very positive effects. Vegetarians have to think about what they eat and where it comes   20
from, and therefore they tend to eat better quality food and less of it. As a result, vegetarians are often slimmer than omnivores and less prone to arteriosclerosis and colon cancer—caused by fatty red meats. Vegetarians feel they live a more sustainable lifestyle, with less impact on the natural world. Still, vegans and   25
vegetarians have their struggles. Many restaurants have meat in just about every dish, including soups and salads, making it a challenge to eat out. Ads and consumer culture also push vegetarians to eat meat. And vegetarians have to be careful to find proteins that can replace those that others get from eating   30
meat.

The vegetarian lifestyle offers numerous physical and spiritual benefits to a person who chooses it. But the lifestyle isn't for everyone. People with poor impulse control will have a hard time resisting society's penchant for eating meat. Besides that,   35
growing children and adolescents must be careful to get enough of the proteins and fats they need to keep growing. The vegetarian lifestyle doesn't work for everyone, but some people wouldn't have it any other way.

Creating an Opening Paragraph

The opening paragraph should capture the reader's attention, provide any necessary information about the topic, and state your thesis. Here are four strategies for beginning your essay.

- **Start with an interesting quotation:**
  "We've spent thousands of years getting to the top of the food chain, so why go back to eating leaves?"
- **Begin with a startling fact:**
  For more than four millennia, the "meat of the Orient" hasn't been meat at all, but soybeans.
- **Share an anecdote:**
  When I decided to become a vegetarian, my friends looked at me as if I had joined a cult.
- **Begin with a question:**
  How many animals does the average American eat in a year?

Developing the Middle Paragraphs

Write your middle paragraphs based on the planning you did on pages 346–347. Here are some reminders to help you develop this part.

- Be sure to follow the pattern of arrangement you established for your essay.
- Then present your specific causes and effects in the best possible order.
- Add details as necessary to make all of your ideas clear and complete.

Forming a Closing Paragraph

The closing paragraph should summarize the key points made in your essay and provide a final idea about the topic.

- **Summarizing thoughts:**
  The vegetarian lifestyle offers numerous physical and spiritual benefits to a person who chooses it. But the lifestyle . . .
- **Final idea:**
  The vegetarian lifestyle doesn't work for everyone, but some people wouldn't have it any other way.

Write Write your first draft, using your planning (pages 346–347) and the information above as a guide.

LO7   Revising the Writing

Revising your first draft involves adding, deleting, rearranging, and reworking parts of your writing. Revising often begins with a peer review of your work.

Peer Review

Sharing your writing at various stages is important, especially when you review and revise a first draft. The feedback that you receive will help you change and improve your essay.

Peer Review Sheet

Essay title: _Herbivore, Carnivore, or Omnivore?_

Writer: _Randy Lee_

Reviewer: _Sondra King_

1. Which part of the essay seems to work best—opening, middle, or closing? Why?

   The middle: The explanations of the causes and effects are very clear

   and detailed.

2. Which part of the essay needs work—opening, middle, or closing? Why?

   The closing: The reference to spiritual benefits needs to be analyzed

   more fully.

3. Which cause-effect details caught your attention? Name three.

   a. _Rejection of modern American eating habits_

   b. _Americans on average eat 44% of their calories in fat._

   c. _Vegetarians need to be careful about getting enough protein._

4. Write two other details that might be included.

   a. _Information about the long-term effects of a vegetarian diet_

   b. _The vegetarian diet versus a diet including fish or poultry_

5. Identify a phrase or two that show the writer's level of interest.

   Every vegetarian is unique. Vegetarians seek . . . a more sustainable lifestyle.

Respond   Complete a response sheet like the one above after reading the first draft of a classmate's essay. Then share the sheet with the writer. (Keep your comments helpful and positive.)

Using a Variety of Details

Your essay will be stronger if you use a variety of details to support your point. Different types of details provide different types of support.

- **Facts** ground your essay in reality.
    > The US Department of Agriculture recommends that people "go lean on protein" and eat even less fat.
- **Statistics** quantify facts.
    > However, the average American eats 16 percent of calories in proteins and 44 percent in fat.
- **Quotations** from an expert lend support to your point.
    > Chris Woolston of the Consumer Health Interactive says, "Fatty, unbalanced, and oversized: That, in a nutshell, is the American diet."
- **Anecdotes** share an experience from real life.
    > After a week without meat, some vegetarians report that the smell of cooking hamburger makes them sick.

Revising in Action

Read aloud the unrevised and revised version of the following excerpt. Note how adding facts and statistics makes the essay much stronger.

Other vegetarians reject modern American eating habits, with too much meat and too few vegetables. Vegetarians seek a better diet and a more sustainable lifestyle.

> The US Department of Agriculture recommends that people "go lean on protein" and eat even less fat. However, the average American eats 16 percent of calories in proteins and 44 percent in fat.

Revise Improve your writing, using the following checklist and your classmate's comments on the response sheet. Continue revising until you can check off each item in the list.

Using a Revising Checklist

Ideas
- ☐ **1.** Do I focus on an interesting lifestyle choice?
- ☐ **2.** Do I trace the causes and effects of the lifestyle choice?
- ☐ **3.** Do I include a variety of details?

Organization
- ☐ **4.** Does my essay have an effective opening, middle, and closing?
- ☐ **5.** Have I used one paragraph for causes and the other for effects?

Voice
- ☐ **6.** Do I sound knowledgeable about and interested in my topic?

LO8 Editing the Writing

The main work of editing is correcting your revised first draft.

Correcting Comma Splices and Run-On Sentences

To correctly join two sentences, you need to use a comma and a coordinating conjunction (*and, but, or, nor, for, so, yet*). If you omit the conjunction, you have an error called a comma splice. If you omit both the comma and the conjunction, you have a run-on sentence.

Comma Splice:	Video games are fun, they shouldn't take over your life.
Run-On:	Video games are fun they shouldn't take over your life.
Corrected:	Video games are fun, **but** they shouldn't take over your life.

Practice Correct the following comma splices and run-on sentences by using both a comma and a coordinating conjunction.

1. I enjoy many types of video games, my friends and I play together.
2. Sometimes we are in the same room often we play together online.
3. We like first-person shooters mostly online role-playing games are also fun.
4. Some games are designed to be addictive, it's important to keep perspective.
5. Balancing life and games is crucial, you can't just live in the game.
6. Game technology is always changing it's exciting to see what they invent next.
7. Motion-capture games get you moving some people exercise to them.
8. Other games have social aspects we talk to each other over the Internet.
9. Games are like other aspects of life too much of a good thing is too much.
10. Games should be social, they should not replace having friends.

Apply Read your cause-effect essay and watch for comma errors. If you find any, correct them. (For more information, see pages 536–539.)

Correcting Sentence Fragments

A complete sentence has a subject and a verb and expresses a complete thought. If a group of words is missing a subject or a verb (or both) or does not express a complete thought, it is a fragment. Fix fragments by supplying what is missing.

> **Missing a subject:** Love to play video games.
> **Complete sentence:** **My friends and I** love to play video games.
>
> **Missing a verb:** Bill and I especially.
> **Complete sentence:** Bill and I especially **are game fanatics.**
>
> **Missing subject and verb:** Every weekend for hours at a time.
> **Complete sentence:** **We play games** every weekend for hours at a time.
>
> **Incomplete thought:** When we should be studying.
> **Complete sentence:** When we should be studying, **the temptation to play is greatest.**

Practice Fix each fragment below by rewriting it and supplying what is missing. Use your imagination to provide details.

1. Found a new game online

   _____

2. After we've played all afternoon

   _____

3. Until two in the morning

   _____

4. Everyone, including my little brother

   _____

5. Whenever somebody wants to quit

   _____

Apply Read your essay, watching for sentence fragments. Fix them by providing what is missing—a subject, a verb, a subject and a verb, or a complete thought.

auremar, 2013 / Used under license from Shutterstock.com

Marking an Essay

Before you finish editing your revised essay, practice editing the following model.

Practice   Read this cause-effect essay, looking for problems listed in the checklist on the next page. Then correct the model using the marks listed below. One correction has been done for you.

Staying in Step

People have many different ways to stay in shape, from jogging to   *1*
swimming to bike riding. Different people gravitate toward different
types of exercise. Recently, when I was trying to (chose) a type of exercise,
I decided on walking. Many factors made me choose walking over other
forms of exercise walking has changed my life in a number of ways.   *5*

Walking appealed because of its simplicity, safety, cost, and sociability.
While other types of exercise require special equipment or special training
walking is an activity I do every day anyway. I've been walking since I
was 1-year-old. It requires only normal cloths, comfortable shoes, and a
sidewalk. Walking also ain't dangerous like swimming, and walking isn't   *10*
hard on the knees like joging. To walk, I don't have to belong to a special
club or rent any special equipment. And when I walk, I walk with friends,
and we talk.

Walking regularly has helped me a lot. First of all, I've dropped ten
pounds, I also toned up my legs and the most important muscle of all, my   *15*
heart. Beyond these benefits, walking has gave me a chance to talk with
best friends about all kinds of things. It has brung us closer. Walking also
connects me to my community. Many people stop me and say they see me
walking and feel they know me. I also like the way that walking connects
me to Nature and Weather. Rain or shine, I feel it when I'm walking.   *20*

So you can keep your fancy weight machines and thigh busters. I
choose walking because it is simple, safe, cheap, and fun. Walking has
rewarded me with health and happiness walking is a habit that could
benefit many people.

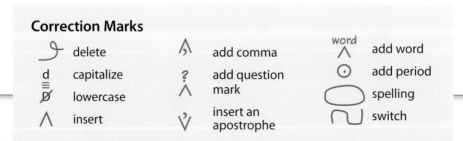

Correction Marks

✄ delete	⋏ add comma	*word* ∧ add word	
d̲ capitalize	? add question	⊙ add period	
∅ lowercase	∧ mark	⬭ spelling	
∧ insert	⌄ insert an apostrophe	⎍ switch	

Using an Editing Checklist

Now it's time to correct your own essay.

Edit Create a clean copy of your revised essay and use the following checklist to search for errors. Continue working until you can check off each item in the list.

Words

☐ 1. Have I used specific nouns and verbs? (See page 146.)

☐ 2. Have I used more action verbs than "be" verbs? (See page 147.)

Sentences

☐ 3. Have I varied the beginnings and lengths of sentences? (See page 149.)

☐ 4. Have I combined short, choppy sentences? (See page 149.)

☐ 5. Have I avoided improper shifts in sentences? (See pages 544–545.)

☐ 6. Have I avoided fragments and run-ons? (See pages 532–535, 538–539.)

Conventions

☐ 7. Do I use correct verb forms (*he saw,* not *he seen*)? (See page 588.)

☐ 8. Do my subjects and verbs agree (*she speaks,* not *she speak*)?
(See pages 516–525.)

☐ 9. Have I used the right words (*their, there, they're*)?

☐ 10. Have I capitalized first words and proper nouns and adjectives?
(See page 626.)

☐ 11. Have I used commas after long introductory word groups? (See page 638.)

☐ 12. Have I punctuated dialogue correctly? (See pages 209–210.)

☐ 13. Have I carefully checked my spelling?

Adding a Title

Make sure to add an attention-getting title. Here are three simple strategies for writing titles.

■ Ask a question:

Why Eat That Stuff?

■ Use the word "or":

Herbivore, Carnivore, or Omnivore

■ Repeat the sounds of letters:

Staying in Step

Create Prepare a clean final copy of your essay and proofread it.

> "You must get good at one of two things: sowing
> in the spring or begging in the fall."
> —Jim Rohn

Enrichment: Reading

In the first part of this section, you will read and react to a cause-effect essay entitled "Spanglish Spoken Here." As you read this essay, use the steps in the reading process as your guide. In the second part, you will find a number of writing ideas to choose from to write a cause-effect essay of your own.

About the Author

Janice Castro is an assistant professor at Northwestern University's journalism school. She served as a reporter, writer, and editor at *Time* magazine for more than 20 years and has freelanced for many other publications.

Prereading

Change is a common theme in cause-effect essays. The essay on pages 337–338 examines the changes caused by deforestation. The essay on pages 342–343 discusses the changes caused by the reign of Elizabeth I. The essay that follows examines a form of English resulting from population changes. List two or three changes you have observed, experienced, or read about. (Fast-melting Arctic ice is an example.)

_____

_____

_____

_____

CONSIDER THE TRAITS ——

As you read the essay, focus first on the **ideas**—the main idea, the causes and effects, and the details that explain them. Also note the author's **voice**—her special way of speaking to the reader. Then ask yourself if these traits combine to produce a satisfying and meaningful reading experience.

What do you think?

How does the quotation at the top of the page relate to causes and effects? What point is Jim Rohn trying to make?

Identify Before you read, answer these three questions:

1. What do the title, the opening paragraph, and the first few lines of other paragraphs tell you about the text?

   _____

2. What might be the author's purpose?

   _____

3. What questions would you like answered in your reading?

   _____

Reading and Rereading

This essay, which first appeared in *Time* magazine, focuses on a hybrid or special form of English spoken in parts of the United States with large Hispanic populations. The text contains many interesting examples of this language.

As you read, make it your goal to (1) identify the main idea and (2) pay careful attention to the causes and effects in the text. Consider using a cause-effect chart (page 346) to help you keep track of the causes and effects in the selection.

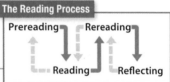

The Reading Process — Prereading, Rereading, Reading, Reflecting

Spanglish Spoken Here

In Manhattan a first grader greets her visiting grandparents, happily exclaiming, "Come here, sientate!" Her bemused grandfather, who does not speak Spanish, nevertheless knows she is asking him to sit down. A Miami personnel officer understands what a job applicant means when he says, "Quiero un part time." Nor do drivers miss a beat reading a billboard alongside a Los Angeles street advertising CERVEZA—SIX-PACK!   *5*

This free-form blend of Spanish and English, known as Spanglish, is common **linguistic** currency wherever concentrations of **Hispanic** Americans are found in the US. In Los Angeles, where 55 percent of the city's 3 million inhabitants speak Spanish, Spanglish is as much a part of daily   *10*
life as sunglasses. Unlike the broken-English efforts of earlier immigrants from Europe, Asia, and other regions, Spanglish has become a widely accepted conversational mode used casually—even playfully—by Spanish-speaking immigrants and native-born Americans alike.

Consisting of one part Hispanicized English, one part Americanized   *15*
Spanish and more than a little fractured **syntax**, Spanglish is a bit like a Robin Williams comedy routine: a crackling line of cross-cultural **patter** straight from the melting pot. Often it enters **Anglo** homes and families through the children, who pick it up at school or at play with their young

1

Hispanic **contemporaries**. In other cases, it comes from watching TV; many 20
an Anglo child watching Sesame Street has learned uno dos tres almost as
quickly as one two three.

Spanglish takes a variety of forms, from the Southern California
Anglos who bid farewell with the utterly silly "hasta la bye-bye" to the
Cuban-American drivers in Miami who parquean their carros. Some 25
Spanglish sentences are mostly Spanish, with a quick detour for an
English word or two. A Latino friend may cut short a conversation by
glancing at his watch and excusing himself with the explanation that he
must "ir al supermarket."

Many of the English words transplanted in this way are simply handier 30
than their Spanish counterparts. No matter how distasteful the subject, for
example, it is still easier to say "income tax" than impuesto sobre la renta.
At the same time, many Spanish-speaking immigrants have adopted such
terms as VCR, microwave, and dishwasher for what they view as largely
American phenomena. Still other English words convey a cultural context 35
that is not **implicit** in the Spanish. A friend who invites you to lonche most
likely has in mind the brisk American custom of "doing lunch" rather than
the languorous afternoon break traditionally implied by almuerzo.

Mainstream Americans exposed to similar **hybrids** of German, Chinese
or Hindi might be mystified. But even Anglos who speak little or no Spanish 40
are somewhat familiar with Spanglish. Living among them, for one thing,
are 19 million Hispanics. In addition, more American high school and
university students sign up for Spanish than for any other foreign language.

Only in the past ten years, though, has Spanglish begun to turn into
a national slang. Its popularity has grown with the explosive increases in 45
US immigration from Latin American countries. English has increasingly
collided with Spanish in retail stores, offices, and classrooms, in pop music
and on street corners. Anglos whose ancestors picked up such Spanish
words as rancho, bronco, tornado, and incommunicado, for instance, now
freely use such Spanish words as gracias, bueno, amigo, and por favor. 50

Among Latinos, Spanglish conversations often flow easily from
Spanish into several sentences of English and back again. "It is done
unconsciously," explains Carmen Silva-Corvalan, a Chilean-born associate
professor of linguistics at the University of Southern California, who
speaks Spanglish with relatives and neighbors. "I couldn't even tell you 55
minutes later if I said something in Spanish or in English."

Spanglish is a sort of code for Latinos: the speakers know Spanish, but
their hybrid language reflects the American culture in which they live.
Many lean to shorter, clipped phrases in place of the longer, more graceful
expressions their parents used. Says Leonel de la Cuesta, an assistant 60
professor of modern languages at Florida International University in
Miami: "In the US, time is money, and that is showing up in Spanglish
as an economy of language." Conversational examples: taipiar (type)
and winshi-wiper (windshield wiper) replace escribir a maquina and
limpiaparabrisas. 65

Major advertisers, eager to tap the estimated $134 billion in spending
power wielded by Spanish-speaking Americans, have ventured into

Spanglish to promote their products. In some cases, attempts to sprinkle
Spanish through commercials have produced embarrassing gaffes. A
Braniff airlines ad that sought to tell Spanish-speaking audiences they
could settle back en (in) luxuriant cuero (leather) seats, for example,
inadvertently said they could fly without clothes (encuero).

    A fractured translation of the Miller Lite slogan told readers the
beer was "Filling, and less delicious." Similar blunders are often made
by Anglos trying to impress Spanish-speaking pals. But if Latinos are
amused by mangled Spanglish, they also recognize these goofs as a sort of
friendly acceptance. As they might put it, no problema.

linguistic
concerning languages

Hispanic
a person of Latin American descent living in the USA

syntax
the ordering of words into phrases and sentences

patter
rapid speech

Anglo
a Caucasian

contemporaries
belonging to the age

implicit
clearly conveyed, though not directly expressed

hybrid
a mixture of two or more backgrounds

Reflecting

Practice After your reading, answer these questions. Then share your responses with your classmates.

1. What is the main idea? *Hint*: Refer to the second paragraph.

2. What causal connection is suggested in the main idea? (See page 335.)

3. What main causes and effects are discussed?

Vocabulary Practice

Identify   Define the following words by using context clues and your understanding of word parts. Also list the clues or word parts that help you define each term. (See pages 34–37 and 668–676 for help.)

1. **bemused**   (line 2)

   _____

   _____

2. **languorous**   (line 38)

   _____

   _____

3. **gaffes**   (line 71)

   _____

   _____

4. **inadvertently**   (line 74)

   _____

   _____

Drawing Inferences

Explain   Answer these two questions to help you draw inferences from the text. (See pages 30–32 for help.) Consider adding your own observation as well.

1. What does Spanglish tell you about the development of languages?

   _____

   _____

2. Why is the development of Spanglish a good thing? A bad thing?

   _____

   _____

3. (Your own observation)

   _____

   _____

Writing

What follows are possible writing activities to complete in response to the reading. Use the writing process (pages 106–111) to help you develop your writing.

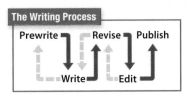

Prewriting

Choose one of the following writing ideas as a starting point for a piece of writing, or decide upon an idea of your own making related to the reading.

Writing Ideas

1. **Writing to Learn:** In a personal blog or journal entry, explore your own experiences with Spanish or another second language.
2. **Essay Writing:** Write a cause-effect essay about one of the changes you identified on page 356.
3. Write a cause-effect essay about another one of the topics that you listed on page 346.
4. Write a cause-effect essay related to one of the photographs in this book.
5. Explore the importance of English in education, business, and entertainment. (This topic will require some research.)

When planning . . .

Refer to pages 346–347 to help you plan your essay. Also use these tips.

- Choose a topic you know well or can easily learn about.
- Consider questions that your readers may have about the topic.
- Carefully study the causes and effects of your topic before you decide on the appropriate pattern of arrangement for your essay.

Writing and Revising

Refer to pages 348–351 to help you write and revise your first draft. Also use the tips that follow.

When writing . . .

- Clearly identify whether you are discussing causes or effects.
- Add a variety of details to explain the causes and effects.

When revising . . .

- Fix any gaps in thought or any unclear parts.
- Decide whether your essay will interest your readers. If not, reconsider your opening strategy, add an interesting fact or two, and so on.

Editing

Refer to pages 352–354 and to the checklist on page 355 when you are ready to edit your essay.

Reflecting on Cause-Effect Writing

Answer the following questions about your reading and writing experiences in this chapter.

1. Why are cause-effect essays a common form of writing in textbooks?

   _____

2. What is your favorite essay in this chapter? Explain.

   _____

3. Which reading strategy seems the most helpful? Explain.

   _____

4. What are the most important things to remember when writing a cause-effect essay? Name at least two.

   _____

5. What basic patterns of arrangement can you use to shape a cause-effect essay?

   _____

6. What do you like best about your cause-effect essay?

   _____

7. What is one thing you would like to change about it?

   _____

Key Terms to Remember

When you read and write cause-effect essays, it's important to understand the following terms.

- **Causes**—the reasons for an action or a condition
- **Effects**—circumstances brought about by a cause or an action
- **T-chart**—a graphic organizer used to list causes and effects
- **Causal connection**—the link between the causes and the effects of a topic, usually identified in the thesis statement

13

"What lies behind you and what lies in front of you pales in comparison to what lies inside you."
—Ralph Waldo Emerson

Comparison

The photograph below is full of contrasts: glass versus painted brick, straight lines versus curves and slashes, an industrial wall versus an explosion of color. The photograph also contains some surprising comparisons. The building and the mural both serve the neighborhood, and they are both the products of craftsmanship.

Essays that examine similarities and differences are called comparison essays. They help the writer and the reader understand subjects more completely, and you will find these essays in most textbooks. For example, a political science text may compare and contrast political parties, and a health text may explore gender differences.

In the first part of this chapter, you will learn about this form and read and react to professional examples. In the second part, you will develop a comparison essay of your own.

Learning Outcomes

LO1 Understand comparison.

LO2 Learn reading strategies (recognizing common patterns and transitions).

LO3 Read and react to a professional comparison.

LO4 Read and react to a second professional comparison.

LO5 Plan a comparison essay.

LO6 Write the first draft.

LO7 Revise the writing.

LO8 Edit the writing.

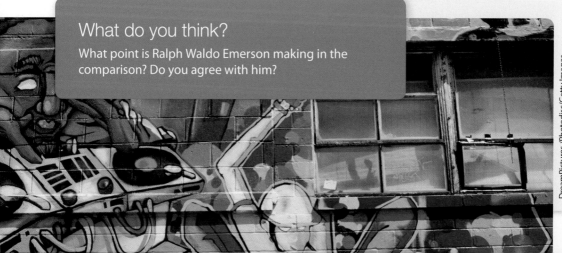

What do you think?

What point is Ralph Waldo Emerson making in the comparison? Do you agree with him?

DreamPictures /Photodisc/Getty Images

"People will always make comparisons."
—Don DeLillo

LO1 Understanding Comparison

People must have a deep-seated need to rank things. Why else would there be so many top-ten lists? For example, professional sports are filled with such lists: the ten best players, the ten most exciting games, and the ten worst defeats. In the entertainment realm, you'll find lists of the top-ten revenue-producing movies, the ten greatest rock concerts, and so on. And meteorologists rank the ten worst hurricanes, the ten hottest temperatures on record, and on and on.

Compiling lists like these requires analysis—the process of breaking down information to understand it better. And making comparisons is the most important form of analysis used to rank things. Without making comparisons, how could a meteorologist identify the ten worst hurricanes, or a historian rate the most important Civil War battles?

The effectiveness of any ranking depends on the points of comparisons that are made. For a ranking of the best baseball players, a researcher would have to use worthy points of comparison, such as batting averages and on-base percentages. When ranking hurricanes, a meteorologist would need to consider wind velocity, resulting damage, and so on. As you study any ranking, always ask yourself if it is the result of meaningful comparisons. And, of course, ask the same question when you read comparison essays.

Comparing Versus Contrasting

To be specific, comparisons deal with the similarities between subjects, and contrasts deal with their differences. Some comparison essays may focus primarily on the similarities between the subjects; others may focus more on their differences. Still others may present a balanced analysis—equal numbers of similarities and differences. It all depends on the information the writer has discovered—and the points of comparison he or she makes. Note: "Comparison essay" and "comparison-contrast essay" are often used interchangeably; they essentially refer to the same thing.

INSIGHT

Related types of analysis include cause-effect and classification. These two forms require you to carefully examine the subjects, just as when making comparisons.

Identify Identify one type of entertainment and one academic field that interests you. Then name a possible top-ten list for each topic as well as two or three possible points of comparison for ranking the top-ten lists. Share your work with your classmates.

Entertainment Type
- Top-ten list
- Points of comparison

Academic Field
- Top-ten list
- Points of comparison

Reading

Comparison essays offer readers a special challenge because the writing focuses on two (or more) primary subjects, not just on one. The strategies below will help you understand this type of essay.

LO2 Learning Reading Strategies

Recognizing Common Patterns

Knowing the different patterns of organization used in comparison essays will help you follow the main ideas in the text.

- **Point-by-point:** Some comparison essays are organized point by point. That is, each subject is addressed according to different points of comparison.
- **Subject-by-subject:** Other comparison essays discuss one subject in the first part and the other subject in the second part.
- **Similarities and differences:** Still other essays address the similarities between the subjects in the first part and the differences in the second part.

INSIGHT
A writer may use a variation on one of the patterns, following it in general, but not exactly from start to finish.

Point-by-Point	Subject-by-Subject	Similarities and Differences
Beginning	Beginning	Beginning
Point 1 — Subject 1 / Subject 2	Subject 1	Similarities
Point 2 — Subject 1 / Subject 2		
Point 3 — Subject 1 / Subject 2	Subject 2	Differences
Ending	Ending	Ending

Recognizing Transitions

As you read comparison essays, watch for transitions or linking words that alert you to specific comparisons and contrasts.

Transitions that show comparisons

also	both	in the same way	much as	likewise
much like	one way	similarly	another way	as

Transitions that show contrasts

although	even though	by contrast	but	however
on the one hand	on the other hand	otherwise	though	

LO3 Reading and Reacting to a Professional Comparison

In this selection, the authors compare and contrast the two hemispheres or halves of the brain. Using the reading process will help you gain a full understanding of the text.

About the Authors

Dennis Coon earned a doctorate in psychology from the University of Arizona. He has taught psychology for many years and authored *Introduction to Psychology* and *Psychology: A Journey,* as well as the text that includes this essay. **John Mitterer** earned a doctorate in cognitive psychology from McMaster University in Canada, and he currently teaches at Brock University, also in Canada. He has contributed to many textbooks and support materials in the field of psychology.

Preread   Before you read, answer these questions:

1. What do the title, first paragraph, and headings tell you about the text?

_____

2. What do you already know about the topic?

_____

3. What do you expect to learn?

_____

Read and Reread   As you read, make it your goal to (1) identify the main idea, (2) pay careful attention to the different functions of the two hemispheres, and (3) reread any parts as needed. Use a graphic organizer such as a T-chart to help you keep track of the different functions of the left brain and right brain.

The Reading Process

Prereading   Rereading

Reading   Reflecting

Hemispheric Specialization

In 1981, Roger Sperry won a Nobel Prize for his remarkable discovery   *1*
that the right and left brain hemispheres perform differently on tests of
language, perception, music, and other capabilities. . . .

Right Brain/Left Brain . . . The brain divides its work in interesting
ways. Roughly 95 percent of us use our left brain for language (speaking,   *5*

writing, and understanding). In addition, the left hemisphere is superior in math, judging time and rhythm, and coordinating the order of complex movements, such as those needed for speech.

In contrast, the right hemisphere can produce only the simplest language and numbers. Working with the right brain is like talking to a *10* child who can say only a dozen words or so. To answer questions, the right hemisphere must use nonverbal responses, such as pointing at objects.

Although it is poor at producing language, the right brain is especially good at perceptual skills, such as recognizing patterns, faces, and melodies, putting together a puzzle, or drawing a picture. It also helps you *15* express emotions and detect the emotions that other people are feeling (Borod et al., 2002; Stuss & Alexander, 2000).

Even though the right hemisphere is nearly "speechless," it is superior at some aspects of understanding language. If the right side of the brain is damaged, people lose their ability to understand jokes, irony, *20* sarcasm, implications, and other nuances of language. Basically, the right hemisphere helps us see the overall context in which something is said (Beeman & Chiarello, 1998).

One Brain, Two Styles In general, the left hemisphere is involved mainly with *analysis* (breaking information into parts). It also processes *25* information sequentially (in order, one item after the next). The right hemisphere appears to process information holistically (all at once) and simultaneously (Springer & Deutsch, 1998).

To summarize further, you could say that the right hemisphere is better at assembling pieces of the world into a coherent picture; it sees *30* overall patterns and general connections. The left brain focuses on small details. The right brain sees the wide-angle view; the left zooms in on specifics. The focus of the left brain is local, the right is global (Hubner & Volberg, 2005).

From Coon/Mitterer. *Psychology*, 12E. © 2012 Wadsworth, a part of Cengage Learning, Inc. Reproduced by permission.

Reflect   After you complete your reading, answer these questions. Share your responses with your classmates.

1. What is the main idea?

_____

_____

_____

2. What pattern of organization do the authors use? (See page 365.) *Hint:* The basic pattern is established under the first heading and repeated under the second heading.

_____

_____

3. What key similarities and differences between the hemispheres are provided?

_____

_____

_____

4. What is the purpose of this essay? (Circle one.) Explain your choice.

   to entertain   to persuade   to inform   to humor

_____

_____

5. What questions do you still have about the topic?

_____

_____

6. How would you rate this essay and why?

   Weak ★ ★ ★ ★ ★ Strong

_____

_____

Vocabulary Practice

Identify   Define the following words by using context clues. (See pages 34–35.)

1. **hemispheres**   (line 2)

   clues: _____

   definition: _____

2. **perceptual**   (line 14)

   clues: _____

   definition: _____

3. **nuances**   (line 21)

   clues: _____

   definition: _____

Drawing Inferences

Explain   Answer the following questions to help you draw inferences from the selection. (See pages 30–32 for help.) Consider adding your own observation as well.

1. What conclusion can you draw about the human brain after reading this text?

   _____

   _____

2. What makes this information important or useful?

   _____

   _____

3. (Your own observation)

   _____

   _____

LO4 Reading and Reacting to a Second Professional Comparison

In this selection the author compares the ways in which American and Chinese cultures create a different sense of space and place. Use the reading process to help you gain a full understanding of the text.

About the Author

Yi-Fu Tuan was born in China and received his university education in England and the United States. He earned a PhD in geography from the University of California, Berkeley, in 1957. Tuan has taught at universities in Canada and the US, the last of which was the University of Wisconsin.

Preread   Before you read, answer these questions:

1. What do the title and the first few lines in the paragraphs tell you about the text?

   _____

2. What do you already know about the topic?

   _____

3. What questions to you hope to have answered?

   _____

Read and Reread   As you read, make it your goal to (1) identify the main idea, (2) note the differences between the two societies in terms of place and space, and (3) study the ending paragraph. Use a graphic organizer such as a T-chart or Venn diagram (page 375) to help you keep track of the contrasts between the topics.

The Reading Process

Prereading   Rereading

Reading   Reflecting

Chinese Place, American Space

Americans have a sense of space, not of place. Go to an American home   1
in **exurbia**, and almost the first thing you do is drift toward the picture
window. How curious that the first compliment you pay your host inside
his house is to say how lovely it is outside the house! He is pleased that
you should admire his vistas. This distant horizon is not merely a line   5
separating earth from the sky; it is a symbol of the future. The American
is not rooted in his place, however lovely: his eyes are drawn by the
expanding space to a point on the horizon, which is his future.

By contrast, consider the traditional Chinese home. Blank walls
enclose it. Step behind the **spirit wall** and you are in a courtyard with   *10*
perhaps a miniature garden around a corner. Once inside his private
compound, you are wrapped in an **ambiance** of calm beauty, an ordered
world of buildings, pavement, rock, and decorative vegetation. But you have
no distant view: nowhere does the space open out before you. Raw nature in
such a home is experienced only as weather, and the only open space is the   *15*
sky above. The Chinese is rooted in his place. When he has to leave, it is
not for the promised land on the terrestrial horizon, but for another world
altogether along the vertical, religious axis of his imagination.

The Chinese tie to place is deeply felt. Wanderlust is an alien sentiment.
The Taoist classic *Tao Te Ching* captures the ideal of rootedness in place with   *20*
these words: "Though there may be another country in the neighborhood so
close that they are within sight of each other and the crowing of cocks and
barking dogs in one place can be heard in the other, yet there is no traffic
between them; and throughout their lives the two people have nothing to
do with each other." In theory if not in practice, farmers have ranked high   *25*
in Chinese society. The reason is not only that they are engaged in a "root"
industry of producing food but that, unlike **pecuniary** merchants, they are
tied to the land and do not abandon their country when it is in danger.

Nostalgia is a recurrent theme in Chinese poetry. An American reader
of translated Chinese poems may well be taken aback—even put off—by   *30*
the frequency, as well as the sentimentality, of the **lament** for home. To
understand the strength of this sentiment, we need to know that Chinese
desire for stability and rootedness in place is prompted by constant threat
of war, exile, and the natural disasters of flood and drought. Forcible
removal makes the Chinese keenly aware of their loss. By contrast,   *35*
Americans move, for the most part, voluntarily. Their nostalgia for
hometown is really longing for a childhood to which they can return: in the
meantime the future beckons and the future is "out there," in open space.

When we criticize American rootlessness, we tend to forget that it is
a result of ideals we admire, namely social mobility and optimism about   *40*
the future. When we admire Chinese rootedness, we forget that the word
"place" means both a location in space and position in society: to be tied
to place is also to be bound to one's station in life, with little hope of
betterment. Space symbolizes hope; place, achievement and stability.

Yi-Fu Tuan, "Chinese Place, American Space." Reprinted by permission of the author.

exurbia
a region beyond the
suburbs

spirit wall
a wall around a courtyard,
to keep out evil spirits

ambiance
a feeling or mood
associated with a place

pecuniary
involved with money

lament
to long for, mourn

Reflect   After you complete your reading, answer the questions that follow. Then share your responses with your classmates.

1. What comparisons and/or contrasts are made between the two topics? Name at least three of them.

   _____

   _____

   _____

2. What pattern of organization does the author use throughout most of the text? (See page 365.)

   _____

   _____

3. What is the main idea?

   _____

   _____

   _____

4. What types of details does the author include—facts, statistics, examples, explanations, quotations, analysis, and/or anecdotes?

   _____

   _____

5. What questions do you still have about the topic?

   _____

   _____

   _____

6. How would you rate this essay and why?

   Weak ★ ★ ★ ★ ★ Strong

   _____

   _____

Vocabulary Practice

Identify Define the following words by using context clues and your understanding of word parts. Also list the clues or word parts that help you define the terms. (See pages 34–37 and 668–676 for help.)

1. **wanderlust**   (line 19)

   _____

   _____

2. **nostalgia**   (line 30 & 37)

   _____

   _____

3. **rootedness**   (line 34 & 42)

   _____

   _____

4. **rootlessness**   (line 40)

   _____

   _____

Summarize the Text

Explain Summarize the text to show your understanding of information. Remember that a summary is usually no more than a third as long as the original. (See page 25 for help.)

_____

_____

_____

_____

_____

Writing

In your own essay, you will compare and contrast two places that you know well. Use the writing process to help you do your best work. (See pages 106–111.)

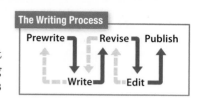

The Writing Process

Prewrite   Revise   Publish
Write   Edit

LO5   Planning a Comparison Essay

These two pages will help you gather your thoughts about your topic before you actually begin writing.

Selecting a Topic

Because you will be using subject-by-subject organization in your essay, choose two places with interesting contrasts.

Select For each general heading, identify two specific places you know enough about to compare and contrast. Then select the two places you would most like to write about in your essay.

Businesses	1. _____	2. _____
Neighborhoods	1. _____	2. _____
Restaurants	1. _____	2. _____
Rooms	1. _____	2. _____

INSIGHT _____

As you review your list, choose the places that offer the most interesting, thought-provoking comparisons.

Describing the Places

Select Identify details about the two places by answering the following questions.

1. What three adjectives best describe each place?
   Place 1:
   Place 2:

2. What is the main feature of each place?
   Place 1:
   Place 2:

3. What is the feeling you get in each place?
   Place 1:
   Place 2:

4. Why do you want to write about these places?
   Place 1:
   Place 2:

Perig, 2013 / Used under license from Shutterstock.com
Kasza, 2013 / Used under license from Shutterstock.com

Gathering Details

You can use a T-chart to gather details for your own essay. Another useful organizer for this purpose is the Venn diagram. A Venn diagram shows the similarities and differences between the subjects. See the example that follows.

Venn Diagram

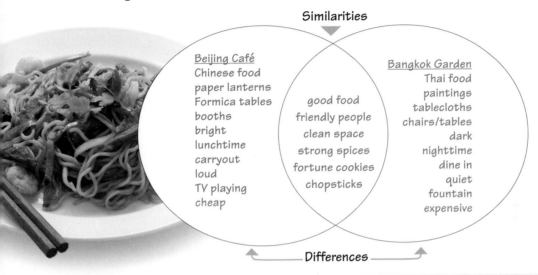

Similarities

Beijing Café
Chinese food
paper lanterns
Formica tables
booths
bright
lunchtime
carryout
loud
TV playing
cheap

good food
friendly people
clean space
strong spices
fortune cookies
chopsticks

Bangkok Garden
Thai food
paintings
tablecloths
chairs/tables
dark
nighttime
dine in
quiet
fountain
expensive

Differences

Gather Complete a T-chart or a Venn diagram with details that show the similarities and differences between your two subjects. At the top of your graphic organizer, name each subject. Then list your details in the appropriate spaces.

Tip

If you have trouble identifying enough interesting details, try writing freely and rapidly about each place to see what you can discover. If that doesn't help, consider choosing different subjects.

Writing a Thesis Statement

After collecting details for your essay, you are ready to write a thesis statement. This statement should name your topic and identify an important point of comparison between them.

Topic		Key Point of Comparison		Thesis Statement
Beijing Café, Bangkok Garden	**+**	The difference in cuisine is only the start.	**=**	The difference between the Beijing Café and the Bangkok Garden only starts with the cuisine.

Create Develop a thesis statement for your comparison essay using the formula above as a guide. If necessary, write two or three versions until your statement says what you want it to say.

LO6 Writing the First Draft

Creating a first draft puts all of your planning into concrete form. Provided below is another student essay that is organized subject by subject.

Read Read the essay, noting how the writer created an effective opening and closing for the subject-by-subject comparison.

Two Tastes of Asia

Opening paragraph

What's the difference between Chinese and Thai food? That's what I wondered when a Thai restaurant opened just down the street from my favorite Chinese restaurant. Soon, I had two favorites. The difference between the Beijing Café and the Bangkok Garden only starts with the cuisine.

Middle paragraph: Subject 1

The Beijing Café has been my favorite because of its inexpensive food and bright, busy atmosphere. The Chinese food is excellent, from the sizzling Chairman Mao's chicken to the extra spicy Szechuan vegetables, and lunch portions are priced below $5. Such prices mean the restaurant has basic decorations like paper lanterns and a utilitarian interior, with Formica tables and plastic booths. The fluorescent lights overhead make the place bright, and the constant traffic of people on lunch break makes the place a loud, busy hangout.

Middle paragraph: Subject 2

The Bangkok Garden offers a completely different experience. The Thai food is similar to Chinese food, but with coconut milk and different spices. The prices, though, are higher, partly because Bangkok Garden is more of a dinner place. The walls are covered in elegant paintings and tapestries, and candles give a warm glow to cloth-covered tables. As a result, the Bangkok Garden is a quieter spot, more for dates than for high-schoolers on a lunch break.

Closing paragraph

Both restaurants have great food and friendly staff, and both offer chopsticks and fortune cookies. When I'm hungry at lunchtime and need a quick, inexpensive, and delicious meal, I go with friends over to the Beijing Café. And when I'm hungry at dinner time and want a romantic dinner, I head to the Bangkok Garden. At first, it seemed a waste to have a Chinese restaurant and a Thai restaurant so close together, but they are more different than they are alike.

Creating an Opening Paragraph

The opening paragraph needs to capture the reader's attention and introduce your thesis statement. Here are some strategies for beginning your essay.

- **Start with a surprising statement.**
  My two favorite restaurants feature food from the other side of the world.
- **Begin with a question.**
  What's the difference between Chinese and Thai food?
- **Use a quotation.**
  "You will soon have two favorites," the fortune cookie read.
- **Share an anecdote.**
  The first time I walked into Bangkok Garden, I was nervous. . . .

Developing the Middle Paragraphs

Refer to your T-chart or Venn diagram on page 375 to help you develop the middle paragraphs. Use one paragraph to address one of the subjects and the other paragraph to address the second subject. Write a topic sentence for each paragraph. Here are some other reminders to help you develop this part.

- Use transitions as needed to connect ideas, but be careful not to overuse them.
- Address each subject with plenty of specific details.
- Arrange the details in each middle paragraph in a sensible way—logically, by location, or by importance.

Forming a Closing Paragraph

The closing part of your essay should provide summarizing thoughts about the subjects. Then consider offering a final idea about the subjects.

- **Summarizing thoughts:** Both restaurants have great food and friendly staff, and both offer chopsticks and fortune cookies.
- **Final idea:** At first, it seemed a waste to have a Chinese restaurant and a Thai restaurant so close together, but they are more different than they are alike.

Write Write your first draft, using your planning (pages 374–375) and the information above and on the previous page as a guide.

LO7 Revising the Writing

Revising your first draft involves adding, deleting, rearranging, and reworking parts of your writing. Revision often begins with a peer review.

Peer Review

Sharing your writing at various stages is important, but it is especially important when you review and revise a first draft. The feedback that you receive will help you improve your essay.

Essay title: _____

Writer: _____

Reviewer: _____

1. Which part of the essay seems to work best—opening, middle, or closing? Why?

    _____

    _____

2. Which part of the essay needs work—opening, middle, or closing? Why?

    _____

    _____

3. Which contrasting points about the two subjects caught your attention? Name three.

    a. _____

    b. _____

    c. _____

4. Name two favorite details.

    a. _____

    b. _____

5. Identify a phrase or two that show the writer's level of interest.

    _____

Respond   Complete a response sheet like the one above after reading the first draft of a classmate's essay. Then share the sheet with the writer. (Keep your comments helpful and positive.)

Adding Sensory Details

Your essay will be stronger if you *show* the similarities and differences, not just *tell* about them. Consider the sensory details listed below and used in the essay on page 376. Build your own chart of sensory details to enhance your writing.

Senses	Sensory Details
Sight -----------	paper lanterns, bright, fluorescent
Hearing ---------	sizzle, loud, traffic
Smell -----------	chicken, Szechuan vegetables
Taste -----------	extra spicy
Touch -----------	plastic booths

Revising in Action

Read aloud the unrevised and revised version of the following excerpt. Note how adding sensory details makes the description much richer.

> The Chinese food is excellent, from the ⋀*sizzling* Chairman Mao's chicken to the ⋀*extra spicy* Szechuan vegetables, and lunch portions are priced below $5. Such prices mean the restaurant has basic decorations ⋀*like paper lanterns* and a utilitarian interior, with ⋀*Formica* tables and ⋀*plastic* booths. . . .

Revise   Improve your writing, using the following checklist and your partner's comments on the response sheet. Continue revising until you can check off each item in the list.

Using a Revising Checklist

Ideas

☐ 1. Do I compare two places?

☐ 2. Do I include sensory details that make the places come to life?

Organization

☐ 3. Does my opening capture the reader's interest and present a thesis statement?

☐ 4. Have I used a subject-by-subject pattern in the middle part?

☐ 5. Have I used transitions to connect my sentences?

☐ 6. Does my closing sum up the comparison and contrast effectively?

Voice

☐ 7. Do I sound knowledgeable about and interested in my subjects?

☐ 8. Is my interest obvious to the reader?

LO8 Editing the Writing

The main work of editing is correcting your revised first draft.

Correcting Subject-Verb Agreement

A verb must agree in number with the subject of the sentence. If the subject is singular, the verb must be singular. If the subject is plural, the verb must be plural. When a sentence has two or more subjects joined by *and,* the verb should be plural. When a sentence has two or more subjects joined by *or* or *nor,* the verb should agree with the last subject.

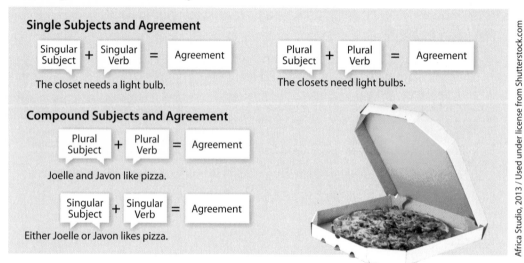

Single Subjects and Agreement

Singular Subject + Singular Verb = Agreement

The closet needs a light bulb.

Plural Subject + Plural Verb = Agreement

The closets need light bulbs.

Compound Subjects and Agreement

Plural Subject + Plural Verb = Agreement

Joelle and Javon like pizza.

Singular Subject + Singular Verb = Agreement

Either Joelle or Javon likes pizza.

Africa Studio, 2013 / Used under license from Shutterstock.com

Practice   Correct the subject-verb agreement errors by deleting the wrong forms and writing the correct verbs above.

1. My old car have a stick shift and are really loud above 55 mph.
2. My new car are an automatic.
3. Both the new car and the old car is ice blue.
4. The new one are a Prius, but the old one are a Taurus.
5. The Prius have four speakers, but the Taurus have just two.
6. Either the Prius or the Taurus were built in the United States.
7. The Prius and the Taurus has front-wheel drive.
8. My brother wants the Prius, but either he or my sister get the Taurus.
9. A car become your best friend when you commute.
10. Both my brother and my sister needs a car for their jobs.

Apply   Read your comparison essay and watch for agreement errors. If you find any, correct them. (For more information, see pages 516–519.)

Agreement with *I* and *You*

The pronouns *I* and *you* sometimes take plural-form verbs, even though they are singular. Review the examples below.

Agreement Formulas

> Plural verbs agree with *I* and *you*.

Correct: I look and see you. You smile at me.

> Most singular verbs do not agree with *I* and *you*.

Incorrect: I looks and sees you. You smiles at me.

Note: The pronoun *I* takes the singular verbs *am* and *was*. Do not use *I* with *be*.

> The singular verbs *am* and *was* agree with *I*.

Correct: I am happy. I was wanting to help. I am eager. I am ready.

> The verbs *be, are, is,* and *were* do not agree with *I*.

Incorrect: I are happy. I were wanting to help. I is eager. I be ready.

Practice Correct the subject-verb agreement errors by deleting the wrong forms and writing the correct verbs above.

1. I keeps a balcony garden at my apartment.
2. You is tasting some of the fruits I grows in my garden.
3. I be especially good at growing tomatoes.
4. You looks surprised that I grows tomatoes on a balcony.
5. I has pots for scallions, carrots, and radishes, too.
6. I thinks you is the first person, besides me, to eat from my garden.
7. You has never tasted such tomatoes, has you?
8. I be proud of this garden, as you knows from my expression.
9. You seems amazed that I raises such good produce on a balcony!
10. I works hard, but I enjoys it.

Apply Read your comparison essay and watch for agreement errors with *I* and *you*. If you find any, correct them. (For more information, see pages 520–521.)

Marking an Essay

Before you finish editing your revised essay, practice editing the following model.

Practice Read this comparison essay, looking for problems listed in the checklist on the next page. Then correct the model using the marks listed below. One correction has been done for you.

A Commuter's Best Friend

spend
I ~~spends~~ much of my day in my car, an ice-blue Toyota Prius. Its a   *1*
hybrid, which means it's much better for my commute to school than my
old Taurus. Still, I loved that old beater. It carried me safely and faithfully.
Through many winters. Aside from being the same color, my new Prius and
my old Taurus couldn't be more different.   *5*

The Taurus was a fifteen-year-old workhorse it had four doors, room
for six, and a trunk to hold all their stuff. The interior is no-frills, with
manual windows, a stereo and tape deck, and two speakers. Nothing was
digital. In its last years, the Taurus been leaking every fluid I put in it, but
still it soldiered on—getting probably twenty miles to the gallon.   *10*

The Prius is brand new and a little delicate. It weighs about half as
much as the Taurus, and though it has four doors, it really has room only
for four people. It has power everything and a GPS navagation system. As
I back up the Prius the digital console even shows me a picture of what's
behind me. this hybrid is super quiet in the city and gets about twice the   *15*
mileage of the Taurus.

I think cars have souls, and my taurus was a good friend to me. It read
me a lot of books on tape, and it never left me stranded when I needed it.
I'm still getting used to this Prius, and I hope we'll be friends, too. Heaven
knows, we spend plenty of time together.   *20*

Correction Marks

⟋	delete	⌄	add comma	*word* ⋀	add word
d ≡	capitalize	? ⋀	add question mark	⊙	add period
⌀	lowercase	⌄	insert an apostrophe	⌒	spelling
⋀	insert			⌐⌐	switch

Using an Editing Checklist

Now it's time to correct your own essay.

Edit Prepare a clean copy of your revised essay and use the following checklist to look for errors. Continue working until you can check off each item in the list.

Words

- ☐ **1.** Have I used specific nouns and verbs? (See page 146.)
- ☐ **2.** Have I used more action verbs than "be" verbs? (See page 147.)

Sentences

- ☐ **3.** Have I used sentences with varying beginnings and lengths? (See page 149.)
- ☐ **4.** Have I combined short, choppy sentences? (See page 149.)
- ☐ **5.** Have I avoided improper shifts in sentences? (See pages 544–545.)
- ☐ **6.** Have I avoided fragments and run-ons? (See pages 532–535, 538–539.)

Conventions

- ☐ **7.** Do I use correct verb forms (*he saw*, not *he seen*)? (See page 588.)
- ☐ **8.** Do my subjects and verbs agree (*she speaks*, not *she speak*)? (See pages 516–525.)
- ☐ **9.** Have I used the right words (*their, there, they're*)?
- ☐ **10.** Have I capitalized first words and proper nouns and adjectives? (See page 626.)
- ☐ **11.** Have I used commas after long introductory word groups and to set off extra information? (See pages 638 and 642.)
- ☐ **12.** Have I carefully checked my spelling?

Adding a Title

Make sure to add an attention-getting title. Here are three simple strategies for creating one.

- ■ Use a phrase from the essay:

  Cars Have Souls

- ■ Point to a similarity or difference:

  Great Food, Worlds Apart

- ■ Use the word "versus":

  Pink Versus Black

Create Prepare a clean final copy of your essay and proofread it.

> "You can't compare me to my father. Our similarities are different."
> —Dale Berra

Enrichment: Reading

On pages 385–387 you will find the selection entitled "Liberalism and Conservatism" to read and react to. As you read this selection, be sure to follow the steps in the reading process. The reading activities are followed by a number of writing ideas to choose from to write a comparison piece of your own.

About the Authors

Steffen W. Schmidt is professor of political science at Iowa State University. He has published 12 books and more than 122 journal articles. He also has a political talk show on WOI Public Radio. **Mack C. Shelley II** is professor of political science at Iowa State University. He has served as coeditor of *Policy Studies Journal* and has numerous publications on public policy. **Barbara A. Bardes** is professor *emerita* (retired but retaining her professional title) of political science. She has written extensively on public opinion, foreign policy, and on women and politics. **Lynne E. Ford** is professor of political science and associate provost (administrator) for curriculum and academic administration at the College of Charleston. She has authored many articles and books on women and politics.

Prereading

There is a good chance that you know people whose background, beliefs, and interests are quite different from your own. A classmate may have come from a different country, or a fellow employee may follow different traditions and beliefs. Then again, there may be political or social differences between you and someone in your family.

List two or three individuals that you know quite well and differ with in significant ways (taste in clothing, political beliefs, approach to relationships, etc.).

_____

_____

_____

What do you think?

Explain what you think Dale Berra means in the quotation above. Can it be possible that a father and son can have "similarities that are different"? Explain.

Identify   Before you read, answer these three questions:

1. What do the title and first few lines in each paragraph tell you about the text?

_____

2. What do you already know about the topics?

_____

3. What questions do you have about them?

_____

Reading and Rereading

This text comes from the textbook *American Government and Politics Today*. As you will see, the authors provide a modern and historical discussion of the two topics, liberalism and conservatism. Some of the historical facts may surprise you.

As you read, make it your goal to (1) identify the main idea, (2) pay careful attention to the differences between the two topics, and (3) reread any parts as needed for clarification. Consider using a T-chart to keep track of the differences between the two topics, liberalism and conservatism.

The Reading Process

Prereading → Rereading

Reading → Reflecting

Liberalism and Conservatism

The set of beliefs called **conservatism** includes a limited role for the   *1*
government in helping individuals. These values usually include a strong
sense of patriotism. Conservatives believe that the private sector probably
can outperform the government in almost any activity. Believing that
the individual is primarily responsible for his or her own well-being,   *5*
conservatives typically oppose government programs to redistribute
income or change the status of individuals. Conservatism may also include
support for what conservatives refer to as traditional values regarding
individual behavior and the importance of the family.

The set of beliefs called **liberalism** includes **advocacy** of government   *10*
action to improve the welfare of individuals, support civil rights, and
tolerance for social change. American liberals believe that government
should take positive action to reduce poverty, to **redistribute** income from
wealthier classes to poorer ones, and to regulate the economy. Those who
espouse liberalism may also be more supportive of the rights of women and   *15*
gays and diverse lifestyles. Liberals are often seen as an influential force
within the Democratic Party, and conservatives are often regarded as the
most influential force in the Republican Party.

While political candidates and commentators are quick to label candidates and voters as "liberals" and "conservatives," the meanings of these words have evolved over time. Moreover, each term may represent a quite different set of ideas to the person or group that uses it.

Liberalism. The word liberal has an odd history. It comes from the same root as liberty, and originally it simply meant "free." In that broad sense, the United States as a whole is a liberal country, and all popular American ideologies are variants of liberalism. In a more restricted definition, a liberal was a person who believed in limited government and who opposed religion in politics. A hundred years ago, liberalism referred to a philosophy that in some ways resembled modern-day **libertarianism**. For that reason, many libertarians today refer to themselves as classical liberals.

How did the meaning of the word liberal change? In the 1800s, the Democratic Party was seen as the more liberal of the two parties. The Democrats of that time stood for limited government and opposition to **moralism** in politics. Democrats opposed Republican projects such as building roads, freeing the slaves, and prohibiting the sale of alcoholic beverages. Beginning with Democratic President Woodrow Wilson (served 1913–1921), however, the party's economic policies began to change. President Franklin Delano Roosevelt won a landslide election in 1932 by pledging to take steps to end the Great Depression. Roosevelt and the Democratic Congress quickly passed several measures that increased federal government intervention in the economy and improved conditions for Americans. By the end of Roosevelt's presidency in 1945, the Democratic Party had established itself as standing for positive government action to help the economy. Although Roosevelt stood for new policies, he kept the old language—as Democrats had long done, he called himself a liberal.

Outside the United States and Canada, the meaning of the word liberal never changed. For this reason, you might hear a left-of-center European denounce US President Ronald Reagan (served 1981–1989) or British Prime Minister Margaret Thatcher (served 1979–1990) for their "liberalism," meaning that these two leaders were enthusiastic advocates of **laissez-faire** capitalism.

Conservatism. The term conservatism suffers from similar identity problems. In the United States and Western Europe, conservatives tended to believe in maintaining traditions and opposing change. Conservatives were more likely to support the continuation of the **monarchy**, for example. At the end of World War II, Senator Robert A. Taft of Ohio was known as "Mr. Conservative," and he steadfastly opposed the Democratic Party's platform of an active government. However, he was not a spokesperson for conservative or traditional personal values.

Today, conservatism is often considered to have two quite different dimensions. Some self-identified conservatives are "economic conservatives" who believe in less government, support for capitalism and private property, and allowing individuals to pursue their own route to achievement with little government interference. Recent presidential 65 campaigns have seen great efforts to motivate those individuals who might be called "social conservatives" to support Republican candidates. Social conservatives are much less interested in economic issues than in supporting particular social values, including opposition to abortion, support for the death penalty or the right to own firearms, and opposition 70 to gay marriage. Given these two different dimensions of conservatism, it is not surprising that conservatives are not always united in their political preferences.

From Schmidt/Shelley/Bardes/Ford, *American Government and Politics Today*, 2013-2014 Edition, 16E. © 2014 Cengage Learning.

conservatism
a set of beliefs calling for a limited role of the government in helping individuals

liberalism
a set of beliefs calling for a significant role of the government in helping individuals

advocacy
the act of pleading or arguing for a cause or position

redistribute
to divide something among a group in a different way

espouse
to adopt or support something as a belief or cause

libertarianism
a political philosophy that emphasizes the individual and free will

moralism
the act or practice of criticizing the conduct or behavior of others

laissez-faire
operating with little interference from the government

monarchy
a form of government ruled by a monarch, using a king or a queen

Reflecting

Practice   After you complete your reading, answer the following questions. Then share your responses with your classmates.

1. What is the main idea of the selection? Is this idea directly stated or implied? (See page 52.)

   _____

   _____

2. What organizational pattern do the authors employ? (See page 365.)

   _____

   _____

3. What significant differences between the two topics are provided? Name two or three.

   _____

   _____

   _____

   _____

4. How has liberalism clearly changed over the years? Conservatism?

   _____

   _____

   _____

5. What questions, if any, do you still have about either topic?

   _____

   _____

6. How would you rate this selection and why?

   Weak ★ ★ ★ ★ ★ Strong

   _____

   _____

Vocabulary Practice

Identify Use context clues to define or explain the following words. (See pages 34–35 for help.)

1. **sector** (line 3)

   clues: _____

   definition: _____

2. **tolerance** (line 12)

   clues: _____

   definition: _____

3. **variants** (line 26)

   clues: _____

   definition: _____

Drawing Inferences

Explain Answer the following questions to draw inferences from the text. (See pages 30–32 for help.) Consider making your own observation as well.

1. How can you best use this information?

   _____

   _____

2. What strong feelings do you have with either set of beliefs and why?

   _____

   _____

3. (Your own observation)

   _____

   _____

Writing

What follows are possible writing activities to complete in response to the reading. Use the writing process (pages 106–111) to help you develop your writing.

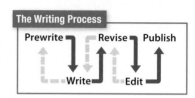

The Writing Process

Prewrite ➡ Revise ➡ Publish

Write ⬅ Edit

Prewriting

Choose one of the following writing ideas to write a comparison essay. Or decide upon an idea of your own making related to the reading.

Writing Ideas

1. **Writing to Learn:** Create an imaginary dialogue between you and someone with a different political or social belief system. Keep the discussion going as long as you can.

2. **Essay Writing:** Develop a comparison essay between two individuals in politics, sports, or entertainment.

3. Write a comparison between you and one of the individuals that you identified on page 384.

4. Develop a comparison essay about another two topics that you identified on page 374.

5. Compare libertarianism to either liberalism or conservatism. This will require some research.

When planning . . .

Refer to pages 374–375 to help you plan your essay. Also use these tips.

- Choose subjects that are specific enough for an essay and that you know a lot about.

- Carry out some primary and/or secondary research to learn more about your subjects. (See pages 428–432.)

Writing and Revising

Refer to pages 376–379 to help you write and revise your first draft. Also use the tips that follow.

When writing . . .

- Include opening, middle, and closing parts in your essay. Each part has a specific role. (See page 377.)
- Keep your reader in mind. Your goal should be to engage the reader with interesting and thoughtful information.

When revising . . .

- Ask yourself if your essay contains any dead spots that either need more details or should be cut back.
- Decide if any parts are confusing or cause you to stumble. Rewrite these parts as needed.
- Determine if you have organized your details in the best way.

Editing

Refer to pages 380–382 when you are ready to edit your essay for style and accuracy. Use the checklist on page 383 as your final editing guide.

Reflecting on Comparison Writing

Answer the following questions about your reading and writing experiences in this chapter.

1. What is your favorite essay in this chapter? Explain.

_____

2. Which reading strategy in the chapter seems the most helpful? Explain.

_____

3. What is the most important thing that you have learned about reading comparison essays?

_____

4. What do you like the most about the comparison essay that you wrote in this chapter? Explain.

_____

5. What is one thing that you would like to change about your essay?

_____

6. What is the most important thing that you have learned about comparison writing?

_____

7. What is the hardest thing about this type of writing? The easiest?

_____

Key Terms to Remember

When you read and write comparison essays, it's important to understand the following terms.

- **Comparing**—showing how two or more subjects are similar
- **Contrasting**—showing how two or more subjects are different
- **Points of comparison**—the special elements or features used to make a comparison (size, strength, appearance, and so on)
- **Patterns of organization for comparison essays**—point by point, subject by subject, and similarities and differences (See page 365.)

14

> "Nothing is as frustrating as arguing with someone who knows what he's talking about."
>
> —Sam Ewing

Argumentation

One definition of *argument* is "a quarrel or dispute," as when a brother and a sister engage in a shouting match. As you well know, heated words are exchanged in this type of argument. Another definition of *argument* is "a discussion aimed at demonstrating truth or falsehood." Levelheadedness is important in this type of argument.

This chapter focuses on reasonable arguments that let the facts speak for themselves. A well-crafted argumentative essay informs and explains. It prompts logical thinking rather than emotion, guiding the reader toward informed conclusions about important, sometimes controversial issues.

In this chapter, you will learn about the working parts of argumentation and read and react to two professional argumentative texts. Then you will read and react to a student essay and develop an argumentative essay of your own.

Learning Outcomes

LO1 Understand argumentation.

LO2 Learn reading strategies (identifying the main parts and understanding the voice).

LO3 Read and react to a professional argument.

LO4 Read and react to a second professional argument.

LO5 Plan an argument essay.

LO6 Write the first draft.

LO7 Revise the writing.

LO8 Edit the writing.

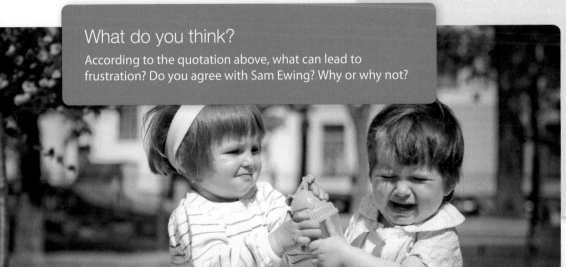

What do you think?

According to the quotation above, what can lead to frustration? Do you agree with Sam Ewing? Why or why not?

Aliaksei Lasevich, 2013 / Used under license from Shutterstock.com

LO1 Understanding Argumentation

In ancient Greece and Rome, anyone lucky enough to receive an education was trained in argumentation. The belief was (and still is) that those who develop argumentative skills become clear thinkers and leaders. Believe it or not, the basic structure used to build arguments in those ancient civilizations is still used today.

An argument is only as good as the thoughts and ideas that go into it. A strong argument develops a logical or reasonable claim (thesis) with solid evidence. It recognizes important opposing points of view and either concedes or counters them. And overall, it provides a meaningful and logical examination of an issue. Arguments, of course, are made about issues in which people have differing points of view. There's nothing to argue about if everyone agrees on something.

Arguments are weakened by logical fallacies or false statements. These appear unintentionally in quickly fashioned persuasive texts, or intentionally in manipulative arguments, such as advertisements: "Temptrol is the best cold medicine in the world!" or "One call to my law office will take care of all of your bankruptcy problems!"

> "Argument is meant to reveal the truth, not to create it."
> —Edward de Bono

Argumentation Versus Persuasion

The main purpose of persuasion is to be convincing. A campaigning politician trying to gain votes through persuasion will very likely appeal more to the voters' personal interests—"Follow me. I can fix the economy!"—than to logic and reason. A thorough, logical argument may be persuasive, but that is not its main purpose. Its main intent is to prove the strength and validity of a certain line of thinking. A judge's logical explanation of a decision is a form of argumentation.

INSIGHT

The difference between a claim and evidence is the difference between opinion and facts. A claim states an opinion, and evidence provides factual support.

Identify Find two examples each of argumentation and of persuasion. For each one, identify the subject and provide a one- or two-sentence explanation of its content. Check online, in newspapers, in magazines, and on billboards for ideas.

Argumentation	Persuasion

Reading

Reading argument essays requires a close examination of the main claim and supporting details. This section provides valuable reading practice.

LO2 Learning Reading Strategies

Identifying the Main Parts

Once you identify the three parts of an argument discussed below, you can judge whether or not the argument has value or merit.

Main claim: The main claim (or thesis) generally appears early in the essay, usually in one of the opening paragraphs, after background information about the topic. A claim takes a stand or presents a viewpoint about the topic:

- Two internships should be required before graduation.
- Special taxes should be placed on gas-guzzling SUVs.

Evidence: A claim succeeds or falls based on its supporting evidence. The evidence in a strong argument can be checked, backed up, and relied upon. Common types of evidence include the following (also see pages 65–66):

- **Facts and statistics:** According to a 2011 study by the DNR, a murky bottom predicts an algae cover greater than 80 percent.
- **Examples:** Wind causes algae to wash up on the beaches.
- **Expert testimony:** Sarah Follet, a water resource official, stated, "There are . . ."

Counterarguments: A strong argument addresses opposing points of view, either conceding or countering them. Many opposing points of view are introduced with words or phrases such as *admittedly, granted, it is true that, I accept that, no doubt,* and *so on.*

- **Opposing point of view:** It is true that the appearance of the algae is limited to late summer, and according to some people, it occurs only if the weather is very still and hot.
- **Counter:** In saying this, people are simply ignoring the problem. The algae will still be there regardless of the weather, just waiting to bloom.

Understanding the Voice

Voice refers to the author's writing personality and attitude toward the topic and the reader. Use these questions as a guide for judging voice in an argument.

- Does the author seem honest and sincere?
- Does he or she make a realistic claim?
- Does he or she seem respectful and understanding?
- Does he or she focus on issues rather than personalities?
- Does the author engage the reader, rather that lecture him or her?

LO3 Reading and Reacting to a Professional Argument

In this selection the author addresses his new opinion about the death penalty. Use the reading process and the strategies on the previous page to help you gain a full understanding of the text.

About the Author

Lance Morrow has been a professor of journalism at Boston University and a journalist and essayist for *Time* magazine. He is also the author of several nonfiction books

Preread   Before you read, answer these questions:

1. What do the title, the first few paragraphs, and the final few paragraphs tell you about the text?

2. What is your position related to the topic?

3. What do you expect to learn?

Read and Reread   As you read, make it your goal to (1) identify the author's main claim, (2) follow his reasoning and argument, and (3) reread any parts as needed. Consider annotating the text (page 20) and taking notes (page 22) as you read.

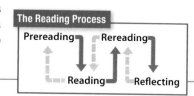

The Reading Process

Prereading → Rereading → Reading → Reflecting

Why I Changed My Mind on the Death Penalty

Christina Marie Riggs, a nurse in Arkansas and a single mother, killed her two children—Justin, 5, and Shelby Alexis, 2—by giving them injections of **potassium chloride** and then smothering them with a pillow. She wrote a suicide note, and apparently tried to kill herself with an overdose of 28 antidepressant tablets. She survived.   5

Or she did until last night, when the state of Arkansas put Riggs to death by lethal injection at the state prison in Varner. She was the first woman to be executed in Arkansas since 1845.

     1

The state of Arkansas played the part of **Jack Kevorkian** in a case of assisted suicide. Christina Riggs said she wanted to die. She had dropped all legal appeals. She wanted to be with her children in heaven. Just before Riggs died, she said, "I love you, my babies." Some people said she had killed them because she was severely depressed. The prosecutor, on the other hand, called her "a self-centered, selfish, premeditated killer who did the unspeakable act of taking her own children's lives." *15*

So where do we stand on capital punishment now? (And, incidentally, isn't it grand that we seem to be overcoming, at the speed of light, our reluctance to execute women? Bless you, **Gloria Steinem**.)

Review the state of play:

Deterrence is an unreliable argument for the death penalty, I think, *20* because deterrence is unprovable.

The fear of executing the wrong man (a more popular line of **demurral** these days) is an unreliable argument against all capital punishment. What if there are many witnesses to a murder? What if it's Hitler? Is capital punishment OK in cases of unmistakable guilt? George W. *25* Bush [when governor] says that he reviews each case to make sure he is absolutely certain a person did it before he allows a Texas execution to go ahead.

I have argued in the past that the death penalty was justified, in certain brutal cases, on the basis of the social contract. That is: Some *30* hideous crimes demand the ultimate punishment in order to satisfy the essentially civilizing deal that we make with one another as citizens. We forgo individual revenge, deferring to the law, but depend upon a certainty that the law will give us a justice that must include appropriate harshness. I favored the Texas folk wisdom: "He needs killing." If the law fails in that *35* task, I said, and people see that evil is **fecklessly** tolerated, then the social contract disintegrates. Society needs a measure of **homeopathic** revenge.

But I have changed my mind about capital punishment.

I think the American atmosphere, the American imagination (news, movies, books, music, fact, fiction, entertainment, culture, life in the *40* streets, **zeitgeist**) is now so filled with murder and violence (gang wars, random shootings not just in housing projects but in offices and malls and schools) that violence of any kind—including solemn execution—has become merely a part of our cultural routine and joins, in our minds, the passing parade of stupidity/**psychosis**/chaos/entertainment that Americans *45* seem to like, or have come to deserve. In **Freudian** terms, the once forceful (and **patriarchal**) American **Superego** (arguably including the authority of law, of the presidency, of the military, etc.) has collapsed into a great dismal swamp of **Id**.

And in the Swamp, I have come to think, capital punishment has lost   *50*
whatever cautionary social force it had—its exemplary meaning, its power
to proclaim, as it once arguably did, that some deeds are, in our fine and
virtuous company, intolerable.

I think those arguing in favor of capital punishment now are indulging
in a form of **nostalgia**. Capital punishment no longer works as a morality   *55*
play. Each execution (divorced from its moral meaning, including its
capacity to shock and to warn the young) simply becomes part of the great
messy pageant, the vast and voracious stupidity, the Jerry Springer show
of American life.

Maybe most of our moral opinions are formed by emotions and   *60*
aesthetic reactions. My opinion is this: Capital punishment has lost its
moral meaning. Having lost its moral meaning, it has become as immoral
as any other expression of violence. And therefore we should stop doing it.

potassium chloride
an odorless salt used in
some state executions

Jack Kevorkian
doctor who fought for
terminal patients' right to
die

Gloria Steinem
spokesperson for the
women's movement

deterrence
measures taken to prevent
hostile actions

demurral
hesitation or objection

fecklessly
carelessly

homeopathic
a medical treatment to
create immunity by small,
repeated exposure

zeitgeist
the spirit of a cultural time
period

psychosis
insanity involving a break
with reality

Freudian
related to the theories
of Sigmund Freud, a
psychiatrist

patriarchal
ruled by a patriarch (man)

Superego
sense of moral
responsibility, conscience

Id
instinctual drives

nostalgia
longing for the past

aesthetic
artistic sense of beauty

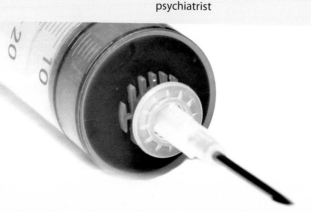

Reflect After you complete your reading, answer these questions. Share your responses with your classmates.

1. What is the author's main claim, and where in the essay does he state it?

   _____

   _____

   _____

2. What evidence does the author provide to support his claim? Provide two examples.

   _____

   _____

   _____

3. What, if any, opposing points of view does the author address? Does he concede or counter them?

   _____

   _____

   _____

4. What questions, if any, do you still have about the topic?

   _____

   _____

   _____

5. How would you rate this paragraph and why?

   Weak ★ ★ ★ ★ ★ Strong

   _____

   _____

Vocabulary Practice

Identify   Define the following words using context clues and your understanding of word parts as a guide. Also list the words or word parts that help you define each term. (See pages 34–37 and 668–676 for help.)

1. **premeditated**   (line 14)

_____

_____

2. **intolerable**   (line 53)

_____

_____

3. **voracious**   (line 58)

_____

_____

Drawing Inferences

Explain   Answer the questions below to help you draw inferences from the text. (See pages 30–32 for help.) Consider adding one of your own observations as well.

1. How does the writer's argument stack up against your own opinion about the topic?

_____

_____

2. What generalization can you make about capital punishment in this country?

_____

_____

3. (Your own observation)

_____

_____

LO4 Reading and Reacting to a Second Professional Argument

This selection comes from the book *Nickel and Dimed*, in which the author Barbara Ehrenreich discovered through firsthand experiences the difficulties experienced by the working poor. Use the reading process to help you gain a full understanding of the text.

About the Author

Barbara Ehrenreich is a journalist, author of many books, and activist for health care, women's rights, and economic fairness.

Preread Before you read, answer these three questions:

1. What do the title, the first paragraph, and the first sentences of other paragraphs tell you about the text?

_____

2. Who might be the author's intended audience?

_____

3. What do you expect to learn in this selection?

_____

Read and Reread As you read, make it your goal to (1) identify the main claim, (2) follow the supporting evidence, and (3) study the ending paragraphs. Consider annotating the text (page 20) and/or taking notes (page 22) as you read.

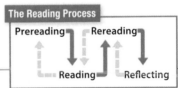

The Reading Process

Prereading · Rereading

Reading · Reflecting

The High Cost of Being Poor

There are people, concentrated in the **Hamptons** and Beverly Hills, who   *1*
still confuse poverty with the simple life. No cable TV, no altercations with
the maid, no summer home **maintenance** issues—just the basics like family,
sunsets, and walks in the park. What they don't know is that it's expensive
to be poor.   *5*

In fact, you, the reader of **middling** income, could probably not afford
it. A new study from the Brookings Institute documents the "ghetto tax,"
or higher cost of living in low-income urban neighborhoods. It comes at you

from every direction, from food prices to auto insurance. A few examples
from this study, by Matt Fellowes, that covered 12 American cities: *10*

- Poor people are less likely to have bank accounts, which can be
  expensive for those with low balances, and so they tend to cash their
  pay checks at check-cashing businesses, which in the cities surveyed,
  charged $5 to $50 for a $500 check.
- Nationwide, low-income car buyers, defined as people earning less   *15*
  than $30,000 a year, pay two percentage points more for a car loan
  than more affluent buyers.
- Low-income drivers pay more for car insurance. In New York,
  Baltimore and Hartford, they pay an average $400 more a year to
  insure the exact same car and driver risk than wealthier drivers.   *20*
- Poorer people pay an average of one percentage point more in mortgage
  interest.
- They are more likely to buy their furniture and appliances through
  pricey rent-to-own businesses. In Wisconsin, the study reports, a
  $200 rent-to-own TV set can cost $700 with the interest included.   *25*
- They are less likely to have access to large supermarkets and hence
  have to rely on the far more expensive, and lower quality offerings, of
  small grocery and convenience stores.

I didn't live in any ghettoes when I worked on *Nickel and Dimed*—a trailer
park, yes, but no ghetto—and on my average wage of $7 an hour, or about   *30*
$14,400 a year, I wasn't in the market for furniture, a house, or a car. But
the high cost of life, when, slipping into social-worker mode, I chastised a
coworker for living in a motel room when it would be so much cheaper to rent
an apartment. Her response: Where would she get the first month's rent and
security deposit it takes to pin down an apartment? The lack of that amount   *35*
of capital—probably well over $1,000—condemned her to paying $40 a night
at the Day's Inn.

Then there was the problem of sustenance. I had gone into the project
imagining myself preparing vast quantities of cheap, nutritious soups and
stews, which I would freeze and heat for dinner each day. But surprise: I   *40*
didn't have the **proverbial** pot to pee in, not to mention spices or Tupperware.
A scouting trip to K-Mart established that it would take about a $40 capital
investment to get my kitchenette up to speed for the low-wage way of life.

The food situation got only more challenging when I, too, found myself
living in a motel. Lacking a fridge and microwave, all my food had to come   *45*
from the nearest convenience store (hardboiled egg and banana for breakfast)
or, for the big meal of the day, Wendy's or KFC. I have no nutritional

complaints; after all, there is a veggie, or flecks of one, in Wendy's broccoli and cheese baked potato. The problem was financial. A double cheeseburger and fries is lot more expensive than that **hypothetical** homemade lentil stew. *50*

There are other tolls along the road well-traveled by the working poor. If your credit is lousy, which it is likely to be, you'll pay a higher deposit for a phone. If you don't have health insurance, you may end up taking that feverish child to an emergency room, and please don't think of ER's as socialized medicine for the poor. The average cost of a visit is over $1,000, *55* which is over ten times more than what a clinic pediatrician would charge. Or you neglect that **hypertension**, diabetes, or mystery lump until you end up with a $100,000 problem on your hands.

So let's have a little less talk about how the poor should learn to manage their money, and a little more attention to all the ways that money is being *60* systematically **siphoned** off. Yes, certain kinds of advice would be helpful: skip the pay-day loans and rent-to-pay furniture, for example. But we need laws in more states to stop predatory practices like $50 charges for check cashing. Also, think what some microcredit could do to move families from motels and shelters to apartments. And did I mention a **living wage**? *65*

If you're rich, you might want to stay that way. It's a whole lot cheaper than being poor.

Reprinted by permission of International Creative Management, Inc. Copyright © by Barbara Ehrenreich

Hamptons
wealthy and exclusive section of Long Island

maintenance
keeping in the proper condition

middling
moderate or average

Nickel and Dimed
book by Barbara Ehrenreich detailing her year as a member of the working poor

proverbial
widely referred to

hypothetical
based on a suggested idea

hypertension
high blood pressure

siphoned
to draw money or resources from

living wage
a wage that allows a worker to support a family

Reflect   After you complete your reading, answer the following questions. Then share your responses with your classmates.

1. What is the author's main claim?

   _____

   _____

2. What evidence does the author provide to support her claim? Provide at least three examples.

   _____

   _____

   _____

   _____

3. What, if any, opposing points of view does the author address? Does she concede or counter them? Where in the essay do they appear?

   _____

   _____

   _____

4. What questions do you still have about the topic?

   _____

   _____

5. How would you rate this essay and why?

   Weak ★ ★ ★ ★ ★ Strong

   _____

   _____

Vocabulary Practice

Identify   Use context clues to define or explain the following words. (See pages 34–35 for help.)

1. **altercations**   (line 2)

   clues: _____

   definition: _____

2. **chastised**   (line 32)

   clues: _____

   definition: _____

3. **sustenance**   (line 38)

   clues: _____

   definition: _____

4. **predatory**   (line 63)

   clues: _____

   definition: _____

Drawing Inferences

Explain   Answer these questions to help you draw inferences from the text. (See pages 30–32 for help.)

1. How does the writer's argument stack up against your own opinion about the topic?

   _____

   _____

2. What generalization can you make about the quality of life in this country?

   _____

   _____

Writing

In your own argument essay, you will develop a claim about a debatable topic. Be sure to write about a topic that you truly care about. Use the writing process to help you do your best work. (See pages 106–111.)

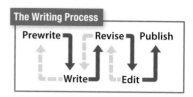

LO5 Planning an Argument Essay

The information on these two pages covers the prewriting tasks that you must complete before developing your first draft.

Selecting a Topic

If you can't think of a topic, browse newspapers, magazines, and the Internet for current issues that people have strong feelings about.

Select   In the space below, list three or four debatable issues you could write about in an essay. Think of issues related to school, your city, the economy, and so on. Circle your favorite topic.

_____   _____

_____   _____

Taking a Position

Once you decide on a topic, consider your initial position or opinion about the issue.

Write   Write down a defensible position statement that introduces the issue and expresses your opinion about it.

_____

_____

Refining a Position

Use the following strategies to develop and refine your opinion:

- Research different positions on your topic.
- Determine if the most compelling evidence supports or opposes your initial position.

Write   If necessary, rewrite your position statement to reflect your research.

Gathering Details

To support your stand or position on an issue, you must gather convincing support to defend it. The following types of details can be used to support your position: facts, statistics, testimonials, and predictions.

Support Chart

Fact	Statistic	Testimonial	Prediction
A shield law is a law that gives reporters protection . . .	Currently 49 states, including California, offer shield laws . . .	"We definitely need to have a shield law, but we also need to have . . ."	Sources may fear being identified and decide against . . .

Gather Fill in a support chart with the research you have gathered about your topic. If you have not found supporting details to fit each category, consider doing additional research.

Fact	Statistic	Testimony	Prediction

Arranging the Details

Order of importance is often used in argument essays. With this pattern of organization, you may present your evidence in one of two ways—either from the most important to the least important, or from the least to most.

Choose Review the evidence that you have collected. Then determine how you will arrange the support—which idea will you develop first, second, and so on. Explain.

Considering Opposing Points of View

Your instructor may want you to address one or two opposing points of view. You can either concede or counter these viewpoints. (See page 395.)

LO6 Writing the First Draft

Creating a first draft puts all of your planning and gathering into concrete form. Provided below is another argument essay to review before you begin writing.

Read Read the following argument essay, paying careful attention to the opening, middle, and closing parts.

A Necessary Protection

Opening paragraph

Back in the summer of 2006, investigative journalists Lance Williams and Mark Fainaru-Wada of the *San Francisco Chronicle* faced a dilemma: either reveal the source who leaked confidential information for their story about steroid use in professional baseball or refuse to name names and be found in contempt of court, a conviction carrying an 18-month prison sentence. At the heart of the matter were shield laws. A shield law is a law that gives reporters protection from being forced to reveal confidential information or anonymous sources in a courtroom. Currently 49 states, including California, offer shield laws of varying degrees. However, Williams and Fainaru-Wada's source was involved in a federal investigation, and no shield laws protect journalists in federal court. This fact must change. Passing a federal shield law is a necessary step to ensure the general public's right to know.

Thesis statement

Support paragraph 1

Some of the most important stories in American history have surfaced due to anonymous whistle-blowers, including the Watergate and Enron scandals. Without a federal shield law, future stories like these may never be told for two reasons. First, sources may fear being identified and decide against leaking a story of corruption or scandal. Second, news organizations may not fulfill their confidential-sources agreements due to the financial responsibility of fighting a case in court. Either one hurts news gathering.

Support paragraph 2

Furthermore, a federal shield law would provide journalists with the basic protections they need to be watchdogs for the general public. It's the responsibility of a free press to frustrate government corruption, corporate misconduct, and threats to public health and safety by unearthing stories. But what if a journalist decides against running an important story with an unnamed source for fear of being subpoenaed?

Closing paragraph

To be certain, a federal shield law should not provide journalists with unlimited protections. If an unnamed source is an imminent threat to national security or could cause bodily harm, the journalist should be compelled to reveal the source. However, in cases where an unnamed source is absolutely necessary, reporters shouldn't have to fear imprisonment for honoring a confidentiality agreement. Trust is the foundation of a source-reporter relationship. Williams and Fainaru-Wada knew this. They decided against revealing their source and would have served jail time if the source had not confessed. But the next journalist might not be so lucky. It's time to pass a federal shield law.

Creating an Opening Paragraph

The opening paragraph or part of your essay should capture the reader's interest, provide background information, and state your position on the topic. Consider these attention-grabbing strategies for your opening paragraph.

- **Start with a brief dramatic story.**
  Back in the summer of 2006, investigative journalists Lance Williams and Mark Fainaru-Wada of the *San Francisco Chronicle* faced a dilemma: either reveal the source who leaked confidential information for their story about steroid use in professional baseball or refuse to name names and be found in contempt of court.

- **Offer a surprising statistic.**
  An American Farmland Trust study estimates two acres of farmland and ranch land is lost to development every minute of every day.

- **Make a personal confession.**
  I can't stand cigarette smoke, but I believe adults should have the freedom to smoke in public.

Developing the Middle Paragraphs

In the middle paragraphs, you should support your claim with the details you gathered on page 407. Here are more tips.

- Present your supporting arguments in the best order. (See page 407.)
- Provide enough information to make each point clear.
- Address any opposing points of view as directed by your instructor. (See page 395.)

Forming a Closing Paragraph

The closing paragraph should restate or reaffirm your position. If appropriate, make a direct or indirect call for the reader to adopt your position. Here are some examples.

- If the United States wants to maintain its fragile southern ecosystem, it should take a hard look at making the importation of Burmese pythons illegal.
- We must build around, not on, farms on the urban edge. Furthermore, we must be more judicious with growth by making already-developed areas more livable.
- It's time to pass a federal shield law.

Write Write your first draft, using the information above and on the previous pages as a guide.

LO7 Revising the Writing

Revising your first draft involves adding, deleting, rearranging, and reworking parts of your writing. Revision begins with a peer review.

Peer Review

Sharing your writing—whether with a friend, classmate, or tutor—is especially important in the revising process.

Peer Review Sheet

Essay title: _____

Writer: _____

Reviewer: _____

1. Which part of the essay seems to work best—opening, middle, or closing? Why?

   _____

   _____

2. Which part of the essay needs work—opening, middle, or closing? Why?

   _____

   _____

3. Do the middle paragraphs support the writer's position statement? How so?

   _____

   _____

4. Does the writer use a variety of support details? Are more needed? Why or why not?

   _____

   _____

5. Does the writer build a convincing argument? Why or why not?

   _____

   _____

Respond Complete this response sheet after reading the first draft of a classmate's essay. Then share the sheet with the writer. (Keep your comments helpful and positive.)

Looking Out for Logical Fallacies

A logical fallacy is a false statement that weakens an argument by distorting an issue, drawing false conclusions, misusing evidence, or misusing language. Below are four common logical fallacies.

Straw Man This logical fallacy distorts an issue by exaggerating or misinterpreting an opponent's position.

> Those who consider themselves caring people can't approve of the death penalty.

Bandwagon Mentality Such a logical fallacy appeals to "popular opinion" by implying that a claim cannot be true because most people oppose it, or must be true because most support it.

> It's obvious to everyone that cockroaches live only in dirty apartments.

Broad Generalization This logical fallacy makes an all-or-nothing claim based on little evidence. The claim will often include an intensifier, such as *all, every,* or *never.*

> All athletes are driven by money.

Impressing with Numbers In this case, a writer attempts to overwhelm the reader with a deluge of statistics, some of which are unrelated to the issue at hand.

> At 35 ppm, CO levels factory-wide are only 10ppm above the OSHA recommendation, which is 25 ppm. Clearly, that 10 ppm is insignificant in the big picture.

Revise Improve your writing using your partner's comments on the response sheet and the following checklist. Continue working until you can check off each item in the list.

Using a Revising Checklist

Ideas

- [ ] 1. Do I take a stand on a debatable issue?
- [ ] 2. Do I support my position with a variety of supporting details?
- [ ] 3. Do I avoid errors in logic (logical fallacies)?

Organization

- [ ] 4. Do I have opening, middle, and closing paragraphs?
- [ ] 5. Have I used transitions to connect my ideas?

Voice

- [ ] 6. Do I sound knowledgeable about and interested in the issue?

LO8 Editing the Writing

The main work of editing is correcting your revised first draft.

Correcting Ambiguous Wording

Ambiguous wording creates uncertainty for the reader. Such wording results in sentences that have multiple meanings. Avoid indefinite pronoun references, incomplete comparisons, and unclear wording.

Vague or Indefinite Pronoun Reference

When it is unclear which word or phrase a pronoun refers to, the wording is ambiguous.

Ambiguous: When Mike moved the lamp onto the wobbly chair, it fell on the floor.

Clear: When Mike moved the lamp onto the wobbly chair, the lamp fell on the floor.

Ambiguous: Monica reminded Misha that she needed to buy a new black dress for the party. *(Who needed to buy a black dress—Monica or Misha?)*

Clear: Monica reminded Misha to buy a new black dress for the party.

Practice Rewrite each sentence so that it does not contain any ambiguous pronoun references.

1. When Andy placed the box of macaroni back on the shelf, it tipped over.

   _____

   _____

2. The professor told Tim that he needed to pursue the research opportunity.

   _____

   _____

3. As Brad drove his motorcycle into the garage, it shook.

   _____

   _____

Apply Read your argument essay and watch for indefinite pronoun references. If you find any, correct them.

Incomplete Comparisons

Don't confuse the reader by leaving out a word or words that are necessary to complete a comparison.

Ambiguous: The head chef said the Kobe steak is tastier. *(The Kobe is tastier than what?)*

Clear: The head chef said the Kobe steak is tastier than the porterhouse.

Unclear Wording

Avoid writing a statement that can have two or more meanings.

Ambiguous: Jill decided to take her sister to a movie, which turned out to be a real bummer. *(It is unclear what was a real bummer—taking her sister to the movie or the movie itself.)*

Clear: Jill decided to take her sister to a movie, but the film turned out to be a real bummer.

Practice Rewrite each of the following sentences so that it does not contain incomplete comparisons or unclear wording.

1. Going bowling is more fun.

_____

_____

2. I can handle Mel's personality better.

_____

_____

3. Vera wanted to complete her economics report after reading the latest research, but she didn't.

_____

_____

Apply Read your argument essay and watch for incomplete comparisons or unclear wording. If you find any examples, correct them.

Marking an Essay

Before you finish editing your revised essay, you can practice by editing the following model.

Practice Read the following argument essay, looking for problems listed in the checklist on the next page. Correct the model using the marks at the bottom of this page.

Ban Burmese Pythons

An invasive species are taking the southern tip of Florida by storm. Thousands of Burmese pythons—giant snakes native to Southern asia—are thriving in the tropical-like environment of Everglades National Park. Their presence in the park is a product of irresponsible pet owners, who intentionally release the snakes into the wild when they become too difficult to care for. as a result, Florida lawmakers have passed a law making it illigal for individuals to own burmese pythons. In order to protect native wildlife and treasured ecosystems of the southern United States, this law should expand nationally.

Reports show some 144,000 pythons have been imported into the United States, many of which end up in homes of irresponsible pet owners. "All of the Burmese pythons that we see in the park are a product of the international pet trade" said Skip Snow, a wildlife biologist at Everglades National Park. The problem is many pet owners doesn't fully understand the responsibility of taking care of a python often the python, which grow up to between 10 and 20 feet becomes too big and to expensive to be kept in a home. In the end, the owner releases the pet into the wild.

It is in the wild where Burmese pythons is causing havoc. The tropical environment of the Everglades provides perfect conditions for the pythons to breed and feed. With no natural competitor the strong and stealthy python is feeding at will on native Everglade's species, Scientists worry the ecological effects could be devastating. Second to habitat loss, invasive species are the leading cause of species endangerment.

To be fair, there are no doubt thousands of responsible pet owners across the United States. But the drawbacks of owning Burmese pythons outweigh the benefits. These species are not meant to be pets. If the United States wants to maintain its fragile southern ecosystem, it should take a hard look at making the importation of Burmese pythons illegal.

1

5

10

15

20

25

Correction Marks

⟋⟍ delete	⋏ add comma	*word* ∧ add word
≡d capitalize	? add question	⊙ add period
∅ lowercase	∧ mark	⌒ spelling
∧ insert	⌄ insert an apostrophe	⇄ switch

Using an Editing Checklist

Now it's time to edit your own essay.

Apply   Create a clean copy of your revised essay and use the following checklist to check for errors. Continue working until you can check off each item in the list.

Words
- [ ] 1. Have I used specific nouns and verbs? (See page 146.)
- [ ] 2. Have I used more action verbs than "be" verbs? (See page 147.)

Sentences
- [ ] 3. Have I varied the beginnings and lengths of sentences? (See page 149.)
- [ ] 4. Have I combined short, choppy sentences? (See page 149.)
- [ ] 5. Have I avoided improper shifts in sentences? (See pages 544–545.)
- [ ] 6. Have I avoided fragments and run-ons? (See pages 532–535, 538–539.)
- [ ] 7. Have I avoided vague pronoun references, incomplete comparisons, and unclear wording?

Conventions
- [ ] 8. Do I use correct verb forms (*he saw*, not *he seen*)? (See page 588.)
- [ ] 9. Do my subjects and verbs agree (*she speaks*, not *she speak*)? (See pages 516–525.)
- [ ] 10. Have I used the right words (*their, there, they're*)?
- [ ] 11. Have I capitalized first words and proper nouns and adjectives? (See page 626.)
- [ ] 12. Have I used commas after long introductory word groups? (See page 638.)
- [ ] 13. Have I punctuated dialogue correctly? (See pages 209–210.)
- [ ] 14. Have I carefully checked my spelling?

Adding a Title

Make sure to add an attention-getting title. Here are three simple strategies for writing titles.

- Use a phrase from the essay:

   America the Developed

- Make a dramatic statement:

   A Necessary Protection

- Use a play on words:

   Ban Burmese Pythons

> "The best argument is that which seems merely an explanation."
> —Dale Carnegie

Enrichment: Reading

On pages 417–419 you will find an argumentative essay entitled "In Praise of the F Word" to read and react to. As you read this essay, be sure to follow the steps in the reading process. The reading activities are followed by writing ideas to choose from to write an argumentative essay of your own.

About the Author

Mary Sherry is a teacher of adult literacy programs. She lives near Minneapolis, Minnesota. Her essay first appeared in *Newsweek* magazine.

Prereading

Seldom does a day go by without a politician, a community leader, or an educator making a new claim about improving our schools. Tougher standards, more hands-on experiences, and smaller classes are three of the many "solutions" that are regularly discussed. List below two or three of your own claims about education. Consider your own experiences in school as well as your own beliefs about higher-level learning and job training.

_____

_____

_____

CONSIDER THE TRAITS

As you read the essay on pages 417–419, focus first on the **ideas**—the main claim, the evidence, and any counterarguments. Then consider the **organization**—the arrangement of the details in the main part of the essay. Also think about the writer's **voice**—her unique way of speaking to the reader. And finally, ask yourself if these traits combine to produce a satisfying reading experience.

What do you think?

According to Dale Carnegie's quotation at the top of the page, a strong argument "seems merely an explanation." What does this idea mean to you?

Identify Before you read, answer these three questions:

1. What do the title and the first sentences of the essay's paragraphs tell you about the text?

   _____

2. Who might be the intended audience?

   _____

3. What do you expect to learn?

   _____

Reading and Rereading

This argumentative essay focuses on a traditional but seldom-used strategy to improve learning in the classroom. Consider your own experiences in school while you read the essay. As you read, make it your goal to (1) identify the main claim, (2) follow the supporting evidence, and (3) study the ending paragraph. Consider annotating the text (page 20) and/or taking notes (page 22) to help you gain a full understanding of the argument.

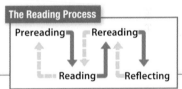

In Praise of the F Word

Tens of thousands of 18-year-olds will graduate this year and be   *1*
handed meaningless diplomas. These diplomas won't look any different
from those awarded their luckier classmates. Their **validity** will be
questioned only when their employers discover that these graduates are
semiliterate.   *5*

Eventually a fortunate few will find their way into educational-repair
shops—adult-literacy programs, such as the one where I teach basic
grammar and writing. There, high-school graduates and high-school
dropouts pursuing graduate-equivalency certificates will learn the skills
they should have learned in school. They will also discover they have been *10*
cheated by our educational system.

As I teach, I learn a lot about our schools. Early in each session I ask
my students to write about an unpleasant experience they had in school.
No writers' block here! "I wish someone would have made me stop doing
drugs and made me study." "I liked to party, and no one seemed to care."   *15*
"I was a good kid and didn't cause any trouble, so they just passed me
along even though I didn't read and couldn't write." And so on.

I am your basic do-gooder, and prior to teaching this class I blamed the poor academic skills our kids have today on drugs, divorce, and other impediments to concentration necessary for doing well in school. But, as I *20* rediscover each time I walk into the classroom, before a teacher can expect students to concentrate, he has to get their attention, no matter what distractions may be at hand. There are many ways to do this, and they have much to do with teaching style. However, if style alone won't do it, there is another way to show who holds the winning hand in the classroom. *25* That is to reveal the **trump card** of failure.

I will never forget a teacher who played that card to get the attention of one of my children. Our youngest, a world-class charmer, did little to develop his intellectual talents but always got by. Until Mrs. Stifter.

Our son was a high-school senior when he had her for English. "He *30* sits in the back of the room talking to his friends," she told me. "Why don't you move him to the front row?" I urged, believing the embarrassment would get him to settle down. Mrs. Stifter looked at me steely-eyed over her glasses. "I don't move seniors," she said. "I flunk them." I was **flustered**. Our son's academic life flashed before my eyes. No teacher had ever *35* threatened him with that before. I regained my composure and managed to say that I thought she was right. By the time I got home I was feeling pretty good about this. It was a **radical** approach for these times, but, well, why not? "She's going to flunk you," I told my son. I did not discuss it any further. Suddenly English became a **priority** in his life. He finished out the *40* semester with an A.

I know one example doesn't make a case, but at night I see a parade of students who are angry and resentful for having been passed along until they could no longer even pretend to keep up. Of average intelligence or better, they eventually quit school, concluding they were too dumb to *45* finish. "I should have been held back," is a comment I hear frequently. Even sadder are those students who are high-school graduates who say to me after a few weeks of class, "I don't know how I ever got a high-school diploma."

Passing students who have not mastered the work cheats them and *50* the employers who expect graduates to have basic skills. We excuse this dishonest behavior by saying kids can't learn if they come from terrible environments. No one seems to stop to think that—no matter what environments they come from—most kids don't put school first on their list unless they perceive something is at stake. They'd rather be sailing. *55*

Many students I see at night could give expert **testimony** on unemployment, chemical dependency, abusive relationships. In spite of these difficulties, they have decided to make education a priority. They are motivated by the desire for a better job or the need to hang on to the one they've got. They have a healthy fear of failure.   *60*

People of all ages can rise above their problems, but they need to have a reason to do so. Young people generally don't have the maturity to value education in the same way my adult students value it. But fear of failure, whether economic or academic, can motivate both. Flunking as a regular policy has just as much merit today as it did two generations ago. We must   *65* review the threat of flunking and see it as it really is—a positive teaching tool. It is an expression of confidence by both teachers and parents that the students have the ability to learn the material presented to them. However, making it work again would take a dedicated, caring conspiracy between teachers and parents. It would mean facing the tough reality that passing   *70* kids who haven't learned the material—while it might save them grief for the short term—dooms them to long-term illiteracy. It would mean that teachers would have to follow through on their threats, and parents would have to stand behind them, knowing their children's best interests are indeed at stake. This means no more doing Scott's assignments for him   *75* because he might fail. No more passing Jodi because she's such a nice kid.

validity
acceptance, judged as having value

semiliterate
having achieved an elementary level of reading and writing

trump card
the winning card; a key resource that gives someone an advantage

flustered
to become nervous

radical
departing from the usual

priority
greatest importance

testimony
a statement by a witness

Reflecting

Practice   After your reading, answer the following questions. Then share your responses with your classmates.

1. What is the author's main claim?

   _____

   _____

2. What evidence does she provide in support of her claim? Give at least two examples.

   _____

   _____

   _____

3. What opposing arguments, if any, are addressed? Does the writer concede or counter them?

   _____

   _____

   _____

4. How would you describe the writer's voice or tone? Does she engage readers or lecture them? Explain.

   _____

   _____

5. What questions do you still have about the claim?

   _____

   _____

6. How would you rate this essay and why?

   Weak ★ ★ ★ ★ ★ Strong

   _____

   _____

Vocabulary Practice

Identify Define the following words using context clues and your understanding of words parts. Also list the words or word parts that help you define each term. (See pages 34–37 and 668–676 for help.)

1. **impediments**   (line 20)

   clues: _____

   definition: _____

2. **composure**   (line 36)

   clues: _____

   definition: _____

3. **conspiracy**   (line 69)

   clues: _____

   definition: _____

Drawing Inferences

Explain Answer the following questions to help you draw inferences from the text. (See pages 30–32 for help.) Consider adding an observation of your own as well.

1. How does the writer's claim match up to your own thinking about the topic?

   _____

   _____

2. What is the strongest opposing argument that you can think of?

   _____

   _____

3. (Your own observation)

   _____

   _____

Writing

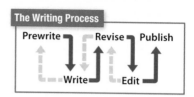

What follows are possible writing activities to complete in response to the reading. Use the writing process (pages 106–111) to help you develop your essay.

Prewriting

Chose one of the following ideas for your writing. Or decide upon an idea of your own making related to the reading.

Writing Ideas

1. **Writing to Learn:** Write a personal blog or journal entry in which you explore your effort (or lack of it) in your high school or college classes.

2. **Essay Writing:** Develop an argument for one of the claims that you identified on page 416.

3. Develop an argument for another debatable issue that you listed on page 406.

4. Rewrite your essay from pages 406–415 by reordering your supporting evidence or by adding a different opposing argument.

5. Write your own argumentative essay for the topic covered in one of the example essays in this chapter.

When planning . . .

Refer to pages 406–407 to help you plan your essay. Also use these planning tips.

- Choose a topic that is debatable and that truly interests you.
- Gather information and evidence that effectively supports your claim.
- Also consider questions the reader may have about the topic.

Writing and Revising

Refer to pages 408–411 to help you write and revise your first draft. Also use the tips that follow.

When writing . . .

- Review the essays in the chapter to see how the writers shaped their ideas.
- Use specific details to explain your ideas.
- Make a strong connection between the opening and closing parts of your essay.

When revising . . .

- Restate weak ideas, making them logical and clear.
- Add any missing key details about the topic.
- Ask yourself if you have engaged your reader.

Editing

Refer to the checklist on page 415 when you are ready to edit your work for style and correctness.

Andresr, 2013 / Used under license from Shutterstock.com

Reflecting on Argument Writing

Answer the following questions about your reading and writing experiences in this chapter.

1. What is the purpose of an argument essay—to inform, to persuade, to entertain, combination of purposes? Explain.

   _____

2. What is your favorite essay in this chapter and why?

   _____

3. What reading strategy seems the most helpful for reading this type of essay? Explain.

   _____

4. How does the writer's voice affect the impact of an argument essay?

   _____

5. What are the key parts of an argument essay?

   _____

6. What basic pattern of organization works well for an argument essay—chronological order, order of importance, logical order?

   _____

7. What do you like best about your argument essay?

   _____

8. What is one thing you would like to change in it?

   _____

Key Terms to Remember

When you read and write argument essays, it's important to understand the following terms.

- **Argumentation**—the process of proving the strength of a certain line of thinking
- **Persuasion**—the process of trying to convince an audience
- **Claim**—the position or thesis developed in an argument essay
- **Evidence**—the facts and details that support the claim
- **Counterarguments**—opposing positions or arguments

Part **III**:

Research

Part III: Research

15

> "Research is formalized curiosity.
> It is poking and prying with a purpose."
> —Zora Neale Hurston

Understanding Research

Who actually conducts research? The simple answer is that everyone does. One person may review reports about the latest cell phones before buying one. Another person may study different careers before choosing a college major. Still another may talk to experienced travelers before planning a trip.

In all of these cases, the people are truly interested in their topics and are pursuing information in their own ways. Of course, when you are assigned an academic research project, the situation is different. Your research must follow guidelines and time lines established by your instructor. Even so, the basic research process is still the same.

In this chapter, you will learn about a key aspect of the research process—using outside sources of information. The knowledge that you gain in this chapter will help you write effective research reports.

Learning Outcomes

LO1 Understand sources of information.

LO2 Evaluate sources of information.

LO3 Cite sources of information.

LO4 Avoid plagiarism.

LO4 Review responsible research.

What do you think?

What does Zora Neale Hurston mean above when she says that research is "poking and prying with a purpose"?

LO1 Understanding Sources of Information

Sources of information fall into two general categories: *primary sources* and *secondary sources*. Primary sources provide information that you collect directly, such as through firsthand experiences. Secondary sources provide information that you collect indirectly, such as through reading books and articles.

> "Research is creating new knowledge."
> —Neil Armstrong

Primary Sources

Listed here are several examples of primary sources of information. Each one involves you directly in the research process.

- Conducting interviews and surveys
- Making observations
- Attending presentations (art exhibits, museum displays, and so on)
- Gaining firsthand experience
- Studying original documents (court records, letters, journals, and so on)

Secondary Sources

Listed here are several examples of secondary sources of information. Each one involves you indirectly in the research process, providing the thoughts and ideas of others.

- Reference books
- Nonfiction books
- Periodicals (magazines and journals)
- Newspapers
- Web sites

The Value of Primary and Secondary Sources

Primary sources of information offer direct meaningful involvement in the research process. Secondary sources enhance understanding by providing expert explanations and analyses of a topic. Your particular research assignment may require you to consult both primary and secondary sources.

Identify List examples of primary and secondary sources of information that you have used recently for academic as well as personal purposes. Share these researching experiences with your classmates.

Primary sources

Secondary sources

_____   _____

Using Primary Sources

Provided below is information about using two common types of primary sources—an interview and an observation.

Conducting Interviews

During an interview you either (1) talk in person with someone who knows about your topic, (2) communicate with someone by phone, or (3) email questions you would like answered by the person.

Advantage: Interviewing allows you to learn about your topic from an expert.

Disadvantage: Interviewing involves lots of preparation, from scheduling to preparing questions.

When conducting an interview, follow these guidelines.

1. **Schedule the interview**—in person, by phone, or online.
2. **List important questions to ask.** Arrange them in a sensible order.
3. **Be polite** during the interview.
4. **Give background information** about yourself and your research.
5. **Listen carefully** to the person's answers.
6. **Be prepared to reword a question** or to ask follow-up questions.
7. **Thank the person** for her or his help.
8. **Review your notes** and contact the person to clarify anything you are unsure about.

Making Observations

Some topics can be studied by watching people, places, events, and things in action. This is a seldom used but valuable form of research.

Advantage: Making observations allows you to experience your topic for yourself.

Disadvantage: Depending on the topic, it may be difficult to schedule or carry out an observation.

When making an observation, follow these guidelines.

1. **Know what you want to accomplish**—your goal.
2. **Learn about your topic** before you observe it.
3. **Get permission to observe** if a location or an event isn't open to the public.
4. **Come prepared with the proper equipment**—pens, notebook, camera, and so on.
5. **Record sights and sounds** as you experience them.
6. **Review your notes** to determine what you have learned.

Using Secondary Sources

Three main types of secondary sources include books, periodicals (magazines and newspapers), and Web sites. Provided below is important information about each type.

Books

Reference books and other nonfiction books are common sources of information. Both can play an important role during a research project.

Reference Books

Reference books are general sources of information, and they are available to you in print and online. Common reference books include encyclopedias, atlases, and almanacs.

Advantage: Reference books serve as a good starting point for research.

Disadvantage: Reference books contain only general information.

When using reference books, follow these guidelines.

1. **Learn about the structure of the reference;** also learn how additional sources of information are provided or indexed.
2. **Understand what the reference covers.**
3. **Use precise words in searches.** For example, the word "vegetarian" will lead to different information than the word "vegan" will.
4. **Take notes on your reading,** using an effective strategy. (See page 472.)
5. **Refer to these notes as needed** during your research.

Nonfiction Books

Nonfiction books have been traditionally a main source of information in college-level research projects. Books are storehouses of information about every sort of topic imaginable.

Advantage: Nonfiction books usually provide far more information about a topic than you will find in reference books.

Disadvantage: Some books may be out of date, and some authors may not be recognized authorities in a particular field of study.

Nonfiction Books (continued)

When using nonfiction books, follow these guidelines.

1. **Learn how the book is put together** and which parts seem important to your research.
2. **Use the reading process** to fully understand the text. (See pages 13–15.)
3. **Take careful notes,** using a proven strategy. (See page 472.)
4. **Identify the source** of your notes (title and author) and the page numbers of the information.
5. **Use quotation marks** to enclose words and ideas taken directly from the text. (See pages 209–210.)
6. **Refer to the notes** as needed during your research.

Periodicals

Periodicals are magazines and journals that are published on a regular basis (often weekly, monthly, or quarterly). Magazines usually focus on general areas of interest. Journals usually address professional areas of study.

> **Advantage:** Periodicals provide up-to-date information.
>
> **Disadvantage:** Magazine articles may be written by people who are not experts in the field; journal articles may be written in a scholarly style that is difficult to understand.

When using periodicals, follow these guidelines.

1. **Learn about the periodical**—its purpose, structure, and so on.
2. **Use the reading process** to fully understand the text. (See pages 13–15.)
3. **Take careful notes,** using a proven strategy. (See page 472.)
4. **Identify the source of your notes** (title and author of the article, page number, title of the periodical, volume number, date).
5. **Use quotation marks to enclose** the exact words that you record. (See pages 209–210.)
6. **Refer to the notes** during your research.

Finding Articles

With so many periodicals available, it can be a challenge to find the most helpful articles. To get started, learn about the search tools your library offers.

Your library may subscribe to EBSCOhost, Lexis-Nexis, or another database service. Use a keyword search with one of these services to find articles on your topic. When you find promising articles, you may be able to print, save, or email them to yourself. If not, look for a print version. Check with your instructor or a librarian for help.

Practice   Learn about the procedure for finding periodicals in your school's library. Test the procedure for a topic of your choice.

Web Sites

The Internet will probably be one of the first places you turn to for beginning your research. Just make sure that it isn't the only place you turn to. Your instructors may, in fact, limit the number of Internet sources you can cite in your research.

Advantage: The Internet provides a vast amount of information that is easy to access.

Disadvantage: The information load can be overwhelming, some sites are unreliable sources, and it's easy to get distracted as you browse the Web.

When using the Internet for research, follow these guidelines.

1. **Check with a librarian** for special online searching options, such as the Library of Congress, EBSCOhost (a database of newspapers, magazines, and journals), and national and state government sites.
2. **Know the basics of Internet searching,** such as using keywords. (See below.)
3. **Review a number of choices** before deciding which ones to use. Finding good information takes time.
4. **Check the reliability** of sites that interest you. (See page 433.)
5. **Take careful notes** (page 472) or annotate copies of the information. (See page 20.)
6. **Identify the key source of your information** (title of the article or Web page, author, name of the Web site, date of posting, and so on. (See page 436.)
7. **Refer to your notes as needed** during your research.

A Guide to Keyword Searching

The success of your Internet search depends on the quality of the keywords you use. Making simple changes to a keyword can provide completely different results.

1. Start by typing in your topic: *salmon, robotics.*
2. Add a word to call up pages containing any of the words: *wild salmon, home robotics.*
3. Enclose the phrase in quotation marks to call up just the pages containing that phrase: *"wild salmon."*
4. Use words such as *and* (+) or *not* (-) to narrow or focus your search: *salmon and harvesting, salmon not farmed,* and so on.

LO2 Evaluating Sources of Information

When you conduct research, be sure that your sources are reliable or trustworthy. The following information will help you check sources for reliability.

Experts and Other Primary Sources

Before deciding to interview an "expert," learn about the person. Does he or she have the education and experience to be an expert? Check with your instructor or a librarian if you are not sure. And during an interview, try to determine the quality of the person's responses.

Books and Other Print Materials

When selecting print material, learn about the author. Does she or he have the proper background? Check the material's publisher and the date of publication to make sure that the information comes from a reputable source and is current. Then, as you read, decide if the information seems fair and balanced, and raises no questions about its reliability. Checking with other sources will help you do this.

Telecasts and Broadcasts

When considering a TV or radio program, be aware that it may address a topic unfairly. Documentaries and straight news reports will be more reliable than certain talk-radio conversations. Always consider the show's intended audience, its sponsors, and the particular broadcaster's approach to news and current events.

Web Sites

Be sure that the author of a site (if identified) is reliable and respected in the field. Also check the type of site: government (.gov), education (.edu), and nonprofit (.org) sites often are more reliable than commercial (.com) sites. In addition, determine if the site presents current information that seems balanced and accurate. If you have questions about a site, check the information against other sources.

Identify Team up with a classmate to answer this question: What are the two most helpful tips on this page?

Special Challenge With the help of your partner, evaluate the effectiveness of two specific sources of information (Web site, magazine article, book) using the information above and on the previous pages as a guide. Share with your classmates what you have learned.

INSIGHT

The quality of a Web site's design or presentation is another clue for determining its reliability. A professional, error-free text with effective graphics is a good sign. Sites with poor design features, many grammatical errors, and broken links signal problems.

LO3 Citing Sources of Information

You must give credit to the sources of ideas or words that you use in your academic essays and reports. Doing so avoids *plagiarism*, which is using the words and thoughts of others without crediting them in your writing. (See pages 438–439.)

Academic research uses a number of different styles for citing sources. For example, the Modern Language Association (MLA) style is generally used for research in the humanities (literature, philosophy, and so on), and the American Psychological Association (APA) style is generally used for research in the social sciences (sociology, psychology, and so on). Check with your instructor before choosing a citation style.

Using MLA and APA Styles

Here are the basic guidelines for using the MLA and APA styles for crediting sources in the text of a research report.

Sources	MLA	APA
Work with one author	*Author name and page number* (Waye 27)	*Author name, year of publication, and page number* (Waye, 2008, p. 27)
Work with two (or three) authors	(Waye and Joniz 27) (Sams, Banks, and Ory 31)	(Waye & Joniz, 2008, p. 27) (Sams, Banks, & Ory, 2010, p. 31)
Work with four (or five) authors	(Waye et al. 27)	(Waye, Joniz, Damik, & Martin, 2008, p. 27)
Work with six or more authors	(Waye et al. 27)	(Waye et al., 2008, p. 27)
Author identified within the sentence	According to Mariah Waye, fishery expert, wild salmon need human help (27).	According to Mariah Waye, fishery expert, wild salmon need human help (2008, p. 27).
Work with no author specified	*First main word(s) of the title and page number* ("Salmon in Crisis" 27)	*First main word(s) of the title, date, and page number.* ("Salmon in Crisis," 2008, p. 27)
Work with no page number specified (as in a Web page)	*Author name only (or first main word[s] of title if no author is specified)* (Waye)	*Author name only (or first main word[s] of title if no author is specified), and date* (Waye, 2008)

Citing Sources Within a Report

You can learn more about basic documentation by studying the passages below from a research report, demonstrating first the MLA style and then the APA style.

MLA Style

Source is cited in the sentence.

According to the United States Consumer Product Safety Commission, almost 25,000 children ages five and under are treated in hospital emergency rooms each year as a result of shopping-cart injuries. The total number of injuries has, in fact,

Title only; this Web site names no author.

risen by more than 30 percent since 2000 ("Secure Children").

B. Potential Injuries

Shopping-cart injuries include cuts, bruises, fractures, internal injuries, and head injuries—even skull fractures. In fact, children have died as a result of shopping-cart falls (Smith

Four authors

et al. 161). For the sake of our customers, Jonesville Home Mart needs to take steps to ensure shopping-cart safety. . . .

C. Solutions

A solution to this problem comes from a sister store in

Single author

Anchorage, which has made safety its motto (Clepper 47). Like this store, Jonesville . . .

APA Style

According to the United States Consumer Product Safety Commission, almost 25,000 children ages five and under are treated in hospital emergency rooms each year as a result of

Online material with no page numbers specified

shopping-cart injuries (2009). The total number of injuries has, in fact, risen by more than 30 percent since 1985 ("Secure Children," 2009).

B. Potential Injuries

Shopping-cart injuries include cuts, bruises, fractures, internal injuries, and head injuries—even skull fractures. In fact, children have died as a result of shopping-cart falls (Smith,

Four authors

Dietrich, Garcia, & Shields, 2010, p. 161). For the sake of our customers, Jonesville Home Mart needs to take steps to ensure shopping-cart safety.

C. Solutions

A solution to this problem comes from a sister store in

Single author

Anchorage, which has made safety its motto (Clepper, 2010, p. 47). Like this store, Jonesville . . .

Creating a Source List

At the end of your report, you must list your sources—either a **works-cited list** (MLA) or a **references list** (APA)—so that your reader can locate them. In both the MLA and APA formats, any source listed must also be cited in your paper, and any source cited in your paper must appear in the source list.

What to Include

Whether your sources are books, magazine articles, pamphlets, or Web sites, the citations should include all of the following elements that are available:

1. **Author name(s)**
2. **Title** (When including two parts of a publication, list the smaller part first.)
   - "Book chapter" / *Book title*
   - "Magazine article" / *Magazine title*
   - "Web-site article" / *Web-site title*
3. **Publication facts** (the date, the place of publication, the publisher; or appropriate Web information)

How MLA and APA Styles Differ

	Author	Title	Publication Facts
MLA	Give the name as it appears on the title page.	Capitalize all important words (see page 630).	Place the date after the publication information, followed by the medium—Print, Web, CD–ROM, etc.
	Waye, Mariah S. *Environmental Watch: Salmon in Danger.* New York: Pudding Press, 2010. Print.		
APA	Use initials for the first and middle names.	Capitalize only the first word in a title, the first word in a subtitle, and any proper nouns. Capitalize titles of periodicals normally.	Place the date after the author's name.
	Waye, M. S. (2010). *Environmental watch: Salmon in danger.* New York, NY: Pudding Press.		

---

works-cited list
list of sources prepared according to MLA style

references list
list of sources prepared according to APA style

MLA Style

Works Cited

Magazine article

Clepper, Irene. "Safety First: Alaska Retailer Attracts Customers
with Safe-and-Sound Seminars." *Playthings* 97 (2010): 46-47.
Print.

Web article

"Secure Children Properly in Shopping Carts." Texas Medical
Center. 2009. Web. 22 Sept. 2010.

Book

Shelov, Steven P., ed. *Caring for Your Baby and Young Child: Birth to
Age 5.* 5th ed. New York: Bantam, 2009. Print.

Article, four authors

Smith, Gary A., et al. "Injuries to Children Related to Shopping
Carts." *Pediatrics* 97 (2010): 161-65. Print.

APA Style (for the same sources)

References

Clepper, I. (2010). Safety first: Alaska retailer attracts customers
with safe-and-sound seminars. *Playthings, 97,* 46-47.

Secure children properly in shopping carts. (2009). Retrieved
September 22, 2010, from http://www.tmc.edu/tmcnews/
06_15_00/page_16.html

Shelov, S. P. (Ed.). (2009). *Caring for your baby and young child: Birth
to age 5.* New York, NY: Bantam.

Smith, G. A., Dietrich, A., Garcia, T., & Shields, B. (2010). Injuries
to children related to shopping carts. *Pediatrics, 97,* 161-165.

INSIGHT ―――――――――――――――――――――――――
See the report on pages 464–466 for a complete research report using
MLA documentation style. A research report using APA style requires
a title page and an abstract, a brief summary of the report that readers
can review to see if the material is of interest to them.

LO4 Avoiding Plagiarism

The article below and the explanations on the following page demonstrate different types of plagiarism. Use this information as a guide to check your own work and to avoid plagiarizing the sources you've used.

People in Need

On a chilly February afternoon, an old man stands on a city sidewalk and leans against a fence. In his hands a sign reads: "Will work for food. Please help!" Imagine, for a moment, the life this man leads. **He probably spends his days alone on the street begging for handouts, and his nights searching for shelter from the cold. He has no job, no friends, and nowhere to turn.**

wrangler, 2013 / Used under license from Shutterstock.com

Most Americans would like to believe that cases like this are rare. However, the National Coalition for the Homeless estimates that as many as 3 million people in this country share this man's condition. Who are these people we call "the homeless," and what factors have contributed to their plight?

According to Pastor Joel Warren, the director of the Greater Mission Shelter in San Angela, most of the homeless are unemployed males, and from 40 to 60 percent have alcohol or drug-related problems. Warren notes that the image of the typical homeless person is changing. He says that the average age of the homeless has dropped from fifty-five to thirty in the last ten years. National studies have also shown that this population is changing.

A recent study by the United States Conference of Mayors found that one-third of the homeless population consists of families with small children, and 22 percent of the homeless have full- or part-time jobs. Statistics seem to show that more and more of the homeless are entire families who have simply become the victims of a bad economy.

Common Types of Plagiarism

The highlighted examples of plagiarism below are linked to the original article on page 438 from which the information was taken.

Copying Text

A writer includes sentences word-for-word from the original source without giving credit.

> It's not hard to imagine what life is like for a homeless person. **He probably spends his days alone on the street begging for handouts, and his nights searching for shelter from the cold. He has no job, no friends, and nowhere to turn.** Such a life is becoming all too familiar to many because of the poor economy.

Forgetting Quotation Marks

A writer includes the exact words from a source without enclosing them in quotation marks.

> Many people have no real connection with a homeless man like the one just described, and so they do not think much about this serious problem. In "People in Need," Anna Morales states that **most Americans would like to believe that cases like this are rare. However, the National Coalition for the Homeless estimates that as many as 3 million people share this man's condition.** Still, many of us seem to live in places far removed from the homeless.

Restating Ideas Without Citing Them

A writer restates a specific passage from an original article or book without identifying the source.

> **The economy has changed the profile of the homeless population. Studies indicate that families with young children now make up more than 30 percent of this population. In addition, more and more homeless have part-time or full-time jobs.**

LO5 Reviewing Responsible Research

Answer the questions below to review the concepts covered in this chapter.

Understand Sources of Information   Define or explain the two types of sources and the particular advantage, or value, of each. See pages 428–432.)

- Primary Sources

  _____

- Secondary sources

  _____

Explain two possible problems with using the Internet for research. (See page 432.)

_____

_____

Evaluate Sources of Information   Explain how you can determine the reliability of two of the following sources: an expert, a book, a TV program, a Web site. (See page 433.)

_____

_____

Cite Sources of Information   Explain what it means to cite sources of information within your writing. (See pages 434–437.)

_____

_____

Identify the two common documentation styles. (See page 434.)

_____

What is a source list, and what is its purpose? (See page 436.)

_____

Avoid Plagiarism   Define the term "plagiarism." (See pages 438–439.)

_____

Explain how you can avoid plagiarism in your writing. (See page 439.)

_____

16

Vladkol, 2013 / Used under license from Shutterstock.com

"There is a great difference between knowing and understanding; you can know a lot about something and not really understand it."
—Charles F. Kettering

Summarizing

You learned earlier in this text that writing about your reading assignments is one of the best ways to understand them. (See page 26.) The physical act of writing—recording one word after another—brings your thoughts into focus. So when you write about your reading, you are bringing the ideas in the text into focus. Academic reading and writing go hand in hand: Reading introduces new information, and writing about it helps you learn and understand it.

Summarizing a reading assignment is an especially effective form of writing to learn. It is the process of identifying and explaining the most important ideas in the text. Writing a summary tells you how well you understand the material and also helps you remember what you have read. Along with taking notes and recording your personal thoughts and feelings, summarizing is an excellent way of becoming actively involved in your reading.

Learning Outcomes

LO1 Understand summarizing.
LO2 Learn reading strategies.
LO3 Read and react to a summary.
LO4 Write a summary.
LO5 Practice additional summary writing.

What do you think?

Charles F. Kettering says there is a difference between knowing and understanding. What do you think he means by this? Do you agree with him?

LO1 Understanding Summarizing

When you write a summary, you should use your own words, except for any specific, essential words or ideas from the text. Share the main ideas and leave out the details and examples. Your purpose is to report the basic meaning of the reading, offering a sense of the whole rather than a detailed look at the parts.

In one way you practice summarizing every day in conversations with friends, coworkers, and family members. For example, when you talk about a movie, an athletic event, or a concert, you summarize or highlight the most important points using your own words. Summary writing is something like making maple-sugar candy. After boiling the sap, you are left with a rich maple syrup. And after boiling the syrup, you finally get the crystalline maple-sugar candy. This is a reduction process. And that is essentially the process that you follow when you write a summary—reducing a longer piece of writing to its crystalline form.

> "I hear and I forget; I see and I remember; I write and I understand."
> —Chinese Proverb

Summary Versus Paraphrase

A paraphrase, also written in your own words, does not reduce a text to its basic meaning. Rather, it explains the full meaning of a challenging reading. Because a paraphrase often includes explanations or interpretations, it can actually be longer than the original. A summary, by contrast, provides a brief explanation of the main ideas in the text and should be about one-third the length of the original.

Identify Telling friends about a movie is one example of informal summarizing. List three or four other examples of summaries that commonly occur in your conversations.

1. _____

2. _____

3. _____

4. _____

INSIGHT

A typical one- or two-page essay can be summarized in one well-formed paragraph. The first sentence in a summary is the topic sentence. The sentences that follow must support the topic sentence.

Reading

Summarizing is an important learning tool in all of your class work, especially for report and research assignments. But to summarize a text, you need to understand it in its original form. The strategies below will help.

LO2 Learning Reading Strategies

Using a Table Diagram

Part of the challenge when reading a text is keeping track of the main idea and key supporting points. A graphic organizer called a table diagram works well for this purpose. Identify the thesis, or main idea, of the reading on the table top and list the key supporting points underneath. Then refer to this information as you write a summary of the text.

Table Diagram

Thesis or main idea

supporting points	supporting points	supporting points	supporting points

Understanding the Structure of Writing

Most informational texts are shaped in the following way: The first part introduces the topic and states the thesis or main idea. The middle paragraphs support and develop the thesis. The closing part usually reviews what has been said and may offer an additional idea or two. Keeping this structure in mind should help you find the key information in a text.

Beginning

Middle

Ending

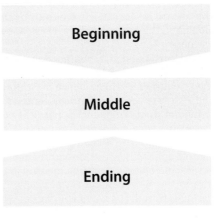

ajt, 2013 / Used under license from Shutterstock.com

LO3 Reading and Reacting to a Summary

In order to read and react to a summary, you must first read and react to the original text. The text below is followed by a model summary.

Read   Read this excerpt from an article entitled "Religious Faith Versus Spirituality" by Neil Bissoondath. In this passage, the author defines and explores spirituality. Use the reading process to help you fully understand the text. (See pages 13–15.)

About the Author
Neil Bissoondath is an award-winning author who was born in Trinidad and later immigrated to Canada. He was born into the Hindu tradition but is not a religious person.

Religious Faith Versus Spirituality

Spirituality is the individual's ability to wonder at, and delight in, the indecipherable, like a baby marveling at the wiggling of its own toes. It is to be at ease with speculation, asking the unanswerable question and accepting that any answer would necessarily be incomplete, even false. It is recognizing that if scientific inquiry has inevitable limits, so too do religious explanations, which base themselves on unquestioning acceptance of the unprovable: neither can ever fully satisfy. *1*

A sense of the spiritual comes from staring deep into the formation of a rose or hibiscus and being astonished at the intricate delicacy of its symmetry without needing to see behind its perfection of form the fashioning hand of a deity. *10*

It comes from watching your child being born and gazing for the first time into those newly opened eyes, from holding that child against your chest and feeling his or her heartbeat molding with yours.

It comes from gazing up into the sparkling solitude of a clear midnight sky, secure in the knowledge that, no matter how alone you may feel at moments, the message of the stars appears to be that you most indisputably are not. *15*

At such moments, you need no dogma to tell you that the world seen or unseen, near or distant, is a wonderful and mysterious place. Spirituality, then, requires neither science nor religion, both of which hunger after answers and reassurance—while the essence of spirituality lies in the opening up of the individual to dazzlement. Spirituality entails no worship. *20*

At the very moment of my mother's cremation, her brother, trapped thousands of miles away in England by airline schedules, got out his photographs of her and spread them on his coffee table. He reread her old letters and spent some time meditating on the life that had been lived—his way, at the very moment flames consumed her body, of celebrating the life and saying farewell, his way of engaging with the spiritual. *25*

Neil Bissoondath, "Religious Faith Versus Spirituality." Reprinted by permission of the author.

Reflect   Answer the questions below about the passage on page 444. Then discuss your responses with your classmates.

1. What is the main idea or thesis of the text? In what part of the text is it stated? (See pages 52–64.)

_____

2. What key points in the middle paragraphs explain or develop the thesis? Consider listing them on a table diagram. (See page 443.)

Table Diagram			
Thesis or main idea			
supporting points	supporting points	supporting points	supporting points

3. How does the closing paragraph demonstrate the author's definition of spirituality?

_____

4. How would you rate this passage and why?

   Weak ★ ★ ★ ★ ★ Strong

_____

5. What questions, if any, do you still have about the topic?

_____

Drawing Inferences

Explain   Answer the questions below to help you draw inferences from the text. (See pages 30–32 for help.)

1. What conclusions can you draw about the author? Do you think he is a scientist, a religious man, a free thinker, a man with a lot of uncertainty?

_____

2. According to the author, how do science and religion have limits?

_____

Read   Carefully read the following summary of the text about spirituality. Notice that it is not more than one-third the length of the original text.

Summary of the Text

In this passage from "Religious Faith Versus Spirituality," author Neil Bissoondath explores spirituality. He says that a spiritual person marvels at life and understands that science and religion do not have all the answers. In the same way, a spiritual person needs no scientific explanations or regular worship to know that the world is magical. According to Bissoondath, spirituality shows itself in many ways, as in enjoying the beauty of flowers. Upon the death of the author's mother, an uncle, who was unable to attend the cremation, demonstrated his spirituality by meditating about his sister and her life.

Reflect   Answer the following questions about the summary. Then share your responses with your classmates.

1. What main idea is provided in the topic sentence of the summary?

2. What supporting information is provided in the body or middle sentences? Name three ideas.

3. What idea is provided in the closing sentence?

4. What details, if any, would you add or take out? Explain. (See your answer to the second question on page 445.)

5. Does the writer of the summary use his own words for the most part? If so, why do you think this is important?

6. Does the summary help you understand the original passage? Explain.

INSIGHT

When you are writing a summary for a report or research paper, make a note of the original source (title of the text, author, page number, and so on). This will make it easier for you to acknowledge or cite the source in your actual report. (See pages 434–435.)

LO4 Writing a Summary

In this part of the chapter, you will write a summary of your own following the guidelines presented in this section.

Read To get started, read and react to the article below by Roper Seip. Use the reading process to help you gain a complete understanding of the text. (See pages 13–15.)

About the Author

A former stand-up comedian, **Roger Seip** is now a nationally known motivational speaker for organizations such as Harley Davidson, Northwestern Mutual, and the National Association of Realtors. This article comes from the "Freedom Personal Development Blog" at www.deliverfreedom.com.

Sorry, What's Your Name Again? 6 Steps to Relieve the Most Common Memory Worry

If you live in fear of forgetting people's names, sometimes within mere seconds of being introduced to them, you're not alone. Surveys show that 83% of the population worries about their inability to recall people's names. Ironically, while most of us hate having our names forgotten or mispronounced, the majority of us claim we just "aren't good at remembering names" or putting faces together with names when we meet people again.

If you have difficulty recalling names, you know that the two most common scenarios are forgetting the name instantaneously upon being introduced to someone new, and failing to recall the name of someone you've met and interacted with in the past and should know but just can't pull up from your memory bank.

Forgetting names becomes more than just an embarrassing social faux pas in sales. Straining to recall a name can so preoccupy you that you are unable to fully pay attention to your client or prospect. He or she may perceive you not only as unfocused and easily distracted, but also as not very bright if you're unable to devote your full attention to him or her. Even worse, if you forget the name of a client with whom you've worked in the past, he or she may view your memory lapse as a betrayal of trust, which can cost you a great deal of money if that client severs the relationship.

Integrating Learning Styles to Improve Name Recall

While common, this frustrating phenomenon of forgetting names can be relatively easy to overcome when you commit to taking steps to improve your memory. The most important key to really effective learning 25 of any kind is understanding that there are three learning styles: visual, **auditory**, and kinesthetic (physically interactive). The more you can apply all three of these styles to a task, the more quickly and solidly you will learn anything.

Practice each of the following steps to improve your name recollection 30 in every sales and social situation.

1. When you're first introduced to someone, look closely at his or her face and try to find something unique about it. Whether you find a distinctive quality or not is **irrelevant**; by really looking for a memorable characteristic in a new face, you're incorporating 35 the visual learning style. And a word of advice: if you do find something that really stands out about someone's face, don't say anything! Within minutes of meeting someone new, it's generally a bad idea to exclaim, "Whoa! That's a huge nose!"

2. The next step **utilizes** both auditory and kinesthetic learning 40 styles. When you meet someone, slow down for five seconds, and concentrate on listening to him or her. Focus on the prospect and repeat his or her name back in a conversational manner, such as "Susan. Nice to meet you, Susan." Also make sure to give a good firm handshake, which establishes a physical connection with the 45 prospect.

3. Creating a mental picture of someone's name incorporates the visual sense again. Many people have names that already are pictures: consider Robin, Jay, Matt, or Dawn to name just a few. Some names will require you to play with them a bit to create 50 a picture. Ken, for example, may not bring an immediate image to your mind, but a "can" is very close. Or you might envision a Ken doll. The point is not to create the best, most creative mental image ever, so don't get caught up in your head during this step of the process, thinking, "Oh, that's not a very good picture. What's a 55 better one?" The worst thing you can do when learning is to stress yourself out and overthink the process. If an image doesn't come to you right away, skip it and do it later. You'll undo all of your good efforts if you're staring dumbly at your prospect, insisting, "Hey. Hold still for a minute while I try to turn your name into a 60 picture!"

4. Once you've identified a mental image that you associate with a person's name, the next step is to "glue" that image to the person's face or upper body. This bridges the gap many people experience between being able to recall faces but not the names that belong 65 to those faces. If you met a new prospect named Rosalind, for example, you might have broken her name down into the memorable image of "rose on land." Now you must create a mental picture that will stick with you as long as you need it and pop into your head every time you meet her; this should be something fun, 70 even a little odd, that will bring "rose on land" to mind when you see her face. You might imagine her buried up to her neck in earth, with roses scattered around her, for example. Because you created the image, it will come up next time you see her and enable you to recall her name. 75

5. At the end of the conversation, integrate auditory learning by repeating the prospect's name one more time, but don't ever overuse someone's name in an effort to place it more firmly in your mind. Use the prospect's name only right at the beginning of the conversation, and then again at the end; if you feel like you can 80 do so naturally, you might insert someone's name once or twice in a natural fashion during the course of the conversation, too. But if you've ever had a **stereotypically** pushy salesperson use your name a dozen times in a five-minute conversation, you know how annoying, even weird, this can be, so don't overdo it. 85

6. Writing is a form of kinesthetic learning—you're getting a part of your body involved in the learning process—so if you're really serious about wanting to remember people's names for the long term, keep a name journal or a log of important people you meet, and review it periodically. 90

Roger Seip, "Sorry, What's Your Name Again? 6 Steps to Relieve the Most Common Memory Worry," *Freedom Personal Development Blog*, July 27, 2009. www.deliverfreedom.com

auditory
involving hearing
irrelevant
not applicable

utilize
to put to use
stereotypically
conforming to a general
pattern or characteristic

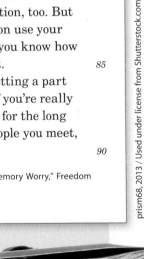

Reflect   Answer the following questions about the reading. Your responses to these questions will help you write your summary.

1. What is the main idea or thesis of the text? (See pages 52–64.)

   _____

2. What key points in the middle paragraphs explain or develop the thesis? Consider listing them on a table diagram. (See page 443.)

Table Diagram			
Thesis or main idea			
supporting points	supporting points	supporting points	supporting points

3. How does the structure of the text help you identify the key points?

   _____

4. How would you rate this essay and why?

   Weak ★ ★ ★ ★ ★ Strong

   _____

Vocabulary Practice

Identify   Define the following words by using context clues and your understanding of word parts. Also list the clues or word parts that help you define each term. (See pages 34–37 and 668–676.)

1. **incorporating**   (line 35)

   _____

2. **integrate**   (line 76)

   _____

3. **periodically**   (line 90)

   _____

Writing Guidelines

The following guidelines will help you write a paragraph summary of an essay or extended passage.

Planning Your Summary

Most of your prewriting and planning will occur when you read and react to the text. During your planning . . .

- Name the thesis or main idea of the text.
- Identify the key points that support the thesis.

> **INSIGHT**
>
> In academic texts, each middle paragraph often addresses one key supporting point. This point is usually stated in the topic sentence.

Writing the First Draft

Remember that you are writing a paragraph, starting with a topic sentence and following with supporting ideas. As you write your first draft . . .

- Use your own words as much as possible.
- Start with a topic sentence, naming the title, author, and topic of the text.
- Continue with the key points that explain the thesis. (Avoid specific details.)
- Arrange your ideas in the most logical order.
- Add a closing sentence, if one seems necessary.

Revising the Writing

Remember that your summary should address just the essential information from the original text. As you review your first draft . . .

- Determine if it identifies the main idea of the text.
- Decide if you've limited yourself to key supporting information.
- See if your summary reads smoothly and logically.
- Determine if you've used your own words, except for key ideas. (See the next page.)

Editing the Writing

Be sure that your summary is clear and accurate if you are turning it in for evaluation. As you edit your revised summary . . .

- Check that you've used complete sentences.
- Check for spelling, capitalization, and punctuation errors. Pay special attention to titles and quoted material. (See the next page.)
- Check for proper usage and grammar. (See pages 483–661.)

Write Write a paragraph summary of the text on pages 447–449, using the information above as a guide. Be prepared to refer to the original text many times as you develop your writing.

A CLOSER LOOK at Revising and Editing

Revising

The information that follows will help you check your summary for (1) recognizing the source and (2) identifying exact ideas from the text.

Recognizing the Source Follow your instructor's guidelines for identifying the source of your summary (if you are turning it in for evaluation). The following example shows you how to identify the title and author in the topic sentence of your summary.

- In this passage from "Religious Faith Versus Spirituality," author Neil Bissoondath explores spirituality. . . .

Identifying Exact Ideas from the Text In your summary, you may find it necessary to include a few exact ideas or specialized words from the original text. When this type of information is taken directly from the text, enclose it within quotation marks.

- **Exact idea:** The author describes himself as "soaring with a lightness I'd never known before" after the ceremony.
- **Specialized word:** One teacher recognized as a master teacher serves as a "standard-bearer" for all great teachers.

Editing

This information will help you correctly capitalize and punctuate titles and quoted materials.

Capitalizing Titles Capitalize the first and last words in a title and all important words in between. Do not capitalize words such as *a, for, by, in, and,* and *the* if they occur within the title. (See pages 630–631 and 632–633 for more.)

- **Title:** Chinese Space, American Space *(All the words are important so they are all capitalized.)*
- **Title:** Catcher in the Rye *("In" and "the" occur within the title so they are lowercased.)*

Punctuating Titles Use quotation marks to set off the titles of chapters, essays, articles, and so on. Italicize or underline the titles of books, magazines, newspapers, Web sites, and so on.

- **Title of an Essay:** "Chinese Space, American Space"
- **Title of a Book:** *Catcher in the Rye*

Placement of Other Punctuation Place commas and periods inside quotation marks. Place question marks or exclamation marks inside the quotation marks when they punctuate the quotation and outside when they punctuate the sentence.

- **Placement of a Comma:** In this passage from "Religious Faith Versus Spirituality," author Neil Bissoondath explores spirituality. *(Commas and periods are always placed inside the quotation marks.)*

- **Placement of a Question Mark:** The essay "Yes, Accidents Happen. But Why?" analyzes the causes of accidents. *(The question mark punctuates the quotation, so it is placed inside the quotation marks.)*

- Have you read "Spanglish Spoken Here"? *(The question mark punctuates the entire sentence, so it is placed outside the quotation marks.)*

Check Be sure to use the information on these two pages to help you revise and edit your summary, correctly capitalizing and punctuating titles and quoted material.

carlosseller, 2013 / Used under license from Shutterstock.com

LO5 Practicing Additional Summary Writing

This section includes two texts that you can use for additional summary-writing practice. Always read and react to the text before writing your summary.

First Text

`Read` Read the following passage from a health text entitled *An Invitation to Health* by Dianne Hales. In this passage, Hales explores weight-loss diets. Use the reading process to help you understand the text. (See pages 13–15.)

Weight-Loss Diets

The diet debates over low-fat versus low-carbohydrate versus high-protein have raged for years. Which is best? Several studies over recent years found little difference in the ultimate results. The largest-ever controlled study of dietary methods reached a clear conclusion: It doesn't matter whether you count **carbohydrates**, protein, or fat—as long as you eat less.   *1*   *5*

In the study, more than 800 overweight men and women were assigned to one of four diets, each loosely based on popular weight-loss programs, such as the Atkins high-protein diet and Dean Ornish's low-fat approach. Here is how they compared in terms of **macronutrients**:   *10*

- High fat, high protein: 40 percent fat, 25 percent protein, 35 percent carbohydrates.

- High fat, modified protein: 40 percent fat, 15 percent protein, 45 percent carbohydrates.

- Low fat, high protein: 20 percent fat, 25 percent protein, 55 percent carbohydrates.   *15*

- Low fat, average protein: 20 percent fat, 15 percent protein, 65 percent carbohydrates.

Each participant consumed about 750 calories less than normal, but all ate at least 1,200 calories a day. After six months every diet group had lost about the same amount of weight, regardless of the weight-loss plan,   *20* for an average of 13 pounds per person. About 15 percent lost more than 10 percent of their body weight by the end of the two-year study. Those who lost the most attended more counseling sessions and followed the diets *25* more closely than others.

Most of the dieters regained some of the weight they shed, although on average the volunteers were nine pounds lighter and their waistlines two inches smaller at the end of two years. They also reduced their risk factors for cardiovascular disease and diabetes. *30*

Although people lose weight on any diet that helps them eat less, most dieters lose only about 5 percent of their initial weight. However, even a modest weight loss can lower **cardiovascular** risk factors, such as blood pressure, total cholesterol, and elevated blood **glucose**.

From Hales, *An Invitation to Health*, 7E. © 2012 Cengage Learning.

carbohydrates
one component of food that includes sugars, starches, and fibers

macronutrients
the three main components of food: protein, carbohydrates, and fats

cardiovascular
of, relating to, or involving the heart and the blood vessels

glucose
the main type of sugar in the blood and the main source of energy for the body's cells

Reflect Answer the questions below about the text on pages 454–455. Then discuss your responses with your classmates.

1. What is the main idea or thesis of the text? (See pages 52–64.)

_____

2. What key points in the middle paragraphs explain or develop the thesis? Consider using a table diagram to list these points. (See page 443.)

Table Diagram			
Thesis or main idea			
supporting points	supporting points	supporting points	supporting points

3. How would you rate this text and why?

   Weak ★ ★ ★ ★ ★ Strong

_____

4. What did you learn about the topic? Name at least two things.

_____

5. What questions, if any, do you still have about the topic?

_____

Drawing Inferences

Explain Answer the following questions to help you draw inferences from the text. (See pages 30–32 for help.)

1. What makes the dieting process so frustrating?

_____

2. Why are there so many diets to choose from?

_____

Write Write a summary of this text, using your responses above and the information on page 451 as a basic guide.

Second Text

Read   Read the following passage from *Living in the Environment* by G. Tyler Miller, Jr., and Scott E. Spoolman. In this passage, the authors explore the democratic process in relation to decisions made about the environment. Use the reading process to help you understand the text. (See pages 13–15.)

Democracy Does Not Always Allow for Quick Solutions

Democracy is government by the people through elected officials and representatives. In a *constitutional democracy,* a constitution (a document recording the rights of citizens and the laws by which a government functions) provides the basis of government authority and, in most cases, limits government power by **mandating** free elections and guaranteeing the right of free speech.

Political institutions in most constitutional democracies are designed to allow gradual change that ensures economic and political stability. In the United States, for example, rapid and destabilizing change is curbed by a system of **checks and balances** that distributes power among three branches of government—*legislative, executive,* and *judicial*—and among federal, state, and local governments.

In passing laws, developing budgets, and formulating regulations, elected and appointed government officials must deal with pressure from many competing **special-interest groups**. Each of these groups advocates passing laws, providing subsidies or tax breaks, or establishing regulations favorable to its cause, while attempting to weaken or repeal laws, subsidies, tax breaks, and regulations unfavorable to its position. Some special-interest groups such as corporations are profit-making organizations. Others are nongovernmental organizations (NGOs), most of which are nonprofit, such as labor unions and environmental organizations.

The design for stability and gradual change in democracies is highly desirable. But several features of democratic governments hinder their

ability to deal with environmental problems. For example, problems   *25*
such as climate change and **biodiversity** loss are complex and difficult to
understand. Such problems also have long-lasting effects, are interrelated,
and require integrated, long-term solutions that emphasize prevention.
But because local, state, and national elections are held as often as every
2 years, most politicians spend much of their time seeking reelection and   *30*
tend to focus on short-term, isolated issues rather than on long-term,
complex, and time-consuming problems.

One of our greatest challenges is to place more emphasis on long-term
thinking and policies and to educate political leaders and the public about
the need for long-range thinking and actions. Another problem is that   *35*
many political leaders, with hundreds of issues to deal with, have too little
understanding of how the earth's natural systems work and how those
systems support all life, economies, and societies. Again, there is an urgent
need to educate politicians and voters about these vital matters.

From Miller, *Living in the Environment*, 17E. © 2012 Cengage Learning.

mandating
requiring
checks and balances
a system that prevents any
one branch of government
from exerting too much
power

special-interest groups
groups, both profit-making
and nonprofit, who try to
influence public policy by
lobbying members of the
legislature

biodiversity
the number and variety of
organisms (forms of life)
found in a geographical
region

Reflect   Answer the questions below about the text on pages 457–458. Then discuss your responses with your classmates.

1. What is the main idea or thesis of the text? (See pages 52–64.)

_____

2. What key points in the middle paragraphs explain or develop the thesis? Consider listing them on a table diagram. (See page 443.)

Table Diagram

Thesis or main idea

supporting points	supporting points	supporting points	supporting points

3. How would you rate this text and why?

Weak ★ ★ ★ ★ ★ Strong

_____

4. What did you learn about the topic? Name at least two things.

_____

5. What questions, if any, do you still have about the topic?

_____

Drawing Inferences

Explain   Answer the following questions to help you draw inferences from the text. (See pages 30–32 for help.)

1. Why should you be glad that you live in a democracy?

_____

2. What reform may be necessary in the democratic process and why?

_____

Write   Write a summary of this text, using your responses above and the information on page 451 as a basic guide.

Reflecting on Summary Writing

Answer the following questions about your summary-writing experiences in this chapter.

1. Why is summary writing valuable?

   _____

2. How is careful reading connected to effective summary writing?

   _____

3. What are three important things to remember when writing a summary?

   _____

4. Which of the reading strategies is most helpful when it comes to aiding your summary writing? Explain.

   _____

5. What do you like most about the summary you wrote in this chapter? Explain.

   _____

6. What one thing would you like to change in your summary?

   _____

7. When will you use summary writing in the future?

   _____

Key Terms to Remember

When you write summaries, it's important to understand the following terms.

- **Summary**—the core of a text presented in a condensed form
- **Paraphrase**—a form of summary writing with explanations and interpretations; may be as long as or longer than the source text
- **Table diagram**—a graphic organizer for identifying the thesis and key supporting points in a text

17

> "Somewhere, something special
> is waiting to be known."
> —Carl Sagan

Research Report

Everyone has at least one favorite pastime or interest. You may, for example, have a special interest in hair design and enjoy talking about the latest styles with your friends. Or you may follow the NASCAR circuit and need little prompting to talk about the latest standings. Then again, you may be attracted to music, movies, gaming, or working out. Your choices are endless.

Writing a research report is a similar experience: A topic interests you, and after learning enough about it, you share what you have learned. While the research described in the first paragraph is pure enjoyment, the research you do for an assigned report may seem a little more like work. However, both types reward you with an understanding of the world around you.

In this chapter, you will read and react to a research report and then write one of your own. In the process, you will learn about a number of important strategies that will help you with research writing in all of your classes.

Learning Outcomes

LO1 Understand research.
LO2 Learn reading strategies.
LO3 Read and react to a research report.
LO4 Plan a research report.
LO5 Write a research report.
LO6 Revise and edit a report.

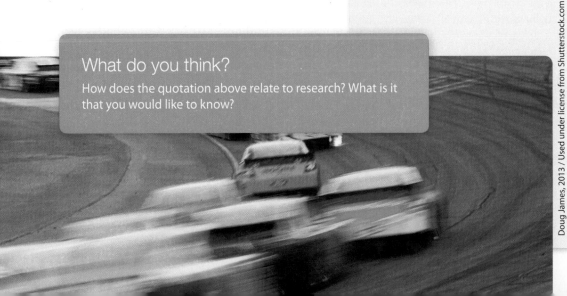

What do you think?

How does the quotation above relate to research? What is it that you would like to know?

LO1 Understanding Research

When an instructor asks you to write a research report, he or she is asking you to do two things: (1) become knowledgeable about a topic and (2) share this information in a clear, organized paper.

> "All my knowledge comes from research."
> —Stan Sakai

A research report is a carefully planned form of informational writing, usually two to three or more pages long. It will cite information from books, periodicals, Web sites, interviews, or observations following MLA, APA, or another recognized documentation style. (See pages 434–437.) It may also include graphics—charts, diagrams, maps, or photographs. Each instructor will have specific guidelines for researching your topic and compiling your report.

The Internet serves as an easy first source of information, accessing an unlimited number of resources almost immediately. Unfortunately, all of this information can overwhelm you. Effective research requires the ability to narrow your choices by recognizing the difference between quality and questionable sources of information. (See page 433.)

Since a research report is an extended writing assignment, it requires careful planning and patience. During the first part of the process, you need to learn about your topic. During the second part, you need to plan and write your report. Your instructor may provide a timetable for accomplishing your work; if not, you'll need to establish your own timetable. (See page 468.)

Research Report Versus Research Paper

In a research *report,* you collect, organize, and compile information about a topic. You share important facts and details from reliable sources in order to enhance or expand upon your own ideas. In a research *paper,* you select a topic that is open for debate, research it, and develop a position based on your own thinking and findings. In short, a research report shares information, and a research paper defends or develops a point of view. You will write both during your college career.

INSIGHT

While report writing is common in school, it is also common in the workplace. Depending on your job, you may be asked to write a marketing report, a budget report, a safety report, and so on. Such reports require careful research and clear writing.

Identify List two or three personal interests that you could discuss authoritatively with friends and classmates. Share your list with your classmates. Be prepared to identify a few interesting ideas related to one of these interests.

1. _____

2. _____

3. _____

Reading

Research reports, always full of information, require careful reading. The strategies that follow will help you gain a thorough understanding of the reports that you read.

LO2 Learning Reading Strategies

Using an Organized List

The purpose of reading a report is to learn about a particular topic. Using an organized list is one strategy that will help you keep track of all the supporting information. The graphic to the right shows how this simple strategy works.

Understanding the Writer's Approach

When reading a report, it may be helpful to understand the writer's basic approach. Often a writer presents information objectively, letting the facts and details speak for themselves. Sometimes a writer takes a subjective approach, including personal thoughts and feelings throughout. Objective reports are written in the third person (*he, she, it, they,* and so on), subjective reports in the first person (*I, me,* and *we*). These two passages show the difference:

Organized List

Report topic/thesis:

1. Main idea or topic sentence of the first middle paragraph
   + (Key supporting points)
   +
   +

2. Main idea or topic sentence of the second middle paragraph
   +
   +
   +

3. Main idea or topic sentence of the third middle paragraph (and so on)

Tip: If needed, add another level of detail under the (+) key supporting points introduced by another symbol (-).

- **Objective:** Squatters often live by simple, straightforward rules. Rule number one is keep the lights off to avoid being noticed. Rule number two is don't bother people when they are sleeping. Rule number three involves . . .

- **Subjective:** I chose to investigate a funeral home to cure myself of the grim-reaper syndrome. When I walked inside Vander Furniture Store/Funeral Home, I half expected to see a well-dressed, evil individual standing by a counter, sharpening his sickle . . .

INSIGHT

Writers who are especially involved in their research will likely include personal thoughts and feelings in their reports. Their reports may seem more like personal stories. However, both the subjective and the objective report have their place and value.

LO3 Reading and Reacting to a Research Report

Read Read the following report that explores a new form of agriculture called vertical farming. The report follows MLA documentation style. Use the reading process to help you fully appreciate and understand the text. (See pages 13–15.)

Steifle 1

Maurice Steifle
Professor Dakota Hinton
Life Sciences 101
19 February 2012

> **The title is centered.**

Agriculture Must Grow Up

> **The opening paragraph includes a thesis statement.**

Imagine living in the middle of New York City, right next to a farm. This farm is located in a skyscraper made of stacked greenhouses. And you can shop there for fresh fruits and vegetables. Does this sound unrealistic? It isn't. It's a real possibility, considering recent developments in agriculture. Vertical farms may be a main source of fresh food for city dwellers in the future.

> **The paper is double spaced throughout.**

A key spokesperson for vertical farming is Dickson Despommier, a professor at Columbia University in New York City. At *Verticalfarm.com,* he talks about new agricultural techniques. By 2050, 80 percent of all people will live in cities, and the world's population will have increased by 3 billion. To feed everyone will require a lot of new farmland. A logical solution is to farm vertically in urban areas, right where the food is needed. In his book *The Vertical Farm,* the professor proposes stacked greenhouses for growing food (Despommier 3-9).

> **Middle paragraphs give details to support the thesis statement.**

The *Economist* reports that vertical farming makes good sense. First of all, vertical farms need no soil. Crops are grown hydroponically, in a solution of essential minerals dissolved in water. The roots of plants absorb nutrients directly from this liquid. Second, since crops are grown in a controlled environment, few pesticides or herbicides are needed. That's good news for the environment. Third, everything is recycled, so vertical farming uses far less water and nutrients than

Steifle 2

traditional farms use. Finally, vertical farms will provide food to local areas, which saves on transportation costs ("Does It Really Stack Up?").

Two key technologies already exist for vertical farming— greenhouses and hydroponics. The *Economist* mentions a number of experiments already in place. For example, the South Pole Growth Chamber is a semi-automated hydroponic facility that produces food for scientists and technicians working in Antarctica. The Science Barge in New York has also been growing food hydroponically ("Does It Really Stack Up?"). Another example is Plantlab, a 10-year-old company in the Netherlands that has grown strawberries, corn, and beans on three floors, all underground (Kretschmer and Kollenberg).

Closer to home, Joe Heineman and Johanna Hearron-Heineman have been growing butter lettuce on two floors of an old building in Racine, Wisconsin. As the *Milwaukee Journal Sentinel* reports, the couple uses treated wastewater from tilapia fish tanks to grow the lettuce. In this building, they hope to produce the same amount of lettuce that would take 40 acres of traditional farmland to grow. The couple also wants to grow a half million pounds of tomatoes in a rooftop greenhouse (Herzog).

The idea of vertical farming on a grand scale, however, still needs work. There are no stacked greenhouses yet, as Despommier has envisioned them. As a matter of fact, environmental scientists and engineers have serious questions about the efficiency of vertical farming.

The *Economist* explains one main concern: "Light has to be very tightly controlled to get uniform production of very high-quality food," says British engineer Peter Head. Often this means using expensive artificial light. Dr. Ted Caplow, a pioneer in rooftop greenhouses, believes vertical farming will work only if it uses natural light ("Does It Really Stack Up?"). Vertical farms also need power for heating and cooling. In Racine, the Heinemans say that lighting and temperature control

---

Text cues indicate where borrowed ideas begin.

Parenthetical citations show the sources of borrowed ideas.

The exact words of a source are placed in quotation marks.

Steifle 3

are expensive. It costs 40 cents worth of electricity for every head of lettuce, which sells for $1.50. Joe Heineman hopes to cut this cost in half (Herzog). As it is, the electric bill for vertical farming could wipe out the savings in transportation costs.

The *Economist* mentions ideas for addressing these concerns. In single-story structures, for example, movable trays can give plants the best exposure to natural and artificial light. The magazine also shares Dr. Caplow's idea for farming in existing multistory buildings: "plants growing around edges of the building, sandwiched between two glass layers and rotating on a conveyor." Another idea is rooftop gardens, which get the best natural light, as Peter Head explains. Members of the Science Barge project have started a business to create a huge commercial rooftop farm in Queens. Powered by solar panels, it will produce 30 tons of vegetables per year ("Does It Really Stack Up?").

Whether urban farming ultimately follows the Despommier model or takes some other form, it looks like it will become an important part of the urban landscape. What the pioneers in the field learn today may lead to multileveled, integrated systems that can feed large cities in a cost-effective way. Greenhouses may one day reach into the sky.

> The conclusion revisits the thesis statement.

Steifle 4

> A separate page lists works cited in the report.

> Sources are formatted with hanging indentation.

Works Cited

Despommier, Dickson. *The Vertical Farm*. New York: St. Martins, 2010. Print.

---. *Verticalfarm.com*. Np., n.d. Web. 31 Jan. 2012.

"Does It Really Stack Up?" *Economist* 11 Dec. 2010: 15-16. Print.

Herzog, Karen. "Urban Farm in Racine Is No Fish Tale." *Milwaukee Journal Sentinel* 15 July 2010: B3. Print.

Kretschmer, Fabian, and Malte E. Kollenberg, "Can Urban Agriculture Feed a Hungry World?" *Spiegel.de*. Spiegel Online, 22 July 2011. Web. 31 Jan. 2012.

Reflect Answer the questions below about the report on pages 464–466. Then discuss your responses with your classmates.

1. What is the main idea or thesis in this report? (See pages 52–64.)

   _____

2. How is the thesis supported or developed? Consider using an organized list to identify the key details in each middle paragraph. The number of key supporting points (+) may vary from paragraph to paragraph. (See page 463.)

Organized List
Report topic/thesis: _____
1. _____
+
+ + +
2. _____
+ + +
3. _____
+ + +

3. What is the main purpose of this report—to entertain, to inform, or to persuade?

   _____

4. For the most part, does the writer approach the topic objectively or subjectively? Explain. (See page 463.)

   _____

5. How would you evaluate the sources of information cited in this report? Are they up to date? Do they seem reliable? (See pages 433.)

   _____

6. How would you rate this report and why?

   Weak ★ ★ ★ ★ ★ Strong

   _____

7. What did you learn from this report? Name two important things.

   _____

8. What questions do you still have about the topic?

   _____

Writing

A research report requires a lots of planning, which takes time. You won't write an effective report if you wait until the last minute to start your work. Be sure to use the writing process to do your best work.

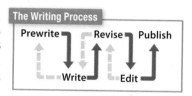

LO4 Planning a Research Report

In this section you will get ready to write, and your first tasks involve making a work schedule and selecting a topic.

Scheduling Your Work

Follow the schedule or timetable that your instructor provides. If you must make your own schedule, use the timetable below, as a guide. It gives you approximately three weeks to complete the assignment, but you may adjust the schedule as necessary.

Research Timetable

1. Prewriting and planning (4 or 5 days)

2. Writing the first draft (2 or 3 days)

3. Revising (3 days)

4. Editing (2 days)

5. Preparing a final copy (1 day)

Plan   Prepare a timetable for your report.

Research Timetable

1. _____

2. _____

3. _____

4. _____

5. _____

Selecting a Topic

Write your report about a new trend or development in energy, agriculture, technology, health, careers, or so on.

Identify For two or more of these categories, list three possible subjects for your report. One idea has been provided under each heading. (You may add other categories.)

energy	agriculture	technology	health	careers
wind power	vertical farming	tablet computers	concussions in sports	interior design

Choose Carefully review your lists of topics before choosing one. It may help to talk about your ideas with a classmate. Also consider the points below. Finally, circle the topic you want to write about.

Be sure that . . .

- the topic is well suited to your interests.
- the topic is neither too general nor too specific. (*Alternative energy sources* is too general; *biking to school* may be too specific.)
- you can find enough information about the topic.
- you have enough time to research and write about this topic.

Explain In a few sentences, explain the reason for your topic choice. Doing this will help you establish a focus for your research.

_____

_____

_____

Researching Your Topic

Effective research begins with questions that will direct you as you gather information about your topic.

Establishing a Starting Point

You can establish a starting point for your research by identifying what you already know about the topic and what you need to learn about it.

List   In a chart like the one below, list things that you already know about the topic and things you would like to find out.

Topic: _____	
Things I Know	**Things I Need to Find Out**

Forming Research Questions

As a guide for your research, turn your "Things I Need to Find Out" list into a series of questions. The following chart provides an example research question.

Topic: _Vertical Farming_	
Things I Need to Find Out	**Research Questions**
examples of vertical farming	Where is vertical farming being used?

Identify   Write four to six important questions about your topic. As you conduct your actual research, you may add more questions to your list, depending on what you discover.

Research Questions

_____

_____

_____

Identifying Your Sources

Once you have formed a series of questions, you can begin your research. Always follow your instructor's guidelines for the number and types of resources to consult. (See pages 434–437.) Whether you refer to books, periodicals, Web sites, or so on, determine first that your sources are current and reliable. (See page 433.)

Complete Fill in a chart like the one below with sources of information that seem promising for your research. (You may or may not use all of the different types listed below.) Include enough information—title, author, key page numbers, location, and so on—so that you can easily find or refer to each source. This list is often called a **preliminary bibliography.**

Sources for My Research Report

Web sites	
Articles (from journals, magazines, and newspapers)	
Books	
People to interview	
Places to visit	

INSIGHT

Plan any interviews and visits right away so that you can benefit from these valuable primary sources. (See page 429.)

preliminary bibliography an early list of resources for your research

beaucro, 2013 / Used under license from Shutterstock.com

Taking Notes

As you read and learn about your topic, take notes on key points and record important quotations. No matter what form your notes take—note cards, notebook, computer file—follow these guidelines.

- Write each question at the top of a note card or page of your notes.
- Number your note cards or pages to keep track of them.
- Take notes on key information that answers each question.
- Use your own words, except for direct quotations or special information.
- Write the source and the page number (if appropriate) of the information you record.

Sample Notes

Where is vertical farming being used?   ③

- a modified form in Racine (parts of two floors in an old building)
- Joe Heineman and Johanna Hearron-Heineman grow butter lettuce and raise tilapia.
- use treated fish water to nourish the lettuce (hydroponics)
- hope to produce lettuce same as 40 acres, also half mill. lbs. tomatoes on rooftop

Joe: "We're a green business." "Water is a scarce resource, and we use a tenth of what soil-based farms use."

Karen Herzog, "Urban Farm in Racine Is No Fish Tale." Milwaukee Journal Sentinel. July 15, 2010. B3.

Record Take notes as you read, following the guidelines above. Use you own words as much as possible. Put word-for-word quotations in quotation marks.

Focusing Your Research

After gathering information, you are ready to form a thesis statement and organize your notes before you begin writing your report.

Writing a Thesis Statement

A thesis or focus statement identifies the main point of your report and dictates the best way to organize the supporting information. The following formula will help you write this statement.

Topic		**Main Point About Topic**		**Thesis Statement**
Vertical farming	**+**	main source of food for future cities	**=**	Vertical farms may be a main source of fresh food for city dwellers in the future.

Form After reviewing your notes, write a thesis statement for your report using the formula above as a guide. If necessary, write two or three versions and then choose the best one.

Topic   **Main Point About Topic**   **Thesis Statement**

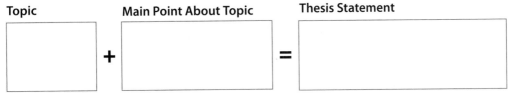

Organizing Your Notes for Writing

Next, organize your notes into groups that deal with each main supporting point. The information in the report on pages 464–466 was grouped into the following categories.

- spokesperson
- history
- advantages
- early experiments
- disadvantages
- alternatives

Name Identify the categories of supporting information for your report. *Remember:* Your main research questions basically become the key supporting points in your report.

Afterward, check the order of your categories. If they are not in the best or most logical order, rearrange them.

Creating an Outline

An outline serves as a blueprint for your report. It identifies the main ideas and details in the order that you want to include them in the body of your report. Outlines can be general or detailed, depending on your personal choice and your instructor's guidelines.

List your main ideas (categories) using Roman numerals (I, II, III), key supporting points using capital letters (A, B, C), and further details using numbers (1, 2, 3). Here is the first part of an outline for the report on pages 464–466.

I. A key spokesperson—Dickson Despommier, a professor at Columbia (NY)

    A. Talks about new agriculture techniques

        1. By 2050, 80% of people living in cities

        2. Three billion increase in world's population

        3. Will need a lot of new farmland

    B. Vertical farming a logical solution

        1. Hydroponics—no soil needed

        2. Controlled environment—fewer pesticides

INSIGHT

Topic outlines such as this example use words and phrases; sentence outlines use complete sentences.

Create Develop an outline for the body of your report, using the information above as a guide. (You don't need to outline the beginning or ending paragraphs.)

I. _____

    A. _____

        1. _____

        2. _____

        3. _____

    B. _____

        1. _____

        2. _____

LO5 Writing a Research Report

Writing your first draft allows you to connect all of your information and thoughts about the topic. You can improve your writing later during the revising and editing steps, so don't take time now to make your report perfect. The following information will help you develop each main part of your report.

Creating an Opening Paragraph

Your opening paragraph, must (1) gain the reader's interest, (2) introduce your topic, and (3) state your thesis. (See the opening paragraph on page 464 for an example.) Here are three strategies for gaining the reader's interest.

- **Create an inviting image or mental picture:**
  Imagine living in the middle of New York City, right next to a farm. This farm is located in a skyscraper made of stacked greenhouses.
- **Make a dramatic statement:**
  By 2050, 80 percent of all people will live in cities, and the world's population will have increased by 3 billion.
- **Ask an important question:**
  In the future, how will it be possible to feed our rapidly increasing world's population?

Developing the Middle Paragraphs

Your middle paragraphs must explain and develop your thesis. Use your outline and notes as a guide for writing these paragraphs. Here are a few additional tips.

- Turn each main idea in your outline—Roman numerals (I, II, III)—into a topic sentence.

  > **Main idea:** A key spokesperson—Dickson Despommier, a professor at Columbia (NY)

  > **Topic sentence:** A key spokesperson for vertical farming is Dickson Despommier, a professor at Columbia University in New York City.

- Develop each paragraph with the details under the main points (I, II, III) in your outline and related details in your notes.
- If a paragraph seems too long, separate the information into two paragraphs.
- Use your own words as much as possible, and always give credit for direct quotations and specific facts and details that you include. (See pages 434–435.)
- Be objective, unless your instructor allows you to include personal thoughts and feelings. (See page 463.)

A CLOSER LOOK at Writing: Integrating Quotations

Reports may contain quotations to support but not replace the writer's own ideas. Here are a few strategies for their use:

- **Use quotations to back up a main point.**
  The magazine also shares Dr. Caplow's idea for farming in existing multistory buildings: "plants growing around the edges of the building, sandwiched between two glass layers and rotating on a conveyor." Another idea is . . .

- **Use quotations to add the thoughts of an expert.**
  . . . one main concern: "Light has to be very tightly controlled to get uniform production of very high-quality food," says British engineer Peter Head. Often this means . . .

Writing a Closing Paragraph

The final paragraph should tie up any loose ends and leave the reader with a clear understanding of the importance of your topic. Here is a strategy for forming a closing paragraph.

- **Restate and expand on the key point in your report:**
  Whether urban farming ultimately follows the Despommier model or takes some other form, it looks like it will become an important part of the urban landscape.
- **Emphasize the value or importance of the topic:**
  What the pioneers in the field learn today may lead to multileveled, integrated systems that can feed large cities in a cost-effective way.
- **Reconnect with the opening:**
  Greenhouses may one day reach into the sky.

Write Write your first draft using your planning (pages 468–474) and the information on the previous pages to guide you. After you complete your first draft, compile a source list for your report. *Remember*: This page lists the sources that you have cited in your report. (See pages 436–437.)

LO6 Revising and Editing a Report

Revising the first draft involves adding, deleting, rearranging, and reworking parts of your report. Revision can begin with a peer review.

Peer Review

Sharing your writing at various stages is important, but it is especially important when you review and revise a first draft. The feedback that you receive will help you change and improve your report.

Peer Review Sheet

Report title: _____

Writer: _____

Reviewer: _____

1. Which part of the report seems to work best—opening, middle, or closing? Why?
   _____
   _____

2. Which part of the report needs work—opening, middle, or closing? Why?
   _____
   _____

3. Do the middle paragraphs clearly explain and develop the topic? Explain.
   _____
   _____

4. Does the report cite effective sources? Explain?
   _____
   _____

5. Do you have a clear understanding of the topic after reading this report? Explain.
   _____
   _____

6. Identify phrases or ideas (two or three) that show the writer's interest?
   _____
   _____

Respond Complete a peer-review sheet like this one after reading the first draft of a classmate's report. Then share the sheet with the writer. (Keep your comments helpful and positive.)

Revising

Besides asking a classmate to review your report, you need to carry out a careful review of your own. These reminders will help.

REVISING GUIDELINES

First, get the big picture.

- **Read your report from start to finish.** This will give you an overall sense of your writing.
- **Compare your first impressions against your classmate's comments (page 477).** How are they similar? Different?

Next, focus on the main parts.

- **Consider your beginning.** Does it gain the reader's attention, introduce your topic, and state your thesis, the main point of your report?
- **Review your middle paragraphs.** Do they support or explain your thesis, and are they arranged in a logical order?
- **Consider your closing.** Does it provide important final ideas about your topic?

Then focus on specific features.

- **Check your writing for voice.** Do you sound informed and interested in your topic?
- **Consider your reporting style.** Do you, for the most part, use your own words in your report?
- **Check for proper citation.** Have you followed an accepted documentation style to give credit to your sources? (See pages 434–435.)
- **Consider the flow of your ideas.** Does your draft read smoothly from start to finish?
- **Review your works-cited or references page.** Does it list the sources you have cited in your report following the proper documentation style? (See pages 436–437.)

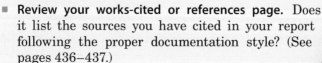

A CLOSER LOOK at Revising: Checking for Proper Citation

When citing sources in your report, be sure to check with your instructor's guidelines and with the information on pages 434–435. Also study the paragraphs below from the model report.

The name of the Web site signals the start of cited information and identifies the specific source. The book title indicates a shift to a new source. A parenthetical citation signals the end of the borrowed information. (Both sources have the same author; note how they are listed in the works cited.)

The name of a newspaper signals more borrowed information.

A parenthetical citation identifies the author's name.

This paragraph of general summary needs no citation.

A key spokesperson for vertical farming is Dickson Despommier, a professor at Columbia University in New York City. At *Verticalfarm.com,* he talks about new agricultural techniques. By 2050, 80 percent of all people will live in cities, and the world's population will have increased by 3 billion. To feed everyone will require a lot of new farmland. A logical solution is to farm vertically in urban areas, right where the food is needed. In his book *The Vertical Farm,* the professor proposes stacked greenhouses for growing food (Despommier 3-9).

Closer to home, Joe Heineman and Johanna Hearron-Heineman have been growing butter lettuce on two floors of an old building in Racine, Wisconsin. As the *Milwaukee Journal Sentinel* reports, the couple uses treated wastewater from tilapia fish tanks to grow the lettuce. In this building, they hope to produce the same amount of lettuce that would take 40 acres of traditional farmland to grow. The couple also wants to grow a half million pounds of tomatoes in a rooftop greenhouse (Herzog).

The idea of vertical farming on a grand scale, however, still needs work. There are no stacked greenhouses yet, as Despommier has envisioned them. As a matter of fact, environmental scientists and engineers have serious questions about the efficiency of vertical farming.

Revise Improve your writing, using the information on pages 477–478 as a guide. To do your best work, be prepared to revise some parts of your report several times.

Editing

After completing revising, editing becomes important. During the editing step, you check your writing for style and correctness. The guidelines that follow will help.

EDITING GUIDELINES

First, concentrate on your sentences.

- **Consider their readability.** Do your sentences read smoothly from one to the next?
- **Check them for variety.** Do your sentences start in different ways? Do they vary in length?
- **Consider their correctness.** Watch for fragments, run-ons, and comma splices. (See pages 532–539.)

Next, focus on word choice.

- **Consider your nouns.** For the most part, do you use specific nouns like *Science Barge* and *Columbia University*?
- **Check your verbs.** Do you avoid the "be" verbs (*is, are, was,* and *were*) in most of your sentences, choosing active verbs like *imagine* and *absorb*?

Then concentrate on conventions.

- **Check for correct verb forms.** For example, use *he saw,* not *he seen; she brought,* not *she brung.* (See page 588.)
- **Consider subject-verb agreement.** For example, use *she speaks,* not *she speak.* (See pages 516–525.)
- **Check for commonly misused words.** For example, use *their, there, they're; your, you're;* and *it's, its* correctly.
- **Look for capitalization problems.** Capitalize the first words of sentences and quotations as well as specific names. (See page 626.)
- **Check for punctuation problems.** Use correct end punctuation after sentences, commas in compound sentences, apostrophes to show possession, and so on. (See pages 635–661.)
- **Carefully check citations.** Follow the correct documentation style, including proper capitalization and punctuation, when citing sources in your report (within the text and at the end). (See pages 434–437.)

Marking a Report

Practice   Before editing your own report, edit the following page from a research report that follows MLA style. Use the information on page 480 as your guide, and mark any changes with the correction symbols shown.

Romero 1
Carlos Romero
Mrs. Becker
Science 8
February 11, 2011

Wolves in Wisconsin

The gray wolf is one of the most controversial animal species in North America in no state is this more evident than in Wisconsin. A great number of gray wolves roamed the northern woods of this state from the time of the retreating glaciers to the 1950s, when the wolf population all but disappeared. Today, however, gray wolves is back in Wisconsin. There return is an ecological triumph, but it also brings up old concerns. Hunters and farmers worry about the impact of wolves on deer populations and livestock, and state environmental officials say the wolf population is too large to manage. Decisions concerning these key issues will determine the future of gray wolves in wisconsin ("Wolves").

Evidence of gray wolves (Canis lupus) in Wisconsin traces back 10,000 years The wolves thrived in the thick forest habitat of northern Wisconsin, where retreating glaciers formed many lakes and streams. By the 1800s, there were believed to be between 3,000 and 5,000 wolves living in the state (Wydeven). Around this same time, many European settlers arrived in the area. These settlers who were mostly hunters and farmers feared that the wolves would diminish the deer population and endanger their livestock. Consequently, Wisconsin passed bounty laws, which paid hunters up to $20 for every wolf killed ("Wolves"). The law was revoked in 1957, but the damage is already done. Hundreds of wolves were killed, and the survivors took refuge in Minnesota and Michigan. By 1960, there were no gray wolves in Wisconsin ("Wolves").

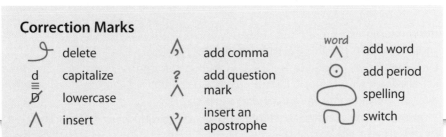

Correction Marks

℘ delete	⅋ add comma	⋏ᵂᵒʳᵈ add word
d̲ capitalize	? add question	⊙ add period
ᴅ̸ lowercase	⋀ mark	spelling
⋀ insert	ᶜᵛ insert an apostrophe	switch

Edit and Write   Edit a clean copy of your revised report using, the information on page 480 as your guide. Then prepare a final copy of your report, following the formatting guidelines and documentation style requested by your instructor. Proofread this copy before submitting it.

Reflecting on Research Writing

Answer the following questions about your reading and writing experiences in this chapter.

1. What is the purpose of a research report—to inform, to persuade, or to entertain? Explain.

   _____

2. What is the difference between a research report and a research paper?

   _____

3. Which reading strategy seems most helpful when reading a report? Explain.

   _____

4. What do you like the most in the model report? The least?

   _____

5. What do you like the most in your own report?

   _____

6. What is one thing that you would like to change?

   _____

7. What are two important things that you learned about writing a research report?

   _____

Key Terms to Remember

When you read and write reports, it is important to understand the following terms.

- **Research report**—a carefully planned form of informational writing, ranging in length from two or three pages on up
- **Documentation guidelines**—rules to follow for giving credit for the ideas of others used in a report; commonly MLA *(Modern Language Association)* or APA *(American Psychological Association)*
- **Citations**—sources cited or referred to in research; occur within the text and in a listing at the end of the report
- **Organized list**—an outline-like graphic used to keep track of the information in a report
- **Writer's stance**—the writer's approach to her or his reporting; either objective *(sticking to the facts)* or subjective *(including personal reflections)*

Part IV:

Sentence Workshops

Part IV: Sentence Workshops

18

> "We cannot always build the future for our youth,
> but we can build our youth for the future."
> —Franklin Delano Roosevelt

Sentence Basics

As you know, sentences are built from some very simple parts—nouns, verbs, and modifiers. Every sentence has, at its base, the pairing of a noun and a verb, or a few of them. The other words in the sentence merely modify the noun and verb.

These are sentence basics—the building blocks of thought. With these blocks, you can build tiny towers or magnificent mansions. It all comes down to understanding how to put the pieces together and deciding what you want to create. This chapter can help.

Learning Outcomes

LO1 Subjects and Verbs (Predicates)
LO2 Special Types of Subjects
LO3 Special Verbs (Predicates)
LO4 Adjectives
LO5 Adverbs
LO6 Prepositional Phrases
LO7 Clauses
LO8 Real-World Application

What do you think?

How do we "build our youth for the future," as Franklin Delano Roosevelt suggests in the quotation above? What part do language and writing play in building our youth?

Losevsky Pavel, 2013 / Used under license from Shutterstock.com

LO1 Subjects and Verbs (Predicates)

The subject of a sentence tells what the sentence is about. The verb (predicate) of a sentence tells what the subject does or is.

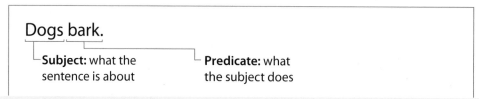

Dogs bark.

Subject: what the sentence is about

Predicate: what the subject does

Simple Subject and Simple Predicate

The **simple subject** is the subject without any modifiers, and the **simple predicate** is the verb and any helping verbs without modifiers or objects.

The black and white Schnauzer barked all day long.

simple subject simple predicate

Complete Subject and Complete Predicate

The **complete subject** is the subject with modifiers, and the **complete predicate** is the predicate with modifiers and objects.

The black and white Schnauzer barked all day long.

complete subject   complete predicate

Implied Subject

In commands, the subject *you* is implied. Commands are the only type of sentence in English that can have an **implied subject**.

(You)   Stop barking!
implied subject   complete predicate

Inverted Order

Most often in English, the subject comes before the predicate. However, in questions and sentences that begin with *here* or *there*, the subject comes after the predicate.

subject   subject
Why are you so loud?   Here is a biscuit.
predicate   predicate

Creating Subjects and Verbs (Predicates)

Identify/Write For each sentence below, identify the simple subject (SS) and simple predicate (SP). Then write a similar sentence of your own and identify the simple subject and simple predicate in the same way.

1. For thousands of years, humans bred dogs.

   _____

2. All dog breeds descended from wolf ancestors.

   _____

3. At the end of the Ice Age, humans lived nomadically with their dogs.

   _____

4. Ever since that time, dogs enjoyed going for walks.

   _____

Identify/Write For each sentence below, identify the complete subject (CS) and complete predicate (CP). Then write a similar sentence of your own and identify the complete subject and complete predicate in the same way.

1. An Irish wolfhound stands as tall as a small pony.

   _____

2. Wolfhounds were bred to hunt their ancestors.

   _____

3. Wolfhounds also were used for hunting boar.

   _____

4. Why are boars extinct in Ireland?

   _____

5. There were too many wolfhounds.

   _____

simple subject	complete subject	implied subject
the subject without any modifiers	the subject with modifiers	the word *you* implied in command sentences
simple predicate the verb and any helping verbs without modifiers or objects	**complete predicate** the predicate with modifiers and objects	

LO2 Special Types of Subjects

As you work with subjects, watch for these special types.

Compound Subjects

A **compound subject** is two or more subjects connected by *and* or *or*.

My <u>sister and I</u> swim well. <u>Terri, Josh, and I</u> love to dive.
   compound subject   compound subject

"To" Words (Infinitives) as Subjects

An **infinitive** can function as a subject. An infinitive is a verbal form that begins with *to* and may be followed by objects or modifiers.

<u>To become a park ranger</u> is my dream.
     infinitive subject

"Ing" Words (Gerunds) as Subjects

A **gerund** can function as a subject. A gerund is a verb form that ends in *ing* and may be followed by objects or modifiers.

<u>Hiking</u> builds strong calves.   <u>Hiking the Appalachian trail</u> is amazing.
 gerund subject   gerund subject

Noun Clause as Subject

A **noun clause** can function as a subject. The clause itself has a subject and a verb but cannot stand alone as a sentence. Noun clauses are introduced by words like *what, that, when, why, how, whatever,* or *whichever.*

<u>Whoever hikes the trail</u> should bring replacement boots.
  noun clause subject

<u>Whatever you need</u> must be carried on your back.
 noun clause subject

CONSIDER THE TRAITS

Note that each of these special subjects still functions as a noun or a group of nouns. A sentence is still, at root, the connection between a noun and a verb.

Say It

Pair up with a partner and read each sentence aloud. Take turns identifying the type of subject—compound subject, infinitive subject, gerund subject, or noun-clause subject. Discuss your answers.

1. You and I should go hiking sometime.
2. To reach the peak of Mount Rainier would be amazing.
3. Whoever wants to go should train with mountaineering.
4. Hiking the Rockies at altitude is challenging.

Creating Special Subjects

Identify/Write For each sentence below, identify the complete subject as a compound subject (CS), infinitive (I), gerund (G), or noun clause (NC). Then write a similar sentence of your own and identify the complete subject in the same way.

1. Planning for success is the key to success. _____

2. To complete the course in two years is my main goal. _____

3. The fan and the air conditioner are running. _____

4. Working through our differences won't be easy. _____

5. A donut, a cup of coffee, and good conversation make my morning. _____

6. Lifting the ban on street parking will help the neighborhood. _____

7. To live life to its fullest is not as easy as it sounds. _____

8. Whoever finds the money will keep it. _____

9. Are Hannah, Michelle, and Sharissa going? _____

10. Whenever he arrives is the starting time. _____

compound subject	gerund	noun clause
two or more subjects connected by *and* or *or*	a verb form that ends in *ing* and is used as a noun	a group of words beginning with words like *that, what, whoever,* and so on; containing a subject and a verb but unable to function as a sentence
infinitive		
a verb form that begins with *to* and can be used as a noun (or as an adjective or adverb)		

LO3 Special Verbs (Predicates)

As you work with predicates, watch for these special types.

Compound Predicates

A **compound predicate** consists of two or more predicates joined by *and* or *or*.

I watched and laughed. My cat stalked, pounced, and tumbled.
compound predicate   compound predicate

Predicates with Direct Objects

A **direct object** follows a transitive verb and tells what or who receives the action of the verb.

I pointed the laser. My cat saw the spot. He batted it and nipped the ground.
direct object   direct object   direct objects

Predicates with Indirect Objects

An **indirect object** comes between a transitive verb and a direct object and tells to whom or for whom an action was done.

I gave him a rest. My cat shot me a puzzled look.
indirect object   indirect object

Passive Predicates

When a predicate is **passive**, the subject of the sentence is being acted upon rather than acting. Often, the actor is the object of the preposition in a phrase that starts with *by*. To make the sentence **active**, rewrite it, turning the object of the preposition into the subject.

Passive

My cat was exhausted by the game.
subject   passive verb   object of the preposition

Active

The game exhausted my cat.
subject   active verb   direct object

Say It

Pair up with a partner and read each sentence aloud. Take turns identifying the sentence as active or passive. If the sentence is passive, speak the active version out loud.

1. My cat was mesmerized by the laser.
2. The light danced in his paws.
3. The laser glowed red on the wall.
4. The light was chased all down the hallway by my cat.

Creating Special Predicates

Identify/Write For each sentence below, write and label any compound predicate (CP), direct object (DO), and indirect object (IO). Then write a similar sentence of your own and identify the compound predicate and direct or indirect object in the same way.

1. Our pet rabbits hopped and thumped. _____

2. The lop-ear leaped the gate. _____

3. I gave her a carrot. _____

4. She crouched and nibbled. _____

5. The lion sniffed and bounded. _____

6. I gave him some dried banana. _____

7. Those rabbits give me hours of entertainment. _____

Identify/Write For each passive sentence below, write and label the simple subject (SS), the simple predicate (SP), and the object of the preposition *by* (O). Then rewrite each sentence, making it active. (See "Passive Predicates" on the previous page.)

1. The rabbits are fed by my sister. _____

2. Their cages are cleaned by her as well. _____

3. She is seen by them as their food goddess. _____

---

compound predicate
two or more predicates joined by *and* or *or*

direct object
a word that follows a transitive verb and tells what or who receives the action of the verb

indirect object
a word that comes between a transitive verb and a direct object and tells to whom or for whom an action was done

passive
the voice created when a subject is being acted upon

active
the voice created when a subject is acting

LO4 Adjectives

To modify a noun, use an adjective or a phrase or clause acting as an adjective.

Adjectives

Adjectives answer these basic questions: *which, what kind of, how many, how much.*

To modify the noun **athletes,** ask . . .

Which athletes? ⟶ college athletes

What kind of athletes? ⟶ female athletes

How many athletes? ⟶ ten athletes

> ten female college athletes

Adjective Phrases and Clauses

Phrases and clauses can also act as adjectives to modify nouns.

To modify the noun **athletes,** ask . . .

Which athletes? ⟶ athletes who are taking at least 12 credit hours

What kind of athletes? ⟶ athletes with a 3.0 average

> The administration will approve loans for athletes with a 3.0 average who are taking at least 12 credit hours.

INSIGHT

It's less important to know the name of a phrase or clause than to know how it functions. If a group of words answers one of the adjective questions, the words are probably functioning as an adjective.

Pete Saloutos, 2013 / Used under license from Shutterstock.com

Pair up with a classmate to find adjectives—words, phrases, or clauses—that modify the nouns below. Take turns asking the questions while the other person answers.

1. **Sports**
   Which sports?
   What kind of sports?
   How many sports?

2. **Classes**
   Which classes?
   What kind of classes?
   How many classes?

Using Adjectives

Answer/Write For each noun, answer the questions using adjectives—words, phrases, or clauses. Then write a sentence using two or more of your answers.

1. **Tournaments**

   Which tournaments?_____

   What kind of tournaments? _____

   How many tournaments? _____

   Sentence: _____

   _____

2. **Opponents**

   Which opponents? _____

   What kind of opponents? _____

   How many opponents? _____

   Sentence: _____

   _____

3. **Victories**

   Which victories? _____

   What kind of victories?_____

   How many victories?_____

   Sentence: _____

   _____

LO5 Adverbs

To modify a verb, use an adverb or a phrase or clause acting as an adverb.

Adverbs

Adverbs answer these basic questions: *how, when, where, why, how long, and how often.*

To modify the verb **dance,** ask . . .

How did they dance? ⟶	danced vigorously
When did they dance? ⟶	danced yesterday
Where did they dance? ⟶	danced there
How often did they dance? ⟶	danced often

> Yesterday, the bride and groom often vigorously danced, there in the middle of the floor.

Adverb Phrases and Clauses

Phrases and clauses can also act as adverbs to modify verbs.

To modify the verb **dance,** ask . . .

How did they dance? ⟶	danced grinning and laughing
When did they dance? ⟶	danced from the first song
Where did they dance? ⟶	danced all around the room
Why did they dance? ⟶	danced to celebrate their wedding
How long did they dance? ⟶	danced until the last song

> Grinning and laughing, the bride and groom danced all around the room from the first song until the last song to celebrate their wedding.

CONSIDER SPEAKING AND LISTENING

Read the last sentence aloud. Though it may look imposing on the page, it sounds natural, probably because adverbs and adjectives are a common part of our speech. Experiment with these modifiers in your writing as well.

Using Adverbs

Answer/Write   For each verb, answer the questions using adverbs—words, phrases, or clauses. Then write a sentence using three or more of your answers.

1. Ran

How did they run? _____

When did they run? _____

Where did they run? _____

Why did they run? _____

How long did they run? _____

How often did they run? _____

Sentence: _____

_____

2. Jumped

How did they jump? _____

When did they jump? _____

Where did they jump? _____

Why did they jump? _____

How long did they jump? _____

How often did they jump? _____

Sentence: _____

_____

LO6 Prepositional Phrases

One of the simplest and most versatile types of phrases in English is the **prepositional phrase**. A prepositional phrase can function as an adjective or an adverb.

Building Prepositional Phrases

A prepositional phrase is a preposition followed by an object (a noun or pronoun) and any modifiers.

Preposition	+	Object	=	Prepositional Phrase
at		noon		at noon
in		an hour		in an hour
beside		the green clock		beside the green clock
in front of		my aunt's vinyl purse		in front of my aunt's vinyl purse

As you can see, a propositional phrase can be just two words long, or many words long. As you can also see, some prepositions are themselves made up of more than one word. Here is a list of common prepositions.

Prepositions

aboard	back of	except for	near to	round
about	because of	excepting	notwithstanding	save
above	before	for	of	since
according to	behind	from	off	subsequent to
across	below	from among	on	through
across from	beneath	from between	on account of	throughout
after	beside	from under	on behalf of	'til
against	besides	in	onto	to
along	between	in addition to	on top of	together with
alongside	beyond	in behalf of	opposite	toward
alongside of	but	in front of	out	under
along with	by	in place of	out of	underneath
amid	by means of	in regard to	outside	until
among	concerning	inside	outside of	unto
apart from	considering	inside of	over	up
around	despite	in spite of	over to	upon
as far as	down	instead of	owing to	up to
aside from	down from	into	past	with
at	during	like	prior to	within
away from	except	near	regarding	without

INSIGHT

A preposition is pre-positioned before the other words it introduces to form a phrase. Other languages have post-positional words that follow their objects.

Using Prepositional Phrases

Create For each item below, create a prepositional phrase by writing a preposition and an object (and any modifiers). Then write a sentence using the prepositional phrase.

1. | Preposition | $+$ | Object (and any modifiers) |

   Sentence: _____

2. | Preposition | $+$ | Object (and any modifiers) |

   Sentence: _____

3. | Preposition | $+$ | Object (and any modifiers) |

   Sentence: _____

4. | Preposition | $+$ | Object (and any modifiers) |

   Sentence: _____

5. | Preposition | $+$ | Object (and any modifiers) |

   Sentence: _____

prepositional phrase
a group of words beginning with a preposition and including an object (noun or pronoun) and any modifiers

LO7 Clauses

A clause is a group of words with a subject and a predicate. If a clause can stand on its own as a sentence, it is an **independent clause**, but if it cannot, it is a **dependent clause**.

Independent Clause

An independent clause has a subject and a predicate and expresses a complete thought. It is the same as a simple sentence.

Clouds piled up in the stormy sky.

Dependent Clause

A dependent clause has a subject and a predicate but does not express a complete thought. Instead, it is used as an **adverb clause**, an **adjective clause**, or a **noun clause**.

An adverb clause begins with a subordinating conjunction (see below) and functions as an adverb, so it must be connected to an independent clause to be complete.

Consider Speaking and Listening

In each example below, read the dependent clause out loud. (The dependent clause is in red.) Can you hear how each dependent clause sounds incomplete? Read it to another person, and the listener will probably say, "What about it?" These clauses depend on a complete thought to make sense.

after	as long as	given that	since	unless	where
although	because	if	so that	until	whereas
as	before	in order that	that	when	while
as if	even though	provided that	though	whenever	

Even though the forecast said clear skies, the storms rolled in.

An adjective clause begins with a relative pronoun *(which, that, who)* and functions as an adjective, so it must be connected to an independent clause to be complete.

I don't like a meteorologist who often gets the forecast wrong.

A noun clause begins with words like those below and functions as a noun. It is used as a subject or an object in a sentence.

how	what	whoever	whomever
that	whatever	whom	why

I wish he had known what the weather would be.

Using Clauses

Identify/Write For each sentence below, write and label any adverb clauses (ADVC), adjective clauses (ADJC), or noun clauses (NC). Then write a similar sentence of your own and identify the clauses.

1. I wonder why weather is so unpredictable.

2. Storms still surprise meteorologists who have years of experience.

3. Many different factors determine what will happen in the sky.

4. Until we can track all factors, we can't predict perfectly.

5. Whoever gives a forecast is making a guess.

6. Since weather is so uncertain, predictions have percentages.

7. A 50 percent chance of rain means that there is a 50 percent chance of fair weather.

8. When air crosses a large lake, it picks up moisture.

9. Because of lake-effect rain, Valparaiso is called "Vapor Rain Snow."

10. Buffalo gets whatever moisture Lake Erie dishes up.

---

independent clause
a group of words with a subject and predicate that expresses a complete thought

dependent clause
a group of words with a subject and predicate that does not express a complete thought

adverb clause
a dependent clause beginning with a subordinating conjunction and functioning as an adverb

adjective clause
a dependent clause beginning with a relative pronoun and functioning as an adjective

noun clause
a dependent clause beginning with a subordinating word and functioning as a noun

LO8 Real-World Application

Identify In the email below, write and identify simple subjects (SS), simple predicates (SP), and dependent clauses (DC).

Send	Attach	Fonts	Colors	Save As Draft

To: Terri Bell

Subject: Revision Suggestions

Hi, Teri: *1*

I enjoyed your article, "What Is New in *BattleTown 2*," which you submitted for publication on MMORPNews2.com. We like your article but request a few revisions before we send contracts.

This is a quick rundown of our revision suggestions: *5*

1. The opening could be more gripping. The title works well to grab the reader's interest, but the opening feels flat. Perhaps you could provide a glimpse of new features of game play, or even give a scenario that wasn't possible in *BattleTown 1*.

2. A direct quotation from Todd Allen would strengthen the center section. *10* Though you allude to your interview on many occasions, Todd never speaks for himself, and he is a definite name in the industry.

3. Can you get permission to use the visuals? AssemblyArts would love the free publicity, but you need written permission to include the screenshots.

If you could make these changes, we would be very interested in publishing *15* your article. Once I see the revised piece, I can send a contract for you to sign.

Thanks,

Richard Prince

Expand Answer the adjective and adverb questions below. Then expand the sentence using some of the words, phrases, and clauses you have created.

The agent called.

Which agent? _____

What kind of agent? _____

Called *when?* _____

Called *how?* _____

Sentence: _____

19

> "A complex system that works is invariably found to have evolved from a simple system that works."
> —John Gaule

Simple, Compound, and Complex Sentences

Most leaves have a central stem with veins extending from it. Sometimes this structure forms a simple oval, but at other times, two or more ovals connect to form a compound leaf. And the shape of some leaves is complex, as if a number of leaves were fused together.

Sentences are similar. All have a noun and a verb, but some stop at this simple structure. In other cases, two or more sentences combine to make a compound sentence. And when a sentence has one or more dependent clauses fused to it, it becomes complex.

This chapter shows how to create simple, compound, and complex sentences. As with leaves, variety makes sentences beautiful.

Learning Outcomes

LO1 Simple Sentences

LO2 Simple Sentences with Compound Subjects

LO3 Simple Sentences with Compound Verbs

LO4 Compound Sentences

LO5 Complex Sentences

LO6 Complex Sentences with Relative Clauses

LO7 Real-World Application

What do you think?

Which type of leaf is most beautiful—a simple, compound, or complex leaf? Why?

raresirimie, 2013 / Used under license from Shutterstock.com

LO1 Simple Sentences

A **simple sentence** consists of a subject and a verb. The subject is a noun or pronoun that names what the sentence is about. The verb tells what the subject does or is.

Rachel sang.
subject verb

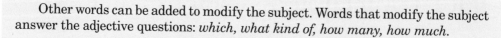

Modifiers

Other words can be added to modify the subject. Words that modify the subject answer the adjective questions: *which, what kind of, how many, how much.*

My new roommate Rachel sang. *(Which Rachel do you mean?)*

Other words can also modify the verb. These words and phrases answer the adverb questions: *how, when, where, why, to what degree,* and *how often.*

Rachel sang in the shower at the top of her lungs.
(Where and how did Rachel sing?)

Direct and Indirect Objects

The verb might also be followed by a noun or pronoun that receives the action of the verb. Such a word is called the **direct object**, and it answers the question *what* or *whom?*

Rachel sang "I Need a Hero." *(What did Rachel sing?)*

Another noun or pronoun could come between the verb and the direct object, telling *to whom* or *for whom* an action is done. Such a word is the **indirect object**.

I gave her a picture of Chuck Norris.
(I gave a picture of Chuck Norris to whom?)

simple sentence
a subject and a verb that together form a complete thought

direct object
a noun or pronoun that follows a verb and receives its action

indirect object
a noun or pronoun that comes between a verb and a direct object, telling *to whom* or *for whom* an action is done

Say It

Team up with a partner and follow these steps: One of you speaks the sentence aloud, and the other asks the question in italics. Then the first person says the sentence again, inserting an answer.

1. We sang songs. *(Where did you sing songs?)*
2. The song was our favorite. *(Which song was your favorite?)*
3. Rachel sang. *(What did Rachel sing?)*
4. I sang a song. *(To whom did you sing a song?)*

Creating Simple Sentences

Create Provide a noun for a subject and a verb for a predicate. Then write a sentence with the noun and verb, adding details that answer the questions asked.

1. | Subject | Verb |

Which? _____

Simple sentence: _____

2. | Subject | Verb |

What kind of? _____

Simple sentence: _____

3. | Subject | Verb |

When? _____

Simple sentence: _____

4. | Subject | Verb |

Where? _____

Simple sentence: _____

LO2 Simple Sentences with Compound Subjects

A simple sentence can have a **compound subject** (two or more subjects).

A Simple Sentence with Two Subjects

To write a simple sentence with two subjects, join them using *and* or *or*.

One Subject: Lee worked on the Rube Goldberg machine.
Two Subjects: Lee and Jerome will add the lever arm that tips the bucket.
Lee or Jerome will add the lever arm that tips the bucket.

One Subject: Ms. Claymore will help them attach the flywheel.
Two Subjects: Ms. Claymore and her aide will help them attach the flywheel.
Either Ms. Claymore or her aide will help them attach the flywheel.

A Simple Sentence with Three or More Subjects

To write a simple sentence with three or more subjects, create a series. List each subject, placing a comma after all but the last, and place an *and* or *or* before the last.

Three Subjects: Jerome, Lee, and Sandra are finishing the machine soon.
Five Subjects: Jerome, Lee, Sandra, Ms. Claymore, and her aide will enter the machine in a contest.

NOTE: When a compound subject is joined by *and*, the subject is plural and requires a plural verb. When a compound subject is joined by *or*, the verb should match the last subject.

Ms. Claymore and her aide need to submit the entry form.

Ms. Claymore or her aide needs to submit the entry form.

CONSIDER THE TRAITS

A compound subject does not make the sentence compound. As long as both (or all) of the subjects connect to the same verb or verbs, the sentence is still considered simple.

Say It

Speak each of the following sentences out loud.
1. Jerome *loves* the Rube Goldberg project.
2. Jerome *and* Sandra *love* the Rube Goldberg project.
3. Jerome *or* Sandra *works* on it every day after school.
4. Jerome, Sandra, *and* Lee *have* contributed most.
5. Jerome, Sandra, *or* Lee *has* contributed most.

Using Compound Subjects

Create Write subjects for each of the boxes provided. Then write a sentence that includes the subjects as a compound subject using *and* or *or*.

1. | Subject | Subject |

Simple Sentence: _____

2. | Subject | Subject |

Simple Sentence: _____

3. | Subject | Subject | Subject |

Simple Sentence: _____

4. | Subject | Subject | Subject |

Simple Sentence: _____

5. | Subject | Subject | Subject | Subject |

Simple Sentence: _____

6. | Subject | Subject | Subject | Subject |

compound subject
two or more subjects in a simple sentence

LO3 Simple Sentences with Compound Verbs

A simple sentence can also have two or more verbs (predicates). Remember that the predicate tells what the subject is doing or being, so as long as both predicates connect to the same subject, the sentence is still a simple sentence.

A Simple Sentence with Two Verbs

To create a **compound predicate** with two parts, join two verbs using *and* or *or*.

One Verb: The band rocked.

Two Verbs: The band rocked and danced.

Remember that the predicate includes not just the verbs, but also words that modify or complete the verbs.

One Predicate: The band played their hit single.

Two Predicates: The band played their hit single and covered other songs.

A Simple Sentence with Three or More Verbs

To create a compound predicate with three or more parts, list the verbs in a series, with a comma after each except the last, and the word *and* or *or* before the last.

Three Verbs: The singer crooned, wailed, and roared.

Five Verbs: The fans clapped, screamed, danced, cheered, and swayed.

If each verb also includes modifiers or completing words (direct and indirect objects), place the commas after each complete predicate.

The crowd members got to their feet, waved their hands back and forth, and sang along with the band.

Using Compound Predicates

Create   For each subject below, create predicates. Then write a simple sentence that joins the compound predicates with *and* or *or*.

1. The reporters

Predicate

Predicate

2. The police

Predicate

Predicate

3. The manager

Predicate

Predicate

4. The bouncer

Predicate

Predicate

Predicate

Petr Malyshev, 2013 / Used under license from Shutterstock.com

compound predicate
two or more predicates in a simple sentence

LO4 Compound Sentences

A **compound sentence** is made out of simple sentences joined by a coordinating conjunction: *and, but, or, nor, for, so,* or *yet.*

Compound of Two Sentences

Most compound sentences connect two simple sentences, which are also called independent clauses. Connect the sentences by placing a comma after the first sentence and using a coordinating conjunction after the comma.

Two Sentences: We ordered pizza. I got just one piece.

Compound Sentence: We ordered pizza, but I got just one piece.

Compound of Three or More Sentences

Sometimes, you might want to join three or more short sentences in a compound sentence.

Three Sentences: Tim likes cheese. Jan likes veggie. I like pepperoni.

Compound Sentence: Tim likes cheese, Jan likes veggie, and I like pepperoni.

You can also join the sentences using semicolons. Authors sometimes use this approach to describe a long, involved process or a flurry of activity.

Tim ate the cheese pizza; Jan ate the veggie pizza; Ray showed up and ate the pepperoni pizza; I got back in time for the last slice.

NOTE: Remember that a compound sentence is made of two or more complete sentences. Each part needs to have its own subject and verb.

CONSIDER THE TRAITS ───────────────────────

The word *and* indicates that the second clause provides additional information. The words *but, or, nor,* and *yet* create a contrast. The words *for* and *so* indicate that one clause is the cause of the other.

Creating Compound Sentences

Write   Write a simple sentence for each prompt; then combine them as a compound sentence.

1. What pizza do you like? _____

   What pizza does a friend like? _____

   Compound Sentence: _____

   _____

2. Where do you go for pizza? _____

   What other place do people go? _____

   Compound Sentence: _____

   _____

3. Who likes thin crust pizza? _____

   Who likes pan pizza? _____

   Who likes stuffed pizza? _____

   Compound Sentence: _____

   _____

4. What is the weirdest pizza? _____

   What is the grossest pizza? _____

   What is the stinkiest pizza? _____

   Compound Sentence: _____

   _____

5. When do you eat pizza? _____

   When do your friends eat pizza? _____

   When does your family eat pizza? _____

   Compound Sentence: _____

   _____

compound sentence
two or more simple sentences joined
with a coordinating conjunction

LO5 Complex Sentences

A **complex sentence** shows a special relationship between two ideas. Instead of connecting two sentences as equal ideas (as in a compound sentence), a complex sentence shows that one idea depends on the other.

Using a Subordinating Conjunction

You can create a complex sentence by placing a subordinating conjunction before the sentence that is less important. Here are common subordinating conjunctions:

after	before	so that	when
although	even though	that	where
as	if	though	whereas
as if	in order that	till	while
as long as	provided that	'til	
because	since	until	

CONSIDER SPEAKING AND LISTENING

Read the example complex and compound-complex sentences aloud. Despite their daunting names, these sentences aren't that complicated. You use them all the time in speech. Experiment with them in your writing.

The subordinating conjunction shows that this sentence depends on the other sentence and can't stand without it.

Two Sentences: We played strong offense. We won the football game.

Complex Sentence: Because we played strong offense, we won the football game.

We won the football game because we played strong offense.

NOTE: The subordinating conjunction goes at the beginning of the less important clause, but the two clauses could go in either order. When the dependent clause comes second, it usually isn't set off with a comma.

Compound-Complex

You can create a **compound-complex sentence** by placing a subordinating conjunction before a simple sentence and connecting it to a compound sentence.

Simple Sentence: I threw two touchdowns.

Compound Sentence: Jake kicked the extra points, and the other team couldn't catch up.

Compound-Complex: After I threw two touchdowns, Jake kicked the extra points, and the other team couldn't catch up.

Creating Complex Sentences

Write Write a simple sentence for each prompt. Then select a subordinating conjunction from the facing page, place it at the beginning of one sentence, and combine the two sentences into a single complex sentence.

1. What did you play? _____

   Did you win or lose? _____

   Complex sentence: _____

   _____

2. Who did you play? _____

   Why did you play the opponent? _____

   Complex sentence: _____

   _____

3. Who won the game? _____

   Why did that side win? _____

   Complex sentence: _____

   _____

4. Where did you play? _____

   Where else could you have played? _____

   Complex sentence: _____

   _____

5. What surprised you? _____

   Why did it surprise you? _____

   Complex sentence: _____

   _____

6. How long did you play? _____

   When did you stop? _____

   Complex sentence: _____

   _____

complex sentence
a sentence with one independent clause and
one or more dependent clauses

compound-complex sentence
a sentence with two or more independent
clauses and one or more dependent clauses

LO6 Complex Sentences with Relative Clauses

In a complex sentence, one idea depends on the other. You've seen how a dependent clause can start with a subordinating conjunction. Another type of dependent clause starts with a relative pronoun.

Relative Clauses

A **relative clause** is a group of words that begins with a **relative pronoun** *(that, which, who, whom)* and includes a verb and any words that modify or complete it:

Relative Clauses:	that leads into the garden
	which usually leans against the shed
	who planted the scallions
	whom I asked to help me weed

Each relative clause above has a subject and a verb, but none of the clauses is a complete sentence. All need to be connected to a complete sentence.

Complex Sentences:	I followed the path that leads into the garden.
	I looked for the shovel, which usually leans against the shed.
	We have many onions thanks to a friend who planted the scallions.
	I worked with Tina, whom I asked to help me weed.

That and *Which*

The pronoun *that* signals that the information after it is necessary to the sentence. The pronoun *which* signals that the information is not necessary, so the clause is set off with a comma.

That: The scallions that we planted this spring taste strongest. (*That* defines the scallions.)

Which: I love scallions, which I eat raw or fried. (*Which* does not define the scallions but just adds more information about them.)

Who and *Whom*

The pronoun *who* is the subject of the relative clause that it introduces. The pronoun *whom* is a direct object of a clause it introduces.

Who: I helped the woman who harvested scallions. (*Who* is the subject.)

Whom: I thanked the woman whom I helped. (*Whom* is the direct object.)

Using Relative Clauses

Create   For each item, write a relative clause beginning with the pronoun provided. Then write a complex sentence that includes the relative clause. In case you need a topic idea, think of a party you have attended or one that you would like to attend.

1. Relative clause: _that_ _____

   Complex sentence: _____

   _____

2. Relative clause: _who_ _____

   Complex sentence: _____

   _____

3. Relative clause: _which_ _____

   Complex sentence: _____

   _____

4. Relative clause: _whom_ _____

   Complex sentence: _____

   _____

5. Relative clause: _that_ _____

   Complex sentence: _____

   _____

6. Relative clause: _which_ _____

   Complex sentence: _____

   _____

INSIGHT

In some languages, if the relative pronoun is the object of the clause it introduces, another pronoun is inserted in the clause: *I liked the gift that my boss gave* it *to me.* In English, no additional pronoun is inserted: *I liked the gift that my boss gave to me.*

relative clause
a group of words that begins with a relative pronoun and includes a verb but cannot stand alone as a sentence

relative pronoun
a word *(that, which, who, whom)* that relates a relative clause with another word in the sentence

LO7 Real-World Application

Rewrite Read the following message about a meeting. Note how every sentence is a simple sentence. Rewrite the message, combining sentences into some compound or complex sentences and improving the flow.

Dear Mr. Lindau:

You asked about the Monday production meeting. I will summarize it. The production staff met with the editors. The writers explained their new project. It focuses on twenty-first-century skills. The writers presented two chapters. They will become a prototype.

The new project needs to be visual. It should appeal to students and teachers. The design needs to make text accessible. The writing has an open quality. It still feels academic. The book should be available for sale in the fall. A teacher's edition will follow.

The designers are beginning work on a prototype. The writers continue to create chapters.

Dear Mr. Lindau:

_____

_____

_____

_____

_____

_____

_____

_____

_____

_____

CONSIDER THE WORKPLACE

Using a variety of sentences in workplace writing will help ideas flow and will present a polished image.

20

> "My idea of an agreeable person is a person who agrees with me."
>
> —Benjamin Disraeli

Agreement

When two people agree, they can work together. They have the same goals and outlook, and they can become a team.

Subjects and verbs are much the same. If the subject is plural, the verb needs to be as well, or they can't work together. Pronouns also need to agree with their antecedents in terms of number. Without agreement, these words fight each other, and instead of conveying ideas, they disrupt communication.

This chapter focuses on the agreement between subjects and verbs and between pronouns and antecedents. It also tackles other pronoun problems. After you work through the exercises here, you'll find it easy to write agreeable sentences.

Learning Outcomes

LO1 Subject-Verb Agreement

LO2 Agreement with Two Subjects

LO3 Agreement with *I* and *You*

LO4 Agreement with Indefinite Pronouns

LO5 Pronoun-Antecedent Agreement

LO6 Other Pronoun Problems

LO7 Real-World Application

What do you think?

What makes a person agreeable? What makes subjects and verbs agreeable?

LO1 Subject-Verb Agreement

A verb must **agree in number** with the subject of the sentence. If the subject is singular, the verb must be singular. If the subject is plural, the verb must be plural.

| singular subject | + | singular verb | = | agreement | | plural subject | + | plural verb | = | agreement |

The truck needs a tune-up.   The trucks need tune-ups.

NOTE: Plural subjects often end in *s*, but plural verbs usually do not. Also note that only present-tense verbs and certain *be* verbs have separate singular and plural forms.

Present:	singular	plural		Past:	singular	plural
	walks	walk			walked	walked
	sees	see			saw	saw
	eats	eat			ate	ate
	is/am	are			was	were

To make most verbs singular, add just an *s*.

run—runs   write—writes   stay—stays

The verbs *do* and *go* are made singular by adding an *es*.

do—does   go—goes

When a verb ends in *ch, sh, x,* or *z,* make it singular by adding *es*.

latch—latches   wish—wishes   fix—fixes   buzz—buzzes

When a verb ends in a consonant followed by a *y,* change the *y* to *i* and add *es*.

try—tries   fly—flies   cry—cries   quantify—quantifies

INSIGHT

The "Say It" activity on the next page will help you become familiar with the subject-verb agreement patterns in English. Practice it aloud, and for added practice, write the sentences as well.

Say It

Read the following sentences aloud, emphasizing the words in italics.
1. The bird *sings*. The birds *sing*. The phone *rings*. The phones *ring*.
2. The person *is*. The people *are*. The child *is*. The children *are*.
3. He *works*. They *work*. She *learns*. They *learn*.
4. The woman *does*. The women *do*. The man *goes*. The men *go*.
5. She *wishes*. They *wish*. He *boxes*. They *box*.

Correcting Basic Subject-Verb Agreement

Write   For each sentence below, write the correct form of the verb in parentheses.

1. A philosophy major _____ about thinking. (know)
2. A philosopher _____ to find philosophical work. (try)
3. An employer rarely _____ to hire philosophers. (wish)
4. But such students _____ able to think (is).
5. My roommate _____ philosophy. (study)
6. He also _____ to study the want ads for jobs. (need)
7. He _____ employers need thinkers. (say)
8. That idea _____ sense. (make)
9. But that idea doesn't _____ people hire him. (make)
10. At his job, he _____ lawn mowers very philosophically. (fix)

Correct   Correct any agreement errors you find by writing the line number and the verb you would change. Cross it out and write the correct present-tense verb.

> The philosopher Plato say the material world aren't the real world.   *1*
> He say we sees shadows on a cave wall. Plato believe in eternal forms of
> perfection. Every real table in the world are patterned after the perfect
> form of a table. In that way, people too is patterned after the perfect form
> of people. Though Plato live more than three hundred years before Jesus,   *5*
> many Christian thinkers likes his concept of eternal forms. The idea fit
> well with the ideas of a soul and a creator. Many modern thinkers, though,
> has the opposite idea. They says that only physical things is real. Plato, of
> course, disagree.

Write   For each plural verb below, write one sentence using the verb in its singular form.

1. fly _____
2. do _____
3. fish _____
4. wax _____

agree in number
match, as when a subject and verb are both singular, or when they are both plural

LO2 Agreement with Two Subjects

Sentences with **compound subjects** have special rules to make sure that they agree.

When a sentence has two or more subjects joined by *and,* the verb should be plural.

plural subject + plural verb = agreement

Jumbo and Dumbo march.

or

When a sentence has two or more subjects joined by *or, nor,* or *but also,* the verb should agree with the last subject.

singular subject + singular verb = agreement

Either Jumbo or Dumbo trumpets.

Not only Jumbo but also Dumbo trumpets.

CJimenez, 2013 / Used under license from Shutterstock.com

Say It

Read the following sentences aloud, emphasizing the words in *italics.*

1. Jumbo *and* Dumbo *perform.* Jumbo *or* Dumbo *performs.*

2. The man *and* woman *dance.* The man *or* woman *dances.*

3. The Democrat *and* the Republican *agree.* The Democrat *or* the Republican *agrees.*

4. Not only Dave *but also* Tim *writes.*

5. The dog, cat, *and* guinea pig *greet* me. The dog, cat, *or* guinea pig *greets* me.

INSIGHT ————————————————————————————

For more practice with compound subjects, see pages 504–505.

Fixing Agreement with Two Subjects

Write   For each sentence below, write the correct form of the verb in parentheses.

1. The acrobat and clown _____ the crowd. (entertain)

2. The acrobat or clown _____ a pie in the face. (get)

3. A trapeze artist and a tightrope walker _____ an ovation. (receive)

4. Not only the acrobat but also the clown _____ highly paid. (are)

5. Neither the lion tamer nor the sword swallower _____ insurance. (have)

6. The human cannonball or the lion tamer _____ the scariest job. (have)

7. Either Todd or Lewis _____ to join the circus. (plan)

8. Thrills and hard work _____ Todd or Lewis. (await)

9. Not only Todd but also Lewis _____ a daredevil. (are)

10. The clowns or the ringmaster _____ each act. (introduce)

Correct   Correct any agreement errors you find by writing the line number and incorrect verb, crossing it out, and writing the correct present tense verb.

> Childhood dreams and fantasies rarely comes true. A firefighter   *1*
> or police officer are what many children dream of being. Imagine a
> world filled with firefighters and police! Neither the accountant nor the
> landscaper figure big in childhood plans. A princess or a wizard are also
> a popular choice for kids. Job openings and pay for both careers is pretty   *5*
> slim. Even the job of astronaut or explorer have become scarce. The trials
> of joblessness and the responsibilities of adulthood conspires to convince
> people to seek other careers. Childhood stars sometimes get "real" jobs, too.
> Johnny Whitaker and Wil Wheaton works with computers. They traded
> childhood dreams for adult ones.   *10*

Write   Write a sentence with a compound subject joined by *and*. Write a sentence with a compound subject joined by *or*. Check subject-verb agreement.

_____

compound subject
two or more subjects that
share the same verb or verbs

LO3 Agreement with *I* and *You*

The pronouns *I* and *you* usually take plural verbs, even though they are singular.

plural verb

Correct: I go to Great America and ride roller coasters. You do too.

singular verb

Incorrect: I goes to Great America and rides roller coasters. You does too.

NOTE: The pronoun *I* takes the singular verbs *am* and *was*. **Do not** use *I* with *be* or *is*.

Correct: I am excited. I was nervous. I am eager to ride the roller coaster.

Incorrect: I are exited. I were nervous. I is eager to ride the roller coaster.

Quick Guide

Using *am, is, are, was,* and *were*

	Singular	Plural
Present Tense	I *am* you *are* he *is* she *is* it *is*	we *are* you *are* they *are*
Past Tense	I *was* you *were* he *was* she *was* it *was*	we *were* you *were* they *were*

INSIGHT

The word *am* exists for one reason only, to go along with the word *I*. There is no other subject for the verb *am*. In academic or formal writing, *I* should never be used with *be* or *is*. Think of René Descartes saying, "I think, therefore I am."

Say It

Read the following word groups aloud, emphasizing the words in *italics*.
1. I *laugh* / You *laugh* / She *laughs* / They *laugh*
2. I *work* / You *work* / He *works* / They *work*
3. I *do* / You *do* / He *does* / They *do*
4. I *am* / You *are* / She *is* / They *are*
5. I *was* / You *were* / He *was* / They *were*

Correcting Agreement with *I* and *You*

Write For each blank below, write the correct forms of the verb in parentheses. (Do not change the tense.)

1. I _____ louder than he _____ . (laugh)

2. You _____ as well as she _____ . (climb)

3. We _____ together, or you _____ alone. (work)

4. Stan _____ silverware, while I _____ pans. (wash)

5. I _____ often, but he _____ rarely. (help)

6. The group _____ on Sunday, but I _____ later. (watch)

7. I _____ first, and she _____ after. (eat)

8. You _____ tired, and I _____ too. (is)

9. Last year, I _____ short, but you _____ tall. (was)

10. You _____ helpful; I hope I _____ also. (is)

Correct Correct any agreement errors you find by writing the line number and incorrect verb. Cross it out and write the correct verb.

> I is starting a class in astronomy, and I wonders if I can borrow your   *1*
> telescope. You rarely uses it anymore, and I needs it to be able to look at
> the moons of Jupiter. My professor says that even a moderate-size telescope
> will show the moons. She have instructions for finding Jupiter. I knows
> how to use the telescope, but if you is afraid I would break it, you could set   *5*
> it up for me.
> Another idea would be for us to stargaze together. I has a place away
> from city lights, and I has lawn chairs and blankets we could use. If you
> agrees to come along and set up the telescope, I agrees to bring snacks for
> us.   *10*
> What do you think? I hopes I'm not asking too much and that you isn't
> mad about the request. I is just excited to see Jupiter's moons, and I thinks
> you might like to see them, too.

Write Write two sentences using "I" as the subject. Then write two more using "you" as the subject. Check your subject-verb agreement.

_____

_____

LO4 Agreement with Singular Indefinite Pronouns

An **indefinite pronoun** is intentionally vague. Instead of referring to a specific person, place, or thing, it refers to something general or unknown.

Singular Indefinite Pronouns

Singular indefinite pronouns take singular verbs:

Singular
someone
somebody
something
anyone
anybody
anything
no one
nobody
nothing
everyone
everybody
everything
one
each
either
neither

Someone cooks every night.

No one gets out of kitchen duty.

Everyone benefits from the chore schedule.

Note that indefinite pronouns that end in *one, body,* or *thing* are singular, just as these words themselves are singular. Just as you would write, "That thing is missing," so you would write "Something is missing." The words *one, each, either,* and *neither* can be tricky because they are often followed by a prepositional phrase that contains a plural noun. The verb should still be singular.

One of my friends is a great cook.

Each of us wants to cook as well as he does.

Remember that a compound subject joined with *and* needs a plural verb, and a compound subject joined with *or* needs a verb that matches the last subject.

Anything and everything taste terrific in his meals.

No one or nothing keeps him from making a wonderful meal.

Say It

Read the following word groups aloud, emphasizing the words in *italics*.

1. No one *is* / Nobody *has* / Nothing *does*

2. Everyone *is* / Everybody *has* / Everything *does*

3. One of my friends *is* / Each of my friends *has* / Either of my friends *does*

Correcting Indefinite Pronoun Agreement I

Write For each sentence below, write the correct form of the verb in parentheses. (Do not change the tense.)

1. Everyone _____ an application. (complete)

2. Somebody _____ to get the job. (have)

3. Each of the jobs _____ available. (are)

4. Neither of the applicants _____ qualified. (are)

5. Either of the prospects _____ to be trained. (hope)

6. Nobody _____ to go home empty-handed. (want)

7. Everybody _____ bills to pay. (have)

8. Someone or something _____ to give. (have)

9. Either of the positions _____ well. (pay)

10. One of my friends _____ for word on the job. (wait)

Write Write sentences using each indefinite pronoun as a subject. Choose present-tense verbs and check subject-verb agreement.

1. Someone _____

_____

2. Nothing _____

_____

3. Neither _____

_____

4. Everyone _____

_____

5. Each _____

_____

6. Anybody _____

_____

indefinite pronoun
a special type of pronoun that does not refer to a specific person or thing

Agreement with Other Indefinite Pronouns

Other indefinite pronouns are always plural, or they have a singular or plural form depending on how they are used.

Plural Indefinite Pronouns

Plural indefinite pronouns take plural verbs:

Many of us follow classical music.

Several are big fans.

Plural
both
few
many
several

Singular or Plural Indefinite Pronouns

Some indefinite pronouns or quantity words are singular or plural. If the object of the preposition in the phrase following the pronoun is singular, the pronoun takes a singular verb; if the object is plural, the pronoun takes a plural verb.

Most of the song thrills us.

Most of the songs thrill us.

Singular or Plural
all
any
half
part
most
none
some

Notice the shift in meaning, depending on the prepositional phrase. "Most of the song" means that one song is mostly thrilling. "Most of the songs" means that all but a few of many songs are thrilling. Here's another startling difference.

Half of the concert features Tchaikovsky.

Half of the concerts feature Tchaikovsky.

In the first example, half of one concert features the Russian master. In the second example, half of many concerts feature Tchaikovsky's music. What a difference one *s* can make!

Say It

Read the following word groups aloud, emphasizing the words in *italics*.
1. Both *are* / Few *have* / Many *do* / Several *were*
2. All of the piece *is* / Any of the pieces *are* / Half of the piece *does*
3. Part of the song *is* / Most of the songs *are* /
   None of the instruments *are* / Part of the instrument *is*

Correcting Indefinite Pronoun Agreement II

`Write` For each blank below, write the correct form of the verb in parentheses. (Do not change the tense.)

1. Several _____ attending, but all of us _____ listening. (are)

2. All of the songs _____ dramatic, but all of the drama _____ intentional. (is)

3. Everyone _____ Tchaikovsky, but few _____ only him. (likes)

4. One of my friends _____ to classical radio; several _____ to Internet radio. (listen)

5. Half of the album _____ symphonies, and half of the symphonies _____ brass fanfares. (feature)

6. Most of us _____ about music, and some of us _____ music, too. (read)

7. Of the music fans, several _____ hard-core, but none of them _____ a composer. (is)

8. One of my friends _____ trombone, and some of my friends _____ piano. (play)

9. Few _____ played in an orchestra, but one of us _____ played in a band. (has)

CONSIDER SPEAKING AND LISTENING

After completing the sentences in the first exercise, say them aloud, emphasizing the underlined verbs.

`Write` Write sentences using each indefinite pronoun as a subject. Choose present-tense verbs and check subject-verb agreement.

1. Part _____

2. Most _____

3. Few _____

4. Several _____

5. Both _____

6. All _____

LO5 Pronoun-Antecedent Agreement

A pronoun must agree in **person**, **number**, and **gender** with its **antecedent**. (The antecedent is the word the pronoun replaces.)

The **woman** brought **her** briefcase but forgot **her** computer.

antecedent + **pronoun** = **agreement**
(third person   (third person
singular   singular
feminine)   feminine)

Quick Guide

	Singular	Plural
First Person:	I, me (my, mine)	we, us (our, ours)
Second Person:	you (your, yours)	you (your, yours)
Third Person:		
masculine	he, him (his)	they, them (their, theirs)
feminine	she, her (her, hers)	they, them (their, theirs)
neuter	it (its)	they, them (their, theirs)

Two or More Antecedents

When two or more antecedents are joined by *and,* the pronoun should be plural.

Kali and Teri filled their baskets with eggs.

When two or more singular antecedents are joined by *or, nor,* or *but also,* the pronoun or pronouns should be singular.

Kali or Teri filled her basket with eggs.

Not only Kali but also Teri filled her basket with eggs.

NOTE: Avoid sexism when choosing pronouns that agree in number.

Sexist: Each child should bring his basket.
Correct: Each child should bring her or his basket.
Correct: Children should bring their baskets.

Correcting Pronoun-Antecedent Agreement

Write   For each blank below, write the pronoun that agrees with the underlined word or words.

1. <u>Ted</u> has written a patriotic poem and _____ will read _____ poem at the Fourth of July festival.

2. <u>Shandra</u> and <u>Shelli</u> will bring _____ lawn chairs to the fireworks display.

3. Either <u>John</u> or <u>Grace</u> will play _____ or _____ favorite marches over the sound system.

4. Not only <u>John</u> but also <u>Dave</u> plays trombone and will bring _____ instrument to play with the band.

5. Each <u>person</u> should bring _____ or _____ own flag.

6. <u>Mayor Jenny White</u> or <u>Congressperson Mark Russell</u> will give the invocation, and then _____ or _____ will introduce the main speaker.

7. <u>Rick</u> and <u>Linda</u> will sing _____ rendition of the national anthem.

8. <u>Acrobats</u> will stroll through the park on _____ ten-foot-tall stilts.

9. Each <u>acrobat</u> will have to keep _____ or _____ balance on uneven ground among running children.

10. <u>Ducks</u> and <u>ducklings</u> in the lake will have to make _____ way to quieter waters when the fireworks begin.

Revise   Rewrite each of the following sentences to avoid sexism.

1. Every acrobat should check his equipment.

   _____

2. Each acrobat must keep her balance.

   _____

3. One of the acrobats left his stilts at the park.

   _____

person	**number**	**antecedent**
the person speaking (first person—*I, we*), the person being spoken to (second person—*you*), or the person being spoken about (third person—*he, she, it, they*)	singular or plural **gender** masculine, feminine, neuter, or indefinite	the noun (or pronoun) that a pronoun refers to or replaces

LO6 Other Pronoun Problems

Missing Antecedent

If no clear antecedent is provided, the reader doesn't know what or whom the pronoun refers to.

Confusing: In Illinois, they claim Lincoln as their own.
(Who does "they" refer to?)

Clear: In Illinois, the citizens claim Lincoln as their own.

Vague Pronoun

If the pronoun could refer to two or more words, the passage is **ambiguous**.

Indefinite: Sheila told her daughter to use her new tennis racket.
(To whom does the pronoun "her" refer, Sheila or her daughter?)

Clumsy: Sheila told her daughter to use Sheila's new tennis racket.

Clear: Sheila loaned her new tennis racket to her daughter.

Double Subject

If a pronoun is used right after the subject, an error called a double subject occurs.

Incorrect: Your father, he is good at poker.

Correct: Your father is good at poker

> **INSIGHT**
>
> Use *my* before the thing possessed and use *mine* afterward: *my cat,* but *that cat is mine.* Do the same with *our/ours, your/yours,* and *her/hers.*

Incorrect Case

Personal pronouns can function as subjects, objects, or possessives. If the wrong case is used, an error occurs.

Incorrect: Them are funny videos.

Correct: They are funny videos.

The list on the right tells you which pronouns to use in each case.

Subject	Object	Possessive
I	me	my, mine
we	us	our, ours
you	you	your, yours
he	him	his
she	her	her, hers
it	it	its
they	them	their, theirs

Correcting Other Pronoun Problems

Write For each blank below, write the correct pronoun from the choices in parentheses.

1. _____ need to help_____ with the taxes.

   (I, me, my, mine)   (you, your, yours)

2. _____ should help_____ and see what_____ needs.

   (you, your, yours)   (she, her, hers)   (she, her, hers)

3. _____ can show _____ that account of _____ .

   (he, him, his)   (I, me, my, mine)   (you, your, yours)

4. _____ gave_____ permission for_____ to see.

   (you, your, yours)   (you, your, yours)   (I, me, my, mine)

5. _____ asked_____ accountant to help _____ .

   (we, us, our, ours)   (we, us, our, ours)   (we, us, our, ours)

Revise Rewrite each sentence below, correcting the pronoun problems.

1. Bob and Josh took his assignment to class.

   _____

2. Lupita needed to visit with Kelly, but she had no time.

   _____

3. Before we climbed in, it collapsed.

   _____

4. They say that a cure for cancer is coming.

   _____

5. Trina and Lois, they bought frozen custard.

   _____

6. Carl asked Tim to cook his lunch.

   _____

ambiguous
unclear, confusing

LO7 Real-World Application

Correct In the email below, correct the agreement errors. Write the line number and any word you would change. Then show the change. Use the correction marks at the bottom of the page.

Send	Attach	Fonts	Colors	Save As Draft

To: Jean Leuinski

Subject: Thank You for Your Recommendation

Hi, Ms. Leuinski: 1

Thank your for recommending me for the position of research analyst at Bismark Laboratories. During the interview last Monday, Dr. Jason Lemark said that she had received your letter and had talked with you by phone. On both occasions, him noted, you described mine work as "well-researched, meticulous,   5 and professional." I deeply appreciates your comments and you trust.

The outcome of the application process could not be more positive. Dr. Lemark are offering not just one job, but two! The first position is the one that I applied for in Bismark's San Diego office. The second position have more responsibility and higher pay, but they is in the company's Houston office.   10

Thanks again for your strong recommendation, Ms. Leuinski! Your positive words clearly affected the decision made by Dr. Lemark and the Research and Development Department. You has my deepest gratitude.

Best wishes,

Rodell
                                                                                                              15

Correction Marks

⌐	delete	⌃	add comma	ʷᵒʳᵈ ∧	add word
d̲	capitalize	?	add question	⊙	add period
⌿	lowercase	∧	mark	⌒	spelling
∧	insert	⌄	insert an apostrophe	⌒	switch

21

> "I say that what we really need is a car that can be shot when it breaks down.'"
>
> —Russell Baker

Sentence Problems

Cars are great when they go, but when a car breaks down, it is a huge headache. There's going to be a look under the hood, a bit of scrabbling beneath the thing, maybe a push, maybe a jack, and probably a tow truck and a big bill.

Sentences also are great until they break down. But you don't have to be a skilled mechanic to fix sentences. This chapter outlines a few common sentence problems and shows how to fix them. You'll be on your way in no time!

Learning Outcomes

LO1 Common Fragments
LO2 Tricky Fragments
LO3 Comma Splices
LO4 Run-On Sentences
LO5 Rambling Sentences
LO6 Misplaced and Dangling Modifiers
LO7 Shifts in Sentence Construction
LO8 Real-World Application
LO9 Real-World Application
LO10 Real-World Application

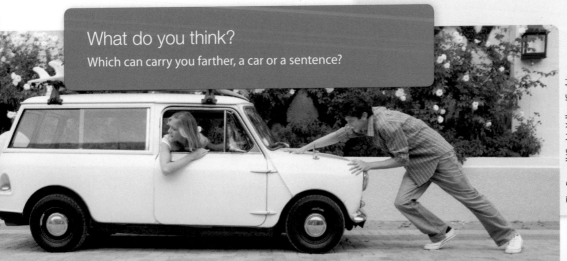

What do you think?
Which can carry you farther, a car or a sentence?

Tim Pannell/Corbis Yellow/Corbis

LO1 Common Fragments

In spoken communication and informal writing, sentence fragments are occasionally used and understood. In formal writing, fragments should be avoided.

Missing Parts

A sentence requires a subject and a predicate. If one or the other or both are missing, the sentence is a **fragment**. Such fragments can be fixed by supplying the missing part.

Fragment:	Went to the concert.
Fragment + Subject:	We went to the concert.
Fragment:	Everyone from Westville Community College.
Fragment + Predicate:	Everyone from Westville Community College may participate.
Fragment:	For the sake of student safety.
Fragment + Subject and Predicate:	The president set up a curfew for the sake of student safety.

Incomplete Thoughts

A sentence also must express a complete thought. Some fragments have a subject and a verb but do not express a complete thought. These fragments can be corrected by providing words that complete the thought.

Fragment:	The concert will include.
Completing Thought:	The concert will include an amazing light show.
Fragment:	If we arrive in time.
Completing Thought:	If we arrive in time, we'll get front-row seats.
Fragment:	Which opened the concert.
Completing Thought:	I liked the bluegrass band which opened the concert.

Say It

Read these fragments aloud. Then read each one again, but this time supply the necessary words to form a complete thought.
1. The student union building.
2. Where you can buy used books.
3. Walked to class every morning.
4. When the instructor is sick.
5. The cop was.

Correct Add words to correct each fragment below. Write the complete sentence on the lines provided.

1. Went to the office.

   _____

2. The photographer, standing at the door.

   _____

3. Will debate the pros and cons of tanning.

   _____

4. Native Americans.

   _____

5. Is one of the benefits of art class.

   _____

Correct The following paragraph contains numerous fragments. Either add what is missing or combine fragments with other sentences to make them complete. Use the correction marks shown below.

> Some people are good at memorizing facts. They piece things together.   *1*
> Like the inside of a jigsaw puzzle. Slowly build a big picture. Others are
> better at grasping overall shapes. Then filling in the middle with facts.
> Either way, have to finish the puzzle.

Correction Marks

delete	add comma	*word* add word
d capitalize	? add question mark	add period
∅ lowercase	insert an apostrophe	spelling
∧ insert		switch

Correct On your own paper or orally, correct the following fragments by supplying the missing parts. Use your imagination.

1. In the newspaper.
2. We bought.
3. The purpose of sociology class.
4. Somewhere above the clouds tonight.
5. Was the reason.

> **fragment**
> a group of words that is missing a subject or a predicate (or both) or that does not express a complete thought

LO2 Tricky Fragments

Some fragments are more difficult to find and correct. They creep into our writing because they are often part of the way we communicate in our speaking.

Absolute Phrases

An **absolute phrase** looks like a sentence that is missing its helping verb. An absolute phrase can be made into a sentence by adding the helping verb or by connecting the phrase to a complete sentence.

Absolute Phrase (Fragment):	Our legs trembling from the hike
Absolute Phrase + Helping Verb:	Our legs were trembling from the hike.
Absolute Phrase + Complete Sentence:	We collapsed on the couch, our legs trembling from the hike.

Informal Fragments

Fragments that are commonly used in speech should be eliminated from formal writing. Avoid the following types of fragments unless you are writing dialogue.

Interjections:	Hey! Yeah!	**Questions:**	How come? Why not? What?
Exclamations:	What a nuisance! How fun!		
Greetings:	Hi, everybody. Good afternoon.	**Answers:**	About three or four. As soon as possible.

NOTE: Sentences that begin with *here* or *there* have a **delayed subject**, which appears after the verb. Other sentences (commands) have an **implied subject** (*you*). Such sentences are not fragments.

Delayed Subject:	Here are some crazy fans wearing wild hats.
Implied Subject:	Tackle him! Bring him down!

Say It

Read these fragments aloud. Then add words to form a complete thought.
1. Are three types of laptop computers.
2. Our instructor explaining the assignment.
3. About three in the morning.
4. Is my favorite Web site.
5. My friend working at a half-priced disk shop.

Complete   Rewrite each tricky fragment below, making it a sentence.

1. Our boisterous behavior announcing our approach.

_____

2. A tidy hedge surrounding the trimmed lawn.

_____

3. The owner's gaze tracking us from the front porch.

_____

4. His dogs barking loudly from the backyard.

_____

5. Our welcome feeling less likely with each step.

_____

Delete   The following paragraph contains a number of informal fragments. Identify and delete each one. Reread the paragraph and listen for the difference.

> Wow! It's amazing what archaeologists can discover from bones. *1*
> Did you know that Cro-Magnon (our ancestors) and Neanderthal tribes
> sometimes lived side by side? Sure did! In other places, when climate
> change drove our ancestors south, Neanderthals took their place.
> Neanderthals were tough and had stronger arms and hands than Cro- *5*
> Magnons had. Neanderthal brains were bigger, too. What? So why aren't
> there any Neanderthals around now? Huh? Well, although Neanderthal
> tribes used spears and stone tools, our ancestors were much better
> toolmakers. Yeah! Also, Neanderthals ate mainly big animals, while Cro-
> Magnon ate anything from fish to pigs to roots and berries. So in the long *10*
> run, Cro-Magnon hominids prospered while Neanderthal tribes dwindled
> away.

absolute phrase
a group of words with a noun and a participle (a word ending in *ing* or *ed*) and the words that modify them

delayed subject
a subject that appears after the verb, as in a sentence that begins with *here* or *there* or a sentence that asks a question

implied subject
the word *you*, assumed to begin command sentences

LO3 Comma Splices

Comma splices occur when two sentences are connected with only a comma. A comma splice can be fixed by adding a coordinating conjunction (*and, but, or, nor, for, so,* or *yet*) or a subordinating conjunction (*while, after, when,* and so on). The two sentences could also be joined by a semicolon (;) or separated by a period.

Comma Splice: The Eiffel Tower was a main attraction at the Paris Exposition, the Ferris wheel was its equivalent at the Chicago Exposition.

Corrected by adding a coordinating conjunction:	The Eiffel Tower was a main attraction at the Paris Exposition, and the Ferris wheel was its equivalent at the Chicago Exposition.
Corrected by adding a subordinating conjunction:	While the Eiffel Tower was a main attraction at the Paris Exposition, the Ferris wheel was its equivalent at the Chicago Exposition.
Corrected by replacing the comma with a semicolon:	The Eiffel Tower was a main attraction at the Paris Exposition; the Ferris wheel was its equivalent at the Chicago Exposition.

INSIGHT

A comma is not strong enough to join sentences without a conjunction. A semicolon can join two closely related sentences. A period or question mark can separate two sentences.

Comma Splice: An engineer named George Washington Gale Ferris planned the first Ferris wheel, many people thought he was crazy.

Corrected by adding a coordinating conjunction:	An engineer named George Washington Gale Ferris planned the first Ferris wheel, but many people thought he was crazy.
Corrected by adding a subordinating conjunction:	When an engineer named George Washington Gale Ferris planned the first Ferris wheel, many people thought he was crazy.
Corrected by replacing the comma with a period:	An engineer named George Washington Gale Ferris planned the first Ferris wheel. Many people thought he was crazy.

Correcting Comma Splices

Correct Correct the following comma splices by adding a coordinating conjunction (*and, but, yet, or, nor, for, so*), adding a subordinating conjunction (*when, while, because,* and so on), or replacing the comma with a semicolon or period. Use the approach that makes the sentence read most smoothly.

1. We set out for a morning hike, it was raining.

2. The weather cleared by the afternoon, we hit the trail.

3. Both Jill and I were expecting wonderful scenery, we were not disappointed.

4. The view of the valley was spectacular, it was like a portrait.

5. We snacked on granola bars and apples, we enjoyed the view.

6. Then we strapped on our backpacks, the final leg of the hike awaited us.

7. The trail became rockier, we had to watch our step.

8. We reached the end of our hike, the sun was setting.

9. We're on the lookout for a new trail, it will be tough to beat this one.

10. We're done with our physical activities, it is time to watch a movie.

Correct Correct any comma splices in the following email message.

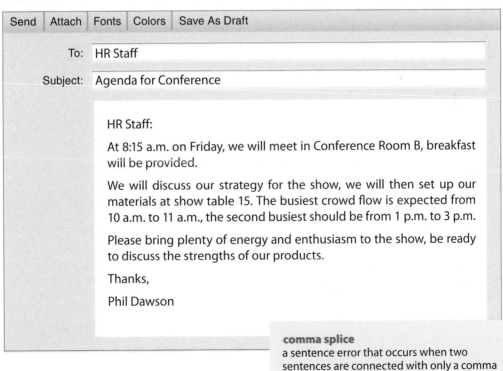

| Send | Attach | Fonts | Colors | Save As Draft |

To: HR Staff

Subject: Agenda for Conference

HR Staff:

At 8:15 a.m. on Friday, we will meet in Conference Room B, breakfast will be provided.

We will discuss our strategy for the show, we will then set up our materials at show table 15. The busiest crowd flow is expected from 10 a.m. to 11 a.m., the second busiest should be from 1 p.m. to 3 p.m.

Please bring plenty of energy and enthusiasm to the show, be ready to discuss the strengths of our products.

Thanks,

Phil Dawson

comma splice
a sentence error that occurs when two sentences are connected with only a comma

LO4 Run-On Sentences

A **run-on sentence** occurs when two sentences are joined without punctuation or a connecting word. A run-on can be corrected by adding a comma and a conjunction or by inserting a semicolon or period between the two sentences.

Run-On: Horace Wilson taught in Tokyo in 1872 he introduced the Japanese to baseball.

Corrected by adding a comma and coordinating conjunction:	Horace Wilson taught in Tokyo in 1872, and he introduced the Japanese to baseball.
Corrected by adding a subordinating conjunction and a comma:	While Horace Wilson taught in Tokyo in 1872, he introduced the Japanese to baseball.
Corrected by inserting a semicolon:	Horace Wilson taught in Tokyo in 1872; he introduced the Japanese to baseball.

CONSIDER THE TRAITS

Here's an additional way to correct a run-on sentence: Turn one of the sentences into a phrase or series of phrases; then combine it with the other sentence.

The first team in Japan was formed in 1878 without a thought about how popular the sport would become.

Run-On: The first team in Japan was formed in 1878 no one knew how popular the sport would become.

Corrected by adding a comma and a coordinating conjunction:	The first team in Japan was formed in 1878, yet no one knew how popular the sport would become.
Corrected by adding a subordinating conjunction and a comma:	When the first team in Japan was formed in 1878, no one knew how popular the sport would become.
Corrected by inserting a period:	The first team in Japan was formed in 1878. No one knew how popular the sport would become.

Correcting Run-On Sentences

Correct   Correct the following run-on sentences. Use the approach that makes the sentence read most smoothly.

1. In 1767 English scientist Joseph Priestley discovered a way to infuse water with carbon dioxide this invention led to carbonated water.

2. Carbonated water is one of the main components of soft drinks it gives soft drinks the fizz and bubbles we enjoy.

3. The first soft drinks in America were dispensed out of soda fountains they were most often found at drug stores and ice-cream parlors.

4. Interestingly, soda was sold at drug stores it promised healing properties.

5. Most of the formulas for American soft drinks were invented by pharmacists the idea was to create nonalcoholic alternatives to traditional medicines.

6. The first carbonated drink bottles could not keep bubbles from escaping it was more popular to buy a soda from a soda fountain.

7. A successful method of keeping bubbles in a bottle was not invented until 1892 it was called a crowned bottle cap.

8. The first diet soda to be sold was known as "No-Cal Beverage" in 1959 the first diet cola hit the stores.

Rewrite   Rewrite the following paragraph, correcting any run-on sentences that you find.

> Arbor Day is an undervalued holiday in America. On this holiday, people are encouraged to plant trees it is celebrated on the fourth Friday of April. It was created by J. Sterling Morton he was President Grover Cleveland's Secretary of Agriculture. The holiday is now observed in a number of other countries.
>
> *1*
>
> *5*

run-on sentence
a sentence error that occurs when two sentences are joined without punctuation *or* a connecting word

kosam, 2013 / Used under license from Shutterstock.com

LO5 Rambling Sentences

A **rambling sentence** occurs when a long series of separate ideas are connected by one *and, but,* or *so* after another. The result is an unfocused sentence that goes on and on. To correct a rambling sentence, break it into smaller units, adding and cutting words as needed.

Rambling: When we signed up for the two-on-two tournament, I had no thoughts about winning, but then my brother started talking about spending his prize money and he asked me how I would spend my share so we were counting on winning when we really had little chance and as it turned out, we lost in the second round.

Corrected: When we signed up for the two-on-two tournament, I had no thoughts about winning. Then my brother started talking about spending the prize money. He even asked me how I would spend my share. Soon, we were counting on winning when we really had little chance. As it turned out, we lost in the second round.

Say It

Read the following rambling sentences aloud. Afterward, circle all of the connecting words (*and, but, so*), and be prepared to suggest different ways to break each rambling idea into more manageable units.

1. I enjoyed touring the hospital and I would enjoy joining the nursing staff and I believe that my prior work experience will be an asset but I also know that I have a lot more to learn.

2. The electronics store claims to offer "one-stop shopping" and they can take care of all of a customer's computer needs and they have a fully trained staff to answer questions and solve problems so there is really no need to go anywhere else.

Correcting Rambling Sentences

Correct Correct the following rambling sentences by dividing them into separate sentences. Afterward, share your corrections with a classmate.

1. The dancer entered gracefully onto the stage and she twirled around twice and then tiptoed to the front of the stage and the crowd applauded.

_____

2. I went to the movies last night and when I got to the theater, I had to wait in a super-slow line and when I finally got to the front, the show I wanted to see was sold out.

_____

3. I like to listen to music everywhere but I especially like to rock out in my car so I scream and dance and I don't care if anyone sees me through the windows.

_____

EDHAR, 2013 / Used under license from Shutterstock.com

CONSIDER EXTENDING

Share your corrections with a classmate. Did you change each rambling sentence in the same way?

Answer Answer the following questions about rambling sentences.

1. How can you recognize a rambling sentence?

_____

2. Why is a rambling sentence a problem?

_____

3. How can you correct one?

_____

rambling sentence
a sentence error that occurs when a long series of separate ideas are connected by one *and, but,* or *so* after another

LO6 Misplaced and Dangling Modifiers

Dangling Modifiers

A modifier is a word, phrase, or clause that functions as an adjective or adverb. When the modifier does not clearly modify another word in the sentence, it is called a **dangling modifier**. This error can be corrected by inserting the missing word and/or rewriting the sentence.

Dangling Modifier: After strapping the cowboy hat to his back, my cat stalked sullenly around the house.
(The cat could strap the cowboy hat to his own back?)

Corrected: After I strapped the cowboy hat to his back, my cat stalked sullenly around the house.

Dangling Modifier: Trying to get the cowboy hat off, the bowl got knocked off the shelf. *(The bowl was trying to get the cowboy hat off?)*

Corrected: Trying to get the cowboy hat off, the cat knocked the bowl off the shelf.

Misplaced Modifiers

When a modifier is placed beside a word that it does not modify, the modifier is misplaced and often results in an amusing or **illogical** statement. A **misplaced modifier** can be corrected by moving it next to the word that it modifies.

Misplaced Modifier: My cat was diagnosed by the vet with fleas.
(The vet has fleas?)

Corrected: The vet diagnosed my cat with fleas.

Misplaced Modifier: The vet gave a pill to my cat tasting like fish.
(The cat tastes like fish?)

Corrected: The vet gave my cat a pill tasting like fish.

INSIGHT

Avoid placing any adverb modifiers between a verb and its direct object.
  Misplaced: I will throw quickly the ball.
  Corrected: I will quickly throw the ball.
Also, do not separate two-word verbs with an adverb modifier.
  Misplaced: Please take immediately out the trash.
  Corrected: Please immediately take out the trash.

Say It

Read the following sentences aloud, noting the dangling or misplaced modifier in each one. Then tell a classmate how you would correct each error.

1. After tearing up the couch, I decided to get my cat a scratching post.
2. I have worked to teach my cat to beg for three weeks.

Correcting Dangling and Misplaced Modifiers

Rewrite Rewrite each of the sentences below, correcting the misplaced and dangling modifiers.

1. I bought a hound dog for my brother named Rover.

2. The doctor diagnosed me and referred me to a specialist with scoliosis.

3. The man was reported murdered by the coroner.

4. Please present the recommendation that is attached to Mrs. Burble.

5. Jack drove me to our home in a Chevy.

6. I couldn't believe my brother would hire a disco DJ who hates disco.

7. We saw a fox and a vixen on the way to the psychiatrist.

8. I gave the secretary my phone number that works in reception.

9. I found a pair of underwear in the drawer that doesn't belong to me.

10. We offer jackets for trendy teens with gold piping.

Correct For each sentence, correct the placement of the adverb.

1. Give quickly the report to your boss.
2. We will provide immediately an explanation.
3. Fill completely out the test sheet.

INSIGHT ——————————————————————————————

When a modifier comes at the beginning of the sentence or the end of the sentence, make sure it modifies the word or phrase closest to it. Ask yourself, "Who or what is being described?"

---

dangling modifier
a modifying word, phrase, or clause that appears to modify the wrong word or a word that isn't in the sentence

illogical
without logic; senseless, false, or untrue

misplaced modifier
a modifying word, phrase, or clause that has been placed incorrectly in a sentence, often creating an amusing or illogical idea

LO7 Shifts in Sentence Construction

Shift in Person

A **shift in person** is an error that occurs when first, second, and/or third person are improperly mixed in a sentence.

Shift in person:	If you exercise and eat right, an individual can lose weight. (The sentence improperly shifts from second person—*you*—to third person—*individual*.)
Corrected:	If you exercise and eat right, you can lose weight.

Shift in Tense

A **shift in tense** is an error that occurs when more than one verb tense is improperly used in a sentence. (See pages 586–593 for more about tense.)

Shift in tense:	He tried every other option before he agrees to do it my way. (The sentence improperly shifts from past tense—*tried*—to present tense—*agrees*.)
Corrected:	He tried every other option before he agreed to do it my way.

Shift in Voice

A **shift in voice** is an error that occurs when active voice and passive voice are mixed in a sentence.

Shift in voice:	When she fixes the radiator, other repairs may be suggested. (The sentence improperly shifts from active voice—*fixes*—to passive voice—*may be suggested*.)
Corrected:	When she fixes the radiator, she may suggest other repairs.

Say It

Read the following sentences aloud, paying careful attention to the improper shift each contains. Then tell a classmate how you would correct each error.

1. David exercises daily and ate well.
2. Marianne goes running each morning and new friends might be met.
3. After you choose an exercise routine, a person should stick to it.
4. Lamar swam every morning and does ten laps.
5. The personal trainer made a schedule for me, and a diet was suggested by her.

Correcting Improper Shifts in Sentences

Rewrite Rewrite each sentence below, correcting any improper shifts in construction.

1. You should be ready for each class in a person's schedule.

2. I work for my brother most days and classes are attended by me at night.

3. When you give me a review, can he also give me a raise?

4. As we walked to school, last night's football game was discussed by us.

5. I hoped to catch the bus until I see it leave.

Correct Correct the improper shifts in person, tense, or voice in the following paragraph. Use the correction marks below when you make your changes.

> Some people are early adopters, which means technology is adopted   *1*
> by them when it is new. Other people are technophobes because you are
> afraid of technology, period. I am not an early adopter or a technophobe,
> but a person has to see the value in technology before I use it. Technology
> has to be cheap, intuitive, reliable, and truly helpful before you start using   *5*
> it. I let others work out the bugs and pay the high prices before a piece
> of technology is adopted by me. But when I decide it is time to get a new
> gadget or program, you buy it and use it until it is worn out. Then I look
> for something else that is even cheaper and more intuitive, reliable, and
> helpful, which is then bought by me.   *10*

Correction Marks

⌐	delete	⅄	add comma	word ∧	add word
d̲	capitalize	?	add question mark	⊙	add period
ø̲	lowercase			⬭	spelling
∧	insert	ⱽ	insert an apostrophe	∿	switch

person
first person (*I* or *we*—the person speaking), second person (*you*—the person spoken to), or third person (*he, she, it,* or *they*—the person or thing spoken about)

voice of verb
whether the subject is doing the action of the verb (active voice) or is being acted upon (passive voice) (See page 584.)

shift in person
an error that occurs when first, second, and third person are improperly mixed in a sentence

shift in tense
an error that occurs when more than one verb tense is improperly used in a sentence

shift in voice
an error that occurs when active voice and passive voice are mixed in a sentence

LO8 Real-World Application

Correct Correct any sentence fragments in the following business memo. Use the correction marks below.

Slovik Manufacturing   *1*

Date: August 8, 2013

To: Jerome James, Personnel Director

From: Ike Harris, Graphic Arts Director

Subject: Promotion of Mona Veal from Intern to Full-Time Graphic Artist   *5*

For the past five months, Mona Veal as an intern in our Marketing Department. I recommend that she be offered a position as a full-time designer. Are the two main reasons behind this recommendation.

1. Mona has shown the traits that Slovik Manufacturing values in a graphic designer. Creative, dependable, and easy to work with.   *10*

2. Presently, we have two full-time graphic designers and one intern. While this group has worked well. The full-time designers have averaged 3.5 hours of overtime per week. Given this fact. Our new contract with Lee-Stamp Industries will require more help, including at least one additional designer.   *15*

If you approve this recommendation. Please initial below and return this memo.

Yes, I approve the recommendation to offer Mona Veal a full-time position.

———

Attachment: Evaluation report of Mona Veal   *20*

cc: Elizabeth Zoe
    Mark Moon

Correction Marks

ℐ	delete	⟋ⵢ	add comma	word ∧	add word
d̲	capitalize	? ∧	add question mark	⊙	add period
ⱷ	lowercase			⌒	spelling
∧	insert	⌄	insert an apostrophe	∼	switch

LO9 Real-World Application

Correct Correct any comma splices or run-on sentences in the following email. Use the correction marks on the previous page.

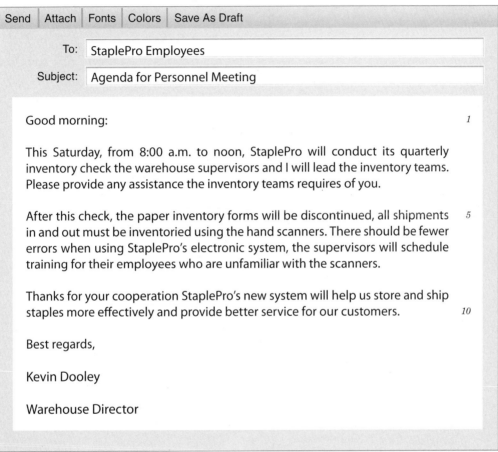

| Send | Attach | Fonts | Colors | Save As Draft |

| To: | StaplePro Employees |
| Subject: | Agenda for Personnel Meeting |

Good morning: *1*

This Saturday, from 8:00 a.m. to noon, StaplePro will conduct its quarterly inventory check the warehouse supervisors and I will lead the inventory teams. Please provide any assistance the inventory teams requires of you.

After this check, the paper inventory forms will be discontinued, all shipments   *5*
in and out must be inventoried using the hand scanners. There should be fewer errors when using StaplePro's electronic system, the supervisors will schedule training for their employees who are unfamiliar with the scanners.

Thanks for your cooperation StaplePro's new system will help us store and ship staples more effectively and provide better service for our customers.   *10*

Best regards,

Kevin Dooley

Warehouse Director

Reflect Reflect on what you have learned about comma splices and run-on sentences by answering the following questions.

1. What is the difference between a comma splice and a run-on sentence?

_____

2. How can you correct comma splices and run-on sentences? (Name at least three ways.)

_____

3. What are three common coordinating conjunctions that you can use to connect two sentences?

_____

LO10 Real-World Application

Correct Correct any dangling modifiers, misplaced modifiers, or shifts in construction in the following email. Use the correction marks below.

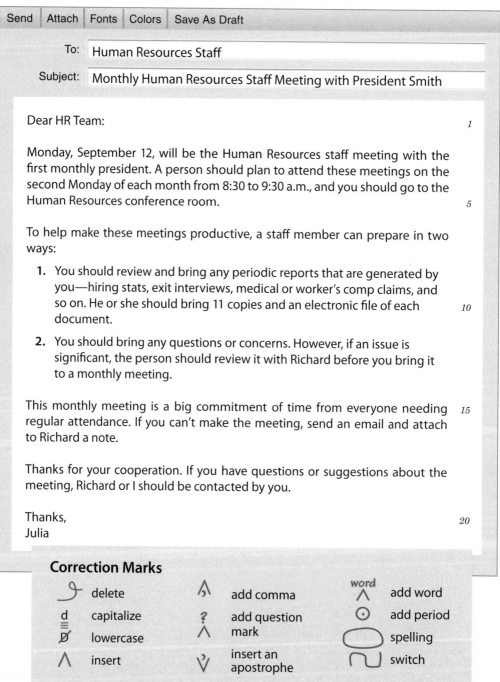

| Send | Attach | Fonts | Colors | Save As Draft |

To: Human Resources Staff

Subject: Monthly Human Resources Staff Meeting with President Smith

Dear HR Team: *1*

Monday, September 12, will be the Human Resources staff meeting with the first monthly president. A person should plan to attend these meetings on the second Monday of each month from 8:30 to 9:30 a.m., and you should go to the Human Resources conference room.   *5*

To help make these meetings productive, a staff member can prepare in two ways:

1. You should review and bring any periodic reports that are generated by you—hiring stats, exit interviews, medical or worker's comp claims, and so on. He or she should bring 11 copies and an electronic file of each *10* document.

2. You should bring any questions or concerns. However, if an issue is significant, the person should review it with Richard before you bring it to a monthly meeting.

This monthly meeting is a big commitment of time from everyone needing *15* regular attendance. If you can't make the meeting, send an email and attach to Richard a note.

Thanks for your cooperation. If you have questions or suggestions about the meeting, Richard or I should be contacted by you.

Thanks,   *20*
Julia

Correction Marks

� delete	⌃, add comma	word ⌃ add word
d̲ capitalize	? add question	⊙ add period
⌀ lowercase	⌃ mark	⬭ spelling
⌃ insert	⌄ insert an apostrophe	⎗ switch

Rewrite The sentences that follow come from church bulletins and are amusing due to misplaced or dangling modifiers or other sentence problems. Rewrite each sentence to remove these problems.

1. Remember in prayer the many who are sick of our church and community.

   _____

2. For those of you who have children and don't know it, we have a nursery downstairs.

   _____

3. The ladies of the church have cast off clothing of every kind. They can be seen in the church basement Saturday.

   _____

4. The third verse of "Blessed Assurance" will be sung without musical accomplishment.

   _____

Write Write the first draft of a personal narrative (true story) in which you share a time when you misplaced or lost something important to you or to someone else. Here are some tips for adding interest to your story:

- Start right in the middle of the action.
- Build suspense to keep the reader's interest.
- Use dialogue.
- Use sensory details (what you heard, saw, felt, and so on).

Afterward, exchange your writing with a classmate. Read each other's narrative first for enjoyment and a second time to check it for the sentence errors discussed in this chapter.

CONSIDER THE WORKPLACE

Journalists and publishers need to be especially careful to avoid mistakes in their writing. But errors in writing reflect badly on all professionals.

April Cat, 2013 / Used under license from Shutterstock.com

Part V: Word Workshops

22

> "If you want to make an apple pie from scratch, you must first create the universe."
>
> —Carl Sagan

Noun

Astrophysicists tell us that the universe is made up of two things—matter and energy. Matter is the stuff, and energy is the movement or heat of the stuff.

Grammarians tell us that thoughts are made up of two things—nouns and verbs. Nouns name the stuff, and verbs capture the energy. In that way, the sentence reflects the universe itself. You can't express a complete thought unless you are talking about matter and energy. Each sentence, then, is the basic particle of thought.

This chapter focuses on nouns, which describe not just things you can see—such as people, places, or objects—but also things you can't see—such as love, justice, and democracy. The exercises in this chapter will help you sort out the stuff of thinking.

Learning Outcomes

LO1 Classes of Nouns
LO2 Singular and Plural Nouns
LO3 Tricky Plurals
LO4 Count and Noncount Nouns
LO5 Articles
LO6 Other Noun Markers
LO7 Real-World Application

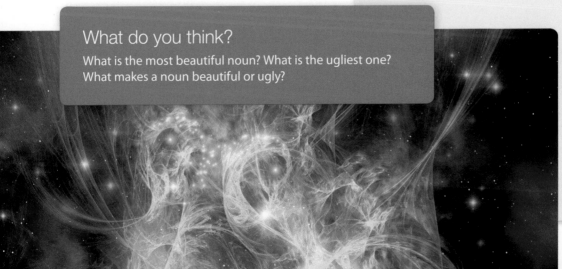

What do you think?

What is the most beautiful noun? What is the ugliest one? What makes a noun beautiful or ugly?

Catmando, 2013 / Used under license from Shutterstock.com

LO1 Classes of Nouns

All nouns are either *common* or *proper*. They can also be *individual* or *collective, concrete* or *abstract*.

Common or Proper Nouns

Common nouns name a general person, place, thing, or idea. They are not capitalized as names. **Proper nouns** name a specific person, place, thing, or idea, and they are capitalized as names.

	Common Nouns	Proper Nouns
Person:	politician	Barack Obama
Place:	park	Yellowstone
Thing:	marker	Sharpie
Idea:	religion	Hinduism

Individual or Collective Nouns

Most nouns are **individual**: They refer to one person or thing. Other nouns are **collective**, referring most commonly to a group of people or animals.

	Individual Nouns	Collective Nouns
Person:	secretary	staff
	catcher	team
	student	class
	daughter	family
Animal:	lamb	herd
	locust	swarm
	wolf	pack
	kitten	litter
	goose	gaggle

Concrete or Abstract

If a noun refers to something that can be seen, heard, smelled, tasted, or touched, it is a **concrete noun**. If a noun refers to something that can't be sensed, it is an **abstract noun**. Abstract nouns name ideas, conditions, or feelings.

Concrete Nouns	Abstract Nouns
judge	impartiality
brain	mind
heart	courage
train	transportation

Using Different Classes of Nouns

Identify In each sentence below, identify the underlined nouns as common (C) or proper (P).

1. William Faulkner wrote about the death of the Old South.

2. His novel *The Unvanquished* tells about the aftermath of the Civil War.

3. He chronicles the end of slavery but also of the genteel class in the South.

4. His novel *Absalom, Absalom!* describes the creation and end of a plantation.

Identify In each sentence below, identify the underlined nouns as individual (I) or collective (CL).

1. Quentin Compson appears often in the collected works of Faulkner.

2. The Compson family is the centerpiece of Yoknapatawpha County.

3. The novel *The Sound and the Fury* tells of the plight of the Compsons.

4. Benjamin Compson watches a group golf in what was once their farm field.

Identify In each sentence below, identify the underlined nouns as concrete (CT) or abstract (A).

1. The Compsons become a symbol of the decline of the South.

2. Faulkner depicts the family with compassion and humor.

3. Other novels tell of other denizens of Faulkner's imagination.

4. Faulkner won the Pulitzer Prize for his novel *A Fable,* set outside the county.

---

common noun
noun referring to a general person, place, thing, or idea; not capitalized as a name

proper noun
noun referring to a specific person, place, thing, or idea; capitalized as a name

individual noun
noun referring to one person or thing

collective noun
noun referring to a group of people or animals

concrete noun
noun referring to something that can be sensed

abstract noun
noun referring to an idea, a condition, or a feeling—something that cannot be sensed

LO2   Singular and Plural Nouns

The **number** of a noun indicates whether it is singular or plural. A **singular** noun refers to one person, place, thing, or idea. A **plural** noun refers to more than one person, place, thing, or idea. For most words, the plural is formed by adding *s*. For nouns ending in *ch*, *s*, *sh*, *x*, or *z*, add an *es*.

	Most Nouns Add *s*		Nouns Ending in *ch, s, sh, x, or z* Add *es*	
	Singular	Plural	Singular	Plural
Person:	sister	sisters	coach	coaches
Place:	park	parks	church	churches
Thing:	spoon	spoons	kiss	kisses
Idea:	solution	solutions	wish	wishes

Same in Both Forms or Usually Plural

Some nouns are the same in both forms, and others are usually plural.

Same in Both Forms		Usually Plural	
Singular	Plural	Plural	
deer	deer	clothes	series
fish	fish	glasses	shears
moose	moose	pants	shorts
salmon	salmon	proceeds	species
sheep	sheep	savings	tongs
swine	swine	scissors	trousers

Irregular Plurals

Irregular plurals are formed by changing the words themselves. That is because the plural form comes from Old English or Latin.

From Old English		From Latin	
Singular	Plural	Singular	Plural
child	children	alumnus	alumni
foot	feet	axis	axes
goose	geese	crisis	crises
man	men	datum	data
mouse	mice	millennium	millennia
person	people	medium	media
tooth	teeth	nucleus	nuclei
woman	women	phenomenon	phenomena

Using Singular and Plural Nouns

Identify For each word, fill in the blank with either the singular or plural form, whichever is missing. If the word usually uses the plural form or is the same in both forms, write an X.

1. crisis _____
2. _____ species
3. child _____
4. automobile _____
5. _____ shears
6. _____ teeth
7. _____ clothes
8. deer _____
9. swine _____
10. phenomenon _____
11. _____ girls
12. _____ millennia
13. man _____
14. fish _____
15. _____ pants
16. _____ moose
17. axis _____
18. boy _____
19. _____ mice
20. goose _____
21. _____ data
22. alumnus _____
23. _____ savings
24. tree _____
25. _____ women

number	**plural**	**irregular plural**
whether a word is singular or plural	referring to more than one thing	a plural noun formed by changing the word rather than by adding *s*
singular		
referring to one thing		

LO3 Tricky Plurals

Some plural nouns are more challenging to form. Words ending in *y, f,* or *fe* and certain compound nouns require special consideration.

Nouns Ending in *y*

If a common noun ends in *y* after a consonant, change the *y* to *i* and add *es*. If the noun ends in *y* after a vowel, leave the *y* and add *s*.

y After a Consonant		*y* After a Vowel	
Singular	Plural	Singular	Plural
fly	flies	bay	bays
lady	ladies	key	keys
penny	pennies	toy	toys
story	stories	tray	trays

Nouns Ending in *f* or *fe*

If a common noun ends in *f* or *fe,* change the *f* or *fe* to a *v* and add *es*—unless the *f* sound remains in the plural form. Then just add an *s*.

v Sound in Plural		*f* Sound in Plural	
Singular	Plural	Singular	Plural
calf	calves	belief	beliefs
life	lives	chef	chefs
self	selves	proof	proofs
shelf	shelves	safe	safes

Compound Nouns

A **compound noun** is made up of two or more words that function together as a single noun. Whether the compound is hyphenated or not, make it plural by placing the *s* or *es* on the most important word in the compound.

Important Word First		Important Word Last	
Singular	Plural	Singular	Plural
editor in chief	editors in chief	bird-watcher	bird-watchers
mother-in-law	mothers-in-law	human being	human beings
professor emeritus	professors emeritus	test tube	test tubes
secretary of state	secretaries of state	well-wisher	well-wishers

Forming Tricky Plurals

Form Plurals For each word below, create the correct plural form.

1. day _____
2. shelf _____
3. middle school _____
4. pony _____
5. bay _____
6. life _____
7. chief _____
8. loaf _____
9. tray _____
10. compact car _____

11. mother-in-law _____
12. ray _____
13. lady _____
14. carafe _____
15. stepsister _____
16. poof _____
17. nose tackle _____
18. party _____
19. son-in-law _____
20. baby _____

Form Plurals In the sentences below, correct the plural errors by writing the correct forms.

1. If I give you two pennys for your thoughts, will you give me two cents' worths?
2. Have you read *The Secret Lifes of Cheves*?
3. The professor emerituses are working on two mathematical prooves.
4. I won't question your believes or insult your wells-wisher.
5. The ladys tried to quiet their screaming babys.
6. Time is sure fun when you're having flys.
7. The compacts car are equipped with remote-access keis.
8. I like chicken pattys but don't like salmons patty.
9. I read about dwarves and elfs.
10. Stack those books on the shelfs above the saves.

compound noun
noun made up of two or more words

Kalim, 2013 / Used under license from Shutterstock.com

LO4 Count and Noncount Nouns

Some nouns name things that can be counted, and other nouns name things that cannot. Different rules apply to each type.

Count Nouns

Count nouns name things that can be counted—*pens, people, votes, cats,* and so forth. They can be singular or plural, and they can be preceded by numbers or articles (*a, an,* or *the*).

Singular	Plural
apple	apples
iguana	iguanas
thought	thoughts
room	rooms

> **INSIGHT**
>
> Many native English speakers aren't even aware of count and noncount nouns, though they use them correctly out of habit. Listen for their use of count and noncount nouns.

Noncount Nouns

Noncount nouns name things that cannot be counted. They are used in singular form, and they can be preceded by *the,* but rarely by *a* or *an*.

This semester, I'm taking **mathematics** and **biology** as well as **Spanish**.

Substances	Foods	Activities	Science	Languages	Abstractions
wood	water	reading	oxygen	Spanish	justice
cloth	milk	boating	weather	English	harm
ice	wine	smoking	heat	Mandarin	publicity
plastic	sugar	dancing	sunshine	Farsi	advice
wool	rice	swimming	electricity	Greek	happiness
steel	meat	soccer	lightning	Latin	health
aluminum	cheese	hockey	biology	French	joy
metal	flour	photography	history	Japanese	love
leather	pasta	writing	mathematics	Afrikaans	anger
porcelain	gravy	homework	economics	German	fame

Two-Way Nouns

Two-way nouns can function as count or noncount nouns, depending on their context.

Please set a **glass** in front of each place mat. (count noun)

The display case was made of tempered **glass**. (noncount noun)

Using Count and Noncount Nouns

Sort Read the list of nouns below and sort the words into columns of count and noncount nouns.

window	aluminum	holiday	health	rain
English	shoe	tricycle	poetry	ice
bowling	plum	Japanese	lawyer	teaspoon

Using Count and Noncount Nouns

Correct Read the following paragraph and correct the noun errors. Write the line number and any words you would change, and then show the change. The first line has been corrected for you.

Our kitchen redesign involved tearing out the plastics that covered   1

the counter and removing the flashings around the edges. We installed

new aluminums to replace the old metals. Also, the cupboard doors, which

used to be made of woods, were replaced by doors made of glasses. We have

a new jar for holding flours and a new refrigerator with a special place   5

for milks and a dispenser for waters. Everything is illuminated by new

lightings, and a larger window lets more sunlights in.

Correction Marks

℈	delete	⍾	add comma	⋏	add word
d	capitalize	?	add question mark	⊙	add period
∅	lowercase			⌒	spelling
∧	insert	⌄	insert an apostrophe	⁓	switch

LO5 Articles

Articles help you to know if a noun refers to a specific thing or to a general thing. There are two basic types of articles—definite and indefinite.

Definite Article

The **definite article** is the word *the*. It signals that the noun refers to one specific person, place, thing, or idea.

> Look at the rainbow.
> (Look at a specific rainbow.)
>
> > NOTE: *The* can be used with most nouns, but usually not with proper nouns.
>
> **Incorrect:** The Joe looked at the rainbow.
>   **Correct:** Joe looked at the rainbow.

INSIGHT

If your heritage language does not use articles, pay close attention to the way native English speakers use *the* when referring to a specific thing. Note, however, that *the* is not usually used with proper nouns naming people or animals.

Indefinite Articles

The **indefinite articles** are the words *a* and *an*. They signal that the noun refers to a general person, place, thing, or idea. The word *a* is used before nouns that begin with consonant sounds, and the word *an* is used before nouns that begin with vowel sounds.

> I enjoy seeing a rainbow.
> (I enjoy seeing any rainbow.)
>
> > NOTE: Don't use *a* or *an* with noncount nouns or plural count nouns.
>
> **Incorrect:** I love a sunshine.
>   **Correct:** I love the sunshine.
>
> > NOTE: If a word begins with an *h* that is pronounced, use *a*. If the *h* is silent, use *an*.
>
> **Incorrect:** I stared for a hour.
>   **Correct:** I stared for an hour.

Using Articles

Identify Add the appropriate indefinite article (*a* or *an*) to each of the words below. The first one has been done for you.

1. __an__ orchard
2. _____ petunia
3. _____ hose
4. _____ honor
5. _____ avocado
6. _____ evening
7. _____ house
8. _____ hour
9. _____ shark
10. _____ eye
11. _____ error
12. _____ opportunity
13. __ honest mistake
14. _____ emblem
15. ____ handkerchief

Correct Write the line number and either delete or replace any articles that are incorrectly used. The first sentence has been done for you.

> the ⟋
> Climate scientists see a shift in a̶ weather. With a increase in the   *1*
> levels of carbon dioxide, the atmosphere traps a heat of the sun. More
> heat in an air means more heat in the oceans. If a ocean gets warmer,
> the storms it creates are more intense. An hurricane could develop to an
> higher category, with stronger winds and a increase in a lightning. A   *5*
> Earth is already an storm world, but with a rise in global temperatures,
> a weather could become more extreme.

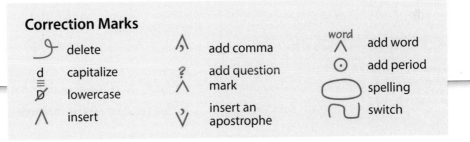

Correction Marks

⟋ delete	⩘ add comma	word ⋀ add word
d̲ capitalize	? ⋀ add question mark	⊙ add period
⌀ lowercase		⌓ spelling
⋀ insert	⋎ insert an apostrophe	⌂ switch

article
the most common type of noun marker (*a, an,* or *the*)

definite article
the word *the*, used to mark a noun that refers to a specific person, place, or thing

indefinite article
the words *a* or *an*, used to mark a noun that refers to a general person, place, or thing

LO6 Other Noun Markers

Possessive Adjective

A **possessive adjective** is the possessive form of a noun or pronoun. Possessive adjectives can be formed by adding *'s* to singular nouns and *'* to plural nouns.

Paul's car is in the shop, but **Taylor's** is fixed.	**Possessive Pronouns**			
Florida's coast is beautiful.		**Singular**		**Plural**
The **Kings'** porch has screens.		Before	After	Before	After
That is **my** pen. This pen is **mine**.	First Person	my	mine	our	ours
	Second Person	your	yours	your	yours
It's **your** choice. The choice is **yours**.	Third Person	his	his	their	theirs
		her	hers	their	theirs
		its	its	their	theirs

Indefinite Adjectives

An **indefinite adjective** signals that the noun it marks refers to a general person, place, thing, or idea. Some indefinite adjectives mark count nouns and others mark noncount nouns.

Each person brought food. **Much** food was set out.

With Count Nouns			**With Noncount Nouns**	**With Count or Noncount**		
each	either	every	much	all	any	more
few	many	neither		most	some	
several						

Demonstrative Adjectives

A **demonstrative adjective** marks a specific noun. The words *this* and *that* (singular) or *these* and *those* (plural) demonstrate exactly which one is meant.

These pickles are from **that** jar.   **This** taste comes from **those** spices.

Quantifiers

A **quantifier** tells *how many* or *how much* there is of something.

With Count Nouns		**With Noncount Nouns**		**With Count or Noncount**		
each	a couple of	a bag of	a little	no	a lot of	most
several	every	a bowl of	much	not any	lots of	all
a number of	many	a piece of	a great deal of	some	plenty of	
both	a few					
nine						

Using Noun Markers

Identify Write the appropriate noun marker in parentheses for each sentence.

1. I brought one of (*my, mine*) favorite recipes, and you brought
   one of (*your, yours*).
2. Is this (*her, hers*) recipe, or is it (*their, theirs*)?
3. How (*many, much*) sugar should I add to the batter?
4. I can't believe the recipe does not use (*any, each*) flour.
5. Next, we should make (*this, these*) casserole.
6. Your face tells me you don't like (*that, those*) idea.
7. After making the dough, we had (*several, a little*) butter left over.
8. We liked (*a number of, much*) the recipes.
9. The best pie of all was (*her, hers*).
10. Let's make sure everyone has a copy in (*their, theirs*) recipe files.

Correct Write the line number and show the changes you would make to correct
any incorrectly used noun markers. The first one has been done for you.

An omelet can contain as few or as ~~much~~ *many* ingredients as you wish.   *1*
Of course, a good omelet starts with three or four eggs. Blend the eggs in
yours biggest bowl and add a couple of milk. Next, you can include much
vegetables. Try fresh ingredients from yours garden. Add a cup of chopped
scallions, fresh tomatoes, or green peppers. And a number of spinach can   *5*
give the omelet a savory flavor. You can also add several meat. Mix in a
couple of bacon or many ham. Or you might include several sausage. Fry
the omelet, fold it, sprinkle it with a couple of cheese, and enjoy!

Correction Marks

↗ delete	⌃ add comma	⌃ add word (*word*)
d capitalize	? add question mark	⊙ add period
⌿ lowercase	⌃ mark	⬭ spelling
⌃ insert	⌄ insert an apostrophe	⊓ switch

possessive adjective
the possessive form of a
noun or pronoun, showing
ownership of another noun

indefinite adjective
an indefinite pronoun
(*many, much, some*) used
as an adjective to mark a
nonspecific noun

demonstrative adjective
a demonstrative pronoun
(*this, that, these, those*) used as
an adjective to mark a specific
noun

quantifier
a modifier that tells *how many*
or *how much*

LO7 Real-World Application

Correct In the email that follows, correct any errors with nouns, articles, or other noun markers. Use the correction marks below.

Send	Attach	Fonts	Colors	Save As Draft

To: Design and Printing Staff

Subject: Internship Program for University Students

Hi, Team: 1

Could you use a assistant—a extra pair of hands at little cost?

The head of the Graphic Arts Department at Northwestern College has asked
us if we'd be interested in developing internships for third-year students in a
university's four-year graphic-arts program.   5

Internships could be the real win-win proposition because interns would
  • work on tasks that you assign.
  • get excellent professional experience by working with you.
  • give us an opportunity to work with potential employees.

Please consider working with an student intern during the fall semester. If you   10
are interested, let me know before January 28.

Thanks for considering these invitation to help future member of a graphic
arts profession.

Melissa

Correction Marks

⌐	delete	⌄	add comma	*word* ∧	add word	
d ≡	capitalize	?	add question	⊙	add period	
∅	lowercase	∧	mark		spelling	
∧	insert	⌄	insert an apostrophe	∩	switch	

23

Pronoun

An old saying goes that clothes make the man. Well, not quite. Just because a suit is standing on a mannequin in the window doesn't mean that a living, breathing, and thinking person is in the room. The clothes are just temporary stand-ins.

Pronouns, similarly, are stand-ins for nouns. They aren't nouns, but they suggest nouns or refer back to them. That's why it's especially important for the pronoun to clearly connect to whatever it is replacing.

This chapter will help you make sure your pronoun stand-ins work well.

Learning Outcomes

LO1 Personal Pronouns

LO2 Pronoun-Antecedent Agreement

LO3 Other Pronoun Problems

LO4 Indefinite Pronouns

LO5 Relative Pronouns

LO6 Other Pronoun Types

LO7 Real-World Application

What do you think?

How could clothes make the man (or woman)? How do pronouns help nouns?

PhotoHouse, 2013 / Used under license from Shutterstock.com

LO1 Personal Pronouns

A **pronoun** is a word that takes the place of a noun or another pronoun. The most common type of pronoun is the **personal pronoun**. Personal pronouns indicate whether the person is speaking, is being spoken to, or is being spoken about.

Person	Singular			Plural		
	Nom.	**Obj.**	**Poss.**	**Nom.**	**Obj.**	**Poss.**
First (speaking)	I	me	my/mine	we	us	our/ours
Second (spoken to)	you	you	your/yours	you	you	your/yours
Third (spoken about) masculine	he	him	his	they	them	their/theirs
feminine	she	her	her/hers	they	them	their/theirs
neuter	it	it	its	they	them	their/theirs

Nom.=nominative case / **Obj.**=objective case / **Poss.**=possessive case

Case of Pronouns

The **case** of a personal pronoun indicates how it can be used.

- **Nominative** pronouns are used as the subjects of sentences or as subject complements (following the linking verbs *am, is, are, was, were, be, being,* or *been*).

  He applied for the job, but the person hired was she.

- **Objective** pronouns are used as direct objects, indirect objects, or objects of prepositions.

  The police officer warned us about them.

- **Possessive** pronouns show ownership and function as adjectives.

  Her lawn looks much greener than mine.

Gender

Pronouns can be **masculine**, **feminine**, or **neuter**.

He showed her how to fix it.

> ## Say It
>
> Read the following aloud.
> 1. *I* am / *You* are / *He* is / *She* is / *It* is / *We* are / *They* are
> 2. Show *me* / Show *you* / Show *him* / Show *her* / Show *them* / Show *us*
> 3. *My* car / *Your* car / *His* car / *Her* car / *Their* car
> 4. The car is *mine*. / The car is *yours*. / The car is *his*. / The car is *hers*. / The car is *theirs*.

Using Personal Pronouns

Select For each sentence below, select the correct personal pronoun in parentheses.

1. *(I, me, my)* love to hang out at the corner coffee shop.
2. *(I, Me, My)* friends and I gather there on Saturday morning.
3. One friend, Zach, is making a film, and *(he, him, his)* asked me to be in it.
4. We read over the lines, and other patrons listened to *(we, us, our)*.

Correct In the following paragraph, correct the pronoun errors. Write the line number and any incorrect pronoun. Cross it out and write a correction beside it.

> Zach, Rachel, and me went to the coffee shop on Saturday afternoon,   *1*
> when them is usually closed. The owners agreed to let we film there. Zach
> rearranged the tables a little to make room for the camera, and him and
> me set up the equipment. The camera rolled, and Rachel and me started
> into our lines. A couple of times, we had to stop because the owners were   *5*
> laughing so much them couldn't hold a straight face. Rachel and me had a
> hard time being straight when it came to ours kissing scene. It went well,
> and her and me got through it in one take.

pronoun
a word that takes the place of a noun or other pronoun

personal pronoun
a pronoun that indicates whether the person is speaking, is spoken to, or is spoken about

case
whether a pronoun is used as a subject, an object, or a possessive

nominative
used as a subject or subject complement

objective
used as a direct object, an indirect object, or an object of a preposition

possessive
used to show ownership

masculine
male

feminine
female

neuter
neither male nor female

LO2 Pronoun-Antecedent Agreement

The **antecedent** is the word that a pronoun refers to or replaces. A pronoun must have the same person, number, and gender as the antecedent, which is called **pronoun-antecedent agreement**.

> third-person   third-person   third-person
> singular feminine singular feminine singular feminine
>
> Colleen thought she would need a lift, but her car started.

Agreement in Person

A pronoun needs to match its antecedent in **person** (first, second, or third).

> third person   second person
>
> **Incorrect:** If people keep going, you can usually reach the goal.
> **Correct:** If you keep going, you can usually reach the goal.
> **Correct:** If people keep going, they can usually reach the goal.

Agreement in Number

A pronoun needs to match its antecedent in **number** (singular or plural).

> singular   plural
>
> **Incorrect:** Each lifeguard must buy their own uniform.
> **Correct:** Lifeguards must buy their own uniforms.
> **Correct:** Each lifeguard must buy her or his own uniform.

Agreement in Gender

A pronoun needs to match its antecedent in **gender** (masculine, feminine, or neuter).

> feminine   masculine
>
> **Incorrect:** Mrs. Miller will present his speech.
> **Correct:** Mrs. Miller will present her speech.

Say It

Speak the following words aloud.
1. First person: *I, me, my, mine; we, us, our, ours*
2. Second person: *you, your, yours*
3. Third person feminine: *she, her, hers; they, them, their, theirs*
4. Third person masculine: *he, him, his; they, them, their, theirs*
5. Third person neuter: *it, its; they, them, their, theirs*

Correcting Agreement Errors

Correct Person Rewrite each sentence to correct the person error.

1. When you go to the multiplex, a person has a lot of movies to choose from.

2. Each of us has to buy their own ticket and snacks.

3. If the viewer arrives early enough, you can see a triple feature.

4. One can be overwhelmed by how many movies you can see.

Correct Number Rewrite each sentence to correct the number error.

5. Each moviegoer chooses what movies they want to see.

6. A snack-counter attendant serves treats, and they also clean up messes.

7. Movie critics give his opinion about different films.

8. A critic shouldn't give away the ending because they would ruin the movie.

Correct Gender Rewrite each sentence to correct the gender error.

9. A critic shouldn't give away the ending because he would ruin the movie.

10. When Wesley Morris critiques a film, she's right most of the time.

11. Anita accidentally left his purse at the theater.

12. The multiplex sits on a hilltop, and she looks like a palace.

antecedent
the word that a pronoun refers to or replaces

pronoun-antecedent agreement
matching a pronoun to its antecedent in terms of person, number, and gender

person
whether the pronoun is speaking, being spoken to, or being spoken about

number
whether the pronoun is singular or plural

gender
whether the pronoun is masculine, feminine, or neuter

LO3 Other Pronoun Problems

Pronouns are very useful parts of speech, but if they are mishandled, they can cause problems.

Vague Pronoun

Do not use a pronoun that could refer to more than one antecedent.

> **Unclear:** Raul played baseball with his friend and his brother.
> **Clear:** Raul played baseball with his friend and his friend's brother.

Missing Antecedent

Avoid using *it* or *they* without clear antecedents.

> **Unclear:** They say humans share 97 percent of DNA with chimps.
> **Clear:** Scientists say humans share 97 percent of DNA with chimps.
>
> **Unclear:** It says in the *Times* that the Democrats back the bill.
> **Clear:** The *Times* says that the Democrats back the bill.

Double Subjects

Do not place a pronoun right after the subject. Doing so creates an error called a **double subject**, which is not a standard construction.

> **Nonstandard:** Rudy and Charlie, they went fishing.
> **Standard:** Rudy and Charlie went fishing.

Usage Errors *(They're, You're, It's)*

Do not confuse possessive pronouns (*your, their, its*) with contractions (*you're, they're, it's*). Remember that contractions use apostrophes in place of missing letters.

> **Incorrect:** Keep you're car in it's own lane.
> **Correct:** Keep your car in its own lane.

CONSIDER SPEAKING AND LISTENING ────────────────────

The pronoun problems on this page may not cause confusion in spoken English. In written English, these problems can derail meaning. Correct them in your writing.

Correcting Other Pronoun Problems

Rewrite Rewrite each sentence to correct the pronoun-reference problems.

1. Sarah asked her sister and her friend to help her move.

2. It said on the news that the accident will cost billions to fix.

3. They say that dark energy takes up 75 percent of the universe.

4. Dan wants his father and his friend to help.

5. They have found a way to make deep-water drilling safer.

6. It says on the parking ticket that I have to pay $50.

Correct In the following paragraph, correct the pronoun errors. Write the line number and any words you would change. Then show how you would change them.

> For 28 years, it reported in the *Weekly World News* all kinds of *1*
> outlandish stories. Often the paper reported about Elvis or the Loch Ness
> monster being spotted and his impromptu concerts for die-hard fans. A
> bat-human hybrid named Bat Boy and an alien named P'lod appeared
> repeatedly in the tabloid, and he even supposedly had an affair with *5*
> Hillary Clinton. Since this was during the Monica Lewinski scandal,
> maybe she was getting back at him. The writers and editors of the *Weekly*
> *World News,* they rarely publicly acknowledged that their stories were
> jokes, but said that he or she had to "suspend disbelief for the sake of
> enjoyment." *10*

Correction Marks

⌐ delete	⁄⋏ add comma	word ⋀ add word
d capitalize	? add question mark	⊙ add period
≡D̸ lowercase	⋀	⊂⊃ spelling
⋀ insert	⋎ insert an apostrophe	⊃⊂ switch

vague pronoun
using a pronoun that could refer to more than one antecedent

missing antecedent
using a pronoun that has no clear antecedent

double subject
error created by following a subject with a pronoun

usage error
using the wrong word (e.g., *they're* instead of *their*)

LO4 Indefinite Pronouns

An **indefinite pronoun** does not have an antecedent, and it does not refer to a specific person, place, thing, or idea. These pronouns pose unique issues with subject-verb and pronoun-antecedent agreement.

Singular Indefinite Pronouns

Some indefinite pronouns are singular. When they are used as subjects, they require a singular verb. As antecedents, they must be matched to singular pronouns.

each	anyone	anybody	anything
either	someone	somebody	something
neither	everyone	everybody	everything
another	no one	nobody	nothing
one			

> Nobody is expecting to see Bigfoot on our camping trip.
>
> Someone used his or her own money to buy a Bigfoot detector at a novelty shop.

Plural Indefinite Pronouns

Some indefinite pronouns are plural. As subjects, they require a plural verb, and as antecedents, they require a plural pronoun.

both	few	several	many

> A few of the campers hear thumps in the night.
>
> Several of my friends swear they can see eyes glowing eight feet off the ground.

Singular or Plural Indefinite Pronouns

Some indefinite pronouns can be singular or plural, depending on the object of the preposition in the phrase that follows them.

all	any	most	none	some

> Most of us are too frightened to sleep.
>
> Most of the night is over already anyway.

INSIGHT ————————————————————————————

For more practice with indefinite pronouns, see pages 522–525.

Correcting Agreement

Correct Rewrite each sentence to correct the agreement errors. (Hint: The sentences are about a group of female campers.)

1. Everyone needs to set up their own tent.

   _____

2. No one are getting out of work.

   _____

3. Anyone who wants to be dry should make sure they have a rain fly.

   _____

4. Nothing are more miserable than a wet sleeping bag.

   _____

5. Few is wanting to end up drenched.

   _____

6. Several wants to go hiking to look for Bigfoot.

   _____

7. Many has doubts that he exists.

   _____

8. A few says they might have dated him in high school.

   _____

9. A Bigfoot hunter should make sure they have a camera along.

   _____

10. Most of the hunters is also going to carry a big stick.

    _____

11. Most of the afternoon are available for different activities.

    _____

12. None of the girls is planning to hike after dark.

    _____

13. None of the food are to be left out to attract
    animals or Bigfoot.

    _____

> **indefinite pronoun**
> a pronoun that does not refer
> to a specific person, place,
> thing, or idea

LO5 Relative Pronouns

A **relative pronoun** introduces a dependent clause and relates it to the rest of the sentence.

who	whom	which	whose
whoever	whomever	that	

| relative clause |
| I would like to meet the person who discovered dark matter. |

Who/Whoever and Whom/Whomever

Who, whoever, whom, and *whomever* refer to people. *Who* or *whoever* functions as the subject of the relative clause, while *whom* or *whomever* functions as the object of the clause.

I am amazed by a person who could imagine matter that can't be seen.

The woman whom I met was named Vera Rubin.

relative clause   **relative clause**

NOTE: In the second **relative clause**, *whom* introduces the clause even though it is the direct object, not the subject *(I met whom).*

That and Which

That and *which* usually refer to things. When *that* introduces the clause, the clause **is not** set off with commas. When *which* introduces the clause, the clause **is** set off with commas.

I saw a documentary that explained about dark matter and dark energy.

The show is *Into the Wormhole,* which is on the Science Channel.

relative clause   **relative clause**

Whose

Whose shows ownership or connection.

relative clause

Morgan Freeman, whose voice is soothing, hosts the show.

NOTE: Do not confuse *whose* with the contraction *who's* (who is).

Using Relative Pronouns

Select   For each sentence, select the correct relative pronoun.

1. Vera Rubin, *(who, whom)* first discovered dark matter, wasn't seeking fame.

2. In the 1960s, she avoided black holes, *(that, which)* were a hot topic.

3. Instead, Rubin focused on the rotation of spiral galaxies, *(that, which)* few other people studied.

4. She expected stars *(that, which)* were on the outside of galaxies would move faster than stars *(that, which)* were near the center.

5. Instead, Rubin discovered the same speed for stars *(that, which)* were in different parts of the galaxy.

6. The only way for the galaxy to move that way would be if it had ten times the mass *(that, which)* was visible.

7. Rubin, *(who, whom, whose)* had never courted fame, became a very controversial figure when she presented her findings about dark matter.

8. Other astrophysicists *(who, whom)* disbelieved her did similar observations and calculations and confirmed her findings.

9. Rubin, *(who, whom, whose)* theory once was radical, became one of the great contributors to modern science.

10. *(Whoever, Whomever)* wrestles with the idea of dark matter should remember that over fifty years ago, one woman was the first to wrestle with the idea.

Write   Write a relative clause for each of these relative pronouns:

1. who	**3.** whom	**5.** which
2. whoever	**4.** whomever	**6.** that

Write a sentence including one of your clauses.

---

relative pronoun
a pronoun that begins a relative clause, connecting it to a sentence

relative clause
a type of dependent clause that begins with a relative pronoun that is either the subject or the direct object of the clause

---

INSIGHT ———————————————————————————
For more practice with relative pronouns, see pages 512–513.

LO6 Other Pronoun Types

Other types of pronouns have specific uses in your writing: asking questions, pointing to specific things, reflecting back on a noun (or pronoun), or intensifying a noun (or pronoun).

Interrogative Pronoun

An **interrogative pronoun** asks a question—*who, whose, whom, which, what.*

> What should we call our band? Who will be in it?

Demonstrative Pronoun

A **demonstrative pronoun** points to a specific thing—*this, that, these, those.*

> That is a great name! This will look terrific on a cover!

Reflexive Pronoun

A **reflexive pronoun** reflects back to the subject of a sentence or clause—*myself, ourselves, yourself, yourselves, himself, herself, itself, themselves.*

> I credit myself for the name. You can credit yourself for the logo.

Intensive Pronoun

An **intensive pronoun** emphasizes the noun or pronoun it refers to—*myself, ourselves, yourself, yourselves, himself, herself, itself, themselves.*

> You yourself love the name Psycho Drummer. I myself couldn't be happier.

Reciprocal Pronoun

A **reciprocal pronoun** refers to two things in an equal way—*each other, one another.*

> We shouldn't fight with each other. We should support one another.

Say It

Speak the following words aloud.
1. Interrogative: *Who* is? / *Whose* is? / *Which* is? / *What* is? / *Whom* do you see?
2. Demonstrative: *This* is / *That* is / *These* are / *Those* are
3. Reflexive: I helped *myself.* / You helped *yourself.* / They helped *themselves.*
4. Intensive: I *myself* / You *yourself* / She *herself* / He *himself* / They *themselves*
5. Reciprocal: We helped *each other.* / We helped *one another.*

Using Other Types of Pronouns

Identify   Indicate the type of each underlined pronoun: *interrogative, demonstrative, reflexive, intensive,* or *reciprocal.*

1. <u>That</u> is why this band needs a road crew.   _____

2. <u>What</u> are we supposed to do without power cords?   _____

3. I <u>myself</u> would not mind playing unplugged.   _____

4. You need to remind <u>yourself</u> that we don't have acoustic guitars.   _____

5. <u>That</u> is the whole problem.   _____

6. The guitars <u>themselves</u> prevent us from playing unplugged.   _____

7. <u>Who</u> could hear an unplugged electric guitar?   _____

8. <u>What</u> person will stand a foot away to listen?   _____

9. <u>This</u> is ridiculous.   _____

10. <u>That</u> won't work as a power cord.   _____

11. I <u>myself</u> am about to quit this band.   _____

12. We should be ashamed of <u>ourselves</u>.   _____

13. We shouldn't blame <u>each other</u>.   _____

14. As a band, we should help <u>one another</u> get through this.   _____

15. Let's buy <u>ourselves</u> another set of cords.   _____

Write   Create a sentence using *myself* as a reflexive pronoun, and a second using *myself* as an intensive pronoun.

1. _____

2. _____

LO7 Real-World Application

Correct   Correct any pronoun errors in the letter that follows. Write the line number and any words you would change. Cross out the word and show the change you would make.

☒ **Psycho Drummer**

12185 W. 22nd Avenue, Elkhorn, WI 53100 Ph: 262.555.7188

1   July 30, 2013

Ms. Marcia Schwamps, Manager
Piedog Studios
350 South Jackson Street
5   Elkhorn, WI 53100

Dear Ms. Schwamps:

One of your recording technicians says that you are looking for session musicians whom could play instruments for other artists. My band-mate Jerome and me would like to offer ours services.

10   Jerome and me are the power duo whom are called Psycho Drummer, a name that refers to Jerome hisself. He is a master percussionist, and him has trained hisself in many styles from heavy metal to rock, pop, jazz, blues, and even classical.

I am the guitarist in Psycho Drummer. I play electric and acoustic
15   (six- and 12-string) guitars as well as electric bass, and I too have trained me in they.

Attached, you will find ours résumés, a list of recent gigs us have played, and a review of we from the *Walworth County Week.*

20   Please consider Jerome and I for work as session musicians at Piedog Studios. We look forward to hearing from yous and would very much appreciate an interview/ audition.

Sincerely,

25   *Terrance "Tear-It-Up" Clark*

Terrance "Tear-It-Up" Clark
Guitarist
Enclosures 3

Correction Marks

Mark	Meaning
ℐ	delete
d̲̲	capitalize
D̸	lowercase
∧	insert
⌃	add comma
?	add question
∧	mark
word ∧	add word
⊙	add period
⬭	spelling
⌇	switch

24

> "Theater is a verb before it is a
> noun, an act before it is a place."
> —Martha Graham

Verb

You've probably heard that a shark has to keep swimming or it suffocates. That's not entirely true. Yes, sharks breathe by moving water across their gills, but they can also lie on the bottom and push water through their gills or let currents do the work. Still, most sharks stay on the move, and when a shark is still, it has to work harder to breathe.

Verbs are much the same way. They like to stay on the move. Most verbs are action words, describing what is happening. Some verbs describe states of being—much like sharks sitting on the bottom, breathing. Either way, though, the verb gives life to the sentence, and often it is a word with big teeth. This chapter gives a view into the compelling world of verbs.

Learning Outcomes

LO1 Verb Classes
LO2 Number and Person
LO3 Voice of the Verb
LO4 Present- and Future-Tense Verbs
LO5 Past-Tense Verbs
LO6 Progressive-Tense Verbs
LO7 Perfect-Tense Verbs
LO8 Verbals
LO9 Verbals as Objects
LO10 Real-World Application

What do you think?
Do you prefer *doing* or *being*? Why?

LO1 Verb Classes

Verbs show action or states of being. Different classes of verbs do these jobs.

Action Verbs

Verbs that show action are called **action verbs**. Some action verbs are **transitive**, which means that they transfer action to a direct object.

Trina hurled the softball.
(The verb *hurled* transfers action to the direct object *softball*.)

Others are **intransitive**: They don't transfer action to a direct object.

Trina pitches.
(The verb *pitches* does not transfer action to a direct object.)

Linking Verbs

Verbs that link the subject to a noun, a pronoun, or an adjective are **linking verbs**. Predicates with linking verbs express a state of being.

Trina is a pitcher.
(The linking verb *is* connects *Trina* to the noun *pitcher*.)

She seems unbeatable.
(The linking verb *seems* connects *She* to the adjective *unbeatable*.)

Linking Verbs

is	am	are	was	were	be	being	been	become
grow	feel	seem	look	smell	taste	sound	appear	remain

NOTE: The bottom-row words are linking verbs if they don't show action.

INSIGHT

If you are mathematically minded, think of a linking verb as an equal sign. It indicates that the subject equals (or is similar to) what is in the predicate.

Ingvar Bjork, 2013 / Used under license from Shutterstock.com

Helping Verbs

A verb that works with an action or linking verb is a **helping** (or auxiliary) verb. A helping verb helps the main verb form tense, mood, and voice.

> Trina has pitched two shut-out games, and today she may be pitching her third. (The helping verb *has* works with the main verb *pitched;* the helping verbs *may be* work with *pitching*. Both form special tenses.)

NOTE: Helping verbs work with verbs ending in *ing* or in past-tense form.

Helping Verbs

am	been	could	does	have	might	should	will
are	being	did	had	is	must	was	would
be	can	do	has	may	shall	were	

Using Verb Classes

Identify/Write For each sentence below, identify the underlined verbs as transitive action verbs (T), intransitive action verbs (I), linking verbs (L), or helping verbs (H). Then write your own sentence using the same class of verb.

1. I <u>love</u> fast-pitch softball, but I rarely <u>pitch</u>.

2. I <u>play</u> first base; it <u>is</u> a pressure-filled position.

3. Runners <u>charge</u> first base, and I <u>tag</u> them out.

4. Double-plays <u>require</u> on-target throws, clean catches, and timing.

5. If a runner <u>steals</u>, the pitcher and second baseperson <u>work</u> with me.

6. We <u>catch</u> the runner in a "pickle" and <u>tag</u> her out.

7. Softball <u>is</u> exciting, and I <u>will</u> play all summer.

8. I <u>look</u> worn out after a game, but I <u>feel</u> completely exhilarated.

---

action verb
word that expresses action

transitive verb
action verb that transfers action to a direct object

intransitive verb
action verb that does not transfer action to a direct object

linking verb
verb that connects the subject with a noun, a pronoun, or an adjective in the predicate

helping (auxiliary) verb
verb that works with a main verb to form some tenses, mood, and voice

LO2 Number and Person of the Verb

Verbs reflect number (singular or plural) and person (first person, second person, or third person).

Number

The **number** of the verb indicates whether the subject is singular or plural. Note that most present-tense singular verbs end in *s*, while most present-tense plural verbs do not.

Singular: A civil war re-enactment involves infantry, cavalry, and artillery units.
Plural: Civil war re-enactors stage amazing battle scenes from the war.

Person

The **person** of the verb indicates whether the subject is speaking, being spoken to, or being spoken about.

	Singular	**Plural**
First Person:	(I) am	(we) are
Second Person:	(you) are	(you) are
Third Person:	(she) is	(they) are

Note that the pronoun *I* takes a special form of the *be* verb—*am*.

Correct: I am eager to see the cannons fire.
Incorrect: I is eager to see the cannons fire.

The pronoun *I* also is paired with plural present-tense verbs.

Correct: I hope to see a bayonet charge.
Incorrect: I hopes to see a bayonet charge.

In a similar way, the singular pronoun *you* takes the plural form of the *be* verb—*are, were.*

Correct: You are in for a treat when the battle begins.
Incorrect: You is in for a treat when the battle begins.

Correct: You were surprised at how steady the horses were in combat.
Incorrect: You was surprised at how steady the horses were in combat.

Using Number and Person

Provide   For each sentence below, provide the correct person and number of the present-tense *be* verb *(is, am, are)*.

1. We _____ at the Civil War encampment.

2. It _____ a gathering of Union and Confederate regiments.

3. You _____ in a uniform of Union blue.

4. I _____ in the gray of the Confederacy.

5. A light artillery brigade _____ a group of mobile cannon.

6. A cavalry regiment _____ a group of mounted soldiers.

7. The camp doctors _____ equipped to do amputations.

8. The medicine they use _____ sometimes worse than the disease.

9. I _____ amazed by all of the tent encampments.

10. You _____ interested in becoming a re-enactor.

Rewrite   Rewrite each sentence below to fix the errors in the number and person of the verb.

1. I jumps the first time a cannon goes off.

   _____

2. The guns blows huge white smoke rings whirling into the air.

   _____

3. The cavalry regiments charges together and battles with sabers.

   _____

4. In the fray, one cavalry officer fall from his horse.

   _____

5. The infantry soldiers lines up in two rows and sends out volleys of bullets.

   _____

6. After the battle, President Lincoln deliver a solemn address.

   _____

number	**person**
singular or plural	whether the subject is speaking *(I, we)*, is being spoken to *(you)*, or is being spoken about *(he, she, it, they)*

David W. Leindecker, 2013 / Used under license from Shutterstock.com

LO3 Voice of the Verb

The **voice** of the verb indicates whether the subject is acting or being acted upon.

Voice

An **active voice** means that the subject is acting. A **passive voice** means that the subject is acted on.

Active: The cast sang the song "Our State Fair."
Passive: The song "Our State Fair" was sung by the cast.

	Active Voice		Passive Voice	
	Singular	Plural	Singular	Plural
Present Tense	I see you see he/she/it sees	we see you see they see	I am seen you are seen he/she/it is seen	we are seen you are seen they are seen
Past Tense	I saw you saw he saw	we saw you saw they saw	I was seen you were seen it was seen	we were seen you were seen they were seen
Future Tense	I will see you will see he will see	we will see you will see they will see	I will be seen you will be seen it will be seen	we will be seen you will be seen they will be seen
Present Perfect Tense	I have seen you have seen he has seen	we have seen you have seen they have seen	I have been seen you have been seen it has been seen	we have been seen you have been seen they have been seen
Past Perfect Tense	I had seen you had seen he had seen	we had seen you had seen they had seen	I had been seen you had been seen it had been seen	we had been seen you had been seen they had been seen
Future Perfect Tense	I will have seen you will have seen he will have seen	we will have seen you will have seen they will have seen	I will have been seen you will have been seen it will have been seen	we will have been seen you will have been seen they will have been seen

Active voice is preferred for most writing because it is direct and energetic.

Active: The crowd gave the cast a standing ovation.
Passive: The cast was given a standing ovation by the crowd.

Passive voice is preferred when the focus is on the receiver of the action or when the subject is unknown.

Passive: A donation was left at the ticket office.
Active: Someone left a donation at the ticket office.

Using Voice of a Verb

Rewrite   Read each passive sentence below and rewrite it to be active. Think about what is performing the action and make that the subject. The first one is done for you.

1. *State Fair* was put on by the community theater group.
   <u>The community theater group put on *State Fair*.</u>

2. The Frake family was featured in the musical. _____

3. Many songs were sung and danced by the cast. _____

4. Pickles and mincemeat were rated by judges at the fair. _____

5. Mrs. Frake's mincemeat was spiked with too much brandy.
   _____

6. The judges of the contest were overcome by the strength of the mincemeat.
   _____

7. Two couples were shown falling in love at the fair. _____

8. The singers were assisted by a stalwart piano player in the orchestra pit.
   _____

9. The first act was climaxed by the song "It's a Grand Night for Singing."
   _____

10. The cast was applauded gratefully by the crowd. _____

Write   Using the chart on the facing page, write a sentence for each situation below.

1. (A present-tense singular active sentence)
   _____

2. (A past-tense plural passive sentence)
   _____

CONSIDER WORKPLACE

In workplace writing, use active voice for most messages. Use passive voice to deliver bad news.

voice	active voice	passive voice
active or passive	voice created when the subject is performing the action of the verb	voice created when the subject is receiving the action of the verb

LO4 Present- and Future-Tense Verbs

Basic verb tenses tell whether action happens in the past, in the present, or in the future.

Present Tense

Present-tense verbs indicate that action is happening right now.

Master musicians and new professionals gather at the Marlboro Music Festival.

Present-tense verbs also can indicate that action happens routinely or continually.

Every summer, they spend seven weeks together learning music.

Present Tense in Academic Writing

Use present-tense verbs to describe current conditions.

Pianist Richard Goode plays beside talented young artists.

Use present-tense verbs also to discuss the ideas in literature or to use historical quotations in a modern context. This use is called the "historical present," which allows writers to continue speaking.

The audiences at Marlboro rave about the quality of the music, or as the *New York Times* says, "No matter what is played . . . the performances at Marlboro are usually extraordinary."

NOTE: It is important to write a paragraph or an essay in one tense. Avoid shifting needlessly from tense to tense as you write.

Future Tense

Future-tense verbs indicate that action will happen later on.

Marlboro Music will launch the careers of many more young stars.

Using Present- and Future-Verb Tenses

Write For each sentence below, supply the present-tense form of the verb indicated in parentheses.

1. Young musicians _____ to Marlboro Music by special invitation. (came)

2. Seasoned professionals _____ them like colleagues, not students. (treated)

3. Musicians _____ side by side for weeks before performing. (worked)

4. The town of Marlboro, New Hampshire, _____ only 987 citizens. (had)

5. Many times that number _____ to the concerts each summer. (came)

Change Replace the verbs in the following paragraph, making them all present tense. Write the line number and the present tense verb.

> A sixteen-year-old cellist named Yo Yo Ma arrived at Marlboro   *1*
> Music. He couldn't believe his fortune to be surrounded by such great
> musicians. He began to play and soon fell in love with music. A festival
> administrator named Jill Hornor also caught his eye, and he fell in love
> with her as well. They were married.   *5*

Write Write a sentence of your own, using each word below in the form indicated in parentheses.

1. thought (present) _____

2. lived (future) _____

3. hoped (present) _____

4. cooperated (future) _____

present tense
verb tense indicating that action is
happening now

future tense
verb tense indicating that action will
happen later

LO5 Past-Tense Verbs

Past-tense verbs indicate that action happened in the past.

When referring to his campaign in Asia Minor, Julius Caesar reported, "I came. I saw. I conquered."

Forming Past Tense

Most verbs form their past tense by adding *ed*. If the word ends in a silent *e*, just add *d*.

help ⟶ helped	love ⟶ loved
look ⟶ looked	hope ⟶ hoped

If the word ends in a consonant before a single vowel and the last syllable is stressed, double the final consonant before adding *ed*.

stop ⟶ stopped	occur ⟶ occur**red**
plan ⟶ planned	refer ⟶ refer**red**

If the word ends in a *y* preceded by a consonant, change the *y* to *i* before adding *ed*.

study ⟶ studied	hurry ⟶ hurried
worry ⟶ worried	carry ⟶ carried

Irregular Verbs

Some of the most commonly used verbs form past tense by changing the verb itself. See the chart below:

Pres.	Past	Pres.	Past	Pres.	Past	Pres.	Past	Pres.	Past	Pres.	Past
am	was, were	come	came	find	found	hear	heard	see	saw	steal	stole
become	became	dig	dug	fly	flew	hide	hid	shake	shook	swim	swam
begin	began	do	did	forget	forgot	keep	kept	shine	shone	swing	swung
blow	blew	draw	drew	freeze	froze	know	knew	shrink	shrank	take	took
break	broke	drink	drank	get	got	lead	led	sing	sang	teach	taught
bring	brought	drive	drove	give	gave	pay	paid	sink	sank	tear	tore
buy	bought	eat	ate	go	went	ride	rode	sit	sat	think	thought
can	could	fall	fell	grow	grew	ring	rang	sleep	slept	throw	threw
catch	caught	feel	felt	hang	hung	rise	rose	speak	spoke	wear	wore
choose	chose	fight	fought	have	had	run	ran	stand	stood	write	wrote

Using Past-Tense Verbs

Write For each verb, write the correct past-tense form.

1. swing _____
2. think _____
3. slip _____
4. reply _____
5. teach _____
6. cry _____
7. sing _____
8. give _____
9. cap _____
10. fly _____

11. type _____
12. cope _____
13. shop _____
14. grip _____
15. gripe _____
16. pour _____
17. soap _____
18. trick _____
19. try _____
20. tip _____

Edit Make changes to the following paragraph, converting it from present tense to past tense. Write the line number and any word you would change. Cross it out and write the change.

> When I am fresh out of college, I get my first job as an assistant *1*
> editor at a sports publisher. At this company, acquisitions editors follow
> trends, talk with authors, and work with them to create a manuscript.
> Developmental editors then work with the manuscript to develop it into
> a worthwhile book. Assistant editors help with all stages of production. *5*
> They edit manuscripts and typemark them. Then they check the galleys—
> or long sheets of printout film that paste-up artists cut and wax to create
> pages. Those are the days of manual layout. Assistant editors have to
> check the paste-up pages for dropped copy. They also proofread and enter
> changes, and check bluelines. Publishing is completely different now, but *10*
> back then, I get my first experience in real-world work. I am glad just to
> have an office of my own.

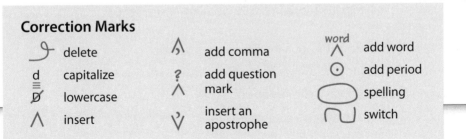

Correction Marks

⌐ delete	⌃ add comma	word ∧ add word
d capitalize	? add question mark	⊙ add period
⌀ lowercase		⬭ spelling
∧ insert	⌄ insert an apostrophe	⤳ switch

past tense
verb tense indicating that action happened previously

LO6 Progressive-Tense Verbs

The basic tenses of past, present, and future tell when action takes place. The progressive tense or aspect tells that action is ongoing.

Progressive Tense

Progressive tense indicates that action is ongoing. Progressive tense is formed by using a helping verb along with the *ing* form of the main verb.

Work habits were changing rapidly.

There are past, present, and future progressive tenses. Each uses a helping verb in the appropriate tense.

For thousands of years, most humans were working in agriculture.

Currently in the West, most humans are working in nonagricultural jobs.

In the future, people will be making their living in unimaginable ways.

Forming Progressive Tense

Past:	was/were	+	main verb	+	ing
Present:	am/is/are	+	main verb	+	ing
Future:	will be	+	main verb	+	ing

INSIGHT

Avoid using progressive tense with the following:

- Verbs that express thoughts, attitudes, and desires: *know, understand, want, prefer*

- Verbs that describe appearances: *seem, resemble*

- Verbs that indicate possession: *belong, have, own, possess*

- Verbs that signify inclusion: *contain, hold*

    Correct: I **know** your name.
    Incorrect: I **am knowing** your name.

Using Progressive-Tense Verbs

Form   Rewrite each sentence three times, changing the tenses as requested in parentheses.

Humans require food, but agribusiness makes food production very efficient.

1. (present progressive) _____

_____

2. (past progressive) _____

_____

3. (future progressive) _____

_____

People provide a product or service, and others pay for it.

4. (present progressive) _____

_____

5. (past progressive) _____

_____

6. (future progressive) _____

_____

The products and services in greatest demand produce the most wealth.

7. (present progressive) _____

_____

8. (past progressive) _____

_____

9. (future progressive) _____

_____

progressive tense
verb tense that expresses
ongoing action

LO7 Perfect-Tense Verbs

The perfect tense tells that action is not ongoing but is finished, whether in the past, present, or future.

Perfect Tense

Perfect tense indicates that action is completed. Perfect tense is formed by using a helping verb along with the past-tense form of the main verb.

> Each year of my career, I have learned something new.

There are past, present, and future perfect tenses. These tenses are formed by using helping verbs in past, present, and future tenses.

> In my first year, I had learned to get along in a corporate structure.

> This year, I have learned new technology skills.

> By this time next year, I will have learned how to be an effective salesperson.

	Forming Perfect Tense		
Past:	had	+	past-tense main verb
Present:	has/have	+	past-tense main verb
Future:	will have	+	past-tense main verb

Perfect Tense with Irregular Verbs

To form perfect tense with irregular verbs, use the past participle form instead of the past tense form. Here are the past participles of common irregular verbs.

Pres.	Past Part.	Pres.	Past Part.	Pres.	Past Part.	Pres.	Past Part.	Pres.	Past Part.	Pres.	Past Part.
am, be	been	dig	dug	fly	flown	hide	hidden	see	seen	stand	stood
become	become	do	done	forget	forgotten	keep	kept	shake	shaken	steal	stolen
begin	begun	draw	drawn	freeze	frozen	know	known	shine	shone	swim	swum
blow	blown	drink	drunk	get	gotten	lead	led	show	shown	swing	swung
break	broken	drive	driven	give	given	pay	paid	shrink	shrunk	take	taken
bring	brought	eat	eaten	go	gone	prove	proven	sing	sung	teach	taught
buy	bought	fall	fallen	grow	grown	ride	ridden	sink	sunk	tear	torn
catch	caught	feel	felt	hang	hung	ring	rung	sit	sat	throw	thrown
choose	chosen	fight	fought	have	had	rise	risen	sleep	slept	wear	worn
come	come	find	found	hear	heard	run	run	speak	spoken	write	written

Using Perfect Tense

`Form` Rewrite each sentence three times, changing the tenses as requested in parentheses.

I work hard and listen carefully.

1. (past perfect) _____

   _____

2. (present perfect) _____

   _____

3. (future perfect) _____

   _____

I gain my position by being helpful, and I keep it the same way.

4. (past perfect) _____

   _____

5. (present perfect) _____

   _____

6. (future perfect) _____

   _____

My colleagues depend on me, and I deliver what they need.

7. (past perfect) _____

   _____

8. (present perfect) _____

   _____

9. (future perfect) _____

   _____

perfect tense
verb tense that expresses
completed action

LO8 Verbals

A **verbal** is formed from a verb but functions as a noun, an adjective, or an adverb. Each type of verbal—gerund, participle, and infinitive—can appear alone or can begin a **verbal phrase**.

Gerund

A **gerund** is formed from a verb ending in *ing,* and it functions as a noun.

Kayaking is a fun type of exercise. (subject)
I love kayaking. (direct object)

A **gerund phrase** begins with a gerund and includes any objects and modifiers.

Running rapids in a kayak is exhilarating. (subject)
I enjoy paddling a kayak through white water. (direct object)

Participle

A **participle** is formed from a verb ending in *ing* or *ed,* and it functions as an adjective.

Exhilarated, I ran my first rapids at age 15. (*exhilarated* modifies *I*)
That was an exhilarating ride! (*exhilarating* modifies *ride*)

A **participial phrase** begins with a participle and includes any objects and modifiers.

Shocking my parents, I said I wanted to go again.

Infinitive

An **infinitive** is formed from *to* and a present-tense verb, and it functions as a noun, an adjective, or an adverb.

To kayak is to live. (noun)
I will schedule more time to kayak. (adjective)
You need courage and a little craziness to kayak. (adverb)

An **infinitive phrase** begins with an infinitive and includes any objects or modifiers.

I want to kayak the Colorado River through the Grand Canyon.

Using Verbals

Identify Identify each underlined verbal by selecting the correct choice in parentheses (gerund, participle, infinitive).

1. <u>Rock climbing</u> is an extreme sport. (gerund, participle, infinitive)
2. I'd like <u>to climb</u> El Capitan one day. (gerund, participle, infinitive).
3. <u>Rappelling down a cliff in Arizona</u>, I almost slipped. (gerund, participle, infinitive).
4. <u>Catching myself</u>, I checked my lines and carabiners. (gerund, participle, infinitive).
5. <u>To fall while climbing</u> could be fatal. (gerund, participle, infinitive).
6. I keep my equipment in top shape <u>to avoid a mishap</u>. (gerund, participle, infinitive).

Form Complete each sentence below by supplying the type of verbal (or verbal phrase) requested in parentheses.

1. My favorite exercise is _____. (gerund)
2. _____ would get me into shape. (gerund)
3. _____ , I could stay in shape (participle)
4. Perhaps I will also try _____ . (gerund)
5. When exercising, remember _____ . (infinitive)
6. _____ , I'll lose weight. (participle)

Write For each verbal phrase below, write a sentence that correctly uses it.

1. to work out _____
2. choosing a type of exercise _____
3. excited by the idea _____

---

verbal
gerund, participle, or infinitive; a construction formed from a verb but functioning as a noun, an adjective, or an adverb

verbal phrase
phrase beginning with a gerund, a participle, or an infinitive

gerund
verbal ending in *ing* and functioning as a noun

gerund phrase
phrase beginning with a gerund and including objects and modifiers

participle
verbal ending in *ing* or *ed* and functioning as an adjective

participial phrase
phrase beginning with a participle and including objects and modifiers

infinitive
verbal beginning with *to* and functioning as a noun, an adjective, or an adverb

infinitive phrase
phrase beginning with an infinitive and including objects and modifiers

LO9 Verbals as Objects

Though both infinitives and gerunds can function as nouns, they can't be used interchangeably as direct objects. Some verbs take infinitives and not gerunds. Other verbs take only gerunds and not infinitives.

Gerunds as Objects

Verbs that express facts are followed by **gerunds**.

admit	deny	enjoy	miss	recommend
avoid	discuss	finish	quit	regret
consider	dislike	imagine	recall	

I miss walking along the beach.
not I miss to walk along the beach.

I regret cutting our vacation short.
not I regret to cut our vacation short.

Infinitives as Objects

Verbs that express intentions, hopes, and desires are followed by **infinitives**.

agree	demand	hope	prepare	volunteer
appear	deserve	intend	promise	want
attempt	endeavor	need	refuse	wish
consent	fail	offer	seem	
decide	hesitate	plan	tend	

We should plan to go back to the ocean.
not We should plan going back to the ocean.

We will endeavor to save money for the trip.
not We will endeavor saving money for the trip.

Gerunds or Infinitives as Objects

Some verbs can be followed by either a gerund or an infinitive.

begin	hate	love	remember	stop
continue	like	prefer	start	try

I love walking by the ocean.
or I love to walk by the ocean.

Using Verbals as Objects

Select For each sentence below, select the appropriate verbal in parentheses.

1. I imagine (walking, to walk) along the Pacific Coast.
2. We want (seeing, to see) whales or dolphins when we are there.
3. I hope (getting, to get) some beautiful shots of the ocean.
4. We should avoid (getting, to get) sunburned when we are on the beach.
5. I enjoy (getting, to get) sand between my toes.
6. Maybe a surfer will offer (showing, to show) me how to surf.
7. We deserve (going, to go) on vacation more often.
8. Later, we will regret not (taking, to take) the time for ourselves.
9. I have never regretted (taking, to take) a vacation.
10. I wish (having, to have) a vacation right now.

Write For each verb below, write your own sentence using the verb and following it with a gerund or an infinitive, as appropriate.

1. quit

2. recall

3. tend

4. volunteer

5. discuss

6. decide

gerund	infinitive
verbal ending in *ing* and functioning as a noun	verbal beginning with *to* and functioning as a noun, an adjective, or an adverb

LO10 Real-World Application

Revise Rewrite the following paragraph, changing passive verbs to active verbs.

> Bedford's school music program should be supported by Grohling Music Suppliers. Our instrument rentals and our sheet-music services have been used extensively by the school system. In these tough economic times, the school should be assisted by us.
>
> _____
>
> _____
>
> _____

Revise In the following paragraph, change future perfect verbs into past perfect verbs. Write the line number and the words you would change. Then show the change.

> We will have provided reduced-cost sheet music to the school system   1
> and will have added used and refurbished instrument rentals. In
> addition, we will have provided best-customer discounts to schools that
> will have rented and bought in volume.

Revise In the following paragraph, correct misused verbals. Write the line number and the words you would change. Then show the change.

> I hope exploring these possibilities with you. We could recommend to   1
> make some of these changes the first year. I admit to have a soft spot for
> student performers. I recall to get my first flute as a student and to begin
> with music then.

25

"Where lipstick is concerned, the important thing is not color, but to accept God's final word on where your lips end."

—Jerry Seinfeld

Adjective and Adverb

The purpose of makeup is to accentuate the beauty that is already in your face. The focus should be on you, not on the mascara, lipstick, foundation, or blush you use.

In the same way, the real beauty of a sentence lies in the nouns and verbs. Adjectives and adverbs can modify those nouns and verbs, bringing out their true beauty, but these modifiers should not overwhelm the sentence. Use them sparingly to make your meaning clear, not to distract with flash. This chapter will show you how to get the most out of those few adjectives and adverbs.

Learning Outcomes

LO1 Adjective Basics
LO2 Adjective Order
LO3 Adjective Questions and Adjectivals
LO4 Adverb Basics
LO5 Placement Adverbs
LO6 Adverbials
LO7 Real-World Application

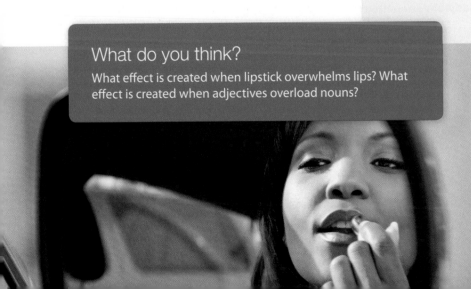

What do you think?

What effect is created when lipstick overwhelms lips? What effect is created when adjectives overload nouns?

LO1 Adjective Basics

An **adjective** is a word that modifies a noun or pronoun. Even **articles** such as *a, an,* and *the* are adjectives, because they indicate whether you mean a general or specific thing. Adjectives answer these basic questions: *which, what kind of, how many/how much.*

Adjectives often appear before the word they modify.

I saw a beautiful gray tabby cat.

A **predicate adjective** appears after the noun it modifies and is linked to the word by a linking verb.

The cat was beautiful and gray.

Proper adjectives come from proper nouns and are capitalized.

I also saw a Persian cat.

Forms of Adjectives

Adjectives come in three forms: positive, comparative, and superlative.

- **Positive adjectives** describe one thing without making any comparisons.

Fred is a graceful cat.

- **Comparative adjectives** compare the thing to something else.

Fred is more graceful than our dog, Barney.

- **Superlative adjectives** compare the thing to two or more other things.

He is the most graceful cat you will ever see.

NOTE: For one- and two-syllable words, create the comparative form by adding *er,* and create the superlative form by added *est.* For words of three syllables or more, use *more* (or *less*) for comparatives and *most* (or *least*) for superlatives. Also note that *good* and *bad* have special superlative forms:

Positive		Comparative		Superlative	
good	happy	better	happier	best	happiest
bad	wonderful	worse	more wonderful	worst	most wonderful
big		bigger		biggest	

Using the Forms of Adjectives

Identify/Write For each sentence below, identify the underlined adjectives as positive (P), comparative (C), or superlative (S). Then write a new sentence about a different topic, but use the same adjectives.

1. The shelter had a <u>Siamese</u> cat with <u>crossed</u> eyes and <u>black</u> feet. _____

2. She was <u>more inquisitive</u> than the other cats. _____

3. Her eyes were the <u>bluest</u> I had ever seen on a cat. _____

4. Her <u>surprising</u> meow was <u>loud</u> and <u>insistent</u>. _____

5. But her name—Monkey—was the <u>most surprising</u> fact of all. _____

Correct Read the paragraph below and correct adjective errors. Write the line number and the word you would change. Then show the change. The first one is done for you.

Some people say dogs are ~~more~~ tamer than cats, but cats have a more   *1*
great place in some people's hearts. Cats were probably first attracted
to human civilizations during the most early days of the agricultural
revolution. The sudden surplus of grains attracted many mice, which in
turn attracted cats. Cats that were the most best mousers were welcomed   *5*
by humans. In time, more cute and more cuddly cats became pets. But
cats have never given up their wildness. Even now, a barn cat that is not
used to human touch can be feraler than a dog.

Correction Marks

⌐ delete	⋏ add comma	⌃ word add word
d̲ capitalize	? add question	⊙ add period
D̶ lowercase	⋀ mark	◯ spelling
⋀ insert	⋁ insert an apostrophe	⎇ switch

adjective
word that modifies a noun or pronoun

articles
the adjectives *a, an,* and *the*

predicate adjective
adjective that appears after a linking verb and describes the subject

positive adjective
word that modifies a noun or pronoun without comparing it

comparative adjective
word that modifies a noun or pronoun by comparing it to something else

superlative adjective
word that modifies a noun or pronoun by comparing it to two or more things

LO2 Adjective Order

Adjectives aren't all created equally. Native English speakers use a specific order when putting multiple adjectives before a noun, and all speakers of English can benefit from understanding this order.

Begin with . . .

1.	articles	a, an, the
	demonstrative adjectives	that, this, these, those
	possessives	my, our, her, their, Kayla's

Then position adjectives that tell . . .

2.	time	first, second, next, last
3.	how many	three, few, some, many
4.	value	important, prized, fine
5.	size	giant, puny, hulking
6.	shape	spiky, blocky, square
7.	condition	clean, tattered, repaired
8.	age	old, new, classic
9.	color	blue, scarlet, salmon
10.	nationality	French, Chinese, Cuban
11.	religion	Baptist, Buddhist, Hindu
12.	material	cloth, stone, wood, bronze

Finally place . . .

13.	nouns used as adjectives	baby [seat], shoe [lace]

Example:

that ruined ancient stone temple
(**1** + **7** + **8** + **12** + **noun**)

John Copland, 2013 / Used under license from Shutterstock.com

INSIGHT

As the introduction indicates, native English speakers use this order unconsciously because it sounds right to them. If you put adjectives in a different order, a native English speaker might say, "That's not how anybody says it." One way to avoid this issue is to avoid stacking multiple adjectives before nouns.

NOTE: Avoid using too many adjectives before a noun. An article and one or two adjectives are usually enough. More adjectives may overload the noun.

Too many:	their first few expensive delicious French bread appetizers
Effective:	their first French bread appetizers

Placing Adjectives in Order

Order   Rearrange each set of adjectives and articles so that they are in the correct order. The first one has been done for you.

1. blue   square   that

_____that square blue_____ button

2. my   Scottish   rugged

_____ kilt

3. plastic   brand-new   few

_____ beads

4. worthless   a   brass

_____ tack

5. classic   many   Kenyan

_____ masks

6. aluminum   soda   Ted's

_____ can

7. key   Catholic   my

_____ chain

8. dilapidated   this   old

_____ shack

9. wool   her   woven

_____ cardigan

10. identical   seven   music

_____ stands

11. young   the   bright

_____ faces

12. last   real   our

_____ option

LO3 Adjective Questions and Adjectivals

Adjectives answer four basic questions: *which, what kind of, how many/how much.*

	Guy
Which?	that guy
What kind of?	cool tattooed guy
How many/how much?	one guy

that one cool tattooed guy

Adjectivals

A single word that answers one of these questions is called an adjective. If a phrase or clause answers one of these questions, it is an **adjectival** phrase or clause.

	Guy
Which?	guy leaning on the Mustang
What kind of?	guy who exudes attitude

Look at that guy, who exudes attitude, leaning on the Mustang.

The following types of phrases and clauses can be adjectivals:

Prepositional phrase:	with his arms crossed
Participial phrase:	staring at something
Adjective clause:	who doesn't even own the Mustang

INSIGHT

Instead of trying to memorize the names of different types of phrases and clauses, just remember the adjective questions. Turn them into a cheer—*which, what kind of, how many/ how much.*

Say It

Partner with a classmate. One of you should say the noun, and the other should ask the adjective questions. Then the first person should answer each question with adjectives or adjectivals.

1. convertibles
   Which convertibles?
   What kind of convertibles?
   How many convertibles?

2. detergent
   Which detergent?
   What kind of detergent?
   How much detergent?

Using Adjectives and Adjectivals

Answer/Write For each word, answer the adjective questions using adjectives and adjectivals. Then write a sentence using two or more of your answers.

1. **Dogs**

    Which dogs? _____

    What kind of dogs? _____

    How many dogs? _____

    Sentence: _____

    _____

2. **Sports**

    Which sports? _____

    What kind of sports? _____

    How many sports? _____

    Sentence: _____

    _____

3. **Proposals**

    Which proposals? _____

    What kind of proposals? _____

    How many proposals? _____

    Sentence: _____

    _____

adjectival
phrase or clause that answers one of the adjective questions and modifies a noun or pronoun

prepositional phrase
phrase that starts with a preposition and includes an object and modifiers

participial phrase
phrase beginning with a participle (*ing* or *ed* form of verb) plus objects and modifiers; used as an adjective

adjective clause
clause beginning with a relative pronoun and including a verb, but not able to stand alone; functioning as an adjective

LO4 Adverb Basics

An **adverb** modifies a verb, a **verbal**, an adjective, an adverb, or a whole sentence. An adverb answers six basic questions: *how, when, where, why, to what degree, how often.*

INSIGHT ————

In the United States, intensifying adverbs such as *very* and *really* are used sparingly. Also, in academic writing, it is considered better to find a precise, vivid verb than to prop up an imprecise verb with an adverb.

Sheri leaped fearlessly.
(*Fearlessly* modifies the verb *leaped.*)

Sheri leaped quite readily.
(*Quite* modifies *readily,* which modifies *leaped.*)

Obviously, she wants to fly.
(*Obviously* modifies the whole sentence.)

NOTE: Most adverbs end in *ly*. Some can be written with or without the *ly*, but when in doubt, use the *ly* form.

loud ⟶ loudly   tight ⟶ tightly   deep ⟶ deeply

Forms of Adverbs

Adverbs have three forms: positive, comparative, and superlative.

■ **Positive adverbs** describe without comparing.

Sheri leaped high and fearlessly.

■ **Comparative adverbs** (*-er, more,* or *less*) describe by comparing with one other action.

She leaped higher and more fearlessly than I did.

■ **Superlative adverbs** (*-est, most,* or *least*) describe by comparing with more than one action.

She leaped highest and most fearlessly of any of us.

NOTE: Some adjectives change form to create comparative or superlative forms.

well ⟶ better ⟶ best   badly ⟶ worse ⟶ worst

Using the Forms of Adverbs

Provide For each sentence below, provide the correct form of the adverb in parentheses—positive, comparative, or superlative.

1. My friend likes to eat _____ (quickly).

2. She eats _____ (quickly) than I do.

3. She eats _____ (quickly) of anyone I know.

4. My brother eats _____ (reluctantly).

5. He eats _____ (reluctantly) than a spoiled child.

6. He eats _____ (reluctantly) of anyone on Earth.

7. I eat _____ (slowly).

8. I eat _____ (slowly) than I used to.

9. I eat _____ (slowly) of anytime in my life.

10. I suppose the three of us eat pretty _____ (badly).

Choose For each sentence, write the correct word in parentheses. If the word modifies a noun or pronoun, choose the adjective form (*good, bad*). If the word modifies a verb, a verbal, an adjective, or an adverb, choose the adverb form (*well, badly.*)

1. My brother went to a (good, well) play.

2. He said the actors did (good, well), and that the plot was (good, well).

3. He even got a (good, well) deal on tickets for (good, well) seats.

4. He wanted (bad, badly) to see this play.

5. The problem was that one patron behaved (bad, badly).

6. He had a (bad, badly) attitude and once even booed.

7. My brother told him to stop, but the guy took it (bad, badly).

8. The ushers did (good, well) when they removed the guy.

9. The audience even gave them a (good, well) ovation.

10. My brother says the overall evening went (good, well).

adverb	positive adverb	superlative adverb
word that modifies a verb, a verbal, an adjective, an adverb, or a whole sentence	adverb that modifies without comparing	adverb that modifies by comparing to two or more things
verbal	**comparative adverb**	
word formed from a verb but functioning as a noun, an adjective, or an adverb	adverb that modifies by comparing with one other thing	

LO5 Placement of Adverbs

Adverbs should be placed in different places in sentences, depending on their use.

How Adverbs

Adverbs that tell *how* can appear anywhere except between a verb and a direct object.

Steadily we hiked the trail. We steadily hiked the trail.	We hiked the trail steadily. **not** We hiked steadily the trail.

When Adverbs

Adverbs that tell *when* should go at the beginning or end of the sentence.

We hiked to base camp yesterday. Today we'll reach the peak.

Where Adverbs

Adverbs that tell *where* should follow the verb they modify but should not come between the verb and the direct object. (NOTE: Prepositional phrases often function as *where* adverbs.)

The trail wound uphill and passed through rockslide debris.
We avoided falling rocks throughout our journey.
not We avoided throughout our journey falling rocks.

To What Degree Adverbs

Adverbs that tell *to what degree* go right before the adverb they modify.

I learned very definitely the value of good hiking boots.

How Often Adverbs

Adverbs that tell *how often* should go right before an action verb, even if the verb has a helping verb.

I often remember that wonderful hike.	I will never forget the sights I saw.

Placing Adverbs Well

Place For each sentence below, insert the adverb (in parentheses) in the most appropriate position. Write the word before the adverb, the adverb, and the word that follows it. The first one has been done for you.

1. In order to scare off bears, we *occasionally* made noise. (occasionally)

2. Bears avoid contact with human beings. (usually)

3. A bear surprised or cornered by people will turn to attack. (often)

4. A mother bear with cubs is likely to attack. (very)

5. If a bear approaches, playing dead may work. (sometimes)

6. Climbing a tree is not the best idea. (usually)

7. Black bears climb trees. (often)

8. Grizzly bears just knock the tree down. (usually)

9. Another defense is to open your coat to look large. (especially)

10. At the same time, try to make a loud noise. (very)

Revise In the paragraph below, move adverbs into their correct positions. Write the line number, the word before the adverb, the adverb, and the word after it.

> Spotting wildlife is one often of the highlights of a hiking trip. Deer   *1*
> appear in fields occasionally, and lucky hikers might glimpse a bear
> sometimes in the distance. Porcupines, raccoons, and other creatures
> amble out of the woods curiously. Not usually hikers will see mountain
> lions because the cats are ambush predators. Mountain lions attack groups   *5*
> of people rarely and usually avoid human contact. Do keep children from
> behind straggling.

Eric Isselée, 2013 / Used under license from Shutterstock.com

LO6   Adverbials

Adverbs answer six basic questions: *how, when, where, why, to what degree,* and *how often.*

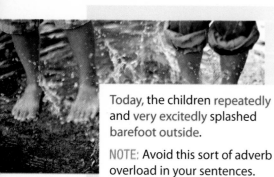

Today, the children repeatedly and very excitedly splashed barefoot outside.

NOTE: Avoid this sort of adverb overload in your sentences.

Children splashed.

How?	splashed barefoot
When?	splashed today
Where?	splashed outside
Why?	splashed excitedly
To what degree?	splashed very excitedly
How often?	splashed repeatedly

© Don Smith, / Getty Images

Adverbials

Often, the adverb questions are answered by **adverbial** phrases and clauses, which answer the same six questions.

Children splashed.

How?	splashed jumping up and down
When?	splashed during the downpour
Where?	splashed in the puddles in the driveway
Why?	splashed for the joy of being wet
To what degree?	splashed until they were drenched
How often?	splashed throughout the storm

During the downpour and throughout the storm, the children splashed, jumping up and down in the puddles in the driveway for the joy of being wet and until they were drenched.

NOTE: Again, avoid this sort of adverbial overload in your sentences.

The following types of phrases and clauses can be adverbials:

Prepositional phrase:	in the puddles in the driveway
Participial phrase:	jumping up and down
Dependent clause:	until they were drenched

Using Adverbials

Answer/Write For each sentence, answer the adverb questions using adverbs and adverbials. Then write a sentence using three or more of your answers.

1. They danced.

How did they dance? _____

When did they dance? _____

Where did they dance? _____

Why did they dance? _____

To what degree did they dance? _____

How often did they dance? _____

Sentence: _____

_____

2. They sang.

How did they sing? _____

When did they sing? _____

Where did they sing? _____

Why did they sing? _____

To what degree did they sing? _____

How often did they sing? _____

Sentence: _____

_____

INSIGHT

The adverb questions can be memorized by turning them into a cheer: *how, when, where, why, to what degree, how often!*

adverbial
phrase or clause that answers one of the adverb questions

LO7 Real-World Application

Correct In the following document, correct the use of adjectives and adverbs. Write the line number and the words you would change. Then show the change.

Clowning Around

1328 West Mound Road
Waukesha, WI 53100
262-555-8180

1   January 6, 2012

Mrs. Judy Bednar
38115 North Bayfield Drive
Waukesha, WI 53100

5   Dear Ms. Bednar:

It's time for a party birthday! You've thought of everything—balloons,
decorations, cake . . . But what about awesomely entertainment? How
many kids are coming, and how much time do you have to keep them
entertained?

10   Fear not. At Clowning Around, we specialize in making every
birthday the funnest and memorablest it can be. For young kids, we
offer balloon colorful animals, magic amazing tricks, and backyard
goofy games. For older kids, we have water wild games and magic
street illusions. And for kids of all ages, we have the most funny
15   clowns, the most bravest superheroes, and the most amazingest
impressionists.

That's right. You can throw a terrific party for your
loved one worrying without about the entertainment—
and paying without a lot either. See the enclosed
20   brochure for our services and rates. Then give us a call
at Clowning Around, and we'll make your party next an
event to remember.

Let's talk soon!

Dave Jenkins

25   Dave Jenkins
CEO, Clowning Around

Enclosure: Brochure

Correction Marks

Mark	Meaning
ℐ	delete
d̲̲	capitalize
ɸ̸	lowercase
∧	insert
∧̓	add comma
? ∧	add question mark
word ∧	add word
⊙	add period
⏝	spelling
⏞	switch

26

"A family is a unit composed not only of children but of men, women, an occasional animal, and the common cold."

—Ogden Nash

Conjunction and Preposition

A family is a network of relationships. Some people have an equal relationship, like wives and husbands or brothers and sisters. Some people have unequal relationships, like mothers and daughters or fathers and sons. And the very young or very old are often considered dependent on those in their middle age.

Ideas also have relationships, and conjunctions and prepositions show those relationships. When two ideas are equal, a coordinating conjunction connects them. When two ideas are not equal, a subordinating conjunction makes one idea depend on the other. And prepositions create special relationships between nouns and other words.

Conjunctions and prepositions help you connect ideas and build whole families of thought.

Learning Outcomes

LO1 Coordinating and Correlative Conjunctions
LO2 Subordinating Conjunctions
LO3 Common Prepositions
LO4 *By, At, On,* and *In*
LO5 Real-World Documents

What do you think?
What equal relationships do you have? What dependent relationships do you have?

AISPIX, 2013 / Used under license from Shutterstock.com

LO1 Coordinating and Correlative Conjunctions

A **conjunction** is a word or word group that joins parts of a sentence—words, phrases, or clauses.

Coordinating Conjunctions

A **coordinating conjunction** joins grammatically equal parts—a word to a word, a phrase to a phrase, or a clause to a clause. (A clause is basically a sentence.)

Coordinating Conjunctions						
and	but	or	nor	for	so	yet

Equal importance: A coordinating conjunction shows that the two things joined are of equal importance.

Rachel and Lydia enjoy arts and crafts.
(*And* joins words in an equal way.)

They have knitted sweaters and pieced quilts.
(*And* joins the phrases *knitted sweaters* and *pieced quilts*.)

I tried to knit a sweater, but the thing unraveled.
(*But* joins the two clauses, with a comma after the first.)

Items in a series: A coordinating conjunction can also join more than two equal things in a series.

Rachel, Lydia, and I will take a class on making mosaics.
(*And* joins *Rachel, Lydia,* and *I*. A comma follows each word except the last.)

We will take the class, design a mosaic, and complete it together.
(*And* joins three parts of a compound verb.)

Correlative Conjunctions

Correlative conjunctions consist of a coordinating conjunction paired with another word. They also join equal grammatical parts: word to word, phrase to phrase, or clause to clause.

Correlative Conjunctions				
either/or	neither/nor	whether/or	both/and	not only/but also

Stressing equality: Correlative conjunctions stress the equality of parts.

Not only Rachel but also Lydia has made beautiful quilts.
(*Not only/but also* stresses the equality of *Rachel* and *Lydia*.)

Using Coordinating and Correlative Conjunctions

Correct For each sentence below, write the best coordinating conjunction in parentheses.

1. I would like to learn knitting (but, for, or) crocheting.

2. Lydia, Rachel, (and, nor, yet) I enjoy making cloth with our hands.

3. We have different talents, (or, so, yet) we teach each other what we know.

4. Lydia is best at knitting, (nor, but, for) I am best at tatting.

5. Rachel is our weaver, (but, yet, so) she is the loom master.

6. Each week, Lydia, Rachel, (and, but, or) I meet to share our works.

7. We want to broaden our skills, (and, or, yet) it's hard to learn something new.

8. I like needlepoint, Rachel likes quilting, (and, nor, so) Lydia likes construction.

9. Come join us one day, (and, for, so) we love to teach beginners.

10. We'll show you our work, (but, nor, for) you'll decide what you want to learn.

Write Create sentences of your own, using a coordinating conjunction (*and, but, or, nor, for, so, yet*) as requested.

1. joining two words: _____

2. joining two phrases: _____

3. creating a series: _____

4. joining two clauses (place a comma after the first clause, before the conjunction): _____

Write Create a sentence using a pair of correlative conjunctions:

_____

CONSIDER THE TRAITS

When two ideas correlate, they work together. They co-relate. Thinking in this way can help you remember the term *correlative conjunctions*.

conjunction	**coordinating conjunction**	**correlative conjunction**
word or word group that joins parts of a sentence	conjunction that joins grammatically equal components	pair of conjunctions that stress the equality of the parts that are joined

LO2 Subordinating Conjunctions

A **subordinating conjunction** is a word or word group that connects two clauses of different importance. (A clause is basically a sentence.)

Subordinating Conjunctions					
after	as long as	if	so that	till	whenever
although	because	in order that	than	unless	where
as	before	provided that	that	until	whereas
as if	even though	since	though	when	while

Subordinate clause: The subordinating conjunction comes at the beginning of the less-important clause, making it subordinate (it can't stand on its own). The **subordinate clause** can come before or after the more important clause (the **independent clause**).

Summer is too hot to cook inside. I often barbecue.
(two clauses)

Because summer is too hot to cook inside, I often barbecue.
(*Because* introduces the subordinate clause, which is followed by a comma.)

I often barbecue because summer is too hot to cook inside.
(If the subordinate clause comes second, a comma usually isn't needed.)

Special relationship: A subordinating conjunction shows a special relationship between ideas. Here are the relationships that subordinating conjunctions show:

Time	after, as, before, since, till, until, when, whenever, while
Cause	as, as long as, because, before, if, in order that, provided that, since, so that, that, till, until, when, whenever
Contrast	although, as if, even though, though, unless, whereas

Whenever the temperature climbs, I cook on the grill.
(time)

I grill because I don't want to heat up the house.
(cause)

Even though it is hot outside, I feel cool in the shade as I cook.
(contrast)

Using Subordinating Conjunctions

Write For the blank in each sentence, provide an appropriate subordinating conjunction. Then write what type of relationship it shows.

1. _____ I marinated the chicken, I put it on the grill.
   (time, cause, contrast)

2. Grilling bratwurst is tough _____ the
   grease causes big flames.   (time, cause, contrast)

3. _____ of trichinosis, pork should not be pink inside.
   (time, cause, contrast)

4. I like grilling chicken _____ my favorite food is steak.
   (time, cause, contrast)

5. I grill my steak rare_____ the FDA recommends well-done.
   (time, cause, contrast)

6. Some people use barbecue sauce _____
   I prefer marinades.   (time, cause, contrast)

7. I use a gas grill _____ it is fast and
   convenient.   (time, cause, contrast)

8. Purists use only charcoal _____ it creates a nice flavor.
   (time, cause, contrast)

9. _____ I was in Texas, I had great brisket.
   (time, cause, contrast)

10. _____ brisket can be tough, this was tender.
    (time, cause, contrast)

Write Create three of your own sentences using subordinating conjunctions, one for each type of relationship.

1. time: _____

2. cause: _____

3. contrast: _____

subordinating conjunction	subordinate clause	independent clause
word or word group that connects clauses of different importance	word group that begins with a subordinating conjunction and has a subject and verb but can't stand alone as a sentence	group of words with a subject and verb and that expresses a complete thought; it can stand alone as a sentence

LO3 Common Prepositions

A **preposition** is a word or word group that shows a relationship between a noun or pronoun and another word. Here are common prepositions:

Prepositions

aboard	back of	except for	near to	round
about	because of	excepting	notwithstanding	save
above	before	for	of	since
according to	behind	from	off	subsequent to
across	below	from among	on	through
across from	beneath	from between	on account of	throughout
after	beside	from under	on behalf of	'til
against	besides	in	onto	to
along	between	in addition to	on top of	together with
alongside	beyond	in behalf of	opposite	toward
alongside of	but	in front of	out	under
along with	by	in place of	out of	underneath
amid	by means of	in regard to	outside	until
among	concerning	inside	outside of	unto
apart from	considering	inside of	over	up
around	despite	in spite of	over to	upon
as far as	down	instead of	owing to	up to
aside from	down from	into	past	with
at	during	like	prior to	within
away from	except	near	regarding	without

Prepositional Phrases

A **prepositional phrase** starts with a preposition and includes an object of the preposition (a noun or pronoun) and any modifiers. A prepositional phrase functions as an adjective or adverb.

> The Basset hound flopped on his side on the rug.
> (*On his side* and *on the rug* modify the verb *flopped*.)
>
> He slept on the rug in the middle of the hallway.
> (*On the rug* modifies *slept*; *in the middle* modifies *rug*; and *of the hallway* modifies *middle*.)

CONSIDER THE TRAITS

A prepositional phrase can help break up a string of adjectives. Instead of writing "the old, blue-awninged store," you can write "the old store with the blue awning."

Using Common Prepositions

Create   For each sentence, fill in the blanks with prepositional phrases. Create them from the prepositions on the facing page and nouns or pronouns of your own choosing. Be creative!

1. Yesterday, I ran _____ .

2. Another runner _____ waved at me.

3. I was so distracted, I ran _____ .

4. The other runner then ran _____ .

5. We both had looks of surprise _____ .

6. I leaped _____ .

7. The other runner jogged _____ .

8. Then we both were _____ .

9. The incident _____ was a lesson.

10. The lesson was not to run _____ .

Model   Read each sentence below and write another sentence modeled on it. Note how the writer uses prepositional phrases to create specific effects.

1. The coupe shot between the semis, around the limousine, down the tunnel, and up into bright sunlight.

   _____

2. I will look for you, but I also look to you.

   _____

3. Before the freedom of the road and the fun of the trip, I have finals.

   _____

4. Walk through the hallway, down the stairs, through the door, and into the pantry.

   _____

preposition	prepositional phrase
word or word group that creates a relationship between a noun or pronoun and another word	phrase that starts with a preposition, includes an object of the preposition (noun or pronoun) and any modifiers; and functions as an adjective or adverb

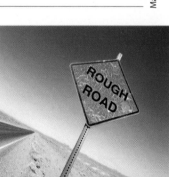

Mark Sayer, 2013 / Used under license from Shutterstock.com

LO4 *By, At, On,* and *In*

Prepositions often show the physical position of things—above, below, beside, around, and so on. Four specific prepositions show position but also get a lot of other use in English.

Uses for *By, At, On,* and *In*

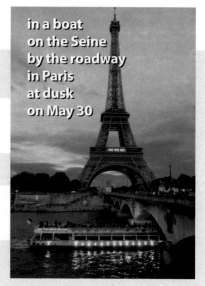

in a boat
on the Seine
by the roadway
in Paris
at dusk
on May 30

By means "beside" or "up to a certain place or time."

> by the creek, by the garage
>
> by noon, by August 16

At refers to a specific place or time.

> at the edge, at the coffee shop
>
> at 6:45 p.m., at midnight

On refers to a surface, a day or date, or an electronic medium.

> on the table, on the T-shirt
>
> on July 22, on Wednesday
>
> on the computer, on the DVD

In refers to an enclosed space; a geographical location; an hour, a month, or a year; or a print medium.

> in the hall, in the bathroom
>
> in Madison, in France
>
> in a minute, in December, in 2014
>
> in the magazine, in the book

INSIGHT

Native English speakers follow these rules without thinking about them. Listen to the way native speakers use *by, at, on,* and *in,* and practice their use until it seems second nature.

Say It

Team up with a partner. Have the first person read one of the words below, and have the second person use it in a prepositional phrase beginning with *by*, *at, on,* or *in.* The first person should check if the form is correct. (Some have more than one correct answer.) Then you should switch roles.

1. the den
2. June 23
3. 9:33 p.m.
4. the MP3 player
5. the corner

6. Pittsburgh
7. the counter
8. the diner
9. sunset
10. the newspaper

Using *By, At, On,* and *In*

Circle For each sentence, write the correct preposition in parentheses.

1. The guests arrived (by, on, in) 7:30 p.m., so we could eat (at, on, in) 8:00 p.m.
2. Put your suitcase (by, at, on, in) the trunk or (by, at, on) the rooftop luggage rack.
3. I looked for the new album (by, at, on, in) a music store, but could find it only (by, at, on, in) the Internet.
4. We waited (by, at, on, in) the lobby for a half hour, but Jerry didn't show up or even call (by, at, on, in) his cell phone.
5. Three people standing (by, at, in) the corner saw a traffic accident (by, at, on) the intersection of 45th and Monroe.
6. (By, At, On, In) April 1 of 2012, many pranksters may post apocalypse hoaxes (by, at, on, in) the Internet.
7. Let's meet (by, at, on) the convenience store (at, on, in) 7:00 p.m.
8. Place your order form (by, at, on, in) the postage-paid envelope, write your return address (by, at, on, in) the envelope, and post it.
9. A cat lay (by, at, on) the windowsill and looked me (by, at, on, in) the eye.
10. (At, On, In) noon of January 7, the school's pipes (at, on, in) the basement froze and caused flooding.

Write Write a sentence that uses all four of these prepositions in phrases: *by, at, on, in.*

_____

_____

_____

LO5 Real-World Application

Revise Read the following email, noting how choppy it sounds because all of the sentences are short. Rewrite the email. Connect some of the sentences using a coordinating conjunction and a comma, and connect others using a subordinating conjunction. You can also change other words as needed. Reread the email to make sure it sounds smooth.

Subordinating Conjunctions

after	as long as	if	so that	till	whenever
although	because	in order that	than	unless	where
as	before	provided that	that	until	whereas
as if	even though	since	though	when	while

Coordinating Conjunctions

| and | but | or | nor |
| for | so | yet | |

| Send | Attach | Fonts | Colors | Save As Draft |

To: dkraitsman@delafordandco.com

Subject: Completed Photo Log

Attach: Photolog.doc

Dear Deirdra: 1

Attached, please find the photo log. The log shows all photos on the Web site. Some photos are from Getty Images. Others are from Shutterstock. A few are from Corbis. All photos have been downloaded. The downloads have the right resolution.   5

I hope you are pleased with the log. It includes permissions details. It also shows the resolution. I included a description of each photo.

I am available for more work. I could compile another photo log. I could also do the permissions work on these photos. I do writing and editing as well.

Thank you for this project. I look forward to hearing from you.   10

Thanks,

Roger Haverson

Photo Editor

Correct Read the following party invitation, noting the incorrect use of the prepositions *by, at, on,* and *in.* (See page 620.) Correct the errors by deleting the prepositions and replacing them. Use the correction marks on page 612.

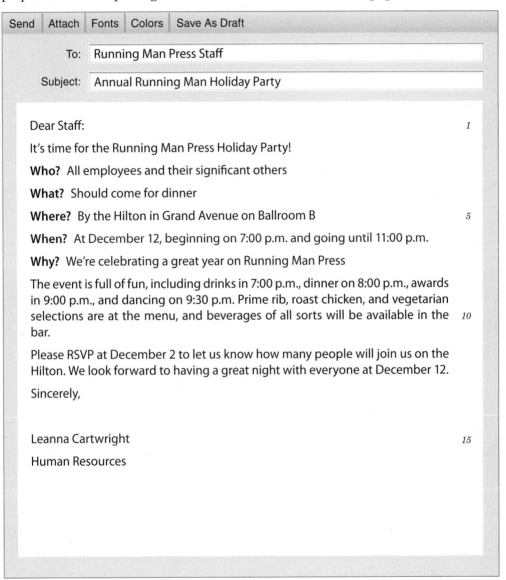

Send	Attach	Fonts	Colors	Save As Draft

To: Running Man Press Staff

Subject: Annual Running Man Holiday Party

Dear Staff: *1*

It's time for the Running Man Press Holiday Party!

Who? All employees and their significant others

What? Should come for dinner

Where? By the Hilton in Grand Avenue on Ballroom B   *5*

When? At December 12, beginning on 7:00 p.m. and going until 11:00 p.m.

Why? We're celebrating a great year on Running Man Press

The event is full of fun, including drinks in 7:00 p.m., dinner on 8:00 p.m., awards
in 9:00 p.m., and dancing on 9:30 p.m. Prime rib, roast chicken, and vegetarian
selections are at the menu, and beverages of all sorts will be available in the *10*
bar.

Please RSVP at December 2 to let us know how many people will join us on the
Hilton. We look forward to having a great night with everyone at December 12.

Sincerely,

Leanna Cartwright   *15*

Human Resources

CONSIDER THE WORKPLACE

Correct use of *by, at, on,* and *in* will mark you as a writer comfortable with English.

Part VI: Punctuation and Mechanics Workshops

27

> "Conventions are subject to the vagaries of time and fashion. . . . The writers of the Constitution capitalized words in the middle of sentences."
> —Mitchell Ivers

Capitalization

Why is the word *mom* capitalized in "Did Mom call?" and not in "Did my mom call?" Why is *river* capitalized in "the Ohio River" but not in "the Ohio and Missouri rivers"? These are just two of the vagaries when it comes to proper capitalization in our language. As you review this chapter, you will find others.

One of the best ways to learn about the unexpected changes in capitalization is to become a reader and writer yourself. Combine regular reading and writing with the practice in this chapter and you will be well on your way to mastering correct capitalization. You can also use this chapter as a reference whenever you have questions about capitalization. Each left-hand page provides an easy-to-use set of rules and examples.

Learning Outcomes

LO1 Basic Capitalization
LO2 Advanced Capitalization
LO3 Other Capitalization Rules
LO4 Other Capitalization Rules II
LO5 Real-World Application

What do you think?

Why do you suppose that we pay so much attention to the rules of capitalization? Why don't we capitalize common nouns in the middle of sentences?

LO1 Basic Capitalization

All first words, proper nouns, and proper adjectives must be capitalized. The following guidelines and examples will help explain these rules.

Proper Nouns and Adjectives

Capitalize all proper nouns and all proper adjectives (adjectives derived from proper nouns). The chart below provides a quick overview of capitalization.

Quick Guide: Capitalization at a Glance

Days of the week	Saturday, Sunday, Tuesday
Months	March, August, December
Holidays, holy days	Christmas, Hanukkah, President's Day
Periods, events in history	the Renaissance, Middle Ages
Special events	Tate Memorial Dedication Ceremony
Political parties	Republican Party, Green Party
Official documents	Bill of Rights
Trade names	Frisbee disc, Heinz ketchup
Formal epithets	Alexander the Great
Official titles	Vice President Al Gore, Senator Davis
Official state nicknames	the Garden State, the Beaver State
Planets, heavenly bodies	Earth, Mars, the Milky Way
Continents	Asia, Australia, Europe
Countries	France, Brazil, Japan, Pakistan
States, provinces	Montana, Nebraska, Alberta, Ontario
Cities, towns, villages	Portland, Brookfield, Broad Ripple
Streets, roads, highways	Rodeo Drive, Route 66, Interstate 55
Sections of the United States and the world	the West Coast, the Middle East
Landforms	Appalachian Mountains, Kalahari Desert
Bodies of water	Lake Erie, Tiber River, Atlantic Ocean
Public areas	Central Park, Rocky Mountain National Park

First Words

Capitalize the first word in every sentence and the first word in a direct quotation that is a full sentence.

Professional sports has become far too important in the United States.

Yvonne asked, "**Why** do baseball players spit all of the time?"

Correcting Capitalization

Practice A   If a word in the sentences below should be capitalized, write the word and place capitalization marks (≡) under any letters that should be capitalized.

1. Musician louis armstrong helped make jazz popular to american and european audiences.

2. Armstrong grew up in new Orleans in a rough neighborhood called the "battleground."

3. he was sent to reform school because he fired a gun in the air on new year's eve.

4. Upon his release, he visited music halls like funky butt hall to hear king oliver play.

5. Oliver gave armstrong his first real cornet, and he played with oliver's band in storyville, a red-light district in New orleans.

6. He also played with the allen brass band on the strekfus line of riverboats.

7. In 1919, Armstrong left new Orleans for Chicago and played with kid orv.

8. He really began to make a name for himself in the creole jazz band that played at Lincoln gardens in Chicago.

Practice B   Read the following paragraph. If a word should be capitalized, write the line number and the word. Place capitalization marks (≡) under any letters that should be capitalized in proper nouns, proper adjectives, or first words.

My great-grandfather Erv grew up in Racine, Wisconsin, during *1*
the great depression. He lived in two different houses on villa street just
south of the downtown area. Erv attended Holy Name Catholic school and
Franklin school when he was a kid. His dad, my great-great-grandfather,
came from Poland and started out by selling hot dogs at north beach. *5*
Because money was scarce, great-grandfather's family sometimes had only
corn on the cob for dinner. After high school, he enlisted in the US navy,
but was turned down because of poor eyesight. He then joined the army
and fought in Europe during world war II. when Erv returned to Racine,
he went to work at massey harris, a company that made tractors. *10*

INSIGHT —————————————————————————————
Different languages use capitalization differently. For example, German capitalizes not just proper nouns but all important nouns. Compare and contrast capitalization styles between your heritage language and English.

LO2 Advanced Capitalization

Sentences in Parentheses

Capitalize the first word in a sentence that is enclosed in parentheses if that sentence is not combined within another complete sentence.

I need to learn more about the health care system in Canada. (**Missy** just married a guy from Toronto.)

NOTE: Do *not* capitalize a sentence that is enclosed in parentheses and is located in the middle of another sentence.

Missy's husband (his name is Andre) works in a family business.

Sentences Following Colons

Capitalize a complete sentence that follows a colon when that sentence is a formal statement, a quotation, or a sentence that you want to emphasize.

Seldom have I heard such encouraging words: **The** economy is on the rebound.

Salutation and Complimentary Closing

In a letter, capitalize the first and all major words of the salutation. Capitalize only the first word of the complimentary closing.

Dear Governor Walker: **Sincerely** yours,

Sections of the Country

Words that indicate sections of the country are proper nouns and should be capitalized; words that simply indicate directions are not proper nouns.

The **Southwest** is suffering from a drought. *(section of country)*

I live a few blocks **southwest** of here. *(direction)*

Languages, Ethnic Groups, Nationalities, and Religions

Capitalize languages, ethnic groups, nationalities, religions, Supreme Beings, and holy books.

African	**Navajo**	**Islam**	**God**	**Allah**
Jehovah	the **Koran**	the **Book of Exodus**		the **Bible**

Correcting Capitalization

Practice A If capitalization is incorrect in any sentence below, write the word and place capitalization marks (≡) under any letters that should be capitalized.

1. The high plains is a subregion in the great plains.

2. Golda Meir once said this about women: "whether women are better than men I cannot say—but I can say they are certainly no worse."

3. The hopi indians come from a group of people called pueblo.

4. My dad is already planning for his retirement. (what will he do with so much free time?)

5. Many people from Mexico prefer the term Mexican American more than hispanic or latino.

6. Don't visit the deep south in August unless you like stifling heat and humidity.

7. The third largest religion, hinduism, does not have a single founder or a single sacred text.

8. My mechanic made a bad day even worse: he told me that my car needed four new tires.

Practice B Read the following paragraph. For any capitalization errors, write the line number and the word and place capitalization marks (≡) under any letters that should be capitalized.

> From 1943-1954, the midwest was blessed with the All American Girls   *1*
> Professional Baseball League. There were teams in Racine, Kenosha,
> Rockford, south Bend, Fort Wayne, grand Rapids, and Minneapolis. The
> league filled an entertainment need created by World War II: many men,
> especially minor-leaguers, were serving overseas. The women wore dress   *5*
> uniforms with knee-high woolen socks. (they must have been careful about
> sliding.) The women became heroines for young girls all across the country,
> from new England to the west coast.

Practice C Write each word and place capitalization marks (≡) under any letters that should be capitalized.

1. kleenex tissue   3. the koran   5. holiday   7. asian

2. memorial day   4. sherwood forest   6. tissue paper   8. the middle east

LO3 Other Capitalization Rules I

Titles

Capitalize the first word of a title, the last word, and every word in between except articles *(a, an, the)*, short prepositions, *to* in an infinitive, and coordinating conjunctions. Follow this rule for titles of books, newspapers, magazines, poems, plays, songs, articles, films, works of art, and stories.

The Dark Knight (movie)	*Washington Post* (newspaper)
"What a Wonderful World" (song)	"Death Penalty's False Promise" (essay)
Comedy of *Errors* (play)	*Gulliver's Travels* (novel)

Organizations

Capitalize the name of an organization or a team and its members.

Habitat for Humanity	Libertarian Party
The Bill & Melinda Gates Foundation	Chicago Cubs
Special Olympics	Phoenix Suns

Abbreviations

Capitalize abbreviations of titles and organizations.

MD	PhD	NAACP	CE	BCE	GPA

Letters

Capitalize letters used to indicate a form or shape.

S-curve	T-shirt	R-rated	C-section

INSIGHT ————————————————————

Note that the American Psychological Association has a different style for capitalizing the titles of smaller works. Be sure you know the style required for a specific class.

Correcting Capitalization

Practice If any words are incorrectly capitalized in the sentences below, write the word and place capitalization marks (≡) under any letters that should be capitalized.

1. To me, *a midsummer night's dream* is one of Shakespeare's best plays.

2. The San Francisco giants used to play in Candlestick park.

3. I enjoyed reading *city of thieves,* a novel by David Benioff.

4. Do you know the song "don't drink the water" by dave matthews?

5. My brother splattered some paint on my favorite Chicago white sox t-shirt.

6. Newman's own foundation donates to charities all net royalties and profits it receives from Newman's own products.

7. Javier Lopez, an old friend from the neighborhood, earned a phd in history.

8. Perhaps the least known of the beatles is George Harrison; I love his song "while my guitar gently weeps."

9. The movie *the kids are all right* is r-rated according to the *Denver post.*

10. Anna Quindlen's article "uncle sam and aunt samantha" first appeared in *newsweek.*

11. People attend aa (alcoholics anonymous) meetings to support each other as they battle their alcoholism.

Practice B Read the paragraph below. If any words are incorrectly capitalized, write the word and place capitalization marks (≡) under letters that should be capitalized.

> An article in last week's *standard press* promoted the city's farmer's *1*
> market. The market, held every Thursday afternoon, is sponsored by the
> Brighton chamber of commerce. The vendors, who must reside within
> the local area, sell everything from fresh produce to tie-dyed t-shirts. In
> addition, organizations such as the american red cross and Brighton little *5*
> league have informational booths at the market. A special feature is the
> live entertainment supplied by rainbow road, a local folk rock band. They
> play a lot of Bob Dylan, singing favorites like "blowin' in the wind."

LO4 Other Capitalization Rules II

Words Used as Names

Capitalize words like *father, mother, uncle, senator,* and *professor* only when they are parts of titles that include a personal name or when they are substitutes for proper nouns (especially in direct address).

Hello, **Representative** Baldwin. (*Representative* is part of the name.)

It's good to meet you, **Representative**. (*Representative* is a substitute for the name.)

Our **representative** is a member of two important committees.

Who was the volleyball **coach** last year?

We had **Coach Snyder** for two years.

I met **Coach** in the athletic office.

NOTE: To test whether a word is being substituted for a proper noun, simply read the sentence with a proper noun in place of the word. If the proper noun fits in the sentence, the word being tested should be capitalized. Usually the word is not capitalized if it follows a possessive—*my, his, our, your,* and so on.

Did **Mom** (Yvonne) pick up the dry cleaning? (*Yvonne* works in the sentence.)

Did your **mom** (Yvonne) pick up the dry cleaning? (*Yvonne* does not work in the sentence; the word *mom* follows *your.*)

Titles of Courses

Words such as *technology, history,* and *science* are proper nouns when they are included in the titles of specific courses; they are common nouns when they name a field of study.

The only course that fits my schedule is **Introduction to Oil Painting.** (title of a specific course)

Judy Kenner advises anyone interested in **oil painting.** (a field of study)

Web Terms

The words *Internet* and *World Wide Web* are capitalized because they are considered proper nouns. When your writing includes a Web address (URL), capitalize any letters that the site's owner does (on printed materials or on the site itself).

When doing research on the **Internet**, be sure to record each site's **Web** address (URL) and each contact's **email** address.

Correcting Capitalization

Practice A If a word in the sentences below needs to be capitalized, write the word and place capitalization marks (≡) under any letters that should be capitalized.

1. Every summer, pastor Bachman leads the youth group on a hike around lake geneva.

2. Claude Dickert, our current mayor, writes blog entries on About brighton, the city's official web site.

3. At the celebration, dad asked senator ryan about health care.

4. The easiest course I ever took in high school was called leisure reading.

5. When I'm on the internet, I use google to answer all kinds of questions.

6. Whenever mom talks about politics, she eventually criticizes our local congressman.

7. My night course, contemporary history, is always packed because professor scharfenburg presents such interesting lectures.

8. When it comes to shopping for books, I often go to amazon.com for ideas and information.

9. Our instructor had us bookmark grammar girl, a web site that provides grammar tips and practice.

10. Make an appointment with the dean if you want to drop cultural geography.

Practice B If a word in the paragraph below needs to be capitalized, write the line number and the word. Then place capitalization marks (≡) under any letters that should be capitalized.

Internet art does not consist of existing pieces of artwork digitized to   *1*
be seen using a web browser. Instead, it is art that is created on or with
the net, and it comes into being using web sites, email options, virtual
worlds such as second life, and so on. Steve Dietz, formerly the curator of
the Walker art center, defines internet art as art that has "the internet   *5*
as a necessary condition of viewing/participating/experiencing." Martin
Wattenberg has created a Web site called idea line, which provides "a time
line of net artwork" to help people experience this type of art.

LO5 Real-World Application

Correct   If capitalization errors occur in the email below, write the line number and the word and correct the capitalization. Place capitalization marks (≡) under letters that should be capitalized. (If a letter is capitalized and shouldn't be, put a lowercase editing mark (/) through the letter.)

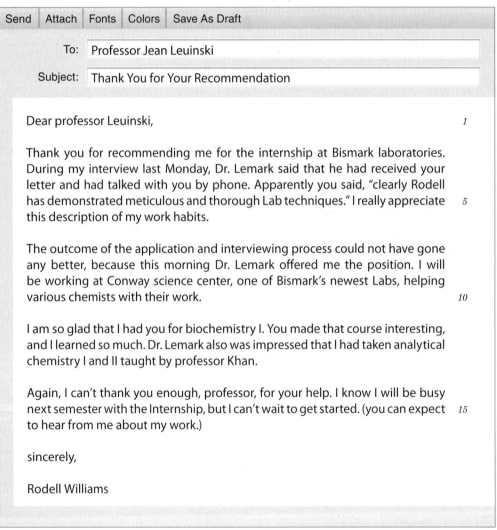

| Send | Attach | Fonts | Colors | Save As Draft |

To: Professor Jean Leuinski

Subject: Thank You for Your Recommendation

Dear professor Leuinski,   1

Thank you for recommending me for the internship at Bismark laboratories. During my interview last Monday, Dr. Lemark said that he had received your letter and had talked with you by phone. Apparently you said, "clearly Rodell has demonstrated meticulous and thorough Lab techniques." I really appreciate   5
this description of my work habits.

The outcome of the application and interviewing process could not have gone any better, because this morning Dr. Lemark offered me the position. I will be working at Conway science center, one of Bismark's newest Labs, helping various chemists with their work.   10

I am so glad that I had you for biochemistry I. You made that course interesting, and I learned so much. Dr. Lemark also was impressed that I had taken analytical chemistry I and II taught by professor Khan.

Again, I can't thank you enough, professor, for your help. I know I will be busy next semester with the Internship, but I can't wait to get started. (you can expect   15
to hear from me about my work.)

sincerely,

Rodell Williams

Special Challenge   Write one sentence in which you use the same regional or directional word twice—with the word correctly capitalized in one case and correctly lowercase in the other case.

28

> "The writer who neglects punctuation, or mispunctuates, is liable to be misunderstood for the want of merely a comma. "
>
> —Edgar Allan Poe

Comma

When you speak, you communicate with much more than words. You pause, raise or lower your pitch, change your tone or volume, and use facial expressions and body language to get your point across.

When you write, you can forget about pitch or volume, facial expressions or body language. You're left with the tone of your words and with the pauses that you put in them. Commas give you one way to create a soft pause. They help to show which words belong together, which should be separated, and which line up in parallel. Commas are key to being understood.

In this chapter you will learn about the conventional use of commas. Understanding the correct comma usage is an important step in becoming a college-level writer.

Learning Outcomes

LO1 In Compound Sentences and After Introductory Clauses

LO2 With Introductory Phrases and Equal Adjectives

LO3 Between Items in a Series and Other Uses

LO4 With Appositives and Other Word Groups

LO5 Real-World Application

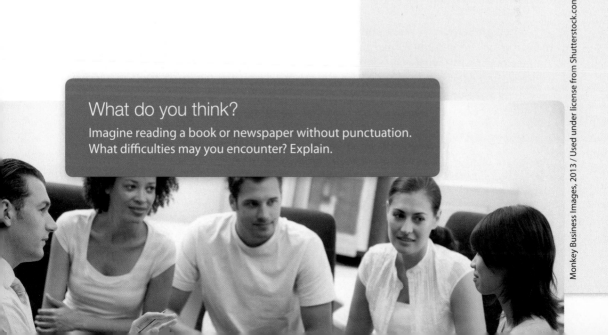

What do you think?

Imagine reading a book or newspaper without punctuation. What difficulties may you encounter? Explain.

Monkey Business Images, 2013 / Used under license from Shutterstock.com

LO1 In Compound Sentences and After Introductory Clauses

The following principles will guide the use of commas in your writing.

In Compound Sentences

Use a comma before the coordinating conjunction *(and, but, or, nor, for, yet, so)* in a compound sentence.

Heath Ledger completed his brilliant portrayal as the Joker in *The Dark Knight*, **but** he died before the film was released.

NOTE: Do not confuse a compound verb with a compound sentence.

Ledger's Joker became instantly iconic and won him the Oscar for best supporting actor. *(compound verb)*

His death resulted from the abuse of prescription drugs, but it was ruled an accident. *(compound sentence)*

After Introductory Clauses

Use a comma after most introductory clauses.

Although Charlemagne was a great patron of learning, he never learned to write properly. (adverb dependent clause)

When the clause follows the independent clause and is not essential to the meaning of the sentence, use a comma. This comma use generally applies to clauses beginning with *even though, although, while,* or some other conjunction expressing a contrast.

Charlemagne never learned to write properly, **even though he continued to practice.**

NOTE: A comma is *not* used if the dependent clause following the independent clause is needed for clarity.

CONSIDER THE TRAITS

Make sure to use both a comma and a coordinating conjunction in a compound sentence, or you will create a comma splice or a run-on.

Correcting Comma Errors

Correct If the clause on each side of the coordinating conjunction could stand alone as a sentence, add a comma. Write the words before and after the comma, showing the comma between them. Write "correct" if the conjunction separates word groups that can't stand alone.

1. Catherine had questions about her class schedule so she set up an appointment with her academic adviser. _____

2. I was going to play in the sand volleyball league but it conflicted with my work schedule. _____

3. Trisha picked up some groceries and stopped by the bank. _____

4. I normally don't listen to jazz music yet I love going to summer jazz concerts in the park. _____

5. Should I finish my essay a day early or should I go to my friend's house party? _____

6. Kevin has a job interview at the advertisement agency and he hopes he can make a good impression. _____

7. Creativity is his best quality but leadership is not far behind. _____

Correct If an introductory clause needs to be followed by a comma, write the words before and after the comma, showing it between them. If no comma is needed, write "correct."

1. Even though digital books are the craze I prefer paperbacks. _____

2. Although the crab dip appetizer was delicious my entrée left something to be desired. _____

3. Because I'm starved for time online shopping is a convenient alternative to mall shopping. _____

4. I toggled through radio stations while I waited at the tollbooth. _____

5. Erin worried about giving her speech even though she had practiced for weeks. _____

LO2 With Introductory Phrases and Equal Adjectives

After Introductory Phrases

Use a comma after introductory phrases.

In spite of his friend's prodding, Jared decided to stay home and study.

A comma is usually omitted if the phrase follows an independent clause.

Jared decided to stay home and study **in spite of his friend's prodding.**

You may omit a comma after a short (four or fewer words) introductory phrase unless it is needed to ensure clarity.

At 10:32 p.m. he would quit and go to sleep.

To Separate Adjectives

Use commas to separate adjectives that equally modify the same noun. Notice in the examples below that no comma separates the last adjective from the noun.

You should exercise regularly and follow a **sensible, healthful** diet.

A good diet is one that includes lots of **high-protein, low-fat** foods.

To Determine Equal Modifiers

To determine whether adjectives modify a noun equally, use these two tests.

1. Reverse the order of the adjectives; if the sentence is clear, the adjectives modify equally. (In the example below, *hot* and *crowded* can be switched, but *short* and *coffee* cannot.)

   Matt was tired of working in the **hot, crowded** lab and decided to take a **short coffee** break.

2. Insert *and* between the adjectives; if the sentence reads well, use a comma when *and* is omitted. (The word *and* can be inserted between *hot* and *crowded*, but *and* does not make sense between *short* and *coffee*.)

Correcting Comma Errors

Correct If a comma is needed after the introductory phrase, write the words before and after the comma, with it between them. If no comma is needed, write "correct."

1. Before you send the email make sure you reread it for errors in clarity. _____

2. In accordance with the academic code plagiarism is deemed a major offense. _____

3. After hitting the 10-mile jogging plateau Heather felt a great rush of adrenaline. _____

4. Heather felt a great rush of adrenaline after hitting the 10-mile jogging plateau. _____

5. Thankfully DeMarcus stopped the leak before it could do any real damage. _____

6. Based on his past experience Wilson decided against going to the concert. _____

7. To train for the triathlon Brent altered his diet. _____

8. At the end of the day Erin recorded her favorite show. _____

Correct For each sentence below, determine whether or not a comma is needed to separate the adjectives that modify the same noun. Write the two adjectives with the comma between them. Write "correct" if a comma is not needed.

1. I'm expecting this to be a **rocking after** party. _____

2. There's nothing like the **warm emerald** water off the Florida Gulf Coast. _____

3. The exercise program included a **calorie-burning cardio** session. _____

4. My **surly economics** professor is one of a kind. _____

5. I'm in desperate need of a **relaxing summer** vacation. _____

6. Marathon runners favor **light comfortable** shorts. _____

LO3 Between Items in a Series and Other Uses

Between Items in Series

Use commas to separate individual words, phrases, or clauses in a series. (A series contains at least three items.)

Many college students must balance studying with **taking care of a family, working, getting exercise, and finding time to relax.**

Do not use commas when all the items are connected with *or, nor,* or *and.*

Hmm . . . should I study **or** do laundry **or** go out?

To Set Off Transitional Expressions

Use a comma to set off conjunctive adverbs and transitional phrases.

Handwriting is not, **as a matter of fact,** easy to improve upon later in life; **however,** it can be done if you are determined enough.

If a transitional expression blends smoothly with the rest of the sentence, it does not need to be set off.

If you are **in fact** coming, I'll see you there.

To Set Off Dialogue

Use commas to set off the words of the speaker from the rest of the sentence. Do not use a comma before an indirect quotation.

"Never be afraid to ask for help," advised Ms. Kane.

"With the evidence that we now have," Professor Thom said, **"many scientists believe there could be life on Mars."**

To Enclose Explanatory Words

Use commas to enclose an explanatory word or phrase.

Time management, **according to many professionals,** is an important skill that should be taught in college.

Correcting Comma Errors

Correct   Indicate where commas are needed. Write the words before and after the comma, showing the comma between them.

1. I considered becoming a lawyer; however law school wasn't for me.

2. "Don't give up, don't ever give up" advised the late Jim Valvano.

3. Calvin Harris's music is infused with electronic beats, catchy lyrics and a pop-friendly sound.

4. Western Wisconsin as opposed to Illinois is relatively hilly.

5. In Boston I visited Fenway Park the U.S.S. *Constitution,* and Old North Church.

6. Thomas as you may have noticed is eager to share his vast knowledge of random facts.

7. In regard to public transportation, you may decide between the subway buses or taxicabs.

8. "While it certainly offers a convenient alternative to paper maps" said Emilie "my car's navigational system more often gets me lost."

9. Avocados the key ingredient of guacamole are a good source of fiber.

10. Secondly determine if weather price or transportation will factor into your decision.

Correct   Indicate where commas are needed. Write the line number and the words before and after the comma, showing the comma between them.

> On an early summer morning in July I sat slumped in a terminal   *1*
> at JFK airport, reminiscing about my time in Washington D.C. It had
> been a fun trip. I visited all the usual landmarks, including the Lincoln
> Memorial, Arlington National Cemetery and the Smithsonian Institute.
> However my favorite landmark was Mount Vernon the home and former   *5*
> estate of President George Washington. It's easy to see why Washington
> adored the location. The estate located in Alexandria, Virginia, is nestled
> above the Hudson River. Besides Washington's plantation home, the estate
> also included a distillery a blacksmith shop and acres of farmland. If you're
> ever in Washington D.C., I highly recommend a trip to Mount Vernon.   *10*

LO4 With Appositives and Nonrestrictive Modifiers

To Set Off Some Appositives

A specific kind of explanatory word or phrase called an **appositive** identifies or renames a preceding noun or pronoun.

Albert Einstein, **the famous mathematician and physicist,** developed the theory of relativity.

Do not use commas if the appositive is important to the basic meaning of the sentence.

The famous physicist **Albert Einstein** developed the theory of relativity.

With Some Clauses and Phrases

Use commas to enclose phrases or clauses that add information that is not necessary to the basic meaning of the sentence. For example, if the clause or phrase (in boldface) were left out of the two examples below, the meaning of the sentences would remain clear. Therefore, commas are used to set off the information.

The locker rooms in Swain Hall, **which were painted and updated last summer,** give professors a place to shower. (nonrestrictive clause)

Work-study programs, **offered on many campuses,** give students the opportunity to earn tuition money. (nonrestrictive phrase)

Do not use commas to set off necessary clauses and phrases, which add information that the reader needs to understand the sentence.

Only the professors **who run at noon** use the locker rooms. (necessary clause)

Using "That" or "Which"

Use *that* to introduce necessary clauses; use *which* to introduce unnecessary clauses.

Campus jobs **that are funded by the university** are awarded to students only. (necessary)

The cafeteria, **which is run by an independent contractor,** can hire nonstudents. (unnecessary)

Correcting Comma Errors

Correct Indicate where commas are needed in the following sentences. Write the words before and after the comma and show the comma between them. If no commas are needed, write "correct."

1. The U.S.S. *Constitution* a wooden-hulled ship named by George Washington is the world's oldest floating commissioned naval vessel.   _____

2. Gordon Ramsay the fiery chef and television star specializes in French, Italian, and British cuisines.   _____

3. Hall of Fame baseball player and notable philanthropist Roberto Clemente died in a plane crash while en route to Nicaragua to deliver aid to earthquake victims.   _____

4. The concert hall which is on the corner of Meridian Ave and 1st Street is expected to revitalize the downtown district.   _____

5. Press passes that allow for backstage access are given out to special media members.   _____

6. John Quincy Adams who later became the sixth president of the United States authored the Monroe Doctrine in 1823.   _____

Write The following sentences contain clauses using *that*. Rewrite the sentences with clauses using *which*, and insert commas correctly. You may need to reword some parts.

1. The mechanical issue that delayed the flight should be corrected within 25 minutes.

   _____

2. The wind farm that was built along I-95 is scheduled to double in size by 2016.

   _____

3. Scholarships that are sponsored by the Kiwanis Club are awarded to local high school students.

   _____

> **appositive**
> a noun or noun phrase that renames another noun right beside it

LO5 Real-World Application

Correct Indicate where commas are needed in the following email message. Write the line number and the words before and after the comma, showing it between them.

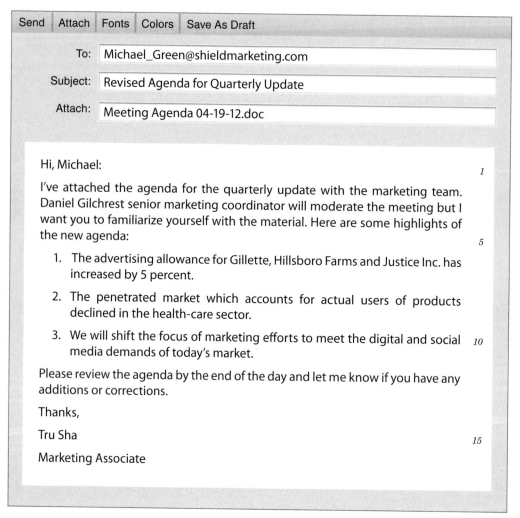

Send	Attach	Fonts	Colors	Save As Draft

To: Michael_Green@shieldmarketing.com

Subject: Revised Agenda for Quarterly Update

Attach: Meeting Agenda 04-19-12.doc

Hi, Michael: *1*

I've attached the agenda for the quarterly update with the marketing team. Daniel Gilchrest senior marketing coordinator will moderate the meeting but I want you to familiarize yourself with the material. Here are some highlights of the new agenda: *5*

1. The advertising allowance for Gillette, Hillsboro Farms and Justice Inc. has increased by 5 percent.

2. The penetrated market which accounts for actual users of products declined in the health-care sector.

3. We will shift the focus of marketing efforts to meet the digital and social   *10* media demands of today's market.

Please review the agenda by the end of the day and let me know if you have any additions or corrections.

Thanks,

Tru Sha   *15*

Marketing Associate

CONSIDER THE WORKPLACE

Correct comma use is critical for clear business communication.

29

"Sometimes people give [book] titles to me,
and sometimes I see them on a billboard."
—Robert Penn Warren

Quotation Marks and Italics

Broadway is plastered with billboards five stories high and is jammed with marquees that flash in the night. They advertise plays and movies, books and magazines, albums and TV shows—all in spotlights or neon trying to make people take notice.

In writing, there are no spotlights, there is no neon. Instead of writing the names of plays, movies, books, and so forth in giant, flashing letters, writers set them off with *italics*. This chapter will show you how to correctly punctuate titles of works big and small and words used as words.

Learning Outcomes

LO1 Quotation Marks
LO2 Italics
LO3 Real-World Application

What do you think?

How are quotation marks and italics like flashing lights in writing? How are they different?

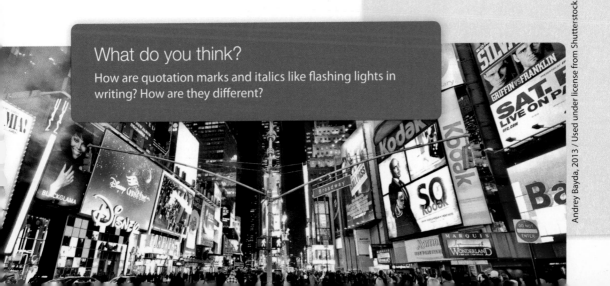

LO1   Quotation Marks

To Punctuate Titles (Smaller Works)

Use quotation marks to enclose the titles of smaller works, including speeches, short stories, songs, poems, episodes of audio or video programs, chapters or sections of books, unpublished works, and articles from magazines, journals, newspapers, or encyclopedias. (For other titles, see page 648.)

Speech:	"Ain't I a Woman?"
Song:	"California Girls"
Short Story:	"The Tell-Tale Heart"
Magazine Article:	"Is Google Making Us Stupid?"
Chapter in a Book:	"The Second Eve"
Television Episode:	"The Empty Child"
Encyclopedia Article:	"Autoban"

Placement of Periods and Commas

When quoted words end in a period or comma, always place that punctuation inside the quotation marks.

"When you leave the kitchen," Tim said, "turn out the light."

Placement of Semicolons and Colons

When a quotation is followed by a semicolon or colon, always place that punctuation outside the quotation marks.

I finally read "The Celebrated Jumping Frog of Calaveras County"; it is a hoot!

Placement of Exclamation Points and Question Marks

If an exclamation point or a question mark is part of the quotation, place it inside the quotation marks. Otherwise, place it outside.

Shawndra asked me, "Would you like to go to the movies?" What could I say except "That sounds great"?

For Special Words

Quotation marks can be used (1) to show that a word is being referred to as the word itself; (2) to indicate that it is jargon, slang, or a coined term; or (3) to show that it is used in an ironic or sarcastic sense.

(1) The word "chuffed" is British slang for "very excited."
(2) I'm "chuffed" about my new computer.
(3) I'm "chuffed" about my root canal.

Using Quotation Marks

Correct   For the following sentences, write down words that should be in quotation marks, and show the marks.

1. Tim loves the short story Cask of Amontillado by Edgar Allan Poe.

2. Stephen King's short story The Body was made into a movie.

3. Anna Quindlen wrote the article Uncle Sam and Aunt Samantha.

4. Lisa told Jennie, Tonight is the pizza and pasta buffet.

5. Jennie asked, Isn't it buy one, get one free?

6. Was she thinking, That's a lot better than cooking?

7. Here is the main conflict of the story To Build a Fire: man versus nature.

8. I read an article entitled The Obese Fruit of Capitalism; it suggested that our modern obesity epidemic demonstrates the tremendous achievements of fast food and agribusiness.

9. What does the word hypertrophy mean?

10. I was thrilled to receive the unexpected bill.

Write   Write a sentence that indicates the actual meaning of each sentence below.

1. The fully loaded logging truck "tiptoed" across the one-lane bridge.

_____

_____

_____

2. Enjoy our "fast" and "friendly" service.

_____

_____

_____

3. We had a "fun" time at our IRS audit.

_____

_____

_____

LO2 Italics

To Punctuate Titles (Larger Works)

Use italics to indicate the titles of larger works, including newspapers, magazines, journals, pamphlets, books, plays, films, radio and television programs, movies, ballets, operas, long musical compositions, CDs, DVDs, software programs, and legal cases, as well as the names of ships, trains, aircraft, and spacecraft. (For other titles, see page 646.)

Magazine: *The Week*   **Newspaper:** *Chicago Tribune*

Play: *Cat on a Hot Tin Roof*   **Journal:** *Nature*

Film: *Casablanca*   **Software Program:** *Final Draft*

Book: *Death's Disciples*   **Television Program:** *Doctor Who*

For a Word, Letter, or Number Referred to as Itself

Use italics (or quotation marks—see page 646) to show that a word, letter, or number is being referred to as itself. If a definition follows a word used in this way, place that definition in quotation marks.

The word *courage* comes from the French word *cour,* which means "heart."

In the handwritten note, I couldn't distinguish an *N* from an *M.*

For Foreign Words

Use italics to indicate a word that is being borrowed from a foreign language.

The phrase *et cetera ad nauseum* is a Latin phrase meaning "and so on until vomiting."

For Technical Terms

Use italics to introduce a technical term for the first time in a piece of writing. After that, the term may be used without italics.

Particle physicists are seeking the elusive *Higgs boson*—a subatomic particle thought to provide mass to all other particles. The Higgs boson has become a sort of Holy Grail of quantum mechanics.

NOTE: If a technical term is being used within an organization or a field of study where it is common, it may be used without italics even the first time in a piece of writing.

Using Italics

Correct   For the following sentences, write down or underline words that should be in italics.

1. One of my favorite novels is *The Curious Incident of the Dog in the Night-Time* by Mark Haddon.

2. Have you seen the amazing movie *Memento*?

3. The name of the *paso doble* dance comes from the Spanish word for "double step."

4. In 1945, the bomber called the *Enola Gay* dropped the first atomic bomb, a weapon predicted in 1914 in the H. G. Wells novel *The World Set Free*.

5. She always has a real *joie de vivre*.

6. To look at the PDF, you need Adobe Reader or Adobe Acrobat.

7. In this context, the words *profane* and *profanity* do not refer to swearing but simply to things that are not divine.

8. The television show *Project Runway* pits fashion designers against each other.

9. In the musical *A Funny Thing Happened on the Way to the Forum*, the slave Pseudolus spells out his hope to be *F – R – E – E*.

10. The enlargement of muscles through weight lifting is known as *hypertrophy*.

Write   Write three sentences, each demonstrating your understanding of one or more rules for using italics.

1. _____

_____

_____

2. _____

_____

_____

3. _____

_____

_____

LO3 Real-World Application

Practice If a word in the following email should be italicized or in quotation marks, write the line number and the word and show the correct punctuation.

Send	Attach	Fonts	Colors	Save As Draft

To: Will McMartin

Subject: Metrameme Author Bio

Hi, Will: 1

Here is the author bio you requested from me to be published in my next book,
War Child:

John Metrameme has published over a dozen novels, most recently the historical
epic Sons of Thunder and the romp Daddy Zeus. He has written articles also for   5
The Atlantic and The New Yorker, and his short story Me and the Mudman won
the Rubel Prize. Metrameme is perhaps best known for his novel Darling Buds
of May.

In his spare time, Metrameme enjoys acting in productions at his community
theater. He played himself in the three-man show The Complete Works of   10
William Shakespeare (Abridged). He also starred as Kit Gill in No Way to Treat a
Lady and as Jonathan in Arsenic and Old Lace.

Will, please let me know if you need anything more from me.

Thanks,

John   15

Correction Marks

⌿	delete	⅄	add comma	word ∧	add word
d	capitalize	? ∧	add question mark	⊙	add period
∅	lowercase			⟳	spelling
∧	insert	⌄	insert an apostrophe	⊓	switch

30

Other Punctuation

Work is important, of course. Progress. Motion. Getting somewhere. And yet, sometimes it's important to pause and take a breath. Breaks allow you to work even more effectively afterward.

Written materials need pauses and breaks, too. It doesn't have to be a full stop (a period); maybe something softer will do. Semicolons, colons, and dashes can give the reader just the right break to be refreshed and to set out again. This chapter covers these three punctuation marks as well as the useful hyphen.

Learning Outcomes

LO1 Apostrophes for Contractions and Possessives

LO2 Semicolons and Colons

LO3 Hyphens

LO4 Dashes

LO5 Real-World Application

LO6 Real-World Application

What do you think?

Do you deserve a break? What kind? What kind of break does this sentence deserve if any?

Yuri Arcurs, 2013 / Used under license from Shutterstock.com

LO1 Apostrophes for Contractions and Possessives

Apostrophes are used primarily to show that a letter or number has been left out or that a noun is possessive.

Contractions

When one or more letters are left out of a word, use an apostrophe to form the contraction.

> **INSIGHT**
>
> Pronoun possessives *do not use* apostrophes: *its, whose, hers, his, ours.*

don't
(*o* is left out)

he'd
(*woul* is left out)

would've
(*ha* is left out)

Missing Characters

Use an apostrophe to signal when one or more characters are left out.

class of '16
(*20* is left out)

rock 'n' roll
(*a* and *d* are left out)

good mornin'
(*g* is left out)

Possessives

Form possessives of singular nouns by adding an apostrophe and an *s*.

Sharla's pen

the man's coat

The Pilgrim's Progress

Singular Noun Ending in *s* (One Syllable)

Form the possessive by adding an apostrophe and an *s*.

the boss's idea

the lass's purse

the bass's teeth

Singular Noun Ending in *s* (Two or More Syllables)

Form the possessive by adding an apostrophe and an *s*—or by adding just an apostrophe.

Kansas's plains

or

Kansas' plains

Plural Noun Ending in *s*

Form the possessive by adding just an apostrophe.

the bosses' preference

the Smiths' home

the girls' ball
(*girls* are the owners)

> **INSIGHT**
>
> The word before the apostrophe is the owner.

Plural Noun Not Ending in *s*

Form the possessive by adding an apostrophe and an *s*.

the children's toys

the women's room

Forming Contractions and Possessives

Write For each contraction below, write the words that formed the contraction. For each set of words, write the contraction that would be formed.

1. you're _____

2. John is _____

3. would have _____

4. she'd _____

5. you would _____

6. shouldn't _____

7. I had _____

8. they are _____

9. we've _____

10. it is _____

Rewrite Rework the following sentences, replacing the "of" phrases with possessives using apostrophes.

1. I'm going to the house of Jeremy.

_____

2. The ice cream of the corner stand is amazing.

_____

3. The pace of the track star is impressive.

_____

4. I like the early work of the Rolling Stones.

_____

5. The persona of Texas is well represented in the slogan "Everything is bigger in Texas."

_____

6. The paintings of the artist were outstanding.

_____

7. I discovered the best pizza spot of Portland.

_____

8. She reviewed the notes of Kimbra.

_____

9. The contractor assessed the structure of the house.

_____

10. The position of the politician on health care remained firm.

_____

contraction
word formed by joining two words, leaving out one or more letters (indicated by an apostrophe)

LO2 Semicolons and Colons

Semicolons and colons have specific uses in writing.

Semicolon

A **semicolon** can be called a soft period. Use the semicolon to join two sentences that are closely related.

> The mosquitoes have returned; it must be August in Wisconsin.

Before a Conjunctive Adverb

Often, the second sentence will begin with a conjunctive adverb *(also, besides, however, instead, meanwhile, therefore)*, which signals the relationship between the sentences. Place a semicolon before the conjunctive adverb, and place a comma after it.

> The outdoor mosquito treatment was rated for six weeks; however, it lasted only four.

With Series

Use a semicolon to separate items in a series if any of the items already include commas.

> Before the party, I'll cut the grass and treat the lawn; buy a bug zapper, citronella candles, and bug spray; and get ready to swat and scratch.

Colon

The main use of a **colon** is to introduce an example or a list.

> Here's one other mosquito treatment: napalm.
> I have one motto: No bug is going to use my blood to reproduce!

After Salutations

In business documents, use a colon after **salutations** and in memo headings.

> Dear Ms. Alvarez: To: Tawnya Smith

Times and Ratios

Use a colon to separate hours, minutes, and seconds. Also use a colon between the numbers in a ratio.

> 8:23 a.m.   4:15 p.m.   14:32:46   The mosquito-person ratio is 5:1.

Using Semicolons and Colons

Correct Rewrite the following sentences, adding semicolons and commas as needed.

1. Mosquitoes here are a nuisance however in some places they are deadly.

2. Malaria kills many in Africa and South America it is carried by mosquitoes.

3. Each year, mosquito-borne illnesses affect 700 million victims many of them die.

4. Mosquitoes breed in stagnant water they need only a small amount.

5. Ponds would produce more mosquitoes however, many fish eat mosquito eggs and larva.

6. A female mosquito inserts her proboscis, injects an anti-clotting agent, and draws blood into her abdomen then she uses the blood proteins to create her eggs.

7. A mosquito bites you and gets away afterward she uses your blood to create more little horrors.

8. Bats rely on mosquitoes for much of their food frogs and birds eat them as well.

9. A friend of mine says a bug zapper does not get rid of mosquitoes it only reduces the "mosquito pressure."

10. The oldest known mosquito was trapped in amber in the Cretaceous period 73 million years ago perhaps it inspired the dinosaur mosquito in *Jurassic Park*.

Correct Rewrite the following sentences, adding colons as needed.

1. Mosquitoes in Egypt can carry a deadly disease yellow fever.

2. Here's the real shame the mosquitoes don't catch the disease.

3. Thankfully, mosquitoes don't pass along one terrible disease AIDS.

4. A mosquito can, however, pass along another nasty payload parasites.

5. Millions die per year because of one critter the mosquito.

6. A world without mosquitoes would be utterly different for one species Homo sapiens.

semicolon	colon	salutation
a punctuation mark (;) that connects sentences and separates items in some series	a punctuation mark (:) that introduces an example or list and has other special uses	the formal greeting in a letter; the line starting with "Dear"

LO3 Hyphens

A **hyphen** joins words to letters or to each other to form compounds.

Compound Nouns

Use hyphens to create **compound nouns**.

city-state	fail-safe	fact-check	one-liner	mother-in-law

Compound Adjectives

Use hyphens to create **compound adjectives** that appear before the noun. If the adjective appears after, it usually is not hyphenated.

peer-reviewed article   an article that was peer reviewed
ready-made solution   a solution that is ready made

NOTE: Don't hyphenate a compound made from an *-ly* adverb and an adjective, or a compound that ends with a single letter.

newly acquired songs   grade B plywood

Compound Numbers

Use hyphens for **compound numbers** from twenty-one to ninety-nine. Also use hyphens for numbers in a fraction and other number compounds.

twenty-two	fifty-fifty	three-quarters	seven thirty-seconds

With Letters

Use a hyphen to join a letter to a word that follows it.

L-bracket	U-shaped	T-shirt	O-ring	G-rated	x-ray

With Common Elements

Use hyphens to show that two or more words share a common element included in only the final term.

We offer low-, middle-, and high-coverage plans.

Using Hyphens

Correct   Rewrite the following sentences, adding hyphens as needed.

1. The United Nations secretary general ruled the vote fifty fifty.

   _____

2. I replaced the U bend and made a new P trap under the sink.

   _____

3. He guessed the board was three eighths inch thick.

   _____

4. Would you like to purchase low , medium , or high deductible insurance?

   _____

5. The double decker sandwich includes low fat ham and fat free mayonnaise.

   _____

6. The ham is low fat, and the mayonnaise is fat free.

   _____

7. In your graph, make sure to label the x and y axes.

   _____

8. The sales tax percentage is at an all time high.

   _____

9. My father in law is an attorney at law.

   _____

10. The T shirt showed the x ray of a rib cage.

    _____

---

hyphen
a short horizontal line (-) used to form compound words

compound noun
a noun made of two or more words, often hyphenated or spelled closed

compound adjective
an adjective made of two or more words, hyphenated before the noun but not afterward

compound numbers
two-word numbers from twenty-one to ninety-nine

LO4 Dashes

Unlike the hyphen, the **dash** does more to separate words than to join them together. A dash is indicated by two hyphens with no spacing before or after. Most word-processing programs convert two hyphens into a dash.

For Emphasis

Use a dash instead of a colon if you want to emphasize a word, phrase, clause, or series.

Donuts—they're not just for cops anymore.

There's only one thing better than a donut—two donuts.

I like all kinds of donuts—fritters, crullers, and cake donuts.

To Set Off a Series

Use a dash to set off a series of items.

Elephant ears, Danish, funnel cakes—they just aren't as cool as donuts.

They have many similarities—batter, frosting, and sugar—but where's the hole?

With Nonessential Elements

Use a dash to set off explanations, examples, and definitions, especially when these elements already include commas.

The hole—which is where the "dough nut" got its name originally—is a key component.

To Show Interrupted Speech

Use a dash to show that a speaker has been interrupted or has started and stopped while speaking.

"I'd like a—um—how about a fritter?"

"You want an apple—"

"Yes, an apple fritter, well—make it two."

INSIGHT

In most academic writing, use dashes sparingly. If they are overused, they lose their emphasis.

Using Dashes

Correct Rewrite the following sentences, adding dashes where needed.

1. Which would you prefer a cruller, a glazed donut, or a long john?

2. I love a nice blintz basically like a crepe but from Eastern Europe.

3. Donuts or do you prefer the spelling "doughnuts" are yummy.

4. "Could I have a dozen of Do you have a sale on donuts or on" "Today our sale is on wait, let me check yes, on donuts. Get a dozen for $3.00."

5. Batter, hot fat, frosting, sprinkles that's how you make a donut.

6. Making your own donuts is fun fattening, too!

7. A deep-fat fryer basically a deep pot filled with oil is needed to make donuts.

8. Let the donut cool before taking a bite extremely hot!

9. Decorate your donut with frosting, cinnamon, jelly whatever you want.

10. Don't eat too many donuts you'll end up with one around the middle.

Correct Write your own sentence, correctly using dashes for each of the situations indicated below:

1. For emphasis:

   _____

2. To set off a series:

   _____

3. With nonessential elements:

   _____

dash
long horizontal line that separates words, creating emphasis.

LO5 Real-World Application

Correct The following letter sounds too informal because it contains too many contractions. For any contractions you find, write the line number and full form of the word. Also, if you find any errors with apostrophes, write the line number and show the correct punctuation.

REDLAND STATE BANK

October 13, 2013   *1*

Phillip Jones
2398 10th Ave.
Westchester, NY 10959

Dear Mr. Jones: *5*

This letter's a response to your inquiry about financing your housing
project. I enjoyed discussing your project and appreciated your honesty
about your current loan.

As of today, we've decided to make a commitment to your project. I've
enclosed Redland State Banks' commitment letter. Please take time to   *10*
read the terms of agreement.

If there's any part you don't understand, don't hesitate to call or email us.
We'd be happy to answer any questions. As always's, we look forward to
serving you.

Sincerely,   *15*

Melinda Erson

Melinda Erson
Loan Officer

Enclosure: Commitment Letter

Correction Marks

✜ delete	⌃ add comma	⌃ add word (word)
d capitalize	? add question mark	⊙ add period
⌿ lowercase	⌃	⌒ spelling
⌃ insert	⌄ insert an apostrophe	⌇ switch

LO6 Real-World Application

Correct Rewrite the following email message, inserting semicolons, colons, hyphens, and dashes where necessary.

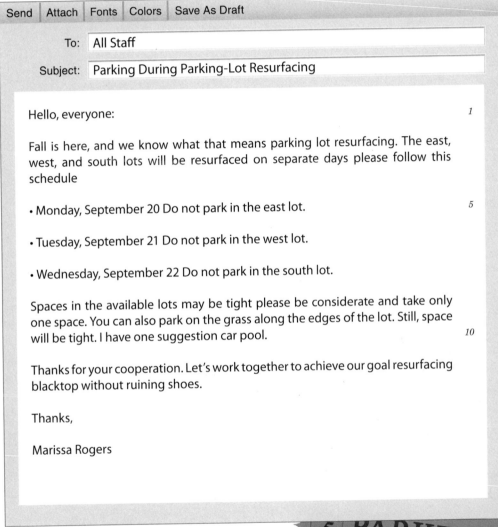

| Send | Attach | Fonts | Colors | Save As Draft |

To: All Staff

Subject: Parking During Parking-Lot Resurfacing

Hello, everyone: 1

Fall is here, and we know what that means parking lot resurfacing. The east, west, and south lots will be resurfaced on separate days please follow this schedule

• Monday, September 20 Do not park in the east lot.   5

• Tuesday, September 21 Do not park in the west lot.

• Wednesday, September 22 Do not park in the south lot.

Spaces in the available lots may be tight please be considerate and take only one space. You can also park on the grass along the edges of the lot. Still, space will be tight. I have one suggestion car pool.   10

Thanks for your cooperation. Let's work together to achieve our goal resurfacing blacktop without ruining shoes.

Thanks,

Marissa Rogers

Appendix, Glossary, and Index

Understanding the Reading Process

When reading academic texts, be sure to use the **reading process** to gain a full understanding of the material. This graphic shows the reading process in action. The arrows show how you may move back and forth between the steps.

The Reading Process

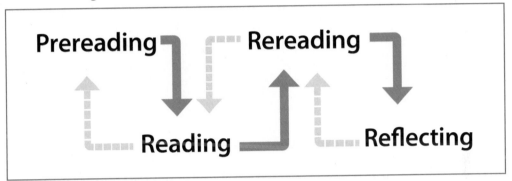

Key Terms to Remember

To use the reading process, you must understand each step in the process.

- **Prereading**—Becoming familiar with the text by reviewing the title, headings, etc.
- **Reading**—Reading the text once for a basic understanding, using a reading strategy such as note taking
- **Rereading**—Completing additional readings as needed until you have a clear understanding of the material
- **Reflecting**—Evaluating your reading experience: *What have you learned? What questions to you still have?*

For additional information, see pages 13–15.

Understanding the Writing Process

When completing a writing assignment, be sure to use the writing process to help you do your best work. This graphic shows the writing process in action. The arrows show how you may move back and forth between the steps.

The Writing Process

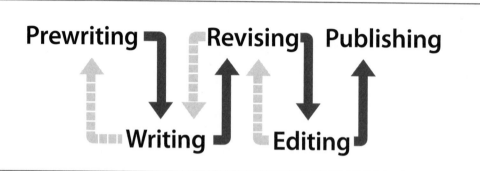

Key Terms to Remember

To use the writing process, you must understand each step in the process.

- **Prewriting**—Starting the process by analyzing the assignment, selecting a topic, gathering details, and finding a focus
- **Writing**—Writing a first draft using your prewriting as a guide
- **Revising**—Improving the content of a first draft
- **Editing**—Checking for style, grammar, mechanics, and spelling
- **Publishing**—Preparing your writing to share or submit

For additional information, see pages 106–111.

Understanding the Structure of Paragraphs and Essays

Paragraphs and essays follow a three-part structure. Knowing the purpose of each part will help you understand reading assignments and develop your own writing.

Three-Part Structure

Paragraph Structure

Topic Sentence

- Names the topic and focus

Body Sentences

- Provide supporting sentences
- Follow a pattern of organization

Closing Sentence

- Wraps up the paragraph

Essay Structure

Opening Part

- Introduces the topic
- Provides background information
- Identifies the main point or thesis

Middle Part

- Supports or develops the main point
- Follows one or more patterns of organization

Closing Part

- Summarizes the key ideas
- Restates the thesis
- Provides final thoughts or analysis

For additional information, see pages 80–81 and 112–117.

Understanding Strong Writing

The checklist below serves as a guide to strong writing. Your writing will be clear and effective when it can "pass" each point. This checklist is especially helpful during revising, when you are deciding how to improve your writing.

A Guide to Strong Writing

Ideas

☐   **1.** Does an interesting and relevant topic serve as a starting point for the writing?

☐   **2.** Is the writing focused, addressing a specific feeling about or a specific part of the topic? (Check the thesis statement.)

☐   **3.** Are there enough specific ideas, details, and examples to support the thesis?

☐   **4.** Overall, is the writing interesting and informative?

Organization

☐   **5.** Does the writing form a meaningful whole—with opening, middle, and closing parts?

☐   **6.** Does the writing follow a logical pattern of organization?

☐   **7.** Do transitions connect ideas and help the writing flow?

Voice

☐   **8.** Does the writer sound informed about and interested in the topic?

☐   **9.** Does the writer sound sincere and genuine?

Word Choice

☐ **10.** Does the word choice clearly fit the purpose and the audience?

☐ **11.** Does the writing include specific nouns and verbs?

Sentence Fluency

☐ **12.** Are the sentences clear, and do they flow smoothly?

☐ **13.** Are the sentences varied in their beginnings and length?

Conventions

☐ **14.** Does your writing follow the rules of the language?

For additional information, see pages 131–160.

Using a Peer Review Sheet

Sharing your writing at various stages is important, but it is especially important when you review and revise a first draft. The feedback that you receive will help you change and improve your essay.

Peer Review Sheet

Essay title: _____

Writer: _____

Reviewer: _____

1. Which part of the essay seems to work best—opening, middle, or closing? Why?

   _____

   _____

2. Which part of the essay needs work—opening, middle, or closing? Why?

   _____

   _____

3. Do the middle paragraphs clearly present each step of the process? Explain.

   _____

   _____

4. Do you understand the process after reading the essay?

   _____

   _____

5. Identify a phrase or two that show the writer's level of interest.

   _____

   _____

Understanding Word Parts

The next nine pages include common prefixes, suffixes, and roots. Many of our words are made up of combinations of these word parts.

Prefixes

Prefixes are those "word parts" that come *before* the root words (*pre* = before). Depending upon its meaning, a prefix changes the intent, or sense, of the base word. As a skilled reader, you will want to know the meanings of the most common prefixes and then watch for them when you read.

a, an [not, without] amoral (without a sense of moral responsibility), atypical, atom (not cuttable), apathy (without feeling), anesthesia (without sensation)

ab, abs, a [from, away] abnormal, abduct, absent, avert (turn away)

acro [high] acropolis (high city), acrobat, acronym, acrophobia (fear of height)

ambi, amb [both, around] ambidextrous (skilled with both hands), ambiguous, amble

amphi [both] amphibious (living on both land and water), amphitheater

ante [before] antedate, anteroom, antebellum, antecedent (happening before)

anti, ant [against] anticommunist, antidote, anticlimax, antacid

be [on, away] bedeck, belabor, bequest, bestow, beloved

bene, bon [well] benefit, benefactor, benevolent, benediction, bonanza, bonus

bi, bis, bin [both, double, twice] bicycle, biweekly, bilateral, biscuit, binoculars

by [side, close, near] bypass, bystander, by-product, bylaw, byline

cata [down, against] catalog, catapult, catastrophe, cataclysm

cerebro [brain] cerebral, cerebrum, cerebellum

circum, circ [around] circumference, circumnavigate, circumspect, circular

co, con, col, com [together, with] copilot, conspire, collect, compose

coni [dust] coniosis (disease that comes from inhaling dust)

contra, counter [against] controversy, contradict, counterpart

de [from, down] demote, depress, degrade, deject, deprive

deca [ten] decade, decathlon, decapod (10 feet)

di [two, twice] divide, dilemma, dilute, dioxide, dipole, ditto

dia [through, between] diameter, diagonal, diagram, dialogue (speech between people)

dis, dif [apart, away, reverse] dismiss, distort, distinguish, diffuse

dys [badly, ill] dyspepsia (digesting badly), dystrophy, dysentery

em, en [in, into] embrace, enslave

epi [upon] epidermis (upon the skin, outer layer of skin), epitaph, epithet

eu [well] eulogize (speak well of, praise), euphony, euphemism, euphoria

ex, e, ec, ef [out] expel (drive out), ex-mayor, exorcism, eject, eccentric (out of the center position), efflux, effluent

extra, extro [beyond, outside] extraordinary (beyond the ordinary), extrovert, extracurricular

for [away or off] forswear (to renounce an oath)

fore [before in time] forecast, foretell (to tell beforehand), foreshadow

hemi, demi, semi [half] hemisphere, demitasse, semicircle (half of a circle)

hex [six] hexameter, hexagon

homo [man] Homo sapiens, homicide (killing man)

hyper [over, above] hypersensitive (overly sensitive), hyperactive

hypo [under] hypodermic (under the skin), hypothesis

il, ir, in, im [not] illegal, irregular, incorrect, immoral

in, il, im [into] inject, inside, illuminate, illustrate, impose, implant, imprison

infra [beneath] infrared, infrasonic

inter [between] intercollegiate, interfere, intervene, interrupt (break between)

intra [within] intramural, intravenous (within the veins)

intro [into, inward] introduce, introvert (turn inward)

macro [large, excessive] macrodent (having large teeth), macrocosm

mal [badly, poorly] maladjusted, malady, malnutrition, malfunction

meta [beyond, after, with] metaphor, metamorphosis, metaphysical

mis [incorrect, bad] misuse, misprint

miso [hate] misanthrope, misogynist

mono [one] monoplane, monotone, monochrome, monocle

multi [many] multiply, multiform

neo [new] neopaganism, neoclassic, neophyte, neonatal

non [not] nontaxable (not taxed), nontoxic, nonexistent, nonsense

ob, of, op, oc [toward, against] obstruct, offend, oppose, occur

oct [eight] octagon, octameter, octave, octopus

paleo [ancient] paleoanthropology (pertaining to ancient humans), paleontology (study of ancient life-forms)

para [beside, almost] parasite (one who eats beside or at the table of another), paraphrase, paramedic, parallel, paradox

penta [five] pentagon (figure or building having five angles or sides), pentameter, pentathlon

per [throughout, completely] pervert (completely turn wrong, corrupt), perfect, perceive, permanent, persuade

peri [around] perimeter (measurement around an area), periphery, periscope, pericardium, period

poly [many] polygon (figure having many angles or sides), polygamy, polyglot, polychrome

post [after] postpone, postwar, postscript, posterity

pre [before] prewar, preview, precede, prevent, premonition

pro [forward, in favor of] project (throw forward), progress, promote, prohibition

pseudo [false] pseudonym (false or assumed name), pseudopodia

quad [four] quadruple (four times as much), quadriplegic, quadratic, quadrant

quint [five] quintuplet, quintuple, quintet, quintile

re [back, again] reclaim, revive, revoke, rejuvenate, retard, reject, return

retro [backward] retrospective (looking backward), retroactive, retrorocket

se [aside] seduce (lead aside), secede, secrete, segregate

self [by oneself] self-determination, self-employed, self-service, selfish

sesqui [one and a half] sesquicentennial (one and one-half centuries)

sex, sest [six] sexagenarian (sixty years old), sexennial, sextant, sextuplet, sestet

sub [under] submerge (put under), submarine, substitute, subsoil

suf, sug, sup, sus [from under] sufficient, suffer, suggest, support, suspend

super, supr [above, over, more] supervise, superman, supernatural, supreme

syn, sym, sys, syl [with, together] system, synthesis, synchronize (time together), synonym, sympathy, symphony, syllable

trans, tra [across, beyond] transoceanic, transmit (send across), transfusion, tradition

tri [three] tricycle, triangle, tripod, tristate

ultra [beyond, exceedingly] ultramodern, ultraviolet, ultraconservative

un [not, release] unfair, unnatural, unknown

under [beneath] underground, underlying

uni [one] unicycle, uniform, unify, universe, unique (one of a kind)

vice [in place of] vice president, viceroy, vice admiral

Numerical Prefixes

Prefix	Symbol	Multiples and Submultiples	Equivalent	Prefix	Symbol	Multiples and Submultiples	Equivalent
tera	T	10^{12}	trillionfold	centi	c	10^{-2}	hundredth part
giga	G	10^{9}	billionfold	milli	m	10^{-3}	thousandth part
mega	M	10^{6}	millionfold	micro	u	10^{-6}	millionth part
kilo	k	10^{3}	thousandfold	nano	n	10^{-9}	billionth part
hecto	h	10^{2}	hundredfold	pico	p	10^{-12}	trillionth part
deka	da	10	tenfold	femto	f	10^{-15}	quadrillionth part
deci	d	10^{-1}	tenth part	atto	a	10^{-18}	quintillionth part

Suffixes

Suffixes come at the end of a word. Very often a suffix will tell you what kind of word it is part of (noun, adverb, adjective, and so on). For example, words ending in -*ly* are usually adverbs.

able, ible [able, can do] capable, agreeable, edible, visible (can be seen)

ade [result of action] blockade (the result of a blocking action), lemonade

age [act of, state of, collection of] salvage (act of saving), storage, forage

al [relating to] sensual, gradual, manual, natural (relating to nature)

algia [pain] neuralgia (nerve pain)

an, ian [native of, relating to] African, Canadian, Floridian

ance, ancy [action, process, state] assistance, allowance, defiance, truancy

ant [performing, agent] assistant, servant

ary, ery, ory [relating to, quality, place where] dictionary, bravery, dormitory

ate [cause, make] liquidate, segregate (cause a group to be set aside)

cian [having a certain skill or art] musician, beautician, magician, physician

cule, ling [very small] molecule, ridicule, duckling (very small duck), sapling

cy [action, function] hesitancy, prophecy, normalcy (function in a normal way)

dom [quality, realm, office] freedom, kingdom, wisdom (quality of being wise)

ee [one who receives the action] employee, nominee (one who is nominated), refugee

en [made of, make] silken, frozen, oaken (made of oak), wooden, lighten

ence, ency [action, state of, quality] difference, conference, urgency

er, or [one who, that which] baker, miller, teacher, racer, amplifier, doctor

escent [in the process of] adolescent (in the process of becoming an adult), obsolescent, convalescent

ese [a native of, the language of] Japanese, Vietnamese, Portuguese

esis, osis [action, process, condition] genesis, hypnosis, neurosis, osmosis

ess [female] actress, goddess, lioness

et, ette [a small one, group] midget, octet, baronet, majorette

fic [making, causing] scientific, specific

ful [full of] frightful, careful, helpful

fy [make] fortify (make strong), simplify, amplify

hood [order, condition, quality] manhood, womanhood, brotherhood

ic [nature of, like] metallic (of the nature of metal), heroic, poetic, acidic

ice [condition, state, quality] justice, malice

id, ide [a thing connected with or belonging to] fluid, fluoride

ile [relating to, suited for, capable of] missile, juvenile, senile (related to being old)

ine [nature of] feminine, genuine, medicine

ion, sion, tion [act of, state of, result of] contagion, aversion, infection (state of being infected)

ish [origin, nature, resembling] foolish, Irish, clownish (resembling a clown)

ism [system, manner, condition, characteristic] heroism, alcoholism, Communism

ist [one who, that which] artist, dentist

ite [nature of, quality of, mineral product] Israelite, dynamite, graphite, sulfite

ity, ty [state of, quality] captivity, clarity

ive [causing, making] abusive (causing abuse), exhaustive

ize [make] emphasize, publicize, idolize

less [without] baseless, careless (without care), artless, fearless, helpless

ly [like, manner of] carelessly, quickly, forcefully, lovingly

ment [act of, state of, result] contentment, amendment (state of amending)

ness [state of] carelessness, kindness

oid [resembling] asteroid, spheroid, tabloid, anthropoid

ology [study, science, theory] biology, anthropology, geology, neurology

ous [full of, having] gracious, nervous, spacious, vivacious (full of life)

ship [office, state, quality, skill] friendship, authorship, dictatorship

some [like, apt, tending to] lonesome, threesome, gruesome

tude [state of, condition of] gratitude, multitude (condition of being many), aptitude

ure [state of, act, process, rank] culture, literature, rupture (state of being broken)

ward [in the direction of] eastward, forward, backward

y [inclined to, tend to] cheery, crafty, faulty

Roots

A *root* is a base upon which other words are built. Knowing the root of a difficult word can go a long way toward helping you figure out its meaning— even without a dictionary. For that reason, learning the following roots will be very valuable in all your classes.

acer, acid, acri [bitter, sour, sharp] acrid, acerbic, acidity (sourness), acrimony

acu [sharp] acute, acupuncture

ag, agi, ig, act [do, move, go] agent (doer), agenda (things to do), agitate, navigate (move by sea), ambiguous (going both ways), action

ali, allo, alter [other] alias (a person's other name), alibi, alien (from another place), alloy, alter (change to another form)

alt [high, deep] altimeter (a device for measuring heights), altitude

am, amor [love, liking] amiable, amorous, enamored

anni, annu, enni [year] anniversary, annually (yearly), centennial (occurring once in 100 years)

anthrop [man] anthropology (study of mankind), philanthropy (love of mankind), misanthrope (hater of mankind)

anti [old] antique, antiquated, antiquity

arch [chief, first, rule] archangel (chief angel), architect (chief worker), archaic (first, very early), monarchy (rule by one person), matriarchy (rule by the mother)

aster, astr [star] aster (star flower), asterisk, asteroid, astronomy (star law), astronaut (star traveler, space traveler)

aud, aus [hear, listen] audible (can be heard), auditorium, audio, audition, auditory, audience, ausculate

aug, auc [increase] augur, augment (add to; increase), auction

auto, aut [self] autograph (self-writing), automobile (self-moving vehicle), author, automatic (self-acting), autobiography

belli [war] rebellion, belligerent (warlike or hostile)

bibl [book] Bible, bibliography (list of books), bibliomania (craze for books), bibliophile (book lover)

bio [life] biology (study of life), biography, biopsy (cut living tissue for examination)

brev [short] abbreviate, brevity, brief

cad, cas [to fall] cadaver, cadence, caducous (falling off), cascade

calor [heat] calorie (a unit of heat), calorify (to make hot), caloric

cap, cip, cept [take] capable, capacity, capture, reciprocate, accept, except, concept

capit, capt [head] decapitate (to remove the head from), capital, captain, caption

carn [flesh] carnivorous (flesh eating), incarnate, reincarnation

caus, caut [burn, heat] caustic, cauterize (to make hot, to burn)

cause, cuse, cus [cause, motive] because, excuse (to attempt to remove the blame or cause), accusation

ced, ceed, cede, cess [move, yield, go, surrender] procedure, secede (move aside from), proceed (move forward), cede (yield), concede, intercede, precede, recede, success

centri [center] concentric, centrifugal, centripetal, eccentric (out of center)

chrom [color] chrome, chromosome (color body in genetics), chromosphere, monochrome (one color), polychrome

chron [time] chronological (in order of time), chronometer (time measured), chronicle (record of events in time), synchronize (make time with, set time together)

cide, cise [cut down, kill] suicide (killing of self), homicide (human killer), pesticide (pest killer), germicide (germ killer), insecticide, precise (cut exactly right), incision, scissors

cit [to call, start] incite, citation, cite

civ [citizen] civic (relating to a citizen), civil, civilian, civilization

clam, claim [cry out] exclamation, clamor, proclamation, reclamation, acclaim

clud, clus, claus [shut] include (to take in), conclude, claustrophobia (abnormal fear of being shut up, confined), recluse (one who shuts himself away from others)

cognosc, gnosi [know] recognize (to know again), incognito (not known), prognosis (forward knowing), diagnosis

cord, cor, cardi [heart] cordial (hearty, heartfelt), concord, discord, courage, encourage (put heart into), discourage (take heart out of), core, coronary, cardiac

corp [body] corporation (a legal body), corpse, corpulent

cosm [universe, world] cosmic, cosmos (the universe), cosmopolitan (world citizen), cosmonaut, microcosm, macrocosm

crat, cracy [rule, strength] democratic, autocracy

crea [create] creature (anything created), recreation, creation, creator

cred [believe] creed (statement of beliefs), credo (a creed), credence (belief), credit (belief, trust), credulous (believing too readily, easily deceived), incredible

cresc, cret, crease, cru [rise, grow] crescendo (growing in loudness or intensity), concrete (grown together, solidified), increase, decrease, accrue (to grow) crit [separate, choose] critical, criterion (that which is used in choosing), hypocrite

cur, curs [run] concurrent, current (running or flowing), concur (run together, agree), incur (run into), recur, occur, precursor (forerunner), cursive

cura [care] curator, curative, manicure (caring for the hands)

cycl, cyclo [wheel, circular] Cyclops (a mythical giant with one eye in the middle of his forehead), unicycle, bicycle, cyclone (a wind blowing circularly, a tornado)

deca [ten] decade, decalogue, decathlon

dem [people] democracy (people-rule), demography (vital statistics of the people: deaths, births, and so on), epidemic (on or among the people)

dent, dont [tooth] dental (relating to teeth), denture, dentifrice, orthodontist

derm [skin] hypodermic (injected under the skin), dermatology (skin study), epidermis (outer layer of skin), taxidermy (arranging skin; mounting animals)

dict [say, speak] diction (how one speaks, what one says), dictionary, dictate, dictator, dictaphone, dictatorial, edict, predict, verdict, contradict, benediction

doc [teach] indoctrinate, document, doctrine

domin [master] dominate, dominion, predominant, domain

don [give] donate, condone

dorm [sleep] dormant, dormitory

dox [opinion, praise] doxy (belief, creed, or opinion), orthodox (having the correct, commonly accepted opinion), heterodox (differing opinion), paradox (contradictory)

drome [run, step] syndrome (run-together symptoms), hippodrome (a place where horses run)

duc, duct [lead] produce, induce (lead into, persuade), seduce (lead aside), reduce, aqueduct (water leader or channel), viaduct, conduct

dura [hard, lasting] durable, duration, endurance

dynam [power] dynamo (power producer), dynamic, dynamite, hydrodynamics

endo [within] endoral (within the mouth), endocardial (within the heart), endoskeletal

equi [equal] equinox, equilibrium

erg [work] energy, erg (unit of work), allergy, ergophobia (morbid fear of work), ergometer, ergonomic

fac, fact, fic, fect [do, make] factory (place where workers make goods of various kinds), fact (a thing done), manufacture, amplification, confection

fall, fals [deceive] fallacy, falsify

fer [bear, carry] ferry (carry by water), coniferous (bearing cones, as a pine tree), fertile (bearing richly), defer, infer, refer

fid, fide, feder [faith, trust] confidante, Fido, fidelity, confident, infidelity, infidel, federal, confederacy

fila, fili [thread] filament (a single thread or threadlike object), filibuster, filigree

fin [end, ended, finished] final, finite, finish, confine, fine, refine, define, finale

fix [attach] fix, fixation (the state of being attached), fixture, affix, prefix, suffix

flex, flect [bend] flex (bend), reflex (bending back), flexible, flexor (muscle for bending), inflexibility, reflect, deflect

flu, fluc, fluv [flowing] influence (to flow in), fluid, flue, flush, fluently, fluctuate (to wave in an unsteady motion)

form [form, shape] form, uniform, conform, deform, reform, perform, formative, formation, formal, formula

fort, forc [strong] fort, fortress (a strong place), fortify (make strong), forte (one's strong point), fortitude, enforce

fract, frag [break] fracture (a break), infraction, fragile (easy to break), fraction (result of breaking a whole into equal parts), refract (to break or bend)

gam [marriage] bigamy (two marriages), monogamy, polygamy (many spouses or marriages)

gastr(o) [stomach] gastric, gastronomic, gastritis (inflammation of the stomach)

gen [birth, race, produce] genesis (birth, beginning), genetics (study of heredity), eugenics (well born), genealogy (lineage by race, stock), generate, genetic

geo [earth] geometry (earth measurement), geography (earth writing), geocentric (earth centered), geology

germ [vital part] germination (to grow), germ (seed; living substance, as the germ of an idea), germane

gest [carry, bear] congest (bear together, clog), congestive (causing clogging), gestation

gloss, glot [tongue] glossary, polyglot (many tongues), epiglottis

glu, glo [lump, bond, glue] glue, agglutinate (make to hold in a bond), conglomerate (bond together)

grad, gress [step, go] grade (step, degree), gradual (step-by-step), graduate (make all the steps, finish a course), graduated (in steps or degrees), progress

graph, gram [write, written] graph, graphic (written, vivid), autograph (self-writing, signature), graphite (carbon used for writing), photography (light writing), phonograph (sound writing), diagram, bibliography, telegram

grat [pleasing] gratuity (mark of favor, a tip), congratulate (express pleasure over success), grateful, ingrate (not thankful)

grav [heavy, weighty] grave, gravity, aggravate, gravitate

greg [herd, group, crowd] gregarian (belonging to a herd), congregation (a group functioning together), segregate (tending to group aside or apart)

helio [sun] heliograph (an instrument for using the sun's rays to send signals), heliotrope (a plant that turns to the sun)

hema, hemo [blood] hemorrhage (an outpouring or flowing of blood), hemoglobin, hemophilia

here, hes [stick] adhere, cohere, cohesion

hetero [different] heterogeneous (different in birth), heterosexual (with interest in the opposite sex)

homo [same] homogeneous (of same birth or kind), homonym (word with same pronunciation as another), homogenize

hum, human [earth, ground, man] humus, exhume (to take out of the ground), humane (compassion for other humans)

hydr, hydra, hydro [water] dehydrate, hydrant, hydraulic, hydraulics, hydrogen, hydrophobia (fear of water)

hypn [sleep] hypnosis, Hypnos (god of sleep), hypnotherapy (treatment of disease by hypnosis)

ignis [fire] ignite, igneous, ignition

ject [throw] deject, inject, project (throw forward), eject, object

join, junct [join] adjoining, enjoin (to lay an order upon, to command), juncture, conjunction, injunction

juven [young] juvenile, rejuvenate (to make young again)

lau, lav, lot, lut [wash] launder, lavatory, lotion, ablution (a washing away), dilute (to make a liquid thinner and weaker)

leg [law] legal (lawful; according to law), legislate (to enact a law), legislature, legitimize (make legal)

levi [light] alleviate (lighten a load), levitate, levity (light conversation; humor)

liber, liver [free] liberty (freedom), liberal, liberalize (to make more free), deliverance

liter [letters] literary (concerned with books and writing), literature, literal, alliteration, obliterate

loc, loco [place] locality, locale, location, allocate (to assign, to place), relocate (to put back into place), locomotion (act of moving from place to place)

log, logo, ogue, ology [word, study, speech] catalog, prologue, dialogue, logogram (a symbol representing a word), zoology (animal study), psychology (mind study)

loqu, locut [talk, speak] eloquent (speaking well and forcefully), soliloquy, locution, loquacious (talkative), colloquial (talking together; conversational or informal)

luc, lum, lus, lun [light] translucent (letting light come through), lumen (a unit of light), luminary (a heavenly body; someone who shines in his or her profession), luster (sparkle, shine), Luna (the moon goddess)

magn [great] magnify (make great, enlarge), magnificent, magnanimous (great of mind or spirit), magnate, magnitude, magnum

man [hand] manual, manage, manufacture, manacle, manicure, manifest, maneuver, emancipate

mand [command] mandatory (commanded), remand (order back), mandate

mania [madness] mania (insanity, craze), monomania (mania on one idea), kleptomania, pyromania (insane tendency to set fires), maniac

mar, mari, mer [sea, pool] marine (a soldier serving on shipboard), marsh (wetland, swamp), maritime (relating to the sea and navigation), mermaid (fabled sea creature, half fish, half woman)

matri [mother] maternal (relating to the mother), matrimony, matriarchate (rulership of women), matron

medi [half, middle, between, halfway] mediate (come between, intervene), medieval (pertaining to the Middle Ages), Mediterranean (lying between lands), mediocre, medium

mega [great, million] megaphone (great sound), megalopolis (great city; an extensive urban area including a number of cities), megacycle (a million cycles), megaton

mem [remember] memo (a reminder), commemoration (the act of remembering by a memorial or ceremony), memento, memoir, memorable

meter [measure] meter (a metric measure), voltameter (instrument to measure volts), barometer, thermometer

micro [small] microscope, microfilm, microcard, microwave, micrometer (device for measuring small distances), omicron, micron (a millionth of a meter), microbe (small living thing)

migra [wander] migrate (to wander), emigrate (one who leaves a country), immigrate (to come into the land)

mit, miss [send] emit (send out, give off), remit (send back, as money due), submit, admit, commit, permit, transmit (send across), omit, intermittent (sending between, at intervals), mission, missile

mob, mot, mov [move] mobile (capable of moving), motionless (without motion), motor, emotional (moved strongly by feelings), motivate, promotion, demote, movement

mon [warn, remind] monument (a reminder or memorial of a person or an event), admonish (warn), monitor, premonition (forewarning)

mor, mort [mortal, death] mortal (causing death or destined for death), immortal (not subject to death), mortality (rate of death), mortician (one who prepares the dead for burial), mortuary (place for the dead, a morgue)

morph [form] amorphous (with no form, shapeless), metamorphosis (a change of form, as a caterpillar into a butterfly), morphology

multi [many, much] multifold (folded many times), multilinguist (one who speaks many languages), multiped (an organism with many feet), multiply

nat, nasc [to be born, to spring forth] innate (inborn), natal, native, nativity, renascence (a rebirth, a revival)

neur [nerve] neuritis (inflammation of a nerve), neurology (study of nervous systems), neurologist (one who practices neurology), neural, neurosis, neurotic

nom [law, order] autonomy (self-law, self-government), astronomy, gastronomy (art or science of good eating), economy

nomen, nomin [name] nomenclature, nominate (name someone for an office)

nov [new] novel (new, strange, not formerly known), renovate (to make like new again), novice, nova, innovate

nox, noc [night] nocturnal, equinox (equal nights), noctilucent (shining by night)

numer [number] numeral (a figure expressing a number), numeration (act of counting), enumerate (count out, one by one), innumerable

omni [all, every] omnipotent (all-powerful), omniscient (all-knowing), omnipresent (present everywhere), omnivorous

onym [name] anonymous (without name), synonym, pseudonym (false name), antonym (name of opposite meaning)

oper [work] operate (to labor, function), cooperate (work together)

ortho [straight, correct] orthodox (of the correct or accepted opinion), orthodontist (tooth straightener), orthopedic (originally pertaining to straightening a child), unorthodox

pac [peace] pacifist (one for peace only; opposed to war), pacify (make peace, quiet), Pacific Ocean (peaceful ocean)

pan [all] panacea (cure-all), pandemonium (place of all the demons, wild disorder), pantheon (place of all the gods in mythology)

pater, patr [father] paternity (fatherhood, responsibility), patriarch (head of the tribe, family), patriot, patron (a wealthy person who supports as would a father)

path, pathy [feeling, suffering] pathos (feeling of pity, sorrow), sympathy, antipathy (feeling against), apathy (without feeling), empathy (feeling or identifying with another), telepathy (far feeling; thought transference)

ped, pod [foot] pedal (lever for a foot), impede (get the feet in a trap, hinder), pedestal (foot or base of a statue), pedestrian (foot traveler), centipede, tripod (three-footed support), podiatry (care of the feet), antipodes (opposite feet)

pedo [child] orthopedic, pedagogue (child leader; teacher), pediatrics (medical care of children)

pel, puls [drive, urge] compel, dispel, expel, repel, propel, pulse, impulse, pulsate, compulsory, expulsion, repulsive

pend, pens, pond [hang, weigh] pendant pendulum, suspend, appendage, pensive (weighing thought), ponderous

phil [love] philosophy (love of wisdom), philanthropy, philharmonic, bibliophile, Philadelphia (city of brotherly love)

phobia [fear] claustrophobia (fear of closed spaces), acrophobia (fear of high places), hydrophobia (fear of water)

phon [sound] phonograph, phonetic (pertaining to sound), symphony (sounds with or together)

photo [light] photograph (light-writing), photoelectric, photogenic (artistically suitable for being photographed), photosynthesis (action of light on chlorophyll to make carbohydrates)

plac [please] placid (calm, peaceful), placebo, placate, complacent

plu, plur, plus [more] plural (more than one), pluralist (a person who holds more than one office), plus (indicating that something more is to be added)

pneuma, pneumon [breath] pneumatic (pertaining to air, wind, or other gases), pneumonia (disease of the lungs)

pod (see ped)

poli [city] metropolis (mother city), police, politics, Indianapolis, Acropolis (high city, upper part of Athens), megalopolis

pon, pos, pound [place, put] postpone (put afterward), component, opponent (one put against), proponent, expose, impose, deposit, posture (how one places oneself), position, expound, impound

pop [people] population, populous (full of people), popular

port [carry] porter (one who carries), portable, transport (carry across), report, export, import, support, transportation

portion [part, share] portion (a part; a share, as a portion of pie), proportion (the relation of one share to others)

prehend [seize] comprehend (seize with the mind), apprehend (seize a criminal), comprehensive (seizing much, extensive)

prim, prime [first] primacy (state of being first in rank), prima donna (the first lady of opera), primitive (from the earliest or first time), primary, primal, primeval proto [first] prototype (the first model made), protocol, protagonist, protozoan

psych [mind, soul] psyche (soul, mind), psychiatry (healing of the mind), psychology, psychosis (serious mental disorder), psychotherapy (mind treatment), psychic

punct [point, dot] punctual (being exactly on time), punctuation, puncture, acupuncture

reg, recti [straighten] regiment, regular, regulate, rectify (make straight), correct, direction

ri, ridi, risi [laughter] deride (mock, jeer at), ridicule (laughter at the expense of another, mockery), ridiculous, derision

rog, roga [ask] prerogative (privilege; asking before), interrogation (questioning; the act of questioning), derogatory

rupt [break] rupture (break), interrupt (break into), abrupt (broken off), disrupt (break apart), erupt (break out), incorruptible (unable to be broken down)

sacr, sanc, secr [sacred] sacred, sanction, sacrosanct, consecrate, desecrate

salv, salu [safe, healthy] salvation (act of being saved), salvage, salutation

sat, satis [enough] saturate, satisfy (to give pleasure to; to give as much as is needed)

sci [know] science (knowledge), conscious (knowing, aware), omniscient (knowing everything)

scope [see, watch] telescope, microscope, kaleidoscope (instrument for seeing beautiful forms), periscope, stethoscope

scrib, script [write] scribe (a writer), scribble, manuscript (written by hand), inscribe, describe, subscribe, prescribe

sed, sess, sid [sit] sediment (that which sits or settles out of a liquid), session (a sitting), obsession (an idea that sits stubbornly in the mind), possess, preside (sit before), president, reside, subside

sen [old] senior, senator, senile (old; showing the weakness of old age)

sent, sens [feel] sentiment (feeling), consent, resent, dissent, sentimental (having strong feeling or emotion), sense, sensation, sensitive, sensory, dissension

sequ, secu, sue [follow] sequence (following of one thing after another), sequel, consequence, subsequent, prosecute, consecutive (following in order), second (following "first"), ensue, pursue

serv [save, serve] servant, service, preserve, subservient, servitude, conserve, reservation, deserve, conservation

sign, signi [sign, mark, seal] signal (a gesture or sign to call attention), signature (the mark of a person written in his or her own handwriting), design, insignia (distinguishing marks)

simil, simul [like, resembling] similar (resembling in many respects), assimilate (to make similar to), simile, simulate (pretend; put on an act to make a certain impression)

sist, sta, stit [stand] persist (stand firmly; unyielding; continue), assist (to stand by with help), circumstance, stamina (power to withstand, to endure), status (standing), state, static, stable, stationary, substitute (to stand in for another)

solus [alone] soliloquy, solitaire, solitude, solo

solv, solu [loosen] solvent (a loosener, a dissolver), solve, absolve (loosen from, free from), resolve, soluble, solution, resolution, resolute, dissolute (loosened morally)

somnus [sleep] insomnia (not being able to sleep), somnambulist (a sleepwalker)

soph [wise] sophomore (wise fool), philosophy (love of wisdom), sophisticated

spec, spect, spic [look] specimen (an example to look at, study), specific, aspect, spectator (one who looks), spectacle, speculate, inspect, respect, prospect, retrospective (looking backward), introspective, expect, conspicuous

sphere [ball, sphere] stratosphere (the upper portion of the atmosphere), hemisphere (half of the earth), spheroid

spir [breath] spirit (breath), conspire (breathe together; plot), inspire (breathe into), aspire (breathe toward), expire (breathe out; die), perspire, respiration

string, strict [draw tight] stringent (drawn tight; rigid), strict, restrict, constrict (draw tightly together), boa constrictor (snake that constricts its prey)

stru, struct [build] construe (build in the mind, interpret), structure, construct, instruct, obstruct, destruction, destroy

sume, sump [take, use, waste] consume (to use up), assume (to take; to use), sump pump (a pump that takes up water), presumption (to take or use before knowing all the facts)

tact, tang, tag, tig, ting [touch] contact, tactile, intangible (not able to be touched), intact (untouched, uninjured), tangible, contingency, contagious (able to transmit disease by touching), contiguous

tele [far] telephone (far sound), telegraph (far writing), television (far seeing), telephoto (far photography), telecast

tempo [time] tempo (rate of speed), temporary, extemporaneously, contemporary (those who live at the same time), pro tem (for the time being)

ten, tin, tain [hold] tenacious (holding fast), tenant, tenure, untenable, detention, content, pertinent, continent, obstinate, abstain, pertain, detain

tend, tent, tens [stretch, strain] tendency (a stretching; leaning), extend, intend, contend, pretend, superintend, tender, extent, tension (a stretching, strain), pretense terra [earth] terrain, terrarium, territory, terrestrial

test [to bear witness] testament (a will; bearing witness to someone's wishes), detest, attest (bear witness to), testimony

the, theo [God, a god] monotheism (belief in one god), polytheism (belief in many gods), atheism, theology

therm [heat] thermometer, therm (heat unit), thermal, thermostat, thermos, hypothermia (subnormal temperature)

thesis, thet [place, put] antithesis (place against), hypothesis (place under), synthesis (put together), epithet

tom [cut] atom (not cuttable; smallest particle of matter), appendectomy (cutting out an appendix), tonsillectomy, dichotomy (cutting in two; a division), anatomy (cutting, dissecting to study structure)

tort, tors [twist] torture (twisting to inflict pain), retort (twist back, reply sharply), extort (twist out), distort (twist out of shape), contort, torsion (act of twisting, as a torsion bar)

tox [poison] toxic (poisonous), intoxicate, antitoxin

tract, tra [draw, pull] tractor, attract, subtract, tractable (can be handled), abstract (to draw away), subtrahend (the number to be drawn away from another)

trib [pay, bestow] tribute (to pay honor to), contribute (to give money to a cause), attribute, retribution, tributary

turbo [disturb] turbulent, disturb, turbid, turmoil

typ [print] type, prototype (first print; model), typical, typography, typewriter, typology (study of types, symbols), typify

ultima [last] ultimate, ultimatum (the final or last offer that can be made)

uni [one] unicorn (a legendary creature with one horn), unify (make into one), university, unanimous, universal

vac [empty] vacate (to make empty), vacuum (a space entirely devoid of matter), evacuate (to remove troops or people), vacation, vacant

vale, vali, valu [strength, worth] valiant, equivalent (of equal worth), validity (truth; legal strength), evaluate (find out the value), value, valor (value; worth)

ven, vent [come] convene (come together, assemble), intervene (come between), venue, convenient, avenue, circumvent (come or go around), invent, prevent

ver, veri [true] very, aver (say to be true, affirm), verdict, verity (truth), verify (show to be true), verisimilitude

vert, vers [turn] avert (turn away), divert (turn aside, amuse), invert (turn over), introvert (turn inward), convertible, reverse (turn back), controversy (a turning against; a dispute), versatile (turning easily from one skill to another)

vic, vicis [change, substitute] vicarious, vicar, vicissitude

vict, vinc [conquer] victor (conqueror, winner), evict (conquer out, expel), convict (prove guilty), convince (conquer mentally, persuade), invincible (not conquerable)

vid, vis [see] video, television, evident, provide, providence, visible, revise, supervise (oversee), vista, visit, vision

viv, vita, vivi [alive, life] revive (make live again), survive (live beyond, outlive), vivid, vivacious (full of life), vitality

voc [call] vocation (a calling), avocation (occupation not one's calling), convocation (a calling together), invocation, vocal

vol [will] malevolent, benevolent (one of goodwill), volunteer, volition

volcan, vulcan [fire] volcano (a mountain erupting fiery lava), volcanize (to undergo volcanic heat), Vulcan (Roman god of fire)

volvo [turn about, roll] revolve, voluminous (winding), voluble (easily turned about or around), convolution (a twisting)

vor [eat greedily] voracious, carnivorous (flesh eating), herbivorous (plant eating), omnivorous (eating everything), devour

zo [animal] zoo (short for zoological garden), zoology (study of animal life), zodiac (circle of animal constellations), zoomorphism (being in the form of an animal), protozoa (one-celled animals)

The Human Body

capit	head	gastro	stomach	osteo	bone
card	heart	glos	tongue	ped	foot
corp	body	hema	blood	pneuma	breathe
dent	tooth	man	hand	psych	mind
derm	skin	neur	nerve	spir	breath

For additional information, see page 36.

Glossary

A

abstract
something that can't be sensed (seen, heard, etc.); a feeling or idea

abstract nouns
nouns referring to ideas or conditions that cannot be sensed

academic sentences
usually longer sentences with multiple layers of meaning; reveal careful thought on the part of the writer

academic voice
the tone or style used in most textbooks and professional journals; formal and serious

action verb
word functioning as a verb that expresses action

active voice
the voice created when a subject is acting

adjective
a word that modifies a noun or pronoun

adjective phrase or clause
a dependent clause functioning as an adjective

adverb
word that modifies a verb, an adjective, an adverb, or a whole sentence

adverb clause
a dependent clause functioning as an adverb

agree in number
when subject and verb are both singular or both plural

ambiguous
unclear or confusing

annotate
to add comments or make notes in a text

antecedent
the noun or pronoun that a pronoun refers to or replaces

APA
American Psychological Association; provides documentation guidelines for the social sciences

appositive
a noun or non phrase that renames another noun right beside it; usually set off by commas

apostrophe
a punctuation mark (') used to show that a letter or number has been left out or that a word is possessive

argumentation
a discussion or course of reasoning aimed at demonstrating truth or falsehood; relies on logic and sound reasoning

article
common noun markers (*a, an,* or *the*)

audience
the intended reader of a text

auxiliary verbs
helping verbs used with the main verb to indicate tense and other things

B

base word (root)
the word part or base upon which other words are built (*help* is the base for the word *helpful*)

"be" verb
forms of the verb "be" *(is, are, was, were)*; function as linking verbs

C

causal connection
the link between the causes and effects of a topic; usually identified in the thesis statement

causes
the reasons for an action or a condition

chronological
organized by time

citations
sources referred to in research; occur within the text and in a listing at the end of the report

claim
the position or thesis developed in an argument essay

classification
the act of arranging or organizing according to classes or categories

closing
the final part of writing; a closing sentence in a paragraph, a closing paragraph (or two) in an essay

cluster
a strategy to generate ideas graphically; used to select topics and to gather details about a topic

colon
a punctuation mark (:) that introduces an example or list

comma splice
a sentence error that occurs when two sentences are connected with only a comma

common noun
a general noun, not capitalized

comparison-contrast
showing how two or more subjects are similar and different

complete predicate
the predicate with modifiers and objects

complete subject
the subject with modifiers

complex sentence
a sentence with an independent and dependent clause

compound adjective
an adjective made of two more words, hyphenated before the noun but not afterward (*ready-made meals*)

compound-complex sentence
a sentence with two or more independent clauses and one or more dependent clauses

compound noun
noun made up of two or more words (*editor in chief*)

compound predicate
two or more predicates joined by *and* or *or*

compound sentence
two or more simple sentences joined with a coordinating conjunction

compound subject
two or more subjects connected by *and* or *or*

concrete nouns
nouns referring to something that can be sensed

conjunction
word or word group that joins parts of a sentence

content
the ideas and meaning developed in a piece of writing

context
the part of a text that surrounds a particular word; helps determine the word's meaning

contraction
word formed by joining two words, leaving out one or more letters (indicated by an apostrophe)

conventions
the rules governing the standard use of the language

coordinating conjunction
conjunction that joins grammatically equal parts

correlative conjunctions
pair of conjunctions that stress the equality of the parts that are joined

count nouns
nouns that name things that can be counted (*pens, votes, people*)

counterarguments
opposing positions or arguments

cycle chart
a graphic organizer that identifies the steps in a recurring process

D

dangling modifiers
a modifying word, phrase, or clause that appears to modify the wrong word

dash
long horizontal line (—) that separates words or ideas, creating emphasis

declarative sentence
a sentence that expresses a basic statement

deductive thinking
following a thesis (main idea) with supporting reasons, examples, and facts

definite article
the word *the*

definition
the formal statement or explanation of a meaning of a word

delayed subject
a subject that appears after the verb

demonstrative adjective
a demonstrative pronoun (*this, that, those*) used as an adjective

dependent clause
a group of words with a subject and verb that does not express a complete thought

description
a written creation of an image of a person, place, thing, or idea

dialogue
conversation between two or more people

direct object
a word that follows a transitive verb

documentation guidelines
rules to follow for giving credit for the ideas of others used in a report; MLA and APA provide two common sets of documentation rules

double negative
the nonstandard use of two negatives to express a single negative idea (*I can't hardly sleep*)

double preposition
the nonstandard use of two prepositions together (*off of*)

double subject
error created by following a subject with a pronoun

E

editing
checking revised writing for style, grammar, punctuation, capitalization, and spelling errors

effects
circumstances brought about by a cause or an action

essay
a short piece of writing that uses facts and details to support a claim (thesis)

example
details that demonstrate or show something

exclamation mark
a punctuation mark (!) used at the end of an exclamatory sentence or a word that indicates strong emotion

exclamatory sentence
a sentence that expresses strong emotion

F

feminine
female

first draft
a first attempt to develop writing

focus
a particular part or feeling about a topic that is emphasized in a piece of writing; usually expressed in a thesis statement

formal English
a serious, straightforward style used in most academic writing; objective (sticks to the facts)

fragment
a group of words that does not express a complete thought

freewriting
a prewriting strategy involving rapid, nonstop writing; helps in selecting a topic and gathering details about it

future tense
verb tense indicating that action will happen later

G

gathering grid
a graphic organizer used to identify or gather different types of defining details

gender
masculine, feminine, neuter, or indefinite

gerund
a verb form that ends in *ing* and is used as a noun

graphic organizers
clusters, lists, charts, and other visuals that help writers explore and arrange ideas

H

helping (auxiliary) verb
verbs that work with a main verb to form different tenses and so on

hyphen
a short horizontal line (-) used to form compound words (*in-service*)

I

ideas
the first and main trait of writing; includes the main idea plus supporting details

idiom
a common expression whose meaning is different from its literal meaning (*hit the roof*)

illogical
without logic; senseless, false, or untrue

illustration
the act of clarifying or explaining in writing

implied subject
the word assumed to begin command sentences

indefinite article
the words *a* or *an*

indefinite adjective
an indefinite pronoun (*much, some*) used as an adjective

indefinite pronoun
a pronoun such as *someone* or *everything* that does not refer to a specific person or thing

independent clause
a group of words with a subject and verb that expresses a complete thought

indirect object
a word that comes between a transitive verb and a direct object

inductive thinking
presenting specific details first and concluding with the thesis (main point)

inferences
a logical conclusion that can be made about something that is not actually said or stated in a text

infinitive
a verb form that begins with *to* and can used as a noun (or as an adjective or adverb)

informal English
a relaxed style used in most personal essays; subjective (contains the writer's thoughts and feelings)

interrogative sentence
a sentence that asks a question

italics
a special type style like *this* used to identify titles of books, movies, etc.; functions the same as underlining

items in a series
three or more words, phrases, or clauses that are grammatically the same; set off by commas

interjection
a word or phrase that expresses strong emotion

intransitive verb
action verb that does not transfer action to a direct object

irregular verb
a verb in which the principal parts are different words (*give, gave, given*)

K

KWL
a reading strategy identifying what the reader knows, wants to learn, and eventually learns

L

levels of detail
details that contain differing levels of clarifying support

line diagram
a graphic organizer used to identify the main idea and examples in writing

linking verb
verb that connects the subject with a noun or another word; "be" verbs (*is, are, was, were*) are linking verbs

listing
a strategy used to gather ideas for writing

M

main idea (main point)
the idea that is developed in a piece of writing

masculine
male

misplaced modifier
a modifying word, phrase, or clause that has been placed incorrectly in a sentence

MLA
Modern Language Association; provides documentation guidelines for use in the humanities (literature, history, philosophy, etc.)

N

narration
the sharing of a story; a personal narrative shares a true story

neuter
neither male nor female

nominative case
used as a subject or a subject complement

noncount noun
nouns that name things that cannot be counted (*ice, plastic, sunshine*)

noun
a word that names a person, place, thing, or idea

noun clause
a dependent clause that functions as a noun

noun phrase
a noun plus its modifiers

number
singular or plural

O

objective
sticking to the facts; uninfluenced by personal feelings

objective case
used as a direct object, an indirect object, or an object of a preposition

organization
the second important trait; deals with the arrangement of ideas

organized list
an outline-like graphic used to keep track of the information in a report and other forms of writing; customized for personal use

outline
an orderly graphic representation of ideas, following specific rules for arrangement

P

paragraph
a distinct division of writing containing a topic sentence, body sentences, and a closing sentence; usually develops one specific topic

paraphrase
a form of summary writing with explanations and interpretations; may be as long or longer than the source text

participle
a verb form ending in *ing* or *ed* and functioning as an adjective

passive voice
the voice created when a subject is being acted upon

past tense
verb tense indicating that action happened earlier

perfect tense
verb tense that expresses completed action

person
whether the pronoun is speaking, being spoken to, or being spoken about

personal voice
sounds informal and somewhat relaxed; subjective (including the writer's thoughts and feelings)

persuasion
a form of discourse attempting to convince an audience; may appeal to emotion as well as logic

phrase
a group of words that lacks a subject or predicate or both

plagiarism
using the words and thoughts of others without crediting them; intellectual stealing

plot
the different parts of a story that create suspense

plural
referring to more than one thing

points of comparison
the special elements or features used to make a comparison (size, strength, appearance, etc.)

possessive
used to show ownership

predicate
the part of the sentence that tells or asks something about the subject

predicate adjective
adjective that appears after a linking verb

prefix
word parts that come before the base word (*un* is a prefix in *unwind*)

prepositional phrase
a group of words with a preposition, an object, and any modifiers

prereading
becoming familiar with a text by reviewing the title, heading, etc.

present tense
verb tense indicating that action is happening now

prewriting
starting the writing process by analyzing the assignment, selecting a topic, gathering details, and finding a focus

primary sources
information collected directly, such as through firsthand experiences

process
a series of actions, steps, or changes bringing about a result

progressive tense
verb tense that expresses ongoing action

pronoun
word that takes the place of a noun or another pronoun

proper adjective
an adjective based on the name of a specific person, place, thing, or idea; capitalized

proper noun
the specific name of a person, place, thing, or idea; capitalized

publishing
preparing writing to share or submit

purpose
the reason for writing (to inform, to entertain, to persuade, etc.)

Q

question mark
a punctuation mark (?) used an the end of an interrogative sentence (question)

quotation
the specific thoughts or words of other people used in writing

quotation marks
punctuation marks ("") that set off certain titles, special words, and the exact words spoken by someone

R

rambling sentence
a sentence error that occurs when a long series of separate ideas are connected by one connecting word after another

reading
the second step in the reading process; getting a basic understanding of the text

reading process
a process helping a reader gain a full understanding of a text

rereading
part of the reading process; consists of additional readings and analysis after the first reading

research report
a carefully planned form of informational writing, ranging in length from two or three pages and up

revising
improving the content of a first draft

relative clause
a dependent group of words beginning with a relative pronoun and a verb

relative pronoun
a word—*that, which, who, whom*—that introduces a relative clause

root (base word)
the word part (base) upon which other words are built (*help* is the base in *helpful*)

run-on sentence
a sentence error when two sentences are joined without punctuation or a connecting word

S

satiric voice
the use of humor, fake praise, or sarcasm (ridicule) to make fun of someone or something

secondary sources
information gained through reading what others have learned about a topic

semicolon
a punctuation mark (;) that connects sentences and separates items in some series

sensory details
specific sights, sounds, smells, textures, and tastes

sentences
the thoughts that carry the meaning in discourse; one of the key traits

sequencing
the following of one thing after another

shift in person
when first, second, and/or third person are improperly mixed in a sentence

shift in tense
more than one verb tense improperly used in a sentence

simple predicate
the verb and any helping verbs without modifiers or objects

simple sentence
a complete thought (containing a subject and a verb)

simple subject
the subject without any modifiers

singular
referring to one thing

spatial
organization related to location; often used in descriptions

SQ3R
a reading strategy consisting of survey, question, read, recite, and review

Standard English
English considered appropriate for school, business, and government

story line
the parts of a plot or story; includes exposition, rising action, climax, and resolution

STRAP strategy
a strategy to analyze writing and writing assignments

subject
the part of a sentence that tells who or what the sentence is about

subject complement
as word that follows a linking verb and renames or describes the subject

subjective
including a writer's personal thoughts and feelings

subordinate clause
word group that begins with a subordinating conjunction and has a subject and verb but can't stand alone as a sentence

subordinating conjunction
word or word groups that connect clauses of different importance

summarizing
the process of presenting the core of a text in a condensed form

suffix
a word part coming after a base word (*ful* is a suffix in *healthful*)

T

T-chart
A graphic organizer used to list causes and effects

tense
tells whether the action (verb) happens in the past, present, future, etc.

thesis statement
the statement of the main idea or focus of an essay; usually appears early in the text (often at the end of the first paragraph)

time line
a graphic organizer used to list ideas or events in chronological order

topic sentence
the statement of the main idea in a paragraph

transitions
words and phrases that link ideas in writing

transitive verb
action verb that transfers action to a direct object

traits
the main elements or features in writing; includes ideas, organization, voice, word choice, sentences, and conventions

U

usage error
using the wrong word (*they're* instead of *their*)

V

Venn diagram
a graphic organizer (two intersecting circles) used to identify similarities and differences for comparative writing

verb
A word that expresses action or a state of being

verb phrase
the main verb and any auxiliary verbs

verbal
a construction formed from a verb but functioning as a noun, adjective, or adverb (gerund, participle, or infinitive)

voice
the personality or tone in a piece of writing; one of the traits

W

word choice
the choice of words in a piece of writing; one of the traits

writing (the first draft)
the first attempt to develop a piece of writing; one of the steps in the writing process

writing process
a series of steps to follow to develop a piece of writing; includes prewriting, writing, revising, editing, and publishing